Renovating Old Houses

Renovating Old Houses

Bringing New Life to Vintage Homes

George Nash

The Taunton Press

The Taunton Press, Inc.,
63 South Main Street, PO Box 5506,
Newtown, CT 06470-5506
e-mail: tp@taunton.com

Editor: David Schiff
Cover design: Susan Fazekas
Interior design: Carol Petro
Layout: Carol Petro
Illustrator: Lee Hov, Ron Carboni
Photographer: George Nash, except where noted

Library of Congress Cataloging-in-Publication Data

Nash, George, 1949-
    Renovating old houses : bringing new life to vintage homes / George Nash.
        p. cm.
    ISBN-13: 978-1-56158-535-9
    ISBN-10: 1-56158-535-1
    1. Dwellings--Remodeling. 2. Dwellings--Maintenance and repair. I.
Title.
    TH4816 .N3623 2003
    690'.837--dc21

                                        2003011967

Printed in the United States of America
10 9 8 7

The following manufacturers/names appearing in *Renovating Old Houses* are trademarks: Amofoam®, Bakelite®, BAND-AIDS®, Bilco®, B-I-N®, Bituthene®, Coleman®, Fernco®, Formular®, GE®, Geocel®, Griffolyn®, Griptite™, Gypsolite®, Kilz™, Larsen®, Madison®, Masonite®, Miraflex®, Owens Corning®, Phenoseal®, Pressuretrol®, Qest®, Rocklath®, Sakrete®, Sheetrock®, Simpson Strong-Tie™, Sonotubes®, Spackle®, Structolite®, Styrofoam®, Tu-Tuf®, Tyvek®, Vise-Grip®, Volvo®, WD-40®, W.R. Grace Ice and Watershield®, Watco®, Wonder Bar®

Disclaimer

Although the author and the publisher have made every attempt to ensure the accuracy and safety of the information presented herein, he and they make no claim that it is complete or that it complies with every relevant code. Furthermore, because the author and publisher have no control over how the reader chooses to use the information presented in this book nor can establish the reader's proficiency or physical condition, they are not responsible for mishaps or other consequences that may result from the reader's use of this book. Please be careful and remember with old houses, as in everything, "perseverance furthers."

For my mom, my first and fiercest promoter

Acknowledgments

It's been over ten years since the first edition of this book appeared. During that time the enterprise of renovating old houses has moved out of the backwaters and into the mainstream of the building industry. This is good in that people have come to appreciate the value of old houses, both structurally and spiritually.

It's also good that reproduction hardware, lighting and plumbing fixtures, floorings, ceilings, and many other building products specific to old houses that were not available when I first began working with old houses are now widely available. And previously near-moribund crafts like ornamental plastering and slate and standing-seam roofing are enjoying a renaissance. At the same time, the success of the renovation movement, which underwrites television shows and dedicated magazines, shows that old houses are just as susceptible to the pitches of brand-name marketers and fashionable galliflummery as the rest of the building industry.

So it is with this new edition: The packaging is definitely glossier and more attractive, but there's a lot more than just pretty pictures. I've added new material and expanded old material, fixed mistakes and cleaned up confusions, and—I hope—made the contents even more practical and useful than the first edition. I've also tried to add, wherever there was space, a bit of historical background. One of the reasons people like living in old houses is, after all, to have a connection with the past.

I thank Peter Chapman and all the people at The Taunton Press for their support of this project and for their high production values and fairness to their authors. They are a rarity in the all-too-often exploitative world of publishing.

Thanks again to everyone who let me into their homes to take photographs. And, especially, I thank Peter and Rebecca Whitmore of Milton, Vermont—who still haven't changed a thing—for allowing me to photograph in color this time what was done in black and white before. And to Kevin and Becky Walters of Fairfax, Vermont, for letting me use the photographs of their heroic renovation project.

I'd also like to thank my editor, David Schiff, for his insights and plain hard work. The task of trimming and slimming the new manuscript to fit between its allotted covers without watering down its content or doing violence to its continuity was truly daunting. I am extremely grateful that he accomplished it so well.

I am as susceptible to houses as some people are susceptible to other human beings. Twice in my life I have fallen in love with one. Each time it was as violent and fatal as falling in love with a human being.

—Katherine Butler Hathaway,
The Journals and Letters of the Little Locksmith

To all of us who just can't help it, who would still rather live in an old house even after fixing one up, remember the words of the poet:

He who loves an old house never loves in vain.

—Isabel La Howe Conant, "Old House"

Contents

Introduction

This square home, as it stands in unshadowed earth between the winding years of heaven, is, not to me, but of itself, one among the serene and final uncapturable beauties of existence: that this beauty is made between hurt but invincible nature and the plainest cruelties and needs of human existence.

—James Agee and Walker Evans, *Let Us Now Praise Famous Men*

WHY BUY AN OLD HOUSE?

What is it about old houses? What strange spells do they cast, so that otherwise perfectly rational human beings are compelled against all sanity and sense to commit large amounts of energy, money, and time to their rebuilding?

Is it economics? In an era of inflated real-estate prices, fewer and fewer people can afford the up-front costs of a new or completely remodeled house. The "handyman's special" (real-estate agent's euphemism for "crumbling disaster") ostensibly offers home ownership to first-time buyers on a limited budget or enterprising individuals a chance to make a good return on an investment. Of course, the low purchase price will be offset by the cost of remodeling, but this can theoretically be spread out over a long time—ideally, cash flow might keep pace with repairs. But even with that low purchase price, an old house, when all the costs of remodeling are finally tallied, will typically cost as much as, if not more than, a comparable new house.

Is it then a matter of aesthetics, the charm of a bygone style? Splendid manse or humble farmhouse, old houses seem to embody a suitability that is conspicuously absent in their modern counterparts. Even if it's still standing a century from now, a split-level tract house will never be an "old house." Why should this be? According to Jonathan Hale, author of *The Old*

Golden Section ratios and 30-60-90 triangles within the facades of classic late-eighteenth- and early-nineteenth-century houses give them their visually appealing sense of balance and proportion.

Way of Seeing (Houghton Mifflin, 1994), the answer is proportion. The windows and other visual elements that make up the facades of old houses, particularly those built before 1830, are organized by regulating lines in a kind of fugue on the fabled "Golden Section" of classical architecture. It has long been argued that because this ratio (1:1.618) is consonant with the proportions of the human body and ubiquitous throughout the natural world, buildings that incorporate it inevitably seem "just right." Apparently, somehow, somewhere along the road to modernity, we lost that innate sense of pleasing design. We forgot the old way of seeing.

However, although the contrast between a hand-built old house and the developer-assembled product of today is obvious, it is not fundamental. The success of present-day custom builders proves that pride in workmanship is still economically viable. You can build yourself an "old" house from scratch, with the Golden Section as its template. You can make it traditional, down to the last details of the woodwork and hardware, without the shortcomings of comfort, convenience, and utility that plague their prototypes. Design is part of it, but there's more to the mystery than pleasing proportion.

People who work with and live in old houses use fuzzy words like *feel, aura,* and *essence* to justify their obsession. These are aesthetic categories that attempt to describe the perception of beauty, the way that so many old houses almost seem to live a life of their own, breathing in slow, subtle rhythms of shifting lines and weathering wood. As do all living things, a house achieves a delicate equilibrium, a precariously maintained and constantly changing relationship to time, the seasons, and its people. It responds to the care (or neglect) given it—growing, changing, adding windows and doors, sprouting porches and sheds as the years progress.

And when its people depart, a house begins to die. The process occurs with a grace, beauty, and terrible simplicity. The tilt and sag of the walls, the weathered shades of clapboard and peeling paint, the tired angles of the roof, all give mute expression to the ebb and flow of the lives once harbored within.

An Act of Resurrection

For me, it is this spiritual dimension, above all, that makes the renovation of old houses so deeply satisfying. To bring back a house to useful life, immersing oneself in the grain and texture of an earlier way of living in the process, is ultimately an act of resurrection of both the house and its owners.

Although the old-house restorer may undertake a profoundly spiritual journey, the path is full of physical details. Like all heroic quests, it is fraught with pitfalls and perils, both real and imagined. On the mundane level, this translates into lots of work, time, and money. Because purchase price is obviously a function of the neighborhood and the condition of the house, determining how much work the house needs and how to go about doing it make up the crux of the matter. No matter how astutely you may have examined the structure for defects, you are guaranteed to have missed some. It's quite likely you'll discover not only rotted beams but also windowsills eaten clear through the sheathing boards, a roof as watertight as an old bucket used for target practice, and a torrent deep enough to float a river raft pouring through the foundation wall every time it rains.

You will soon find that as bad as you thought the place might be, the reality is much worse. Your original estimate of time and money needed to restore the house to bare livability will increase by a factor of three. This money will disappear into largely invisible, and therefore ungratifying, structural repairs. And winter will be coming on early this year.

Like wood smoke from the cooking fire that has been absorbed into the plaster, the rooms and walls of old houses are suffused with the spirits of former inhabitants. All old houses are full of ghosts.

You probably knew all this at the outset, knew that the place really was in terrible shape even as you were poking your finger through the dry-rotted beams and telling yourself, yes, there will have to be some minor repairs here, and yes, perhaps the cracks in the foundation need some patching, or is it pointing. And, of course, that ghastly linoleum on the floors will have to go, but the plaster seems sound enough, just a patch of Spackle ought to fix it up fine . . . So potent is the spell of the old place, that you simply ignore your reservations and common sense, even as the real-estate agent is thanking the stars for city slickers.

And so you sign a mortgage but also body and soul, spouse and children over to an idea that will soon become a joy and a burden, a black hole that devours every molecule of your time, money, and spirit. Yet even when you discover that the only thing keeping the place from blowing away is the weight of the mouse droppings in the attic, you wouldn't have it any other way. If this is the case, you might be one of those old-house people, a peculiar kind of maniac who is one part ability, one part inventiveness, two parts determination, three parts romanticism, and six parts damn foolishness.

CONSCIOUS RENOVATION: PHILOSOPHIES DEFINED

There are basically three approaches to working with old houses: preservation, renovation, and remodeling (or, as some would have it, "remuddling"). These are distinguished by the degree of alteration (or violence) to the existing structure considered permissible and the amount of importance attached to historical fidelity.

This old farmhouse needs a lot of work to rescue it from years of neglect, yet its undeniable character might justify the expense of major renovation.

Preservation

The umbrella of preservation, encompassing both restoration and conservation, covers the most conservative (some might argue sensitive) end of the spectrum. Preservationists believe that there are thousands of old houses that have a far more enduring importance to society as educational examples and tools than they do as dwelling places for any one family or as investments for any one group or individual at any one time. Since so few of these historically important houses can be protected through outright acquisition by preservation societies, preservationists argue that the lack of a legal mandate to preserve old houses does not absolve private homeowners of their moral responsibility to do so.

The number of surviving American homes built before 1850 in original (or even "modernized") condition is dwindling much faster than the realization is growing of how much important historical and social information is bound up in them. Through the process of *seriation* (the correspondence of particular details and structures to a specific chronological period),

The round tower and curved porches make this house a worthy candidate for preservation. Public funding and tax credits can make the difference between preserving historically significant structures and losing them to remodeling or development.

An architectural record worthy of preservation: Roman numerals, consisting only of straight lines, were designed to be easily cut with a chisel, so framers often used them to label mating pieces before assembly, such as this rafter–collar beam joint.

architectural historians are just starting to trace the evolution of specific features and construction techniques. To do this effectively requires a large stock of original unaltered old houses. In this light, even seemingly minor details of fairly ordinary old houses could be historically significant. Thus if the owners of an architecturally important house make an irreversible change to suit their personal needs or tastes, they will destroy the opportunity for anyone else to learn from that house. They could even permanently erase information considered important by future scholars.

Personally, I think the concept of "old house" is too slippery to assign a cut-off date of 1850. The Shingle-style houses built in the 1930s in Berkeley, California, are now "old" and architecturally significant. The day will doubtless come when preservationists decry the desecration of historically important examples of southern California tract houses. Accordingly, the most important test for any proposed change to any historic old house is *reversibility*. If the change

cannot be undone later, it should be avoided. If this is impractical, the original features and changes should be documented on film and/or videotape, with measured drawings and written or taped descriptions: Documentary overkill is an invaluable aid to future researchers.

Ultimately, preservationists hold that if a prospective buyer finds a particular old house absolutely charming in its ambiance but feels that it needs drastic changes in floor plan, window size, and interior finishes to make it livable, he or she has an obligation to history and society not to buy it. They argue that it is immoral to impose irreversibly one's personal tastes and needs on the fading fabric of history. Such people should seek a house more suited to their sensibilities or build a "new old home" instead.

Within the preservationist camp, there are some nuances of methodology that are confusing enough to merit further discussion. Although it can be argued that in a strict technical sense preservation can be distinguished from conservation, the difference is so subtle that the terms can be used almost interchangeably. At most it's a distinction of fine degree: Just as conserves are a jam made from whole fruit and preserves are a jam made from mashed fruit, a conservationist is perhaps more insistent on leaving the existing structure intact than is a preservationist, whose primary interest is in historical continuity. Whereas a preservationist might paint over existing trimwork with modern latex paint, nevertheless preserving the underlying paint strata, a conservationist would be more likely to oppose the use of any but the traditional calcimine or whitewash formulas.

Restoration

Restoration is in no way synonymous with either preservation or conservation. It refers instead to the historical investigation and precise technical processes by which a structure is stripped of all later additions and returned to its original condition. Thus restoring an early-eighteenth-century village home would require the removal of its nineteenth-century porch, no matter how well that addition harmonized with the core house. Likewise, for trimwork, the restorationist would carefully remove each layer of paint down to the earliest and would repair or replace any damaged surfaces with materials and methods that duplicated the originals. This most conservative and demanding branch of preservation is usually reserved for historically significant, museum-quality examples of a particular architectural style—and has little relevance for the average homeowner.

If you are contemplating the purchase of a truly important old house, a specimen of a rare and perhaps endangered species, you have a responsibility at least to preserve (if you cannot afford to restore) it for future generations. To this end, consult a professional conservationist

With some minor reconstructive work on the porch and routine maintenance, this otherwise well-preserved Victorian summerhouse could be restored to its original condition. (Photo by Jane L. Waterman)

Renovate or restore? Restoring this historic log cabin would require removing the existing roof and replacing it with hewn or pole rafters and wood shingles lain over open lathing, which would have been used on the original. Likewise, the restorer would try to duplicate the recipe for the original chinking. The renovator would leave the roof intact and probably stuff fiberglass insulation between the logs before chinking them with a durable acrylic stucco.

Generic nineteenth-century farmhouses seldom have historically significant features and are excellent candidates for renovation. The foundation of this house has already been replaced and new steel roofing has been installed. This house does have one odd feature—the "coffin window" often found in northern New England, reputed to be used to move a coffin in and out of upstairs bedrooms, which were otherwise accessible by only a narrow staircase.

This quirky but charming Victorian cottage would benefit from the removal of the architecturally inappropriate porch stoop. Similarly, the wrought-iron porch roof supports should be replaced with turned or otherwise suitably detailed square or round wood posts.

or architectural historian before making any but the most superficial changes. And, at the very least, educate yourself about the concerns and issues unique to preservation by doing some reading and research. You can contact your state's historical preservation office on how to proceed or refer to the technical preservation bulletins issued by the National Park Service, which can be obtained from their regional offices. If you aren't comfortable with the obligations of this trusteeship, be reasonable and don't buy the house. There is no shortage of quaint, charming, antebellum farmhouses and Victorian townhouses perfectly ripe for renovation without destroying an irreplaceable heirloom.

Renovation

Because renovation presupposes that one is free to adapt the old to the new, to preserve or uncover the spirit while changing the form to suit personal needs, the mere mention of the word is enough to raise the hackles of preservationists. Living in a restored house is a little like collecting antiques or old bottles, which, whatever their merits, can be carried to extremes.

It's a question of personality, I suppose, whether one wishes to live in a museum. The restored house ignores those elements of antique design that may be impractical or unsuitable to modern living. For example, even though an earthen cellar floor may be historically important, it is a prime cause of excessive household humidity and structural rot. Likewise, few people would be willing to sacrifice the comfort and convenience of central heating, adequate insulation, or modern electrical systems for historical authenticity.

Renovators are not afraid to make changes. Whereas a preservationist might insist that broad expanses of decayed original plaster be repaired or restored with new material mixed and applied according to traditional recipes and finishes, a renovator would more likely remove the plaster entirely, replacing it with modern materials that would more or less duplicate the original texture. Likewise, a renovator would suffer no qualms over installing thermally efficient modern windows (as long as they duplicated the look or feel of the original sashes) or from sanding and then refinishing old floorboards with polyurethane varnish instead of the original shellac. Removing interior walls to open up a cramped, confining floor plan or adding a dormer to a low attic ceiling would not automatically be problematic.

For a renovator, a house is never a monument, never fixed in time. In this respect, at least, the modern owner is carrying on the tradition of the previous owners who, adding and subtracting new wings, porches, walls, and windows, worked to adapt the house to their needs and circumstances. But as you contemplate these revisions, you must never forget that, even though an unexceptional old house may not contain historically important features, it usually does contain some exceptionally fine and beautiful antique fittings and fixtures whose loss through rampant and indiscriminate renovation would be both regrettable and unnecessary.

The difference between renovation and preservation, and the root of much internecine conflict, is that the latter is precise, a science, if you will, whereas the former is poetic—and dangerously indeterminate. Because preservationists must observe the canons of historical fidelity, stylistic options and the very real potential for historical home-icide are limited. But the problem with renovation is that it's one thing to admonish a homeowner not to do violence to the spirit of an old house in the rush to change it and another to define exactly what that means and how to accomplish it. How does one divine the spirit of a place before disturbing its bones? How do the new owners listen to the heartbeat of the house and match their own to it? The very vagueness of the words renovators use to describe their approach is infuriating. They are meaningless to anyone who isn't already receptive to such a way of thinking, to those who don't already speak the language.

The most instructive examples of sensitive renovation are necessarily negative. Somehow, examples of what one shouldn't do seem better able to suggest what one should do. *The Old-House Journal* features monthly photos of "remuddling" that are especially egregious examples of insensitive and clumsy architectural faux pas. Additions (and subtractions) are perhaps the most common offenses. Vinyl siding does not mate well with Federal-style brick. Porches, not decks, belong on the front of farmhouses; if you must have a deck, put it on the back of the house where it can't be seen from the road. Although solariums and greenhouses were a common feature of elegant Victorian mansions, adding a contemporary sunroom to an old house without having it appearing tacked on is not easy.

Matching the trim is a key element of success for any addition. Even without the full-blown gingerbread fretwork of the high Victorian or

A remodeler might replace this period wall-mount lavatory and lighted mirror with a modern vanity and valence light, thereby sacrificing authenticity and character to convenience. An old house with intact original plumbing and lighting fixtures is a bonus. Reproductions can be costly.

This nineteenth-century village home has been disastrously compromised by insensitive remodeling. The new windows are shockingly disproportionate. Removal of the original front porch heightens the imbalance, while the cheap aluminum storm door, cinder block steps, and vinyl siding manage to destroy any surviving shreds of aesthetic integrity.

A case of particularly egregious remuddling: There has to be a better solution to the problem of providing wheelchair access than this singularly infelicitous shed-roofed entry with its sloping blank wall. Granted, a gable-roofed ell would have been much more costly; but it would not have trashed the facade of this 1860s farmhouse.

Gothic style, the cornices of a simple rustic farmhouse are much more complex than modern style dictates. Nevertheless, failure to carry existing detailing over to new work because it costs too much guarantees an aesthetic abomination. Replacement windows that don't match the historical style of the original house are another frequently bungled area.

Rehabilitation, which is the adaptation of a structure for a purpose (typically commercial) different from that for which it was originally intended, is the radical wing of renovation. It's also an excellent example of recycling. Buildings that otherwise would be economically unusable and slated for demolition can be put to other profitable and even pleasing uses. A dilapidated factory block becomes a key element in a revitalized city core when it is reincarnated as a shopping mall or low- or middle-income housing.

Remodeling

Remodelers don't believe in ghosts. Depending on their sensitivity, or lack of it, remodelers will not hesitate to gut the entire house at the first sign of a bulge in the ceiling and wrap every available surface in drywall and texture paint. Because the object is to standardize materials and methods, maximize profit, and eliminate variables, a remodeler's tool of choice is invariably the wrecking bar. Remodelers are seduced by the advertising industry, which markets the images that fuel the successive waves of modernization that have caused the literal vandalizing of countless old homes. Like most products of mass culture, the fashions of remodeling have proved ephemeral. Who today would panel their rec rooms with knotty pine? Does anyone still cover the insides of their houses with barn boards?

I confess my sympathies lie somewhere between liberal preservation and conservative renovation. Except for those few houses in which a plaster ceiling is distinguished by ornamental medallions and cornice castings of historical value, which are worthy of professional restoration, my feeling about old (unsound) plaster, for example, is to replace it rather than repair it. And, given the cost of traditional wet-wall plastering, I'm willing to accept drywall as a substitute.

But I'm not one to lose sleep over strict historical verisimilitude: For example, I wouldn't object to 1930s light fixtures in a 1900 home (but I would definitely take out the 1960s swag light over the kitchen table.) All kinds of anachronistic juxtapositions occur naturally in the life of old houses and, within reason, are a good part of their charm. Although I agree with the need for preserving truly historical houses both out of simple respect for the past and as objects of study, how many of them are needed is an open question. There are many places (such as Colonial Williamsburg) that provide living examples of the evolution of public and domestic buildings. Every town has a historical society that encourages the recognition and preservation of old houses. Special zoning designations and tax incentives can also prevent the depletion of traditional styles, at least for exterior facades. All these preservation and rehabilitation trends should be nourished, if only for the sake of raising general historical awareness.

But people need places to live. And, as they have always done, people will change their houses as they live in them. Outside of a costume party or stage play, we don't wear whalebone corsets or waistcoats anymore. Likewise, I don't think we should be forced to fit into houses that no longer suit the modes of a less formal age

Like it or not, it's not possible to legislate good taste or mandate that only appropriately sensitive individuals be entrusted with the ownership of historic homes. A pluralistic and highly commercialized society shares no cultural consensus on what a house should look like or, even more important, on the value of the past and the desirability of preserving its vessels. There is some consolation in the fact that at least older houses are being recycled rather than left to fall down, uninhabited and pristine examples of historical architecture.

A MANUFACTURER'S WARNING AND LIMITED WARRANTY

Some people might feel that this is a dangerous book. The information it contains is powerful stuff. It's possible someone who is not in tune with a preservation or sensitive renovation philosophy, following the letter of the methods but ignoring the spirit, could damage some significant part of our architectural heritage. Although my book will help professionals and amateurs alike decide what, when, and how to deal with the many problems unique to preserving or renovating an old house, it can't do anything more

Camps are the second homes of the working class, typically built with the cheapest materials and shoddiest methods; they are usually uninsulated and lack any real foundations. This row of generic camps cannot be hurt by extensive remodeling—this is a good example of how a handyman's special can form the nucleus of a sound house.

Better that this unusual Greek Revival had fallen into the hands of a remodeler than succumb to neglect.

than try to make people aware of the special responsibilities that come with old-house ownership. I believe that a course of sensitive renovation offers the least harmful and most economical and emotionally satisfying cure for the ills of most old houses—most of the time. I hope the cautions expressed here and in the following chapters will alert the reader to cases that deserve heroic measures. Please, before you pick up the wrecking bar, take the time to research the history of your house or hire a professional to do it for you. You'll want your ghosts to join comfortably with the community that stays behind after you pass through.

Old Houses Are Idiosyncratic

The information presented in this book is powerful because it is specific to old houses. There are guidebooks on every aspect of the building trade, but there is very little actual crossover between the methodology and mindset of new construction and that of renovation. Most standard instruction is predicated on ideal situations, where wood is uniform in thickness, walls are square, doors are plumb, and foundations are firm. This may not seem all that important until you try to fit a rectangular sheet of plywood into a trapezoidal corner.

In new work, the craftsperson proceeds in logical and rectilinear order. The actual work is relatively simple and even resembles the clear line drawings in the textbooks. The order of an old house is not that coherent. Not only must you deal with someone else's mistakes but you'll confront large imponderables and unsolvable dilemmas as well. Houses a century or more old typically feature a heavy-timber post-and-beam frame that is as individual and arbitrary as its builders. Beyond that, an old house settles and shifts through years of use, and often abuse, into a totally idiosyncratic entity. Walls lean, floors sag, major beams are rotted or missing. Any existing mechanical systems or insulation are at best inadequate. There may be a logic underlying the

Renovation is often a matter of dealing with the consequences of neglect. There are certainly plenty of them showing on the outside of this old farmhouse.

carpenter's nightmare of crumbling walls and patchwork roofing, but it has to be teased out.

What You'll Need

Fortunately, you don't have to be a structural detective or an accomplished carpenter to rebuild your old house. With a little help from an occasional professional and a lot of reading, you can learn as you go, matching your skills to the job, stretching your abilities to the task. I do presuppose a familiarity with tools and a working knowledge of basic carpentry. I also presuppose that you have the determination to tackle some difficult and tedious jobs for the simple satisfaction of their completion.

Renovation demands inordinate amounts of perseverance for what may seem to be nebulous rewards. It's a good thing that we seldom realize just how difficult the job can be; otherwise, we might prudently turn aside and thereby miss the opportunity to test our mettle. For these reasons, I'll also attempt to chart the psychic waters of the renovation process, waters that are seldom clear or calm. Many a marriage, many a self-image, has run aground on the rocks of rebuilding. All too often, homeowners are caught in a whirlpool of obsession, and the work at hand becomes more important than the reason it is being done. You'll have to keep a firm hand on the tiller of self as you run this passage.

What We'll Cover

Although the information in this book is based on my experiences in rural northern New England, it is nevertheless applicable to older houses in just about any region of the country. The rural focus is not meant to be exclusive. Indeed, in many areas, since the available stock of classic farmhouses is just about used up, what's left tends to be expensive. Fortunately, not everyone wants to live back in the "pucker-bush," so village and suburban homes are increasingly attractive candidates for renovation.

Wood-frame structures also make up a large part of the housing stock in smaller cities. And, in many big cities, formerly abandoned historic brownstones are now at the forefront of a back-to-the-ghetto land rush. Blighted urban war zones are rapidly being converted into fashionable neighborhoods. Without becoming embroiled in the politics of gentrification, I would say that these areas offer great opportunities to the potential renovator, especially one who buys before the development wave gathers momentum. But those who are rebuilding houses in the cities or suburbs may have to contend with problems of a bureaucratic nature that we rustics are not yet cursed with. In fact, local ordinances and mortgage lenders may effectively bar anyone but licensed contractors from doing

Wood-frame houses in villages and small cities are often prime candidates for affordable renovation.

This Victorian home is impeccably renovated. (Photo by Jane L. Waterman)

any renovation work at all. In such cases, the information in this book will at least allow you to evaluate a prospective purchase, outline the scope of the work, and help you communicate with your contractor.

In all modesty, even this book won't answer all your questions. My aim is to arm you with a conceptual understanding enhanced with sufficient, but by no means exhaustive, detail, so that you can avoid getting into serious trouble. Sometimes, the best hands-on approach is a little hand holding. Fortunately, there is also a large body of knowledge that is part of the oral and manual tradition, learned by and passed on

through generations of carpenters. A goodly part of it is totally contradictory, being based on the personal experience of whomever you might be talking to at the moment.

Each situation requires its own strategy. This is particularly true in rural areas where old houses have been continually propped up and patched together by their inhabitants, who are often making do with the place their great-grandfather's father hewed the beams for. Just about any old country carpenter knows something about the problems of preserving houses and barns from the ravages of difficult weather and hard years; he's had to do it on his own place or the neighbor's. That this pool of knowledge has remained largely inaccessible to the novice builder is no surprise; it is unknown to more than a few modern trade-school carpenters as well. These old-timers are still very much alive, working back in the hills where time shambles along like a tired horse on a dusty summer road. By asking around, you might find someone who's done it before or has a fair idea of how to go about doing whatever it is that needs to be done.

I know a fellow who is a bridge between two cultures, a dairy farmer starved out of farming who turned to carpentry, father of eight children, who in his own words was "born too late for a big family and too early for birth control." As a young man he owned five hundred acres of prime farmland. Now he owns a house on a village lot. The rest he sold off to a succession of wealthy newcomers from down country, whose houses he built. What makes him so special is his keen awareness of what he has lost. It is a thing you can almost touch, an aura that provides an eerie counterpoint to the humor with which he customarily faces the world about him.

We were wondering once how things had come to such a state, and he told me how people got by in his father's time. They didn't have much, but they didn't need much either. They always seemed to have enough. But when the boys came back from the wars, they brought with them the itch to have some of those things they had seen out there. It was easy to sell a few cows and make a payment on the new pickup truck, the television set. The things his father had valued just didn't seem that important anymore. One by one, they left the farm for the big money and easy life in construction. Once they got a taste of it, by God, they were bound and determined to spend it. What they couldn't see was that they were spending their heritage, their spiritual capital, as well. Once started, things

seemed to run in one direction only. More and more, the old ways were tossed aside and simply forgotten like the rubbish heap at the edge of the sugar woods.

Old houses are a bit like my old friend, tossed aside and forgotten. They are a bridge between the ways of what seems to us a slower and more harmonious time and our own shallow frenzy. In some ways, too, I hope this book is a bridge between these cultures. The renovation of old houses is more than an investment, more than a handyman's challenge or a shortcut to home ownership. It is a spiritual undertaking as well.

In closing, I offer a thought from John F. Kelly's classic treatise *Early Domestic Architecture of Connecticut* (Dover, 1963), as one answer to the question that opened this book.

Consciously or unconsciously, man looks with satisfaction upon that which is substantially and enduringly built. It is primarily, or at least largely, this sense of sheer structural value which makes us admire the pyramids, the temples of Greece, the mighty cathedrals of the thirteenth century. The same instinct infallibly communicates to every observer, even the most casual, the bluff and rugged strength of our old houses; and he who knows these ancient dwellings more intimately, perhaps through having been fortunate enough to live in one of them, is keenly and sensitively responsive to the security, the abundance of strength which they embody.

The sensitive renovator will always strive to preserve the hard-won character of an old house while balancing the need for changes that will ensure its utility for the present generation. The best treatment for this mudroom might be to leave it alone.

Evaluating a House before You Buy

*"Do you see, Pooh? Do you see, Piglet? Brains first and then Hard Work.
Look at it! That's the way to build a house" said Eeyore proudly.*

—A. A. MILNE, *THE HOUSE AT POOH CORNER*

The dividing line between a diamond-in-the-rough and a broken-down wreck is not always easy to
discern and not in any way absolute or even particularly useful. Whether a house is worth "saving" or
not often depends more on the vision and quirks of its owner than on any clear structural mandate.

I remember quite well that leaden April morning, the front end of our ancient van clanking in protest as we climbed the steep washboard road through the forest, where stale snow still clung to the dark places, climbed to where the woods shrank back from the dull, matted fields to reveal the ridges rolling away to the mountains at the end of the valley, like some moldering purple blanket that had lain out by the garden all winter. And there it sat, at the end of a sparsely graveled drive, dwarfed by a pair of towering cottonwoods.

The clapboards had weathered to a filigree of grain and fissure, which to us seemed the purest distillation of poetry. The front of the house leaned opposite of the back, the dormer slouched, and even from a distance we could see that the chimney was crumbled. The porch quivered uneasily underfoot as we pushed our way into the kitchen, where plaster hung from the ceiling in leprous patches of decay. The floors tilted through so many planes, we began to feel seasick. There was at least 2 ft of water in the basement, and a portion of the foundation wall (made of loose stones) had tumbled inward. We bought the house that very day, for what seemed to us quite a bargain price—the very first place we saw, the very first day we went looking. And 30 years and many thousands of dollars later, I'm quite sure it could happen again. But this time, I'd know better what price to offer the real-estate agent.

WHERE TO BEGIN

Some places are just *there*. In all the universe, at that moment this is your particular place. No amount of rational temporizing will change the destiny that has already begun to unfold. There is some deep congruence between your innermost self and the molecules of the old house. You have no choice but to buy the place. You were meant for each other. On the surface of your mind, you tell yourself the obvious, that the place is in terrible shape, it needs way too much work, only a fool would buy it, but within, you are already setting out the window boxes on the sills, and the tea kettle is singing on the stove.

Just about any old house has the power to perturb the spirit, but not always on your personal frequency. You'll need some sort of filtering device to weed out all but the strongest vibrations. It's a commonplace that a marriage needs more than the first flush of passion to sustain itself. Likewise, even if it's love at first sight, you shouldn't buy an old house without conducting a thorough investigation, even into its most uninviting corners. At least then you'll know the extent of the work that lies ahead and whether it's an ordeal you wish to undertake. But how do you do this?

Most books about buying old houses advocate a checklist of some sort, the idea being that if enough items appear on the wrong side of the list, you should look for another place. Such checklists are undeniably useful (I offer one myself at the end of this chapter). But, according to most of these schemata, a house with major structural defects, such as a cracked or heaved-in foundation, rotted sills, or leaning and bowed walls, is immediately disqualified from further consideration. Although it's true that these kinds of defects call for expensive and time-consuming repairs, I don't agree that they necessarily rule out purchase. Instead, they might serve as a bargaining chip when negotiating the price.

Is It Worth Saving?

Any house can be fixed if you spend enough time and money, but unless you are one of those people who have more dollars than sense, you should know the difference between problems so bad they make renovation unfeasible and problems that are formidable but worth the effort. That said, unless a house has actually started to collapse or its frame has rotted to powder or been digested by termites, there is rarely an old house so derelict that it isn't worth saving. This is especially so when an owner substitutes sweat equity for contracted labor.

The great divide of structural evaluation falls on the line between the absolute and the optional, the distinction between structural repairs that must be done to preserve the integrity of the house or, indeed, make it minimally habitable and cosmetic renovations that can be done as circumstances permit. But there are degrees of urgency even within the absolute category. For example, you could live with a poor foundation or rotting sills for several years, but a defunct furnace, inadequate water system, or badly leaking roof requires immediate attention.

Except in very unusual cases, most structural defects are not life threatening, nor do they rule out interim habitation until repairs are complete. After all, unless the place has been long abandoned, another family was living in it just before you showed up. Problems that are immediately obvious even to the untrained eye are the raison d'être of the handyman's special. The information and checklist in this chapter help you find the less obvious but often more significant defects, perhaps allowing you to bargain the price down to what you can afford. The subsequent chapters guide you in planning and doing the actual repairs. Learning to discriminate between merely cosmetic and truly critical problems helps you decide whether your infatuation with any particular house has a chance of maturing into a successful and satisfying long-term relationship.

INSPECTING THE EXTERIOR

Your evaluation should always begin with the exterior of the house. Stand back some distance and look at its shape. Sight along the ridgeline of the roof. Does it sag noticeably in the middle or is it straight? Do the eaves hump upward or curve outward? Then step in closer and sight down the walls. Do they bow, dip, or hump? Do the end walls lean, or do the corners appear to tilt?

A house is a physics equation writ large in a script of stone and wood. Essentially, its frame is a series of interconnected triangles. The stability of the house structure depends on maintaining the integrity of each corner angle. In structural terms, this translates into proper bracing and the uniform transfer of internal and external stresses.

The dip in the line of the attached shed shows foundation settlement.

The curves in this roofline show that the underlying framing is too light and the pitch is too low to withstand the heavy snow loads of local winters.

Dating an Old House

Every old house is an anthology of stories, an intriguing mix of documentary fact and occasional fiction. Learning to read these stories can be an enjoyable pursuit that increases the pride of ownership and the sense of historical continuity.

The question that is foremost, of course, is "When was it built?" Sometimes the answer is on the disclosure statement. The date of the construction may have already been established or researched by the previous owner. Even so, you may wish to delve beyond the surface to discover the name of the original owner and his or her descendants or perhaps the name of the architect or builder if you suspect historical stature, to learn the history of changes and additions to the shape of the house.

Even without its massively columned pediment, the extreme symmetry of the facade identifies this magnificent house as an example of the Greek Revival style that swept the country from the 1820s to the 1840s.

The barge board detailing and tall narrow windows at the roof rakes are hallmarks of the Carpenter Gothic style that was popular from the 1840s until the late 1860s.

While a whiff of the late Gothic period persists in the steeply pitched gable roof, the elaborate, almost Italianate detailing of the cornices and the decorative shingle siding mark this house as Late Victorian (c. 1880–1890s).

Beginning in the 1890s and lasting through the 1920s there was a revulsion against the perceived excesses of the Victorian style. This change in taste expressed itself in various "revival" styles and, most famously, in the Craftsman style. This house is an amalgam of Tudor Revival and Craftsman elements: The half-timbered dormer gable is Tudor Revival and the prominent front porch, low bungalow-type roof, and exposed rafter tails are hallmarks of the Craftsman style.

When the old house is located in a rural village, a first, although not necessarily most reliable, source of background information is the neighbors or perhaps the previous owners. The old-timer next door may not only recite the lineage of the house's inhabitants back to the beginning but also regale you with tales of their foibles and feuds. If there are any skeletons in the closets, they'll be set to dancing. Of course, there's always the likelihood that this history is actually the spinnings of local legend, told and retold until worn to seeming truth.

ARCHITECTURAL STYLE

Lacking confirmed documentation, a passing acquaintance with the vocabulary of period architectural styles is sufficient to venture an immediate rough estimate. Most people can distinguish a seventeenth-, eighteenth-, and nineteenth-century house with a roadside glance. Beyond this, it gets confusing.

Architectural historians have variously divided the evolution of the American home into about a half dozen major periods of roughly a half century each. These large brackets are more

This eclectic, more or less Shingle-style cottage incorporates a potpourri of stylistic elements typical of the first quarter of the twentieth century.

ognized. Although there's no need to master the pedantic minutiae of architectural history, there is pleasure in looking at old houses with an educated eye. This is reason enough to study one of the many illustrated taxonomies of domestic architec-

This running crack occurred because there is no steel lintel over the cellar window, not because of foundation settlement. The discolored mortar joints are evidence of a fruitless repair of an earlier crack. The crack below the cellar window is a surface crack in the stucco veneer most likely caused by moisture penetration from the wood window frame.

The triangle of the roof is lifted above the earth by walls that are joined to the ground through the foundation. The frame, however, is not seamless, being broken by joints and fasteners, but the forces that operate on it are; thus stresses can concentrate at any number of structurally weak points. These places act as hinges, causing failure. Furthermore, the house rests on a foundation that ideally distributes its weight on the ground equably. All too often, portions of the foundation settle or shift more than others, and the house frame naturally follows suit. Rotted sill beams have the same effect as settled foundations.

Deformation of the frame, either through foundation settlement or failure of structural members, disrupts the balance, causing the house to lean, bend, or sag. The effect is amplified throughout the structure, as unbalanced loads try to reestablish a new equilibrium.

In a masonry structure (which has no frame and no give), the results of foundation settlement are immediately obvious: A stepped crack in the brickwork running the height of the wall is a potentially serious problem. In a wood-framed house, shifts of the frame and foundation are telegraphed through the skin of the walls, where the effects can be seen in the finish siding, like the swelling of a broken bone. Because a wood frame is flexible, these defects may not be obvious at first glance. The subtle warnings of bows and sags can be overlooked in the excitement of an initial favorable impression. Nevertheless, if the failure is not repaired or further settlement arrested, the static equilibrium of the structure will continue to decay, and the condition will gradually worsen. As the house inexorably moves from the vertical toward the

A Square and Level House Is a Sound House

A house frame is made of triangles. No triangle leg can lengthen or shorten unless another breaks.

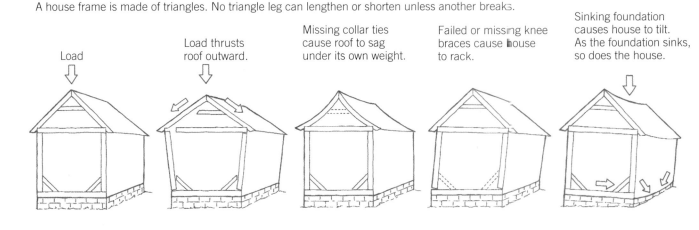

Load

Load thrusts roof outward.

Missing collar ties cause roof to sag under its own weight.

Failed or missing knee braces cause house to rack.

Sinking foundation causes house to tilt. As the foundation sinks, so does the house.

horizontal, a critical point is reached, and the triumph of gravity is realized in a moment of sudden collapse. Your house is likely to be somewhere along this curve of accelerating decline. Reversing the direction is a question of knowing where and how hard to push.

Checking for Square and Level

The drawing on the facing page shows how racking forces operating on a house can lead to its collapse. The point is that a square and level house is a sound house: The roofline should be straight, the corners should appear to line up with each other and look vertical when you sight down along the walls. The walls themselves should inhabit a single plane; bows, sags, and other free-form curves are sure signs of structural failure. Because clapboards or wood shingles were originally installed level, their present orientation clearly reveals hidden problem areas. The lines can also reveal a history of structural changes. For example, when a window appears level but is not parallel with the clapboards, it

has to be a later addition, installed after that section of the building settled.

What hidden problems do these tilting clapboards, leaning walls, and sagging rooflines manifest? As mentioned earlier, something has to give before things start to move. Because there is a fair amount of play in a braced timber frame, over a long enough time such houses tend to lean away from the direction of the prevailing winds. Sometimes structural beams or joists were cut, improperly notched, or even removed during a bout of careless earlier remodeling. The installation of indoor plumbing or the demolition of a fireplace is often the culprit in such cases of home-icide. Sometimes entire bearing walls have been removed or windows have been cut into walls without providing the requisite support.

Chronic seepage from a leaking roof, rotted flashing, or backed-up gutters can rot the beams that support the rafters—when these pull apart, the entire house is twisted by the misplaced load. Sometimes the framing is simply not strong enough to withstand the weight of the

The art of structural evaluation requires an ability to read the lines of a building. Here, the bowed facade and skewed clapboards are signs of structural trouble.

The gaps between these clapboards and at the window casing are signs of serious foundation settlement.

years. Or the addition of a second story, too many layers of old roofing, a heavy cast-iron bathtub, or even a waterbed adds the unbearable one straw too many. Finally, just because a house is old is no guarantee that it was well built.

Obvious Foundation Problems

Although final confirmation must wait until you inspect the cellar, now is a good time to check the exposed part of the foundation wall for cracks and other signs of settlement. The wall should not bow out or in from the line of the building. Bulkheads or cellar entries are common trouble spots. Unless properly footed to prevent frost damage, these walls can push the main foundation wall in. Dry-laid or mortared stone walls and granite slab walls should be sound, with no obvious gaps, or loose or fallen stones. The ground should slope away from the walls, and downspouts should not empty directly against them. Otherwise, water will flow back

Even a rather innocuous crack can lead to serious problems over time. Water has been seeping into the wall and will eventually undermine it. The vines trap moisture against the siding, fostering rot. Invading the crevices between the foundation stones, they will eventually dislodge the stones.

The grade was sloped down to make headroom for a cellar entry, but the foundation itself was not deepened. Frost heave has cracked the mortar joints between the stones.

Frost heave in saturated soil (lacking a gutter, the roof runoff falls next to the wall) is slowly pushing this granite ashlar wall into the cellar.

against the foundation where it can seep into the cellar, undermine the footings, or freeze and push against the wall. Minor regrading can be done with a shovel and wheelbarrow, but anything more extensive calls for heavy machinery. While you're at it, check for the presence of window wells: These are typically the source of water-related foundation problems. Even when well above grade, cellar vent windows, framed before the availability of preservative-treated wood, are most likely to be decayed and in need of replacement.

Checking for Termites

If you live in the northern tier or Rocky Mountain states, termite infestation will not be a problem, but in most other areas of the country these insects are a serious threat to structural integrity. Examine the foundation carefully for the characteristic earthen tubes that these insects build from the soil up the foundation walls to edible wood. (The actual infestation will be hidden within the walls, safe from casual detection.)

Unlike the common *subterranean termite*, which nests in the soil and forages only in your woodwork, the *drywood termite*, a species native to southern California, Arizona, and Florida, both nests and feeds in wood and so leaves no telltale soil tube. Instead look for accumulations of tiny (1/25 in.) hard fecal pellets on surfaces or entrance holes covered by a thin brownish seal. Also suspect any areas where wood structure is in direct contact with the soil or less than the required 8 in. above it or where wood is otherwise constantly damp. Such areas can also conceal an infestation of *dampwood termites*. Because this species leaves no tubes or detritus, the best protection and control is to keep wood from getting soaked in the first place. Where termites are endemic, ask for a certificate of termite inspection before you sign any sales agreement.

All wood siding should be at least 8 in. above grade. In direct contact with the ground, these shingles have rotted away. So has the underlying sill, causing the building to settle, exposing more shingles and wall structure to rot.

Checking for Ants, Bees, and Beetles

Northerners are not entirely secure from the threat of wood-chewing insects. Carpenter ants belie their name; they excavate long galleries and nests along the grain of wood sills and joists. These large black ants (1/4 in. to 3/4 in. long) need moist wood to survive, so infestations are likely wherever water is held against a wall, as, for example, under a porch pillar, behind a ledger, at a leaking pipe penetration, or where wood is in direct contact with earth. Because moisture also tends to collect in cracks where several timbers join together, nests are often found in these hard-to-repair places.

The ants can usually be seen entering and leaving their tunnels on foraging expeditions. Piles of coarse sawdust (frass) are also a sign of their handiwork. Fortunately, ant infestations are a lot easier to control than termites and usually a lot less damaging. Drying up the source

Moisture trapped between a porch railing post (at left of door) and the siding boards allowed the initial entry of carpenter ants. Once the ants reached the heavy timber sill under the threshold, they riddled it with galleries until only a thin tissue of timber remained.

of the moisture is the first step. Poisoning the queen is the second.

Carpenter bees are big bumblebees (about the size of a licorice lozenge) that bore through siding boards to nest behind the walls. They need a big door to accommodate their bulk. Look for entrance holes about ⅜ in. in diameter. These bees can become very aggressive when defending their nest, a fact you are likely to discover when you remove clapboards or old trim that conceal their lair. Fortunately, unlike honeybees, the colonies are sparsely settled. They are easily eradicated by spraying ordinary wasp killer aerosol into the nest opening. Wait until early evening when all the bees are sure to have turned in for the night.

The name *powder-post beetle* is commonly applied to several species of wood-boring insects. Open-pored hardwoods like oak, ash, and hickory are vulnerable to attack by *lyctid beetles*. The larvae eat their way through the wood, depositing a fine floury frass on the surface, while the egg-laying adults pepper it with tiny (¹⁄₃₂-in. to ¹⁄₁₆-in.) exit holes. Besides the oaken beams of colonial-era timber frames, lyctid beetles have a taste for furniture, flooring, and paneling.

Anobiid beetles tunnel through both softwoods and hardwoods, exhuming frass and pellets through ¹⁄₁₆-in. to ⅛-in. holes. The condition of the frass indicates whether the infestation is active or has died out. Yellowed, caked frass means an inactive infestation; light-colored powdery frass is a sign of an active one.

Increasing ventilation or fixing plumbing leaks to reduce the moisture content of the affected wood, especially in dank cellars, can sometimes control infestations of both types of beetles. Stripping the bark left on half-round log floor joists will also deprive borers of their shelter. Failing this, professional whole-house fumigation with extremely nasty chemicals is the last resort. If you see obvious signs of widespread and current insect activity, find another house or at least have a professional pest inspection done to determine the severity of the problem before you sign a sales contract.

Structural Decay

Even more than insects, wood-digesting fungi are responsible for structural decay in every area of the country. Unfortunately, rotted beams or sills aren't normally visible from the outside of the house. If there is enough sound wood left to support the framing above (when less than half the thickness of a sill has rotted), the damaged portions can be hacked out and filled in with new wood. Where sections have collapsed or crumbled away, causing settlement of the structure above, sill replacement is a must. Sills under thresholds are especially prone to rot. So are walls behind steps, junctions between porch roofs and house walls, and any other place chronically exposed to water and snow. Fortunately, repairing such localized decay, although tedious, does not require a great outlay of materials and is not especially difficult.

Decaying exterior siding is a danger sign; there's a good chance that the underlying sheathing and the sills are at least partially affected.

The design of this inset entry left the threshold particularly vulnerable to moisture. The ensuing rot destroyed the underlying sill beam. The angled door bottom reflects the wall settlement.

Watch Out for Buttress Walls

In an attempt to shore up a heaved wall or to prevent surface water and wind infiltration, builders of an earlier generation would sometimes pour a sloped concrete wall directly against the old stone foundation. Because these "buttress" walls seldom extended more than a few inches below grade, they were usually pushed up by frost action, taking the wall stones with them. (Dig down the face of the wall with a hand shovel to establish the wall's depth.) Even worse, the concrete was typically poured right up against the siding. A more ideal incubator for rot than the unprotected joint between mortar and wood is hard to imagine.

Any foundation featuring this kind of wall is immediately suspect. Probe the siding boards with an ice pick to test for soundness. If the pick penetrates the boards easily, sill replacement is almost certainly necessary.

Seen through a telephoto lens, this chimney is in bad shape. So is the flashing that should seal the areas where it meets the roof.

In cold climates, antique lime mortar tends to weather faster on the north side of the chimney. Over time, the chimney can develop a pronounced lean. (Photo by Jane L. Waterman)

The Chimney

If the lines of the house look straight, the sills intact, and the foundation solid, the house is probably structurally sound. The chimney is the only other significant (translation: expensive) structural problem you are likely to encounter. At the very least, any chimney should project at least 2 ft. above the ridge of the roof and any roof or overhanging trees within 10 ft. of it. A stubby chimney will draw poorly and be subject to downdrafting. Use a telephoto lens or binoculars to conduct a close-up investigation without clambering onto the roof.

Look for the obvious signs of decay: a noticeable lean, large cracks, missing or broken bricks, voids in the mortar, a missing or deteriorated cap. The portion of the chimney exposed to the weather above the roofline usually falls apart long before the rest. Sometimes the entire chimney will be unsafe. Note the condition of the flashing where the chimney penetrates the roof. Try to see if it has a clay tile flue liner, which is

required by code and common sense. The liner should project an inch or two above the mortar or brickwork cap. The size of the chimney can indicate the presence of a liner. If the chimney has only four bricks per course, it is definitely unlined. The smallest flue liner (8 in. by 8 in.) requires at least six-brick coursing. But many unlined chimneys also have six-brick coursing.

Because the safety of the chimney depends on the integrity of its flues, your initial from-the-ground inspection should be augmented by an internal exam. You'll need to peer down into the chimney from the roof or up into it from the cellar or fireplace (see chapter 12). Unless you know for certain that the chimney was cleaned by a professional chimneysweep after the last heating season, plan to have it done before you fire up the furnace. A reliable sweep will also inspect your chimney and give you a written report on its condition. If the chimney fails to meet code and the repairs needed to bring it into compliance are extensive, it will have to be torn down and rebuilt or retrofitted with a stainless-steel or proprietary concrete flue liner. Except for relining a straight-run flue with stainless-steel pipe, this isn't a job for the do-it-yourselfer.

The Roof

While looking up at the chimney, note the condition of the roof. First, ascertain the type of roofing material. If it's asphalt shingles, try to count how many layers of old shingles the roof is carrying. If it's just one, you could lay new roofing directly atop the old. But adding another layer of shingles to a roof already carrying two or three layers of asphalt can overload the rafters and cause the roof to sag. (Your local building code may prohibit laying new shingles over more than one existing layer anyway.)

ASPHALT SHINGLES Asphalt roofing has a relatively short life, particularly in harsh climates. Despite manufacturers' warranties that range from 20 years to 30 years, the Insurance Institute for Property Loss Prevention (IIPLP) assigns asphalt shingles a 17-year average life span.

Signs that a roof has outlived its useful life span (not counting leaks, of course) include shingles worn so thin they've lost their protective mineral surface, wood or tarpaper showing between the cutouts, large areas of cracked and buckled shingles, and numerous patches and tarred-over spots. Unless the house has been reroofed within the last 15 years, you can expect to do so within the next few. And if a leaking roof has been haphazardly patched or ignored for a long time, expect to replace rotten roof boards as well as shingles. Stripping and replacing asphalt-shingle roofing is a job you can readily do yourself. The materials themselves are relatively inexpensive (about $40 per 100 sq. ft. of coverage for standard-grade three-tab shingles, underlayment, drip edge, and nails) and the labor, while physically demanding, isn't especially difficult.

Shingles last and stay watertight longer on a steeply pitched roof. The shingles on this mansard roof will typically outlast the shingles on the flatter roof above. They are certainly in better shape than the paint and the surrounding trim boards.

WOOD SHINGLES Wood shingles and shakes in need of replacement will appear crumbly, with many splits in individual shingles. In shady areas under tree canopies, colonies of moss and lichen on wood shingles hold water and promote decay. The only difference between replacement of wood and asphalt shingles is that wood shingles are both more expensive and more labor intensive to apply.

SLATE SHINGLES Although slate roofing lasts a very long time, it eventually erodes (acid rain hastens the process). Individual slates fall or break long before the entire roof requires replacement. Also, except for copper or lead, flashing metals like galvanized steel corrode much faster than slate weathers. Minor repairs to a slate roof, although a bit tricky, are not so difficult as to be beyond the skills of the homeowner. The same general considerations also apply to tile and cement-shingle roofs.

METAL ROOFING   There are two problems that all metal roofs share: leaking seams and corrosion. As sheets of corrugated-steel roofing constantly contract and expand with changes in temperature, the nails that hold them to the roof are pulled up. With standing-seam or soldered sheet-metal roofs, the seams can split or pull apart. Galvanized steel eventually rusts. *Terne metal* (lead-copper alloy-coated steel) and tin-coated steel roofing must be kept painted to last. Rusted but still-sound galvanized-steel roofing can be restored to years of useful life if it's brushed clean and given a coat of asphalt- or metallic-based roof paint. However, asphalt-based coatings will hasten, rather than retard, corrosion on standing-seam or soldered flat-seam metal roofing. These must be repainted with a rust-inhibiting metal enamel or red lead paint. Replacement of standing- or flat-seam metal roofing is expensive and must be done by skilled professionals.

With your telescopic lens, make an initial assessment of the associated metalwork. This includes evaluating any ornamental cresting and finials; flashing at end walls, eaves, and valleys (where roof slopes intersect); flashing boots at the soil vent stack and other plumbing penetrations; and gutters and downspouts. Improperly installed or failed flashing is a major cause of leaks. Check for missing elements; rust; loose joints and attachments; tears and splits; and cracked rubber, tarred, or leaded seals. Unless the flashing metal is long-lasting (and repairable) copper or lead, plan to replace it when you replace the roofing. Plugging leaks with "black goop" should be used only as a temporary fix to tide you over until such time as you can redo the roof. Asphalt cement patches don't last and look sloppy.

Walls, Windows, and Trim

As you inspect the outside of the house, bear in mind that a fresh coat of paint can be something like an undertaker's cosmetic act: Beneath the neat white clapboards and trim black shutters of that perfectly quaint country cottage, sills are rotting away and water is seeping into walls. An unscrupulous seller can temporarily hide the effects of a leak instead of fixing the problem at its source.

"For lack of a nail the kingdom was lost." Thermal expansion and wind have pried this metal roofing loose, allowing water to sneak behind the rake trim board. If not corrected, the encroaching rot could eventually eat through the entire cornice and into the walls.

Paint that has had a chance to ripen, as it were, can tell you something about conditions within the wall cavities. A properly insulated wall should retard the migration of interior moisture to the outside. Since paint (especially oil-based) film is relatively impermeable, escaping water vapor loosens its bond to the siding and the paint blisters. Repainting won't fix the problem, which is noticeably worse where interior moisture is high (such as in bathrooms).

Look at the siding for traces of painted-over small round plastic or wood plug inserts or regular lines of puttied and patched nail heads, evidencing the removal and reinstallation of a course of clapboards: proof that the wall cavities were blown full of cellulose or fiberglass insulation from the outside. While "blowing blind" isn't especially efficacious (it's almost impossible to find and fill every hidden cavity between the often erratically framed studs of an old house), it's still the fastest and cheapest (and therefore preferred) method of insulation contractors. If no other measures are taken to deal with moisture movement, blowing walls full of insulation can actually hasten their decay. Blistering typically shows up on the outside walls of bathrooms, laundries, and kitchens, where high humidity is endemic.

Blackish mildew stains, greenish blooms of algae or moss, or discrete patches of peeling paint on a wall or around window and door trim are signs of chronic dampness. The source of the moisture should be nearby and obvious. Look for leaking gutters, cornices, or end-wall flashing; open joints or failed caulking; water spilling from an adjacent roof or splashing off the ground; and shrubs or trees growing too close to the foundation. Bare wood that does not have a chance to dry out will soon rot.

A new coat of paint can temporarily hide the rot that has gradually been destroying the clapboard at the base of this wall.

Water and wood don't mix: Roof intersections tend to trap snow and funnel water or backsplash against wood walls and trim. The chronic exposure encourages the growth of mildew and algae, eventually rotting the wood.

THE CORNICE The various elements of decorative trim at the edges of the roof that make up the cornice serve as more than mere embellishment. The eaves (bottom edge of the roof) and the rake overhangs (sides of the roof at the gable end walls) are intended to keep rainwater from running down the walls and against the foundation. Leaking joints or rotted trim allows water to seep in to the walls, where it will cause serious structural damage. Squirrels, birds, bats, and wasps can also sneak into the attic through holes in a rotted cornice. The relative inaccessibility of decorative trim elements ("gingerbread" trim) high up on the rakes and cornice peaks almost guarantees neglect to the point of ruin. The expense and trouble of finding or duplicating

Siding: Repair or Replace?

Even though most of these clapboards are still sound, the building has settled and racked so much that they have been literally torn off the wall. Before they can be repaired or replaced, a new foundation is needed to arrest the movement and lift the bottom edge of the structure above the ground.

Asphalt-composition, cement–asbestos (shown here), aluminum, or vinyl siding may mask a hidden treasure. These materials were often applied directly over the original clapboard siding, which, other than needing a new coat of paint, might still be quite sound.

You can repair a few split clapboards without removing them or replace cracked wood shingles (see p. 212), but it's a pretty tricky job to remove deteriorated clapboards or wood shingles without damaging their immediate neighbors if they are also badly weathered. If the damage is confined to a discrete area (such as the first courses just at the sills or a decayed area where a porch or dormer wall joins the main structure or a wall with a harsher weather exposure), you can replace the siding piecemeal, over time, as budget and circumstance or later alterations allow.

If all the siding is so badly split and warped that you can see through to the underlying sheathing, it's long past its useful life span. Plan on wholesale replacement. Because clapboards are expensive and labor intensive to install, re-siding an entire house is costly, whether you do it yourself or contract it out.

the often-unique patterns of the original woodwork complicate repair or replacement.

Reconstructing a cornice, especially at the return (the junction of rake, eaves, and corner board trim elements) is a demanding and finicky job that requires high-grade, expensive wood. All too often, original exterior trim has been partly or even entirely replaced with a bastardized and slapdash version by insensitive (or insolvent) remodelers or buried beneath vinyl or aluminum siding. Check the soffits (the underside of the cornice) at the eaves for vent openings. Unless retrofitted within the last 30 years of so, chances are, there won't be any. Soffit venting is required to vent an insulated attic properly in all climate zones and to prevent destructive ice

ASPHALT-IMPREGNATED FIBERBOARD SIDING

Be wary of houses clad with "Insulbrick," mineral-surfaced asphalt-impregnated fiberboard panels (16 in. to 24 in. wide and 48 in. long) embossed with a brick or stone pattern. Applied directly over weathered wood siding, this early-twentieth-century siding was marketed as the ultimate in modernity, convenience, and durability. Although a 50-year life span was not uncommon, the siding tended to leak along the seams. The ½-in.-thick vegetable fiber backing can soak up water like a sponge and rot the underlying walls.

CEMENT-ASBESTOS SHINGLES

Throughout the 1930s and 1940s, many houses were clad with cement-asbestos shingles (look for hard grayish, flat or ridged-patterned tiles that are ¼ in. thick and about 1 ft. sq.). Although brittle and vulnerable to impact damage, they're fireproof, freeze–thaw stable, and virtually maintenance free. They'll basically last forever. Individual cracked shingles can be safely repaired or replaced. While these shingles are no longer manufactured, it's still possible to buy originals from specialty roofing suppliers; you can also use new gypsum–cement replacements.

"Insulbrick" and other asphalt-impregnated fiber sidings were the early-twentieth-century homeowner's version of "maintenance-free" aluminum siding. Unfortunately, they tend to leak along the seams and rot the underlying walls.

If the shingles are in good shape, there's one very good reason to leave them alone. Although not considered hazardous under Environmental Protection Agency (EPA) and Occupational Safety and Health Administration (OSHA) standards, owing to the regulatory hysteria surrounding all matters asbestos, most state environmental policies do not permit anyone but a licensed asbestos-abatement contractor to remove and dispose of cement–asbestos siding and roofing. Professional removal can be *very* expensive.

Damage from a leak at the junction of the wood gutter and the rake fascia trim has progressed into the cornice return. Small leaks and open joints ignored eventually cause serious damage.

Anatomy of Window Trouble

Unless kept well painted, windows rot wherever wood contacts wood on a surface that can hold water.

Rot area

Gaps between siding and trim allow water infiltration.

Brittle or missing putty

Cracked glass

Uncaulked joint permits leakage

Rot area

Missing or deteriorated drip-cap flashing

Drip cap

Head casing

Casing

Sash (upper)

Glazing

Sash (lower)

Muntins

Rot area

Sill

dams in the snowbelt. Venting an existing soffit without damaging it can be a challenge even for a skilled carpenter. As with all exterior trim, professional repair and replacement are costly.

WINDOWS   While you're still poking around the outside of the house, scrutinize the windows. It's likely the glass will need reglazing, a tedious but inexpensive job. If the putty between the glass and the sash (the wood frame) has dried out and cracked, water and wind can infiltrate. Sashes left unpainted for too long will typically rot at their bottom corners and where they rest against the windowsill. The joints between the windowsill and the side casings also create a rot-prone water trap.

Often, water will seep behind the sill and into the sheathing boards or especially behind an improperly flashed drip cap at the top of the window. The accumulated effect of this water can cause considerable damage to the sheathing and even rot the framing and sills behind the sheathing, necessitating extensive reframing and rebuilding of the windows. Rotted wood can be

An unchecked leak between the casing and sill allowed water to penetrate behind the trim and into the wall sheathing, which eventually rotted. Blown-in cellulose insulation exacerbated the problem by holding water like a sponge.

Time and neglect have already stripped most of the original paint from this magnificent Victorian entry. The woodwork and the granite threshold are still sound. Restoration involves mainly sanding, sealing, and refinishing.

dug out and replaced with epoxy putty (similar to automotive body filler) or drilled and injected with an epoxy consolidant before being sanded and painted over.

DOORS What's true for windows is also true for doors. Because thresholds are even more exposed to wear and weather than windowsills, they are one of the most common vectors of rot. Furthermore, a door that has a warped frame or split panels is no longer weathertight. Unless an old door is an architectural treasure (in which case it should be protected by a storm door), replacing it may make more sense than restoring it. Consider using relatively inexpensive but very energy-efficient steel doors for utility entries, and reserve the expensive, finely crafted wood door for the main entry.

Windows: Repair or Replace?

Old double-hung windows are anything but airtight, and aluminum storm windows sacrifice beauty for utility, so it may seem advisable to install new energy-efficient replacement units where fuel costs are high and the existing windows are in poor shape. Old windows can be replaced piecemeal, as budget permits. But it usually makes more sense and costs less to rebuild your old windows than to replace them, especially for a historic house. Your local millwork or cabinet shop can make replacement sashes to match the original. Retrofitted weatherstripping reduces air leakage.

Attachments and Landscape Features

The final stage in the exterior inspection is to evaluate any attached sheds, ells, porches, and outbuildings. These were often made of inferior materials and lackadaisically tacked on to the main structure at some later date. Even if originally well constructed, their upkeep is more likely to be neglected than the rest of the building. In any case, they are often rotting or resting on a heaved, tumbledown, or inadequate foundation. Note the juncture between the addition and the house proper: A noticeably tapering gap between the two indicates settlement.

PORCHES The joint between a porch roof and the side walls of the main structure is also a possible source of leaks and hidden structural rot, which often shows up as a sagging or water-stained ceiling. Because porch floors are exposed directly to the weather, the framing that supports them is often rotted.

Porch columns, posts and railings, and decorative brackets and other trim are especially vulnerable to deterioration, especially since the tedium of their upkeep means that it's typically ignored. The same is true for wooden and cast-iron fences. The cost of replacing or rebuilding either can be shocking. Fortunately, a wood fence is an ideal do-it-yourself project.

TREES AND SHRUBS Shrubs and trees growing too close to the house trap moisture against the walls and roof. Leaves and needles also clog gutters, and tree roots can lift or crack foundation walls. Overhanging trees interfere with the draft of any nearby chimneys and can attract lightning strikes. (If the roof has a lightning-protection system, check the integrity of the connections at the lighting rods and splices and that it runs unbroken to the ground rod; see pp. 43-45.) Removing a large tree near a building or one that leans toward it is not a job for the weekend chainsaw warrior.

The rot originating between the bottom of this porch post and the floorboards continued into the structural joists. As the post sinks into the crumbling joist, it pulls the roof downward. The difficulty of blocking water infiltration at such junctures is a strong argument for using treated lumber.

INSPECTING THE INTERIOR STRUCTURE

If your external examination hasn't daunted your spirits or revealed any overwhelming problems, proceed to an internal inspection. Don't be distracted by the freshly refinished wide floorboards, the delightful reproduction wallpaper, and all the other cosmetic details the real-estate agent will be pointing out.

The cellar of an old house is the place of childhood terror—of damp, nameless dread, dark corners, mold, and spiders.

Problems in the Cellar

The place to begin your quest is in the cellar, where, more than anywhere else, the true condition of the house is revealed. As you descend the stairs, note their condition: Are the treads sound? Or do they tremble with each halting step? Does the staircase rest on solid rock or melt into muck and mold? Is the staircase steep and narrow? Can you negotiate it safely or without striking your head on a beam? Is there enough space to rebuild a safer set?

In the cellar proper, is there ample enough headroom to permit efficient use or only more-or-less adequate access to the mechanical systems and the underbelly of the house? Does the depth of the cellar vary significantly from one place to another with rock ledge exposed? Is there a crawl space too shallow to actually crawl into? Deepening a cellar accessible only to hand shoveling and a wheelbarrow or bucket brigade calls for a commitment to character building

TIP

Checking the Cellar

When you inspect the cellar, don't forget to bring along the house inspector's two most important tools: a flashlight and an ice pick or awl. Most old houses lack adequate or even working subterranean lighting. In any case, you'll need both tools to inspect the sills and floor joists. ■■ ■■ ■■

Untreated wood in direct contact with concrete will eventually rot. In the case of this cellar stair stringer, the process was exacerbated by the lack of a vapor retarder under the old floor slab and flooding during frequent power outages when the sump pump was inoperative.

Foundation Types

Until the early twentieth century when poured-in-place concrete or concrete block foundations came into use, cellar walls were of masonry construction (in the building trades *masonry* refers to any coursed material: brick, block, or stone).

As a rule of thumb, the older or humbler a house, the more likely it would be to rest on rude walls of irregular dry-laid fieldstone (*rubble* in the mason's parlance). Their inside faces were frequently parged with mortar above grade to block the wind. The cellar of a more prosperous or conscientious homeowner would be laid up with select stone, carefully fitted and mortared in place. And for the house of a very well-heeled owner, the walls would be of coursed and mortared ashlar (quarriewd and faced rectangular stone). Because it readily absorbs moisture, ordinary brick (or sandstone ashlar) was infrequently used in the belowgrade portion of a wall. But it was widely used above grade both for a finished appearance and to seal out cold winds.

Throughout the Northeast and New England, massive granite, bluestone (schist), or marble slabs—8 in. to 12 in. thick, 4 ft. to 8 ft. long, and 2 ft. high—set on top of a standard rubble wall shouldered the sills of many house. Sometimes, the inside face of these ashlar foundation caps was given a brick veneer or the treatment was extended along the full height of the wall. On the other hand, what appears to be a heavy slab cap wall might be only a thin facing over brick or rough stone.

Sometimes what appears from inside the basement to be a smooth-faced mortared stone wall neatly capped with brickwork is only the facade of a double-wall foundation. Look for brick or stonework that runs up to the floorboards in between the floor joists with no visible sill beam. A foundation showing stone on the outside and mortared brick on the inside is another tip-off. In such cases, the stonework bears the building load and the brickwork seals out wind and cold.

Unfortunately, double-laid walls are no more watertight than single walls. To add to the confusion, the sill beams may also be doubled; the inside sill carrying the floor joists and the outside bearing the wall studs and roof load. If the outside sill rots away, the walls of the house will settle past its floors.

The original mortared rubble foundation capped with brick above grade is at the right. A concrete wall was sistered against the portion at the left and capped with a concrete block pony wall. Because the wall was never excavated to install drainpipes, water is still visibly seeping into the cellar between and beneath the stones and concrete.

At first glance, this cellar wall appears to be solid and stable mortared stone with a brick cap. But the stone visible behind the missing brick at the left shows the wall to be of double-faced construction, with nonbearing brick on the cellar side and a rubble stone foundation on the outside.

and backbreaking numbness beyond the ken of the average mere mortal.

Floor joists less than 8 in. above bare dirt are probably at least partially rotten. Any repairs will necessitate taking up the floors or digging out the foundation to excavate under the building. Inaccessible crawl spaces are typically found under a former summer kitchen or coach house shed or tool room converted to living space. Their foundations are likely to be shallow and of haphazard and rickety rubble that doesn't extend below the frost line. The sill beams, if not portions of the actual exterior wall, often rest at or below grade with only a thin rind of sound wood remaining.

FOUNDATION PROBLEMS Is the basement floor underwater? If it is, go no farther. Look for another place, unless you are prepared literally to sink your money into a new foundation and/or a footing drain system.

For reasons that are explained in detail in chapter 3, water (or rather, drainage) problems are the main cause of foundation failure. And water in the cellar is almost always a sign of drainage problems. At the very least, it can be caused when runoff from a heavy rainstorm saturates the soil outside the foundation and percolates through the walls. Sometimes, regrading to direct water away from the house and installing subsurface drainpipes can alleviate the problem. Despite promotional claims to the contrary, there is little evidence that most of the hydraulic-cement compounds and basement sealers touted to stop water seepage from the inside actually work. If the water is coming in *from* outside the wall, the remedy must be applied *to* the outside of the wall.

Examine the foundation. Are the walls original or an obviously later repair? Do they appear sound? If the walls are masonry or concrete, are there any major cracks that could be a sign of ongoing settlement or heaving. If there are cracks, are they still active or have they stabi-

Leave it and love it: Rather than abandon the lot, the nineteenth-century developers of this property chose to build their foundation on top of the steeply sloping bedrock that doubles as the cellar floor.

lized? Are sections of the walls bowed or tilted? If the walls are stone, have more than a few stones fallen out or have entire sections collapsed? Is the mortar (if any) sound or is it crumbly?

If a stone wall is leaky but otherwise stable (that is, not falling into the cellar), it may be possible to add outside drainage without removing or disturbing the wall.

EARTH FLOORS Architects recommended covering the cellar floor with concrete as far back as the 1850s. Even with good exterior drainage or a low seasonal water table, an earth-floored cellar is problematic. Although it appears dry, it's actually exhaling large quantities of water vapor into the house, raising the humidity and contributing to health and structural problems. In the days before insulation and fairly tight construction this might have been less of a problem and more of a benefit since the indoor air of drafty old houses was too dry anyway. So long as the foundation was watertight, providing good ventilation during the summer months could prevent harmful moisture buildup from an earthen cellar floor. But a more effective and permanent solution would be to lay down a polyethylene vapor barrier and cover it with crushed stone or concrete.

IS IT WORTH FIXING? If there are serious problems with the foundation, here's where the demon must be squarely faced. How badly do you want this particular house? Can you find or afford another? Will you have the time and money for the repairs? Although you won't have to fix the foundation immediately, you will have to fix it eventually. And this work must be done before any other work. Only reroofing has a higher priority.

Can your budget accommodate a major foundation repair or wholesale replacement? Since every foundation is different, it's impossible to estimate costs by any running-foot rule of thumb. As a former foundation doctor, I'd ballpark jacking up a typical 24-ft. by 32-ft. farmhouse, removing the existing wall, and replacing it with a poured-concrete foundation at $15,000 to $25,000; more if replacement of rotted sills and siding complicates things. Concrete subcontractors charge a premium for work under existing structures, since it's much more awkward and slower—as much as double their standard cubic-yard-in-place rate for new construction. Since labor is the main component of any foundation and/or sill repair job, doing it yourself can save a significant part of that cost.

Replacing a foundation wall is hard, dirty work that will consume a great deal of time and give you back very little visible reward. Hiring outside help is expensive. No contractor in his or her right mind will give a firm or low bid, because the variables are too unpredictable.

This is where any reasonably sane person would stop; not pass "Go"; and look for a kinder, gentler house to obsess over. But then, what if the price of the house has been substantially discounted to reflect the condition of the foundation? And what if you are one of those dauntless individuals for whom the thought of major foundation surgery excites a little more than it terrifies? If so, continue on with your inspection.

PROBING FOR ROT Check the sills for soundness, insect damage, and rot. So-called dry rot is actually caused by a fungus nourished by exposure to moisture and lack of ventilation. If unchecked, the soft dark streaks that are the first signs of infection eventually progress to a crumbly reddish charcoal. Besides the exterior face, the underside of the sills where they contact the masonry are most vulnerable to decay. Use an ice pick or carpenter's awl to probe the depth of the damage. Replacing a sill is not as expensive or difficult as replacing a foundation, but it's nothing you'd want to do for a hobby either.

Because the old-timers seldom took the time to strip the bark off log joists, an advance force of wood-boring beetles secured the beachhead for the invading dry-rot fungus. The weakened joist must be replaced or strengthened by sistering a new one along side it. But first, the cellar must be dried out and kept well ventilated to arrest the progress of the fungus.

Signs of Seasonal Water Problems

Sometimes basement water problems are seasonal. Ideally, you should do your house hunting in the spring, when the underground water table is at its highest. Any moisture problems will be hard to miss. Sometimes the infiltration is intermittent, occurring only during or shortly after a heavy rainfall (the cause may be lack of gutters or improper grading rather than groundwater seepage). Although standing water usually disappears after a spell of dry weather, basement water problems always leave telltale signs:

■ Dark stains on a concrete floor and/or stains or mineral deposits on the walls.

■ High-water marks or rot on posts.

■ An earth floor that that looks like a mudflat after the tide has gone out—smoothed over with grainy deposits.

■ Dank or musty odor.

■ A sump pit or operating sump pump in the lowest, dankest corner. A sump pump can also indicate a solved water problem as long as there is a means of conducting the infiltrating water to the sump.

■ Concrete floors with shallow drain troughs formed along the walls or a line of clay tiles set in a shallow trench filled with crushed stone and draining into an outside cistern or drywall are indications of earlier and sometimes successful attempts to solve basement water problems.

Water draining into the cellar through the window opening has scoured the whitewash off the foundation stones. Even worse, soil saturation has begun to push the wall inward. The solution is to slope the outside grade away from the wall and install gutters to divert roof runoff.

Examine the floor joists, girders, and underside of the floorboards. If these too are substantially rotted, it may more sense to look for a better house than to repair the damage. On the other hand, if the foundation is basically sound, replacing or repairing even a substantial number of rotted joists and subflooring shouldn't put you off (so long as the problem is rot, not insect damage), especially if the house has other features that seduce you into discounting this defect. But don't worry too much about settled or rotted cellar posts and the sagging floors they're no longer supporting. It is not difficult or expensive to replace cellar posts and to straighten sagging floors.

BULKHEAD AND CELLAR WINDOWS Check to see if there is a cellar bulkhead. Sometimes there isn't one, which makes it a lot harder to use the cellar. An old wooden bulkhead is likely to be fairly rotten (because it's difficult to build doors that are watertight). A prefabricated steel bulkhead (Bilco® door) is often poorly anchored to its foundation, particularly if it is a mortar bed on top of rubble stone. Unless the bulkhead walls have heaved and pushed in the cellar walls, repairs are not particularly difficult.

Caved-in or cracked bulkhead walls must be dug out and replaced, even if they haven't yet begun to damage the main foundation. Good drainage and frost-heave protection are of critical importance in preventing a reoccurrence of the problem. There should also be a door between the bulkhead and the cellar proper. Expect wood door frame, door, and stair treads to be rotten and in need of replacement with pressure-treated material. A full bulkhead replacement can cost several thousand dollars.

Also check any cellar windows. These will likely be in poor condition and candidates for replacement. New insulated and screened cellar window units that can be easily opened for cross-ventilation during summer months cost $60 to $100 each. They should be attached to a pressure-treated wood frame that's mortared into the original opening. Measure the opening to make sure that the replacements will fit without having to chop out the masonry.

The Attic

Once you're done in the cellar, head up to the attic to continue your structural evaluation. Is the attic accessible by a stairwell or just a hatch in the ceiling? Converting an unfinished attic is just about the most economical way to gain extra living space, even if you have to restructure hallways and rooms to include a set of stairs. In any case, be sure to poke your head up through the hatch.

When water and frost heave combine to destroy a bulkhead, the adjoining foundation wall goes with it. Here, the ashlar has fallen into the cellar and there's a dip in the clapboards— both indicate foundation settlement.

ROOF SHEATHING AND FRAMING Shine your light on the underside of the roof boards. If you can see metal roofing or asphalt shingles in wide gaps between the boards, count on removing the roofing and replacing the sheathing. Note the thickness and spacing of the rafters. Pole rafters and hewn or sawn timber rafters should be at least 6 in. in diameter or cross section when spaced 4 ft. or more on center. Ordinary 2x dimension lumber should be spaced no less than 2 ft. on center. Sagging rafters must be stiffened by jacking new timbers into place alongside the old or adding extra rafters in between the spans.

Check for signs of leakage—daylight showing through the roof is one of the more obvious. So are mottled water stains or a lush fungus garden on the roof boards or plate beams and rafters. The attic should also have a gable louver or window at each end for ventilation.

THE CHIMNEY Does the chimney appear sound below the roof or is it a candidate for demolition? Creosote stains on the brickwork are a sign of dangerously eroded mortar. Chalky white stains are caused by water, usually from a leak at the roof flashing.

THE ATTIC FLOOR Is the attic floored or capped with insulation? How much insulation and of what type? Because attic floorboards are the same age as the house proper and are often not nailed to the joists, they make perfect replacement boards for floors throughout the rest of the house. Chances are good that any fiberglass batt or loose-fill insulation laid between the floor joists won't be thick enough. In cold climates, 12 in. of fiberglass (R-30) is the minimum. The fill or batts should not block the roof overhangs either. If there's no insulation in the attic, neither in the floor nor in the ceiling, there probably isn't any in the downstairs walls either, since the attic is the easiest and most cost-efficient part of the house to insulate.

This is an unsafe chimney. The abundant creosote stains on the bricks indicate that the mortar has deteriorated, allowing creosote condensing on the unlined brick flue to seep through.

The Rest of the House

Once the cellar and attic have been scrutinized, you can look around the rest of the house. As you came up the stairs, were they narrow and steep, with turns and landings? Can you imagine moving a chest of drawers or your antique bed frame up them? Is there a way to improve on them without tearing the entire house apart?

WALLS AND CEILING SURFACES Note the condition of the wall and ceiling finishes. Are plastered walls and ceilings sound and firmly attached? Bulges, loose, fallen, or crumbling spots or a mottling of fine cracks like the skin of a cantaloupe are signs of failed plaster. Sometimes a phyllo dough–like layer of brittle

Water stains, especially on ceilings, are a serious concern, because plaster cannot withstand persistent wetting. Efflorescence, powdery dry bubbles deposited when salts are brought to the surface of plaster by water, is another sign of ruined plaster that will have to be replaced.

Hairline cracks and straight cracks, especially above doors, are endemic and usually do not indicate serious structural problems. But large running cracks in the walls are a sign that the house has undergone or is still actively settling. The movement must be arrested for a repair to last.

wallpaper is all that maintains the illusion of solidity. Push gently on the paper; the wall shouldn't yield.

If there is any ornamental plasterwork, such as cornices and ceiling medallions, is it intact or are portions pulling away or missing? Successfully restoring or replacing ornamental plaster is one of those arts that are simple in theory and frustratingly difficult in execution.

Plaster: Repair or Replace?

The fundamental question with plaster is "Can it be salvaged or should it be gutted?" Isolated cracks and leprous patches are readily repairable, and even sagging ceilings can be reattached as long as the failure wasn't caused by water penetration. Likewise, cracked and peeling walls have traditionally been repaired with canvas lining cloth as a base for painting or wallpaper. Several varieties of canvas and fiberglass lining cloths are still manufactured for that purpose. But removal is usually the most sensible, if not always the most desirable, approach when the greater parts of walls or ceilings are decrepit. If insulation and rewiring are also on the agenda, it's a lot harder to justify repair over removal.

If expert results are more important than personal experience, hire a specialist. Otherwise, renovation suppliers now stock reproduction carved moldings, cornices, and medallions made of high-density foam plastic suitable for do-it-yourself installation that, after painting, are indistinguishable from plaster originals.

Age does not necessarily guarantee a plaster finish. Invented in England in the late 1880s, gypsum wallboard or drywall (*Sheetrock* is a registered trade name of the product produced by United States Gypsum) began its rapid eclipse of plaster's 4,000-year reign in 1945. Thus there's a good chance that your home's old-fashioned plaster may have already been replaced with modern drywall during one of the many remodeling frenzies that swept the country throughout the 1950s and into the early 1970s. The makeover may have been motivated by the same reasons that would justify it today: Drywall is undeniably a quick and economical fix for crumbling plaster or walls damaged by extensive wiring and plumbing updates.

CEILING COVERUPS Ceilings of pressed tin or acoustical tiles were often used to hide crumbling plaster. Acoustical tiles are also notorious for lowering the high ceilings typical of nineteenth-century houses. This crime was more likely to have been perpetuated in the name of modernization than it was for concealing a new plumbing drain. Since some early acoustical ceiling tiles contain asbestos, removal could be problematic.

THE FLOORS Are the original floorboards exposed or, more likely, buried under strata of vinyl tiles, linoleum, carpet, or hardwood strip flooring? Hardwood flooring must be applied over a solid subfloor, typically the original wide-board old-growth softwood boards. Upstairs, those same boards might be left uncovered, disguised by an iron-tough layer of gray or dark red paint.

Wall-to-wall carpeting or vinyl sheet flooring glued to thin plywood or hardboard underlayment may hide perfectly serviceable tongue-and-groove yellow pine or Douglas fir flooring, once considered too common and unfashionable to keep up. Your rescue efforts will release the warm glow of time-burnished wood unmatchable and prohibitively expensive in new wood today.

For houses with forced-air heat, you can usually view a cross section of the floor by lifting up a convenient floor grate. Sometimes the original floors will be exposed in a back room. It's also frequently possible to hazard a good guess at the nature of a hidden floor from the cellar, where the underside of the finish floor is visible in gaps between the subfloor boards. If you see plywood instead, you can assume that the original floor had probably rotted out and was taken up. Finally, it's also possible that there's simply no practical way to know what treasure may hide under the current floor until you take it up.

FIREPLACES Examine any fireplaces. Look or feel up inside the throat to find the damper and try to open it. If the fireplace has not been used for a long time, there could be enough debris on top of the damper that it must be patiently wiggled to open. Try to look up the flue (you may need a mirror and bright flashlight) to see if the chimney is unobstructed and if it is safely lined. Check the fireback and hearth for burnt-out, missing, and crumbled brick. Rebuilding a firebox can certainly be a do-it-yourself job. But restoring a historic chimney without damaging it requires a skilled mason with experience in conservation techniques.

FIXTURES Finally, note the type and condition of kitchen and bath fixtures. Almost any faucet can be fixed. Reconditioning old faucets will cost a lot less than replacing them with reproductions. Are there any good or restorable antique fixtures? The original faucets and fittings, hard-

ware, doorknobs, hinges, mortise locks, switch plates, light or gas fixtures, woodwork, stair parts, raised-panel doors, lavatories, bathtubs, water closets, and antique cast-iron radiators—all irreplaceable functional treasures—are too often thrown out during hasty renovations.

Although the bathroom it inhabits is fairly bleak, this antique tiolet is an irreplaceable treasure.

An old house that still has its original hardware is a treasure trove indeed. Whether architectural salvage or reproduction, quality old-fashioned hardware of any sort can be expensive. Having the originals on hand can save you thousands of dollars. (The mortise lock-set and knob in this door would cost $80 to $110 alone. The hinges and the door itself bring the total cost of a replacement up to about $400.)

TIP
Before You Buy

If you find that a new septic system is needed, the sale should be contingent on the owner's furnishing a permit for an on-site sewage-disposal system or a favorable soil percolation test report (usually referred to as a *perc test*) by a licensed engineer accompanied by an approved system design. Ideally, the costs of engineering, testing, and permits should be borne by the owners, but these are sometimes items for negotiation. ■■■ ■■■ ■■■

It's unusual to find cast-iron sewer and drainpipe that are so well maintained. The brass plug is for accessing the clean-out wye.

THE MECHANICAL SYSTEMS

At this point you have done a thorough examination of the house's skin and bones. If you are still in love with the place, it's time to dig into its guts by inspecting the waste disposal, plumbing, electrical, and heating systems, which means heading back down to the cellar.

Checking a Sewer System

As you grope about in the cellar's murk, look for the house drain, typically a 4-in.- to 6-in.-diameter cast-iron pipe that exits at the foundation wall or cellar floor and connects (via the house sewer, or *lateral*) to the municipal sewer or some kind of on-site disposal system (preferably a working septic tank).

Sometimes the gray water (drainage from sinks and laundry) and the black water (drainage from the toilets) will use separate lines, with gray water being routed illegally into a drywell or convenient ditch. Somewhere before the house drain exits the basement, a clean-out wye should be evident. Sometimes these are installed in a well under the floor or even completely covered over with concrete.

OBSOLETE TRAPS If the cleanout is inaccessible, or even absent, unclogging a plugged drain gets a lot more complicated. Depending on the age of the plumbing and on local plumbing practice, the house drain may also be fitted with a trap where it joins the lateral. Before modern venting systems were developed, health officials understandably required a "building trap" to be installed between the house drain and public sewer lateral as a secondary defense against the invasion of your home by rats and noxious and highly flammable sewer gas. The trap was buried outside the foundation wall and connected to an abovegrade air vent/cleanout. At a later date, the building trap was moved into the cellar floor

and the air inlet run through the foundation wall at the sill. Two cleanouts side by side in the cellar floor are a clue that your plumbing system is blessed with this now outlawed and antiquated setup.

Pay particular attention to where the house drain exits through or under the cellar wall. Look for any cracks in the wall that might indicate foundation settlement. Over time, a leaking drain will wash soil (and support) out from under the wall. Invading tree roots, frost heave, or even the weight of a settling house is a possible cause.

Checking a Septic System

The required sales disclosures must specify whether the house is connected to a municipal sewer and water system or if it has on-site disposal and supply. Don't settle for "I think so." Generally, lenders require an approved and operating water and waste disposal system before they will approve a mortgage. Although a water meter is an obvious sign of municipal supply, its presence doesn't preclude connection to an on-site waste-disposal system.

When properly constructed and maintained, septic systems are a safe, reliable, inexpensive, and ecologically sound means of waste disposal (much more so than municipal sewers and treatment plants). Does the house have a septic tank and leach field? It's still possible to find houses that simply dump their raw sewage into a stone-filled pit in the ground (drywell) or an open or covered lagoon (cesspool). In most cases, these unhealthful and inadequate systems exist only because they were grandfathered in under newly adopted health codes, generally with the requirement that they be replaced by systems meeting the new regulations if the property changes hands or is renovated. More likely, however, the system somehow slipped past the permitting process either through oversight or outright deception before the regulations were tightened up.

TANK COMPOSITION AND LOCATION If there is an existing septic system, find out whether the tank is steel or concrete. Steel tanks don't last as long and can collapse. What is the tank's capacity? A 1,000-gal. tank is standard for a four-person household. For in-sink garbage disposals, the tank and field size must be at least 50 percent greater.

Just where are the tank and leach field? If you are excavating a foundation or moving heavy equipment around the property, you don't want to sever the sewer pipe, collapse a tank or compact the leach field. Since septic tanks should be pumped out at least once every 2 years to 5 years as part of routine maintenance to prevent system failure, it helps to know where the tank is. Try to find out when this service was last performed. You might also negotiate with the seller to pay for pumping out the tank.

If you happen to notice a wet area with lush vegetation and the odor of sewage in the general vicinity of where the leach field should be, you have (you hope) a septic tank or (pray you don't) leach-field problem. If you're lucky, the problem might be too much water in the tank. Check the capacity.

Also, sometimes roof drains were connected to the house sewer. (This isn't legal, but it's been done anyway, especially in cities where there is no easy way to get rid of the runoff.) Dumping chemicals—such as drain cleaners, paint thinner, and photographic wastes—down the drain wreaks havoc with the bacterial populations in the septic tank. Waste will then pass undigested into the leach field, plugging up the absorption beds and eventually causing the sewer to drain slowly or back up.

If the problem is not traceable to blockage in the sewer line before the tank or to a tank filled with indigestible grease and cooking oils, you've got a nonfunctioning leach field. Pumping the tank will not fix it. The only cure is to dig up the field and replace it. This is usually a very expen-

sive proposition and could trigger a regulatory nightmare if it turns out that the present system doesn't meet or can't be brought up to current requirements.

Checking the Rest of the Plumbing System

Exploring the plumbing system of an old house is a lot like interpreting the finds of an archaeological dig. The entire evolutionary record of domestic plumbing systems can be read in the successive accretions of new materials and methods on older ones. Thus there are really only two causes at the root of almost any problem that might plague the old house plumbing system: obsolete or unserviceable materials still in use; and illicit changes grafted onto functioning systems by ignorant handymen or unlicensed contractors.

Old houses offer some truly bizarre examples of creative plumbing. The kink shows why the code does not allow black polyethylene pipe to be used for drainage. The uselessness of electrical tape as a leak stopper is evidenced by the bucket beneath this masterpiece of the do-it-yourself plumber's art.

TIP
Public Sewer Connection

If a house presently served by an on-site system is located in a neighborhood slated for connection to a municipal sewer, you will probably be hit with an up-front connection charge or a steep property tax hike. Real-estate agents are usually privy to this sort of thing, but unless a buyer's broker represents you, don't expect the agent to let you in on it. Inquire at the local planning office. ■■ ■■ ■■

What to Do with Lead Pipe

Lead pipe has been used in both drainage and water-supply systems from the time of the ancient Romans up into the 1940s. Any lead water lines should be immediately replaced if they are still in use. Lead releases highly toxic soluble oxides that you don't want in your drinking water. For the same reason, sweat-soldering water pipes with lead–tin alloy has recently been outlawed.

Although lead drainpipes pose no immediate health hazard, they should eventually be replaced, as they do contribute to heavy-metal pollution of ground water and sewage. Look for a soft dull gray metal that shows bright when scratched with a penknife. Check the incoming connection at the water meter (or main shutoff at the foundation wall). The supply from the street or well may be the only lead line left in your system. It's rare to find a lead water main lateral still in use in a municipal system, but it happens. Your water company should have records of when the house was connected, what type of pipe was in use at the time, and when it was replaced. In rural areas, it's more likely to find lead pipe still in use, particularly in houses that draw their water from a gravity-feed spring. Any such lines must be dug up and replaced with polyethylene.

IS THERE VENTING? You can safely assume that any professionally plumbed house meets the code requirements in force *at the time that the work was done.* The problem is that both the plumbing code and plumbing technology have changed greatly over the 150 years since indoor plumbing became common. For example, although the earliest plumbing codes mandated fixture traps for protection against sewer gas, it wasn't until much later that they recognized the need for proper venting of the drain lines to prevent siphoning of the traps. Thus it's possible that the fixtures of an old house may not be properly vented. Because of the difficulty and expense of retrofitting vent lines in existing walls, it's even more likely that fixture drains added later won't have any vents at all. There should be rooftop vent-pipe penetrations in the vicinity of underlying bathrooms, kitchens, and laundries.

Another structural problem with old plumbing systems is the loss of trap seal by evaporation in little-used fixtures such as cellar floor drains. (Floor drains don't always empty into the house sewer—some run into the outside footing drains or directly into a dry well instead. These aren't trapped.) Topping off the trap was once a monthly household chore. Codes now require an automatic primer to keep such traps full. If you smell a foul odor emanating from the bathtubs or sinks of a house that hasn't been lived in for some months, the cause is likely to be a dried-out trap. If the problem doesn't disappear when you fill it back up, then you've got a serious vent problem somewhere, which must be addressed if the house is to be safely habitable.

CAST-IRON PIPE Properly installed high-quality cast-iron drainpipe can last a very long time; copper and brass last even longer. Eventually, even the best cast iron will rust from the inside. Corrosive minerals in the water, grease buildup that slows flushing action, settlement that traps water, and low-grade material in manufacture hasten the process. If the original cast-iron drains are more than a century old they may be nearing the end of their useful life. Look for makeshift patches that might cover a rusted-out leak. Tap the pipe with a hammer: A ringing tone is the sound of healthy pipe; a dull thud means terminal rust.

Check that the drain lines are properly supported with anchor straps or threaded hangers to maintain the necessary pitch for good drainage. Sagging pipes can clog, rust, or leak between their joints. Check leaded joints for signs of leakage. Drainpipes must be airtight to prevent the escape of sewer gas into the cellar. Inspect copper or brass tubing for buildup of

Where dissimilar metals are joined, electrogalvanic action will cause corrosion. This brass faucet is rusting the iron nipple. Over time, the joint could spring a leak. Wrapping the threads with Teflon tape will reduce corrosion.

bluish green deposits, which could indicate pinhole leaks caused by internal corrosion. Acidity in the water is the culprit. The pipes will have to be replaced and the water conditioned.

CHECK FOR DISSIMILAR METALS Note any connections between dissimilar metals; copper or brass mated with iron will corrode very quickly, as will copper pipes hung from steel straps or copper straps secured with steel nails. Galvanized drainpipes are even more likely to be clogged with corrosion than cast-iron ones.

CHECK THE WATER PRESSURE Depending on the age of the plumbing and the hardness of the water, much, if not all, of the iron pipe may be ripe for replacement. If you have iron pipe (check by seeing if a magnet sticks to it) and you note low water pressure when you open the faucets at a fixture, suspect corroded pipes. A knocking sound (*water hammer*) that accompanies the flow is also a symptom.

Pressure drop can have other causes. To confirm the diagnosis, disassemble the pipe at a convenient union joint. If the occlusion has reduced the inside diameter by half or more, the pipe needs to be replaced. Because you can safely

assume that any and all galvanized pipes will eventually need replacing, it's more efficient and less costly to rip them out all at once (pressure drop or not). However, if your time and cost budgets dictate a triage system, you can opt to do the job piecemeal or postpone it indefinitely if you can live with the present system's anemic flow.

COPPER PIPE Mineral buildup is much less likely and a lot slower in copper pipe. Low pressure at the fixture is thus probably a symptom of undersize piping. The hallmark of a low-end plumbing installation was the exclusive use of ½-in. tubing instead of ¾-in. distribution lines feeding ½-in. fixture laterals. Opening the tap at a fixture on the first story or closer to the main will drop the pressure at a fixture on the second story or farther down the line. In private systems, the pump may not deliver enough pressure for adequate flow at the faucet.

Copper tubing is more vulnerable to freezing than is iron pipe. If the water supply is shut off, look for bulges, splits, or soldered joints that have pulled apart.

Plumbing systems, especially drainage, grow by accretion. The original installation of bell-and-spigot cast-iron and copper would be prohibitively expensive today. Changes and extensions are made with inexpensive and easy to use chlorinated polyvinyl chloride (CPVC) pipe.

Antiquated Plumbing: Repair or Replace?

Typically, illegal fixes and fudges of uninformed homeowners cause the worst plumbing problems. Rather than trying to make sense of a tangle of corroding, mismatched, undersize pipes, nonexistent or bizarre venting, and missing shutoff or drain valves, it's quite tempting to tear the whole mess out and replace it with a safe, orderly, and legal system. Unless you can do all the work yourself (and do it well enough to satisfy your local plumbing inspector), given the expense of a professional whole-house replumb, it's probably better to live with what you can and fix only as much as you need to. Wholesale replacement is an attractive alternative only when you intend to gut the entire house anyway.

GAS PIPES Don't mistake black-iron pipe (BIP), which may appear dull and rusty brown, for water-supply pipe. BIP is used exclusively for gas (either natural or propane). It will rust, especially in damp locations. Interior rusting is a serious problem, which is one reason why horizontal gas lines are slightly pitched and vertical drops fitted with a drip leg (a.k.a. *dirt pocket*) to collect any condensate.

Galvanized iron pipe is almost universally prohibited for gas, ostensibly because the zinc coating might flake off and plug the line, a fear that has since been proved groundless. Copper tubing was once prohibited as well. However gas no longer contains the corrosive sulfur compounds that were once a cause of concern. The point is that plumbing codes change much more slowly than plumbing technology and can sometimes enshrine prejudice as fact. If your local code allows it, galvanized iron is actually better for gas piping than BIP, as there's less chance of it ever rusting. It should, however, be painted yellow so as not to be mistaken for water piping.

Checking the Water Supply

The property description generally lists the water source. Drilled deep wells are usually the most reliable, whereas springs can be questionable both in terms of safety and reliability. Mortgage lenders have traditionally assumed that municipal water supplies are safe, although that assumption may be subject to revision as increasing numbers of public water systems are found to be contaminated. In some areas of the country, the water must be tested for bacteriological contamination before the house can be occupied or sold. In other areas, the seller must report only whether or not the water was tested and if it passed.

For drilled wells, try to find out when and by whom the well was installed, and its recovery rate. Depending on depth, 3 gal. per minute should be adequate. The well drillers have the information on file if the owner doesn't know or remember. (Some states maintain a registry of private wells with data furnished by well drillers.) Check the well casing. It should project at least 1 in. above grade to prevent contamination.

The well head cap should be tight and the pump wire protected by plastic or steel conduit. The submersible pumps used in deep wells (more than 100 ft.) are generally trouble free and long lived, unless the well has been pumped dry once too often or was the victim of a lightning strike. There is little you can do to check the condition of the pump other than to see that it works.

For shallow wells (25 ft. or less), look at the source. Is the spring lined with concrete tiles or is it just a wooden box or stone-lined pit? Is the supply pipe to the house buried deep enough not to freeze? Is it galvanized iron or rustproof polyethylene? Is there a shutoff on the line where it enters the cellar? Does that shutoff work? (You cannot repair a soldered joint if water is still dripping through the pipes.)

For some inexplicable reason, this ancient jet pump is still pushing water into the pressure tank. The pump motor is a recent replacement. Note the woefully undersize ½-in.-diameter polyethylene pipe that is the main distribution line.

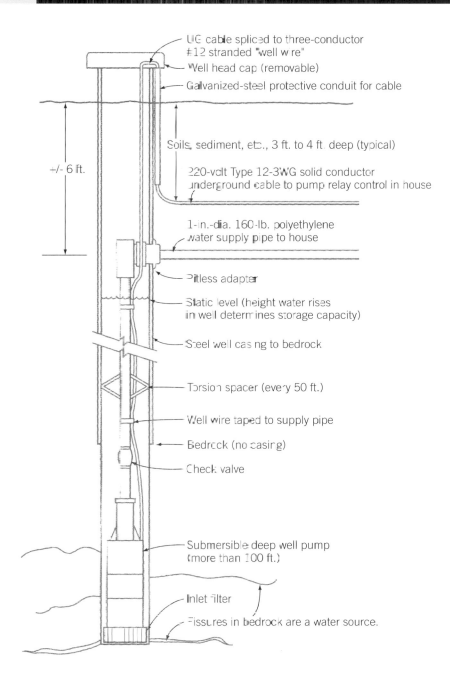

Typical Deep Well Installation

UG cable spliced to three-conductor #12 stranded "well wire"

Well head cap (removable)

Galvanized-steel protective conduit for cable

Soils, sediment, etc., 3 ft. to 4 ft. deep (typical)

+/- 6 ft.

220-volt Type 12-3WG solid conductor underground cable to pump relay control in house

1-in.-dia. 160-lb. polyethylene water supply pipe to house

Pitless adapter

Static level (height water rises in well determines storage capacity)

Steel well casing to bedrock

Torsion spacer (every 50 ft.)

Well wire taped to supply pipe

Bedrock (no casing)

Check valve

Submersible deep well pump (more than 100 ft.)

Inlet filter

Fissures in bedrock are a water source.

WELL PUMPS Pumps for wells up to 100 ft. deep are usually located in the basement, sometimes in an outside well pit (these can be vulnerable to surface contamination), or—outside the snow belt—in a pump house. Examine the pump: Is it corroded, showing signs of leakage or does it appear in good working order? Have someone open a tap (assuming the water supply is connected) and run the water long enough to start the pump while you watch the pressure gauge. If the pump seems to run for quite a while before it reaches operating pressure or kicks on as soon as a tap is opened, the piston washers (of an old-fashioned piston pump) or the impellers (for centrifugal and jet pumps) could be bad or the check valve at the pump or the foot valve at the bottom of the well may be stuck open. These kinds of relatively minor problems are owner fixable.

Replacing a burned-out or frozen pump can also be a do-it-yourself job, albeit an expensive one. If the pump connects to an old-fashioned galvanized-iron pressure tank instead of a modern bright blue diaphragm-type tank, waterlogging (see p. 371) could be the problem. Because the problem is inherent in the design, plan to replace rather than to repair an old-style pressure tank, even if it's currently working.

SPRING WATER Sometimes, the household water enters the cellar by gravity from a spring located above the house. Unless the source is high enough above the point of use, the pressure may be too low to run a dishwasher or washing machine or to provide a comfortable shower on the second floor. If it hasn't already been done, you'll have to add a pump to boost the pressure.

Water-Treatment Systems

If the water pressure tank is connected to a tank about the size of a welding gas cylinder and another about the size of a garbage can, you're looking at an ion-exchange water softener. At the very least, this indicates that there's a hard-water problem (excessive levels of dissolved calcium and magnesium). Look for empty water-softener salt bags. Evidence (either on the tank labeling, an attached owner's manual, or an empty bag) of potassium permanganate, means that the tank is an oxidizing filter type and that there is a problem with iron and manganese (possibly with hard water or sulfur as well).

The good thing about finding a water-treatment appliance in the cellar of an old house is that it means someone has tried to deal with the problem instead of ignoring it to the detriment of the piping and water heater or boiler and the health of the household. The bad thing is that you now have another expensive piece of equipment to baby-sit. Purifier filters and salt levels must be properly maintained and replaced at regular intervals if any of these systems are to work properly and safely. Replacing a failed water-treatment system is a major expense, even if you do the work yourself. Also, just because there is a treatment system, doesn't mean it's the right kind for the problem. Testing the performance of the unit requires a professional.

This is a fairly typical installation for hard water. The brine tank that holds the conditioning salt is in the foreground. The softening unit is directly behind it. The blue tank in the background is the pressure tank for the pump.

Naturally pressurized (artesian) wells and some springs are so prolific that they have a constant overflow. If this is allowed to drain across the floor (as was often done in old dirt-floor cellars), the moisture buildup will encourage mildew and rot. Also, to provide a convenient and frost-proof water source in the days before piped-in supplies, cellars were often dug directly over a spring. Any overflow needs to be drained to the outside.

At the other extreme, a basement cistern (a large, covered concrete or stone tank) is sometimes used as a reservoir for springs with low recovery rates. These are more commonly employed in arid regions to store rainwater collected by a system of downspouts from the roof. Water from roof-collection systems should not be used for drinking without proper filtration.

THE HEATING SYSTEM

If it weren't for the description in the disclosure documents furnished by the real-estate agent, most neophyte amateur house inspectors would be clueless as to which type of heating system that big metal cabinet lurking in the basement might be part of or what kind of fuel it burns, let alone how to check its condition.

The difference between a furnace and a boiler is easy enough to see. A furnace is basically a combustion chamber that heats and circulates air. You'll recognize it by its crown of metal air ducts. A boiler is a combustion chamber that heats and circulates water, so its signature is a medusa-like tangle of pipes. Beyond that, it starts to get complicated. A boiler can heat water for circulation as liquid or as steam. The difference between a hot-water boiler and a steam boiler and the attendant piping is not immediately obvious to the casual observer.

Turn on a Tap

When you leave the cellar at the end of your inspection, open a sink tap, let the water run for a minute or so, and then note the volume, color, odor, and taste. Water that smells like rotten eggs (sulfur), rust stains on the fixture basins (iron), or blue-green stains on taps and drain strainers (acidity) are obvious signs of unsatisfactory water. But some of the worst problems such as bacterial, chemical, or heavy-metal contamination leave no sensible clues. If you have any cause to suspect the water quality, obtain a sampling kit from the town health officer and have the water tested.

Both furnaces and boilers can burn wood, coal, oil, LP or natural gas, or even a combination of wood and fossil fuel. Furnaces can also use electricity as fuel. But not all fuels can be used with equal efficiency, and each type of combustion imposes its own venting requirements that can affect the safety and performance of the chimney.

Furthermore, some boilers are equipped to heat hot water for domestic use as well, either by an internal jacket or by an external storage tank equipped with a heat exchanger. Or the boiler may be dedicated to space heating only, with domestic hot water provided by a separately fueled water heater. Because hot air is a much less efficient heat exchange medium than hot water, houses heated by furnaces inevitably use freestanding domestic water heaters. Finally, in rural areas, old houses heated solely by wood stoves and, therefore, unencumbered by a central heating plant, are not at all uncommon. (See chapter 12 for more information on the various types of heating systems.)

TIP

Pipe Freeze

Heat tapes and insulation wrapped around water pipes in the cellar; daylight visible through walls; and insulation stuffed into the cracks between stones, under sills, and around windows are sure signs of a very cold basement, a hard-to-heat house, and the nagging danger of pipe freeze-up. ▮▮▮ ▮▮▮ ▮▮▮

Note the condition of the furnace or boiler. If you're fortunate, there will be a tag or placard showing the installer's or service contractor's name, the date of the last servicing, and the test results. If this information is not on the premises or otherwise addressed by the disclosure statement, get the name of the fuel dealer from the real-estate agent or the seller and inquire about the condition of the heating system.

If recent service records don't exist, assume it's been a long time since the furnace has had a tune-up. While you definitely need to arrange for one before the heating season begins, it may also be a good idea to hire a burner serviceman to inspect an oil-burning furnace or boiler for safety and performance before you close the sale. A well-tuned oil burner that is less than 10 years old should be able to achieve 80 percent efficiency. Older burners, particularly ones that have been converted from coal to oil, will be doing very well if they reach 70 percent to 75 percent. If the test instruments show lower readings, the burner is in need of a tune-up.

Unlike oil burners, older gas burners have almost no moving parts and burn much cleaner. They normally give years of trouble-free service with no additional maintenance other than a biennial cleaning of the exchanger. But over the last 15 years, oil burners have become more efficient and cleaner and gas-burning furnaces have become more complicated, increasing the opportunity for service problems. The first generation of high-efficiency (80 percent to 90 percent) gas furnaces (condensing furnaces) earned the nearly universal opprobrium of servicemen because of their congenital inability to work outside of the laboratory. It is only since the mid-1990s that reliable high-performance gas boilers and furnaces have become a reality.

Upgrading insulation and tightening up the house will save more energy and money than tinkering with the furnace will. A professional

The presence of uninsulated pipes is the first clue that this is a hot water boiler. (Steam pipes are always heavily insulated.) The second give-away is the (green) electric circulator pumps (for each heating zone). The oil storage tank visible in the background makes determining the fuel type a no-brainer as long as it's actually connected to the boiler.

energy audit to determine the most cost-effective energy-conservation strategy for your particular house is also a good idea (see chapter 8). In the meantime, if the fuel cost for the previous season isn't shown on the disclosure form, ask the seller what it might have been. You might get an honest answer if the heating plant is fairly new and the house adequately insulated.

Other than figuring out what type of system it is and if the furnace runs and the heat rises to the radiators or floor registers, there is little a nonprofessional can tell about the condition or overall performance of a heating system, at least on an initial inspection. If the house is being shown in the winter, the furnace will be running anyway (unless you are looking at an abandoned house). During warm weather turn the thermostat way up and see if the furnace responds.

Water Heaters

If domestic hot water is not provided by a tankless coil in the boiler or by an indirect storage tank, find and inspect the water heater. If the seller doesn't know how old it is or there isn't an attached dated installation tag, your local plumbing and heating supplier may be able to establish its age from its make, model, and serial number. Water heaters are considered to have a service life of 7 years to 12 years, depending on the type of liner and the hardness of the water. Stone-lined tanks (read the label) are the longest lasting. Glass-lined tanks are better than galvanized steel, which barely lasts 5 years.

For electric heaters, remove the inspection covers at the side to look for rust and leakage around the element fittings. With gas-fired heaters, remove the burner access plate at the base of the heater; turn on your flashlight and look for rust or leaks on the bottom of the tank. Check the flue pipe for corrosion. Check also that the heater is properly grounded. For some reason, it almost never is. For both fuel-burning and electric types, there should be a heavy copper "jumper" clamped between the hot- and the cold-water pipes and (for gas-fired heaters) to the gas drop pipe. For electric models, the power cable should have a bare copper ground conduc-

Water heated by the boiler circulates through an exchanger inside this tank to heat potable water for domestic use. House water and boiler water are never mixed. An indirect heater of this type is a separate heating zone and thus requires its own circulator pump.

Aging Furnaces: Repair or Replace?

It usually doesn't pay to replace a functioning, albeit inefficient, older furnace with a more efficient new one until the old furnace is ready for the scrap heap. The pay-back period is just too long to justify the investment. Fortunately, there are quite a few intermediate and cost-effective fixes you can employ to upgrade the present unit until then.

The normal service life is about 20 years; a 30-year-old furnace or boiler is just waiting to die. There's no harm in waiting for it to do that. Be mindful that you must budget for a new heating plant sooner or later and bargain with the seller accordingly. And also be aware that the old thing is most likely to give up the ghost when it's running—that is, on the coldest night of the year.

Although this tank was installed by a licensed plumber, it wasn't done very smartly and it doesn't meet current plumbing or electrical codes. The supply and outlet pipes should be connected to the heater with union fittings, and a first-class installation would have included shutoff valves on each line. The installation is also electrically unsafe because there is no grounding jumper across the pipes to the metal of the tank.

tor fastened to the top of the heater by a green screw. Old cable often lacks the ground wire.

Check also that the water heater flue (or the flue of any combustion appliance or woodstove) is properly vented. Since the definition of what is and what isn't proper is one of those subjects on which the codes can't seem to agree, don't rely on what you might read in a book (even this one). Get the local truth from your local code enforcement officer.

The Chimney Base

Finally, examine the chimney base. Open the clean-out door(s). A neglected flue will be packed with soot, cinders, ash, or creosote, which must be removed before you can use the opening as an inspection port for the chimney flue. This won't be necessary if the clean-out services a fireplace ash pit. As you check out the chimney, be aware that old-timers often vented two fireplaces on different floors into the same chimney. The very real possibility of combustion gases from the lower unit downdrafting into the house through the upper is the reason that code prohibits appliances on different floors from sharing flues.

THE ELECTRICAL SYSTEM

Faulty old wiring cannot be ignored. While any new work you undertake must conform to the current National Electrical Code (NEC), the code is decidedly ambiguous about what pre-existing wiring can and cannot be grandfathered. Thus your local electrical inspector has a lot of leeway when interpreting the rules. In general though, there is agreement throughout the electrical industry that work that was never legal in the first place must be corrected if discovered. Work that was legal at the time it was done but is no longer is a gray area. However, a condition that is clearly hazardous to health and safety, such as rotted insulation at a light fixture, definitely must be corrected. The guiding principle is that there is no requirement to replace old work just because it is old; the requirement is to correct any existing deficiencies that could be life-threatening. The wiring in many old houses is in hazardous condition.

An amatuer electrician "horror show:" Not only is the switch wired outside a protective enclosure completely illegal and hazardous, but the cables feeding the boxes are not protected or secured by connector clamps.

Because there is an outside chance that a licensed electrician who has performed corrective work on an old house could be held liable should it burn down or if an occupant is electrocuted, even though the cause of the injury was unrelated to the work, most electricians understandably favor ripping everything out and starting over rather than making piecemeal repairs to somebody else's mess.

As a homeowner, you can legally wire or rewire your own residence. But any work you do must meet code and pass inspection. If you live "out back of beyond" where electrical inspectors don't go, it's still wise to meet code for safety's sake alone even if no one will ever look your work over. In some jurisdictions, it may be less trouble to hire a licensed electrician than to go head-to-head with an inspector who thinks amateurs shouldn't fool around with electricity. And in others, mortgage lenders may require licensed contractors, not only for rewiring but also for any work.

There are reasons enough for many otherwise competent and confident old-house aficionados to draw the line at do-it-yourself wiring. But such caveats notwithstanding, there are still many fixes that a conscientious and reasonably competent old-house owner can successfully undertake. If there's only a circuit or two to move or rearrange, it's worth doing yourself just for the experience. And, if you decide to rip out the walls and gut the wiring, installing the new system won't be any harder than wiring a new house. But please never forget that an improperly wired house is a fire hazard and carelessly handled, electricity can and does kill. Doing your own wiring is always a job that should be undertaken with caution. You must ask yourself if your knowledge is honestly up to the job. Complicated jobs might best be left to professionals.

Interpreting the Electrical Code

Because the language of the electrical code is incomprehensible to the ordinary mortal, it takes years to develop a good working knowledge of its arcanum and its dialect as spoken by your local inspector. Whatever you do, never be tempted to dismiss code regulations as overkill or useless gobbledygook. What may seem to be an insignificant detail can make the difference between a safe installation and a deadly one. Don't try to tease the meaning out of the oracle on your own; buy an interpretive handbook that does it for you.

Remember too, that the code offers very little clear guidance on the subject of old wiring. While a good home-wiring guidebook may be all you need to stay legal with new construction, the situation in old houses is far from straightforward or obvious. Like everything else about old-house work, adapting, repairing, or upgrading old wiring is fraught with hidden dangers and weird conditions that can befuddle or frustrate even experienced electricians. That said, a good electrician could make sense of the rat's nest of wires and feeds, three-way switches, and other enigmas that may greet you when ripping into a wall, and he or she can have it neatly rewired before you could even figure out which was the hot wire.

The Service Drop

Start your inspection of the electrical system outside by checking the condition of the *service drop*, the overhead cable that runs from the utility pole to the house wall or roof. While unlikely, some houses may still be serviced by an old-fashioned drop consisting of three separate rubber-coated conductors attached to porcelain insulators (or even worse, a two-wire drop). Because the wires are undersize for modern electrical needs and their insulation is most likely cracked or missing, arrange to have the utility company replace it with a new triplex-cable drop immediately.

The electrical system of this old house is grounded to a buried galvanized-iron water pipe, which is no longer legal. On the other hand, bonding the ground for the lightning protection system to the same electrode (the heavier of the two braided copper wires) was illegal at the time it was done but is now permitted.

There's way too much going on in this 60-amp, four-circuit fuse panel. Puzzling out the logic of this electrical spaghetti can short out the brain of even a professional electrician.

Make sure that the overhead service cable doesn't rub against tree limbs or cornice projections. It should be at least 18 ft. above any public roadway, 12 ft. above a driveway, 10 ft. above a sidewalk, 8 ft. above any flat-roofed porches, and 3 ft. above any roof pitch 4 in 12 or greater.

Moving or changing a service drop must be done by your local utility, not by an electrician. Check to make sure that the service drop *attachment insulator* is securely anchored to the house wall and that any *service mast* conduit isn't bent or pulled apart at the joints. The rating of the *service entrance cable* that runs down the wall from the *weatherhead* to the meter box should match the rating of the main breaker in the service panel. Homeowners have been known to upgrade service panels without upgrading the entrance cable.

The plastic insulation jacket should be intact. Old-style cloth-covered rubber insulation should not be so badly frayed that the stranded neutral conductor is visible. Check that the connector at the meter socket is still watertight; likewise where the cable penetrates the house wall.

THE GROUNDING ELECTRODE CONDUCTOR

If your electrical system has been even slightly modernized you should spot a thick (#4) stranded or solid copper wire exiting the house at the service entrance penetration. This is the *grounding electrode conductor,* which should be clamped to a buried copper-clad or galvanized steel rod (the *grounding electrode,* or ground rod, in common parlance). If you can't find an outside ground rod, it's likely that the system is grounded to a buried water pipe where it emerges through the cellar wall. However, this once standard grounding method is no longer allowed.

The Service Panel

Back in the cellar, locate the service entrance panel. This gray steel box is the heart of the electrical system. Depending on when the house was wired and rewired, you may find instead the original four-circuit fuse block at the center of a conglomeration of secondary fuse blocks, subpanels, and switches added willy-nilly in the race to keep up with the increasing electrical needs of modern living. Open the entrance box (or main fuse panel) and try to find its maximum rating, which should be imprinted somewhere on the main breaker, disconnect switch, or fuse block.

Look for the grounding electrode conductor leaving the service panel. If, as is likely, it is bonded to the water pipe, you'll need to run a second conductor to a new electrode buried either in the cellar or outside. (One possibility is to connect the ground to the reinforcing mesh in a new floor slab.) In any case, if the house is serviced by municipal water, look for a jumper across the water meter that ensures the continuity of the ground.

REMOVING THE PANEL COVER Carefully unscrew the panel cover. (It's a good idea to stand on a plank or plastic pail when you do this, especially if the cellar floor is damp earth.)

At this point, you are looking for evidence of obvious problems: water damage, burned or corroded terminals, damaged or loose circuit breakers, charred wiring, and (with fuse panels) higher amperage uses than the circuit's wire size allows. Check also that no extra wires are tapped into the lugs ahead of the main breaker or pull-out fuse block to feed a subpanel. Although

Fuse Box or Breaker Box?

Homeowners often assume that a fuse box means an inferior and unsafe system. An unscrupulous seller or electrical contractor can capitalize on this prejudice and claim to have "upgraded" the electrical system by replacing a functioning "unsafe" fuse panel with a safe-and-modern circuit-breaker panel while having done nothing about the far more dangerous deteriorated or ungrounded wiring.

A fuse panel isn't so much obsolete as it is inconvenient. (Fuse panels are still manufactured.) As long as the panel has adequate circuit capacity, it makes no difference whether it employs plug fuses or magnetic circuit breakers to protect the circuits from overload. In fact, under many circumstances, a fuse is actually a safer overcurrent protection device than a circuit breaker. Breakers can partially fail, refuse to open, or malfunction in a variety of sneaky ways, but a fuse blows only once

In any case, your homeowner's insurance underwriter will require that any fuse sockets that accept old-fashioned Edison-base screw-in fuses (like an ordinary screw-in light bulb base) be fitted with nonremovable type S "fusestat" adapters. These prevent overfusing (for example, replacing a blown 15-amp fuse with a 20-amp fuse), which is just as dangerous as replacing a blown fuse with the traditional penny.

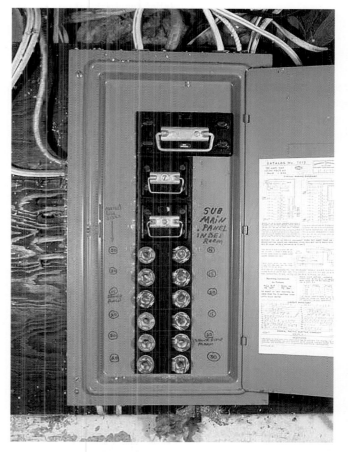

A well-organized and labeled fuse panel like this is even safer than a circuit-breaker panel.

there may be any number of subtle violations or problems that are more or less immediately apparent to an electrician or professional home inspector, you don't need to be concerned with them for this initial inspection. At present, you are more concerned with uncovering any systemic problems (read: "expensive to fix") than you are with flagging every illegality.

THE AMPERAGE A 100-amp service is the bare minimum for today's electrical needs. An acceptable standard for most new construction is now 150 or 200 amps. If you find a 60-amp panel, the entire service entrance will need to be replaced, most likely all the way back to the service drop at the utility pole. This is also a good time to replace an old fuse panel with circuit breakers. Because replacing the service entrance involves disconnecting the meter, specialized tools, and working off ladders near heavy current, many homeowners prefer to leave this part of the renovation to an electrician and limit their own work to rewiring the household circuits.

CHECK FOR CORROSION Check for signs of obvious corrosion. Water can leak into the service panel from an improperly sealed building penetration. A rusting panel box, rusted metal-

jacketed cables, or rusted steel outlet boxes are danger signs. Moisture causes electrical connections to corrode. A corroded connection has increased resistance to current flow. Resistance equals heat, thus the connection can get hot enough to ignite the surrounding material without blowing the fuse. A corroded connection can also cause a faulty ground, which could electrocute you.

KNOB-AND-TUBE WIRING Although there are even more primitive systems, the oldest surviving wiring you might expect to find in an old house today is the knob-and-tube system of individual rubber-coated conductors strung on porcelain insulators that enjoyed wide use from the 1890s into the 1920s. (In some parts of the country, knob-and-tube wiring was actually the preferred system as late as 1940.)

Even today, knob-and-tube wiring is not illegal per se, as long as it is in good condition. You can never safely assume that any knob-and-tube circuit is disconnected. Some of the wires may still carry current, spliced to cables of more recent vintage. The most likely suspects are attic and cellar lighting circuits, where the conductors are accessible and uncovered by insulation or wall finishes.

The problem with knob-and-tube wiring is the same problem that plagues old wiring in general. Rubber was the standard wiring insulating material until after World War II. Since rubber loses its flexibility after only 25 years, the insulation can crack and break off. Thus any surviving knob-and-tube wiring still in use is long past its normal life. If you continue to use knob-and-tube wiring, you might not break any rules, but you are gambling with your safety and your house.

ATTIC CABLE Rubber insulation was also used on the conductors in Attix wire, a cable popular from the early 1900s until about 1920, which was sheathed with the same woven cloth loom tubing used to protect knob-and-tube conduc-

Cambric-insulated cable from the 1930s is routed next to thermoplastic jacketed cable that was installed in the 1950s or 1960s, hinting at two eras of electrical system updates. Remnants of the original loomed wiring dating back to the turn of the last century were found elsewhere in this particular house. The thin yellow and green wires are for powering a 24-volt doorbell system.

tors where they entered an enclosure. Likewise, it was found in early armored cables and *rag-wire,* a primitive form of nonmetallic cable with a painted braided cotton or varnish-impregnated cloth (cambric) covering.

By the late 1940s, the rubber insulation on the individual conductors had been replaced by vinyl chloride plastic (which was invented in 1939). But painted cloth remained in use for the outer sheathing into the early 1960s, after which the plastic-jacketed Romex cable rapidly supplanted it. While rubber-insulated conductors are easy to recognize in Attix cable, it's harder to distinguish some of the later types of ragwire from the transitional plastic-insulated, painted cloth-sheathed cables of the 1940s and 1950s. Remove the cover of a convenient junction box to see what kind of insulation is on the individual wires. Because rubber degrades faster in open air and with heat, any cloth-covered rubber wiring feeding ceiling light fixtures, particularly those in the kitchen (which are typically left on longer), is likely to be seriously deteriorated and most dangerous at the point where it enters the enclosure. Sometimes even the slightest

Armored (BX) cable rusts in damp locations (such as the cellar of an old house). Note also the missing cable clamp. This is particularly dangerous with armored cable, because the steel jacket must be bonded to the box to provide ground continuity.

BX Cable: Is It Safe?

As long as the conductors are insulated with plastic, not rubber, older rust-free BX cable is safe to continue using with one caveat: The steel spiral of BX cable can cause circuit breakers not to trip in response to a short. The problem was overcome in 1959 by adding a thin aluminum strip inside the armor. Nonelectricians typically confuse this with a ground conductor or bonding strip and try to connect it to screw or cable clamps or to splice it to the grounding jumper. It's supposed to just sit there. The point is, old-style BX and new-style circuit breakers are not a safe match.

movement (such as replacing a light bulb) can cause a short circuit or a shock.

BX CABLE Beginning around 1930 and on up into the early 1960s, many houses were wired with BX (a General Electric brand name that slipped into generic usage) galvanized-steel-jacketed armored cable. It is still a code requirement in some cities today. One advantage of armored cable is that the jacket itself is the ground conductor and so no separate conductor is required. Another is that, unlike cloth- or plastic-jacketed cables, BX is impervious to gnawing rodents. However, it is extremely vulnerable to moisture. Check for corrosion wherever the cable enters a steel enclosure and check that the cable clamps are tight and of the kind intended for use with armored cable (they have a screw that tightens down against the armor).

TWO-PRONG OUTLETS Just because you have old-fashioned two-prong outlets doesn't mean you must replace them with modern three-prong ones. The NEC allows the continued use of ungrounded cable and even the replacement of a defective two-prong outlet with another one. But it does not allow you to replace two-prong outlets with three-prong ones, unless you add a continuous ground conductor to the circuit (which is generally impractical unless the cable already contains an unused bare conductor) or you replace the ungrounded outlet with a ground fault circuit interrupter (GFCI) outlet, which is an acceptably safe and quick fix.

Don't presume that just because the previous owner "modernized" the wiring by replacing all the two-prong outlets with three-prong ones that the system is safely grounded. While you might spot a jumper from the outlet's grounding terminal to the box, nothing may have been done to remedy the lack of a ground conductor in the cable itself.

CHECKING FOR POLLUTANTS

In most states, there are four possible sources of house pollution that are considered hazardous enough to require the seller to disclose any knowledge of them to a prospective buyer. These are radon, asbestos, lead paint, and underground storage tanks. For many prospective home buyers there is also a growing concern with chemical contamination of the water or house air, from both on- and off-site sources. The fear is not only for the health of the occupants but also for the often extremely high cost of remediation when a problem is discovered.

Radon

Radon gas is a colorless, odorless, and radioactive by-product of the decay of uranium naturally occurring in association with granite and phosphate rock and also in tailings from uranium mining operations and in reclaimed strip mines. Some building materials such as concrete block and wallboard were also manufactured with radon-bearing minerals. Radon has been found in almost every state in the United States and is estimated to affect at least 10 million homes. No home can be assumed to be immune. A tightly sealed house is more likely to have a dangerous level of radon than a drafty house.

While radon itself is inert, it decays into carcinogenic radioactive heavy-metal "daughters" that bind to inhaled particles. Studies have established a significantly increased risk of lung cancer, especially among smokers and children.

Radon dissolves in water and percolates through the soil to seep into basements through cracks and unsealed penetrations in the foundation or cellar floor, sump pits, or floor drains connected to the foundation drain, where it can build up to unsafe levels. Radon will infiltrate anywhere water can. While a concrete floor offers some resistance, dirt floors are particularly dangerous. Here concentrations can be 10 to 100 times higher. Even more insidiously, radon can be discharged into the home by water from deep-drilled wells. The danger is not so such from drinking the water as it is from breathing the contaminated vapor.

Given the widespread risk, it is only prudent to have a house tested for radon before you buy it. Any disclosure document will state whether the house has been tested for radon and if the results were within acceptable levels. Assuming a previous owner was aware of radon contamination, it can only be hoped he or she took steps to reduce the risk. But there is no guarantee. And neither is there any obligation to test a house for radon in the first place.

As a prospective buyer you could ask the seller to do the test or at least pay for it. But it's more likely that if you want a radon test, you'll have to do it yourself. Inexpensive and easy-to-use home test kits are available at home centers. Because radon levels fluctuate seasonally, the most accurate testing takes place over the course of a year. Since that is impractical for a prospective home buyer, you can get a good indication from the most basic tester, which is a

Radon Entry Routes

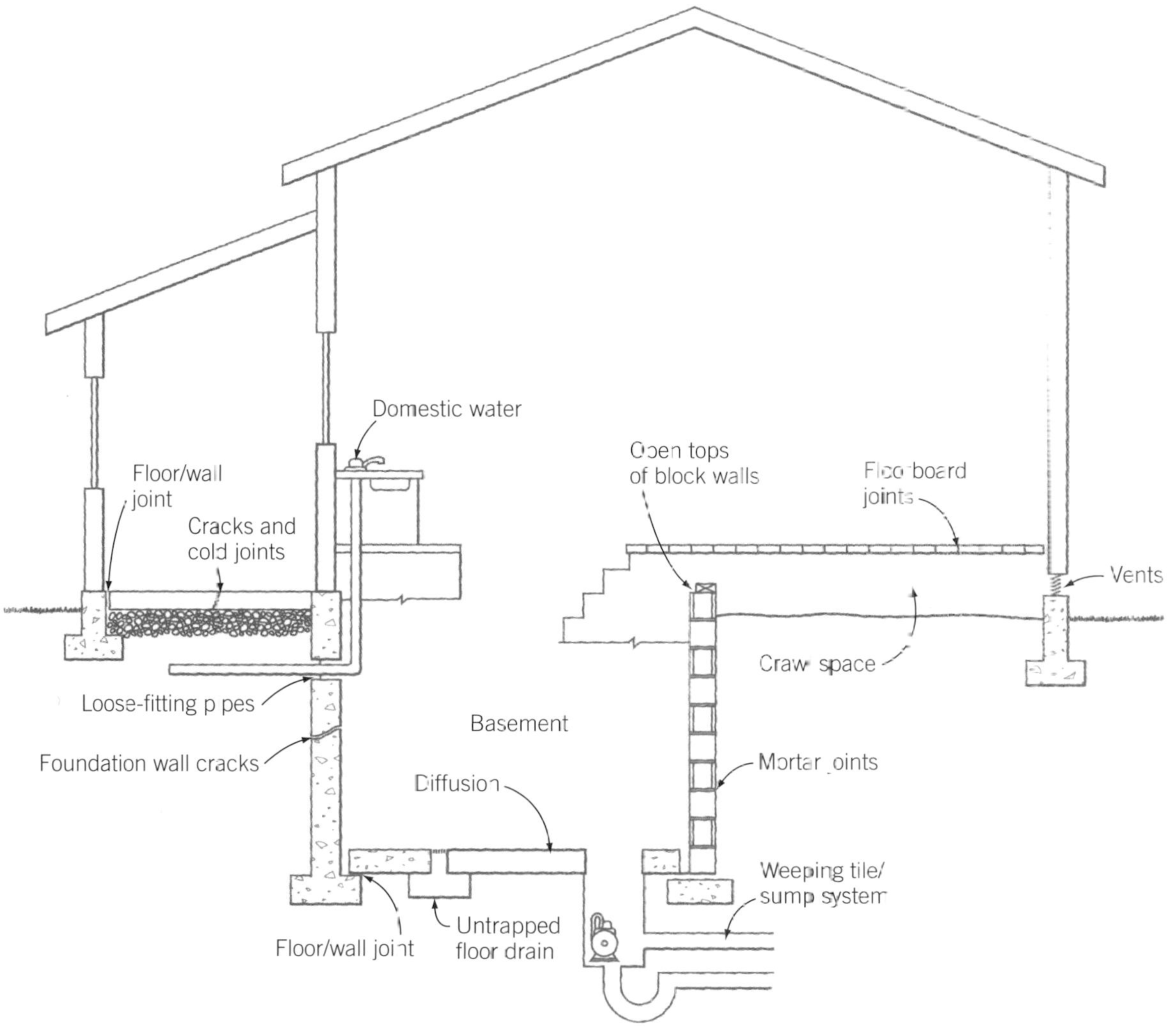

Domestic water

Floor/wall joint

Cracks and cold joints

Open tops of block walls

Floorboard joints

Vents

Loose-fitting pipes

Crawl space

Foundation wall cracks

Basement

Mortar joints

Diffusion

Weeping tile/ sump system

Floor/wall joint

Untrapped floor drain

charcoal canister monitor ($15 to $25, including lab fee).

If testing shows unacceptable radon levels, you can contact a local radon mitigation contractor or search the World Wide Web for information on do-it-yourself mitigation. The EPA or your local health department also has information and a list of contractors. Make sure that the contractor you hire has been licensed under the EPA's Radon Contractor Proficiency

Program. Mitigation strategies involve keeping radon out, exhausting it, or both. Keeping the gas out can involve sealing cracks and installing drain traps or installing gravel, plastic, and concrete over a dirt floor. Exhausting radon can sometime be done with passive venting but sometimes requires continuous-duty fans that actively suck radon out of the ground. Mitigation usually costs between $200 and $2,000.

TIP

Asbestos Help

Unlike asbestos siding or pipe insulation, it's not immediately obvious whether materials like ceiling texture paint or a kitchen floor tile contain asbestos. You'll need to submit a sample for an inexpensive laboratory analysis. Look in the Yellow Pages under "Asbestos—Consulting and Testing." ■■ ■■ ■■

Asbestos

Asbestos is a naturally occurring mineral fiber whose properties as an insulator, binder, reinforcement additive, and fire retardant were exploited in more than 3,000 products, mostly in the building industry, most extensively from the 1940s until the 1970s, and mostly in schools and public buildings. Unfortunately, people who mined and manufactured asbestos had a greatly increased chance of dying from the lung disease asbestosis and from mesotheliomia, a particularly nasty and otherwise rare form of liver cancer. As a result, manufacturing of asbestos-containing materials ceased in 1978.

If a house was built before 1978, there's probably asbestos in it somewhere. The good news is that asbestos is harmful only when it is *friable*. This means it is loose and crumbly and can become airborne so you can breathe it into your lungs. As a result, most asbestos in houses is perfectly fine just where it is. Potentially friable asbestos can be found in boiler and pipe insulation and asbestos fire cloth duct liners. Ceilings that contain asbestos are a major area of concern. Many of the so-called "plastic" paints, such as U.S. Gypsum's Textone, used on textured ceilings from the 1920s until 1977 contained asbestos. Acoustical ceiling tiles and drywall joint compound (also up to 1977) are also sources of friable asbestos. So are some kinds of vinyl floor tiles and the adhesives used to attach them.

There are three levels of approach to asbestos in the home. Each level is more complex and expensive than the last. The first and best strategy is simply to let it be. If the asbestos-containing material is not cracked or crumbling or frayed, handled, sanded, abraded, chipped, cut, or sawn, it's not releasing fibers into the air and isn't a hazard. The material should be monitored to ensure that it remains undamaged and inert.

The second level of action is to cover it up or, in bureaucratese, *encapsulate* it. This is the usu-

Removal of an unused hot-air duct revealed an asbestos liner on the joists and floorboards of this home. Most states allow homeowners to remove such small areas of asbestos themselves, as long as proper precautions are taken.

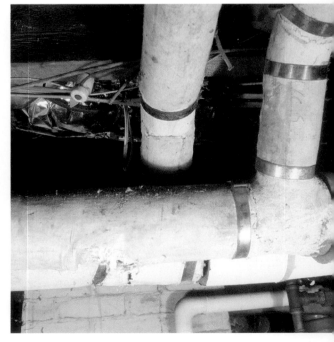

Unless it is actively releasing fibers into the air through a tear, asbestos pipe insulation is best left alone. Rips in the outer covering can be sealed.

ally the best way to deal with asbestos-contaminated vinyl sheet or vinyl tile flooring. As long as you don't sand or scrape asbestos-laced vinyl flooring, the fibers will stay safely bound. Although you could conceivably remove old tiles by applying heat while carefully prying up so as not to break them, there is still the danger of releasing asbestos from scraping the mastic. Instead, cover the old tiles with underlayment and lay down a new floor. Where practical, asbestos pipe insulation can be safely isolated by boxing it in with boards.

The third level is to take it out. Removing more than a small amount of asbestos is almost universally the domain of professional contractors, though some states do allow homeowners to remove asbestos-containing material (contact your state's department of environmental protection to get a clear understanding of what is allowed).

Whether you do-it-yourself or use a professional, safe asbestos removal is a tedious and time-consuming operation. The basic procedures are similar to those employed for handling radioactive waste or biological warfare agents. Proper precautions include turning off heating and cooling to reduce air flow in the house, isolating the work area with polyethylene sheeting, wetting down the asbestos-containing material, wearing protective clothing and a respirator with appropriate cartridge, and thorough cleanup and proper disposal of asbestos-containing materials at a licensed facility.

Lead Paint

Lead, or rather its soluble salts, was an important ingredient in paint since classical antiquity. Until fairly recent advances in paint chemistry made lead pigment obsolete, it was unequaled for the excellence of adhesion, drying, durability, and covering abilities that it imparted to paints. In 1978, the risk of lead poisoning prompted the federal government to ban the use of lead paint in residential housing.

Lead Paint Guidelines

Many health departments initially reacted to the seriousness of lead poisoning by mandating complete removal of lead-based paint. But these days, wholesale or even partial lead-paint abatement is now viewed as needlessly expensive and potentially dangerous overkill. Current guidelines recognize that removal can actually create a worse environmental hazard than the one it was intended to remedy. Thus they recommend *interim control* over removal. The aim is to manage the hazard by stabilizing, by carefully cleaning and maintaining, and—in some cases—by removing limited areas of deteriorating painted surfaces so that no further lead is released and the amount of damage to historic details is minimized.

Lead-based paints were ubiquitous on exterior wood siding and trim, on interior trim, and on the high-gloss wall finishes preferred for kitchens and bathrooms. Lead was also an ingredient in glazing putty and was even sometimes added to improve the covering ability of primitive milk- and water-based paints.

If you have an old house, you have lead paint. But it doesn't necessarily follow that you have a lead paint problem. Like asbestos, which is not a threat until it becomes friable, lead paint causes no ill effects until it deteriorates. Unfortunately, all paint films eventually deteriorate. Painted surfaces inside the house flake off. The paint on the edges of doors, window sashes, and stair treads is abraded by friction. Painted baseboards and other wood trim are bruised by impact in the normal course of domestic life.

The exterior of most houses is routinely repainted at least once every decade. While any surviving layers of lead-based paint are safely buried under at least one recent coat of lead-free paint, lead-laden chips and dust from previous prep work may lie buried in the soil along the house walls or blow into the house through open windows. When these chips or particles are ingested or inhaled, the lead they carry accumulates in the body. Children are much more likely to ingest lead dust than adults are, either by direct hand-to-mouth contact, from chewing on lead-painted surfaces or by playing in lead-contaminated soil.

Because you cannot tell if paint contains lead by looking at it, you have two options: You can assume that it does and treat it that way. Or you can have the paint tested. Since old plaster ceilings were normally painted with lead-free whitewash or calcimine and flat wall finishes normally did not contain lead either, test only the most likely places: Suspect any enameled interior wood trim or hard gloss-finished wall. Doors and window sash and casework almost always have a layer of lead paint somewhere in their accumulated strata. Most painted metal surfaces (such as tin ceilings) and almost all ornamental cast iron was prime-coated with "red lead" (lead tetraoxide). Although a few old varnishes did contain lead, most didn't. But the red or gray paints favored for nineteenth-century bedroom floors in many rural homes certainly do. All exterior paint, except for the whitewash sometimes used on fences and outbuildings, was lead based. Paint is considered to be lead based and hazardous if it contains more than 0.5 percent (5,000 ppm) lead by weight.

There are inexpensive do-it-yourself lead-paint test kits on the market (some are of dubious reliability). A certified risk assessor or lead paint inspector can test for lead either on site or in the lab and evaluate the severity of the hazard and make recommendations for remedial action, based on the age of the occupants who are likely to come in contact with it.

Underground Fuel Oil Storage Tanks

At one time, it was considered the height of modern convenience to bury fuel oil tanks alongside the house. Unfortunately, despite their rust-retardant asphalt coating, apparently as many as half of the underground steel tanks throughout the country have sprung leaks. Because all steel tanks will eventually corrode and any hydrocarbons in the ground water are undesirable, many states moved to prohibit the installations of new residential underground oil tanks and some have even required existing tanks to be removed.

Unfortunately, a leaking underground oil tank is not easy to detect at the surface. Leaks are typically slow enough that there is no obvious increase in oil consumption. Oil seepage into the basement or the foundation drain system is rare. Unless there is a sudden extraordinary increase in fuel usage, most leaks are likely to reveal themselves during foundation or drainage work. Otherwise, when the disclosure lists an underground storage tank, a soil test for contamination may be mandatory. In any case, it is a good idea. Such tests usually cost from $150 to $500.

Other Possible Chemical Contamination

Chlordane is a highly toxic and carcinogenic compound that was widely used as a termiticide until it was banned in 1988. It was typically sprayed on the soil along the foundation walls and under the house in crawl spaces. The compound was absorbed into the soil where, because it does not readily break down, it remained active for up to 20 years or more. Unfortunately, it would move through the soil with runoff water and seep into basements through the foundation walls. Because chlordane is volatile, its fumes could then be drawn into the living spaces when the house was depressurized by the operation of heating appliances, fireplaces, or exhaust fans.

Chlordane carried by surface runoff also contaminated wells and springs. Exposure to chlordane at high levels is lethal. At lower levels, it causes severe nausea, headaches, sterility, neurological problems, and more. Because of its persistence, chlordane-treated soil could be hazardous when working on foundations or in a crawl space. Soils can be tested for chlordane contamination, but mitigation is difficult and costly.

The possibility of chemical contamination of drinking water via surface runoff and aquifer pollution is an increasing concern. At the very least, never assume your water is pure just because it comes from a deep well. There are at least 63,000 organic chemical compounds on the market, most of which are indigestible by microbes. Leaking underground gasoline storage tanks, chemical waste dumps, farm and factory effluent, junkyards, and mining and smelting operations are some of the more obvious sources of potentially very toxic compounds in the ground water.

REAL-ESTATE MATTERS

You can't know if a property is overpriced or underpriced until you gain a feel for the local market. This takes research and time. First, collect all the listings, catalogs, and brochures you can from local real-estate agents. As you look through the multiple listing service (MLS) catalogs, note the difference between the asking price and the actual selling price of properties listed as sold. This will give you some idea of whether you are in a buyer or seller's market. Read the real-estate classifieds in the local papers. By the time you're ready to draw up a list of potential candidates for inspection, you should know what your money can buy.

Spend the next several weekends looking at houses and use the information in this book to make a list of their problems and defects. Eventually, you'll narrow the field down to one or two contenders. At that point, I suggest you hire a local renovator to take a look at the place, review your checklist, and give you a ballpark estimate of the repair cost. This is also a good time to enlist the services of an architectural historian or conservation consultant to determine

Caveat Emptor

Ultimately, the condition of an old house seems to vary in inverse proportion to the financial liquidity of its prospective buyers. Even though the house may categorically fail every structural requirement mentioned in this chapter, it may also be all you can afford to buy. Whatever the disadvantages, at least you can move in and begin acquiring equity rather than paying rent. Don't delude yourself into thinking that house renovation is cheap or easy. It's a bigger, messier, and costlier job than you can imagine.

whether the house has any important features whose preservation could either limit the scope or increase the cost of renovations. Consultations such as these typically run $100 to $300. If they help you negotiate a lower selling price, prevent you from buying a property you can't afford, or save you from getting mired in a project beyond your abilities or from destroying a historically important house, the money will be well spent.

Can You Afford It?

The last consideration, the most pertinent perhaps, to which all the structural criteria are appended is, can you afford it? What terms are available? Will the owner finance all or part? Or will you have to convince strangers at a bank that you are in fact a decent, hardworking, reliable credit risk? Are the monthly payments bearable? You'll need to pay yourself a living wage while working on the house or borrow additional funds to cover renovation costs.

All these evaluations and considerations, all the physical, financial, and personal desiderata, must now be distilled down to a go or a no. Piled onto a heaved-in foundation and rotten sills, and the weight of any other defects, although fairly negligible in themselves, a high asking price may sink your proposed renovation

Obvious problems are not always major problems, but they can be symptoms of serious hidden defects. In this case, the porch is not lifting up. Rather, the house to which it is attached is sinking.

project. If the wiring, plumbing, and heating systems also need replacement, the prudent buyer would look for a better place. Prudence, however, is often overwhelmed by romance, especially when the magic is sweetened with a lowball selling price. If you find yourself already caught up in the spell of the old place and ignoring the obvious truth that somewhere down the road you'll pay for that low price with interest, ask yourself—and answer honestly— "Am I up to it?" As a Clint Eastwood character once said, "A man's got to know his limitations."

Comparison Shopping

Force yourself to look at two or three more likely candidates. Unless you have to stand in line to see the place, you've got time to comparison shop. You can't take a leap of faith if you're wearing overshoes of doubt. If you decide to take the plunge, set up an appointment for the closing with a local lawyer. Then go and visit the place again. Walk around and look at it. Sit under a tall tree and try to feel it as your place. Does it fit? Visit with the house. Sit in the front

room and listen, try to hear its quiet talk of groans and rumbles, let the emptiness fill you, the dust of the world dancing before your eyes in the clear light of the afternoon.

Read through a copy of Les Scher's *Finding and Buying Your Place in the Country* (Guier Books, 1974), to prime yourself for the lawyer. He or she should make certain that there is a clear title—no undischarged mortgages, liens, or attachments or rights-of-way that could in any way hinder the sale or your enjoyment of the property. A policy of title insurance or an abstract should be furnished. Find out if the land has been surveyed and, if not, who bears the cost. Don't make the mistake of thinking that a survey is not all that necessary. A deed generally specifies *x* acres "more or less," to cover any margin of error. That very same clause was in the deed of my own property, which had remained an undivided parcel described as "100 acres, more or less." The survey, done just before I acquired it, showed 68½ acres "more or less." As the former owner, who had been paying taxes on those 100 elastic acres remarked, "There warn't no rebate on the taxes neither."

Now you're ready for the checklist promised at the beginning of this chapter. Besides helping you compare properties, the checklist on the facing page is useful for organizing renovation priorities once you have bought the right house. The items are arranged in order of generally decreasing importance and expense. The topmost items are most influential in determining the reasonableness of the project. Since the degree of difficulty and urgency diminishes from left to right, a cluster of checks in the "poor" column is a darn good excuse to talk yourself out of a potentially disastrous commitment. But, as my farmer neighbor once observed apropos his grandson's fiancée, "Love's blind; follow a hog's butt if it'd a mind to."

Renovation Checklist

Item	Poor*	Passable	Good
Purchase price (high, manageable, a real bargain)			
Foundation (cracks, settlement, leaks)			
Cellar floor (type, water present)			
Crawl space			
Sills (rot, insect damage)			
Structural timbers, joist, visible framing (rot, insect damage)			
Walls and roof (bows, sags, indicating failure)			
Water supply (source, reliability, potability)			
On-site sewage disposal (existing or required? perc test?)			
Plumbing system (waste and supply lines)			
Heating system			
Electrical system (service entrance capacity, circuit wiring condition, number of outlets and fixtures)			
Roofing (type, condition, rot in deck)			
Flashings			
Gutters and downspouts			
Exterior siding (type, condition)			
Exterior trim, paint			

Item	Poor*	Passable	Good
Windows and doors (repair or replace)			
Chimney and flues			
Attachments (porches, sheds, decks)			
Insulation (type, quantity)			
Interior plaster (and other wall and ceiling finishes)			
Woodwork/trim			
Flooring			
Stairs			
Kitchen (cabinetry, appliances)			
Bathroom fixtures			
Water heater			
Outbuildings and barns			
Landscaping, grading, rubbish on site			
Land, acreage, features, general neighborhood			
Public highway access, driveway condition (maintained by town or owner?), off-street parking			
Legal (title, survey, zoning)			
Does it feel right?			

*Poor (needs major work now)
Passable (needs work, but can wait)
Good (does not require any work)

2 Organizing Priorities

Managing the logistics of a major renovation means juggling time, materials, and money. Concentration, experience, and a calm temperament coupled with a sense of humor ensure success and sanity.

A New York lawyer busy with the many chores in closing his place for the winter interrupted his work to say goodbye to his neighbor at a time he thought appropriate for the farmer's schedule. It turned out, as it sometimes does with supposedly taciturn denizens of the hill country, that his neighbor wanted to talk, and after some exchange the lawyer said, "I'm sorry but I've got to go along. Have a hundred things to do."

"You've got a hundred things to do?"

"Well, perhaps not quite," the New Yorker replied, "but it seems that many."

"Let me give you a piece of advice," said the Vermonter, "Do 'em one at a time."

—ALLEN R. FOLEY, *WHAT THE OLD-TIMER SAID*

Rescuing an old house from decay can seem like an overwhelming job. So many disasters clamor for your attention that it's difficult to decide which can safely be ignored and which cannot. Like the hospital emergency room, a renovation needs a triage system to make those necessary choices.

As you worked through the "Renovation Checklist" (p. 59), you probably noticed that the work arranges itself into two major categories: *structural work,* which must be done immediately, and *cosmetic work,* which can be done as time and money allow. Which work fits into which category is frequently self-evident.

STRUCTURAL OR COSMETIC?

I remember a day in June . . . the grass, deep and golden green, parted to let our van up the drive. Like an ark wallowing in the waves, the van rolled to a stop, tired motor hissing. We stretched cramped arms and legs in the warm sunlight. The cicada's song filled the air shimmering around us. In this strong light, the weathered gray clapboards revealed their subtle depths, like the feathers of some huge dull bird. Key in hand, I removed the rusted padlock from the back door—no need; it wasn't hitched to the latch. We were home.

Later, while cooking dinner on a Coleman stove perched on an orange crate in the middle of the bare linoleum floor, we tried to list our priorities—where and how to begin the metamorphosis of house into home. That night, as the rain poured through the ceiling, overflowing our supply of pots and pans, we moved our sleeping bags to the highest corner of the floor. I began to get the idea . . . fixing the roof was in the structural category. So was plugging the hole in the foundation wall through which the runoff cascaded into the cellar. The plaster dripping from the ceiling was only a cosmetic defect.

The point is that structural work is the first link in a logical chain. You can't do any interior or finish work until you've dealt with the foundation, roof, and structural timbers. The messiest jobs, the ones that make the house absolutely unfit for living, should coincide with those times when you are free to set up temporary quarters outside or to leave on vacation while the hired help tears the place apart. Demolition is something you should do only once. Get it over with as quickly as you can so you can restore the house to healthful habitability. If you aren't able to tackle major structural repairs right off, you could do all the interior demolition; rewiring; and whatever plumbing, heating, and insulation are absolutely necessary for health and habitability. But beware of going overboard: Changing the foundation can result in cracked wall finishes, doors and windows that stick open or closed, and partitions and floors that are out of plumb and out of level.

A Seasonal Strategy

Because many structural repairs will expose the vitals of the house to the elements for some length of time, arrange your work schedule so that you perform repairs in warm, dry weather. Nothing is more conducive to an ulcer, frost-bitten fingers, and skyrocketing costs than a house jacked up on timbers in November in a place like Vermont or Minnesota. Allow plenty of time for structural work; it always seems to take longer than estimated, because the links in the chain are never as clear as the metaphor. One muddy timber doesn't always connect to another. If you intend to replace a foundation working nights and weekends, plan on spending an entire summer in mud and dust.

Except for exterior siding and trim or landscaping, most cosmetic work is interior. Save the least disruptive work for winter months, after the house has been footed and roofed and the inside walls gutted. Painting, staining, and roofing, which require warm weather, are ideal summer projects.

Obviously, the border between structural and cosmetic work is not very precise. Nor does the work always fit the ideal season. Renovation projects have a way of unraveling slightly faster than you can knit them together. Schedules are torn apart in the tug of war between what should happen and what did happen. Come September, I'm usually just about caught up with my June work. But it helps to visualize the scope of the work on a sliding scale; the chart on p. 74 sorts projects by the seasons, time available, and estimated costs.

DEVELOPING THE DESIGN

There is one more step before you pick up shovel and house jacks. Your schedule of renovations must be supplemented by, or more precisely,

Ice and mud are equally hard on your enthusiasm and your tools. To save both money and physical discomfort, try to schedule major structural repairs for warm weather.

informed by, a master design plan. This design plan will enable you to meet the challenge of reshaping the house to your needs without doing violence to its structural and spiritual integrity. I am, of course, presupposing that you would not consider "updating" a historic treasure. In that case, design changes are not an option unless they fit within standard preservation guidelines. If you can't comfortably live in lots of tiny rooms with no closets, don't buy a historic house.

A house is a tool for living. And since living is, above all, a personal art, the tool should be shaped to the hand of the user. An ill-fitting house, like a poor hammer, causes psychic blisters. Think of house design in systematic and functional terms. Living is an energy flow, and the layout of a house can

Common Exterior Repairs

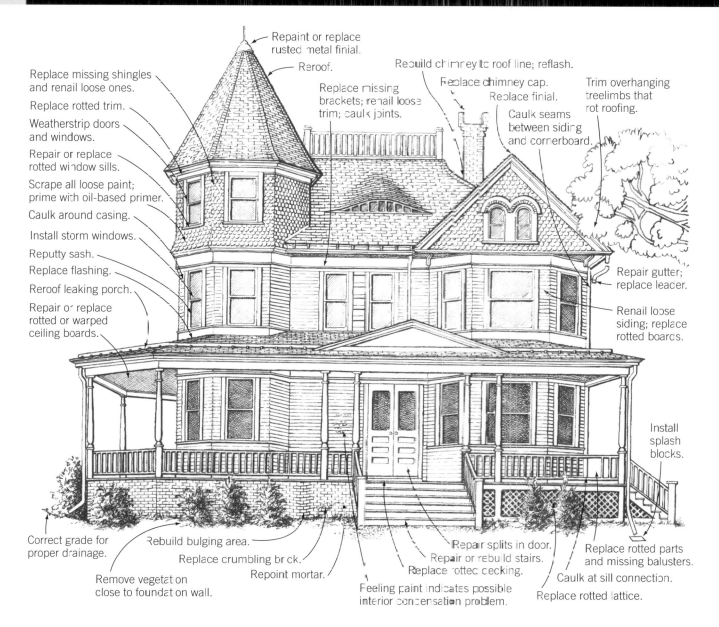

Repaint or replace rusted metal finial.

Reroof.

Rebuild chimney to roof line; reflash.

Replace chimney cap.

Replace finial.

Trim overhanging treelimbs that rot roofing.

Replace missing shingles and renail loose ones.

Replace rotted trim.

Weatherstrip doors and windows.

Repair or replace rotted window sills.

Scrape all loose paint; prime with oil-based primer.

Caulk around casing.

Install storm windows.

Reputty sash.

Replace flashing.

Reroof leaking porch.

Repair or replace rotted or warped ceiling boards.

Replace missing brackets; renail loose trim; caulk joints.

Caulk seams between siding and cornerboard.

Repair gutter; replace leader.

Renail loose siding; replace rotted boards.

Install splash blocks.

Correct grade for proper drainage.

Rebuild bulging area.

Replace crumbling brick.

Repoint mortar.

Remove vegetation close to foundation wall.

Repair splits in door.

Repair or rebuild stairs.

Replace rotted decking.

Feeling paint indicates possible interior condensation problem.

Replace rotted parts and missing balusters.

Caulk at sill connection.

Replace rotted lattice.

influence the current of this flow, alternating between spillways and dams, locks and waterfalls.

Types of Space

As architects will tell you, houses organize themselves into three distinct kinds of space, which are defined by the activities that take place within them. In today's culture of North America at least, the inner, or private, space encompasses such things as sleeping, lovemaking, and bodily care. Family and social activities such as food preparation, dining, and entertaining take place in the outer, public space. (The typical sequestration of the kitchen from the dining room shows that nineteenth-century homeowners did not necessarily share our attitudes about room function.) Finally, there is the middle space, the transition zone between public and private spaces, between inside and outside. This space includes laundry rooms, mudrooms, porches, hallways, and playrooms.

These design concepts can also relate to the cycles of the seasons. As one moves through the year, one moves through space as well. In winter, the family draws together, gathering around the hearth or stove, thinking deep thoughts, sleeping late. In summer, the family wakes early and expands onto porches and lawns. One continually moves from the inner spaces to the outer ones within the sphere of the house itself. A well-designed house will allow graceful transitions and will balance the often-conflicting feeling of

Planning the Work—Structural and Cosmetic

Priority	Scheme	Item	Estimated Cost	Estimated Time	Season*
NOW	STRUCTURAL	1. Foundation 2. Sills 3. Roof repair 4. Chimney repair			SPRING
SOON		5. Sheathing† 6. Windows and doors 7. Gutting interior 8. Rewiring			SUMMER
		9. Replumbing 10. Insulation 11. Heating system			FALL
LATER	COSMETIC	12. Interior changes 13. Interior walls 14. Cabinets, fixtures 15. Floor refinishing			WINTER
		16. Grading, seeding 17. Siding 18. Outbuildings, porches 19. Painting 20. Everything else			NEXT YEAR

*When an item takes up the entire season cycle, all the others merely shift into the next rotation, ad infinitum. Here, the time scheme might be best listed as "mañana."
†If rotten; otherwise leave until later.

Drawing Plans

In the best of all possible worlds, you'll spend the winter before renovation drawing up the master design plan. First, you develop lists and rough sketches of each inhabitant's wants, needs, and fantasies. Then you measure every room and passageway and, using an architect's ruler and graph paper, make a scale drawing of the existing floor plan.

The drawing doesn't have to be (nor will it be) perfectly accurate. But it should show the location of windows, fixed items such as sewer vent stacks and chimneys, the swing of doors, and the run of floor joists and major support beams. Make scaled cutouts of major appliances and furniture pieces, and place them in various combinations on the floor plan. Leave at least a 3-ft.-wide circulation corridor around or between them. (Most people underestimate how much space furniture occupies.) Allow clearance for door swings. Make sure light switches are accessible when the door is opened. Don't forget that pipes and chimneys and stairs shown on the first floor should also show up on the second floor. Use tracing-paper overlays to project changes onto the existing floor plan.

Because there are likely to be things you have overlooked and there may be hidden problems, it's a

good idea to have these drawings evaluated and refined by an architect or designer or a friend in the building business. Although time for leisurely reflection may be a luxury, a well-thought-out design is a necessity. Better to take a week thinking about the changes you'd like to make both in the present and over the long term than to find out later that your renovation needs remodeling. It's a lot easier to correct mistakes with an eraser than with a sledgehammer.

each member of the household about his or her needs for public and private space.

Both graceful transitions and good design can be a hard act to pull off within the confines of an existing structure. The harmonious mating of old and new is one of the most difficult challenges in renovation. Chances are good that additions have already been made sometime over the last century or so, when the former occupants extended the original core house to meet the needs of expanding family or farming operations or to reflect growing prosperity.

Changing Needs, Changing Spaces

The core of this coastal Maine cottage was transported onto its present site in the 1830s. Over the intervening generations, it grew outward, sprouting a dormer and a front porch, which eventually melded into the house proper. In the 1970s, a second bathroom was added, joining the house to its 1900s carriage barn, which was then converted into a guest bedroom. A subsequent owner remodeled that room into a home office. During my tenure in the mid-1990s, I added a second-story bedroom for my teenage daughter and changed the first floor back into a bedroom for my father-in-law.

Dealing with Setback Requirements

Because zoning regulations mandate specific set-backs, a collapsed structure may prove valuable, since you can rebuild within the original foot-print of a building, even if it overshoots setback requirements. If you do decide an addition is needed, check with the zoning board before you get too involved in your design. If it's in a vil-lage, the present structure probably crowds the lot lines already. There may also be a limit to the total additional square footage that you can add even within the original footprint (in effect, a height restriction). One of the benefits of rural

Because local floodplain zoning prohibited expansion of the existing footprint, the living space of this early-nineteenth-century Cape was enlarged by building up. The kneewall at the back of the house was raised, the original roof pitch was increased, dormers were added, and a new gable roof was built over the original shed addition at the back.

Solving a Roof Riddle

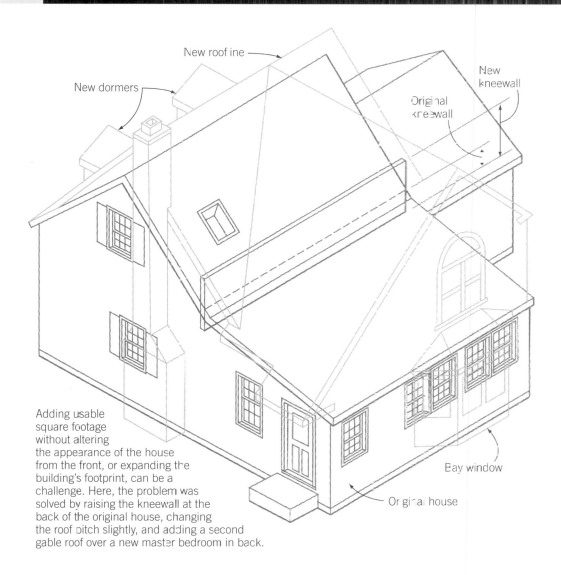

New roof line

New dormers

New kneewall

Original kneewall

Bay window

Original house

Adding usable square footage without altering the appearance of the house from the front, or expanding the building's footprint, can be a challenge. Here, the problem was solved by raising the kneewall at the back of the original house, changing the roof pitch slightly, and adding a second gable roof over a new master bedroom in back.

living is the relative freedom from such bureaucratic annoyances.

Sometimes a house benefits more from subtraction than addition, especially when restoration is a priority. Removing later accretions of inferior workmanship or conflicting styles can do a lot to upgrade and harmonize the appearance of an otherwise unremarkable or ugly house. I don't think one should be fanatical about architectural purity, though. Sometimes the charm of a particular house is its unique style of crazy-quilt patchwork.

APPROACHES TO RENOVATION

Short of tearing the place down to the ground and starting from scratch, what is the best way to untangle this Gordian knot of problems masquerading as a house? What is most efficient is not always the most practical. Rebuilding an old house can be a form of economic strangulation, even suicide. It can also be the only chance you will ever get to have a house of your own. You can work on your house piecemeal while you live in it (the caterpillar approach), or you may want to move out for a while and do the work all at once (the Blitzkrieg approach).

The Blitzkrieg Approach

If you choose the Blitzkrieg approach, consider living in temporary quarters such as a tent, an old house trailer, a camper or a minimally converted outbuilding or garage while rebuilding; house trailers have the advantage of being resalable when the house is ready. I know of a couple who spent their first summer converting a tool shed into a small but serviceable house. Free from the pressure of having to get it all done under a seasonal deadline, they renovated their charming but unlivable farmhouse as time and money allowed. A few years later they

Top: When a restoration is also a renovation: Built early in the twentieth century, the balloon-framed addition with its bulky dormers overpowers the eighteenth-century timber frame it joins. Above: After removing, replacing, repairing, or rebuilding almost every inch from foundation to ridge, the builders restored the original house to its proper prominence. (Photos by Will Calhoun; Kevin Ireton)

moved into the big house and rented out the former shed.

Living in a temporary shelter while rebuilding your dream house goes a long way toward relieving the tensions that inevitably arise during the dust and rubble of renovation. It's also a sensible strategy for using space time and financial windfalls, and allows for wholesale (and therefore more efficient) demolition, especially if the entire house has to be gutted. Interior walls can be removed, wiring and plumbing exposed, and structural weak points repaired as needed. Dormers can be framed or sections of roof removed without fear of damage to household goods.

Whatever is rotten can be replaced while the structure is exposed. Excavation and foundation repair can be done at any time during and after the stripping process. A timber frame will be much easier to straighten if the interior or exterior wall coverings and partitions have been removed—assuming, of course, that they are in need of removal. Each added layer of board or finish, every partition, adds stiffness that must

be overcome if the frame is to shift. Exposing the house's skeleton also makes it easier to decide where to begin and lightens the loads that must be lifted when foundations and sills are replaced. Drafty old sheathing boards can be replaced or covered with modern air-infiltration retarders. In effect, a new house is hung on the old framework of hand-hewn beams, which in some cases may be the only part of the house worth saving.

Blitzkrieg renovation offers the advantage of relatively quick results. Most important, the work can proceed in logical order. Unhampered by having to live around your work or work around your life by having to redo work you did the month or season before as a temporary expedient, you can do it right the first time.

The disadvantage of this approach is that you don't have time for reflection. Your idea of what you require for living space will change and evolve as you live in the house. What seemed like a good idea at the time may prove to be unworkable. A kitchen that seemed spacious to an ex-apartment dweller might be far too small

If a house needs to be gutted, it is a lot more efficient to do it all at once instead of room by room, assuming of course, you can afford to live elsewhere.

to handle the harvest of a serious neo-rustic. The arrival of children certainly requires a complete reorganization. Former urbanites a few seasons removed to the country discover a whole new crop of needs springing up to replace those they had plowed under. Formerly important avocations and responsibilities may wane and their attendant spaces sit unused: Wet laundry may be drying in the media room during the winter while the tiny back room off the kitchen is stuffed to the rafters with the growing stock of garden tools and bags of animal feed. And of course, an all-out assault presupposes adequate reserves of time and money. Lacking both effectively rules out the Blitzkrieg approach.

The Caterpillar Approach

The caterpillar approach—living in the house and renovating it over a period of years—may be your only choice if you don't have the up-front financial assets to buy or build a new house or to renovate an old one.

There are some serious drawbacks to life as a caterpillar. Above all, it's the most expensive and

This owner/renovator literally camped in his attic while rebuilding the house around him. Even after installing new roofing, the tent provided a relatively dust-free refuge amid the ongoing chaos.

demanding way to renovate. Doing a job rapidly and right the first time is inherently more efficient. As a caterpillar, too much of your time is squandered on cleaning up the mess as the house reverts from renovation project to residence at the end of each workday. To maintain even the barest simulacrum of domesticity, the work must be organized by zones that can be quarantined from the flow of family life rather than by job description. For example, you rebuild the back bedroom, gutting the walls, running new wiring down into the cellar, hanging new drywall, painting and finishing the entire room, and so on, before moving on to the next room and repeating the process. It would be far more economical (especially of time) to gut the entire house all at once, and make and clean up a huge mess only once. You could also hire a drywall subcontractor to hang, tape, and finish all the walls within a few days (most won't do just a single room), instead of laboriously botching the job yourself.

If each zone corresponds to a different level of the house, you may be able to increase efficiency and also coordinate the work more easily with the seasons. Start at the top: Rip out the upstairs walls, the plaster and lath, and clean up. Then patch the roof, reshingle it, and frame and close in a dormer. Cover the window rough openings with poly sheeting until you can afford to pay for the new window units. Leave the final finish for the next year. Then start on the foundation. Work on what has rotted until the nights grow crisp. Now is the time to rebuild the chimney. After the new foundation is backfilled, insulate the attic before cold weather sets in. During the winter months, you can finish the upstairs rooms while living on the first level. The following year, you can move upstairs into finished quarters while renovating the first floor.

This house-within-a-house concept allows you to live and work under the same leaky roof with the least amount of disruption. Plan the work in different stages or modules. Try to leave blocks of time open for major jobs (these used to be called vacations) and always leave a refuge or sanctuary, some small undisturbed or finished corner of the house that will allow you to escape from the grime and noise.

The caterpillar approach is probably best suited to self-employed individuals or couples, who will find it somewhat easier to arrange their schedules to accommodate renovation jobs that refuse to fit into weekends or to set aside larger chunks of time without jeopardizing their employment. The temptation is to spread yourself too thin, to commit to a large project, and then spend all of your time working to pay for it while you try to sandwich the actual work into weekends and nights. But you can easily get caught on a dizzying seesaw of working on the place until the bills are too large to ignore and then working elsewhere until you have enough to go back into debt. In the meantime, you'll never get a chance to live in the house.

As trying as the process will be, there is some compensation for living in the house while renovating it. You'll be able to reflect on the progress and to adapt to circumstances as they arise. For example, you may have planned to panel the bedroom walls with plasterboard when you get around to it next winter only to come across a great deal on pine boards that fall. Gaps in the workflow leave room for serendipity to slip in. You can take advantage of flea-market finds and salvage materials. There's more opportunity for creative improvisation. Plans and designs do not necessarily need to be a done deal. You may decide to add an attached woodshed after a winter spent chipping frozen logs out of a snow bank.

A plastic curtain isolates work areas from the living areas.

Baby Steps

Rebuilding an old house is too great an undertaking to be digested whole. It must be thoroughly chewed. The objective is chopped, like spaghetti for a 2-year-old, into small, manageable bites. Focusing on limited goals helps maintain a sense of proportion—you are not so likely to be overwhelmed and swallowed by The Goal. The reason for enduring this ordeal is easier to keep in sight. Enjoy and savor the process in and of itself, as a vehicle for self-discovery, not as an accounting of steps taken to reach the horizon.

Once, an old-timer I used to work with was watching me slam and jam a block of wood into a space too small for it. I was determined to stretch that opening rather than re-cut the block. I guess he finally lost patience because he turned to me and said, "What's your hurry? You'll be doing this for the rest of your life. You might's well slow down and enjoy it, you damn fool!"

And so it goes for as long as it must, a rhythm of seasonal breaths, in and out, in and out, until one day the burden of things to be done mysteriously vanishes. Like a bucket that has sprung a leak, there is not much more to carry. You feel empty, strange. Suddenly, work is no longer a reflex; you have to ask yourself, what am I going to do this weekend? What needs to be done? The days have expanded; your evenings are your own. Your legs spongy, you begin to move with an unaccustomed lightness of purpose.

HIRING A CONTRACTOR

Should you hire a contractor? For many homeowners, by reason of temperament, skill, or economy, the answer is an obvious no. But others, especially those with limited skills, confidence, or experience, might feel certain jobs are best left to professionals. You might, for example, hire out the heaviest, dirtiest work and reserve the more pleasurable projects for yourself. Because time and money exist in a rough

A new foundation and new sill— but somehow the satisfaction of knowing that at least your house will stand safely and that whatever else you do rests on a firm footing simply isn't dramatic enough.

equilibrium, paying for work with your outside income may be more economical than staying home and blundering through it yourself.

Suppose you want to take an active role in the renovation of your house and, mindful of potential savings, are thinking about being your own contractor? Just as no professional contractor makes a commitment without an accurate estimate of labor and materials, you must make an equally precise estimate of your available resources. Ask yourself:

- How much time can you allow for the job?
- When can you spare it?
- What technical skills and general building skills do you have?
- What tools and equipment do you have or need?
- How well can you communicate with trades people?
- How much do you know about renovation, and how much do you want to learn?

A contractor is someone who is paid to stay awake at night and worry about the job. How much is this worth to you? Contractors are often little more than errand-runners, checking off endless lists of things to do, problems to solve, and kinks to straighten—all within a tight financial and temporal framework. How obsessive are you? Experience is what enables a good contractor to make informed choices, and the lack of it is perhaps the greatest stumbling block to successful do-it-yourself contracting. A beginner is at a disadvantage evaluating job progress or anticipating the next unforeseen problem. Learning from your mistakes is effective, but it is also expensive. The skills and techniques may not be very complicated, but the

translation from reading about a task to doing it is not always a direct or simple affair—books don't leak, pipes do.

Do You Really Have the Time?

A contractor has the time to do the job. And supervising a large-scale renovation is a full-time job, not a sideline that can be crammed into a few hours before work, an odd afternoon, weekends, or nights (those moments should be reserved for the rest of life). It's the contractor who has to smooth things out when the plumber is angry with the drywall installers and the carpenters can't stand the way the owner is always hanging around asking questions. It's the contractor's job to work as late as necessary to finish drawing a cornice detail, to listen to the weather forecast to see if frost will hamper the concrete pour scheduled for tomorrow morning. Do you have the time to do all this? Can you afford not to?

Types of Contracts

If you decide to go the contractor route, do your homework on how to select and work with one. Pay particular attention to the type of contract offered.

FIXED PRICE The fixed price, or lump-sum, contract is most familiar, but it is least-suited to renovation. Here, the contractor simply agrees to perform the specified work for a fixed amount—period, no surprises. If costs run over, the contractor eats them; if they come in under his estimate, he pockets the windfall. Caught between the rock of fixed costs and the hard place of fixed price, there are built-in incentives to push productivity and keep costs low to increase profits. Ideally, this contract should benefit the client. But because there is no way to recoup costs of oversights, mistakes, or unforeseen events (all of which characterize renovation

work), the slush factor in the fixed price must be quite large if the temptation to cut corners, pad changes, and squeeze extras to make up the losses is to be avoided. Because of this, lump-sum contracts must be especially clear as to what is included and what is an extra.

COST PLUS In theory, the cost-plus contract offers the lowest price. The contractor's percentage for profit and overhead, as agreed on in advance, is added to the sum of the invoiced charges for materials, subcontractors, and labor. The contractor, ensured of a reasonable profit, does not have to finagle the price to cover surprises and run-of-the-mill disasters. However, our national experience with defense contractors reveals the flaw in this arrangement—the temptation to milk the job for more time than it's worth is hard to resist. Although it leaves a lot to trust and goodwill, this type of contract is well suited to reconstruction of rotten sills and walls, where there are often too many variables to allow a meaningful bid.

THE NOT-TO-EXCEED HYBRID I've found that a combination of the preceding contracts—the not-to-exceed contract—works best. Here, the contractor bills for the actual cost of the work plus a percentage for overhead/profit up to a maximum figure, at which the price becomes fixed. Should the total costs be less than the maximum, the customer saves the difference. Should they exceed it, the contractor absorbs the overrun. Of course, an opportunistic contractor can inflate the not-to-exceed figure and then milk the job or fudge labor costs to push against the limits. Here's where competitive bidding—submitting plans and specs to several contractors for their bids—limits dishonesty to tolerable levels.

Whether you are acting as your own contractor or hiring a professional, foundation repair almost always requires the services of an excavation subcontractor.

BECOMING AN EMPLOYER If you decide to hire labor by the hour, you are no longer legally a contractor but an employer and, as such, are subject to various federal and state regulations. See an accountant for advice; you could also pose your hypothetical case to your state Department of Employment before proceeding. Becoming a short-term employer could turn out to be a great deal of trouble and expense. It's a lot easier to find a hungry general contractor willing to work for an hourly wage and perhaps a small percentage to cover wear and tear on tools and equipment. Whoever you hire, he or she should expect to furnish you with a certificate of insurance to protect you from liability suits. If you hire individual carpenters instead of a subcontractor with crew, each carpenter should furnish proof of insurance.

Knowing When to Show and When to Go

Once the work is under way, keep in touch. But don't be obtrusive. Carpenters and other trades people tend to get nervous when the owner is standing around. Sometimes they become so self-conscious about making a mistake and try so hard to avoid one, that they make mistakes. And the contractor or foreman is loath to draw attention by correcting someone in front of the owner. A proven means of winning worker confidence is to show up on Friday afternoon with the paychecks and the beer. But even if you do bring the doughnuts, don't make a habit of visiting during coffee break. Workers instinctively react with resentment to this intrusion into their most intimate territory. There's a substratum of awkwardness in the hierarchy of worker and worked-for that can never be resolved, no matter how nice a person you are.

You have to trust your contractor's experience, but you shouldn't be a victim of his malfeasance. If you sense a problem developing, talk about it, after hours or aside from the crew. If something they're doing doesn't make sense, ask about it. If the answer rings false, ask someone else. It could be that you misjudged and picked the wrong contractor. If this is so, stop and clear the matter up. And if you feel justified in so doing, don't hesitate to let him go, right then and there. The situation will only get messier if you let things continue askew.

Owners—some motivated by a desire to save money and others by a wish for greater involvement in, and simple fascination with, the building of their homes—will ask to help out or work along with the crew. Since the owners rarely have the skill or time to mesh with the builder's timetables or quality standards, their participation is seldom a good idea.

SPECIFYING "BY OWNER" There are cases, however, where an owner might be a tradesperson or sufficiently skilled to undertake an area of the job that would otherwise be subcontracted out. This can be specified as "by owner" in the contract, and an allowance is factored into the bid. But such cases are rare. More often than not, the owners will ask how much they can save if they do the painting or staining. The wise contractor will answer, "Nothing," and explain that since it is his name that will be on the finished product, he would prefer having control of the outcome. Or he may allow the owner to perform these functions so long as the contract specifies his right to complete or continue them at cost-plus if they are not completed within the necessary time frame.

This is tricky stuff. Usually, only good friends or builders working for other builders will have the necessary rapport to pull it off. Scheduling can be difficult. For example, weekends or long summer evenings are the best time for the owners to stain clapboards, pick up rubbish, stack lumber, or fetch materials to the job site for the next day's work. A fair contractor should compensate for the value of this behind-the-scenes, after-hours help by generosity in the client's favor when figuring up the allowances for job overruns and extras. Or, if the contribution is substantial, have the owner bill him for hours worked at a rate commensurate with his or her skill level and deduct that amount from the contract payment.

STAY AWAY DURING THE DAY Owners on the job site during the workday are a distraction at best. Never try to borrow a carpenter's tools for any reason, unless specifically invited to do so. Carpenters are scrupulously careful about the protocols of such things among themselves—it's one of the ways harmony is maintained. It can cost you dearly to interfere with it.

Hiring a contractor should be no more difficult than hiring a lawyer, accountant, or any

The Fudge Factor

Despite any impressions to the contrary, carpentry is an inexact art. No one builds perfectly, at least not anyone you can afford to hire. Mistakes are a given. The best builders make precious few and know how to fix the ones they do make. Every job has a built-in allowance for "fudge," for covering over or correcting mistakes.

My experience indicates that about 2 percent of the total labor cost is part of that recipe. With a fixed-price contract, the contractor eats it all. If you are paying cost-plus or hiring help by the hour, you can expect a taste too. But you shouldn't have to pay for a three-course meal. Unless caused by poor planning or changes after the fact on your part, major errors should be repaired by the builder at his own expense, not yours. If it's the contractor's fault, it's the contractor's obligation to make it right. An honest builder will absorb the damage without even mentioning it, and simply deduct the time spent straightening things out from the time you are billed.

other professional. Like them, a good contractor has spent 10 or more years learning the trade and survived in an intensely competitive environment. A solid reputation takes years to cultivate. Only a fool would destroy it for a quick buck at their client's expense. Only fools believe that their misdeeds will escape unnoticed. Granted, there are some outright crooks and con artists who do manage to successfully hoodwink unsuspecting and trusting clients. But most of them don't last long, and everybody down at the village lumberyard knows who they are. Most successful contractors survive because, given enough time, honesty and competence do go hand in hand. But, perhaps because people entrust their deepest and most personal dreams to their contractor's care, they are so often quick to shout thief when something is lost in the translation.

ARCHITECTS AND DESIGNERS

If you're capable of doing your own renovation work, chances are you won't need to hire an architect or a designer to tell you what you need to do. Here's the difference between them: Architects are licensed professionals who have completed a graduate level course of study and real-life apprenticeship before passing their certification exam. Designers do the same things as architects, but they are less expensive since they don't have licenses or know how to build skyscrapers and post offices.

Consulting with either a designer or an architect may be invaluable before or during your renovation. These people can spot serious structural problems in your plans before they become a reality. By simply reviewing your rough sketches, a designer or architect can make recommendations that could save you hundreds, even thousands, of dollars and can offer suggestions that dramatically affect the comfort and utility of your home ("Instead of that addition, how about opening up this space, changing that traffic flow . . .").

Also, depending on your local code, site conditions, and the scope of your renovations, you may need a structural engineer's stamp of approval before you can obtain a building permit. Likewise, the design or alteration of an on-site sewage disposal system almost always falls under the aegis of a licensed civil engineer.

The Design—Build Option

If you've hired a contractor, do you also need to hire an architect to supervise your contractor? Or should you hire a contractor who can also furnish you with designs? There are arguments in favor of both options. Armed with the power of creative vision, the architect is supposed to transmute your wishes into a work of art, written in the language of builders (plans and specs), while acting as your agent to ensure the contractor's compliance with the contract terms. The unspoken assumption is that contractors are in need of supervision to secure their honesty or enforce their competence.

Although it is true that there are still contractors with the aesthetic awareness of a mud puddle (as there are designers and architects who wouldn't recognize a hammer if it were thrown at them), the separation between white and blue collars is no longer clear-cut. Today, most renovators also offer some level of design services. For most residential projects smaller in scale than an opera house, the designer/builder is probably the most economical alternative to the traditional client/architect/contractor triad. Just like an architect, a good designer/builder will have the communication skills and insight to interpret your ideas and translate them into a plan that reconciles budget and dreams. The emphasis is on translation, not adulteration (architects are sometimes suspected of forgetting that they work for the client and not vice versa). Unlike most architects, the designer/builder will have solid hands-on experience with how to implement those plans. And because the person using the drawings is the one who drew them, there's one less level of potential misunderstanding between the client and contractor and one fewer professional to pay.

A Vermonter had bought an old, run-down farm and had worked very hard getting it back in good operating condition. When it was back in pretty good working shape, the local minister happened to stop by for a call. He congratulated the farmer on the result of his labors, remarking that it was wonderful what God and man could do when working together.

"Ayeh," allowed the farmer, "p'raps it is. But you should have seen this place when God was running it alone."

—ALLEN R. FOLEY, *WHAT THE OLD-TIMER SAID*

This shaky stone foundation capped by a buttress wall is badly in need of replacement. (Photo by Kevin Walters)

Despite their aura of invincible durability, even the most brutish sill beams left lying in the moist embrace of earth will soon rot, returning to the ground from which they sprang. Holding wood and earth apart while anchoring them to one another, the stones of a foundation postpone that inevitable reunion. It's only when I reflect on the astounding effort it takes to maintain this precarious equilibrium in a cold and moist place like northern New England that the idea of renovating old houses in a place like Arizona begins to seem hugely appealing. All that labor and expense earmarked for preserving a hole in the ground could be spent on things that make a visible difference instead!

THE FORCES OF EARTH AND WATER

A house is heavy. The foundation is supposed to spread the load over a suitably wide area. If the earth is unstable, the foundation can and will settle with dire consequences for the house above. In warm climates where houses are built on slabs, piers, or shallow footings, foundations are likely to stay put so long as the bearing soil is adequate. But even in stable soils, a cellar is inherently unstable. The weight of the soil pushing against the cellar wall will, in time, tend to push it in at its base.

An old-fashioned timber-frame house resists soil pressure in two ways: First, the continuous heavy sill beams and the sheer weight of the frame anchor the house at the top of the wall, stiffening the wall. Second, the wide footprint of formidable boulders at the base of its outwardly flared rubble stone foundation affords the greatest resistance at the point of greatest pressure. Unless braced by a floor slab, the modern concrete wall, which, around 1898 began to replace rubble stone, is actually more vulnerable at this pressure point. On the other hand, it is stronger at its top. Bolted to the sills of a stick frame, a concrete wall is less likely to slide out from under the house than rubble stone. Because the mortar joints of stone, brick, or unreinforced

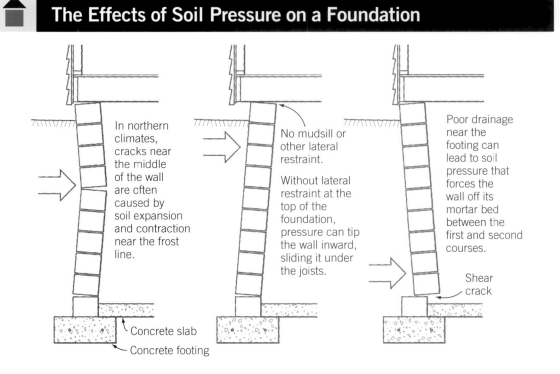

The Effects of Soil Pressure on a Foundation

In northern climates, cracks near the middle of the wall are often caused by soil expansion and contraction near the frost line.

No mudsill or other lateral restraint.

Without lateral restraint at the top of the foundation, pressure can tip the wall inward, sliding it under the joists.

Poor drainage near the footing can lead to soil pressure that forces the wall off its mortar bed between the first and second courses.

Shear crack

Concrete slab

Concrete footing

concrete block have little resistance to lateral forces, tall and relatively narrow masonry walls are more prone to failure than either bulky dry-laid stone or cast concrete walls. Walls that were not securely attached to the house sill or otherwise restrained can also tip inward in response to lateral pressure from frost and soil compaction as when a heavy truck backs onto an abutting driveway.

The weight of soil pressing against the foundation is not, by itself, likely to damage a well-laid and securely anchored foundation. But under the right conditions, water in the soil can easily destroy a foundation. Depending on their porosity, soils are saturated to varying degrees with subsurface water. This water table fluctuates seasonally in response to variations in precipitation. Especially during spring, cellars can lie beneath the crest of the water table. The situation is complicated by surface water (rainwater or snowmelt). As it pours off the eaves or drains toward the house along the ground, water saturates the soil around the house and eventually seeps down the foundation wall.

Hydrostatic Pressure

Whatever the source, water that ponds up against a cellar wall exerts a force (hydrostatic pressure) strong enough to push through the microscopic pores in solid concrete, causing a damp basement or "weeping" joints in masonry and, under extreme circumstances, buckling the wall. Think about it: Water weighs 62.4 lb. per cubic foot. This may not seem like much, since concrete can withstand pressures of several thousand pounds per square inch. But hydrostatic pressure is exerted laterally as well as vertically, which means that if the soil surrounding a cellar is typically saturated over a large enough area, the actual pressure against a wall can easily exceed the elastic limit of poured concrete. The deeper the foundation, the stronger the pressure.

Whether acting in concert or as sole agents, poor drainage, unstable soil, and/or frost heave have caused this stone foundation to crack.

Given the preponderance of wet soils throughout a good part of the country, it would seem that the old-fashioned dry-laid stone foundation stands the best chance of long-term survival. Granted, the fissures between the stones would let water percolate, if not visibly trickle, through the wall, easing any hydrostatic pressure. But, as we know, damp cellars give rise to their own particular set of evils. While there are a number of both traditional and modern drainage techniques to deal with such infiltration, the problem is that soil is also washing into the cellar through those open joints. Over time, the ground level outside the wall settles, the trickle becomes a torrent, and eventually the undermined stones fall into the cellar.

Frost Heave

Furthermore, in cold climates, when water held in poorly drained clay or silty soils freezes, it expands, exerting tremendous pressure in all directions like millions of tiny screw jacks. Because there is less resistance at the ground line, the soil moves upward with the ice. Or, when a cellar offers the opportunity, the soil expands sideways. Obviously, any foundation that doesn't reach below the frost line (the depth of average maximum frost penetration) will rise and fall on the swells of frost heave. Even when deep enough, a foundation lacking proper drainage is vulnerable in both directions. Frost typically forms in pockets called *ice lenses,* which expand in all directions. Ice lenses can exert

destructive lateral pressure on a wall, which typically results in vertical cracks near the middle. They can also adhere to the wall itself and exert an upward force at the same time, causing long horizontal cracks, with the top portion of the wall kicked inward.

No wall, stone or concrete, can withstand the onslaught; it is only a matter of time before the foundation buckles, cracks, and heaves in. Dry-laid rubble-stone walls are actually more susceptible to frost heave than a cast or mortared smooth-surfaced wall. A relatively small lens that adheres to a projecting stone in a rubble wall tends to pluck it out, whereas a monolithic wall offers less purchase and takes more force to move.

Diverting Water

The best protection against both hydrostatic pressure and frost heave is prevention. The grade (the ground next to the house) should slope away from the house. Gutters and downspouts should collect roof runoff and discharge it at a distance from the foundation. In modern

Unreinforced concrete block walls are particularly vulnerable to soil pressure. (Photo by Donald Cohen)

construction, the foundation wall is damp-proofed on the outside, a perforated drainpipe covered with crushed stone is laid along the footings, and the excavation is backfilled with porous material that allows water to drain away, preventing any buildup of hydrostatic pressure on the wall. In effect, the water table can never rise above the level of the drain tile. And because the soil next to the house isn't holding any water, it can't freeze and heave.

Vitrified clay drain tiles were in use as far back as the first quarter of the nineteenth century. But the labor involved in hand or horse-powered excavation and hauling of materials was formidable, so it's not surprising few houses were equipped with drains or that the trenches around the cellar were backfilled with native soil rather than more porous gravel drawn from a distance. Dry-laid stones were sometimes parged with concrete or pointed with mortar to retard water infiltration. But unless the cellar had been dug in well-drained sandy or gravelly soil, a damp cellar was unavoidable.

Basement Springs

For convenience, the cellars of many old houses were deliberately dug over a spring. Not only did this guarantee a year-round freezeproof water supply but it also saved digging and expensive piping for an outside well. In theory, any overflow (some springs flow continuously) would drain through the wall to an outlet away from the house. But sometimes the overflow pipe is clogged, rotted, or missing, and the water just trickles out into the cellar. A new overflow pipe, routed through the cellar wall to an existing or retrofitted foundation drain or into a cellar sump pit, will dry up this quagmire.

One might wonder then, in the absence of well-drained soils or adequate foundation drainage systems, why any old houses built in cold climates still stand at all. Fortunately, the heavy snow cover typical of most Northern winters acted like an insulating blanket to retard downward frost penetration. And heat escaping

Water in the Cellar: Problems and Remedies

Problems

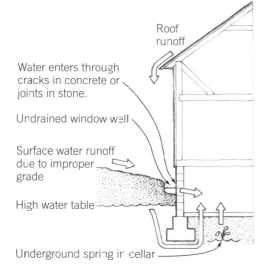

Roof runoff

Water enters through cracks in concrete or joints in stone.

Undrained window well

Surface water runoff due to improper grade

High water table

Underground spring in cellar

Remedies

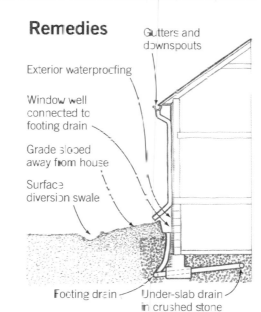

Gutters and downspouts

Exterior waterproofing

Window well connected to footing drain

Grade sloped away from house

Surface diversion swale

Footing drain

Under-slab drain in crushed stone

from the cellar through the foundation walls thawed the earth next to them. Of course, when the house was abandoned, or otherwise left unheated, the cellar would freeze and frost could penetrate beneath the foundation from inside to pry it upward. This is often the cause of a cracked and bulging concrete cellar floor.

In less rigorous climates, old cellars weren't pushed in by waterlogged soils because the loose stones allowed water to enter. Over time, most old foundations shifted as parts of the wall were undermined or stones loosened. In those cases, a common mistake was to pour concrete against the inside of the cellar to block seepage. Of course, blocking the seepage increased the

hydrostatic pressure, causing the walls to give way faster. On the other hand, even in somewhat drier or more stable soils, the buildup of moisture in an unventilated cellar promotes the growth of wood-attacking fungi and insects, which cause structural rot. Whatever the condition or the climate, it's the rare old house that doesn't exhibit some sign of foundation damage or the kinds of water problems that will eventually cause foundation trouble.

SOLVING WATER-INFILTRATION PROBLEMS

It's important to distinguish between problems caused by the infiltration of surface runoff and problems caused by a high water table. Runoff troubles can often be cured easily, whereas water-table problems are seldom resolved without resort to heroic (and expensive) measures. As mentioned previously, when the grade doesn't slope away from the foundation on all sides, surface water flows toward the house. Likewise, roof runoff works down along the foundation wall and through any cracks or pores into the cellar. So-called "dry" walls of stones laid without mortar will usually start to weep after a heavy rain. Rivulets are often visible at the height of the downpour. The mortar joints of concrete block walls are susceptible to this sort of infiltration; even poured concrete walls are not impervious.

Swales and French Drains

If enough surface water percolates down to the bottom of the foundation, water will ooze up between the wall and floor slab, and puddles will form on the cellar floor. If you were to walk around the exterior perimeter of such a house, you'd notice sunken areas and what appear to be small tunnels formed where the surface water has seeped through the foundation wall. A few

Collecting Water

French Drain

French drains collect and transport water. Sometimes the discharge is into a drywell rather than above ground.

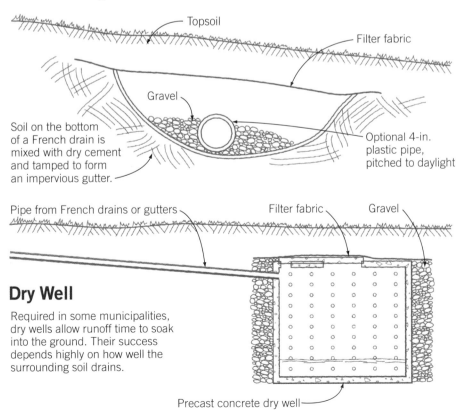

Topsoil

Filter fabric

Gravel

Soil on the bottom of a French drain is mixed with dry cement and tamped to form an impervious gutter.

Optional 4-in. plastic pipe, pitched to daylight

Pipe from French drains or gutters

Filter fabric

Gravel

Dry Well

Required in some municipalities, dry wells allow runoff time to soak into the ground. Their success depends highly on how well the surrounding soil drains.

Precast concrete dry well

wheelbarrow loads of clay soil spread over these spots and compacted will build up the grade and allow runoff to flow away from the house. If the grade pitches toward the foundation, a swale (a grassed-in shallow trough) should be cut into the slope. The swale itself must be pitched to channel water away from the house. Because of the sheer volume of material to be redistributed, this is bulldozer work.

A French drain is an alternative to swales that leaves the surface contour intact. It's basically a subsurface swale filled with a drain tile and crushed stone. The native soil at the bottom of the trench is made somewhat impervious to water by tamping dry cement into it. A layer of filter fabric keeps soil particles out of the porous gravel or crushed stone covering the drain pipe.

Gutters and Downspouts

Gutters (or eaves troughs, as they are somewhat more mellifluously called) and downspouts can help prevent water infiltration by catching roof runoff and diverting it away from the house. The downspout should never drain directly onto the ground because this can merely compound the problem by increasing the water flow at the foundation. Instead attach an extension to the downspout so that it discharges onto a splash block at least 4 ft from the wall or onto undisturbed soil, not backfill.

Problems with Cellar Windows and Window Wells

Wood-framed windows were commonly set in the foundation walls of old houses to admit light (but not necessarily ventilation) into the cellar. When the abovegrade elevation wasn't sufficient to allow the window, a pit was dug against the wall and lined with stone or brick (nowadays, preformed corrugated galvanized steel is most often used). However, located within inches of the ground, the wood sash and

TIP

Gutter Alternative

In the northern United States, gutters and downspouts tend to fill up with ice, splitting seams or backing up under the shingles or into the house walls, thus many homes are built without them. A layer of heavy plastic covered with coarse gravel or a band of pavement along the eaves (basically a continuous splash block) can be an effective alternative to gutters, as long as the bottom of the wall sheathing is at least 2 ft. above grade. ■■ ■■

A simple trough effectively diverts roof runoff away from the foundation and is also less likely to clog or ice up. (Photo by Kevin Walters)

Water draining back under this cellar window eventually caused the foundation wall to collapse inward. Resetting the fallen window is the least of the problems.

Vinyl cladding and pressure-treated wood sash and case work ensure that this cellar vent window will resist the moisture endemic to its exposure. The manufactured unit is set in a site-built frame installed in a new foundation wall.

Ventilating Louvers

One way to alleviate the problem of belowgrade windows is to replace them with a cast-aluminum screened ventilating louver. These are sized to fit into the space otherwise occupied by a standard 8-in. by 16-in. concrete block. Although simple to install, these louvers won't provide natural light and are best suited to walls under porches where light wouldn't penetrate anyway or where there is not sufficient clearance above grade to install a proper foundation window. Modern operable insulated-glass cellar windows admit both light and air. (A window that opens is "operable," one that can't is "fixed.")

To install a louver, remove the old window and scrub the opening clean with a wire brush. Then wet down the old masonry and fill in the opening with solid or cored concrete block or bricks and stones as needed. Bed the louver into mortar sloped to drain at the base and sides. If possible, provide at least two vents along each wall for cross ventilation. In winter, close the vents and stuff a piece of rigid foam or fiberglass insulation against them.

frame were especially vulnerable to moisture. Rare is the window that has not rotted away, leaving a conduit for the entrance of wind, insects, and vermin. Even worse, except for those few cases in which some kind of functioning drainage was provided, the window wells usually channeled surface runoff back against the foundation wall.

The ruin of many a foundation can be traced back to its window wells and the soggy soil that allowed frost to pluck stones out of the undermined wall until it collapsed into the cellar. While replacing a rotted cellar window with a new unit or even a ventilating louver is fairly easy, retrofitting a caved-in window well with proper drainage entails a backbreaking session with a *banjo* (carpenter's slang for a spade shovel) or the hiring of a mini-backhoe.

REPLACING A ROTTED CELLAR WINDOW Pry out the rotted window and its frame. Replace any rotted wood blocking between the head of the window and the house sill with new treated lumber as needed. If possible, size the new window unit to be slightly smaller than the original opening. If no close match is available, fill the opening with masonry to fit. You do not want to enlarge an opening in granite ashlar or poured concrete. (Once you start pulling out bricks and stones, you can end up with a lot bigger opening than you intended.)

The new window typically consists of a vinyl-coated sash set in an uncased treated wood frame that can be bedded in mortar directly (best for irregular rubble or ashlar stone walls). Otherwise, with regular masonry (such as brick, block, or concrete) cut and nail treated-wood casing boards to the frame. Anchor the unit by nailing through the head jamb into the house sill or blocking, and secure the casings to the wall with construction adhesive and a few masonry anchors. Fill any gaps between the frame and the opening with expanding foam caulk.

RETROFITTING A WINDOW WELL Dig out the bottom of the window well and, if site conditions allow, extend a shallow trench out to daylight (see the drawing at right). Lay a short length of perforated pipe into the well (the ends should be capped) and tee it into solid drainpipe to create an outlet. If extending the trench to daylight is impractical, tee the drain into another perforated pipe at the outlet end (ends likewise capped). Cover this pipe and the bottom of the window well with crushed stone and backfill the trench. This mini-drywell will diffuse runoff into the soil at a safe distance from the wall. Otherwise, the drainpipe could be connected to an existing footing drain (which involves a lot of digging) or to the drain that will eventually be installed with a new foundation.

Waterproofing inside Cellar Walls

Hydraulic cements and various epoxy or latex-based waterproofing paints applied to the inside of the foundation walls might cure occasional seepage caused by surface runoff. If the joints between dry-laid stones are first stuffed with mortar (the technique is called *pointing* or *tuck pointing*) and large-scale irregularities are smoothed over, it's possible to stop further leakage by parging the walls with cement stucco, applied in two ⅜-in.-thick coats, and sealing with a hydraulic cement coating such as Thoroseal.

Dampen the stucco (or block wall) before applying the sealer and keep it damp for 2 or 3 days so it will cure to maximum strength. According to the manufacturer, Surewall, a fiber-reinforced coating used to bond dry-laid concrete block, is waterproof. It might be a better choice for parging stone walls. Because each waterproofing compound is unique, be sure to read the manufacturer's recommendations carefully and select a product intended for your specific need. Although these cements are up to 10 times more costly than ordinary mortar,

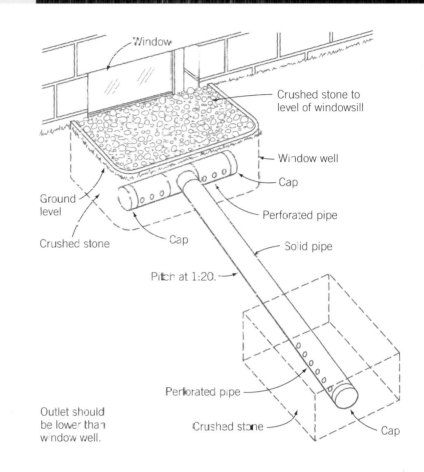

Quick Fix to Improve Window-Well Drainage

Window / Crushed stone to level of windowsill / Window well / Cap / Ground level / Perforated pipe / Crushed stone / Cap / Solid pipe / Pitch at 1:20. / Perforated pipe / Crushed stone / Cap / Outlet should be lower than window well.

they're still cheaper than excavating and sealing the wall from the outside.

SEALING THE JOINT BETWEEN WALL AND FLOOR When water is oozing up between the wall and the floor slab, a stucco coat alone won't stop the leak. The standard recommendation is to use hydraulic cement to seal the joint between wall and floor. To do this, cut a ¾-in.-deep channel into the floor slab where it butts the wall. Ideally, for greater bond strength, the profile should form an angled key that is wider at the bottom than at the top, but because the concrete chips out in irregular chunks, this is seldom possible. A rented hammer drill with a chisel blade makes this tedious job a lot easier.

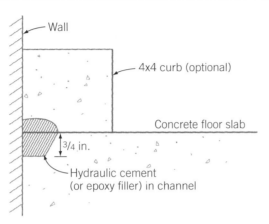

**Water Sealing
the Joint between
Floor Slab and Wall**

Wall

4x4 curb (optional)

Concrete floor slab

3/4 in.

Hydraulic cement
(or epoxy filler) in channel

Hydraulic Cements: Do They Really Work?

Although some contractors and homeowners have claimed success in stopping leakage with hydraulic cements, most writers on the subject take a more jaundiced view of their efficacy. I've had success using hydraulic cement to seal weeping mortar joints in a concrete block pony wall that consists of two or three course of blocks atop a poured concrete frost wall. But its utility seems to diminish with depth (and increasing hydrostatic pressure).

In any case, depending on hydraulic cements to keep your cellar dry is like relying on caulking to keep your boat afloat. Although they can require major excavation and expense, structural safeguards (such as foundation drains and external damp-proofing) will work at least as long as the house is standing, and I prefer them to hydraulic cement stop gaps. There are a few contractor-applied specialized epoxy crack fillers that do successfully plug leaks. Like the consolidants used to repair rotten structural timbers, the resin is injected into the crack with a special pump. When cured, the repair is guaranteed to be stronger than the concrete. But at roughly $40 per lineal foot, such results aren't cheap.

If you pack the joint with successive layers of hydraulic cement, allowing each to set before adding the next, shrinkage will be reduced. (This also keeps the filler from slumping out of a vertical joint.) Some contractors then form and pour a 4-in. by 4-in. curb over the joint (mixing a latex bonding agent into the concrete to improve adhesion) for added insurance against leakage. An alternative is to waterproof the patch with a two-part epoxy sealer, which has excellent adhesion but is otherwise too costly for large areas.

Interior Drainage Systems

There are several variously successful proprietary, contractor-installed internal foundation drainage systems and a few do-it-yourself versions. These basically consist of some type of steel or polyvinyl chloride (PVC) gutter glued to the floor at the base of the wall to intercept water coming through the walls and drain it into a sump or to the exterior footing drain.

The problem with most baseboard drains is that they require a fairly smooth floor and regular wall surface. An earth-floored cellar and/or a rubble-stone wall provide neither. If the water problem is long standing, chances are good that some previous owner already undertook a flood-control program. This may be nothing more than raising the furnace and other vulnerable machinery on concrete blocks up above flood crest. Or it may be a shallow trench scooped out against the walls that drains to a sump at the lowest point of the cellar or to a pipe through the foundation that reaches daylight at the drainage ditch along the road. Trenching does drain off some water, but much of it soaks into the dirt boosting the humidity to ideal levels for wood-eating fungus.

Installing a Sump Pump

The ideal sump pit is simply a concrete-lined box, about 18 in. square and 2 ft. or 3 ft. deep. To make a sump, dig the hole about 1 ft. wider than the finished pit. Form and pour 4-in.-thick walls (a good use for leftover concrete from wall pours). These should extend to the eventual finished floor height, which will be about 1 in. lower than the surrounding floor for better drainage. Nail 1x1 strips to the top of the inside form to make a lip for an optional cover. Backfill with gravel and cover the bottom of the pit with a few inches of coarse stone.

Set the base of the sump pump on the stone and connect the outlet to a 1½-in. PVC or corrugated plastic pipe run up the wall and out through the sill. Install a check valve (a one-way valve) at the pump to keep water from flooding back down into the sump after the pump turns off. A pressure-treated plywood or cast-concrete cover notched to fit around the pump shaft and accouterments will keep debris out of the pit. (Where radon infiltration is a problem, the pump body must be enclosed and all penetrations sealed tight to the sump cover.)

Typical Sump Pump Installation

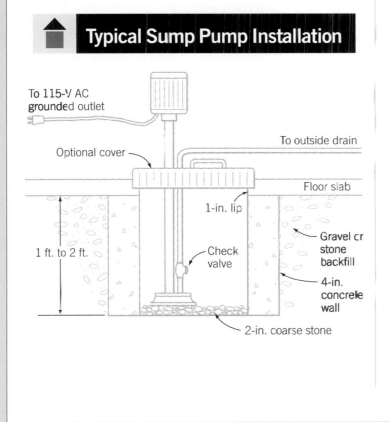

To 115-V AC grounded outlet

Optional cover

To outside drain

Floor slab

1-in. lip

1 ft. to 2 ft.

Check valve

Gravel or stone backfill

4-in. concrete wall

2-in. coarse stone

Modern technology isn't always the most efficient solution: The underslab terra-cotta tiles that carried off the constant seepage of water in the cellar of this c. 1900 house originally drained to an outlet at grade through the tile visible in the right hand corner of the sump. Eventually, the outlet was closed off and an electric sump pump was installed. Unfortunately, whenever there is a power outage, the cellar floor floods in less than 1 hour. A battery-powered backup pump would be a good idea.

Drying Out a Damp Cellar

Earth Floor

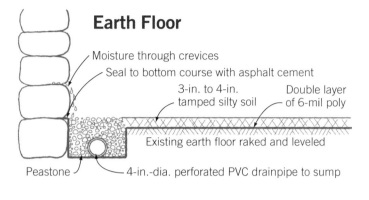

Moisture through crevices
Seal to bottom course with asphalt cement
3-in. to 4-in. tamped silty soil
Double layer of 6-mil poly
Existing earth floor raked and leveled
Peastone
4-in.-dia. perforated PVC drainpipe to sump

Peastone Floor

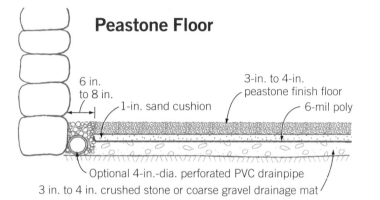

6 in. to 8 in.
1-in. sand cushion
3-in. to 4-in. peastone finish floor
6-mil poly
Optional 4-in.-dia. perforated PVC drainpipe
3 in. to 4 in. crushed stone or coarse gravel drainage mat

Wood Floor

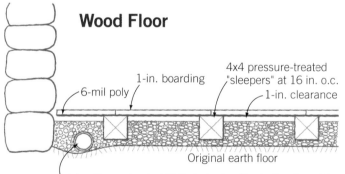

6-mil poly
1-in. boarding
4x4 pressure-treated "sleepers" at 16 in. o.c.
1-in. clearance
Original earth floor
4-in.-dia. perforated PVC drainpipe (in shallow trench)

CREATING A DRY CELLAR FLOOR

In the era before refrigeration, home freezers, and basement furnaces, the cellar played a critical role in the preservation of not only food but also household comfort. As the ambient air temperature rises during spring and summer, the earth also warms, but much more slowly. At 5 ft. or 6 ft. below ground—that is, at the bottom of your cellar—it is much cooler than at the earth's surface. Thus the cellar helped cool the house during the hottest part of the year.

As temperatures drop throughout the fall and winter, the latent heat stored below grade during the warm months is slowly released into the cellar. This phenomenon of *thermal lag* kept the cellar from freezing. Because of these relatively moderate temperature fluctuations, the cellar was an ideal storage area for root vegetables, apples, smoked meats, canned items, and such household staples as dandelion wine and hard cider. Unfortunately, this moist, cool environment was also an ideal incubator for mold. Insufficient ventilation coupled with water vapor released by the earth fostered the growth of wood-devouring fungi. Any wooden objects in direct contact with an earth floor would rot. Metal objects rusted, which is why concrete pads were poured under furnaces and water heaters.

If your cellar still has an earth floor, you don't necessarily have to pour a concrete floor over it to dry the cellar out. There are several intermediate options. If the floor remains basically dry throughout the year, it can be left as is. If seepage (other than at the base of the cellar wall) is endemic, you could cover the floor with peastone (stone crushed to ½-in. pieces) or even boards. But whatever your choice, you must install a polyethylene vapor retarder membrane to block the buildup of excessive humidity and its attendant ills that are the otherwise inevitable consequence of living above an earth-floored cellar.

Modifying an Earth Floor

When, as is most likely the case, there is seepage through crevices in the foundation wall but not from the floor itself, no under-floor drainage is necessary. Instead, clean and grade any existing trench running along the base of the wall or dig a new 4-in.- to 6-in.-deep trench to intercept the water and channel it to a sump or out under the footings before it runs out over the floor. Rake the earthen floor clean, leveling it as much as possible.

Cover the bare earth with a double layer of 6-mil polyethylene, overlapping the seams at least 1 ft. and running the edges across the bottom of the trenches and up onto the walls. Cut around any concrete blocks or support posts and then temporarily remove them to slip an overlapping poly patch under them. Fill the drain trenches with crushed stone. (For added insurance, you can dig the trench 6 in. to 10 in. deep and lay in 4-in.-diameter PVC drainpipe as well.) Then spread and tamp 3 in. to 4 in. of clean silty soil over the poly. The polyethylene will retard vapor transport and keep the new floor and the cellar dry.

Laying a Peastone Floor

In cellars with standing water, first lay down a 3-in. to 4-in. drainage mat of crushed stone or coarse gravel and then cover it with polyethylene, stopping the poly membrane 6 in. to 8 in. short of the cellar walls. (This funnels any water coming through the cellar wall into the underlying drainage mat.) Although the continuous

drainage mat makes an actual trench unnecessary, perforated pipe laid along the perimeter of the wall will speed the conduction of water from the matt and into a sump pit or daylight drain. (If the barrier had been laid over the earth instead and a slab was later poured on top of the peastone, water could pond up in the matt or saturate the earth beneath the barrier and undermine the floor.) Pack 1 in. of sand on top of the poly to cushion it against puncture; then spread 3 in. to 4 in. more peastone to finish the floor.

Getting the peastone into the cellar is the easy part. Distributing it from the bulkhead or window openings (before the windows are installed) takes a lot of back-busting shovel work. (Photo by Kevin Walters)

Laying a Wood Floor

Where site conditions make pouring concrete impractical or too costly and something smoother and easier to maintain than a peastone floor is desirable, consider a wood floor. As before, spread a peastone or gravel drainage mat over the earth and install perforated drainpipe. Set 4x4 pressure-treated "sleepers" level in the peastone, leaving about 1 in. of their depth above the stone. Lay the poly vapor retarder over the sleepers. Then nail painted tongue-and-groove 1x6 spruce floor boards (ideal) or rough-sawn hemlock 1x10s (quick and cheap) to them. Substituting pressure-treated ¾-in. boards or 1-in. decking will yield an effectively rotproof floor for about twice the cost of untreated wood. A wood floor can be left permanently or can be taken up and replaced with a poured slab at some later date.

Any of these options will produce a dry and serviceable cellar floor. But if you opt for a concrete floor instead, set a form board about 6 in. out from the base of the foundation wall to stop the slab and leave the resulting stone-filled trench uncovered to drain any water that seeps through the walls. (If there is a functioning exterior footing drain, interior drains should not be needed and the floor can abut the wall directly.)

Pouring a Concrete Floor

Beginning around the mid-nineteenth century, as the parlor stove and open hearth were supplanted by the coal-fired furnace, concrete floors became increasingly common, at least in the best homes. In conjunction with a vapor retarder, pouring a concrete floor slab can turn a dank and uninviting cellar into a dry and useful basement. (I like to distinguish between cellars and basements; it's like the difference between a dungeon and a living room.)

PREPARING THE FLOOR Before pouring a concrete floor, prepare the cellar by first removing whatever is movable. If the furnace and water heater are not already on concrete pads or blocks, lever them up to finished floor height with a crowbar or 2x4 while you slip the right number of bricks or blocks underneath. Lighter utilities, like the water pump and pressure tank, can be temporarily hung from the ceiling.

Unless you use pressure-treated wood, support posts cast in concrete will rot. It's best to set them on precast footings no more than 1 in. below finish floor height. Paint the bottom end and sides of the posts with wood preservative or asphalt cement. You can remove most of the support posts until the concrete sets up—the floors will sag noticeably, but as long as no one walks on them and you move heavy furniture like the piano away from the middle of the room, they won't collapse. Dig the floor about 4 in. deeper where the posts will bear. Unless you have to rebuild the stair anyway, trim the bottom edges of the stair stringers to fit the new floor height. Pick up all loose material, stones, bark chips, and other debris with a rake or coarse broom.

TAMPING THE FLOOR The floor should be compacted from years of use. Settle any loose areas with a hand tamper, which is nothing more than a heavy cast-iron plate mounted on a handle that you pound up and down. Gas-powered compactors are more effective and faster, but the exhaust fumes are apt to poison you and stink up the house for days, even with all the windows open. When the air becomes blue with smoke, it's time to take a literal breather. Lower any noticeably high spots with a shovel, and spread and compact this fill to bring up the low spots.

Spread a 4-in. layer of clean gravel or peastone over the earth grade and compact it. Here you'll have no choice but to choke and suffer with the gas-powered compactor. Exhaust fans can help.

Concrete Slab Floor for a Dry Cellar

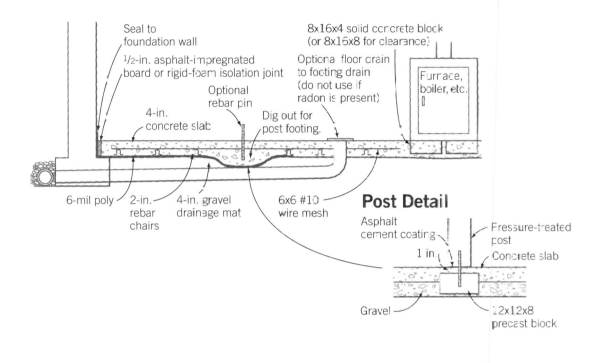

Seal to foundation wall

1/2-in. asphalt-impregnated board or rigid-foam isolation joint

8x16x4 solid concrete block (or 8x16x8 for clearance)

Optional floor drain to footing drain (do not use if radon is present)

Furnace, boiler, etc.

Optional rebar pin

4-in. concrete slab

Dig out for post footing.

6-mil poly

2-in. rebar chairs

4-in. gravel drainage mat

6x6 #10 wire mesh

Post Detail

Asphalt cement coating

Pressure-treated post

1 in.

Concrete slab

Gravel

12x12x8 precast block

INSTALLING A DRAIN Because a floor slab turns the cellar into a potential swimming pool, it's also a good idea to add a floor drain in case your plumbing leaks or the washing machine overflows. If your local code allows, connect this drain (which should be trapped and provided with a cleanout) to the house sewer drain. Otherwise, run it into the exterior perimeter footing drain. Boring a drain line through an existing footing is a lot of work. The alternative is to dig a sump pit.

ESTABLISHING SLAB LEVEL Assuming that all under-slab water problems have been solved, mark a point on the wall 4 in. above the prepared gravel base, which should be nearly flush with the top of the footing. With a transit level or water level, shoot that point around the perimeter and snap a chalkline between the marks. If you're working against an existing stone wall, drive stakes into the floor and stretch a string between them to indicate floor level in front of the wall. With a helper, stretch strings

across the cellar from wall to wall and look for any obvious high or low spots under the string that need further leveling. These strings will also help establish grade when working around posts, furnace slabs, or any other difficult areas. (The same technique is used to set the slope for a floor drain.)

INSTALLING A VAPOR RETARDER AND REINFORCEMENT MESH Lay the 6-mil polyethylene vapor retarder over the prepared gravel base. Carefully cut around existing pads or footing blocks if you cannot slip the plastic under them. Then lay 6-in. by 6-in. wire reinforcement mesh. Use steel rebar "chairs" to support the mesh at the proper height (i.e., in the middle of the slab). Don't use stone or brick shims, because they can weaken the slab. Use a bolt cutter to fit the mesh around posts and other obstructions. Bend the cut ends over to hook adjoining pieces of mesh together and bend free ends upward to prevent puncturing the vapor barrier.

BRINGING IN THE CONCRETE One problem remains: How to get the concrete into the cellar. Window openings and a bulkhead are the best places to start pouring. If, as is likely, the truck can reach only one end of the cellar, add a temporary chute built from plywood or boards (if it's lined with metal, the concrete will slide a lot easier) and supported on sawhorses to reach the far end. The concrete company will not supply extension chutes unless you ask for them when you make your order. If the truck cannot reach the cellar, the concrete can be placed with a pumper boom. This raises the cost per yard considerably, but if it's the only alternative to hauling the concrete down a ramp in a wheelbarrow, it's worth it.

Gather some helpers and outfit them with rakes and shovels. Pull the concrete from the chute to the farthest corners first. The mix should be on the wet side for easier spreading and a slower setting time. Distribute the concrete evenly, working back toward the truck. Wear rubber boots. Concrete contains enough lime to eat through leather soles and your feet.

SCREEDING THE CONCRETE Begin screeding (leveling) the surface before the last of the concrete is placed. Ideally, the screed board (a straight length of 2x4 will do, although you can rent stiff but lightweight magnesium screed bars) will reach across the entire width of the area to be leveled; but in a cellar, shorter screeds enable you to work around obstructions. Drive steel stakes around the perimeter and down the middle of the slab, and nail 2x4s to them at floor height before the pour. Use the top edges to set the floor level and as bearing surfaces on which the screed is drawn back and forth. After an area is screeded, pull the stakes and smooth over the holes before the concrete sets up. If a perfectly level floor is not critical, dispense with the screed guides and screed by eyeball level as best you can.

FLOATING THE SLAB Screeding leaves a slightly ridged finish suitable for a barn floor (better traction for the cows) but hard to keep clean. A bull float, which is a magnesium plate attached to an adjustable handle (rent one), is used to smooth the ridges left by screeding. Begin floating immediately after screeding.

TROWELING THE SLAB When the surface water has evaporated and the concrete appears frosted

Long chutes make up for the lack of convenient access for a cellar concrete pour.

Although powered by the same machines, the blades used for floating the slab are different from those used for troweling it. Power floating is an initial step, performed while the concrete is firm enough to bear weight but still soft enough to show footprints, as shown here. The final power troweling, which imparts a polished finish, is done when the concrete no longer takes imprints. (Photo courtesy Portland Cement Association)

Good Enough

I remember the day I poured my own cellar floor. By noon, the temperature was already in the low 90s, as was the humidity. The job resembled a scene from Dante's *Inferno*: Three near-naked bodies, clad in rubber boots and cut-off shorts, sweating and grunting, tugging at a sluggish puddle with shovels and hoes. The cellar was a Turkish bath; the concrete was setting too fast. My glasses fogged in, the light bulbs glimmered dully through the heavy dew. But there was no stopping, not yet. The concrete was stiffening almost as fast as we could place it. In broad, rough strokes I smoothed the pour with a length of 2×4. "Good enough for a cellar hole, this ain't the Taj Mahal!" And we left it just like that—no screed, no float— and escaped blinking into the shimmering daylight.

(or sugared) it is ready for troweling. The concrete will be hard enough to bear your weight but still soft enough to take an imprint. Working from 1-ft.-sq. plywood kneeling boards, smooth off any ridges and fill any low spots left by the bull float. The kneelers shouldn't sink more than ¼ in. into the surface. Otherwise, let the concrete set up a little more.

Steel troweling gives a hard, polished finish. But steel troweling by hand is incredibly tedious. And, because concrete gives off enough heat while setting to turn a cellar into a sauna, it's not a job for the faint-hearted. A power trowel does a lot better job with much less effort. Unfortunately, it runs on gas, but in this case I'd either leave the floor with a bull-float finish or brave the fumes with a respirator. If you do rent a power trowel, be sure to get a set of blades for finishing as well as floating. Concrete ready for power troweling will have set to where you can walk on it without leaving an imprint.

EXTERIOR DRAINAGE

When standing water in the cellar lingers throughout the year, disappearing only after a prolonged dry spell, the source is most likely ponding from a high water table and an inadequate or nonexistent foundation drain. Houses built on small and/or level lots don't offer enough slope for the foundation drain's outlet to empty below the footing level, so water typically drains into a municipal sewer or a dry well (stone-filled pit) located somewhere on the property. Occasionally, a wet cellar can be traced to a blocked or broken drain tile or silted-in dry well; dead animals and tree roots are also sources of blockage.

Unfortunately, since foundation drains are seldom accessible to a mechanical cleaner, the cause can be discovered only by excavation. I

Supporting a Stone Foundation Wall

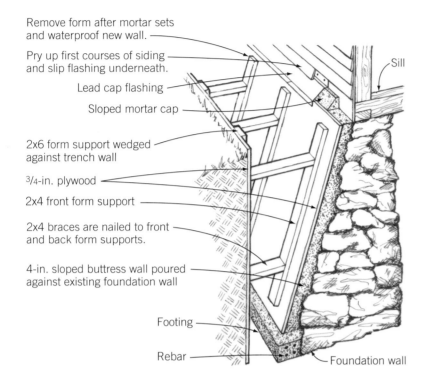

Remove form after mortar sets and waterproof new wall.

Pry up first courses of siding and slip flashing underneath.

Lead cap flashing

Sloped mortar cap

Sill

2x6 form support wedged against trench wall

3/4-in. plywood

2x4 front form support

2x4 braces are nailed to front and back form supports.

4-in. sloped buttress wall poured against existing foundation wall

Footing

Rebar

Foundation wall

remember one particularly stubborn case of floor seepage that was cured only when exposure of the foundation-drain outlet pipe revealed a high spot that was forcing the drainage to flow back into the cellar. Our only clue was the suspiciously small trickle of water that emptied from the drain's outlet.

Even when they do stop the infiltration, waterproofing compounds applied to the inside of the cellar wall can hasten the emergence of long-range problems by allowing hydrostatic pressure to build up against the outside of the wall. Unless coupled with good foundation drainage, correcting grading, fixing window wells, or adding gutters will do little to resolve the underlying cause of chronic water buildup. The only long-term foolproof cure is to add or improve the drainage on the outside of the wall.

Buttressing a Foundation Wall

In theory, a foundation wall is made more or less impermeable to moisture infiltration by an exterior coating of asphalt-based stucco or other damp-proofing material. These materials are easily applied to new concrete walls, but they cannot be used to seal an old stone wall. Even if you could clean enough dirt out of the joints on the ragged outside face of a rubble wall to make a good bond for mortar without collapsing the wall, the bumpy surface would be difficult to parge.

If the wall is structurally sound, it makes more sense to scrub and spray the loose dirt from the stones as best you can (soil prevents a good concrete bond, too) and then pour a 4-in.-thick sister wall against them (see the drawing at left). Although it's possible to form the sloped cap with the pour, it's a lot easier to shape it from mortar with a trowel after the concrete has set and the forms have been stripped. Because the new wall sticks out beyond the siding, you'll have to install a strip of flashing under the first course of siding and seal it to the outside of the concrete. Otherwise, water can collect on top of the sister wall and rot the sills. Another option, particularly recommended for foundations with historic ashlar blocks above grade, is to terminate the sister wall just below grade.

Installing an Exterior Drainage System

Before you lay drainpipe, damp-proof the foundation walls as described on p. 132. Then, with a square-edged shovel, scrape smooth and level the excavation beside the footings and lay perforated pipe, its holes facing sideways, along the footings at their bottom edge (never on top).

Some builders recommend sloping the perforated pipe 1 in. per 20 ft. (½ in. per pipe length) all the way around the building. This might make sense in theory, but in reality it means you'll have to run drain outlets from each corner

Foundation Drainage

Cross Section

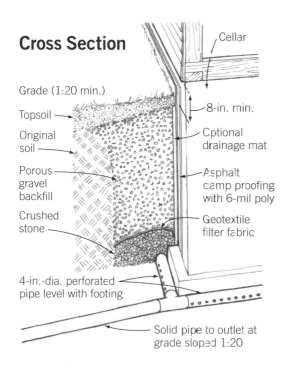

Grade (1:20 min.)

Topsoil

Original soil

Porous gravel backfill

Crushed stone

Cellar

8-in. min.

Optional drainage mat

Asphalt camp proofing with 6-mil poly

Geotextile filter fabric

4-in.-dia. perforated pipe level with footing

Solid pipe to outlet at grade sloped 1:20

Pipes for Foundation Drainage

For drainpipes, 4-in.-diameter perforated PVC pipe is most common—it's light, strong, easily installed, and inexpensive. The Orangeburg asphalt-fiber, cement-asbestos, and clay drainpipes formerly used for footing drains are no longer widely available. Flexible acrylonitrile butadiene styrene (ABS) corrugated plastic pipe, sold in 250-ft. coils, is better suited to draining fields and roadways. It's too "squiggly" to lay level or bridge dips in the footing grade.

of the building or else dig down 5 in. or 6 in. alongside the footing by the time you get to the outlet of a 120-ft.-long perimeter. By laying the pipe level with the bottom of the footing, water will move into it and flow toward the outlet following the path of least resistance, preventing hydrostatic pressure from building up against the wall. Solid pipe is teed in at a convenient point and pitched slightly downward toward an outlet some distance from the foundation.

Cover the pipe with at least 6 in. of 2-in. crushed coarse chestnut stone; lay rosin-coated building paper (not tar paper) or Geotextile filter fabric (more expensive but worth it) over the stone to prevent silting in as the soil settles.

Backfill the trench with gravel to a few inches above finish grade. Porous backfill material conducts both runoff and subsurface water into the drainpipes and eliminates pressure on the wall; the large spaces between gravel particles also

provide plenty of room for ice crystals to expand without creating frost heave. (There are several new matlike filter products on the market that purport to eliminate the need for gravel. However, they are expensive and I'm not sure they work as well as gravel, although I'd certainly consider using a fiberglass insulating/drainage mat against the walls in lieu of polystyrene insulation boards.)

Finally, spread and grade topsoil after the new material has settled (it usually takes a heavy rain) and seed. Close the outlet of the drainpipe with a ¼-in. mesh wire screen (hardware cloth) to keep out rodents.

Good perimeter drainage is the only sure-fire cure for chronic foundation leaks. But if your foundation has suffered from poor drainage for any length of time, water infiltration will probably be the least of your worries (at least where poor drainage goes hand in hand with frost heave). It's more likely that a moisture problem has evolved into a structural problem; sections of wall will have bowed, cracked, heaved, settled, or caved in and part or all of the foundation must be replaced. An excavation solely to retrofit footing drains would be unusual.

The Ground Roof Option

An option that keeps water away from a foundation without the expense of large-scale excavation is to install what University of Illinois research architect William B. Rose calls a "ground roof." This approach works well when surface water seepage rather than a high water table is the primary source of moisture in the cellar and the wall itself is stable (that is, there is no evidence of lateral soil or hydrostatic pressure), particularly in regions with merely middling cold climates.

The topsoil is removed to about 1 ft. below grade and 4 ft. out from the building perimeter. The ground is graded and tamped to slope about 4 in. over that distance. A 4-ft.-wide sheet of 2-in.-thick extruded polystyrene (EPS) rigid foam is broken along one of its 8-in. scoring lines and laid on the slope and up against the foundation as shown in the drawing at left. Ethylene propylene diene monomer (EDPM) roofing membrane, which is more durable than polyethylene, is laid over the foam and up onto the wall, where it is secured with termination bar (used to hold roofing to vertical wall surfaces) and masonry anchors and sealed with polyurethane caulking. A French drain installed under the outside edge of the foam insulation provides extra protection against heavy runoff.

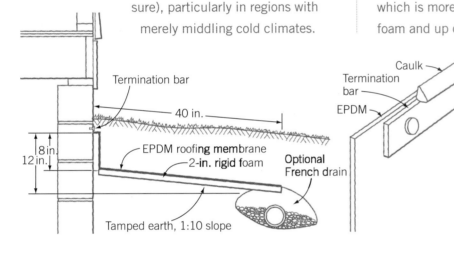

Termination bar

40 in.

8 in.
12 in.

EPDM roofing membrane
2-in. rigid foam

Optional French drain

Tamped earth, 1:10 slope

Caulk

Termination bar

EPDM

REPAIRING FOUNDATION WALLS

Hairline cracks in concrete walls are usually the result of too-rapid curing, improper concrete mixing or placement, or minor settlement. As long as the crack does not appear to be increasing in length or width, it can be repaired with a quick patch of hydraulic cement.

To determine whether a crack is active, tape one side of a piece of paper across the crack and mark the edges of the crack on it. Check before and during winter, in spring and in late summer to see if and how much the edges of the crack have moved relative to the gauge marks. If the movement is greater than $\frac{1}{16}$ in., you have a problem crack. You can also set up a similar crack movement gauge on the outside of the wall. Epoxy a glass microscope slide across the crack. If it breaks, the crack is active and the amount of movement will correspond to the width of the crack between the halves of the slide.

Realigning the Wall

Assuming that good drainage exists (or that you will install it), it's possible to stabilize and patch even large cracks and repair a bowed or kicked-in wall without replacing it. Trench the outside of the foundation wall at least 4 ft. to each side of the crack to relieve the lateral pressure. There's no exact rule: The greater the displacement of the wall sections, the greater the required wall exposure. This done, the damaged sections can be moved back into their original positions; the cracks are closed up using steel jack posts or timbers and screw jacks. (Note that most ordinary hydraulic jacks will not work in the horizontal position—an exception is the hydraulic ram jack, like the kind used for heavy-duty auto-body work and frame straightening. (See

also p.171 for a photo of an alternative shoring technique.) The jacks should push against a timber that spreads the force over the wall. Most likely, the wall on the opposite side of the cellar will be the only practical bearing to jack *from*. Use 6x6 or even 8x8 horizontal timbers to span between the bearing wall and the jacks.

Patching the Crack

Cut a key way into the cellar side of the crack with a cold chisel or a diamond-blade in a circular saw and fill it with hydraulic cement or an epoxy patching compound, such as Thoroseal's Waterplug. Trowel flashing-grade asphalt cement over the immediate area of the crack on the outside and then seal the repair with asphalt foundation coating or (even better and stronger) trowel fiber-reinforced stucco (Blockbond) over the entire wall. Of course, whatever condition caused the wall to crack in the first place must also be corrected if the repair is to be effective. This is one case in which you may have to dig out the rest of the wall to put in the drainage that never was.

As long as soil loading is not excessive, the repair should be perfectly stable when the jacks are released. (Still leave the jacks in place for 2 to 3 days or until after a good rain to allow the backfill to settle.)

Adding Buttress Walls and Pilasters

Long walls often crack vertically near midspan in response to lateral soil pressure. A repair could suffer the same fate as the original wall unless lateral resistance is strengthened by pouring a concrete buttress against the inside of the repaired wall. (For concrete block walls, a concrete-filled block pilaster placed in the center of the wall, against the crack, serves the same purpose.)

These repairs work only when the walls are still relatively intact and the damage is not too extensive. They also work best for poured concrete or concrete-block walls. Brick walls are

As long as the conditions that caused the damage are corrected, it may be possible to repair a cracked foundation wall rather than replace it. Repointing failed mortar joints may be labor intensive, but it's usually cheaper than building a new wall.

often too fragile, and rubble stone (as opposed to cut stone) walls are too irregular.

In the case of block or brick walls, the weight of the house above could collapse the wall when you attempt to move it. It's safer to lift the house just enough to relieve the weight on the wall before you try to push a brick wall back in or rebuild a rubble stone one. Use a jack box, as shown in the drawing below to flatten out a bulging brick or concrete block wall safely.

Fixing Settlement Cracks

When the plane of movement appears to be horizontal rather than vertical, the cause is most likely settlement, not lateral pressure. V-shaped diagonal cracks indicate upward movement of the wall, usually caused by frost penetration of the footings. Pyramidal diagonal cracks are the signature of downward movement, resulting from soil settlement or undermining of the footings by a leaking drainpipe or groundwater seepage. Once the source of the problem is addressed and further settlement arrested, the best thing to do may be to leave the wall alone. Patch the cracks, drive shims between the top of the wall and the sills, and fill gaps with spray-foam insulation. This is probably the best approach for rubble walls that have no footings.

Repairing a Cracked Foundation Wall

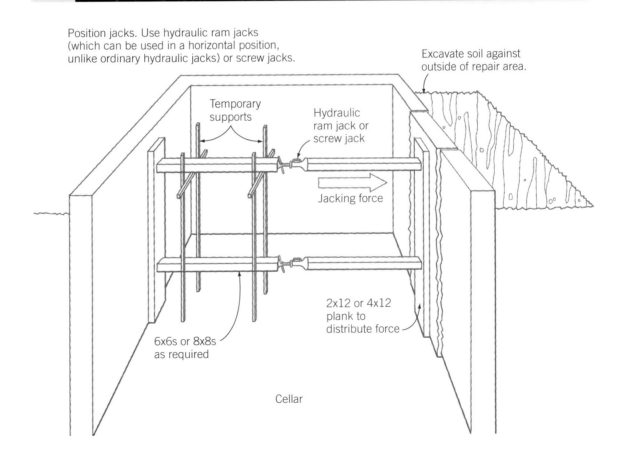

Position jacks. Use hydraulic ram jacks (which can be used in a horizontal position, unlike ordinary hydraulic jacks) or screw jacks.

Excavate soil against outside of repair area.

Temporary supports

Hydraulic ram jack or screw jack

Jacking force

2x12 or 4x12 plank to distribute force

6x6s or 8x8s as required

Cellar

Underpinning a Settled Footing

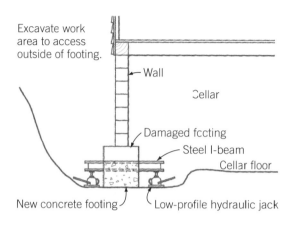

Excavate work area to access outside of footing.

Wall

Cellar

Damaged footing

Steel I-beam

Cellar floor

New concrete footing

Low-profile hydraulic jack

INSTALLING UNDERPINNING Where a settled footing has cracked and pulled the wall down with it, underpinning may be the best cure. Undermine the sunken footing and slide a short steel beam or angle iron through the tunnel. Lift the beam with a pair of low-profile hydraulic jacks to raise the footing and wall section back to its proper height. Place 2x12 pads under the jacks to keep them from sinking in the ground. Depending on the width of the repair, another beam may be required.

Then dig out enough soil from beneath the damaged footing and from under the ends of the intact sections to pour a new footing at least 8 in. thick, casting the beams in the concrete. Leave the repair to cure for at least 3 days and then cut off the projecting beam ends with a torch or grinder, seal them with flashing cement, and fill to grade.

REPLACING FOUNDATION WALLS

When replacing a foundation wall (as opposed to repairing it from the inside), dig a work trench at least 3 ft. wide at the bottom. Slope the sides back to what engineers and building codes call a *safe angle of repose*—in other words, enough of an angle so the side of the trench can't cave in on you. The more stable the soil, the steeper the sides of the cut. If all the walls are to be replaced, trench the entire perimeter.

The trench should extend to the bottom of the existing footings or to where there appears to be more earth than stone for dry-laid walls that don't have footings. If the foundation doesn't go deeper than the frost line, the trench should. If the wall does not need to be completely replaced, it can be effectively extended down below the frost line by pouring a bench

Creating a Bench Footing

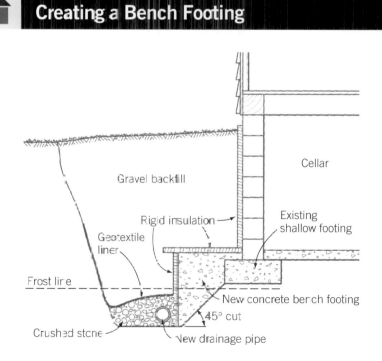

Gravel backfill

Cellar

Rigid insulation

Existing shallow footing

Geotextile liner

Frost line

Crushed stone

New concrete bench footing

45° cut

New drainage pipe

Above: Always provide an outlet to grade when excavating a foundation. Otherwise, even the slightest rainfall will turn the trench into a moat. Not only is your movement hampered but there is also a good chance of losing the wall (and the house). Below: Jacking cribs can settle unevenly or collapse when their earthen bulwarks turn to mud soup.

footing against it (see the drawing on p. 109). (The same technique can be used inside the cellar in lieu of underpinning to stabilize the foundation wall when lowering the cellar floor.) A structural engineer should determine that both the native soil and the existing foundation are stable before you attempt to excavate along the face of an existing footing to extend it below frost line.

Working with a Backhoe Operator

Even under the best of circumstances, digging against a foundation wall is ticklish work. Hire the best backhoe operator you can find—it's not a job to cut your teeth on. Most excavators won't guarantee against cave-in. Some may even ask you to sign a release holding them free from liability if the wall or house does fall down. Take heart, this seldom happens with a good operator, one for whom that cumbersome shovel is a surgically precise extension of hand and mind. Trust your operator, and listen to his advice.

Just the same, it's ultimately you (or your contractor) calling the shots. If you say go, he goes, and if the wall goes with him, well he just works here, mister. If you don't have confidence in your judgment (or in the machine operator's), then hire someone who does to supervise this job. Although failures occur often enough that you should be aware of the possibility, they generally result from foolhardiness and rushing the job. If you proceed slowly and cautiously, you shouldn't fail to detect a potentially serious problem before it happens. Nothing really happens without warning. You learn to listen and feel for the signs. In time you can feel timbers strain as easily as you feel the muscles in your own arms.

Dig as close to the wall as you can. With a poured-concrete wall, this means tight to it but not actually against it. Don't let the bucket get too close to block, brick, or stone walls: These can buckle when pushed. Instead, work alongside the hoe with your hand shovel, pulling the earth that clings to the stones into the ditch for the machine to remove. Don't worry about losing small sections of loose walls. If the sill above is solid, it will span the opening and carry the weight. Simply remove the collapsed wall along with the rest of the rubble.

Dry-laid rubble walls require the most caution. Often the only thing holding them up is the earth you're removing. As mentioned earlier, these walls are pyramidal, with much wider and larger stones at the base. It's easy to mistake an outcrop of the wall for a boulder, and pull the whole thing apart before you know what you're doing.

It takes an experienced heavy equipment operator with a surgeon's touch to safely and comfortably excavate under an existing building. (Photo by Kevin Walters)

Locate Utilities before Digging

In most municipalities there is a toll-free "dig-safe" number you can call to locate buried water, gas, sewer, telephone, and electric lines before you dig. Out in the boondocks, you're usually on your own. In any case, don't dig blind. Go down into the cellar and locate each penetration through the foundation wall (such as sewer line and gas line) by measuring to a fixed point such as the bottom of the sill, an inside corner, or a vent window and then reference your measurements to the outside of the foundation as best you can. Drive stakes along the foundation to mark these points.

When the machine has dug to within 1 ft. or so of the expected pipe or line, dig carefully by hand until you feel the utility line and then clear the dirt around it before resuming with the machine. Experience has taught me to include an assortment of plumbing and electrical couplers and splicing kits in my foundation-job toolkit.

RAISING OR HOLDING A HOUSE

Ultimately, all foundation repairs fall into one of two basic categories: holding the house or raising it. *Holding*, in this sense, refers to lifting the load-bearing sill beams (and any associated carrying beams or girders) just enough to take their weight off one or, at the very most, two adjacent foundation walls at a time (about ½ in. to 1 in. is usually enough). This load is transferred onto some combination of horizontal beams bearing on stacked timber cribs or upright posts. Because the other half the house is still anchored to its foundation, the overall situation is much more stable than if the house were supported by timbers and cribbing alone. The unloaded walls can be safely removed and replaced. Once this is

There is no one best way to jack up a house. Whether to lift from inside or outside the perimeter and whether to hold it in place or raise it higher depend on the particulars of its site and the structural configuration and integrity of its frame and foundation, the equipment and funds on hand, and the owner's design requirements and expertise.

Cribbing, or *cobbing,* is what house movers call the interlocked columns of short timbers that support the jacks and beams that lift and hold the house. A timber crib is, in effect, a kind of temporary pier foundation. As with any foundation, it requires solid bearing on stable soil. The cribbing must remain level as additional tiers are added or the load is shifted.

accomplished, the house is lowered onto the new walls and lifted off the remaining old walls.

If you simply hold the house at its existing level, it's unlikely that a full-height 8-ft. concrete form panel will fit under the sills. Even if it could, there wouldn't be enough clearance between the top of the panel and the underside of the sills to pour and work the concrete into the forms. Instead, the foundation wall must be formed with a 6-ft. panel and topped with a *pony wall* of two or three courses of 8-in. concrete block.

On the plus side, the pony wall approach is the most practical and economical do-it-yourself foundation repair for a full basement. The poured wall gives maximum strength below grade, where it is most needed, and requires almost one third less concrete. Laying two courses of concrete block is not very difficult. Unlike poured concrete walls, where future window openings must coincide with the jacking beams that run under sills, concrete blocks can simply be left out and the opening filled in after the house is lowered onto the new foundation and the timbers are removed.

As distinguished from holding, *raising* is the operation of lifting the entire house off its foundation all at once. With the house carried by steel or heavy timber beams bearing on what may look like alarmingly few timber cribs, all the walls can be removed and replaced in one fell swoop. Usually, this means lifting the house anywhere from 1 ft. to a full story. Because money is saved if enough head and elbow room is gained to dig out, form, and pour a complete full-height foundation without hindrance, raising a house makes the most efficient use of expensive excavation and concrete subcontractors. It's also the only way to prepare a house for transfer to an adjacent foundation.

Raising Is for Pros

Raising a house is not something a novice should attempt. There are two major characteristics that make this a job for professionals. First, when a house is disconnected from its foundation, it can move quite easily, like a boat adrift on its moorings. A strong gust of wind could push it out of alignment, or careless jacking could cause it to slide off its supports. Believe me, there's nothing quite like the thrill of working under a house and feeling it shift sideways as you adjust the jacks.

Second, while this holds true whether the house is raised 1 in. or one story, it's also true that the taller the crib, the more "tippy" it tends to become. Hence, engineering extremely stable and strong cribbing is even more critical for lift-

Hold or Raise?

Because it can be done piecemeal, often with less equipment and certainly with a greater margin of error, the holding method is something a determined homeowner might tackle. But it also takes more time than raising the house, complicates the concrete work, and precludes any major corrections in house level. Furthermore, because machines are repeatedly moved onto and off the site, excavation costs can be considerably higher.

ing a house than for holding it. Setting up these supports and planning the operation requires a solid, almost intuitive, feeling for how the weight of the house is carried by its frame. This can be acquired only by experience.

GET DISCONNECTED As when pulling a car engine, when raising a house, you are obliged to disconnect an awful lot of pipes, ducts, and wires. And if you have to live in the house while repairing it, all those connections must be temporarily reconnected. If for example, you have a hot-water heating system, every riser and return line to and from the radiators must be cut and lengthened. Whether the change in height is temporary or permanent, sewer lines, water supplies, drains, electrical feeds, all must be spliced or rerouted to accommodate it in any case. This could add thousands of dollars to the job in plumber's and electrician's bills. (It isn't an issue if the plumbing and wiring systems are so rudimentary or decrepit that cutting them is the prelude to their replacement.)

DECIDING WHERE TO LIFT Whether you are holding or raising, the structural configuration of the house frame determines where to place the jacks and beams for lifting. With timber frames, the weight of the walls, roof, and upper

Typical Traditional Braced Timber Frame, 1½- to 2-Story House

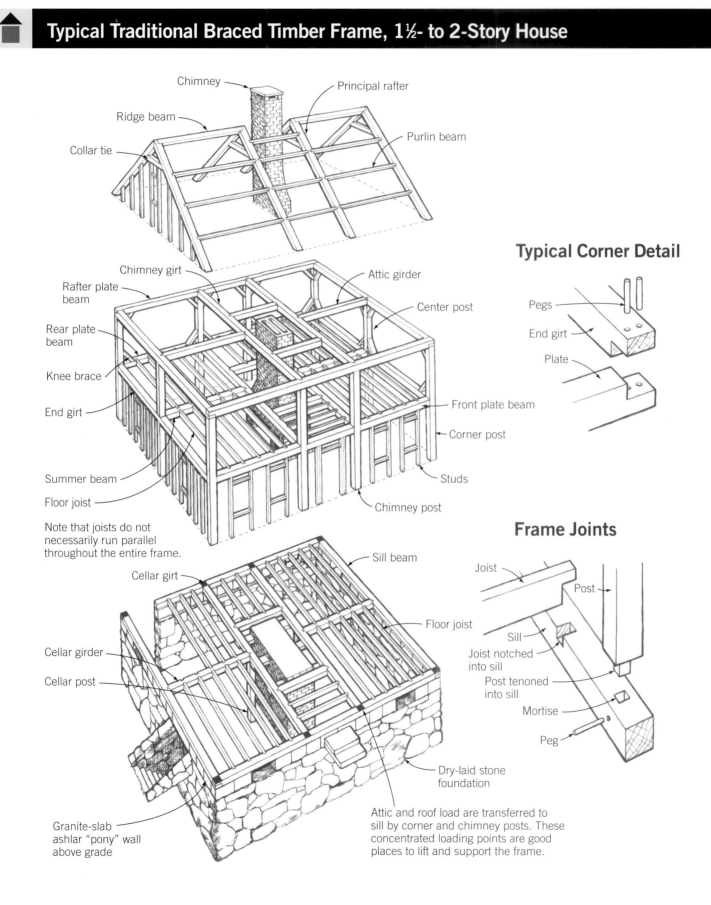

Chimney

Principal rafter

Ridge beam

Purlin beam

Collar tie

Chimney girt

Attic girder

Rafter plate beam

Center post

Rear plate beam

Knee brace

End girt

Front plate beam

Corner post

Summer beam

Studs

Floor joist

Chimney post

Note that joists do not necessarily run parallel throughout the entire frame.

Sill beam

Cellar girt

Floor joist

Cellar girder

Cellar post

Granite-slab ashlar "pony" wall above grade

Dry-laid stone foundation

Attic and roof load are transferred to sill by corner and chimney posts. These concentrated loading points are good places to lift and support the frame.

Typical Corner Detail

Pegs

End girt

Plate

Frame Joints

Joist

Post

Sill

Joist notched into sill

Post tenoned into sill

Mortise

Peg

floors is transferred by braced vertical posts onto continuous sill beams that span the length and breadth of the foundation wall in one or two pieces. The sill beams are typically 8x8s, although 8x12 and larger timbers are not uncommon. Heavy timber girts (also known as *girders*) mortised into the sills and supported by posts at midspan carry the squared timber or half-round log joists that support the floorboards and interior partitions. The girts are sometimes parallel to the length of the house, sometimes perpendicular to it. Interior posts under ceiling girts also distribute weight onto the cellar girts, which are in turn supported by cellar posts.

The floor plan of a stud-frame house follows the same basic layout of the heavy timbered house, but uses lighter framing members that distribute the loads instead of heavy members that concentrate loads at certain points. And joists are nailed, rather than notched into the sills.

PROVIDING SUPPORT UNDER POSTS A basic principle for safe house lifting is to provide support directly under a concentrated load, or as near it as possible. This is what posts and sills do. Thus your temporary supports should shoulder the load carried by the posts. Supporting a sill at midspan, where there may be no significant load, causes the weight carried by a corner or chimney post to put undue strain on the timber.

Sometimes the cellar girts carry part of the wall weight where they are mortised into the sill. Because there are usually vertical posts in the wall above such points, these are good places to lift and support the frame. A jack placed within 1 ft. or 2 ft. of the actual joint is usually sufficient. For example, you may find that a beam placed under the floor joists just inside the sill, when lifted, will raise the sill off the foundation

Because this is a plank frame house, the corner post is not bearing as much weight as it would in a conventional timber-frame. A good thing, in this case, given the obvious lack of solid wood beneath it.

wall, or you may find that only the joists move, taking the floorboards with them. This is most likely to happen when the sills are pinned down by posts supporting girders that carry the floor and roof loads from above. Here, lifting the girders and floor joists simultaneously usually brings the sill up with them.

GABLES SUPPORT LITTLE WEIGHT Unless they include support girders and posts (as described above) or bearing posts for a structural ridge beam that carries the roof load of a cathedral ceiling, the gable ends of the house normally don't carry any great weight and can be raised by lifting the floor joists if they run perpendicular to the gable sill. Usually, especially with stud-framed houses, the inherent stiffness of the gable wall sheathing and framing allow the foundation wall to be removed with no addi-

Most of the time, even a rotted sill is strong enough to hold up the house so that the foundation can be replaced first.

tional support. Because upper-floor framing usually mirrors the layout of the first floor, study the run of cellar–floor framing members to ascertain the best places to support the most weight with the least amount of timber and jacks. The less clutter in your foundation trench, the easier it is to replace the wall.

Even for experts, determining the best place to support the frame is something of a judgment call. Fortunately, there's plenty of opportunity to find out if it's going to work before you risk any serious damage. Although it's possible, beams seldom break spontaneously and without warning, especially if you don't leave long spans unsupported. The loads typical of residential construction are not that great. Groans and creaks are normal. Sagging, twisting, and joints pulling apart are plaintive calls for more support.

SUPPORTING SILLS AND BEAMS The goal is to provide alternative support for the foundation wall and cellar posts that normally support the sills and other structural beams that carry the house. Although preferable, with sound timber sills, it's not critical that jacking beams be directly under a load-bearing post. Placement within 2 ft. to 4 ft. of a corner or middle post will work just as well.

However, structural integrity becomes important when the sills are too rotten to bear any lifting. Jacking will crush a crumbling timber. In this case, the floor platform and the loads of the upper stories and roof must somehow be carried independently of the sills. This can get cumbersome. Some strategies of last resort are detailed on p. 141. When both foundation walls and sills need to be replaced, it's best to restore the wall first and then fix the sill. Most of the time, enough of the sill is relatively intact to afford some purchase for jacking. Because sills typically rot from the outside face inward, the cellar face, into which the floor joists are notched, is probably strong enough to withstand jacking if probing with your awl finds that at least a third to half the sill is still solid. When the sills are completely gone, the jacks must be arranged to lift on the wall instead.

Choosing and Obtaining Jacking Equipment

It takes a lot of timber and other equipment to hold a house and even more to raise it. Some ways are easier and more elegant than others. They may also be more expensive. Professional house movers and jackers use steel beams and heavy timber cribbing. In a typical application, openings are cut or punched through the top of the foundation wall and steel beams, spaced 8 ft.

to 12 ft. apart (depending on load, location of supporting posts and girders, and soundness of sills), are slid under the sills across the width of the house. To reduce the number of cribs and jacks, these beams are often carried on two perpendicular heavier beams and supported on four or six cribs. Hydraulic jacks are set on the cribbing under the lifting beams. Alternating between jacks, the entire house is lifted, a few inches at a time

As each beam is raised, cribbing and shims are added to keep it safely supported. Upon reaching full extension, the jack is lowered to permit the insertion of another crib timber and further lifting. By switching jacks between cribs and adding more timbers, it's possible to raise the house to any desired height. Since the entire house is supported on just a few cribs, all well within the cellar area, the work zone around the foundation wall remains uncluttered.

Hydraulic jacks are centered on the cribbing. Measurements taken from the old piers ensure that the house is lifted evenly.

TIP

Jacking Timbers

Ideally, jacking timbers should be at least as long as the greatest distance you'll need to span, certainly no less than 16 ft. Although there are sawmills that can cut timbers up to 32 ft. long, most cannot handle logs over 24 ft. The timbers should be free of any running splits or bad knots, which will weaken them under load. ▬ ▬ ▬

WOOD BEAMS Wood beams are more practical for low-cost muscle-powered do-it-yourself foundation repair than steel, especially in tight circumstances. (Just try trimming an I-beam with a chainsaw.) Wood is easier to transport and much easier to handle, at least when seasoned. Pounds per foot, a fresh-sawn green hemlock timber weighs almost as much as a steel beam. Although shorter working spans translate into more cribbing, wood beams are always reusable and relatively less expensive.

You might also find good-quality used beams at a salvage yard. While you may know someone with a barn full of antique beams, I'd hesitate to borrow them. Hand-hewn timbers are too precious to drag through the mud, and they're usually full of mortises, which might cause them to break under a concentrated load.

It's best to use 8x8 timbers for heavy lifting; 6x6s are acceptable for lighter loads or upright posts. I prefer solid 8x8 to built-up ones (four 2x8s spiked together). They're about 15 percent stronger and usually less expensive than built-ups of the same length. (Most lumberyards stock 2x8s and 2x10s up to 24-ft.; longer lengths can be special ordered.) But if you can't find a local source for timbers, you can build your own with 2x8 dimension lumber. Layering one or two courses of ½-in. plywood between the planks will increase stiffness. Increasing the depth of a built-up beam compensates for the difference in strength; a built-up 8x10 can carry almost double the load of a solid 8x8. But any jacking timber whose depth is significantly greater than its width has a tendency to flop sideways under load.

You'll also need at least a pickup truck load of cribbing in 3-ft. and 4-ft. lengths. Finding these odd pieces of 6x6s, 8x8s, 2x8s, and 4x12s can be a challenge, too. You might be able to buy or borrow some from a heavy construction yards. Sawmills use a lot of the stuff for lumber storage bunks. Used railroad ties are inexpensive but heavy and difficult to work with. (Creosote-soaked hardwood is hell on a chainsaw.) Their irregular dimensions makes building level cribbing frustrating.

USING HYDRAULIC JACKS Hydraulic jacks are the only jacks you'll need to lift a house. They are compact and stable, lift and lower rapidly and effortlessly, and—unlike screw jacks, which are essentially obsolete—are useful for more than house lifting. They're also relatively inexpensive and easy to find. Hydraulic jacks can be rented. But considering that most foundation jobs spread out over a summer of weekends and other free time, it's definitely cheaper to buy a couple pairs of 20-ton jacks.

Bought or rented, a few steel beams, a pile of timbers, and a truckload of cribbing may be a hefty outlay. Yet, because professional house jacking is almost as labor intensive as the do-it-yourself alternative, your sweat equity will pay for a lot of hardware before you reach the point of diminishing returns, at which it doesn't cost any more to hire a contractor. Both steel and wood beams can be resold at a discount when you're finished with them. And you could use timbers to replace rotted sills or for a barn, shed, or post-and-beam addition. At the very worse, cribbing makes pretty good firewood.

Jacking a House Safely

When working with a hydraulic jack, or any jack for that matter, insert blocking or cribbing under the carrying beam as you raise it. Then, if the hydraulic seal should rupture, causing the jack to lose pressure, or if the jack should suddenly kick out, the timber won't drop enough to hurt anything.

The possibility of failure is real enough that hydraulic jacks should never be left in place under load for any length of time. Lift slightly higher than you need to, block up between the cribbing and the jacking timber, and then release the jack. For an extra margin of safety, use an oversize jack. (I use a 20-ton jack for everything, even when an 8-ton one would be enough.) For wood beams, you'll also need a ½-in. or ¾-in. steel "lifting plate" at least 8 in. square to place between the head of the jack and the timber. This distributes the jacking force evenly across the width of the timber. Without the lifting plate, the head of the jack would penetrate the timber and cause it to split. Here are some additional points to keep in mind to ensure safe and successful house jacking.

Have a solid bearing. Keep your cribbing level and distribute the weight over as large an area as feasible. A crib is a pyramid. Use lifting plates or blocks to distribute the force of the jack. Never use shims to level the base of the cribbing.

Lift straight. If the jack begins to tilt, lower it and shim it to lift plumb or restack and level the cribbing. A loaded jack that slips sideways can kill you.

Block up as you go. This is an important safety precaution. You can't get hurt if nothing can fall.

Listen and look. A house will creak and groan as it is raised. Watch for cracks to open. See if the joists move with the sills or stay in place. Watch to make sure that jacking beams or house timbers aren't bending.

Lift slowly and evenly. If you are holding a house, you need only to relieve the weight on the foundation. In most cases, that means lifting only 1 in. or less. If you are raising a house much higher, do it in small increments, raising each jack an equal amount to avoid stressing timbers past their breaking point. Don't hurry—give the timbers time to settle and adjust to their new positions. Large jobs can take weeks.

Balance the load. Keep the cribbing as close as possible to the lifting points. Avoid lifting from the ends of a beam, leaving the middle unsupported. An 8x8 is not a lever.

Know what is above you. Before you lift, determine where the loads from the upper stories bear on the sills and other timbers in the cellar. Major load-bearing posts or walls often rest above joints between girts and sills or over cellar posts.

Think. Lifting a house out of a hole is a whole lot harder than putting it in there, especially if you happen to be under it when it falls.

Holding a House with Needle Beams

The much greater stiffness of steel beams over wood timbers is used to advantage on this site. The relatively light load of this building is safely carried by a pair of long needle beams resting on cribbing set well outside the footprint of the structure. Setting the beams under the floor joists facilitates the removal of the decayed sills and lower wall sections while giving the backhoe plenty of elbow room for digging out the new crawl space.

Although a rented farm tractor equipped with a bucket loader or the excavator's backhoe provides the most convenient muscle for positioning the needle beams, the beams can also be raised into place incrementally, using a pair of hydraulic jacks and cribbing up as alternating ends of the beam are lifted.

1 The work trench is dug wide enough to accommodate the foundation piers for the new porch. Note that the kitchen-ell sill is almost completely decayed.

2 The ell section of the building is almost entirely supported by a single strategically placed crib. (A steel beam set on cribbing in the middle of the existing cellar was added later when the earth under this crib was excavated for a new crawl space.)

3 Because it never had a proper foundation to begin with, the bottom-most part of the "back house" had basically melted into the ground. Thus long, steel *needle beams* were inserted through the walls under the upper-story floor joists to carry the roof and floor load. The dangling lower walls were cut away, and the structure was jacked up to its original level. The buckled roof and bowed clapboard lines show just how far and how long this section of the structure had been sinking. Setting the cribbing well outside the building footprint allowed unencumbered access for digging the crawl space.

4 The entire ell is carried by three steel beams—two cribbed outside, where there was room enough, and one cribbed inside (barely visible to the left of the door) so that it would not interfere with the piers for the new porch. Note the new frost wall foundation and the new sill ready to be installed.

5 A block wall is laid up under the new sill. Note the openings for extracting the steel beam and for jacking up the new sill. The mechanic's hydraulic floor jack is low enough to fit into the openings. The splice between sill sections is jacked tight before bolting together.

6 The concrete-block section of the new foundation ends at the back house. The new bearing walls are joined to a pressure-treated mudsill set directly on top of the concrete frost wall. After the walls are framed, the jacks will be lowered and the steel beams pulled.

Lifting Beams and Timbers Defined

For purposes of clarity, it's helpful to distinguish between *needle beams* and *carrying beams*. A needle beam is any beam that penetrates a foundation or building wall. A carrying beam does not. Needle beams are almost always used to lift sills or hold plate beams. Carrying beams generally support cellar girts and other principal framing members that carry the floor loads. Likewise, to distinguish wooden beams from steel beams, I refer to the wood ones as *jacking timbers*. As with steel beams, a jacking timber can be used as either a needle beam or a carrying beam.

JACKING THE HOUSE

Reduced to its simplest elements, to lift a wall you slide a long steel or wooden beam under the sill. Crib it on both ends (and, if needed, at midspan) and begin lifting with your jacks until the sill rises off the foundation. Repeat this process at intervals along the wall. Use additional beams and cribbing or vertical posts to raise cellar girts or other floor beams to keep the floor from sagging and stressing the joints or to support any weak points or intersections that carry upper floor loads. Use a 6x6 post balanced on top of a jack or an adjustable steel jack post placed alongside the existing support posts. Add appropriate shims or blocking when the beam lifts off the post and then release the jack to let the beam back down onto the post. If you cannot support a splice or joint directly, you must lift both sides of it, jacking each side a little at a time to avoid twisting the joint.

Jacking as You Remove the Wall

You can combine jacking with wall removal by digging out the wall as you dig the work trench. Starting at a corner (to provide solid support), the backhoe removes about 12 ft. of wall. If the sill is nonbearing, it can be left to dangle while the floor joists and girts are lifted from within the cellar. Otherwise, support this section of sill with a needle beam or carry it directly on cribbing. Another way to provide this support is with braced timber jacking posts. Or you can simply use adjustable steel jack posts, as shown on p. 124.

After the supports are in place, dig the next section of wall and trench and continue adding posts around the wall. If you set the steel jack posts directly under the sill instead of outside, you can leave them in place when the new wall is poured, which greatly simplifies final adjustment and leveling of the house. (Alternatively, one end of a short needle beam can rest on cribbing inside the cellar while the other end bears on the steel post under the sill.) Set any such posts on 1-ft.-sq., 6-in.-thick concrete pads so they too can be incorporated into the footings.

WORKING WITH JACK POSTS When working with jack posts as opposed to needle beams and stable cribbing, remove only one wall at a time. The intact walls are needed to stabilize the house. Jack posts and braced vertical supports are easily overturned by lateral forces. After the new wall is poured and the house lowered back down onto it, the remaining sections of old wall can be replaced.

Choosing a Layout for Jacking Timbers

The more the layout of your jacking timbers resembles the professional house-mover's steel cradle, the more stable and easy to level the house will be. Beams should project at least 1 ft. beyond the outside walls for stability and safety in case the house slips or slides while jacking. Because most houses are at least 24 ft. wide, the requisite 26-ft.- or 28-ft.-long timber is not only

Methods for Jacking the House

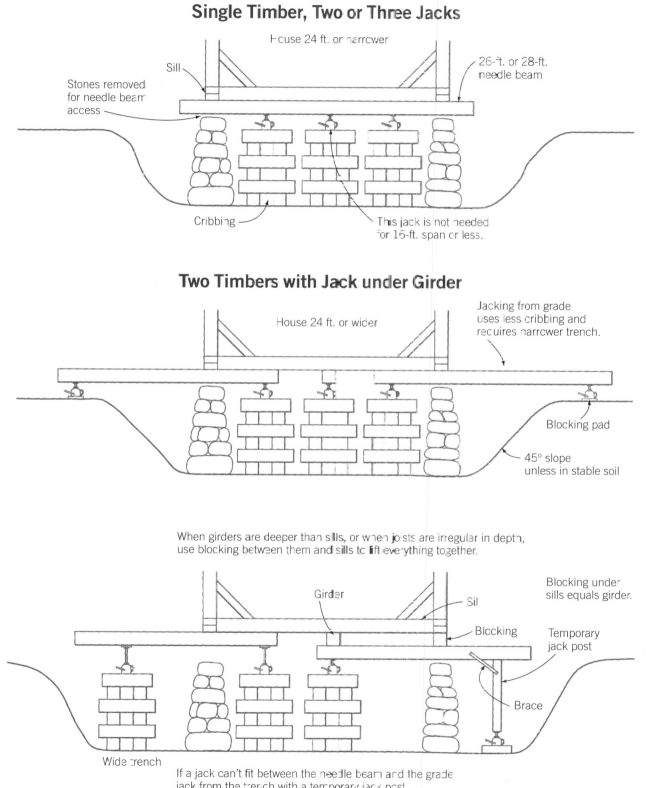

Single Timber, Two or Three Jacks

House 24 ft. or narrower

Sill

26-ft. or 28-ft. needle beam

Stones removed for needle beam access

Cribbing

This jack is not needed for 16-ft. span or less.

Two Timbers with Jack under Girder

House 24 ft. or wider

Jacking from grade uses less cribbing and requires narrower trench.

Blocking pad

45° slope unless in stable soil

When girders are deeper than sills, or when joists are irregular in depth, use blocking between them and sills to lift everything together.

Girder

Sil

Blocking under sills equals girder.

Blocking

Temporary jack post

Brace

Wide trench

If a jack can't fit between the needle beam and the grade, jack from the trench with a temporary jack post.

Steel jack posts normally used for leveling sagging floor beams can also be used to support the sills. These posts will be cast into the concrete wall. (Photo by Kevin Walters)

difficult to procure but almost as challenging to manhandle as a steel beam. Fortunately, as the drawing on p. 123 shows, the do-it-yourself house jacker can use relatively maneuverable 12-ft. to 16-ft. jacking timbers to safely support one, two, or even all four walls.

SUPPORTING A NEEDLE BEAM FROM OUTSIDE THE TRENCH Setting one end of a needle beam at grade level at the edge of the work trench allows you to use two shorter beams to span the entire width of the house instead of one longer beam. It also requires less cribbing. Dig a level platform at the edge of the trench, making it

The Flying House: An Alternative to Excavation

Two cranes are coordinated to lift this house off its old foundation, turn it 180 degrees, and set it onto a new foundation well back from its original site.

Very precise measurements and planning fit the new house to its foundation exactly. The house must be lowered gingerly onto the outlying concrete piers to keep from knocking them askew.

Removing or underpinning an old foundation is time-consuming, dirty, and sometimes difficult work. If your site allows, consider digging a new cellar hole and building a new foundation alongside the old one. Freed of the constraints of working under an existing house, the new foundation will cost less and go up faster. The house can be moved on wood or steel rollers inserted between needle beams, and a timber rollway can be constructed between the two foundations. And, as the photos show, the transfer can be made without resorting to jacks and timbers at all.

deep enough for a jack and its bearing pad to fit under the needle beam. Locate the platform so that the jack sets at a distance away from the wall that's equal to 1½ times the depth of the trench. (You can save a lot of hand shovel work if the backhoe operator places the spoils a few feet beyond that point.) *Never* jack from the very edge of the trench. Stable soils (as judged by an experienced excavation contractor if not an engineer) allow a nearly vertical trench wall instead of the recommended sloped cut, thereby requiring less material to replace during backfilling. Let off the jacks so the needle beam settles the blocking pad into the ground. Raise it again and add new blocking as needed

USING DIAGONAL NEEDLE BEAMS Assuming that the joint under the corner post is solid enough to lift the post with the sills, you could also run needle beams diagonally across the corners of the house to lift two walls with one beam. The wall sheathing and studs usually impart enough rigidity to the frame so that the corner post doesn't require any support. If this isn't the case, refer to pp. 143–145 for information on supporting posts.

THE NEW FOUNDATION

Clear the rubble from under the house and work trench. Throw anything that clutters up the cellar into the trench for the backhoe to scoop away and later bury. Rake the bottom of the trench smooth. If the backhoe operator was worth his pay, the trench bottom should be more or less level. Check it with a transit level. If it doesn't vary more than 1 in. all the way around, you can start to set your footing forms. If there's more of a variation, you'll have to lower the high spots. Even though this might mean a lot of painful hand work, never fill up the low spots—fill that isn't compacted can cause the foundation wall to crack or settle.

Laying Out the Footings

As a rule of thumb, footings in normal silty soils should be twice as wide as the wall and as thick as the wall is wide. Standard residential foundation walls are 8 in. wide; standard footings are 16 in. wide by 8 in. of vertical thickness. In soft clay, increase the footings to 24 in. by 12 in. The bottom of the footing should always be below maximum frost penetration—4 ft. is considered standard in the north, although in the compacted soil under a plowed driveway, it can easily extend to 5 ft. or 6 ft., as should any footing adjoining it.

To align the footings with the sills above, drop a line with a plumb bob (or level and straightedge) from the outside corners of the sill. Mark the corner points with a large spike driven into the ground. Measure 4 in. beyond these spikes (half the width of the wall) and drive another set. Set up batter boards and stretch strings across these outside points to find

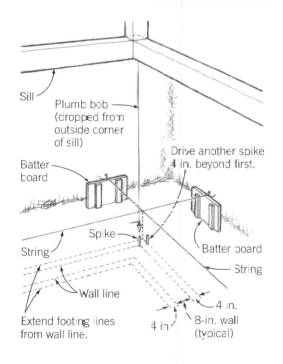

Locating the Footings

Sill

Plumb bob (dropped from outside corner of sill)

Batter board

Drive another spike 4 in. beyond first.

Spike

String

Batter board

String

Wall line

4 in.

Extend footing lines from wall line.

4 in.

8-in. wall (typical)

the outside edges and corners of the footing (and the inside faces of the footing form boards.)

STRAIGHTENING THE SILL Setting the form boards to a string makes for straight footings. Unfortunately, the wall of the old house above is not necessarily straight. It may have more curves than a giant slalom course. Small bows are best ignored; especially when it's the house wall that overhangs the new foundation. But bows greater than 1½ in. are hard to hide, especially if it's the new wall that sticks out beyond the old house.

It's sometimes possible to pull the bow out of a house frame and sill with a come-along and chain (see pp. 166–167) or to push it in with a backhoe bucket. Try this while the sills can still slide on the needle beams.

A string stretched across the bottom of the house wall helps align the footing layout. (Photo by Kevin Walter)

Because there are 4 in. of play in the difference between the footing and wall width, it might seem that as long as the wall doesn't actually overhang the footing, there's nothing to worry about. However, offsetting the wall more than 1 in. or so unbalances the load on the footing enough that it could eventually tilt. Both the footings and the new wall should follow a major bow that refuses to straighten. Plumb down from the trouble spot, mark the deviation with another spike, and set the footing to the adjusted line. Rectilinear perfection is not generally an attribute of the renovated house. Thus footings are aligned with the actual corners of the house rather than squared unto themselves. To do otherwise runs the risk of the wall missing the footing entirely.

Constructing Footing Forms

Lay 2x10 form boards along the string stretched between batter boards. Drive a 2x4 stake against the outside of the form board at one end. Fasten the stake to the board with a double-headed form nail. Drive another stake near the opposite end of the board, level the board between the stakes, and secure. Drive a second nail through each stake to keep it from shifting. Secure additional stakes at 4-ft. to 6-ft. intervals along the form board or wherever it bows off the line. Repeat this procedure, adding form boards until you complete the outside perimeter of the footing form.

REINFORCE THE JOINTS Nail short lengths of plank over each butted joint. When ordering footing boards, remember that the outside dimension of a footing is at least 11 in. longer than the wall (4 in. of footing each end plus two thicknesses of lumber); thus footing forms for a 24-ft. wall require a 12-ft. and a 14-ft. board. Although you could use 1x10 boards (as do many pros), I recommend 2x10 planks because they are easier to lay out straight and level and are less likely to bow under the pressure of the

Footing Form Construction Details

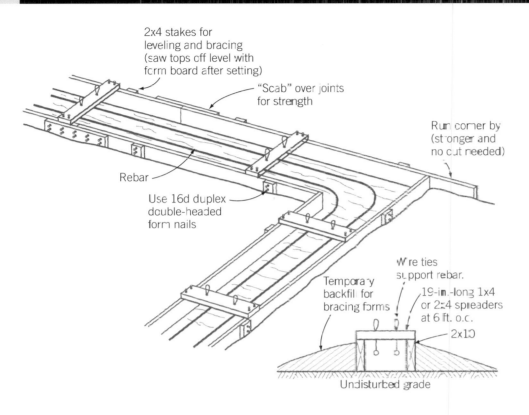

2x4 stakes for leveling and bracing (saw tops off level with form board after setting)

"Scab" over joints for strength

Run corner by (stronger and no cut needed)

Rebar

Use 16d duplex double-headed form nails

Wire ties support rebar.

19-in.-long 1x4 or 2x4 spreaders at 6 ft. o.c.

Temporary backfill for bracing forms

2x10

Undisturbed grade

concrete. It's hard enough to form a straight and level wall without having to fudge it to fit a crooked footing.

INSTALL INSIDE FORM BOARDS Check the boards for level once more after the perimeter is formed. I always use a transit level, because slight humps in 16-ft.-long planks can give a false reading with a 4-ft. level. By the time you go around 128 ft. or so of perimeter, these little discrepancies can add up to forms that are 1 in. or more off level. Since all subsequent measurements are taken from the footings, it's very important that they be level. Some concrete contractors don't bother to level the footings and figure to make up the difference at the top of the wall forms. This is an unnecessarily sleazy way to build a foundation, especially when you can afford to take the time to do it right.

ANCHOR THE FORMS AND INSTALL SPREADERS Cut a 16-in. length of 2x4 as a spreader guide and use it to space off the inside footing form boards. Repeat the staking and leveling process, this time leveling across from the outside form to the inside. Check the finished forms for level a final time. Use the claw of your hammer to scrape out any high spots under the form boards, and make your downward adjustments with a sledgehammer. Upward adjustments are achieved with a lever and rock shims.

Bank the outside with loose dirt to anchor the forms and fill any gaps under their bottom edges but do not fill in any low spots within the actual footing. Trim the tops of the stakes level with the forms. Nail 1x4 spreaders at 6-ft. intervals across the forms to prevent the wet concrete from pushing out the tops. Insert a short length of 4-in. PVC drainpipe through the bottom of the footing for later connection to the cellar floor or interior perimeter drain outlet. Hang two bars of reinforcing steel (rebar) from the spreaders with form tie wire. (Even if not required by code in residential footings, rebar is still a good idea.)

FILL THE FOOTING FORMS AND SCREED THE CONCRETE Fill the forms with concrete and screed with a length of 2x4. Don't worry about

The above-grade portion of this old stone foundation was capped with a new concrete wall. Formwork consisted of plywood braced to the framing and anchored with foundation stones.

Site-Built Forms

Building wall forms from ¾-in. plywood or 1-in. tongue-and-groove boards is a lot of work. But site-built forms are usually the only practical option for replacing short sections of wall. There are several commercially available form-tying systems. Modern *snap ties* are easier to install and align and make a stronger form than the old-fashioned hand-wired forms. Your local supplier can usually help adapt your form design to whatever system it sells. Consult a handbook for details before building any forms. *Audel's Masons and Builders Library* (Theodore Ardel & Co., 1978) is excellent in this regard.

getting it perfectly smooth—a bit of roughness makes a better bond. Before the concrete has set completely, stick 4-ft. lengths of rebar ("dowels") vertically into the footing to tie it to the wall. Most reference manuals suggest that you press 2x2 lengths of wood into the center of the footing to form a keyway, but I've never seen anyone actually do this. Leave the forms in place the next day while you lay out the wall to protect the soft concrete from damage. Remove the forms after 3 days.

Deciding How to Form the Foundation

When it comes to building the forms for your foundation, you have a few choices:

- Hire a concrete contractor to pour the walls. You might also consider having him do the footings. He has all the forms and is good at it. But because he will be working under an existing building, which cramps his style and takes more time, the cost per in-place cubic yard will be more than for standard work. In any case, the cost of the concrete and rebar is 40 percent to 50 percent of the usual contract price.

- Rent forms yourself, which is not always possible and not always cheap.

- Build the forms you need. This is labor intensive and, unlike formwork for a new house that can be recycled into sheathing and framing that you would have to buy anyway, there's likely to be little use for that expensive cement-stained plywood and odd lengths of 2x4s.

- Build a block wall. The materials are cheap and the wall can be done a little at a time to suit your schedule. And block laying is not a particularly difficult skill to master.

Lack of experience alone isn't reason enough not to do your own concrete work. The concentration with which a novice belabors a task often brings about first-quality results. When you don't know what you're getting into, you don't know any shortcuts, so you have to take the long way through. Ultimately, that familiar time/money equation determines your choice. Which do you have more of and which do you value more? Personally, I subcontract out concrete work whenever I can.

Building the Foundation Wall

Start building the wall by dropping the original plumb line that marked the outside corners of the building onto the footings. A chalkline snapped between these corner points marks the edge of the wall itself. If the sill projects over the wall 1 in. or so, the discrepancy can be ignored. But if the sill sits inside of the new wall, water will sit on the shelf and rot the sill. Follow the sill with the wall. Metal flashing inserted under the siding and down over the concrete is an alternative solution.

SELECT AN ENTRANCE Decide if you wish to add a bulkhead or ground-level entrance to the cellar. Bulkheads are used when the grade around the house is more or less level. Fitted with a steel hatchway, a set of stairs, and a tight-fitting interior door, they are energy-efficient and relatively inexpensive. Set pressure-treated 2x4s at the corners of the concrete to provide solid fastening for the door unit, as shown in the top drawing at right. Where the grade drops steeply away from the house, a cellar-floor level entrance is preferable. This makes it easy to use the cellar for storage of outdoor equipment like lawn tractors (useful if you don't have a garage) or to bring in (dry) firewood. The footings should step down below the frost line where the bulkhead wall turns out from the main wall. Otherwise, frost can lift the bulkhead walls and

Two Types of Bulkhead Walls

Cellar Bulkhead Treatment

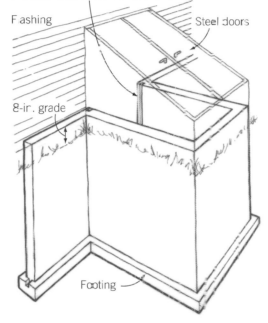

Pressure-treated 2x4 for door anchor

Flashing

Steel doors

8-in. grade

Footing

Open End–Gable Roof Bulkhead Wall

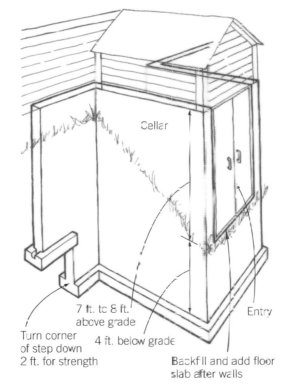

Cellar

Entry

7 ft. to 8 ft. above grade

4 ft. below grade

Turn corner of step down 2 ft. for strength

Backfill and add floor slab after walls

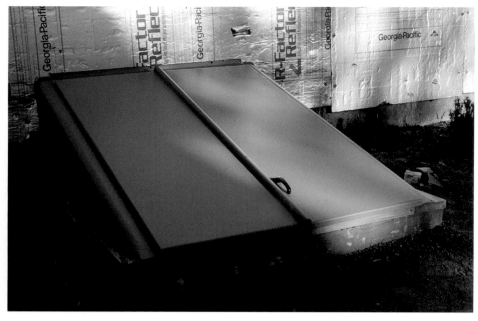

A rotted old wood bulkhead was replaced with a modern steel unit. Proper sealing and flashing against the wall are critical.

ALLOW SPACE FOR THE PONY WALL When holding, rather than raising, the house, allow enough space for the concrete block pony wall plus at least 2 in. of finger space to allow you to slide the top course of block in place. So, for two courses of block, you'll need 18 in. (three courses require 26 in.). A few more inches make it easier to fill the last course with insulation or concrete. For extra strength, I prefer to fill the cores of all foundation block with hand-mixed concrete rather than opt for a small decrease in heat loss by filling with vermiculite insulation. I'd also leave 4-in. rebar pins sticking out of the poured wall to help anchor the blocks. The block cores can be sliced to fit around any pins that are in the way.

INSTALL ANCHOR STRAPS Galvanized steel anchor straps (such as the Simpson Strong-Tie™ MAB15) inserted into the concrete-filled cores tie the foundation to a 2x8 or 2x10 pressure-treated wood mudsill (see the drawing on the facing page. Apply a bead of construction adhesive to help seal the mudsill to the masonry. Because masonry wicks moisture up into wood, building codes no longer allow direct contact between foundation walls and untreated wood.

floor slab and eventually crack or heave the main foundation walls.

Let the wall sit for 4 to 5 days after it is finished and the forms are stripped before easing the house down onto it. Concrete reaches most of its strength in about 1 week. Setting a house down onto a green foundation (new concrete actually does look green until it cures) can cause it to crumble like a dry cookie.

INSTALL THERMAL AND TERMITE SHIELDS
I also insert a layer of sill-seal insulation or ½-in. rigid foam between the mudsill and the old sills. When the house is let back down onto the new foundation, the insulation compresses, forming a tight gasket that seals cracks too small to fill with regular insulation or spray foam. Where termite infestation is endemic, install a termite shield between the sill and the new wall. The shield is simply a 16-in.-wide strip of 20-gauge aluminum, galvanized steel, or copper flashing with its projecting edges bent downward over the top of the perimeter insulation at a 45-degree angle, making it impossible for termites to eat their way into the sills. Copper is the most expensive, but it lasts longer than aluminum or steel and seems worth the price in this case.

Provide Conduits for Utilities

There's one detail that should not be overlooked when setting up the wall forms: Provide sleeves inside the forms to accommodate penetrations through the wall for utilities and the sewer line. A 1-gal. paint can nailed between the walls of the form makes a perfect opening for the cast-iron sewer line. Short lengths of PVC pipe of a diameter larger than the actual utility pipe form sleeves for electric and water lines. Drive them out after the forms are stripped. The actual conduits are sealed to the wall with hydraulic patching cement.

Capping a Concrete Wall with Block

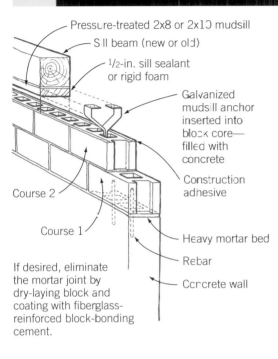

Pressure-treated 2x8 or 2x10 mudsill

Sill beam (new or old)

1/2-in. sill sealant or rigid foam

Galvanized mudsill anchor inserted into block core—filled with concrete

Construction adhesive

Course 2

Course 1

Heavy mortar bed

Rebar

Concrete wall

If desired, eliminate the mortar joint by dry-laying block and coating with fiberglass-reinforced block-bonding cement.

Building Full Block Walls

In my opinion, concrete block foundations perform best in light sandy soils and relatively frost-free zones. The finished wall is nowhere near as resistant to lateral pressures as poured concrete. In silty or clay soils, their longevity absolutely depends on meticulous attention to proper backfilling, foundation drainage, and surface-water control. Check with your local building inspector to see if block foundations are allowed. But a block wall is inexpensive and especially well matched to the on-again, off-again timetable of the part-time renovator. For extra strength, consider using 12-in. core block instead of the standard 8-in. block. As mentioned above, filling the cores with concrete strengthens the wall. The concrete mix should be on the watery side so that it can readily fill all the voids between the overlapping block cores. Inserting rebar into the cores also adds lateral

strength. Consult a good handbook for instructions on laying concrete block.

The working trench can be partially backfilled as soon as the foundation wall is damp proofed and the perimeter drainage installed. But final backfilling should not be attempted until after the house bears on its new wall; the weight braces the top of the wall against the lateral pressure of the backfill against it. Use good coarse gravel (not native soil), and place it carefully. If the trenches are fairly wide, place native

In suitable soils, concrete block foundations offer the advantage of piecemeal construction, which makes them ideal for the part-time foundation renovator. Block is also more forgiving of a novice's gaffes than concrete and does not require any expensive or labor-intensive formwork.

Using Bonding Cement

An easier and structurally sound alternative to a mortared concrete-block pony wall is to coat dry-laid block with a fiberglass-reinforced bonding cement. Sliding blocks into tight spaces under a sill is much easier with block bonding: There's no mortar to knock off the joint as you fit the block. The bonded wall is actually stronger and more water resistant than traditional mortared block. But the labor savings are offset by the expense of the bonding compound.

Foundation Coatings

Asphalt–Rubber Polymer

soil against the bank in steps, (a.k.a. "lifts") alternating with gravel against the wall to reduce the overall amount of gravel backfill. Make sure there are no boulders pressing against the wall.

Damp-Proofing

Contrary to popular perception, the traditional and still widely used asphalt-based foundation coating is not actually waterproof. Although it does block the migration of water through concrete by capillary action, it cannot block water infiltration driven by hydrostatic pressure. Likewise, asphalt coatings won't seal the larger pores in concrete block, so water can get through even without hydrostatic pressure. Hence, these asphalt-based coatings can damp-proof a wall, but they can't make it waterproof. There are compounds, such as *bentonite clay* and certain proprietary membrane systems, that will seal a wall against hydraulic forces; but they are expensive, require meticulous or professional application, and are ultimately unnecessary in all but a few special cases.

When properly installed, a conventional *drain screen* (the fancy name for the venerable practice of backfilling the foundation trench with free-draining porous gravel and/or crushed stone instead of the native soil) completely eliminates hydrostatic pressure. As a result, drain screen coupled with asphalt damp-proofing creates an effective waterproofing system. Take care to seal the little craters (created by snapping off the steel form ties that stick out of the new wall) with flashing-grade asphalt cement to prevent water from seeping between the concrete and the metal. Concrete block walls should be sealed by parging them with a cement stucco undercoat first. Whatever the wall, embedding a sheet of ordinary 6-mil polyethylene into the freshly applied asphalt is also good insurance. Because the plastic is not UV-resistant, it should not be exposed above grade (the asphalt coating isn't UV-resistant either). Leave sufficient slack for the sheet to drape over the footings.

Insulating Foundation Walls

It's now standard practice to insulate foundation walls with rigid extruded polystyrene (XPS) insulation boards. There are two methods to use for old houses. If the foundation is to be replaced, the new wall can be inset 2 in. (the recommended insulation thickness for cold climates) under the sills, as shown in part A of the drawing on the facing page. If the sills are too narrow to overhang, nail a beveled drip cap (ripped from pressure-treated 2x4 stock) to the sill under the first course of siding and butt the foam to it or use preformed metal flashing (see part B of the drawing). Beveling the outside edge of a treated 2x10 mudsill kills two birds with one stone (see part C of the drawing). Note that you'll need a heavy-duty contractor's table saw to rip the boards. In addition to the caulking, seal the joint between the drip cap and the sheathing with a strip of bituthene polymerized asphalt membrane (such as W. R. Grace Ice and Watershield®).

Because XPS is impermeable to vapor diffusion, the panels will effectively damp-proof a foundation. Hence, some experts now suggest that asphalt foundation coatings can be eliminated. But, given their low cost, I don't see any reason not to use them, if only for a backup. Tough and durable cross-laminated polyethylene membrane (such as Tu-Tuf®, Griffolyn®, and Ruffco), draped over the top of the foundation and under the crushed stone of the footing drain, is another newly recommended method of damp-proofing. Ideally, the XPS panels (such as Styrofoam® blue board, Formular® pink board, and Amofoam® green board) should cover the wall from sill to footing. Since most of the heat loss occurs above grade and within the first few feet of the surface, 4 ft. of below-surface coverage is both adequate and cost-effective.

Retrofitting Insulation

Perimeter insulation can be retrofitted to protect an old house, even when the foundation wall is left undisturbed. Dig a 2-ft.-deep narrow trench alongside the wall (soil permitting, this could be hand-shovel work). If the siding is clapboard, remove the first course and add a drip cap, as shown in part D of the drawing at right. For vertical-board siding and wood shingles, make the drip cap channel by cutting along a chalkline with a circular saw set to shallow depth and a 10-degree bevel. Seal the joint between the drip cap and the siding with paintable silicone caulk. Fit the insulation against the wall; backfill.

Although a backhoe can dig and fill trenches quickly and efficiently, it's not the best tool for finish grading. Hire a bulldozer to spread the topsoil (which you, of course, stripped and saved before you started trenching) over the fill. Bulldozer operators can back-drag the surface with the blade, leaving it ready for hand raking and seeding. If there are a lot of stones in the finish material, a tractor-pulled landscape rake (York rake) will drag them into windrows for easier removal. Loosely scattered mulch hay will protect the freshly seeded lawn from birds, wind, and washout until it's established.

Every time you hire a piece of heavy equipment, you pay a moving charge that is equal to at least 1 hour's work: Use the machine to bury stumps, junk, or rubble, regrade the driveway or push some boulders out of the field—use that bulldozer every minute it's on your property and keep it for a few extra hours if you can afford it, rather than call it back at a later date for some small job.

Perimeter Insulation for Foundation Walls

A. Offset Foundation

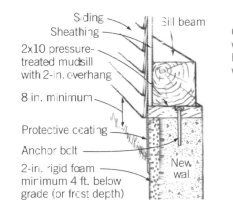

Siding
Sheathing
Sill beam
2x10 pressure-treated mudsill with 2-in. overhang
8 in. minimum
Protective coating
Anchor bolt
2-in. rigid foam minimum 4 ft. below grade (or frost depth)
New wall

B. Drip Cap Over Insulation

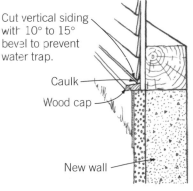

Cut vertical siding with 10° to 15° bevel to prevent water trap.
Caulk
Wood cap
New wall

C. One-Step Mudsill and Drip Cap

Caulk
10° bevel
2x12 or 2x10
Anchor bolt
New wall

D. Perimeter Insulation Retrofit Details

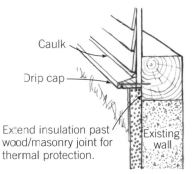

Caulk
Drip cap
Extend insulation past wood/masonry joint for thermal protection.
Existing wall

Beveled pressure-treated drip cap ripped from 2x4 or 2x6 stock and nailed to face of sill or sheathing. (If sheathing is rotten, cut out and extend cap to sill.)

4 The House Frame

Some fifty or fifty-five years ago [mid-1800s] when lumber was more plentiful, it was the common practice to build frame houses, great and small, with solid timbers. . . . The corner posts were usually made out of timbers six or eight inches square with the inner corner hewn out to receive the lath and plaster. Think of doing that kind of work nowadays. . . . though only a lad, we remember the time the trees were being felled in the forest and, after a long wait for the timbers to be squared, they were hauled to the building site, and, after a time for them to season, the carpenters came and, as though but yesterday, we see them under the old apple trees astride the timbers with auger, chisel, and mallet working away from morn till night. . . . Those were days of toil, days of contentment and peace. How different it is now!

—WILLIAM RADFORD, *PRACTICAL CARPENTRY*

The first homes of the early colonists were of necessity crude and temporary affairs, a bare respite from the winter cold while the family got on with the work of clearing and planting. Some settlers simply appropriated the empty wigwams of abandoned Indian settlements. Others built their own. Several decades would pass before any great number of the substantial timber-framed houses we now associate with the early colonial period were built.

Most of the houses built before 1650 would have been considered pitiful hovels even by the standards of the time. Frames, such as they were, consisted of posts anchored in the earth to support a thatched roof. The spaces between them were filled in with wattle and daub, interwoven branches plastered with mud. Chimneys were log cribs, also plastered with mud and mortar. House fires were a constant threat, and the annals of the period are replete with tales of walls washing away in fierce storms and fires leaping from roof to roof.

Although it looks original, this unusual crutched post was actually added during a relatively recent renovation of a 1780s Maine coast farmhouse. It seems fitting because any ship's carpenter moonlighting as a housewright would have been quite familiar with the utility of naturally crutched and curved timbers.

THE EVOLUTION OF AMERICAN HOUSE FRAMES

It was likely with great relief that, as his farm prospered, the settler could afford to hire a master carpenter and crew to build him a proper house, framed with heavy oak beams, like any good English house. During the previous winters he would have felled and hewn the logs. He would also have *riven* (split) stacks of clapboards and roof shingles. But timber framing was an art and a science, the secrets of which had been jealously guarded since the guilds of the Middle Ages. After these well-paid specialists had cut and joined the beams, the farmer and his sons would then shingle and sheathe the house.

The resulting house was substantial enough that European tourists would express their surprise at the comfort they found throughout the settled areas. "Wood was cheap; it took but little more pains to make a subsill forty feet long than to make one twenty feet long; and the houses grew larger and larger after the first settlement was made" (Edward Everett Hale, *Studies in American Colonial Life*, 1895). In Pennsylvania and other regions settled by Germans, the community would work together to raise the barn or house frame. But in New England, house raising, like most other activities, tended to be a private affair.

Timber Frames

Timber frames tend to follow a set pattern (see the drawing on p. 118). The earliest were centered on a massive central fireplace and chimney—the focal point of life in the house. The chimney was thus an integral part of the frame, limiting the layout of the timbers and defining the design of the house. It's not uncommon for the chimney to support the principal girts. This configuration is typical of house frames built from the earliest colonial period up to the end of the eighteenth century.

The widespread use of heating stoves and the introduction of central furnaces around the beginning of the nineteenth century made it possible to omit the large central fireplace and often the chimney girts and summer beam as well. This frame became the direct ancestor of modern layouts. Another significant change was that as oak and chestnut became harder to find, timbers were hewn from spruce. That the original frames were oak was not so much by choice as by chance: oak was a wood already known to English settlers from back home. Spruce was more than strong enough, a lot lighter and easier to work.

Balloon Frames

In 1832, a Chicago businessman constructed the first building that employed a radically different framing system. It made full use of the accurately sized lumber that was suddenly turned out in great quantities by rapidly proliferating circular-saw mills. This lumber, cut from the forests of the great north woods, was shipped over the newly opened railroad network to build the cities that were dotting the treeless Great Plains. The pieces were put together with the cheap machine-made nails that had also become commonly available.

In the balloon frame, studs run continuously from the mudsill to the rafter plate; floor joists

The studs of a balloon framed gable wall usually did not run continuously to the rafters. Instead, they were "fish-plated" (spliced) together.

are nailed to the face of studs and rest on let-in ledger strips. Despite its fragile appearance, this frame is incredibly strong. The principal difference between stud and timber framing is anatomical. The timber frame is modeled on the human skeleton. The bones are large, heavy members; sheathing (the skin) fills in the spaces between, tacked to whatever odd lumber was left over for studding. The balloon frame is analogous to the hard shell of an insect, which is at once skin and bone. The entire frame would collapse were it not for the bracing afforded by the diagonal sheathing boards. (The fact that shoddy or ignorant workmen often laid the sheathing boards horizontally perhaps contributed to the balloon frame's reputation for flimsiness.)

By dispersing great loads over large areas, house design was freed from the rigid requirements of the timber frame. The fanciful confections of the Victorian era were soon forthcoming. The other advantage of balloon framing was that, unlike traditional timber framing, it required no great skill to master and no great time to put together. What more could a burgeoning nation of immigrants ask for? As a contemporary observer remarked "Not mortise nor tenon nor other mysteries of carpentry interfered with the swiftness of its growth." Gervase Wheeler: *Homes for the People, in Suburb and Country*, 1855.

Platform Frames

The balloon frame dominated residential building until after World War II, when the platform, or western, frame—which is the standard for residential construction today—superseded it. The main difference between the two is that in western framing, each story is built on its own platform, whereas in balloon framing the floor platforms are hung on a "ribbon" attached to continuous studs. By using short studs, entire walls could be framed on the platform, even sheathed, and then tilted up, making for even faster and more accurate assembly. In the mid-1950s, plywood sheathing replaced diagonal boarding. Sheathed in plywood, either of these frail-looking stick frames is actually much stronger than the most rugged of traditional timber frames.

Tradition and Suspicion

Even as sawmills began turning out the thin studs and planks of the newfangled balloon frame, tradition-bound old-timers insisted that the only properly built frame was the braced, or full, heavy timber frame of their forefathers. Despite the march of progress elsewhere, in the rural backwaters of New England the old preferences persisted well into the latter half of the nineteenth century. For a long time, it was still cheaper and easier to hew timbers longer than 16 ft. by hand on site rather than transport logs to and from a distant sawmill over poor roads.

Hewn sills, girts, plates, and corner posts were mixed with sawn joists and heavy studding (4x4s or 3x6s set flat-wise, for example) in a hybrid framing system that was common throughout the early years of the twentieth century.

The innovations of mass production did not filter down to rural areas until well into the Victorian era. Even though sawn timbers began supplanting hewn beams in the 1850s, conservative builders remained skeptical of such radical innovations as 2x4 studs. Perhaps they used heavy timbers as insurance, not trusting a doubtful-looking stud wall to bear the weight of centuries. So, at least in the Northeast, chances are good that a house built before 1860 will have a traditional mortise-and-tenon timber frame, and even those built as late as the 1920s will still be more similar to a braced timber frame than a balloon frame.

Structural Logic

When you understand where the loads are concentrated in your house and how they are distributed across a span, repair work is a matter of logic instead of luck. Of course, you should be familiar with the basic elements of house framing.

In a timber-frame house the bulk of the roof and floor platform load is concentrated onto the

Platform Frames Do Rot

Although you might be tempted to think that most platform-framed houses aren't yet old enough to require structural repairs, it takes only about 7 years for wood that's constantly exposed to moisture to rot. Advances in building technology and awareness of moisture problems are no guarantee against decay caused by lack of their utilization. In fact, many homes built during the 1960s and 1970s suffered from misapplied technology that hastened their destruction.

sills at very specific points by the upright posts. The sills and horizontal plate beams anchor the critical knee braces that keep the posts plumb and impart rigidity to the frame. Although it does spread some of the substantial vertical point loads horizontally, most of a sill doesn't actually carry any weight—sills are more bracing than bearing. Obviously, then, all of the sill between posts could be replaced without any jacking other than that required for supporting the floor joists. The problem is how to support the concentrated load carried by a corner or wall post so that the sill directly beneath it can be removed and replaced.

Stick-frame structures (as both balloon and platform framing are called) distribute loads along the entire length of the foundation. One might suppose that this would complicate sill repair, but since the actual portion of the load at any given point is quite small, large pieces of sill and attached framing can be removed with impunity. The lattice of framing, sheathing, siding, and interior walls supports itself as long as some portion of the wall or corner is left to bear

on the foundation. An adjacent section of wall will support the corner of the building while the sill directly under the corner is removed, which is not always the case with timber-framed walls. How much structure can be removed and how little support is required to maintain the stability of a stick-framed house continues to amaze me.

REPAIRING OR REPLACING ROTTED SILLS

Wood won't rot unless it stays moist, and there is no more perfect water trap than the space between the sill and the top of the foundation walls or the back of the sheathing boards. Sometimes houses are too close to the ground—although a good 2 ft. is necessary to avoid damage, standard specs allow the sills to lie a mere 8 in. above grade. Here, the bottom-most boards of the siding rot first, acting like sponges, holding moisture against the sills. Condensation created by improperly insulated walls causes water to run down the vertical members and pool on top of the sills. If constantly exposed to moisture, old timbers will rot sooner than new wood because their natural wood-preserving resins are lost with age. Conversely, when wood is kept dry, it lasts a long time. John Cole and Charles Wing, in *From the Ground Up* (Little Brown, 1976), observe that wooden doors, frames, and furniture buried with their Egyptian owners several thousand years ago are still as strong, functional, and lovely as the day the tombs were closed.

Checking for Rot

A few pages back we suspended our disbelief and raised a house. If we had tried to lift a rotten sill beam, the jack timber would have cut through it like a knife through soft cheese. Over the years, the weight of the house will compress

Because they are at the bottom of the house, sills are closest to the earth and the most vulnerable to decay.

rotted sills like a brick resting on a loaf of white bread. The house begins to sag, twisting and racking when a sinking sill throws it off balance. If the rot can be arrested in its early stages, major repairs will be avoided later.

The condition of the first course of siding boards offers a clue to the state of the underlying sills. If the sheathing boards under the siding are also crumbly, chances are that the rot has progressed into the sill. The building paper covering the sheathing has wonderful wicklike properties that can draw moisture a long way up the wall and keep it there. Remove as many courses of siding as necessary until the sheathing boards appear sound. The areas under windows often have their own veins of rot, which extend downward to meet the rot working upward from the sills. Take off the rotted sheathing to

Sill Test: Poke and Listen

Typically, sills rot from the exterior of the house toward the inside. Poke the cellar side of the sill with an ice pick. If you can push it in more than one quarter of the sill's width, its most likely pretty far gone on its outside, even when hidden beneath apparently sound siding and sheathing boards. (The previous owner may have replaced the siding deliberately to hide the rotted sills.) Sills also rot first and foremost on their bottoms where they suck up water by capillary action from pores in the masonry. To make a rough test for overall soundness from the cellar side, tap the sill with a hammer. A sound sill rings with a high tone; the pitch decreases in proportion to the amount of rot on the outside of the sill.

Not as bad as it looks: Although the corner is gone, the decay does not extend very far along the length of the sill. This is an ideal candidate for in-place repair rather than replacement.

If unchecked, rot will eventually progress from the sills up into the wall studs themselves.

the nearest sound board and expose the sill. Rotted wood is soft and crumbly and stained dark red; sound wood is pale and resists a chisel. A sill that has rotted along its entire bottom face has lost its structural integrity; the building will settle. Replacement is the only practical option.

Repairing a Sill in Place

When only an edge has succumbed to decay, it's usually easier to repair the sill in place rather than replace it. At least half of the old sill must be sound, and the good part should run vertically through the entire sill (that is, it should still be able to carry a load).

REMOVE THE ROTTED AREA Cut vertical kerfs across the rotted area with a reciprocating saw or heavy-duty jigsaw. (The foundation wall will interfere if you make the vertical cuts with a circular saw—set the blade of this tool to the depth of the rot and cut horizontal kerfs to simplify removing the rotted wood.) Clean out the pockets of rot with a chisel until good solid wood is showing, leaving a rectangular excision in the

Removing the granite ashlar and the decayed sheathing boards exposed this badly rotted sill in all its sad glory, providing ample elbow room for replacement. Fiberglass batts stuffed into the cavities will replace the cellulose insulation that has fallen out.

sill. Coat the exposed new wood with a wood preservative such as Cuprinol #10.

INSTALL A DUTCHMAN Cut a block of new wood (a *dutchman*) to fit tightly in the opening; pound it in and secure it with galvanized bugle-head screws or nails. If the cavity is too deep to fill with a single thickness of dimension lumber or board, layer up pieces until the dutchman is flush with the original face. (*Dimension* refers to lumber with a nominal thickness of at least 2 in., such as 2x4s and 2x6s. *Boards* are less than 2 in. in nominal thickness.) If you don't use pressure-treated lumber, coat all faces and edges of the dutchman with wood preservative.

Replacing a Sill

When decay has eaten into the ends of the floor joists or all the way across the bottom of the sill, there's no choice but to replace the whole piece. Sills do carry the ends of the floor joists, but these loads are easily relieved by a jacking timber hung from the joists with a rope sling and then lifted by screw jacks, as shown in the drawing on the facing page. Use vertical 4x4 jack posts under the jacking timber if the distance from the cellar floor to the joists is greater than can be supported with a jacking timber and screw jacks alone.

It makes a huge difference in labor and/or expense whether your goal in sill replacement is restoration or renovation. If your concern is only to restore structural soundness (that is, renovation), the rotted sill can be removed piecemeal and replaced with relatively short sections of treated dimension lumber, set on edge and lapped to make a continuous built-up sill beam. The entire operation can be accomplished without recourse to jacking the frame, other than possibly in the immediate vicinity of a concentrated post load. But where restoration demands the replacement of the original heavy timber sill with like, the entire length of the wall must be

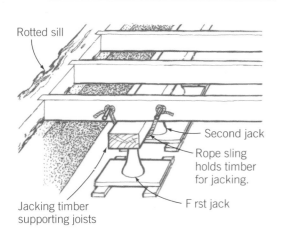

Rotted sill

Second jack

Rope sling holds timber for jacking.

Jacking timber supporting joists

First jack

PREPARE THE JOIST ENDS Cut back the rotted ends of the floor joists to solid wood. If you're lucky and the rot has not eaten very far back into the joists, you can fill the gap by *furring* (building out) the back of the sill beam or rim joist. Otherwise, you'll need to sister new joists onto the truncated ones. If the joists aren't resting directly on the sill, they should be secured to the new rim joist or sill beam with metal joist hangers. The local welding shop can fabricate custom hangers for odd-dimensioned joists and timbers. Purists may wish to mortise the new sill to accept the ends of the joists (when sound), but that's a lot of trouble to go through down in the cellar.

INSERT THE NEW SILL The old sill should be cut to accept a horizontal half-lap joint where it abuts the new. Nail the ends together with 40d spikes driven at an angle or pole-barn nails (long, ring-shanked nails used for joining timbers) driven through the top of the splice. Remove and replace as much sill as you can before repositioning the jacking timbers. Usually, this means a corner and half the length of a wall or to the edge of the first intermediate post.

supported so that the sill can be removed and replaced with one, or perhaps two, new timbers. In that case, jacking is a definite requirement.

REMOVE THE ROTTED SILL Rotted sills are most easily removed piecemeal. Cut the sill into bite-size portions with a chainsaw or reciprocating saw and lever the pieces out with a prybar. If posts are mortised and pegged into the sill, cut through their tenons at the post bottom. Cut through any nails (use a special nail-cutting blade in your reciprocating saw) before attempting to release the sill. This prevents splitting the posts and eases their removal.

PREPARE THE FOUNDATION WALL Clean the surface of the old foundation wall. Uneven stones should be capped level with mortar. This is especially necessary when replacing a sill behind a buttress wall, when the face of the wall is actually higher than the bottom of the sill, creating an ideal water trap. Before the cap sets hard, lay a 2x10 pressure-treated mudsill on the mortar bed and anchor it with 20d galvanized spikes driven through the wood into the mortar.

A half-lap joint not only ties the sills together but also allows them to be lifted as a unit should it be necessary to replace the foundation wall.

Replacing a Rotted Sill

Improper flashing of this buttress wall allowed water to get to the framing. The rot went far enough to require replacement of the entire sill as well as the ends of the floor joists and the wall studs.

1 The damage is obvious once the siding and sheathing boards are removed. The floor joists are supported by a jacking timber slipped into the cellar, and the sill is sawn into pieces for easy removal. The old stone foundation wall is capped with mortar to bring it level with the lip of the buttress wall.

2 A pressure-treated 2x10 mudsill is set on top of the wall and anchored with 20d galvanized spikes driven into the soft mortar. The rotted ends of the joists and wall studs are cut back to sound wood.

3 A band joist is nailed across the face of the floor joists, a treated wood sill is built up under it, and new sole plates are added under the studs. The framing is shimmed out as needed so that the sheathing boards conform to the irregularities in the existing wall. Framing is added between the new sill and the bottom of the old studs.

4 Roughsawn boards match the thickness of the original sheathing boards. Lead flashing prevents water from getting behind the sheathing and under the new sills. Lead conforms well to the irregular surface of the concrete, but must be kept painted to avoid a health hazard.

Replacing a Sill under a Post

The situation is a bit more complicated when the sill directly under a post must also be replaced. As is obvious from the discussion of framing, the post must be supported or its load relieved before the sill can be removed. This is often a judgment call. Most of the time (for single-story structures anyway), the post will just dangle from the beam it supports. Removing the sill won't cause even a slight sag, since the sheathing boards and wall studs will spread out the load to the solid sections already replaced.

RELIEVE THE LOAD Sometimes a post really does carry a substantial load. If the rotted sill under a post appears squashed, it's wise to assume that there's some downward pressure; likewise assume this is the case if, when cutting through the tenon or nails at the bottom of the post, the sawblade pinches tight before the cut is finished. The posts of multistory houses are also much more likely to require support. Relieve the load on the post by lifting the plate beam (the one carried by the post) with a jack placed on the remaining sound sill on either or both sides of the post, or simply make sure that any new sill already installed ends just short of the troublesome post.

USE AS FEW PIECES AS POSSIBLE While it may be practical to piece in short sections of new sill, it's better for structural strength to replace the sills in as few pieces as possible, even if historical integrity is not critical. First lift the post as just described in "Relieve the Load." Then support the plate beam on a braced cradle, as shown in the left drawing below so that you can remove the jack post, allowing unhindered replacement of the rotted sill. Before sliding such cradles through the wall, it is necessary to remove substantial amounts of sheathing and finish siding.

Although a needle beam timber supported by the floor joists requires more setup (see the middle drawing below), only a narrow band of

Three Ways to Brace above a Post

1. A braced cradle carries the plate beam and allows a damaged post or sill section to be replaced. Siding must be removed to slide cradle beams through the wall.

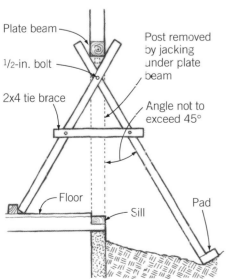

- Plate beam
- 1/2-in. bolt
- 2x4 tie brace
- Post removed by jacking under plate beam
- Angle not to exceed 45°
- Floor
- Sill
- Pad

2. Although more cumbersome, this method supports the plate beam with minimal damage to siding and wall finishes.

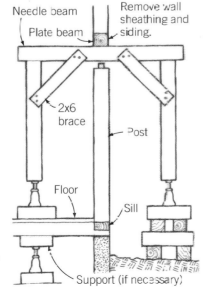

- Needle beam
- Plate beam
- Remove wall sheathing and siding.
- 2x6 brace
- Post
- Floor
- Sill
- Support (if necessary)

3. A timber under adjacent beams can lift a corner post. This method is especially useful where heavy loads are bearing on rotted sills at a corner.

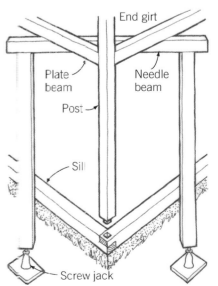

- End girt
- Plate beam
- Needle beam
- Post
- Sill
- Screw jack

Lifting Beams Bear the Load during Sill Replacement

An effective way of relieving the load to allow sill replacement is to shore up the wall with a series of angled lifting beams. This method is particularly useful when replacing the entire length of a sill wholesale.

Remove siding and sheathing boards above the window headers to expose the plate beam (of a single-story structure) or other framing members that support the ceiling joists (of a multistory house). Bolt "lifting beams" to the plate girt or wall studs that carry the ribbon, or rim joist. Beams are ideally 2x12 hardwood planks, one or two per length of wall (structural grade yellow pine or Douglas fir or 3x12 local spruce are alternatives).

Remove the sod and dig pairs of slightly angled cuts about 2 ft. out in front of the foundation wall within 2 ft. or 3 ft. of the ends of each beam. Set 2-ft.-sq. jacking

(Photo by John Crispin Photography)

pads (cross-layered 2x12s and ¾-in. plywood) in each cut. Use hydraulic jacks and angled 4x4 jack posts bearing under the edges of the transverse beams to take the weight off the sills.

sheathing must be removed where the beam goes through the wall. But in any case, sheathing boards nailed across both the post or studs and the sill beam should be removed to ease lifting the post. Also, posts will not lift very far if they are still secured to the sill by their bottom knee braces. These braces should be cut flush with the sill and later renailed.

Use 4x4 or 6x6 posts for the cradles under the plate beams. Brace them firmly against a bearing block outside the house and a block nailed to the floorboards over a joist on the inside. Crib or place a post up under the joists to carry the added stress.

USE A NEEDLE BEAM FOR HEAVY BUILDINGS

A needle beam is more stable than a cradle and thus better suited for repairing heavy buildings. Cribbing can be stacked quite high, as long as it is kept level; the more cribbing and the fewer posts, the greater the stability. Needle beams can also be inserted diagonally under a plate beam and end girt to relieve the load on a corner post (as shown in the right drawing on p. 143).

I've used these methods to carry the roof and upper floor loads while removing entire walls together with their sills. Radical surgery of this sort is called for in situations in which something has caused large areas of a wall to decay, for example, where manure was left piled against a barn or snow was trapped between the wall and a steep slope.

CONSIDER A STEEL JACKING BRACKET If you need to lift a lot of heavily loaded posts (as, for example, when repairing a barn) consider having a steel jacking bracket fabricated at your local welding shop. As shown in the drawing below, the U-shaped bracket is through-bolted to the post and the jack is set beneath the angle-braced flange. If the bracket is wide enough to accommodate the largest post, it can be shimmed to fit narrower ones.

Replacing a Sill in a Stick-Framed House

Sill replacement is much easier in stick-framed houses. Sections up to half the length of a wall can typically be removed without any jacking or lifting beyond whatever it takes to support the floor or ceiling joists. Because the studs hang from the top plate, which, in turn, is nailed to ceiling joists and/or rafters, an entire wall, sheathing, sills, studs and even foundation can be removed or repaired by supporting the roof and floor loads with jacking timbers installed on the inside of the house, as in shown in the drawing on p. 146. Here, the jack placed in the cellar stiffens the floor to support the jacks placed under the ceiling joists, which help carry the roof load where they join the rafters or the plate.

Where the floor joists are still sound and resting firmly on the foundation wall (and not hung or attached to a decayed sill), the basement jacking can be eliminated. Instead, use a 2x12 plank, laid on the first floor and under the jacks perpendicular to the run of the first-floor joists, to distribute the lifting force across as many joists as possible. At gable ends, a jacking or supporting timber is not needed, because the floor joists run parallel to the sill and the wall framing can support its own weight.

Fitting a New Sill

Even with the house raised, fitting a solid-timber replacement sill calls for a combination of brute strength and finesse. Careful measurement ensures that any mortises line up with the existing floor joists. The old-timers used a heavy wooden mallet called a *commander* or *beetle* to persuade a timber into place. A modern sledgehammer will suffice, so long as you tack a pad of 2x stock to the sill to protect it against direct contact with the iron face of the hammer.

Home-Made Post-Lifting Bracket

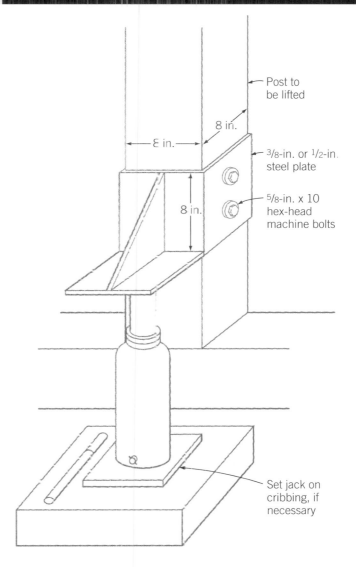

Post to be lifted

8 in.

8 in.

8 in.

3/8-in. or 1/2-in. steel plate

5/8-in. x 10 hex-head machine bolts

Set jack on cribbing, if necessary

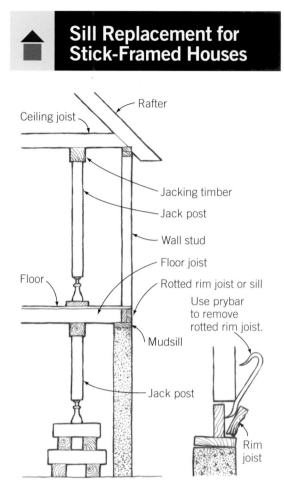

Sill Replacement for Stick-Framed Houses

- Rafter
- Ceiling joist
- Jacking timber
- Jack post
- Wall stud
- Floor joist
- Floor
- Rotted rim joist or sill
- Use prybar to remove rotted rim joist.
- Mudsill
- Jack post
- Rim joist

REMOVE THE RIM JOIST After exposing the damage, pull the rotted rim joist (which is part of the stud-frame equivalent to a timber sill) free from the floor joists with a prybar or pinchbar. You'll probably find it a lot easier to remove the rim joist if you first saw through the nails that secure it to the floor joists and sole plate. Likewise, if you use a cat's paw to remove any nails that tie the floor joists to the mudsill (or saw them through), the bottom edges of the floor joists won't split when the mudsill is ripped out. Cut the mudsill into manageable sections, especially at any sill anchor bolts. Before installing pressure-treated wood replacement framing, brush wood preservative on all sound old surfaces, particularly the end grain.

FUR OUT THE SILLS, IF NECESSARY

Replacement sills laid straight along a wall may not always line up with the framing above. New sheathing boards and studs aren't likely to match the irregular thickness of old ones. Rather than try to curve an 8x8 sill or to saw boards to fit, use tapered shims, beveled clapboards, or varying layers of that renovator's standby, the cedar shingle, to fur out the new work to the old. The wedges are added vertically and/or horizontally, depending on where cosmetic compensation is needed. The object is for the finish siding to approximate a flat plane rather than a waveform. How this illusion is created is not critical. When large areas of sheathing boards must be replaced, it's usually quicker to remove all the boards from the entire wall and resheathe with plywood rather than to match new boards to old.

The rotted timber sill of this barn was replaced with a pressure-treated mudsill pinned to the original concrete foundation wall. The decayed stud ends were cut back to sound wood and sistered onto short lengths of 2x stock.

With an old house, there's a good chance that you aren't the first to attempt repairs. Previous owners may have already shored up a bad foundation or replaced rotted sills. But while the earlier work may have halted the damage, it may not have restored the house to its original level. In other words, you might have a solid house sitting on a tilted foundation. The choice to live with it or correct it depends less on structural necessity than on how much your chair and table legs must be sawn off to fit the room.

Having established the highest point of the foundation (which is usually the original level of the house), you may wish to lift up the rest of the house to more or less match it. Through a combination of lifting floor joists and/or carrying beams and jacking under corner posts, it's usually possible to align the sills with the rest of the house. Additional concrete grout can be poured into the gap and later capped off like a

Prybar, Pinchbar, or Crowbar?

Prybars are smaller than pinchbars, which are what most people call crowbars. Crowbars are 5 ft. or 6 ft. long, straight with a pointed end, and used for heavy-duty levering. Pinchbars, also known as wrecking bars, are for pulling big spikes and for levering, ripping, and tearing. Prybars, or flatbars, are for ordinary nail pulling and light-duty levering, as opposed to the smaller cat's paw, which is for extracting nails just enough so they can be removed with a prybar or hammer claw. Mini-prybars are sometimes helpful for extracting nails from clapboards.

After the new sill was installed, the wall studs were furred out to bring the plywood sheathing flush to the original rough-board sheathing. The clapboards and sheathing above the windows were removed to accommodate a transverse lifting beam.

buttress wall, or pressure-treated wood shims and planks can be added as required, depending on the regularity of the existing foundation wall.

REPLACING OR REPAIRING ROTTED POSTS

Rot is hardly confined to sills alone. Corner posts are especially vulnerable to decay, fed by water seeping behind ill-fitting or uncaulked corner trim boards. All posts tend to rot from the bottom up. Although a horizontal sill can suffer a good deal of decay without its function being seriously impaired, a vertical load-bearing post cannot. Despite the very great compressive strength of wood parallel to its grain, a weakened post, because of the weight it carries, is potentially dangerous. A rotted post is similar to

A 2x4 and shingle wedges support this corner post until the sill can be replaced. The decayed face of the post has been excised and will be filled with new wood. The exposed electrical cable emphasizes the need for caution when hacking away at decayed wood.

a cardboard mailing tube stood on end. It will support a lot of weight if you balance it carefully, but should the balance shift or the end of the tube dent, the whole thing will immediately collapse.

Replacing a Post

As mentioned earlier, it's often possible to remove a post without any jacking or lifting of plate beams, because the adjoining wall sheathing and studs provide more than enough support. Simply cut the post free of its knee braces and pull the nails from the sheathing boards that cover it (this assumes that the interior walls have been removed or at least cut back from the damage zone). Saw through the tenons at top and bottom and lever the post free. If you wish to cut a tenon in the new post to fit the existing plate beam, mortising instead of toenailing it in place, remove the stub of the old tenon by drilling out the wooden pegs (called *trenails* or *trunnels*) if they won't pull or drive out. Because inserting a tenoned post requires lifting the plates, I can't imagine anyone but a fanatical restorationist going to such lengths.

Adding a Scabbed Post

The complete removal and replacement of posts is seldom called for. Most often, a new post is *scabbed* (or sistered) alongside the old one, on either or both sides, depending on the extent of the rot (after the source of the infection has been found and cured). If 4x4 stock is used for the scab post, it will be hidden inside the wall, leaving the old post cosmetically exposed to the interior. Take care to fit repair posts tightly to any knee braces, as only those surfaces in direct contact will actually bear weight.

Replacing the Bottom of a Post

It's also possible to amputate the rotted lower extremity of an otherwise sound post and fill in the gap with a prosthetic section. Where the post must be exposed to view, use a piece of similar but salvaged timber and join it to the remainder with a half-lap joint, as shown in the drawing below. This joint is strong, relatively easy to cut, and handsome. It can look structurally deliberate rather than merely necessary. For added interest, the simple half-lap joint can be mitered at a 45-degree angle, as shown in the drawing. Countersink the heads of the through bolts and plug them with dowel pins.

Repairing Post Connections to Girts and Joists

A single-story frame is actually rather uncommon. Most old houses are framed as one-and-a-half or two stories, with posts running from sill to rafter plate and end-wall girts and floor-joist girts tenoned into them at the second-floor level. This complex joint considerably lowers the

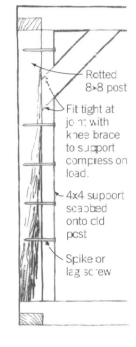

▲ Post Repair

Support the load by scabbing new wood onto rotted posts (find and fix the source of the rot first).

- Rotted 8×8 post
- Fit tight at joint with knee brace to support compression load.
- 4x4 support scabbed onto old post
- Spike or lag screw

▲ Two Joints for Repairing Exposed Posts

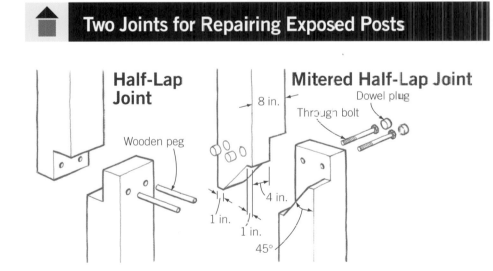

Half-Lap Joint

Wooden peg

Mitered Half-Lap Joint

Dowel plug
Through bolt

8 in.
4 in.
1 in.
1 in.
45°

resistance of the post to outward and downward thrusts, and, if inadequately braced or over-stressed, it can easily fail. If you're lucky, the top portion of the post, having bent outward, will have sheared the tenon pegs, simply pulling the joint apart. This situation is a lot easier to fix than when the post itself snaps off at the peg holes, because the walls can be pulled back in (more on this on pp. 165–171) and the joint repegged.

A sheared post, however, means that a new section must be scarfed in somewhere well below the break. Depending on the extent of the damage, sections of the intersecting girts may also need to be replaced. If appearance is not a problem, consider using custom-fabricated steel supports for splicing and strengthening failed joints. These are much less labor intensive than cutting scarfs and duplicating the old joinery.

Determining the Sag of a Girder

Case 1. Stringing a Girder with Mortised Floor Joists

Sill · Top of foundation wall · String · Use measuring gauge block cut from scrap to align beam with string. · Bowed girder · Floor joist · Floor · Amount of lift needed

Case 2. Stringing a Girder with Floor Joists Carried on Top

No measuring gauge necessary—determine sag by measuring from lowest point of beam to string.

Floor · Sill · Bowed girder · String · Top of foundation wall · Amount of lift needed · Floor joist

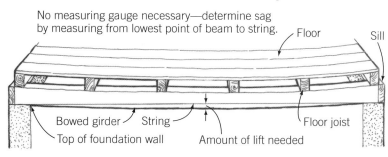

REPAIRING SAGGING FLOORS

With new sills and foundation walls under it, the house will probably not fall down before the next winter. You now can turn your attention to sagging floors and leaning walls. Trusty jack in hand, it's back to the cellar. By now, you've probably come to know every beam and post in that hole by name—some by all kinds of names.

Why Floors Sag

Floors sag because whatever is supposed to be holding them up isn't. Refer to the drawing on p. 114. Joists are the main floor supports. These, in turn, are carried by girts (which nowadays are referred to as girders or sometimes carrying beams). Girts are themselves stiffened by posts that ideally rest on rocks or concrete footings on the cellar floor. Because of the structural limitations of wood construction, joists seldom span the entire width of the building; instead, they end over the girders. Even so, settlement and sag at midspan are quite common with floor joists. Girders also will sag or twist when the support posts beneath them have rotted away or settled into soft earth. Sometimes posts are simply missing. If the load on a girder is too heavy for the number of posts—that is, the span between them is longer than the girder can bridge without sagging—adding extra posts will straighten out the sag.

Gauging the Extent of the Problem

One of the benefits of a complete foundation replacement is that the perimeter of the house at the sills is now (theoretically) level, which provides a convenient reference point for leveling the floors. To determine the amount of sagging, go down into the cellar and stretch a string along the bottom edge of the main girder or carrying beam. The ends should be fixed to blocks nailed at a distance from the bottom of the sills equal to the depth of the maximum sag (as shown in case 1 of the drawing on the facing page). In other words, the string should just touch the lowest point of the girder. The goal is to raise the girder so that the gap between it and the string is constant. Make a measuring gauge from a scrap of board cut to the correct length.

When the bottom of the girder is flush to the bottom of the sills or above the sill, a string stretched at this level will show the amount of lift required directly against the girder itself, without the need for a gauge block (as shown in case 2 in the drawing on the facing page). However, in most situations, this method cannot be used because the joists are mortised into the sides of the girder rather than carried on top of it.

The string method works even if the foundation has not been replaced or the sills brought back up to level. It gives a straight, although not necessarily level, line across the span of the house. The floors may tilt in the same plane, but at least they won't sag.

Raising a Sagging Girder

If the girder needs to be raised and the existing post has settled but is otherwise sound and solidly footed, simply jack alongside the post using a 6x6 and hydraulic jack (don't forget the steel lifting plate over the jack cylinder head). Once the girder is lifted to the desired height plus a hair or two more to allow for settling, insert an appropriately sized block between it and the post (as shown in the drawing below) and back off the jack just enough to pinch the post. Check for plumb and make any fine adjustments with a sledgehammer before completely releasing the jack. Blocks for increasing post height should be cut from dimension lumber or boards wide enough to cover the top of the post and the width of the girder itself. Drive tapered shingle shims for solid bearing on top of uneven posts or under a canted beam.

ADD A PILLOW BLOCK Where two girders butt over a post, additional support is gained by a *pillow block,* which is a short length of timber centered over the post and cantilevered under each side of the splice. Pillow blocks can stiffen a

⬆ Straightening a Girder

A. Use block and shims on a short post to stiffen a continuous girder.

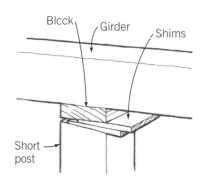

Block · Girder · Shims

Short post

B. Use a pillow block where two girders butt over a post.

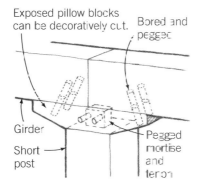

Exposed pillow blocks can be decoratively cut. Bored and pegged

Girder

Short post

Pegged mortise and tenon

Because the top of this post wasn't level, the load was concentrated along its high edge. The resulting shear failure on the shims is graphic proof of the consequences of unbalanced stresses.

sagging girder somewhat by effectively shortening the span. If the amount of shimming required is more than a few inches or if a neat appearance is important, remove the old post and install a new one cut to the correct length.

Adding Extra Posts

Extra posts added under the girder must have solid bearing on the cellar floor. A large, flat stone at least 3 in. thick makes a fine instant footing. Solid or cored concrete blocks don't, since they crack easily. Instead, pour a concrete pad at least 6 in. thick and 16 in. square. An existing floor slab will support a post without additional footings, unless it is carrying an unusually heavy load, in which case it's necessary to break through the slab and excavate a 1-ft. deep by 2-ft. square area and fill it with concrete to floor level. Do this where a slab has cracked and dips noticeably under an existing post.

Additional posts are frequently needed to support the dangling ends of joists or beams that were carelessly cut through for a stairwell

opening, chimney passage, or plumbing drain. Adjustable steel jack posts are often used in place of wood posts.

Stiffening a Sagging Girder

If a forest of posts seems to be growing in your cellar, an alternative is to stiffen the girders themselves by sistering planks along their length (see part A of the drawing on the facing page). Jack the girder from the middle of its span past the level line so that it is crowned.

Cut to length a 2x plank that matches the girder's depth and nail it flush to the top of the girder at each end. Use another jack to raise its middle flush to the crowned edge of the girder. Then nail the stiffener to the girder with 16d or 20d spikes driven 16 in. apart along the length of the girder, three or four to a row. Repeat on the opposite side of the girder. When the jacks are released, the girder should settle to near level. Because it has been prestressed by the crowning, it will resist downward deflection. Sistering can also be used to rebuild and strengthen cracked or rotted girders.

Obviously, planks cannot be sistered to a girder into which floor joists are mortised or nailed. Instead, install an additional timber directly under the sagging girder and shorten the posts to fit after relocating them farther apart (see part B of the drawing on the facing page). The girder can usually be left briefly unsupported while the new timber is jacked into place. To carry heavy loads over long spans, add a continuous girder composed of shorter segments, the butt ends centered on the posts (see part C of the drawing on facing page).

Repairing Floor Joists

Floor joists are frequently damaged by dry rot, as often happens when plumbing fixtures above have leaked for years. Carpenter ants and termites seem to favor these timbers. As suggested for the girders, new joists can be sistered onto

Stiffening a Girder

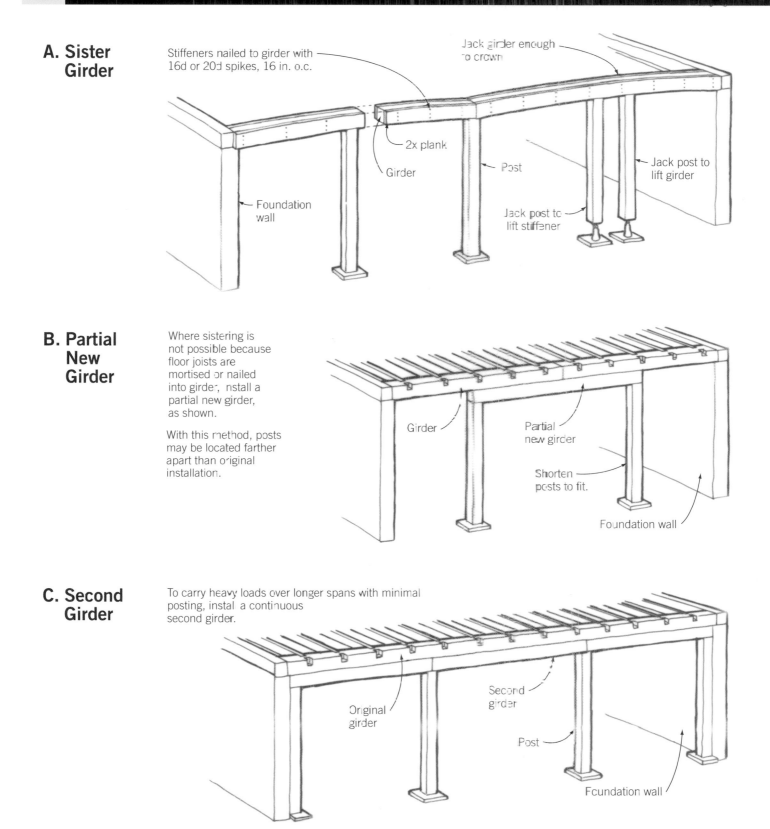

A. Sister Girder

Stiffeners nailed to girder with 16d or 20d spikes, 16 in. o.c.

Jack girder enough to crown

2x plank

Girder

Post

Jack post to lift girder

Jack post to lift stiffener

Foundation wall

B. Partial New Girder

Where sistering is not possible because floor joists are mortised or nailed into girder, install a partial new girder, as shown.

With this method, posts may be located farther apart than original installation.

Girder

Partial new girder

Shorten posts to fit.

Foundation wall

C. Second Girder

To carry heavy loads over longer spans with minimal posting, install a continuous second girder.

Original girder

Second girder

Post

Foundation wall

the old ones and tensioned by jacking after the ends have been nailed. Jacking and sistering may be required in any case to lift a sagging over-stressed or undersize joist back to level. Use string and blocks for calibration.

ADD JOIST HANGERS The new joists likely need steel joist hangers to secure them to the girder or sill. Where joists cross over the girder instead of running into its face, the added joist must be slipped between the flooring and the girder at a slant and then pounded plumb with a sledgehammer.

Replacement joists running perpendicular to other joists also need joist hangers. Chances are that the standard sizes (for rough and planed lumber alike) won't fit your particular joists, especially after sistering. Custom hangers fabricated by your local welding shop, while not exactly cheap, are the best alternatives. Finished flat black, ¼-in. steel hangers can be a pleasing solution to the problems of repairing or supporting exposed beams in the living areas of the house.

Replacing Floor Joists

Where joists have rotted completely, leaving the floorboards above nailed to empty spaces, pry the remains of the joist free, clip off the nails flush to the subfloor and insert a new joist. Jack each end tight to the subfloor and install joist hangers.

In most cases, if the joists have decayed enough to require replacement, the subfloor boards will also be rotted. You'll have to take up enough finish flooring to expose the rotted sub-floor. Cut the boards back to sound wood at the edge of the nearest joist. A 2x4 nailer scabbed alongside this joist will carry the new subfloor boards or plywood. Set new floor joists to accommodate any difference in thickness between the old floorboards and the new, especially if you use plywood instead of boards. If the rot is extensive, it's probably easier to take up the entire floor and reframe it with new joists and new subfloor rather than make piece-meal repairs.

Sometimes, especially when a crawl space instead of a cellar is below, the easiest way to repair or replace rotted joists and sills is to take up the floor above them.

↑ Repairing Split or Sagging Rafters

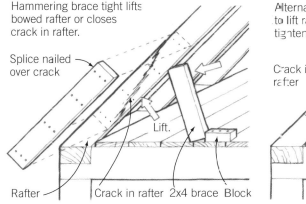

Hammering brace tight lifts bowed rafter or closes crack in rafter.

Splice nailed over crack

Lift.

Rafter   Crack in rafter   2x4 brace   Block

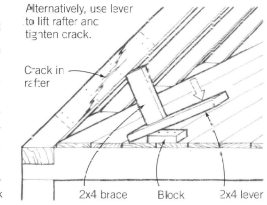

Alternatively, use lever to lift rafter and tighten crack.

Crack in rafter

2x4 brace   Block   2x4 lever

REPAIRING OTHER STRUCTURAL ELEMENTS

Sistering can also be used to repair sagging ceiling joists and cracked rafters, with or without jacking. A 2x4 jammed at an angle to the timber to be straightened (see the drawing above) is a good substitute for a jack if there is no great load to lift. As the brace is hammered tight, the bowed framing member is straightened or a crack is closed tight. Substituting a lever for the hammer gives greater leverage. Once the pieces are correctly realigned, a splice is nailed over the break or a sister is attached.

Repairing Cracked Beams and Joists

After the plaster and lath are stripped from the ceilings and walls, it's not unusual to discover deep cracks running through the exposed beams. These fissures, called *checks* or *shakes,* are caused by uneven drying of the wood and in most cases are not structurally deleterious. Most checks are natural and nothing to worry about, which is a good thing, since there's nothing you can do to prevent them. Timbers soon reach equilibrium and check no further.

↑ Stress at a Joint

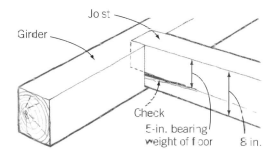

Joist

Girder

Check

5-in. bearing weight of floor   8 in.

But sometimes a timber is stressed so much that it splits along the grain or an existing check deepens. This often happens where the end of the beam has been notched out to make a tenon or a joist has been notched into a girder, as shown in the drawing above. Under load, the unsupported part of the beam or joist splits below the tenon or notch. This crack tends to continue opening down the length of the timber. Although the joist itself may be 8 in. thick, its effective thickness is only that portion actually supported by the girder. The rest of the joist is dead weight and only adds to the stress already on the joint. Thus for an 8-in. beam, only 5 in. actually carries the floor load. The crack follows the line of the joint.

I am of two minds about whether such cracks should be repaired. If a 5-in. joist has held up the floor for a century or more, it will probably continue to do so. Timbered houses were often framed with timbers much larger than an engineering analysis would require. On the other hand, new occupants and new uses may add a greater floor load than the joists can withstand. A piano and several heavy pieces of furniture, or a waterbed or whirlpool bath, could cause joists that supported only a few bushels of onions or old trunks to suddenly fail.

Using Steel Repair Plates

The simplest repair for split beams or joists and separated joints in heavy timbers is a steel repair plate made to order at your local machine shop. Basically, these are just heavy-duty versions of the standard galvanized steel framing anchors, joist hangers, and repair plates sold at the lumberyard. Their actual design depends on the stresses at the failure point and the type of repair. The thickness of the steel varies accordingly from $\frac{3}{16}$ in. to $\frac{1}{2}$ in., as do the fasteners,

Types of Steel Plates Used to Reinforce Timbers

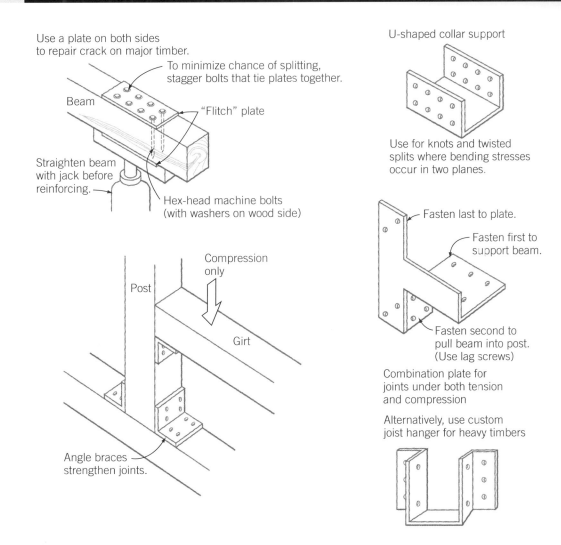

Use a plate on both sides to repair crack on major timber.

To minimize chance of splitting, stagger bolts that tie plates together.

Beam

"Flitch" plate

Straighten beam with jack before reinforcing.

Hex-head machine bolts (with washers on wood side)

U-shaped collar support

Use for knots and twisted splits where bending stresses occur in two planes.

Fasten last to plate.

Fasten first to support beam.

Fasten second to pull beam into post. (Use lag screws)

Combination plate for joints under both tension and compression

Alternatively, use custom joist hanger for heavy timbers

Post

Compression only

Girt

Angle braces strengthen joints.

from ¼-in. to ½-in. lag screws or carriage bolts. Where necessary, grind the welds smooth and paint the plate appropriately for a finished appearance.

JOIST HANGERS To support a split tenon or close a separated joint, fabricate a joist hanger and secure it with ¼-in. to ⅜-in. lag screws after closing the crack with a jack. Drill pilot holes ¹⁄₁₆-in. to ³⁄₃₂-in. smaller than the screw diameter for the lags. Avoid overturning, since the heads can torque off.

LAG SCREWS Lag screws can be used to draw together splits in structural beams that have been jacked closed or—as shown in the top left drawing on the facing page—to pull an opened joint tight. However, don't be surprised if a beam won't draw together very much. It has taken so long to get to its present condition that there's no give left. Stable beams are best left alone. Lag screws, though, can prevent further splitting by relieving strain.

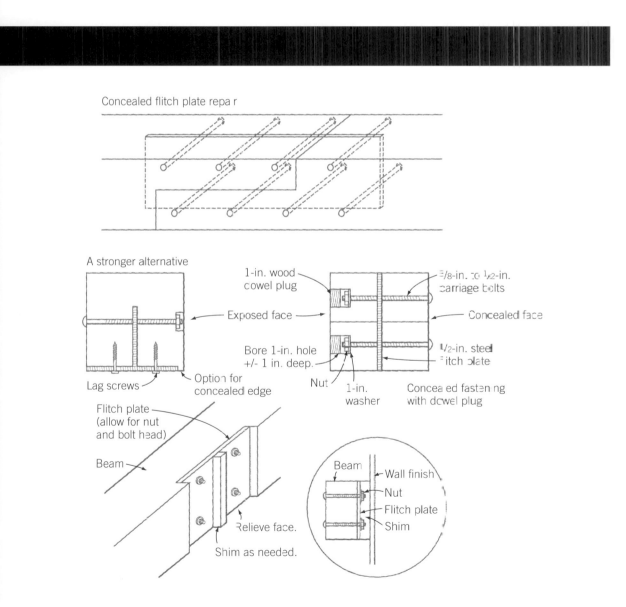

Concealed flitch plate repair

A stronger alternative

Lag screws

Option for concealed edge

1-in. wood dowel plug

Exposed face

Bore 1-in. hole +/- 1 in. deep.

Nut

1-in. washer

⅜-in. to ½-in. carriage bolts

Concealed face

½-in. steel flitch plate

Concealed fastening with dowel plug

Flitch plate (allow for nut and bolt head)

Beam

Relieve face.

Shim as needed.

Beam

Wall finish

Nut

Flitch plate

Shim

TIP

Cutting a Scarf Joint

It is critical that scarf joints be cut accurately. This will be awkward for an existing beam, even after removing sufficient flooring and ceiling to facilitate access. Make a template to transfer the cut lines of the scarf in the existing beam to the new replacement section. ■ ■ ■

SPLICING PLATES Steel ¼ in. splicing plates are useful for repairing cracked timbers or weakened joints. Before fastening a repair plate over a split beam, you should, of course, close the crack tight and straighten the beam with a jack. Major beams, such as rafter plates or girts, require heavy (⅜-in.) *flitch* plates on both sides of the crack, anchored with hex-head machine bolts. (Carriage bolts are used with a single flitch plate, since the bolt head will pull into the wood to resist turning.)

OTHER HARDWARE Timbers that have failed at large knots or where the grain twists around can be stiffened with a U-shaped collar support. Angle braces and combination plates or joist hangers add strength to the joints between girts and posts and are useful for fastening new timbers between existing uprights. Flitch plates are a common cure for a weak or sagging unsupported lap joint (such as a spliced rafter plate beam). If the face of the beam will be covered over, it should be relieved enough so that the repair is

flush with its surface. If the beam will be left exposed, the flitch plate should be concealed in the joint, as shown in the top drawing on p. 157. The carriage bolts are then countersunk, and the holes are plugged with dowels shaped to look like wood pegs.

Joinery for Beam Repair

When considerations of historical verisimilitude or appearance rule out a sistering or flitch-plate beam repair, then a tension scarf joint or a tension/bending scarf joint may be worth the effort, especially if it's the only alternative to replacement of the defective timber. Scarf joints combine structural strength and aesthetic appeal. They are especially practical if only the last few feet of an otherwise sound long beam are rotted or damaged.

SCARF JOINTS Tension scarfs are used to splice beams that must resist only pulling forces, such as an end-wall girt or a rafter collar tie. As the name indicates, tension/bending scarfs resist both pulling and loading (tension and bending) stresses and can be used to repair plate beams and joists. As shown in the drawing at left, the joint includes a wooden key that prevents it from pulling apart.

Sometimes the end of the beam itself is still sound but its tenon has rotted or broken at the post mortise. Drill and chisel out the old tenon from the opposite side of the post and drive a new double tenon through it into a mortise also cut into the girt. Pin it in place, as shown in the top drawing on the facing page. Because you probably can't move the post or the girt to the side, cutting this mortise is quite a job. Except where absolutely necessary, I'd try to avoid this kind of repair.

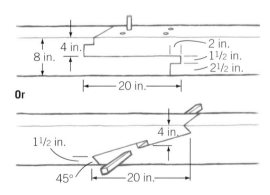

Tension Scarf Joint for Wood Beams

8 in. / 4 in. / 2 in. / 1½ in. / 2½ in. / 20 in.

Or

1½ in. / 4 in. / 45° / 20 in.

Tension/Bending Scarf

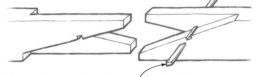

Tapered pegs driven from opposite sides

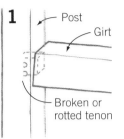

Repairing a Damaged Tenon with the Girt or Post in Place

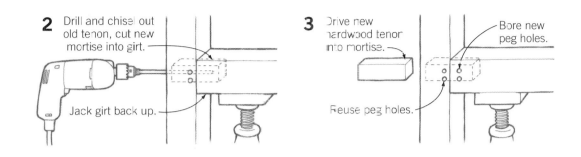

1 Post / Girt / Broken or rotted tenon

2 Drill and chisel out old tenon, cut new mortise into girt. / Jack girt back up.

3 Drive new hardwood tenon into mortise. / Bore new peg holes. / Reuse peg holes.

Repairing Rotted Rafter-to-Plate Joints

The junction of the rafters and the top of the wall (the rafter plate beam) is particularly prone to decay. Water backing up under the shingles from melting ice dams at the eaves or running down the rafters from leaky roofing materials, pools in the mortise in the beam that receives the rafter or, if there is no mortise, on top of the beam where the rafters are nailed to it. As the plate rots away from the rafters, the roof begins to shove out and downward.

If the bottom of the rafter is not to badly rotted, it can be trimmed to fit a new 2x plate nailed on top of the existing plate beam. In modern construction, rafters usually meet plates with a *bird's mouth*—a notch cut consisting of a plumb cut and a level cut. But in many old timber frames—as shown in the drawing at right—the notch is made square to the bottom of the rafter plate while the plate is mortised at an angle to meet the rafter. If both rafter and plate are rotted, cut them both back as shown to make room for a new sister plate. If only the rafter is rotted, the sister plate can span the plate notch, so you need only cut back the rafter. In any case, use L-shaped steel anchors to secure the rafters to the sister plate.

Replacing Rotted Rafter Plates

In most one- and two-story timber frames, the attic floor joists as well as the rafters are joined to the rafter plate. In this case, if the rafter plate

is rotted to the point at which it must be replaced, you have a serious problem that is very difficult to repair. There is little you can do short of removing all the attic joists and holding the roof from the floor or basement below while you remove the plates.

If you are working with a one-and-a-half story house, such as a Cape Cod, replacing the rafter plate is more feasible, because only the rafters are attached to the plate, as shown in the

Repairing Rotted Rafter–Plate Connections

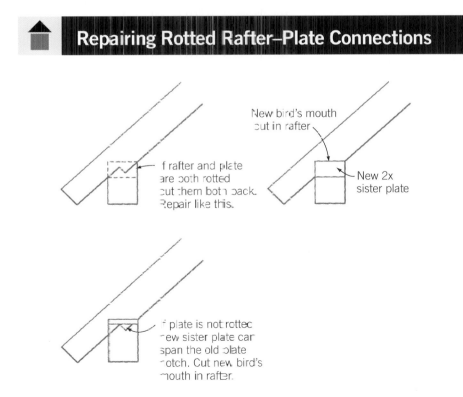

If rafter and plate are both rotted cut them both back. Repair like this.

New bird's mouth cut in rafter / New 2x sister plate

If plate is not rotted new sister plate can span the old plate notch. Cut new bird's mouth in rafter.

Supporting the Roof Load

Case 1. With Collar Ties

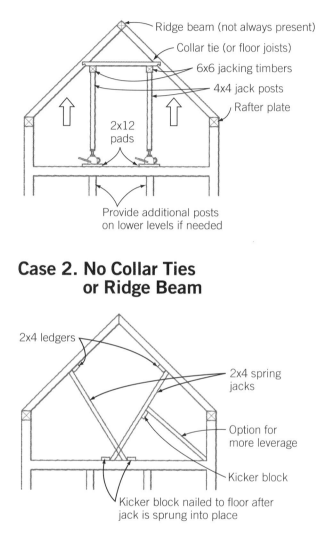

Ridge beam (not always present)

Collar tie (or floor joists)

6x6 jacking timbers

4x4 jack posts

Rafter plate

2x12 pads

Provide additional posts
on lower levels if needed

Case 2. No Collar Ties or Ridge Beam

2x4 ledgers

2x4 spring jacks

Option for
more leverage

Kicker block

Kicker block nailed to floor after
jack is sprung into place

Case 3. Rafters Tied to Ridge Beam

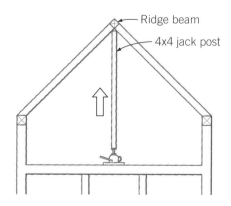

Ridge beam

4x4 jack post

---

drawing at left. Fortunately, most such frames have collar ties, so you can simply run 6x6 jacking timbers under the collar ties. Place jacking posts under the timbers and jacks under the posts. Use 2x12 pads under the jacks. As shown, you may need additional posts on the lower levels.

If there are no collar ties, support the rafters with a 2x4 ledger nailed directly to their underside, as shown in case 2 in the drawing at left. Lengths of 2x6 jammed between this ledger and the floor (*spring jacks*) prevent the roof from slipping outward. If the rafters are tied to a structural ridge beam, then you can simply support the roof with a series of 4x4 jack posts under the ridge beam (see case 3 in the drawing).

DETACH THE ROTTED PLATE Once the rafters and roof load are supported, cut the plate (or the rotted portions of it) into sections between each rafter and pry it free of the sheathing boards that are nailed to it. Likewise, saw through the nails or tenons that join any studs or posts to the underside of the plate. The remaining sections of beam actually pinned to the rafters can then be split apart with a chisel; salvage the pegs for ornamental use.

RECUT THE RAFTERS Take care not to damage any framing for the underside of the cornice boards (the soffit) if it, too, is nailed into the face of the plate. Renailing it won't be possible (there's no room to swing a hammer), but toenailing from the outside can secure the cornice. Since the new plate must slide straight into place between the tops of the posts and studs and the underside of the rafter, there's no room to lift it up and therefore no reason to cut mortises in the top of the replacement beam. Instead, cut a bird's mouth across the bottom of each rafter notch—as shown in the bottom drawing on p. 159—to accept the square edge of the plate. Join the reshaped rafters to the plate with steel framing anchors, as described for repairing rotted rafters.

Epoxy Beam Repairs

The problem with traditional repair techniques like scarfing and splicing, inserting dutchmen and flitch plates, and wholesale beam replacement is that they require a fair amount of woodworking skill and tools, particularly when the problem isn't reinforcement of a broken joint or split but structural repair of a rotten beam. Under certain conditions, an epoxy prosthesis might be preferable to a wooden one.

Epoxy resins are the wonder drugs of old house restoration. Although long familiar to restorers of wooden boats, epoxy wood repair was first used by professional conservators in the 1970s for museum-quality restorations, when preservation of the original elements was less important than cost. Despite the lingering aura of high-tech mystery, there is no reason why an amateur old house doctor can't make a successful epoxy wood repair. In fact, there are some conditions in which epoxy techniques may be the most cost-effective and easiest repair, especially when a replacement for rotted ornamental woodwork may be unavailable or prohibitively expensive to duplicate. While epoxies are definitely pricey ($35 to $50 per gallon for resin; $15 to $25 for hardener), skilled carpentry labor is also expensive.

Understanding How Epoxies Work

Epoxies are two-part systems consisting of a resin and a catalyst that, when mixed together, set into a hard plastic. Manufacturers can vary the chemistry of the resins to impart specific characteristics to the cured product according to the application. Basically, three kinds of epoxy are used for wood repair: low-viscosity consolidants, low-strength patching putties, and high-strength structural epoxies. Depending on the nature of the repair, one or more types may be used in tandem.

CONSOLIDANTS The primary use of consolidants is to stabilize rotted wood in lieu of replacing it. Basically, the process consists of injecting the resin into the wood so that it turns into a dense block of solid plastic. This is usually accomplished by drilling staggered ⅛-in. to ¼-in.

This joint between a cellar girder and a post was mortised into a former sill beam, which had completely decayed. Here, structural epoxy repair might be a better choice than sill replacement alone.

Mix Resin and Hardener Carefully

The success of the chemical reaction that leads to curing of epoxy depends largely on how well the resin and hardener are mixed. Follow the manufacturer's instructions carefully. To ensure accurate proportions, mix consolidant in a clear plastic squeeze bottle with ounce measurements embossed on its side. Shake vigorously for twice as long as the package instructions require. It's also important to maintain the correct temperature, which is between 70°F and 75°F. Squeeze the resin into the bore holes and top off.

Reinforcing Structural Epoxy Repairs

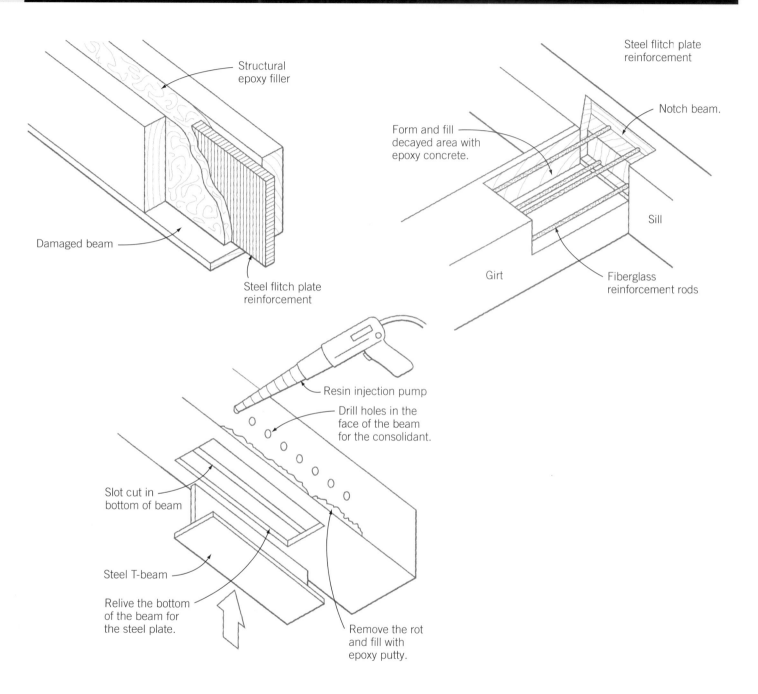

Structural epoxy filler

Damaged beam

Steel flitch plate reinforcement

Steel flitch plate reinforcement

Form and fill decayed area with epoxy concrete.

Notch beam.

Sill

Girt

Fiberglass reinforcement rods

Resin injection pump

Drill holes in the face of the beam for the consolidant.

Slot cut in bottom of beam

Steel T-beam

Relive the bottom of the beam for the steel plate.

Remove the rot and fill with epoxy putty.

holes into the damaged face area at a downward angle. The angled bore hole is required for two reasons: First, angled cuts expose more of the end grain of the wood cells, which is where the epoxy is taken up, and second, the downward slope keeps the epoxy from draining out. (For the same reason, the holes shouldn't go all the way through the wood either.)

The thin penetrating resin has a long cure time (about 8 hours), which allows it to saturate the wood fibers slowly and deeply. When it sets, the crumbled fibers of rotted wood are entombed in plastic, like an insect in amber. (See pp. 222–223 for details on consolidation repairs.)

EPOXY PUTTY Consolidants are too thin to actually fill voids. That function is accomplished with epoxy putty. The process is similar to auto-body repair. (In fact some house restorers actually use relatively inexpensive auto-body filler instead of a product specifically intended for wood repair. This is a mistake; products such as Bondo won't expand and contract with the wood and thus any such patches eventually fall out.) The pastelike material is troweled across the surface and pressed into voids. It can be built up to replace missing decorative details.

STRUCTURAL EPOXIES Like concrete, structural epoxies are formulated to have high compressive strength and require reinforcement when used in tension. Common reinforcement materials include fiberglass rods and plates and steel flitch plates and T-beams. Sometimes, to save costs, as for example when a large void must be repaired, the epoxy is mixed with fillers such as sand or gravel to make an epoxy concrete. The epoxy bonds strongly to both wood and reinforcement to form a composite material that acts as a single structural unit. Any such repair should be carefully engineered to match the components and

the process to the structural requirements. A typical application for structural epoxy is to rebuild the rotted end of a heavy girt or rafter and its joint at a sill or plate.

STEEL AND EPOXY TOGETHER Steel also bonds well with epoxy. When maintaining the original appearance is not a consideration, you can reinforce the rotted end of a wood beam with a steel T-beam. The steel is inserted into a groove cut into the bottom of the beam. (An electric chainsaw is a good tool for this job.) The vertical flange should extend into sound wood. Seal the horizontal flange to the bottom of the beam with a bead of caulking and hold it tight against the wood with a jack post. Drill holes in the beam and inject them with consolidant to bond the steel and wood.

Working Safely with Epoxy

All epoxies are toxic, irritating, and flammable. You don't want to breathe their vapors or get the resin on your skin or in your eyes. When working indoors, wear a respirator with an approved organic vapor cartridge. Wear goggles (especially for overhead applications) or safety glasses and disposable rubber gloves. Wear a dust mask when sanding cured epoxy repairs.

Clean up any spills immediately by wiping with rags or other absorbent materials. Most epoxies are impervious to solvents once they cure. Special epoxy solvent cleaners are very nasty chemicals. Also, because epoxies generate a good deal of heat as they cure, be aware of the possibility of fire in a confined space. Should adjoining wood begin to smolder, cool it down by using a small chemical fire extinguisher.

Repairing a Beam with Structural Epoxy

The process of repairing a rotted beam with structural epoxy is relatively straight-forward. To prepare for the epoxy work, the decayed wood is cut, chipped, and chiseled back to sound wood, leaving a thin shell of wood on two sides to support a form. This shell is stabilized with injected consolidant, as shown in the drawing on p. 162.

1 Holes are bored into the sound end of the beam for inserting the fiberglass reinforcing rods, which extend into the cleaned-out mortise pocket.

2 A plywood form, lined with plastic is tacked to the beam and sealed liquid-tight against its sides with a ribbon of clay. The faces of the excised mortise are coated with latex caulk. (Structural epoxy is inflexible, so the resulting gasket allows for movement with changes in the wood; without it, the joint could fail.)

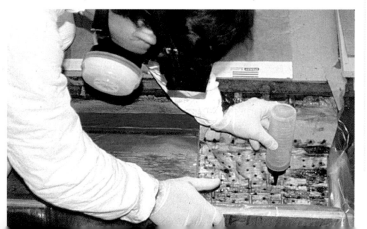

3 The form is filled with epoxy concrete. After it sets and before the form is removed, consolidant is poured into a vertical hole at the edge of the form so that it flows along the rods and out another hole bored into the beam; when cured, it bonds the rods to the wood.

4 The repair is finished. Note the original inscription preserved in the beam.

Considering the Pros and Cons of Epoxy

While there are compelling reasons to use epoxy consolidants and patching putty to repair rotten exterior trim, particularly porch columns, door jambs, window sills, and ornamental details that cannot be easily removed or duplicated, the decision to use epoxy for structural repairs is ultimately a matter of personal preference. Unskilled woodworkers might opt for epoxy. Those with an aversion or sensitivity to chemicals might prefer wood. Personally, I'd rather hack away at wood than hack and cough from fumes.

TRUING UP THE HOUSE FRAME

Even though the foundation is now firm, the sills solid, and the floors more or less level, the roof may still sag and the walls may form odd parallelograms. Missing knee braces, broken joints, cracked timbers, and/or inadequate framing let the house rack under its own weight (dead load), the weight of its inhabitants and furnishings (live load), and in reaction to any forces acting on it, such as wind and snow loads.

How a House Racks and Sags

Although the visible tilt of the walls may have originated in a settled foundation or sill, it does not follow that restoring the base of the house to level will realign the rest of the frame. The pegged mortise-and-tenon joints of a timber frame are much stronger than the nailed joints of a stud frame, but any joint is still the weakest part of the overall structure. As a frame shifts or settles, its joints can be stressed past their strength. This is especially true across the relatively small cross-sectional areas where the knee braces are inserted into girts and sills, and at the corner post-girt mortise mentioned earlier.

When this corner post rotted away, the plate beam dropped and the load-bearing side wall pulled apart from the gable wall and bulged outward. The failed corner will be strengthened with a steel angle plate after the wall is pushed and pulled back in.

When a knee-brace peg shears under stress, the brace becomes unhinged, allowing the post it anchors to move in reaction to that stress, pulling a part of the house along with it. Braces also pull apart when their ends rot. A leaking roof that has caused a corner post to rot at the plate or girt also causes the walls to lean outward as the house pulls apart under the weight of the roof. Sometimes, there simply aren't enough knee braces in the first place. Early housewrights weren't necessarily any more conscientious than contemporary builders. But even the best frames were hard pressed to withstand the "improvements" wrought by subsequent generations of slipshod, haphazard remodelers. I've seen more than one major girt cut through to house a chimney or stairwell.

ASSESS THE TILT Houses tilt in the plane of the gable end, the plane of the roof-bearing walls, or in both directions at once. An "eyeball" level suffices to tell which. The outward lean of a gable wall is almost always attributed to brace failure. But *swayback* (the outward tilt of the roof-bearing walls that pulls the ridgeline down in the center) can occur even without foundation or sill settlement. This usually happens when the collar ties (beams that stiffen the rafters and resist the outward thrust of the roof) are inadequate, are improperly positioned, or were not used at all. It can also be caused by undersize rafters, inadequate wall bracing or framing, excessive dead load (for example, too many layers of roofing material, slate, or other heavy material used with a light-framed roof), or plaster ceilings hung from collar ties doubling as ceiling joists coupled to undersize rafters.

CHECK THE COLLAR TIES AND WALL BRACES

In a one- or two-story house, the attic floor joists resist the outward thrust of the roof load if the rafters are actually fastened directly to them or to a plate just above them. In the case of a one-and-a-half story frame (or cathedral ceiling) the rafter plate is at a considerable height above the attic floor joists; hence the resistance of the floor joists is considerably diminished. While the collar ties that are typical in this arrangement do help prevent bowed rafters by stiffening them at their midspan, they do not, as is commonly supposed, contribute resistance to the outward thrust of the roof against the top of the walls. In fact, the dead load of the ties and the ceiling they sometimes carry actually exacerbates the problem.

It takes a strong and well-braced frame to resist the force of the roof load. Knee braces at principal posts or interior partition walls are essential. Lacking these, over time, the downward—outward thrust of the roof can shear the joints between chimney girts and center posts or floor joists and wall studs. Like a pair of dividers, the angle increases with the spread. However charming this swayback ridge may seem, it's a symptom of an ultimately fatal structural defect. If uncorrected, the frame will become so unstable that a heavy snow, a thaw and rain, then more snow, will burst the walls apart, collapsing the house under the weight of its own roof. Straightening the sag in a roof is really no different from leveling a floor. The loads are a little lighter, but the principles are the same.

Correcting Leaning Walls and Swayback Roofs

Sometimes skewed walls can be pulled back into true alignment with the aid of a come-along. The largest hardware store come-along is probably rated at no more than 2 tons, which is not usually enough to pull a house together unless the house has been stripped down to the bare frame. You might find an extra-heavy-duty come-along at a contractor's equipment rental center or could possibly borrow one from a commercial steel rigger. Besides the come-along itself, you'll need lengths of ¼-in.- to ½-in.-diameter steel cable fitted with thimbles or grab-and-slip hooks and an assortment of slings and chains with hooks and shackle bolts to do the actual pulling.

PULL WITH A COME-ALONG To pull in leaning walls, hook a sling or one end of a cable or chain around the rafter plate alongside a girt. Hook the other end of the cable to the pulling tool. This in turn is hitched to another length of cable, which is attached to a sling hooked around the sill or post. Remove or drill through sheathing boards as needed to allow the cable to pass through the wall. As you begin to pull, the plate may move without the wall following, which means that the post is no longer connected to the beam. In this case, attach a short length of timber over the joint between the plate and post so they both pull together.

TRY TWO COME-ALONGS As the tension increases, the house should start to pull together with a great groaning and creaking. The roof will rise with a heavy shrug. Or perhaps the come-along will reach its limit without any appreciable movement at all. Rather than risk decapitation from the whiplash of a snapped cable, try pulling with two come-alongs running from each plate to the base of the post or sill diagonally opposite. As you begin pulling, watch to see which moves first, the plate or the sill. If the sill moves, you'll need a more stable purchase, such as an 8x8 timber slipped under the sling against the foundation wall and up over the sill and corner post.

LIFT THE RIDGE BEAM Even the increased leverage of two come-alongs by themselves may not be enough to pull the house together. Lifting the ridge beam while simultaneously pulling in the wall plates will ease the load on the come-alongs (see the bottom drawing at right). The support for this jacking must be continuous down to the basement. Begin directly over a girder post and install a jack and lifting post between the first floor and the ceiling joists or girt. Then add another jack and lifting post from the attic floor to the underside of the ridge beam. Use a jacking timber under the rafter peaks if a solid ridge beam is lacking.

Jacking from the attic floor to the ridge without continuous support down through works against the lifting force that should be pulling in the walls. Sometimes, jacking the ridge by itself will pull the walls in without further effort, especially with a balloon-framed house. It's also the best way to straighten out a sagging cathedral ceiling.

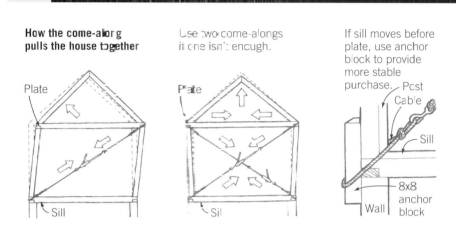

Pulling Crooked Walls Together

How the come-along pulls the house together

Plate

Sill

Use two come-alongs if one isn't enough.

Plate

Sill

If sill moves before plate, use anchor block to provide more stable purchase.

Post

Cable

Sill

Wall

8x8 anchor block

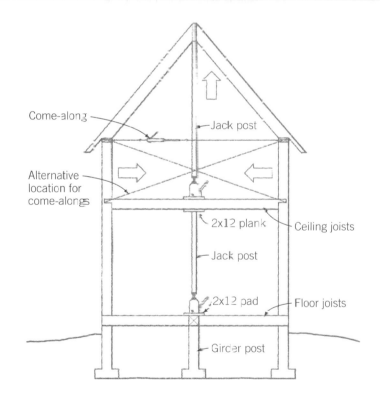

Lifting the Ridge Beam

Come-along

Jack post

Alternative location for come-alongs

2x12 plank

Ceiling joists

Jack post

2x12 pad

Floor joists

Girder post

Half-Lap Dovetail Collar Tie Joint

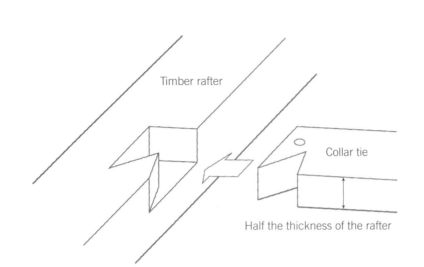

Timber rafter

Collar tie

Half the thickness of the rafter

BRACE PLUMBED WALLS A plumb bob hung from a string fastened to the top corner of the outside wall will show how far the wall needs to move in. So will a 4-ft. level and straightedge placed against the exposed studs or corner posts. After that section of wall is plumb, nail temporary 2x4 knee braces between the upright posts and the sill, plate, and/or girts to help maintain alignment until permanent knee braces are reinstalled, repaired, added, or bolted and nailed securely into place. It's a good idea to pull the walls in just past plumb to counteract their tendency to spring back when the tension is released.

Pull along each major girt or wherever there is a serious bow. Leave 2x4 diagonal braces nailed to blocks on the floor if there is no provision for knee braces in the middle of the wall until the house settles into its new alignment. Otherwise, install permanent let-in diagonal braces in any interior partitions that abut these long walls. Stairwell walls are good places to add such bracing. Incorporate some interior partitions into your renovation if none exist to help brace the frame.

Reinforcing the Rafters

If necessary, stiffen the rafters by adding collar ties before releasing the come-alongs or turnbuckles. Exposed collar ties should be joined to timber rafters with a half-lap dovetail notch.

When the roof pitch is too shallow or the ceiling span too narrow to allow much usable space under standard collar ties, rafters can be stiffened by installing plywood gussets across the peak of the rafters. Use ¾-in. CDX plywood fastened with truss glue and drywall screws on both sides of the rafter pair. Notch the gusset to fit around any ridge beam. Fill the bottom edge of the gap between the gussets with solid wood to provide support for ceiling nailers.

STRAIGHTEN SAGS FIRST Any sags in the rafters should be straightened before you install collar ties or gussets. This may require no more than a 2x4 spring jack jammed up under the midspan of a dimension-lumber rafter. Or it may call for a jack and post under each side of a timber rafter pair. It's best to support as many rafter pairs as possible with jacking timbers installed under both sides of the roof. Of course, posts and jacks should rest on planks laid perpendicular to the run of the floor joists. Use a string on blocks stretched along the run of each rafter or, even better, across the length of the roof to find the required amount of lift. Give the rafters a good crown.

Because collar ties by themselves cannot compensate for undersize rafters, the cure is to sister new, deeper rafter stock alongside the old or to add a new rafter between the existing rafters wherever the span is greater than 2 ft. on center. Many old houses were framed with pole rafters set on 32-in. or even 48-in. centers. Adding rafters between and alongside each irregular pole rafter not only stiffens the roof but also simplifies attic ceiling finish and insulation, should that be part of the plan. Building a kneewall under the bottom third of the rafter

This underbuilt roof was strengthened by sistering the rafters and adding plywood gussets at the ridge. Each rafter pair was jacked at midspan to take out the sag before installing the 2x10s. Because of the low headroom, gussets were used instead of collar ties.

span also stiffens sagging rafters by effectively shortening the overall span. Straighten out the bowed rafters before building the wall and build the kneewall before installing the collar ties. The triangular dead space behind the kneewall can be used for storage.

Truing a Parallelogram

Not all walls lean outward, away from each other. Sometimes the eaves (rafter-bearing) walls lean in the same direction, like a parallelogram. The ridge does not have to be lifted to straighten these walls. Pushing the outward-leaning wall in should push the inward-leaning wall out. A parallelogram is usually the only form that leaning gable end walls take, except for cases in which an end-wall girt-to-post connection has rotted or broken or summer beams have let go at the middle of the house; here both gable walls could push outward at the attic floor level.

Although it is theoretically possible to pull an outward-leaning wall in with a single diagonal come-along from inside the house (see the top drawing on p. 167), it's usually much easier to straighten the wall from outside—pushing is more effective than pulling. Gable walls carry relatively little weight and are perpendicular to the main framing members, so they should straighten with little difficulty. The eaves walls that carry the roof load ordinarily require considerably more persuasion.

TRY JACKING POSTS If you're lucky, you may be able to true up an eaves wall with long jacking posts set diagonally from the rafter plate to pads on a sloped cut in the earth, as described in the sidebar on p. 144. The angle of the jack post relative to the ground is critical: It should be about 45 degrees or less for pushing. Jacking at an angle of about 60 degrees will simultaneously push and lift, whereas angles around 75 degrees to 80 degrees only lift. Since the location of the jacking pads moves farther out from the wall as the angle decreases, the jacking posts must necessarily lengthen. The posts must also become stiffer, since the balance of the stress on a post shifts from compressive toward tensile (or bending) forces as both its length increases and its angle drops off from vertical. In other words, there's a greater chance that the post will bend, twist sideways, or kick out when you apply the jacking force to it.

TRY A TREE Alternatively, a large tree conveniently located near the wall that needs to move outward might provide a firm anchor for a come-along, allowing the wall to be pulled instead of pushed. Lacking suitable trees or other leverage, a tractor might have enough pulling power to move the frame. Or, then again, you might end up just raising the tractor's front end and digging deep ruts in your lawn. Bulldozers and log skidders equipped with winches usually have the horsepower and weight to provide both a firm anchor and a strong pull.

The arm of a backhoe can exert a tremendous amount of pushing force, often more than enough to straighten out a leaning frame. Protect the exterior finish by placing a plank between the hoe and the walls.

Masonry Wall Shoring Techniques

Repair of major bulges in brick or stone walls is usually best left to experienced masons with specialized restoration expertise. Unlike wood walls, masonry structures are very unforgiving of errors in judgment. When masonry joints open

When the building adjoining this masonry party wall was demolished, it took a forest of temporary shoring to keep the brick from collapsing until more permanent reinforcement could be installed.

Strip to the Frame

Truing up a house frame is easiest when the house has been stripped down to the frame. Sheathing and lath and plaster all contribute significantly to the rigidity of the structure. Even if they didn't, the plaster would crack when things began to move. Whatever method you employ, be careful to push, pull, or lift slowly, because chimneys and fireplaces can crack and windows rupture with an explosive force if they are subjected to twisting forces or sudden shock. Leveling and truing a house will, of course, necessitate refitting doors and windows.

or are stressed beyond endurance, they don't just groan and grumble, they fail catastrophically and suddenly—that is, they fall down. When foundation settlement causes a masonry wall to crack and bulge outward, the wall must somehow be pushed and lifted back into place and supported so that the mortar joints can be raked out and repointed after the foundation is underpinned or otherwise stabilized. If you are contemplating undertaking such a repair yourself, I strongly recommend consultation with a structural engineer, house mover, and mason to assess the situation and for help designing an appropriate repair protocol and necessary *shoring* (bracing intended primarily to prevent collapse during repair operations).

Knowing When to Leave Well Enough Alone

Truing and leveling a house take a great deal of trouble, and there comes a point of diminishing returns. My advice is, if the walls lean only a few inches, live with them. By all means add braces and collar ties, level or firm up the foundation, do everything necessary to stabilize the frame against further movement, but don't try to push too hard. When a timber has been in place for a long time, it has taken on whatever shape it needed to stay there. Like old bones, old timbers don't spring back very well. They may break before they will bend. Sometimes, no amount of lifting or pulling force will persuade a beam to budge. You might move the entire wall in 1 ft. or more and not materially affect the shape of a warped beam. It will stay where it wants to.

A house that leans in odd directions does not particularly bother me. As long as the foundation is stable and the frame well braced, it isn't going anywhere. There is something to be said for the delight of skewed walls and corners that

meet in another dimension. It's like living in an M. C. Escher print. Once a house has settled into a comfortable shape, it requires unnatural energy to realign it. Those who feel that the music of the spheres is played on symmetrical strings can pursue the perfection of form and the correction of corners. For myself, I remember the old Chinese saying that only demons travel in straight lines.

When the foundation under the corner of this brick house settled, the pilaster shifted 1 in. off its wall, causing the brickwork to crack and bulge outward. This very simple yet sophisticated shoring technique carried the load of the wall while the pilaster was jacked back onto a reinforced foundation. The shoring then was used to push the wall back into plumb. (Photo by Whitie Gray)

5 The Roof and Gutters

I'm fixing a hole where the rain comes in
To stop my mind from wandering,
Where it will go.

—JOHN LENNON AND PAUL McCARTNEY

S ince the day the first man or woman crawled under an overhanging ledge, creating shelter has entailed the attempt to keep a roof over our heads. Foundation and walls, posts and beams are only the handles of the umbrella. Because water flows downhill, a roof works like the scales of a fish or the feathers of a bird—in one direction only. If the integrity of the overlapping parts is broken, water can work inward under the shingles, through the sheathing, and into the house, where things start to rot.

If your old house roof is leaking, you'll need to decide whether it can be repaired or if the roof needs to be replaced. To help you make this decision, I start by describing the types of roofing you are likely to find on an old house and what your options are for replacement. I don't go into details on how to install a new roof—there are plenty of books available telling you how to do that. Instead, I tell you how to find a leak and how to repair an old roof.

Old houses often have interesting and sometimes obsolete gutter systems that you won't find covered in books focusing on newer houses. So I also describe how to repair, and if necessary, replace the gutters on your old house.

Like a ceremonial headdress, the cut and material of a roof can make a strong impression. Because of its natural color variation and the possibility of intermixing different patterns, slate roofing is particularly adaptable to ornamental treatment.

WOOD SHINGLES

The early colonists soon found that the thatched roofs of their homelands couldn't hold up to the severe storms and heavy snowfalls of North America. Fortunately, a superlative substitute was growing in the surrounding forests. Although metal, clay, and slate were used successfully in some regions, the wood shingle was by far the most popular roofing material used in the United States until the introduction of asphalt composition shingles in the late 1800s.

The earliest shingles were made from bolts split from 2-ft. sections of straight-grained white oak, pine, and cedar that were then riven with a mallet and froe into 1-in.-thick shakes. These were held in a combination vise–stool (a *shingle horse* or *shave horse*) and tapered with a drawknife to make a shingle. Thus the modern resawn wood shingle, made by machine since 1850, looks more like early roofing than the thick and irregular hand-split shakes (indigenous only to the Northwest) used by some misguided restorers attempting to mimic colonial styles. This is a good thing, since shakes cost a lot more, are harder to install, and are more prone to leaks than ordinary wood shingles.

Wood shingles today are manufactured in four grades from eastern white cedar and western red cedar, although cypress and redwood are used where locally plentiful. (Shingles made from pressure-treated yellow pine have also become available recently.) All these woods

TIP

Using Wood Shingles

The choice of whether to reshingle an old wood-shingle roof with new wood or some other material may not be yours to make. Because wood shingles are a potential fire hazard, building codes in many communities (particularly in California) now prohibit their use. In any case, even where permitted, fire-insurance premiums are considerably higher for buildings with wood roofs. ▬ ▬ ▬

(except the yellow pine) are naturally rot resistant, but only the best clear-heart edge-grain grade (#1 Blue Label) is suitable for roofing. Wood shingles cost four to five times as much as asphalt shingles, and their high cost is not offset by any notable longevity. In fact, most wood roofs as applied today will last only 10 years to 15 years, as opposed to the 20 years to 25 years of service you can expect from asphalt shingles.

Old-time wood shingles lasted an average of 40 years for slopes up to 8 in 12 and even 60 years for steeper pitches. One reason for this greater longevity is the shingles themselves. Until the mid-twentieth century, most shingles were cut from old-growth logs that were more rot resistant because of their higher resin content and denser cell structure. Also, since the shingles were split and then shaved, the wood cells would not be torn open as they are by sawing. Another reason was the way the shingles were installed. Wood shingles used to be applied over spaced strips of wood called skip sheathing. The free circulation of air allowed their under-

sides to dry out after a rain and retarded the growth of rot-producing fungi. In modern practice, the shingles are nailed to a solid deck that's covered with tarpaper. Although this makes for a less drafty attic, it also keeps the shingles damp. Furthermore, steeply pitched roofs that quickly shed water have gone out of fashion.

SLATE

Slate is fireproof, attractive, and durable and can easily last a century or more. Unlike most other forms of roofing, it requires no periodic maintenance, such as painting, cleaning, or recoating. Although used as early as 1625 in Virginia, and wherever locally quarried, most of the slate used for roofing was imported from Wales up until about 1850. The heyday of domestically produced slate roofing spanned the latter half of the nineteenth and the early decades of the twentieth centuries. Because several colors and patterns could be mixed together, slate roofing

Traditional skip sheathing, made of 1–3s or 1–4s spaced 5-in. on-center, allows air circulation, helping dry the undersides of wood shingles and thus prolonging their service life. An inlet at the soffit and a ridge vent outlet ensure air circulation. (Photo by Will Calhoun)

Replacing Wood Shingles

Wood shingles leak because they split, allowing water to work under and between courses. Sometimes they rot when not properly ventilated. But most of the damage is caused by the drying effect of direct sunlight. Wood shingles that have outlived their usefulness may appear sound, but when touched, they fall apart. Dried out or rotted, such shingles must be replaced.

The slater's hook/shingle thief is an indispensable tool for repairing wood shingles as well as slate (see the drawing on p. 179). You can usually loosen the shingle by gently lifting it with the tapered edge of the hook. This allows you to slip the hook directly under the nail head and, instead of cutting it, pull out the entire nail as you drive the tool downward. Depending on their condition, wood shingles can be even more infuriating to remove than crumbling asphalt shingles. As a rule of thumb, you can figure on destroying two or three additional shingles for every one you try to replace.

The standard approach is to face-nail the replacement shingle, with either unobtrusive galvanized finish nails sealed with clear caulking or regular shingle nails. The problem with leaving nails exposed is not so much that they might leak, since that can be prevented with caulk or flashing cement, but that they will eventually cause a surface split that will definitely leak.

Fortunately, there is an elegant traditional alternative that works much better: The replacement shingle is slipped into place with its butt end projecting 1 in. below the other shingles in the course. Two shingle nails are driven slightly below the surface of the shingle at a 45-degree angle at the butts of the course above. Then, as you tap the shingle up into line with a wooden block, the angled nails are drawn straight and flush to the surface and hidden about ½ in. under the butts of the overlying shingles.

A quick temporary fix for missing wood shingles is to cut a scrap of asphalt roofing to the same width as the missing shingle, coat it with flashing cement on both sides and slide it up under the edge of the broken shingle.

▲ The Old House Doctor's Wood Shingle Trick

1. Leave butt of replacement shingle 1-in. lower than surrounding shingles.

3. As new shingle is driven into line, the nails move under the butt of the covering shingle—no exposed nails to tar, and no surface cracks to leak.

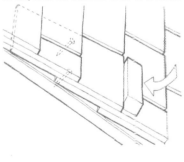

2. Use nailset to drive shingle nails at 45° angle just below butt of overlying shingle.

This roof displays just a few of the color variations available in natural slate.

The color, characteristics, and price of slate depend largely on where it was quarried. The colors of Pennsylvania slate range from blue gray to blue black to black. Pennsylvania slate also tends to have more *ribbons* (bands of rock that differ in color and composition) than slates from other regions. Since ribbons weather faster than the rest of the slate, they're considered defects, like face knots on wood shingles. Slates containing ribbons can be used as long as an overlying shingle covers the ribbon itself or the slate is installed with the ribbon side facing down.

Why Slates Fail

If slate is so durable, then why do so many slate roofs have missing or broken shingles? There are a number of reasons why slate roofs fail. The first has to do with the nature of the material itself. Part of the reason slate roofing became so expensive was that the highest-quality and most easily quarried slate beds were exhausted fairly quickly. Low-quality slates are more porous and tend to absorb water along their grain, which freezes and eventually splits apart the shingles. Some slates have greater concentrations of impurities, such as calcite, a mineral that eventually weathers into gypsum. Since gypsum is expansive, it pushes the slates apart along their cleavage planes. The gypsum leaches to the top and bottom faces of the slate, increasing its porosity and accelerating the rate of delamination.

IMPROPER INSTALLATION It might seem that installing slate shingles should not be any more difficult than wood shingles. But the difference and the difficulty lie in the fact that slates must be nailed to the roof deck exactly right. If the nails are driven too tightly, the shingle will break, if not immediately, then at some time in the future when the nails contract with the cold and are pulled down into the slate. If nailed too loosely, the heads stick up and push against the

complemented the fanciful ornamentation of the high Victorian style. But even then, when labor and materials were far less costly than today, a slate roof indicated the householder's prosperity. Roofing slates were expensive to quarry, transport, and install and, because of their weight, required heavier roof framing, at least on lower-pitched roofs.

For all these reasons, the wood shingle remained the preferred roofing material well into the 1920s, until both it and slate were eclipsed by the asphalt strip shingle. Beginning in the 1970s and driven by a strong demand for upscale renovation, the almost moribund craft of slating has undergone a renaissance. It's once again possible to find roofers with the knowledge and skill to repair or install slate. And quarries in Vermont, New York, Pennsylvania, and Virginia are now producing roofing slate. The high price of new slate has created a strong demand for secondhand slates salvaged from demolished buildings.

TIP

Testing Slate

When using secondhand replacement slates, test them for soundness by tapping with a hammer. A solid slate will ring true, while a worn-out shingle will sound muted. ■ ■ ■

overlying shingles, which eventually crack under the weight of snow and time. The choice of nails is important, too. Ordinary galvanized roofing nails will rust away long before the slate has even begun to weather. Solid copper nails are the only kind that will keep pace with slate. Just the same, the original roofers may have used coated or even steel nails, resulting in a lot of loose or missing slates.

ICE DAMS Another source of damage on old slate roofs is snow and ice buildup at the eaves. As will happen on any roof with an uninsulated attic or unvented soffit, water from snow melting on the warm upper roof refreezes at the cold eaves, forming an ice dam. The added weight of the ice alone, to say nothing of its expansion between the slates, will crack quite a few slates over time. This is the reason for the snow guards that were traditionally installed in the courses above the building line (the point where the plane of the building wall intersects the roof—that is, the borderline between heated attic and unheated eaves). Snow guards were designed to hold snow on the roof above the eaves. A traditional alternative to the snow guard is an eaves flashing consisting of a continuous 36-in.-wide strip of metal that allows ice to slide off instead of building up.

A Realistic Alternative to Natural Slate

A lightweight shingle made from recycled rubber that has an uncanny resemblance to real slate but costs about a third less has recently been introduced to the market. In fact, these synthetic slates —Authentic Roof 2000 (Crowe Building Products)— cannot be distinguished from the real thing until you actually pick them up. The shingles have superior impact resistance and sound-deadening qualities. They are also freeze–thaw stable, do not absorb heat, and have a 50-year warranty. And at 25 percent of the weight, they are a lot cheaper to ship than the real thing.

The individual shingles are 18-in long by 12-in wide with a 6-in. to 7-in. weather exposure and are tapered from ¼ in. at the butt to ⅛ in. at the top. They are marked for easy alignment and are fastened with two ordinary galvanized roofing nails per shingle. Like asphalt shingles, they are cut by scoring with a knife and breaking. Ridge and hip shingles must be heated to bend them to the correct angle. Authentic Roof 2000

Synthetic slate is much easier to install than real slate. There is no danger of breakage from ladders, roof jacks, or overdriven nails. Note the traditional snow guard about to be installed. (Photo courtesy Crowe Industries Ltd.)

can be installed over solid or skip (spaced lath) sheathing. Even without their environmental benefits, thermoplastic polyolefin (TPC) slates seem to be a cost-effective alternative to premium asphalt roofing, true slate, and terne metal.

Repairing Slate Roofs

A concave sprung and toothed copper bib holds the replacement slate in place by friction.

A Chicken Ladder for Working on Slate and Tile Roofs

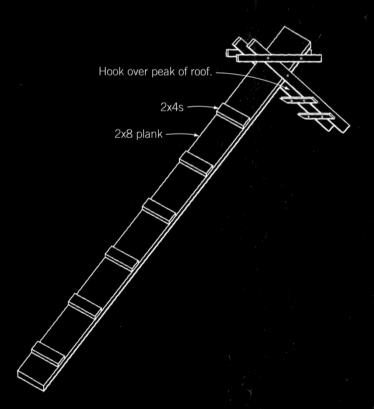

Hook over peak of roof.

2x4s

2x8 plank

Installing or repairing slate shingles requires several specialized tools. The first, and most important, is fairly easy to find at the local hardware or building-supply store. This is the *slater's hook*—also called a "ripper" or (when used for removing wood shingles) a "shingle thief" or "tickle." It's unlikely you'll find a slate cutter (which is the same as a ceramic-tile cutter, only larger) or a slater's stake, knife, or hatchet locally. Fortunately, you can make do without these tools, at least for minor repairs. If you wish to buy them, one mail-order source is John Stortz & Sons.

USE A CHICKEN LADDER

The first challenge when repairing a slate roof is getting up on to it. You cannot walk on slates. Not only will they break but they are extremely slippery. Also, unlike asphalt shingles, you can't bend a slate up to insert a roof jack. Instead, work from a ladder hooked over the ridge. Don't be tempted to use a ladder hook, because its small square tab will break the slates. Instead use a chicken ladder, as shown in the drawing at left.

If the roof is longer than your ladder, or even two sections of ladder tied together, hang the ladder from a stout rope tied to solid support at the base of a chimney or on the ground at the opposite side of the roof. Some roofers also recommend inserting a mover's quilt or heavy blanket under the ladder rungs to cushion the slates.

SEVER THE NAILS AND PULL THE SLATE

To replace a missing or broken slate, slide the hooked end of the slater's hook up under the remains of the broken shingle and feel around until you find the nail shanks. Slide the hook over the nail and, striking the flat part of the tool with your hammer, drive it downward, severing the nail. Repeat with the other nail. Remove the rest of the slate and check that no small chips or nail heads are left underneath. Feel around with the hook. Drive it into the stubs of the nail shanks to remove them. A hacksaw blade slipped under the shingle will also do the job, albeit a lot more slowly. If the slate doesn't pull out, punch a hole in it with the slater's hammer and use it to pull the wedged slate down.

Making a Babbie Repair

Cut a copper repair tab (a "babbie") about 1½ in. wide and slightly longer than the weather exposure of the slate. Use a copper nail to nail this to the course under the shingle you are replacing, so that the babbie projects beyond the bottom edge of the new shingle about ¾ in. Drill or punch (a ⅛-in. nail set works fine) a hole through the slate for the nail. The hole should be countersunk slightly to seat the nail head. Scrape it with a knife or tapered punch if you don't have a slater's punch. Slide the replacement shingle into place and fold the projecting copper tab up over its edge to anchor it.

Replacing a Broken Slate

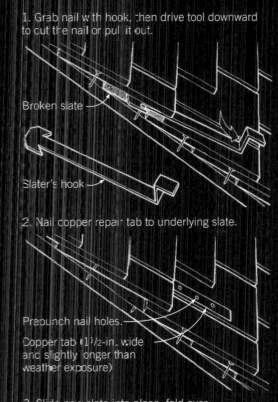

1. Grab nail with hook, then drive tool downward to cut the nail or pull it out.

Broken slate

Slater's hook

2. Nail copper repair tab to underlying slate.

Prepunch nail holes.

Copper tab (1½-in. wide and slightly longer than weather exposure)

3. Slide new slate into place, fold over copper tab to anchor.

These roofers are taking advantage of the skip sheathing to install the slates without having to walk on them or move ladders over them. (Photo by David Heim)

Cement–asbestos shingles are durable. Even after more than a century of service, the roofing on this house is still sound.

POOR FLASHING Finally, although the shingles themselves may have been perfectly installed and of high quality, the metal flashing used to line the valleys, eaves, ridges, and hips might have been less durable. Not everyone could afford copper or lead. Galvanized steel and terne metal were sometimes used instead. Owing to the danger and difficulty of reaching often forbiddingly steep roofs, flashings weren't painted as often as they should have been. Once they rusted, water could work under the shingles and rot some of the decking. No longer held tightly by the nails, the shingles would be forced downward by the pressure of snow and wind. If the metal had been replaced at the right time, the shingles would still be intact.

Installing New Slate Roofing

As a rule of thumb, if more than 20 percent of the slates are damaged, the entire roof should be replaced. Many renovators assume that shingling with slate is so difficult that only highly skilled professional slaters should attempt it or that finding a source of slate will prove impossible. Most commercial roofers feed this misapprehension by insisting that you should remove "all that old stuff" and replace it with a nice modern asphalt shingle (even when nothing more than repairs are needed).

While it's true that you won't find slate roofing down at your local home store, roofing slates are readily available throughout the Northeast and Mid-Atlantic states (and anywhere else you're willing to pay the freight to). If you can lay asphalt or wood shingles, you can lay slate shingles. You don't have to do it fast enough to make a living, just well enough to make a tight and handsome roof.

Preparing the Roof for Slate

Some roofers prefer to lay the slates over skip sheathing, since the slates will dry out faster, decreasing gypsum leaching and prolonging service life. Skip sheathing also provides a convenient and safe toehold for working on the roof without having to drag ladders over the slates. Other slaters prefer a solid-board deck with an underlayment of 30-lb. felt, not as a waterproofing but to cushion the slates.

Chances are, if your rafters carried the old slate roofing without sagging, they'll handle the new one. If the rafters are bowed, they should be beefed up by sistering. Use the next largest nominal dimension (for example, splice a 2x8 onto a 2x6). Standard ⅜-in. slate weighs 750 lb. to 850 lb. per square, (100 sq. ft.), which is about the same as three layers of premium-weight asphalt shingles. Any good carpentry book will contain the tables and formulas for sizing rafters to fit the roof load.

CEMENT–ASBESTOS SHINGLES

Cement–asbestos shingles, which are good for 50 years or longer, share slate's immunity to rot, decay, fire, and weather but at a much more reasonable cost. Produced from the turn of the last century until the end of World War II, this brittle, dull gray, poor-man's slate was heavier and harder to install than asphalt shingles and lacked the pleasing appearance of its prototype. (Cement–asbestos was also a fairly popular low-maintenance siding installed over old wood until aluminum siding was introduced in the 1950s.) The only innate drawback of cement–asbestos roofing and siding is its brittleness, which makes it vulnerable to impact damage and thermal stress. But problems are more likely to be caused by corroded fasteners than by the shingles themselves.

Fortunately, cement–asbestos shingles went out of style long before concern over the health effects of asbestos prohibited their use. While many towns strictly regulate their removal and disposal, the shingles are perfectly safe if left

alone. And, by working carefully to limit breakage, a roofer can remove them safely, one at a time. If you cannot abide otherwise serviceable cement–asbestos roofing (or siding), check with the your state's Environmental Protection Agency office before you renovate.

Asbestos-Free Cement Roofing and Tile Roofing

Asbestos-free cement–fiber roofing came on the market during the 1970s. Modern cement-fiber roofing tiles are much lighter, more colorful, more pleasingly textured, and more durable than their cement–asbestos forebears. These desirable qualities and lower cost make them a logical alternative to natural slate or clay tile roofing. They do have one drawback. Many of the current products are somewhat porous and therefore not freeze–thaw stable, which restricts their use to regions with mild winters.

Popularly associated with the haciendas of the Spanish Southwest, clay tile roofing, both in traditional cylindrical and in flat tiles was used throughout this country from the earliest colo-

Despite its association with warm climes, clay tile roofing has a millennial history in northern Europe. Fashion, not practicality, makes this an unusual roof in Portland, Maine.

nial times up until the 1830s, when it fell out of fashion east of Mississippi and north of Florida. Early colonial tiles were fastened to steep roofs by a wooden peg driven through a hole in the top of the tile that hooked over the edge of the skip sheathing. These pegs would rot long before the tiles weathered away. Iron nails were no better.

Repairing Cement–Asbestos Roofing and Tile Roofing

Many of the techniques used to repair slate roofs are also applicable to cement-asbestos and tile roofing. For all practical purposes, cement shingles are interchangeable with slate, with one difference: The absence of a directional grain makes the cement-asbestos shingles less likely to shatter when scored and snapped to size. Unfortunately, it's the snapping that releases asbestos fibers into the air. If you find yourself having to cut a few shingles in the course of repairs, wear an approved respirator and wet down the shingles. Do all your cutting in one area, out of the wind, and dispose of the debris properly instead of burying it somewhere out back.

Tile roofs can be difficult to repair because it's virtually impossible for an amateur to remove the intricately interlocked tiles used in some styles without damaging them. It's best to make a temporary patch from a piece of asphalt roll roofing until professional help can be obtained. There are some flat tiles that are fastened exactly like slates and are likewise amenable to the slater's hook and copper tab technique. The intersections of tiles with ridges and hips are fairly complicated, and a number of special pieces are needed for finishing these areas.

Clay tile is heir to most of the ills that slates are. They tend to break more often at side walls around dormers and near penetrations and valleys, basically wherever dissimilar materials in close proximity can move and stress the tiles. To cut clay tiles, use a circular saw or chopsaw equipped with a masonry or diamond blade.

Traditional Spanish interlocking tiles and Mission-style barrel tiles are still widely used today throughout the Sunbelt states. Flat clay Williamsburg, or English interlock, tiles are also available as well as a premium Georgian shingle, which is designed to look like wood. As with cement-fiber shingles, if you live in a cold region, make sure any tiles you buy are freeze–thaw stable. If you need to replace a few damaged tiles on an otherwise sound roof, look for dealers in salvaged historic tiles; they may be able to provide you with an exact match.

METAL ROOFING

In 1844, a machine was patented that could form corrugations in flat sheets of rolled iron, making it possible to mass-produce sheets of inexpensive rust-proof galvanized metal roofing. The gold rushes in California (1849) and Australia (1851) provided a huge market for corrugated metal, which was used to cover the roofs and walls of boomtown buildings. Unlike slate or even asphalt, metal roofing of all kinds could be economically shipped over large distances. The advantages of light weight, low cost, and large sheets (nailed to spaced purlins instead of solid decking) and easy, fast, and inexpensive installation are perhaps why corrugated steel roofing is as ubiquitous today in rural areas of the United States and in developing countries as it was on the frontiers of the Wild West and of the Land Down Under. From the post–Civil War period on, cheap corrugated steel has been widely used for roofing commercial buildings, barns, and rural homes.

In the late Victorian period, embossed interlocking galvanized-steel and even pure zinc shingles in a wide variety of patterns and sizes also became popular. The Berridge Manufacturing Co. makes Galvalume metal shingles (made of a proprietary alloy of alu-

Although styled in imitation of individual slates, the steel and zinc shingles of the late nineteenth century were applied in long strips.

The fact that the Spanish-style tiles of this roof are actually metal facsimiles is not at all apparent at first glance.

minum and zinc), prefinished in patterns that reproduce late-Victorian and early-twentieth-century styles. In the late 1990s, a wide variety of metal shingles in styles that mimic classic Mission tiles, slate, wood shakes, and other tiles became available in copper, aluminum, terne, and terne-coated stainless steel. The coatings themselves are guaranteed for 20 years to 50 years. These shingles are not inexpensive.

Types of Metal Roofing

Today, galvanized-steel sheet roofing is manufactured in a wide variety of ribbed and corrugated patterns, none of which is likely to match the style of the old roofing on your house. Fortunately, because of its durability, usable secondhand steel roofing is a fairly common and inexpensive salvage item in many rural areas. If you need a few sheets of a matching style to repair your roof, chances are that you can find them locally.

These roofs can last almost indefinitely, but even the best-grade zinc coating will wear off in

With proper care, a steel roof can last indefinitely. But even the best-grade coating will eventually wear off, exposing the bare steel or (as shown here) causing unsightly stains.

Repairing Metal Roofing

Because it's inexpensive and easy to apply, solvent-based fiber-reinforced asphalt roof coating is the usual, albeit short-lived, cure for rusting or decayed metal roofing or flashing. The coating is somewhat more viscous than foundation coating or cold cement and has some added UV resistance. It is applied straight out of the bucket with a long-handled roofer's mop.

Another type of coating is asphalt emulsion water-soluble gel, which is applied with a coarse paintbrush or wallpaper-paste brush. Depending on the exposure conditions, expect both the fiber-reinforced and the emulsion-type coating to start flaking off within two years to three years and to deteriorate to the point at which you can't ignore it any longer within five years, at most. A third type of roof coating is the thick rubberized asphalt-aluminum coating promoted as a cure-all for mobile-home and RV roof problems. This coating is noncorrosive and does perform marginally better than the others. As an added bonus, its reflective properties keep the roof cooler and protect the asphalt against solar radiation. But at roughly three times the cost of asphalt, the few extra years of peace of mind is dearly purchased.

▮▮ Caulking Joints and Small Holes Sheet-metal roofing laid on a shallow slope (less than 4 in 12) usually leaks along its vertical lapjoints when wind drives rain up under them or capillary action sucks water into them. The only permanent correction is to replace the corrugated roofing with a material suited to low-pitch roofs, such as standing- or soldered-seam metal or even roll roofing.

For a temporary fix, remove the nails along the overlap, lift up the edge of the sheet, and seal it with brushable or caulking-grade acrylic polymer, such as Geocel. Then renail, driving nails next to but not actually in the old nail holes. The idea is to cover as much of the nail hole with the nail head as possible while anchoring the nail itself in solid wood. Finish by caulking the nail. Depending on the slope and climate extremes, the joint may remain watertight for five years or more.

There are a number of premium caulks that possess the flexibility and superior adhesion necessary to withstand the thermal instability of metal-to-metal and metal-to-something-else joints. Silicone or acrylic copolymer caulk, such as Geocel, makes a more durable and reliable patch for small punctures in corrugated sheet roofing than quick-and-dirty asphalt flashing cement.

about 30 years. The exposed bare steel will soon rust and so must be kept painted if it is to last. Note that new galvanized roofing will not accept paint until the coating has weathered for at least a season.

Lightweight corrugated or ribbed steel roofing is economical in the South and West because it requires only minimal roof framing. In the North, it is preferred for its ability to shed snow. Steel sheets can also be used to reroof old shingles without adding excessive weight or tearing off the existing roof.

There are, however, some disadvantages to this seemingly ideal material. Because long vertical seams tend to siphon water, steel roofing can leak if used on roof pitches lower than 4 in 12. When used over heated spaces, such as a house, special precautions must be taken to prevent condensation on the underside of the sheets in cold climates. Because this typically means the

It has been four years since the rusted century-plus-old panels of this steel roof were rejuvenated with a coat of asphalt emulsion paint. The coating is just beginning to show signs of wear and will need to be redone in another year or so.

Patching Larger Holes

Larger holes in roofing sheets, metal valleys, and gutters or eaves flashing require reinforcement and eternal vigilance. Make the patch by embedding fiberglass-reinforcement mesh or asphalt-saturated gutter liner cloth in flashing cement. A piece of the same metal as the roofing, shaped as required, and riveted (or secured with self-tapping sheet metal screws) to the edges of the patch protect the asphalt from UV degradation. Just the same, it's a good idea to check all nonsoldered metal patches in the fall and spring.

Fixing Popped Nails

The relentless contraction and expansion of corrugated-metal roofing tends to pull the nails up over time. Driving them back down doesn't help, since the holes are enlarged as the nails work up. The problem is worse with longer and wider sheets. If renailing with longer and thicker nails doesn't pull the roofing down, try driving the nails at an angle to catch new wood or putting them in different spots altogether. Fill the old holes with caulk and seal any angled nails as well, since the gasket under the nail head works effectively only when driven flat against the roofing.

installation of a vented roof over solid sheathing, the cost and labor savings are less attractive. The biggest drawback, though, is aesthetic. It's fiendishly difficult to cut steel roofing to fit neatly and tightly to valleys, hips, complex roofs, and projections. But for simple gable roofs, such as the Cape-style farmhouse, sheet-steel roofing was and is a good (and authentic) alternative to asphalt shingles.

TIN VERSUS TERNE Once rolling mills became common around the middle of the nineteenth century, tinplate roofing could be cheaply produced. In common parlance, the terms *tinplate* and *tin* are used indiscriminately to describe two distinctly different kinds of metal. True tinplate, or bright tin, is steel coated with pure tin. Copper-bearing steel coated with an alloy of 75 percent to 90 percent lead and 10 percent to

When properly installed and maintained, a standing-seam metal roof will remain watertight and attractive almost forever.

25 percent tin should more properly be called terne plate or leaded-tin.

Terne metal roofing enjoyed a brief but intense vogue during the last 20 years of the 1800s, just before asphalt shingles took hold. Its durability is confirmed by the many tin roofs that have survived to this day. If kept painted, a terne metal roof will easily last a century or more. Lead-coated copper and terne-coated stainless steel both offer the advantage of not needing painting, but at a significantly greater cost. Terne-coated stainless is also more difficult to bend, fold, and cut.

FLAT SEAM VERSUS STANDING SEAM Terne metal was (and still is) used in two different ways: flat seam and standing seam. Square sheets, soldered together on all four edges (with nailing cleats concealed under the flange of the solder joints), were laid on low-pitched roofs, such as on porches, to form an absolutely water-

tight roof. Because the sheets could be cut to fit odd angles, flat-seam tin roofing was ideally suited to the elaborately curved roofs of Victorian verandas. You can find the corroded remains of these squares under the layers of asphalt coating on many an old porch roof today.

To make a standing-seam, long sheets of terne metal (called *pans*) are soldered together at top and bottom and interlocked vertically by an ingenious waterproof joint (the standing seam), which is attached to the roof sheathing with hidden cleats. Standing-seam roofs, painted red, green, silver, or black, are a prominent feature in many small towns and country villages throughout the Northeast and Midwest. Because these roofs are completely watertight and very handsome, contemporary architects have begun to specify them for their upscale clients. This, in turn, has made it easier to find a distributor who carries the material and roofers who can install it. This is a good thing, because all too many old houses lost a distinctive part of their historical character when the old tin roof was torn off and replaced with asphalt strip shingles.

The cost of standard terne metal is about the same as the very best asphalt shingles. But, unlike corrugated sheet roofing, tin roofing has never been cheap to install.

Applying Steel Roofing over Old Asphalt Roofing

Steel roofing can be applied over old asphalt shingles—a convenient solution to the problem of repairing a rotted deck or worn-out shingles with a minimum of effort and expense. But check your local zoning ordinances if you plan to reroof with corrugated steel; some towns actually prohibit its use for residential roofing on the grounds that it lowers neighborhood property values.

Although it's often done, do not nail the steel directly to the shingles. The asphalt will corrode the underside of the metal. Instead, nail the sheets to horizontal wood strips. Use inexpensive roughsawn 1x4 or 2x4 pine or spruce laid 16 in. on center and nailed through the old shingles into the rafters.

Asphalt Roofing

Asphalt first made its appearance around the middle of the nineteenth century as *composition* or *rag* roofing. Basically, a bolt of tar-soaked cloth (hence the "rag"), felt, or paper, it was used to make a watertight covering for the flat-roofed urban buildings that were becoming fashionable at that time.

During the last quarter of the nineteenth century, smooth-surfaced (60-lb.) and mineral-surfaced (90-lb.) roll, or paper, roofing was promoted as a modern, convenient, labor- and cost-saving alternative to traditional wood and slate shingles. Although roll roofing is certainly fast and easy to apply, it also has a short life span (7 years to 15 years). It's hard to believe anyone would find it attractive. Fortunately, asphalt-composition shingles were invented in 1915 before roll roofing had a chance to catch on.

Today, other than for the poorest shacks, sheds, and old factory buildings, roll roofing is used almost exclusively as a liner for valleys and for covering roofs with pitches too low for shingles (slopes between 1 in 12 and 4 in 12). Such low-pitched roofs usually can't be seen from the ground anyway. (The drawing on p. 191 shows which roofing materials are appropriate for different roof slopes.)

Mineral-surfaced roll roofing should not be confused with traditional built-up roofing (BUR; also called *hot mop*), which is still the most widely used covering for flat roofs (roofs with a pitch of 1 in 12 or less). When properly

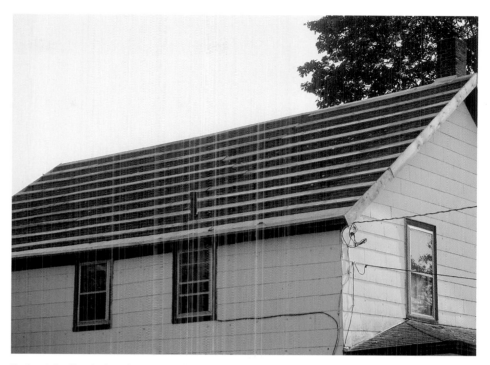

Horizontal nailers isolate the metal roofing from the existing asphalt shingles. The change in roof level is hidden behind a new fascia board. (A simpler option is to overlay the existing fascia with a narrow trim board, as shown in the drawing below.)

Laying Steel over an Existing Roof

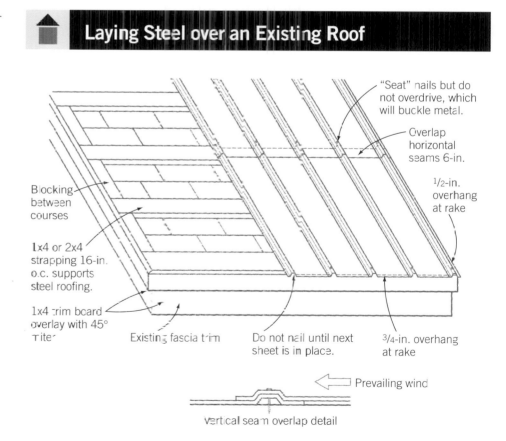

"Seat" nails but do not overdrive, which will buckle metal.

Overlap horizontal seams 6-in.

1/2-in. overhang at rake

Blocking between courses

1x4 or 2x4 strapping 16-in. o.c. supports steel roofing.

1x4 trim board overlay with 45° miter

Existing fascia trim

Do not nail until next sheet is in place.

3/4-in. overhang at rake

Prevailing wind

Vertical seam overlap detail

Patching Built-Up or Roll Roofing

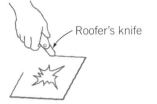

Roofer's knife

Trowel

1. Scrape away gravel and cut out damage. Avoid cutting through underlying felts.

2. Push flashing cement under edges of cutout. Coat entire area with more cement.

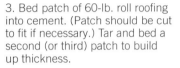

3. Bed patch of 60-lb. roll roofing into cement. (Patch should be cut to fit if necessary.) Tar and bed a second (or third) patch to build up thickness.

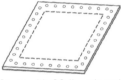

4. Cover with 90-lb. mineral surface roofing patch that overlaps 2 in. on all sides. Coat underside of patch with flashing cement first and nail 1 in. apart.

5. Cover heads of roofing nails with flashing cement. For built-up roofing, coat with cold cement and sprinkle with gravel mix.

installed over a dry deck, this multilayer sandwich of asphalt-saturated felt papers and hot tar (bitumen) topped with a protective gravel finish is very durable (20 years to 40 years). Most problems and leaks occur at the flashings, terminations, and penetrations.

While the homeowner can repair leaks without difficulty, laying down a new hot mop roof is a job best left to professionals. They have the equipment to heat the asphalt and pump or lift it up to the roof.

Ethylene propylene diene monomer (EPDM) membrane roofing is an alternative to asphalt built-up roofing that might be more amenable to the resources of the do-it-yourselfer. A single

layer of this synthetic rubber sheeting can be glued to the roof deck, attached with proprietary nonpenetrating anchors, or even held in place with a gravel overcoat. Proper sealing of the seams is the trickiest and most critical element in making a watertight EPDM roof. Tape, contact cement, and special caulks are typical sealants. Metal termination bars are used to attach the membrane to the edges of the roof and to the flashing at end walls and parapets. EPDM sheets are prone to thermal contraction and expansion and should not be installed taut. Otherwise, the membrane can pull away from fasteners and leak. Follow the manufacturer's installation instructions carefully.

Asphalt-Composition Shingles

The modern asphalt-composition mineral-surfaced shingle is one of the truly significant contributions of technology to building. Although relatively short lived (15 years to 25 years), the shingles are inexpensive and easy to install; provide a reasonably tight seal; and are available in colors, textures, and patterns that can enhance just about any house.

The traditionalist may object to asphalt shingles in favor of wood, slate, or standing-seam roofing; but for most of us, architectural fidelity must take second place to economic reality. Even though a slate or metal roof will be more cost-effective in the long run because it will outlast at least enough asphalt roofs to equal the initial cost difference, the typical renovator on a tight budget is more apt to invest that differential in some other seemingly more deserving project. Besides, asphalt shingles have been around long enough to become familiar. They seem at home with just about any architectural style or period, which is why asphalt shingles account for 85 percent of the roofing installed today.

As you walk down a city street and look at the roofs of the houses, you will observe a variety of shingle types and patterns. The older-style shingles are getting scarcer by the day as they reach the end of their useful life—only a few small regional manufacturers still produce them. There are areas of the country where a particular shingle style may have lingered longer than the others. The old mill towns of the industrial Northeast and Midwest, for example, seem especially rich in unusual shingle styles. Here you will still find the lock-tab shingle, which once enjoyed great popularity because of its wind resistance; this shingle is still ideal for reroofing on top of existing shingles, which won't tele-

graph through as with strip shingles. It's also one of the easiest patterns to apply. Its interlocking, broad T-shape pattern, which resembles brick pavers, looks very much at home on the roof of an old Victorian.

The giant individual and hex-lock shingles are asphalt copies of the slate patterns that they were designed to replace in the 1920s and were often laid directly over the slate. Now these formerly ubiquitous styles are fossils, unearthed when stripping off layers of old shingles before reroofing. But who knows? The revival of the

Common and Obsolete Asphalt Roofing Materials

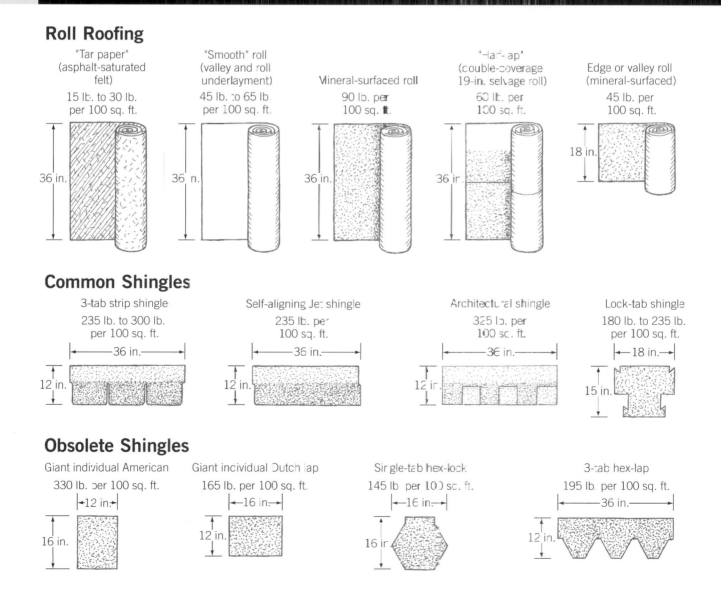

Roll Roofing

"Tar paper" (asphalt-saturated felt)	"Smooth" roll (valley and roll underlayment)	Mineral-surfaced roll	"Half-lap" (double-coverage 19-in. selvage roll)	Edge or valley roll (mineral-surfaced)
15 lb. to 30 lb. per 100 sq. ft.	45 lb. to 65 lb. per 100 sq. ft.	90 lb. per 100 sq. ft.	60 lb. per 100 sq. ft.	45 lb. per 100 sq. ft.
36 in.	36 in.	36 in.	36 in.	18 in.

Common Shingles

3-tab strip shingle	Self-aligning Jet shingle	Architectural shingle	Lock-tab shingle
235 lb. to 300 lb. per 100 sq. ft.	235 lb. per 100 sq. ft.	325 lb. per 100 sq. ft.	180 lb. to 235 lb. per 100 sq. ft.
36 in. / 12 in.	36 in. / 12 in.	36 in. / 12 in.	18 in. / 15 in.

Obsolete Shingles

Giant individual American	Giant individual Dutch lap	Single-tab hex-lock	3-tab hex-lap
330 lb. per 100 sq. ft.	165 lb. per 100 sq. ft.	145 lb. per 100 sq. ft.	195 lb. per 100 sq. ft.
12 in. / 16 in.	16 in. / 12 in.	16 in. / 16 in.	36 in. / 12 in.

Finding Leaks

Before you can fix a leak, you've got to find it. If you know where and when to look and what to look for, visual inspection can locate obvious leaks. An ice dam is the usual culprit when water is running down the inside of a wall during the winter. Water dripping from the soffit boards of a cornice or behind the fascia suggests a problem with the roof overhang or eaves. Because the source of the leak may not always be directly above a dripping ceiling or light fixture, the best time to find a leak is during a rainstorm.

Take a flashlight up into the attic. Starting in the general vicinity of the wet spot, see if you can pinpoint the leak. You may have to pull up wet insulation and trace along rafters or sheathing boards to find it. Try to correlate the leak with an established landmark, such as a vent pipe, chimney, or dormer wall, so you can locate it on the roof after it has dried off. Don't walk on asphalt roofing in hot weather—the shingles become soft enough to tear or smear under your heel. When inspecting slate, tile, or cement roofs, do not walk directly on the shingles, even if the roof pitch is low enough to allow it. Spread your weight across the roofing with a wood ladder. This can be either a home-made chicken ladder or an ordinary wood ladder set on top of an old quilt for extra padding.

CAUSES OF LEAKS

Cracked, broken, missing, and worn-out shingles are only some of the more unmistakable causes of roof leaks. When any of these conditions exposes the wood decking or the nails and top portions of the underlying shingles, a leak is all but guaranteed. Exposure to the weather will eventually dry out asphalt and tar coatings, causing them to crack, blister, and break.

In the snowbelt, overzealous attempts to remove ice and snow buildup at the eaves with shovels and axes are a common cause of leaks. Storm-tossed branches and careless foot traffic can also damage roof shingles.

The source of a leak: Runoff from the unguttered eaves of the main roof has cut a canyon down to the bedrock of the sheathing boards through these otherwise still-solid shingles on the lower roof.

Flashing Leaks

Heat and cold cause wood framing, metal flashing, caulking, brickwork, and roofing materials to expand and contract at different rates. The house settles faster than the chimney. Over the years, all this movement pulls joints apart and cracks seals between walls and roofing, flashing and vents, and chimney and other roof projections. Flashing in particular can prove troublesome. Leaks occur when flashing cement and caulking crack or dry out around vents and ventilators, chimneys, skylights and end walls. And asphalt-based flashing cement will *always* dry out, which is why a good flashing job should not rely on asphalt–cement as its primary defense against leakage.

Flashing metal, especially galvanized iron (and aluminum near saltwater), rusts or corrodes in the most awkward places. Galvanic corrosion, which occurs wherever dissimilar metals

Water seeping behind the flashing exposed by the missing siding at this dormer eventually exited at the soffit and fascia boards. If uncorrected, the rot can lead to structural damage.

contact each other (such as galvanized nails in copper flashing), is another frequent source of leaks. Metal valleys also have a tendency to split or separate at the seams in reaction to thermal stresses. An often-overlooked source of a perplexing leak is a crack in the joint between the flue tile and the chimney cap or even a crack in the cap itself.

Wind Leaks

Sometimes a leak occurs only when the wind blows from a particular direction or with a special ferocity. This was a persistent problem with three-tab shingles until the invention of the Windseal shingle. (A thermoplastic cement strip, which is factory-applied across the backs of the shingles, glues them together after installation.) The shingle edges would blow upward, allowing water to enter underneath. When this happens with slate and wood shingles or modern wind-resistant asphalt roofing, the problem can usually be traced to faulty workmanship or an inappropriate choice of materials.

Poor Materials and/or Workmanship

As shown in the drawing at right, all roofing materials are not suitable for all pitches. Some, such as wood shakes, require strips of asphalt-felt underlayment between courses, which incompetent or unscrupulous roofers may have omitted. Some

corner-cutters will roof with cheaper wood shingles intended for siding. The exposed knots and weaker grain soon cause these shingles to deform—and leak. Wood shingles laid directly over a solid roof deck will also rot, because they need good air circulation to dry out between rains. The worst fault a roofer can commit, either through ignorance or greed, is to lay shingles with a greater weather exposure than recommended for the type of material and slope. Insufficient overlap between courses allows wind-driven rain to penetrate under the shingles. The same is true when strip shingles are used for shallow-pitch roofs (less than 4 in 12). The only cure is to tear off the entire roof and reinstall it properly.

Pitch Limits Choice of Roofing Materials

1. Built-up roofing, hot tar, EPDM membrane systems
2. Roll roofing
3. Soldered-seam flat metal
4. Asphalt shingles with waterproof underlayment
5. Standing-seam metal
6. Corrugated or ribbed metal panels
7. Asphalt shingles
8. Wood shingles with 5-in. exposure
9. Slate and tile with extra framing
10. Wood shakes with 5-in. exposure, wood shingles with 7-in. exposure
11. Wood shakes with 7-in. exposure
12. Slate and tile with ordinary framing

12/12
11/12
10/12
9/12
8/12
7/12
6/12
5/12
4/12
3/12
2/12
1/12

TIP

Distinctive Strip Shingles

Until recently, as old roofs wore out, there was seldom any choice but to replace them with standard modern shingles. Now a few major manufacturers have started to produce either distinctly styled diamond and hexagonal shingles or at least "shaped" strip shingles that evoke the old patterns. For example, IKO Roofing Products has introduced the Royal Victorian scalloped-edge six-tab shingle that harmonizes well with a nineteenth-century renovation. ■ ■ ■

Dutch-lap or the Salem shingle may be waiting only for the next wave of gentrification.

COMMONLY AVAILABLE SHINGLE TYPES

Today, choice is pretty much limited to three basic types. The most common, and the most suitable for old-houses, is the three-tab strip shingle. The overlapping cutouts with their vertical accent suggest the slates on which they were modeled.

The second type is a variation on the three-tab shingle, the tab-less strip shingle (one common brand name is Jet, one of the first of this style to be introduced). These shingles can last 5 years longer, and their self-aligning design allows faster installation than ordinary strip shingles. But tab-less shingles are stylistically more suited to ranch-style tract houses than to old houses, because their strong horizontal lines seem to emphasize every hump and sag in the roof deck.

The third type, the architectural or laminated shingle, combines the speedy application of tab-less shingles with the random pattern and raised profile of wood shingles. This premium shingle, which costs about as much as real wood shingles (although they are much less labor intensive to install), is best applied to steep-pitched roofs, where its rich texture can be appreciated from the ground to the best advantage. Because they consist of two or three layers at the weather exposure, architectural shingles have the longest warranty of any asphalt shingle.

All three styles of asphalt shingles have a layer of thermoplastic cement on the underside that glues the courses together and greatly increases their wind resistance. From the 1940s until the 1970s asphalt shingles had an organic mat made from recycled paper and/or wood fiber (rags were discontinued before World War II). Over time, as the asphalt dried out, these

The venerable lock-tab shingle is easy to install, interesting looking, and ideal for reroofing. Unfortunately, as the presence of the strip shingle patch at top right indicates, it is no longer readily available in many parts of the country.

These antique hex-lock shingles are in amazingly good condition. In some parts of the Midwest, they are being manufactured again, which is fortunate because they are more well suited for reroofing Victorian houses than the lock-tab shingle.

Even without the exaggeration caused by wear, the cutouts of the three-tab strip shingle create a strong vertical shadow line.

Tab-less strip shingles, lacking cutouts, emphasize a horizontal line. One of the drawbacks of these shingles—a tendency to buckle with thermal stress (which cutouts relieve)—is also obvious on this roof.

Architectural, or laminated, shingles combine the speedy application of tab-less shingles with the random pattern and raised profile of wood shingles.

shingles tended to wick up water and slowly rot. Shingles made with inorganic fiberglass mats which are impervious to decay and much more fire resistant, were introduced in the 1970s. They cost a bit more and last about 5 years longer than comparable organic shingles. Presently, they account for over 80 percent of the residential asphalt shingles sold. The only reason organic mat shingles are still manufactured is that fiberglass mats become extremely brittle (and thus hard to install) in cold weather.

REROOFING WITH ASPHALT SHINGLES There are two ways to reroof a house: Remove the old shingles down to the decking or lay new shingles over the old. If the original shingles are not too badly warped and the deck underneath is sound, laying new roofing over old will save time and money (especially the tipping fees at the local landfill).

Asphalt shingles must be applied over a solid base. If roof decking boards are rotted, you'll have to strip off the roof and skin the sheathing with plywood or oriented strand board (OSB). You'll also have to strip the roof if you are replacing wood shingles, slates, or any kind of roofing that was attached to skip sheathing. Nail new sheathing over the skip sheathing. Also, most codes allow no more than three layers of asphalt roofing, so if there are three layers already in place, you will have to strip the roof. One other precaution: Most roofs with a pitch greater than 6 in 12 and framed with at least 2x8 rafters at no more than 2 ft. on center can safely support the weight of up to three layers of asphalt shingles (2 psf or 2.5 psf per layer, depending on the weight per 100 sq. ft. as specified by the manufacturer) If your rafters don't meet these specs you'll have to strip off the old shingles.

Three layers of asphalt is about equal to the dead load of a slate roof, which somewhat belies the argument about the need for extra-heavy roof framing. If there's any doubt about the

Closed valleys tend to trap detritus, which can hasten the decay of the shingles.

Because its protective painted finish has been kept up, this late-nineteenth-century open metal valley, fashioned with short lengths of sheet metal soldered together, has outlived several generations of roofing.

strength of your roof framing, the recommended load for any given configuration can be calculated from tables in any good carpentry textbook. The real objection to reroofing over existing shingles is more a matter of appearance than structural strength. Unless the old roof is carefully prepared by renailing loose and warped shingles and pulling protruding nails, the new shingles will mirror the irregularities in the roof underneath.

VALLEY PROBLEMS

Because they drain the runoff from the watershed of a large portion of the roof, valleys often wear out before the rest of the roofing. This is especially so with woven, or closed, valleys. Here the water-soaked debris trapped by the interlaced shingles hastens their rot. Woven valleys also tend to hold snow longer, which can lead to problems with leaks caused by ice dams.

Although it is considerably more expensive and time-consuming to install, an open metal-lined valley is both more slippery and more resistant to the erosive power of runoff and thus will last longer in regions of heavy rainfall and in the snow belt. (Valleys lined with cheap and flimsy aluminum flashing or mineral-surfaced roll roofing, however, are neither as durable nor as good-looking as copper or painted galvanized steel.) Nevertheless, unless swept clean of debris and (in the case of galvanized steel) kept regularly painted, metal-lined valleys will soon corrode and offer no more protection than shingle-lined valleys. If it has been well maintained, a metal valley liner will outlast several asphalt or wood roofs. If this is the case, the liner is usually left in place or taken up and saved for reuse when the shingles are stripped for reroofing. Asphalt–cement can be used for a short-lived patch, but the only sure cure for a punctured or corroded metal valley liner is a new one. Consult a good roofing book for details on how to lay in a valley.

Sometimes, because of careless installation, a valley flashing doesn't extend far enough up under the shingles to prevent a leak, particularly when ice works up under the shingles and past the metal. As a rule of thumb, no more than one third of the total width of a valley flashing should be exposed. For most purposes, this means that 20 in. is the minimum allowable width of the flashing metal. Cementing the shingles to the valley may help at least temporarily, but the best alternative to replacement is to remove the shingles along the valley and splice new metal to the old. Make a simple interlocking seam and fold it flat. You could also extend the existing valley up under the shingles with an overlaid strip of Bituthene membrane.

Gutters are problematic in cold climates. While they help keep moisture away from the foundation, they also tend to self-destruct or cause leaks when they fill with ice. The conflict is ultimately irresolvable.

GUTTERS

As discussed in chapter 3, water falling from the eaves and pooling along the foundation wall is a major cause of wet cellars. Eaves troughs, or gutters, catch this water at the roof and divert it through a downspout, or leader, away from the building. In regions of heavy seasonal rainfall and mild winters, they are an absolute necessity. But in climates similar to that of northern Vermont, they are so problematic that many builders feel they aren't worth the trouble so long as other measures are employed to divert the roof runoff away from the foundation.

Maintaining Gutters

Most people let their gutters and roofs go without maintenance until a leak becomes too troublesome to ignore. By then, damage has already been done to the roof deck, walls, or ceilings. A simple inspection and cleaning can extend the life of gutter systems and prevent expensive repairs. Make sure leaders drain freely and clean gutters of dead leaves, clotted twigs, and dirt late in the fall before winter sets in. Not only does roof debris plug the entrance to the downspout and dam up the gutters but dead leaves also act like sponges, holding moisture that eventually rots an asphalt liner or corrodes metal.

PREVENTING ICE DAMAGE Preventative maintenance also reduces the likelihood of ice damage. Gutters typically fill up with ice and split apart or facilitate the infiltration of ice into cornices and behind the wall sheathing. The seams of a clogged leader are burst by ice plugs. A free-flowing gutter won't allow ice to build up as quickly as a slow-draining one. Check that the gutter is pitched enough to drain easily. A pitch of 1 in. over 16 ft. is considered adequate.

If the outer lip of the gutter is dropped below the line of the roof slope, snow slides will not tear the gutter off. However, since the amount of the drop will increase with the pitch of the roof, mounting the gutter 5 in. or 6 in. beneath the drip edge for a 12-in-12 roof may look objectionable.

Because ice buildup is basically inevitable anyway, there are a few things you can do to minimize the damage. Double the number of required hangers to help the gutter withstand the weight of the ice. (This won't work with spike-and-ferrule type hangers, which must be driven into the rafter tails.)

If the leader from a gutter on the north side of the house turns the corner to drain down a western wall, it may soak up enough late afternoon sunshine to keep from freezing. Corrugated leaders that do freeze are less likely to split apart than smooth round leaders, since they can expand slightly with the ice. The larger the leader, the less likely it is to clog in the first place. Also, if there is an elbow at the bottom of the leader, relocating it higher up the wall to give the drain extension a good pitch speeds up the flow and discourages ice formation. Finally, half-

round gutters are less likely to suffer ice damage than rectangular-back, ogee-front K-style gutters. Expanding ice tends to ride up the curved profile instead of pushing against corners.

Types of Built-in Gutters

Before the introduction of inexpensive preformed metal gutters in the mid-nineteenth century, the gutters of modest houses were conspicuous only by their absence while those of the well-to-do were typically incorporated into the construction of the cornice. Since any leak would inevitably find its way into the walls of the building proper, it was critical that any such built-in gutter be carefully constructed and well maintained. Until the advent of composition and modern synthetic liners, these gutters were typically lined with costly sheet copper or cheaper tin plate or galvanized iron. Besides the danger of corrosion, metal-lined gutters suffered from thermal stress, which tended to tear apart soldered seams. Elaborate expansion joints were necessary to allow movement while keeping the gutters watertight. Thus it is hardly surprising that built-in gutters quickly fell out of favor. Many were simply boarded over and covered with roofing shingles.

YANKEE GUTTERS In southern New England and throughout the Mid-Atlantic states, it is still fairly common to find gutters built on top of the roof deck just above the eaves, more or less over the soffit at the building line. These so-called Yankee gutters (also called Philadelphia or flush gutters) are little more than a pitched, metal-lined, wooden stop running parallel with the eaves. (Sometimes, appearance was sacrificed for ease of construction and instead of an internally pitched trough, the entire gutter was pitched relative to the eaves.) The rake ends were capped with a wood bracket. The drainspout typically extended straight down through the cornice to connect with the leader on the underside of the soffit. In some old houses, the drains from these

The No-Gutter Option

Ultimately, there is no practical way to build a house that will be secure from every conceivable weather condition. If you have gutters and you live in snow country, you will probably have gutter problems. Some homeowners, fed up with replacing torn-off or broken gutters and leaders or ice melting into cornices simply get rid of them and lay splash blocks along the entire length of the eaves.

Sometimes it seems that the only sensible location for a gutter is a short piece over the front door that can be taken down in the fall. Although a gable-roofed door stoop is a better solution to the triumph of fashion over common sense that results in an unprotected entry placed directly under the eaves, the gutter will at least prevent a chilling downpour when people enter or leave the house. But it won't do much to protect against a dangerous ice avalanche.

Built-in Gutters

Yankee Gutter

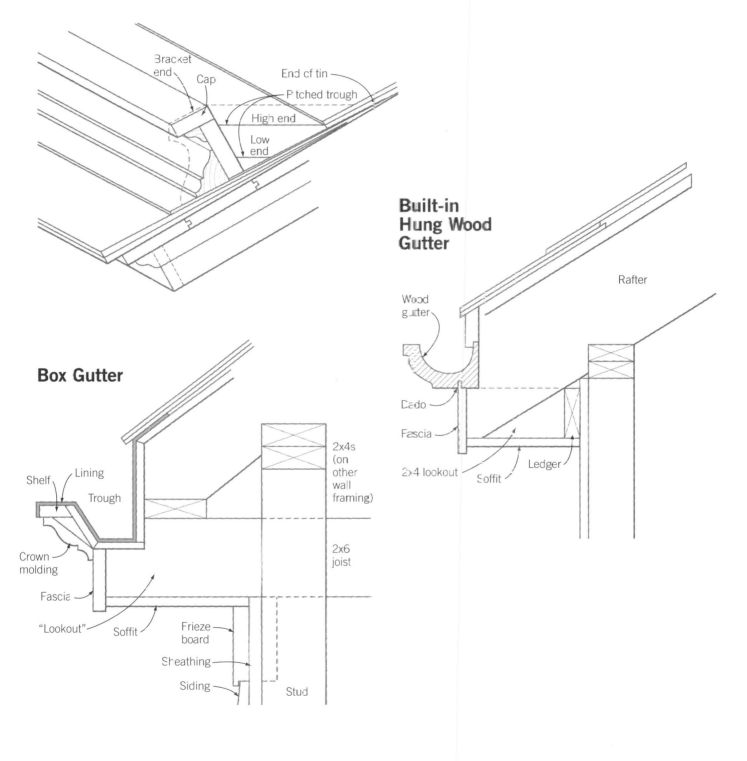

Bracket end
Cap
End of tin
Pitched trough
High end
Low end

Built-in Hung Wood Gutter

Rafter

Wood gutter

Dado

Fascia

2x4 lookout

Ledger

Soffit

Box Gutter

Shelf
Lining
Trough
Crown molding
Fascia
"Lookout"
Soffit
Frieze board
Sheathing
Siding
Stud

2x4s (on other wall framing)

2x6 joist

and other kinds of built-in gutters were actually routed into the wall cavities to conceal them from view. Even without the consideration of how to replace such a downspout should it spring a leak, the potential drawbacks of such a system are so obvious it is a wonder that it was ever employed at all.

Coastal New England is the natural northern limit of the practicality of the Yankee or built-in gutters of all types, since a more ideal environment for a monumental ice dam could not be imagined. This has been the principle objection to Yankee gutters since their inception. However, because a Bituthene underlayment solves the worst part of the ice dam problem, in the interests of maintaining historical authenticity, you may wish to rebuild a rotted Yankee gutter from scratch instead of tearing it off.

BOX GUTTERS Given that the elaborate cornice of an elegant eighteenth- or nineteenth-century house is hardly the place to attach a hung gutter, roof drainage was internalized by concealing it within the cornice structure itself. The resulting box gutter (built-in or sunk gutter) was considered a hallmark of quality construction well into the 1930s. The difference between a Yankee gutter and a box gutter is that the former is constructed on top of the roof deck, independent of the cornice, whereas the built-in gutter is an integral component of it.

Because of this intimate juxtaposition with the structural elements of the house, when a box gutter has leaked for any length of time, serious damage is the usual result. Relining a leaking box gutter may fix the leak, but does nothing to repair the underlying damage. Rafters, plates, wall studs, sheathing, and ceiling joists can all be affected. The entire cornice may have to be rebuilt. As the photo at below suggests, the process can be quite involved.

HUNG WOOD GUTTERS Beginning in the late nineteenth century and until well into the post–World War II years, wood gutters made of clear all-heart Douglas fir, red cedar, or redwood

A neglected leaking box gutter can cause serious damage to the underlying structure. Rebuilding the gutter may require structural repairs of the wall plates and studs, rafter seats, and other frame-bearing members as well as reconstruction of the entire cornice, which, in the case of this elaborate Victorian confection, could be a formidable task.

offered a compromise between the visual elegance of the concealed gutter and the reduced risk of structural damage afforded by the hung gutter. Typically milled with a decorative profile that could double as a crown molding, these gutters were built into the fascia, placing them well outside the building wall. Any damage caused by leaks would not be as great and would be easier to repair.

The inside trough was often milled at a slight pitch to aid drainage while allowing the gutter itself to be installed level against the cornice fascia (or building wall, where the gutter was used in lieu of an extended cornice). Wood gutters were also made with straight troughs. As long as they were kept clean and the downspouts could drain freely, the water would not tend to puddle up to any great extent. No liner was necessary; if the wood was kept painted, the gutters would last as long as the rest of the structure. But frequent cleaning was absolutely critical to ensure good drainage and prevent decay of the paint and eventual rot. Wood gutters are still available and, although pricey, are still employed in top-quality restoration and reproduction work.

Replacing a Yankee Gutter

If the leaking gutter has rotted the roof sheathing or cornice boards, it should be torn off and rebuilt with new wood. At this point, if the cornice would not be architecturally compromised, you should consider installing a standard hung gutter instead. If you choose that option, fill in the missing shingle courses from the top down, slipping each course up under the one above it. Use a chalkline to mark the bottom of each course. If the distance to the newly installed drip edge (in inches) is not divisible by five (the standard exposure for strip shingles), crowd or spread the courses equally to split the difference. This way, you avoid ending up with a 2-in. strip of shingle or uncovered cutouts on the bottom course.

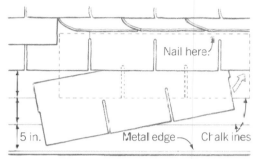

Filling in Shingles at Eaves

Add missing courses from top down. Snap chalkline to mark bottom of each course.

Nail here!

5 in. Metal edge Chalk lines

Compensating for Odd Width

If width doesn't divide evenly by 5, compensate spreading or crowding courses equally.

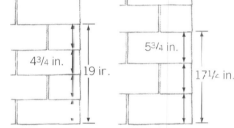

4³/₄ in. 19 in.

5³/₄ in. 17¹/₂ in.

Otherwise, replace any rotten sheathing boards and frame the new stop with treated lumber, as shown in the drawing on p. 250. If historical veracity is not at issue, an EPDM liner is a lot easier to install than metal and more durable than roll roofing. If you do use metal, try to keep the seams to a minimum. Together with a well-insulated, properly vented attic, a Yankee gutter could be an excellent way to capitalize on the insulating properties of a heavy snow cover. With seasonal cleaning and periodic maintenance of the liner, it should last as long as the house itself. Unlike conventional fascia-hung gutters, there's no flimsy trough to buckle or split apart.

as shown in the drawing on p. 250.

TIP

Gutter Liner

Built-in gutters were originally lined with lead, copper, terne, or galvanized iron. But, unless your gutter project is part of a historic restoration, you'll save yourself a lot of trouble if you line it with an EPDM rubber liner instead of metal. Metal liners require expansion joints and/or seams that are best fabricated by a professional roofer or sheet-metal shop. ■■ ■■ ■■

Neglected maintenance allowed the rot that began in this wood gutter to work its way into the cornice of the eaves. Trees that overhang a roof should be cut back to encourage ventilation.

Repairing and Rebuilding Hung Wood Gutters

Wood gutters originally were painted, both on their inside and on their outside. And then, when the paint wore off the trough, someone gave it a nice thick coat of asphalt cement. While this might seem like a good way to waterproof wood, it actually hastens, rather than retards, rot. The wood swells and shrinks as is its wont while the tar becomes increasingly hard and brittle. Water gets trapped in the pockets that eventually form between the wood and tar, starting the decay process.

Ideally, the tar should be removed so that the gutter can be properly treated. But chipping tar, even in cold weather when it's brittle, is slow and frustrating work. Some experts suggest chilling the tar with dry ice. You might consider leaving the tar in place and flooding the cracks with wood preservative or relining them with fiberglass roofer's cloth embedded in aluminized asphalt emulsion or with an EPDM liner.

FIXING SLIGHT ROT Fortunately, or unfortunately, your gutters are just as likely to have been treated with total neglect as with tar. Use a wire brush to thoroughly remove any surviving flakes of tar or loose paint and splintered wood. Slightly rotted gutters are still salvageable: Inject epoxy consolidant into the rotted wood; then rebuild and level any lost wood with epoxy putty. When the gutter is completely dry, saturate the bare wood with an oil-based wood preservative. Wait 2 days and repeat. Let the primer dry for 1 week and then apply one or two finish coats of porch-and-floor enamel or aluminum paint. Expect to repaint the gutters every 4 years or 5 years.

REMOVING ROTTED GUTTERS Hung wood gutters too far gone to reline must be removed. By this point, expect also to replace most of the trim and even some of the underlying wall sheathing. Remove the bed molding that supports the gutter first. Use a pinch bar to separate the gutter from the cornice. You may have to split it apart with a chisel to ease removal. Try to save the wood end blocks that trim the gutter or cut new ones if they are too rotted to remove in one piece.

Wood gutters are quite heavy. Pull carefully with the pinch bar until the back edge is barely hanging from its nails. Then tie one end of the gutter to the roof while you slowly work the other end free and lower it to the ground.

REPLACEMENT OPTIONS There are two options if you can't afford to replace the old wood gutter with a new one (wood-gutter stock is both hard to find and expensive, upward of $5 per foot). Most folks simply use shims or filler boards to rebuild the fascia and install a metal hung gutter. A better alternative, which replicates the look of a classic built-in gutter, is to extend the cornice lookouts or otherwise build out the fascia with 2x stock to make a flat-bottomed shelf that supports a K-style prefinished aluminum gutter.

Metal and Plastic Gutters

Tinsmiths have been making half-round gutters since at least 1821. Terne, tinplate, galvanized steel, and copper were all common gutter and leader materials. The half-round style is more historically appropriate for a nineteenth-century house, whereas the popular K-style, when mated with a crown molding installed below it, fits in nicely with the elaborate classical cornices of eighteenth-century colonials or early-nineteenth-century Greek Revivals. The *K* refers to the pattern designation assigned it in *The Architectural Sheet Metal Manual* published by the Sheet Metal and Air Conditioning Contractors National Association.) This is not, however, how K-style gutters are usually installed. Normally, they are hung directly from the fascia board so that they can be pitched for rapid drainage and, as such, cannot be considered an architectural component of the cornice proper.

Since the 1960s, aluminum and vinyl have almost completely supplanted galvanized steel as the materials of choice for gutter and leader replacement. With the advent of forming machines capable of turning a roll of coil stock into a seamless gutter of any length on site, installation of roof-drainage systems has come into its own as a subcontract specialty. Nevertheless, with the rekindled interest in historic renovation and old house restoration, copper and galvanized-steel half-round styles are once again becoming common. Both metals require soldered joints. At around $0.70 per foot and with a service life of 50 years to 75 years, galvanized-steel half-round is an economical choice for an old house.

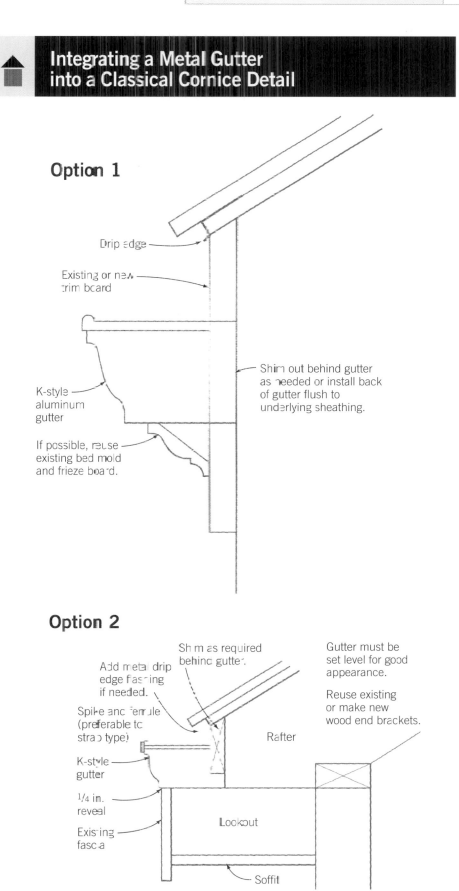

Integrating a Metal Gutter into a Classical Cornice Detail

Option 1

Drip edge

Existing or new trim board

Shim out behind gutter as needed or install back of gutter flush to underlying sheathing.

K-style aluminum gutter

If possible, reuse existing bed mold and frieze board.

Option 2

Shims as required behind gutter.

Gutter must be set level for good appearance.

Add metal drip edge flashing if needed.

Spike and ferrule (preferable to strap type)

Reuse existing or make new wood end brackets.

Rafter

K-style gutter

1/4 in. reveal

Lookout

Existing fascia

Soffit

TIP

Gutter Sizes

Gutters are sized according to the area of the roof surface to be drained. As a rule of thumb, 4-in. gutters will drain up to 750 sq. ft. and 5-in. gutters up to 1,400 sq. ft. If you need a 6-in. gutter, you're probably living in a church. Roofs with more than 1,000 sq. ft. of area require 4-in. downspouting; otherwise, use standard 3-in. pipes. ▬ ▬ ▬

COPPER With copper, historical accuracy and classic beauty come at a premium. Copper gutters are almost as expensive as wood ones. It pains me to think back to all the 100-plus-year-old copper gutters that I helped my grandfather tear down and replace with aluminum or galvanized steel. Today, I think I'd try to resolder split seams rather than sell the copper for scrap as we routinely did back when I was a kid. Granddad would often pay me for helping out by letting me keep the scrap metal. At the end of the summer, we'd take a truckload of old flashing, gutters, and spouting to the junkyard and leave with a small fortune.

GALVANIZED STEEL Galvanized gutters tend to rust first where fast-flowing water erodes the protective zinc coating (for example, at downspout elbows) or where water sits in a chronic puddle. Otherwise, so long as the zinc remains intact or is replaced with rust-inhibiting paint, a galvanized gutter can last a long time, almost as long as copper.

A puddle caused by poor drainage, clotted leaves, or improper pitch probably caused this galvanized steel gutter to rot out.

When a galvanized steel gutter shows just a few rust spots, patching can wheedle another 5 years to 10 years of useful life out of it. (Rusted leaders and elbows won't tolerate this grace period and will have to be replaced.) Clean the rust down to bare metal and paint it with rust-inhibiting enamel. Embed fiberglass reinforcement in asphalt flashing cement to complete the patch. Or make a metal-to-metal patch instead. Form the patch (from copper, for example), and bed it in high-grade silicone caulk. Otherwise, extend the patch so its upstream edge overlays intact zinc (solder won't stick to steel that has lost its zinc coating). Solder it and seal the downstream end with caulk to allow for contraction and expansion. If there are more than a few rusted-out spots, the gutters are ready for replacement.

ALUMINUM Prefinished aluminum gutters and leaders have a baked-on enamel finish that makes them virtually immune to corrosion, even in saltwater climates. These systems are available in over a dozen standard patterns, with corresponding fasteners, hangers, and fittings. Aluminum gutter systems are arguably one of the few justifiably sensible uses of aluminum as a building material.

VINYL Despite their increasing popularity and heavy promotion, I have reservations about the use of vinyl systems. For one thing, they are manufactured from petrochemicals, which might be saved for better uses. For another, all plastics break down eventually with exposure to sunlight, manufacturers' claims notwithstanding. (All building materials wear out eventually. The question is, which ones do it most gracefully? Which would you prefer, weathered wood or degraded plastic?) Vinyl is also more affected by thermal expansion than metals, and provisions to accommodate it are part of the installation. The gutter stock is inexpensive, but the parts and pieces needed to assemble it all are relatively pricey.

Siding, Trim, Windows, and Doors

6

I want a house that has got over all its troubles; I don't want to spend the rest of my life bringing up a young and inexperienced house.

—Jerome K. Jerome

A good portion of the siding and trim had to be replaced or meticulously rebuilt before this house could be prepped for repainting.

A house wears its age on its face. The wrinkles and creases of weathered boards and peeling paint, the arthritic disjointing of cornice and trim, the debilitating diseases of hidden rot— a house shows the weight of life past. But like those beautiful people who fly off to exclusive Swiss clinics for facelifts, old houses, too, can be restored to a semblance of youth. Just as magical unguents, creams, and even surgery stave off the wrinkles of old age for the once-glamorous ingénue, paint, putty, and patching can preserve the good looks of wood siding long past its youthful prime. And, like old dead skin, worn-out wood siding can be replaced with new.

There is nothing exotic to the process, and it need not be expensive. It's fairly necessary for the well-being of the house and can even be fun to do. After the grind of foundation work and roofing, the renovation of an exterior (or interior) wall is a stimulating, pleasurable tonic. Just painting the walls could save a marriage.

Except for houses built in the very early colonial period, when clapboards were nailed directly to wall studs, the exterior walls of most houses have two parts: the outermost siding and the inner layer of sheathing boards. The sheathing boards support the siding, block wind and cold, and make the frame rigid.

Exposure makes a difference. Facing into the prevailing weather, the clapboards on this wall have deteriorated past the point of no return. But the siding on the more protected adjacent wall still has a bit of paint and some life left in it.

Wood Siding

Like feathers or scales, tightly overlapping clapboard or wood shingle siding is designed to shed water. In direct contact with the elements, it endures constant cycles of hot and cold and wet and dry, which will wear down mountains, let alone a house. It is a testimony to the unique durability of wood that it weathers so well and so long.

If kept dry and well aired, unpainted and otherwise unprotected wood will erode before it rots. Outside of the humid subtropical South or the fog-bound temperate rain forests of the Pacific Northwest, the normal movement of air dries and ventilates siding quite well. Likewise, clapboard siding will last almost indefinitely if kept painted and protected from water damage.

The tenacity of a coat of paint is compromised by moisture, both from outside and inside the walls. A painted wall, irrigated by runoff from the eaves or a leaking gutter and shaded by an overhang or vegetation will support a colony of mildew or moss that eats away at the paint film. Meanwhile, moisture migrating through the walls from a humid kitchen or bathroom is lifting the paint off the siding from beneath. Once bubbles and fissures open, water works into the exposed sinews of the wood and accelerates the process of paint failure.

Unfortunately, most homeowners wait until the siding has begun to weather before renewing the paint. If the paint has been allowed to wear too thin or if, as with many houses built before 1725, the siding was never painted at all, the wood will eventually curl and split. Oil-based stains can avert the inevitable if applied after the paint (and before the siding) has worn away. Paint itself will not adhere to weathered wood unless the surface has been prepared by sanding.

As the outermost wood wears away, the nails suck in moisture and start to rust, leaving small cavities to shelter water and rot. The constant shrinking and expanding separate the wood fibers along the grain. As water pries at the fissures, wood leaches away, cracks open wider, and pieces of clapboard break loose, exposing the underlying sheathing to the elements and trapping moisture behind the building paper. More nails pull out as boards warp. The skin becomes loose and flaccid. Like a threadbare overcoat, the clapboards fall apart. The house develops a chronic cold; it is drafty. Water and icy winds penetrate the seams of the house and threaten its structural well-being.

Stick with Wood

When the bill for decades of postponed maintenance and accumulated neglect finally falls due, worn out wood siding must be removed and replaced. There's really no other choice. You can do it little by little, or you can do it all at once. The materials are expensive, and the labor even more so, unless you do it yourself. Fortunately, the task of installing wood siding is not only relatively easy but also satisfying, if undertaken in the proper spirit.

Despite the claims of the synthetic siding industry and its shills down at your local do-it-yourself superstore, replacing old wood with new is far more sensible and economical than ripping it off or entombing it under an aluminum or vinyl straitjacket. In the first place, synthetic sidings are really not as maintenance-free as their promoters would have you believe. Both aluminum and vinyl are much more susceptible to impact damage than wood. Aluminum will scratch and dent. Vinyl will puncture or split. It also turns brittle in extreme cold and can split or shatter if struck. The only way to fix the damage is to replace the piece of siding. But since manufacturers change colors and styles quite frequently, an exact match is unlikely.

Furthermore, the color coating on aluminum eventually wears or peels off, and solid-color vinyl fades with age. Neither material will bear repainting with any great success. Because the 20-year to 40-year manufacturer's warranty is prorated, replacement cost near the end of the

Aluminum siding does not suffer well the inevitable arrows and slings of misfortune; repair is more like automotive bodywork than carpentry.

siding's life span is equal to the initial installation. And the stuff is not so cheap to begin with that you could argue yourself out of real wood for reasons of economy alone.

By contrast, wood siding, even when repainting is neglected, will still look better after 40 years than vinyl or aluminum, and it has at least double if not triple the useful life of the longest-lasting synthetic. When it finally does give up the ghost, it will do it much more gracefully than any synthetic material. Government studies have also shown that synthetic sidings offer little real insulation value. Certainly any energy savings gained are offset by the depletion of nonrenewable resources and environmental damage their manufacture entails.

Hidden Problems with Synthetic Siding

General aesthetic considerations aside, there are two specific reasons why synthetic sidings should not be used with old houses. First, these materials can mask—and even cause—serious structural damage. Because of improper installation that allows water to enter behind the siding, an undetected water problem that was unwittingly covered over, or damage to the old siding caused by nailing siding battens to the house, rot can progressively destroy the underlying structure. In some cases, the siding itself can act as an exterior vapor barrier, trapping condensation beneath it and furthering decay. Hidden from view and protected by the seemingly solid siding, termites and other insects can colonize the walls unmolested.

Even worse, installing aluminum or vinyl siding necessitates the removal or burial of the very details and embellishments that give an old house its distinctive character and aesthetic value. Exterior trim and molding are simplified and visually flattened by the application of stock soffit and cladding material. J-channel moldings and other accouterments of synthetic siding violate window trim proportions. And given the thermal dynamism of aluminum and especially vinyl, minor errors in application can lead to major distortions in appearance. Vinyl also has the annoying habit of creaking as it expands with increasing sunlight.

The J-channel molding used with vinyl and aluminum sidings does not adapt well to curved surfaces. This is just one reason why a clean and elegant fit between those materials and traditional trim details is so difficult to accomplish.

Finally, no matter how many claims to the contrary, vinyl and aluminum clapboards simply do not look like wood, at least not at any distance close enough to matter. Because original materials and historical authenticity increasingly command a premium, installing synthetic sidings can actually reduce resale value, contrary to the established mantra of real-estate agents. Indeed, a potential buyer would do well to suspect that such sidings might actually hide a problem that was never fixed. Is all this worth the trouble of repainting or restaining once every 7 years to 10 years?

GETTING UNDER YOUR HOUSE'S SKIN

There are at least a few fine books that will tell you how to install new wood siding. What you won't find in those books is information about the best way to remove old siding and prepare the walls for new siding. So that's what I focus on in this section. I also discuss how to repair wood siding should wholesale removal be unnecessary.

Old clapboards or wood shingles are easily removed with a flat prybar, working from the top of the wall downward. To reduce "thermal bridging," remove any protruding siding nails rather than hammering them back into the sheathing. Examine the sheathing boards for soundness and replace any rotted ones. Pay particular attention to the areas above and under windows and doors, where water may have worked behind defective flashing or soaked into open joints.

If the drip-cap flashing has rusted out (with luck, the original builders used copper instead of galvanized steel), the sheathing beneath it and under apparently solid window casings will most likely suffer some degree of rot. The wood

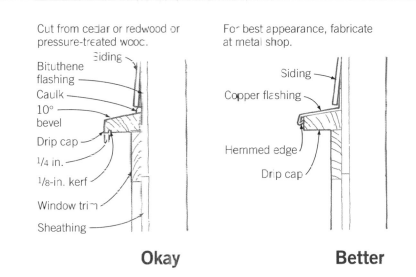

Two Wood Drip Caps for Windows

Cut from cedar or redwood or pressure-treated wood.
Siding
Bituthene flashing
Caulk
10° bevel
Drip cap
1/4 in.
1/8-in. kerf
Window trim
Sheathing

Okay

For best appearance, fabricate at metal shop.
Siding
Copper flashing
Hemmed edge
Drip cap

Better

drip moldings themselves should be sound. Fill any fissures with wood preservative and caulk before repainting. Replace or consolidate badly split or punky wood. The drawing above shows construction details. Sheathing behind the horns of windowsills, under door thresholds, and at the junction of porch roofs and building walls is also especially vulnerable to water damage.

Clearly, the best time to make wholesale changes in the size, number, and arrangement of windows and doors is after the siding has been stripped. This requires advance planning and purchasing, which harks back to the need for a master plan (see chapter 2). There are two other possible strategies worth considering at this point: strengthening the frame and tightening up the building envelope.

Strengthening the Frame

The stability of a braced timber frame depends on the integrity of its knee braces more than it does on the timbers themselves or even the joinery. Horizontal sheathing boards contribute only marginally to racking resistance. A frame that has suffered a fair amount of racking and then withstood the rigors of realignment is apt to be

The ready availability of old-growth lumber explains why eighteenth- and nineteenth-century houses were usually sheathed with wide boards. The diagonal tongue-and-groove board siding visible on this dormer proves that it was added much later, most likely in the early to middle twentieth century.

The discontinuity between the sheathing boards at the windows and door proves that they were later (and considerably smaller) additions.

fairly loose in the joints. Although this might be a desirable state for a practitioner of yoga, it's not one conducive to the long-term stability of a house.

It's not always possible to stiffen the knee braces directly. Quite often, there weren't enough of them to begin with or critical braces were sacrificed to remodeling. The problem can be solved satisfactorily by skinning the old sheathing boards with new ½-in. CDX plywood. This is an especially good idea when you intend to replace all the old windows. Although you can seal the joints between plywood sheets and at building corners with polyethylene tape, thereby eliminating the need to otherwise cover the old sheathing boards with an infiltration retarder (such as Tyvek or Typar housewrap), you'll still need to cover the plywood with coursed 15-lb. tarpaper to make what cutting-edge architects and building engineers call a *drainage plane*—that is, something to keep any

Sheathing the old boards with ½-in. CDX plywood greatly ncreases the structural strength of the rame. It also simplifies nstalling new windows and makes for a tighter wall.

water that leaks beneath the siding out of the building wall proper. Tarpaper is cheaper than housewrap. The tarpaper or housewrap should be cut to fold into window openings as if it were flashing.

Tightening Up the Building Envelope

When boosting structural strength is not a consideration but increasing the insulation value of the building shell is, adding rigid insulating foam boards to the outside may make sense. Just 1 in. of polyisocyanurate foam (R-7) will increase the R-value (resistance to heat transfer) of a fiberglass-filled or blown-in cellulose–filled 2–4 wall cavity by almost 40 percent, without disturbing the finished interior wall or reducing the pleasing reveal of a corner post or ceiling beam. If the existing windows will be left in place, the outside casing boards are simply removed and extensions are added to bring the

Although primarily used as an underlayment for vinyl siding, ½-in.-thick rigid foam insulation can also be used to increase the R-value and air resistance of a wall that will be re-sided with wood clapboards while possibly avoiding the need to build out the trim.

Insulation Concerns

There is some justifiable concern and not a little difference of opinion as to whether insulating the outside of the building wall can increase the severity of internal condensation problems and cause rot in the underside of the siding. This is especially the case if you use the vapor-impermeable aluminum–foil-skinned panels. At the time of this writing, the prevailing wisdom seems to be that you should not use any vapor barrier on the inside wall, except perhaps in a very cold climate, and that the wood siding should be installed over furring strips so that it can dry out in back. When its seams are taped, the foil-faced foam panel serves as both a drainage plane and an infiltration barrier.

jambs flush to the new surface before reinstalling the trim. As with plywood, the joints between the foam panels should also be taped to reduce infiltration.

Using Housewrap

If neither strengthening the frame nor tightening up the building envelope is pursued, and you are simply re-siding over the original board sheathing, you must use housewrap, which serves both drainage plane and infiltration barrier functions, if you want your house to stay tight and dry. I can't think of any better use for this product or a compelling reason to use it anywhere else, despite the ubiquitous ads showing new houses swaddled in the stuff and its recent promotion to code-mandated status. Install the barrier fabric over existing doors and windows, leaving at least an extra inch or so when you cut out the openings. These flanges are then tucked under the casing boards, which must be gently pried up to admit the barrier.

Before the invention of these high-tech spun plastic fabrics, rosin-coated builder's paper was used for the same purpose. Although cheaper (and easier to write on with a pencil or chalk), building paper can actually contribute to structural decay. Being porous, builder's paper absorbs water from a leaking flashing or exposed joint and holds it against the sheathing. Tarpaper was also thought to contribute to rotted walls because it seemed to act as an outside vapor barrier, trapping condensation between itself and the sheathing. Although it's possible that this could happen with an uninsulated house, tarpaper is actually quite vapor permeable and does not cause any problems with well-insulated walls. In fact, it actually makes a more water-resistant drainage plane than housewrap; however the numerous seams that are the result of its 3-ft. width (housewrap is 9 ft. wide) make it a poor air barrier. Since water infiltration into the sheathing is less likely to occur and easier to control than air infiltration, housewrap is preferable to tarpaper. (See chapter 8 for more information.)

Dealing with Buttress Walls

The junction of the siding with a concrete buttress wall is another problem area for siding. Proper installation of flashing is absolutely critical in preventing rot and the inevitable replacement of the sills and other framing members. Blistered or peeling paint and moist siding are sure-fire signs of water damage. Replace all rotted sheathing as necessary. Use pressure-treated boards (shimmed as needed to match the thickness of the existing sound sheathing) for the first courses, where wood is close to masonry.

Correct the pitch of the concrete wall for positive drainage by beveling its edge with a cold chisel or by adding a sloped mortar cap. When the mortar is dry, nail 12-in.-wide lead flashing to the sheathing, allowing the bottom to overlap

Housewrap is a definite requirement when re-siding over old board sheathing. There's one problem with the installation shown here, though: The wrap should have been installed beneath the picture-window mounting flanges rather than on top of them.

To avoid the problems inherent in flashing the base of the wall to a buttressed foundation, the water table on the front wall was built to project out over the foundation. The water table on the adjacent wall is more typical.

and cover the top of the wall. Seal the metal to the concrete with a highly flexible caulking (for example, Geocel). Corner joints are folded and lapped similar to the joint between the base and step flashings of a chimney. The finished flashing should extend at least 6 in. up onto the sheathing, with at least a 1-in. reveal between the top of the wall and the bottom of the first course of siding. Because the exposed lead is accessible to children and pets, it should be given a protective coat of paint.

Wood Shingle Siding

Along the New England coast up into the Maritimes and throughout the Pacific Northwest, cedar shingles have always been a traditional siding. This naturally decay-resistant wood weathers to a soft silvery gray, requiring no other finish or paint. The shingles are durable, watertight, and cost less than clapboards. The only real difference between roof and wall application is the maximum permitted exposure. Because wall shingles are not so

Replacing Individual Clapboards

Clapboards do not always need to be replaced en masse. Sometimes only a few individual pieces are damaged or rotted. It's even possible to repair splits by gently prying them apart, cleaning out any debris with a small brass brush or compressed air, and coating both edges with waterproof resorcinol glue. Use a squeeze bottle or glue syringe. Tack a small wooden block under the butt of the clapboard to force the crack closed until after the glue sets. This is a stronger and more permanent fix than caulk.

To replace a short piece of clapboard, saw through the face of the damaged piece with a fine-toothed backsaw or flush-cut tenon saw. A small, fine-tooth cordless circular saw is another good tool but don't use ordinary circular saws or jigsaws. Power tools are too hard to control, and it's almost impossible to avoid overcutting or splintering the adjacent siding.

Split the clapboard with a chisel. To remove the remaining inch or so wedged up under the next course, carefully try to pull the nails with a small flatbar. If they are too snug, gently pry from beneath the clapboard, loosening it just enough to slip the end of a standard

hacksaw blade (or mini-hacksaw) up under it to cut the nails flush with the sheathing. Then continue the vertical end cuts by pushing a sharp ¼-in. chisel up under the overlying clapboard and carefully extricate the scrap piece. Soak the butt ends with water-repellent preservative and insert back-primed new clapboard.

Because of their greater exposure to moisture, the clapboards at the bottom of the wall usually decay and need to be replaced long before those in more protected spots. Note the rebuilt water table. Maintaining the paint could have avoided or at least postponed the extensive reconstruction.

directly exposed to rain, the exposure can be greater (the rule is half the length of the shingle less ½ in.; thus for a 16-in. shingle, the exposure is 7½ in.). Also, unless the shingles are bone dry, they don't need to be spaced for expansion. When fitted so that their butts just barely touch each other, the natural taper of the shingle from bottom to top provides all the spacing needed while limiting rain and wind infiltration.

Wood shingles are typically butted to trim boards and window casings, although corner-board trim is sometimes omitted and the shingles are mitered or butted together, as shown in the top photo at right. Because shingles taper, they must be cut to fit square against trim boards. A utility knife, a framing square, and a small block or finger plane are the most efficient tools for cutting and trimming wood shingles. A portable table saw kept close at hand on the scaffolding is also helpful, especially for repetitive angles and crosscuts.

Individual damaged wood siding shingles can be replaced in the same way as wood roof shingles (see the sidebar on p. 175).

Some Other Siding Choices

Board-and-batten siding, which often characterizes contemporary "rustic" style as well as sheds, barns, and other rough structures, was actually a distinguishing feature of Andrew Jackson Downing's early Gothic Revival cottages of the 1840s. Planed vertical boards were nailed to horizontal blocking let into the studs or directly to the sheathing boards. The joints between them were covered with thin strips of wood (*battens*), either plain or decoratively beaded, to create an attractive and economical siding. Fitting and cutting are simplified because the corner boards, window casing, and other trim boards are nailed over the boarding. The battens simply butt against the trim. When a board must be spliced, the joint is beveled to shed water.

Woven corners are more common along the West Coast than in the East, where houses are traditionally trimmed out with corner boards instead. If carefully done, a woven corner is both good looking and requires less maintenance (that is, recurrent caulking) than butted corners. As is evident here, the orientation of the overlapped corner pieces alternates between courses.

Board-and-batten siding was a hallmark of the Gothic Revival and Carpenter Gothic styles of the 1840s to 1860s. So was the decorative treatment of the rake fascia, or bargeboard (*vergeboard* is another regional term).

Board-and-Batten Siding

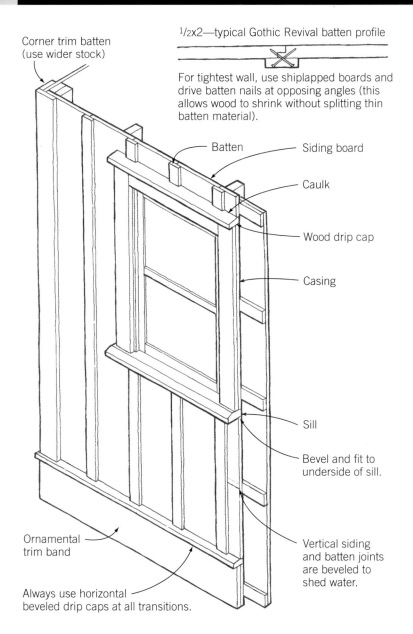

Corner trim batten (use wider stock)

1/2x2—typical Gothic Revival batten profile

For tightest wall, use shiplapped boards and drive batten nails at opposing angles (this allows wood to shrink without splitting thin batten material).

Batten

Siding board

Caulk

Wood drip cap

Casing

Sill

Bevel and fit to underside of sill.

Vertical siding and batten joints are beveled to shed water.

Ornamental trim band

Always use horizontal beveled drip caps at all transitions.

A variety of ornamental banding effects can be created with a minimum of labor and expense. The drawing at left shows some of the details. For a tighter wall, use modern tongue-and-groove or shiplapped boarding instead of square-edged boards, but don't eliminate the battens and ornamental trim. Unadorned vertical board siding is much too contemporary to suit an old house.

Board-and-batten siding can be retrofitted over plywood or foam sheathing with the addition of 1x3 horizontal nailers (also called strapping or furring). Fasten the siding with ring-shank stainless-steel siding nails to prevent rust stains and to minimize movement. To reduce the chances of excessive swelling and shrinkage, which will loosen the siding and cause splits, boards should not be wider than 8 in. Also, if the nails are driven at opposing angles to each other (only two per board), the board will tend to slide down the nail as it shrinks, preventing splits and keeping it tight.

DROP SIDING The steam-powered mills of the post–Civil War years turned out dozens of patterned edge-matched (that is, shiplapped or tongue-and-groove) board sidings that enjoyed great popularity well into the twentieth century. Of the many *drop sidings* (all of which are installed flat directly to the studs to serve as combination siding and sheathing), the "novelty" pattern (also called German or cove pattern), first patented around 1865, is one of the few that still enjoys any significant use today. Its dished-out upper edge enables the joint to shed water when applied horizontally, resulting in a siding that is self-aligning and extremely fast and economical to install. As with board-and-batten siding, the fit to trim boards does not have to be exact, because the boards and casings are applied over the siding. The 8d stainless-steel siding nails are driven through the boards directly into the studding.

SHIPLAP SIDING The drawing at right shows another siding option, which is especially suited for application over 1-in. foam sheathing. Narrow 1x4 or 1x5 shiplapped board, when overlapped clapboard-style, is almost indistinguishable from the real item and much less costly and labor intensive; 10d stainless-steel nails will penetrate the foam and secure the siding to the studs. Because of the extra thickness, corner and casing trim and frieze boards must be at least 1¼ in. thick. If custom milling is unavailable, substitute standard 2x stock instead.

This mock-clapboard siding works best with the narrow brickmold supplied with modern factory-built windows, because the end-nailed siding must catch into the studs beside the window jambs. Old-fashioned flat casings are usually too wide to allow this, unless extra jack studding can be added to the interior wall cavity.

Before there was aluminum or vinyl, there was asphalt shingle siding. These lock-tab shingles were used to quickly cover over clapboards that someone got tired of repainting. The only good thing about asphalt shingle sidings is that they tended to keep the property taxes low.

Two Clapboard-Like Sidings

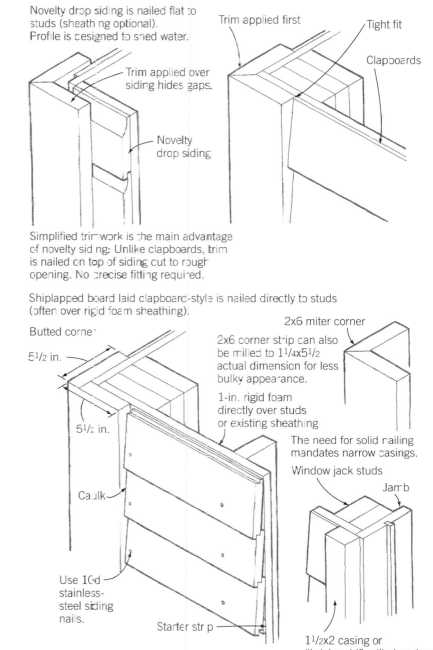

Novelty drop siding is nailed flat to studs (sheathing optional). Profile is designed to shed water.

Trim applied over siding hides gaps.

Novelty drop siding

Trim applied first

Tight fit

Clapboards

Simplified trimwork is the main advantage of novelty siding: Unlike clapboards, trim is nailed on top of siding cut to rough opening. No precise fitting required.

Shiplapped board laid clapboard-style is nailed directly to studs (often over rigid foam sheathing).

Butted corner

5½ in.

5½ in.

Caulk

Use 10d stainless-steel siding nails.

Starter strip

2x6 miter corner

2x6 corner strip can also be milled to 1¼x5½ actual dimension for less bulky appearance.

1-in. rigid foam directly over studs or existing sheathing

The need for solid railing mandates narrow casings.

Window jack studs

Jamb

1½x2 casing or "brickmold" milled casings

Cornice trim is especially vulnerable to water damage. Re-creating the cornice with standard flat boards and cove moldings is a much less expensive option than custom milling to match obsolete molding patterns.

Wherever two boards butt together, a potential water trap is formed. Even when it's painted, end grain can wick water into a board, causing peeling paint and rot. This is a good reason to seal butt joints with paintable caulk. For additional protection, brush a water-repellent wood preservative into cracks and problem areas before caulking or repainting.

REPAIRING AND REPLACING EXTERIOR TRIM

Ideally, missing, damaged, or rotted trim boards are repaired or replaced after the old siding has been removed and before the new siding is installed. Because even sound trim can almost always benefit from a new coat of paint, this is a good time to do it. Repainting the trim before installing the siding also prevents spattered walls and avoids a lot of tedious cutting-in, especially when using two or more colors. Examine existing trimwork for any signs of moisture damage. The source of the leak must be fixed and the wood allowed to dry out before it can be successfully primed and repainted.

If you cannot afford clear or #1 pine for the trim boards, select the best common pine you can, choosing straight boards with only a few tight face knots. Prime them with an exterior-grade shellac-based sealer to prevent the knots from bleeding through the paint (because knots absorb water more readily than the surrounding wood, they are a prime vector of decay). Small holes are best filled with caulk. Plug larger holes and pockets of rot with an epoxy-based wood filler.

Matching Cornice Molding

High above the ground and at the edge of the roof where water and ice marshal their destructive power, the cornice trim is exquisitely vulnerable to both neglect and exposure. As was shown in the previous chapter, this is especially the case when it incorporates a built-in gutter. The elaborate cornices of both classical and Victorian styles expose literally hundreds of lineal feet of running joints to the probing insinuation of water. It's only a matter of time before water breaches a niche left undefended by neglected caulk or paint.

Since the 1980s, there has been a proliferation of specialty suppliers of millwork copied from traditional patterns. You may be able to order an exact match for your molding or other damaged decorative trim from a catalog at a much more reasonable price than the traditional alternative of custom milling at a local shop, where you'll have to pay a setup charge of $75 to $300 on top of the $3 to $5 per lineal foot the molding might cost.

Standard stock can sometimes be artfully combined to re-create the impression of the original in lieu of a perfect copy. For example, sometimes the original molding may almost match a modern off-the-shelf pattern or a melding of two or more stock pieces. With patience and a contour gauge, you might successfully sculpt a stock molding into a reasonable facsimile of the original. If the piece being replaced is small, the match need not be perfect. You won't notice the difference from the ground once the patch is painted in. When all the trim has to be replaced, a flat board, given beveled edges and installed at an angle to a plumb fascia can make a passable substitute for expensive crown molding.

Retrofitting Soffit Vents

The soffit—the underside of the cornice—is another area that frequently demands attention, not because of rot but because of potential problems that are caused by modern insulation methods.

Capping the attic of an old house with insulation causes a problem its old-time builders could not have anticipated. The insulation impedes the otherwise strong convective air movements that carry warm moist air from the house to the outside. Instead, the moisture condenses within the insulation or on the underside of the roof deck, soaking both wood and insulation, which eventually causes rot (more on this in chapter 8). Modern construction practice seeks to prevent condensation by providing a ventilation flow from an inlet on the underside

An unchecked leak in the roofing above has destroyed most of the soffit and a good part of the Italianate bracket that supports and adorns it.

Simple detailing evokes the spirit of a nineteenth-century cornice.

TIP

Watching for Wasps

Keep a can of wasp killer handy when working around cornices; a ladder is no place for fancy dancing. Cover your strategic retreat with the spray and, later in the evening after all the foraging wasps have returned to the hive, launch an all-out assault. Wasps have their ecological niche, but it's better that it be somewhere other than your cornice. ▬▬ ▬▬ ▬▬

A slot cut into the existing soffit board accommodates a retrofitted standard aluminum vent strip.

of the eaves overhang (the soffit vent) to an exhaust vent at the ridge or gable walls and by installing an impermeable barrier on the warm side of the ceiling.

INSTALLING ROUND VENTS Old houses don't have soffit vents. Retrofitting one can be awkward and tricky. The exact method depends on how your particular cornice is put together. The standard but less than satisfactory solution is to drill three or four 2-in. holes through the soffit boards in all the spaces between rafter tails and install a round pop-in aluminum or plastic louver. Not only is there a good chance of breaking your wrist or fingers should the high-torque drill required for the job catch and bind but the total free surface area of the louvers is too small for adequate air flow.

INSTALLING SOFFIT VENT STRIPS If the soffit is composed of at least two boards, it's usually possible to remove one of them. (Remove the one that's easier and will do the least damage to adjoining trim pieces; split the board rather than risk splitting the other cornice members that must remain.) The edge of the remaining board is then pried down enough to admit the flange of a prefabricated aluminum soffit vent strip and then renailed. Rip a new board to fill in the rest of the soffit. This method is the only practical way to retrofit a pitched soffit.

For flat soffits, or where the soffit is a single board that you'd rather not try to remove, make the vent opening by cutting a 2-in.-wide slot down the length of the soffit with a circular saw. The edges of the cut are then pried down to admit the vent strip. If this does not prove possible, make the cut wider and then add a filler strip to each side to hold the vent in place. When painted in, it won't be noticeable from the ground.

DEALING WITH SOFFIT BLOCKAGE Sometimes, opening up the soffit won't create an air channel into the attic space. The space between the rafters is blocked by a board. Depending on the best access, the impediment can usually be removed with a ripping chisel (a heavy prybar or nail puller, which is hammered into a board to split it apart), working either from the vent slot or the attic. The left drawing on the facing page shows a complication found in some timber-frame houses. Here, since the rafters end directly on the plate and the eaves overhang is built against the wall, the plate fills the entire space between the rafters. The solution is to cut diagonal kerfs into the top of the plate with a reciprocating saw and chisel back its leading edge to make an air passage that's at least 1½ in. wide.

In cases where a wood gutter that has been attached to the building wall in lieu of a cornice proper is removed and not reinstalled, the bottom of the roof must be extended to make a proper eaves that can accommodate a soffit as well as fascia. Without this overhang, rainwater from the roof runs directly onto the siding, shortening its life and increasing the probability of water damage. If the wood gutter is left intact, soffit venting is not possible.

NONSTRUCTURAL EPOXY WOOD REPAIRS

Since the 1990s, in situ repair with epoxy consolidants and fillers has emerged from the esoteric provenance of museum conservationists and restoration consultants to become an increasingly popular alternative to removing and replacing rotted or missing ornamental exterior trim such as porch columns, windowsills, railings, cornice work, wood gutters, and more.

Despite its state-of-the-art aura, epoxy wood repair has been around since 1959. But because it can be tricky to work with (unless the mixing instructions are followed carefully and exactly), because the actual repair procedures are considerably more involved than ripping out a piece of rotted wood and cutting a new one to fit back in

Cutting Timber Plate for Air Circulation

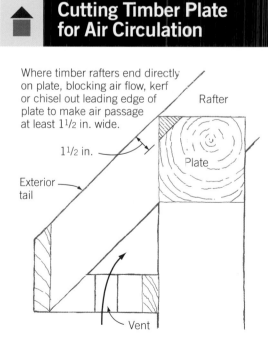

Where timber rafters end directly on plate, blocking air flow, kerf or chisel out leading edge of plate to make air passage at least 1½ in. wide.

1½ in.

Rafter

Plate

Exterior tail

Vent

Retrofitting Soffit Vents

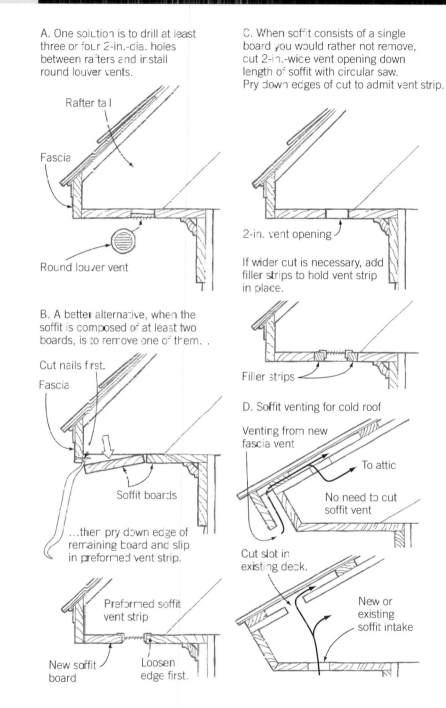

A. One solution is to drill at least three or four 2-in.-dia. holes between rafters and install round louver vents.

Rafter tail

Fascia

Round louver vent

B. A better alternative, when the soffit is composed of at least two boards, is to remove one of them. .

Cut nails first.

Fascia

Soffit boards

...then pry down edge of remaining board and slip in preformed vent strip.

Preformed soffit vent strip

New soffit board

Loosen edge first.

C. When soffit consists of a single board you would rather not remove, cut 2-in.-wide vent opening down length of soffit with circular saw. Pry down edges of cut to admit vent strip.

2-in. vent opening

If wider cut is necessary, add filler strips to hold vent strip in place.

Filler strips

D. Soffit venting for cold roof

Venting from new fascia vent

To attic

No need to cut soffit vent

Cut slot in existing deck.

New or existing soffit intake

Auto Body Repair Anyone?

Automobile body filler (a two-part system based on a polyester resin and a hardening agent and on a fiberglass reinforcement) can be an inexpensive alternative to epoxy for wood repair. Most professional old-house restorers advise against auto body–type fillers on the grounds that the patches don't accommodate changes in the wood as well as epoxy and so will eventually fall out. Others have reported no problems as long as the repair is made on thoroughly dried-out wood and will not be subject to flexing stresses.

A solution of three parts fiberglass-reinforced polyester resin and one part acetone will make an effective consolidant at about 20 percent of the cost of epoxy. I've had excellent results with Bondo brand filler for patching old mortise holes in interior doors.

the hole, and because the materials are expensive (about $64 per gallon), epoxy wood repair has always been something most renovators have read about or heard about rather than actually tried themselves.

Nonstructural Repair for the Nonexpert

The structural epoxy repairs described in chapter 4 certainly qualify as arcane and complex. They should not be entertained without the advice of an epoxy expert and the guidance of a structural engineer. But epoxy repair of nonstructural elements, particularly curved, carved, and nonstock moldings and railing parts, is straightforward, most likely easier, and probably more satisfactory than attempting it in wood. Epoxy fillers are almost always the better choice for fixing small pockets of rot.

If an epoxy repair is to last, whatever caused the problem in the first place must be addressed. If the source of the leak that has caused the rot is not found and fixed, the epoxy patch will probably fall out or the rot will re-infest the sur-

rounding wood. The epoxy may be indestructible, but the substrate to which it adheres has all the original frailties.

After all the loose and crumbling rot has been excavated, the surrounding wood must be allowed to dry out so that it can absorb enough epoxy for the repair to work. In dry weather, this takes a day or two. But when the wood is quite saturated, you may have to coax it along with a heat gun or wrap it in a black plastic tent to protect it from rain, as shown in the sidebar on pp. 222–223.

If you have been able to excise the rot cleanly and the remaining wood is solid, give it a coat of consolidant. Let it dry for a few hours and then mix and apply the epoxy filler while the consolidant is still tacky. Most repairs aren't that simple. The surrounding wood, while not exactly punky is still soft or may harbor unseen rot. Like crevasses, the true depth of fissures and splits may be unknown. Drill a series of ¼-in. holes about 1 in. apart, stopping just short of going all the way through. Blow out the holes with compressed air. Besides enabling you to inject the consolidant deep into the wood, these holes help dry out the wood.

WINDOWS

Like gutters and downspouts in winter, windows are an innately compromised solution to a basic and intractable conundrum of shelter: how to let light in while keeping cold or heat out. That glass succeeds very well at the former and not so well at the latter was obvious long before the energy crisis of the 1970s added *energy-efficient glass* to the homeowner's vocabulary. Traveling through Germany in the late sixteenth century, the French essayist Montaigne complained that the inhabitants had no "defense against the evening dew or the wind except ordinary glass, which was not in any way covered with wood."

Windows: A Little History

Window glass was not manufactured in America until the late 1700s, and few colonists could afford the luxury of glass panes. When it was first imported along with the rest of Georgian fashions around 1720, the rectangular-paned double-hung window was actually "single hung." Its upper sash was fixed. The movable lower sash was propped up with a notched stick or wooden pegs inserted into holes drilled in the jambs.

The true double-hung window, with moveable upper and lower sashes, showed up around 1750, about the same time as the pulley and counterweight balance system for raising and lowering them. The first American glassworks opened in Boston in the 1770s and was soon producing window glass claimed to be the equal of, if not superior to, the best English glass. In the early 1800s, the center of American window-glass manufacture shifted to Pittsburgh, where both coal and sand were plentiful.

Continuing improvements in flat-glass manufacturing brought the cost of glass down and the sizes of window panes up throughout the nineteenth century. The 12-over-12 and 9-over-9 configurations of the Georgian style gave way to the 6-over-6 divided light (to use the formal nomenclature) that was the signature window style of the antebellum farmhouse. By the 1850s, glassmakers were turning out panes as large as 15 in. by 30 in., and the 2-over-2 style became a standard window pattern. When even larger sizes became available after the Civil War, 2-over-1 and 1-over-1 sashes were the order of the day. At the same time, the revival of ecclesiastical stained glass that had begun in the 1830s spurred its use in residential architecture. While architects of the Queen Anne period (1880–1900) played with multicolored and multipaned upper sashes over single-glazed lowers, the Colonial Revival resurrected the 6-over-6 double-hung style, which even today is one of the most popular window patterns.

You don't have to be a fanatical preservationist to realize that careless window treatment is a prime example of remuddling at its worst. During the height of the colonial revival mania, many original Victorian 2-over-2 windows were frequently replaced with 6-over-6 ones in a misguided attempt to make the house look "old-fashioned." Yet the worst sins of the revivalists pale before the excesses of the 1950s and 1960s remodeling boom: Has anyone ever devised a more effective way to obliterate the harmonious proportions of a classic farmhouse than with a picture window?

Windows can help date a house. The frieze-band attic-story windows and the 6-over-6 lights on the first-floor windows are common features of the Greek Revival style of the 1830s and 1840s. But the center-gabled roof and the elliptical fanlight over the entry are characteristics of the transition between Greek Revival and the earlier Adamesque (or Federalist) style. This house more likely dates from 1820 than from 1830.

Step-by-Step Epoxy Wood Repair

Epoxy compounds are ideal for repairing complex rotted wood details in situ. After removing rusted nails and deteriorated wood, holes are drilled into the surrounding area and injected with epoxy consolidant, which is also brushed over the surface. The holes are patched with epoxy filler and smoothed over with a trowel blade dipped in lacquer thinner. After curing, the patch is shaped and sanded and then primed and painted.

Tools for mixing, brushing, and packing include wood tongue depressors, cheap plastic putty knives, disposable paintbrushes and flux brushes, plastic squirt bottles, and recycled plastic containers. Wear three or four pairs of disposable latex gloves so that you can peel them off as they get messy without having to stop and to put on new ones.

1 Dig out any crumbling wood and rusted nails. Heat-absorbent black plastic makes a tent to speed up the drying out of the wood while protecting it from rain and dew. (It can take up to 1 week for the wood to be completely dry.)

2 Inject liquid epoxy consolidant from a squeeze bottle into holes drilled into the surrounding area. Keep injecting consolidant until the holes stay filled.

3 Brush additional consolidant onto the exposed surfaces until they are saturated (until the surface remains glossy). Note the plastic taped to the work area to protect against spills, which are hard to clean up.

4 Knead resin and hardener together on a scrap of plywood.

5 Spread out the freshly mixed filler to increase its *pot life* (working time) and to prevent it from overheating.

6 To conserve expensive epoxy, embed wood "cheaters" in the filler as you make the repair.

7 Pack the repair by hand.

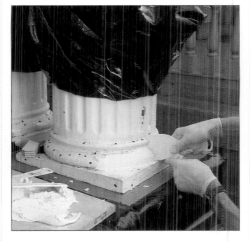

8 Before the putty hardens, sculpt it with a plastic putty knife cut to the appropriate profile of the repair.

9 Protect the repair while it cures overnight with the same plastic tent used to help the wood dry out.

10 Cured epoxy is easy to shape and sand with ordinary woodworking tools.

11 Fill any voids or imperfections with a thinned-down skim coat of epoxy. (Follow the manufacturer's directions.) Prime and paint the finished repair.

At the beginning of the nineteenth century, the indefatigable Count Benjamin Thomas Rumford suggested augmenting this "ordinary glass" with what later came to be called the *storm window.* By mid-century, the biennial ritual of putting up and taking down the storms was well established.

What to do with the windows? Should they be repaired or replaced? Is it possible to live comfortably with old windows? Are traditional wood storm panels, with their attendant maintenance headaches, still a better choice than convenient, but glaringly unhistorical, aluminum triple tracks? Is there any reasonable compromise?

Storm Windows

Windows are always a controversial subject with old houses, and storm windows arouse similar passions. If tradition wins out, then wood storms prevail, at least over triple-track aluminum, which loses on both appearance and energy efficiency (more heat is lost by conduction through the frame than is saved by the extra glazing). A possible alternative is the combination storm–screen insert offered by certain manufacturers. With these, a wooden frame permanently mounted to the edges of the exterior casing provides a thermal break for the removable thin-profile aluminum glazing and screen panels, which are seasonally exchanged.

There are also various so-called invisible storm windows that can be installed either on the outside or inside of the prime window. Basically, all of them consist of glass or acrylic panels that seal magnetically or mechanically to the exterior or interior jambs or casings. The external systems can be fitted with interchangeable screen panels, and the internal solid panels are simply stored for the summer months and replaced with internal screen panels. Besides being unobtrusive, these panels are tighter than conventional storms and can be quickly put up and taken down.

As with almost every other part of an old house, moisture and neglect are the usual suspects responsible for the ruin of old windows. Otherwise, if properly maintained, a wood window can easily last 200 years or more. Fortunately, very few old windows are so far gone that it makes more sense to replace them outright rather than repair or rebuild them. (This is arguably so even if you have to hire a skilled carpenter in lieu of doing it yourself.) There's a lot that can be done to repair and tighten up an old window.

Repair or Replace?

The economics of window replacement are not as straightforward as they might at first appear. Although double glazing reduces *radiation* heat loss by 40 percent compared to single glazing, it offers no inherently greater resistance to *infiltration* heat loss through gaps between glazing and sash or sash and frame. Adding a storm panel to an old window provides the same reduction in radiation heat-loss plus a 40 percent decrease in infiltration. Likewise improving or adding weatherstripping, replacing loose or missing glazing putty and cracked glass, and caulking trim boards will significantly reduce infiltration losses of existing windows.

While the thermal performance of a refurbished single-glazed old window fitted with a tight storm panel can never quite equal that of the best factory-made double-glazed windows, the difference is not so great as to merit the replacement of old windows solely for reasons of improved energy efficiency. The argument for new windows only makes sense when compared to the cost of doing nothing about the old ones or of paying a professional to improve them. Otherwise, you probably won't live long enough to amortize the investment.

On the other hand, the added convenience afforded by new windows can tip the scales in favor of replacement over repair. Modern windows offer the option of spectrally selective coatings that can effectively reduce undesirable heat gain. Triple glazing and inert gas fillings reduce radiant heat loss without the inconvenience of storm windows. Tilt-sashes and pop-out screen panels permit both sides of the window to be easily cleaned from the inside, and modern sash balances and hardware afford effortless operation without compromising weather tightness.

ENERGY EFFICIENCY OR CHARM? The lower heating and cooling bills gained by replacing old, leaky single-glazed windows with modern, tight double-glazed units must be counterpoised against the havoc such radical changes can wreak on the historical authenticity and architectural integrity of an old house. Much of the external charm (for lack of a better word) of an old house is concentrated in its windows. Unfortunately, the sight of so many ill-proportioned and mismatched vinyl-clad windows slapped like bandages over the wounds of a remodeled facade suggests that fidelity to the past does not always take precedence over the bottom line.

While insulated windows that are both energy-efficient and historically compatible are no longer as rare as they once were, they are still considerably more expensive than standard windows suitable only for new homes. This is especially so if you order true divided-light sash instead of the visually tacky "insert" muntins and flat wide-board casings instead of standard narrow brickmold casing or if the manufacturer duplicates your original windows. Living with your old windows and improving them one at a time is one way to balance conservation of energy and conservation of history.

Using Replacement Windows

If you decide to replace your old windows, you have a choice between installing new sash in the existing frame—known as a replacement window—or installing a complete new window unit in the existing rough opening. Replacement windows have the advantage of upgrading performance and energy efficiency without disturbing the original casings, siding, and interior finish. The least expensive replacement windows consist of plastic or metal channels and various trim kits or shims that fur out the original jambs to accommodate standardized modular sashes. Better systems duplicate the original sash and couple it with energy-efficient jamb adapters.

Replacing the entire window makes more sense if you plan to remove the siding or the interior wall finish in any case. Because a new window also includes a new frame, you save the repair of rotted jambs and sills. Also, the seal between the casings of a new window and the wall sheathing can be tighter, providing better protection against moisture and air infiltration. Finally, because sash and tracks are integral, there is less chance of the mechanical problems that often plague replacement windows.

Avoid Vinyl and Aluminum Cladding

Whether replacement window or new window, I wouldn't choose any system that involves exterior vinyl or aluminum cladding. Vinyl is a plastic and will therefore eventually degrade. Whether in 25 years or 75 years, when it does, it can't be rejuvenated with a coat of paint, taken apart and replaced, or given a new lease on life by an epoxy consolidant. Granted, long-term durability is not such an issue with aluminum cladding. But if water somehow works into the wood beneath either cladding, the wood core

TIP

Replacement or New?

There's a lot more labor involved in removing an old window and patching the siding and interior finish than there is in just retrofitting new sash and channels, so unless you do the work yourself, installing replacement windows will be considerably less expensive than replacing windows. Otherwise, there's very little difference in price between a high-quality replacement window and a new window unit. ███ ███ ███

A Double-Hung Window

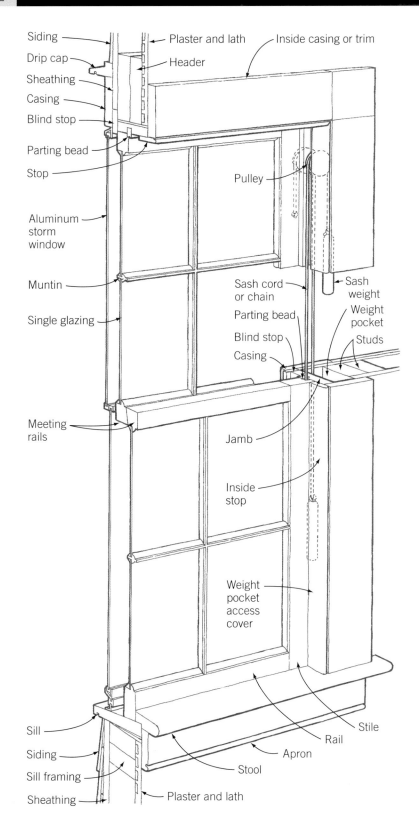

Siding
Drip cap
Sheathing
Casing
Blind stop
Parting bead
Stop
Aluminum storm window
Muntin
Single glazing
Meeting rails
Sill
Siding
Sill framing
Sheathing

Plaster and lath
Header
Inside casing or trim
Pulley
Sash cord or chain
Parting bead
Blind stop
Casing
Sash weight
Weight pocket
Studs
Jamb
Inside stop
Weight pocket access cover
Plaster and lath
Stool
Apron
Rail
Stile

can rot—undetected and unfixable. Furthermore, unlike wood windows, which are nailed through the casings into the sheathing, vinyl and aluminum-clad windows (and extruded windows as well) install with a nailing flange concealed beneath the siding. If there are problems and the window must be replaced, the adjacent siding must come off, too. Nevertheless, judging by the selection available at most lumberyards and home superstores, the all-wood window appears headed for the endangered species list.

Fortunately, since the turn of the millennium, a window built of rigid fiberglass has been introduced to the market. Unlike aluminum and even more so, vinyl, it is thermally stable and structurally stronger than wood, impervious to decay, and paintable. Currently manufactured exclusively by Marvin, the only drawback to the Integrity line is the fairly limited selection of sizes and styles, which might limit their applicability to historic houses.

Sash Repair and Rehabilitation

Although their usual condition would seem to belie the fact, both sashes of a nineteenth-century double-hung window were normally operable (that is, you could easily move them up and down). Ventilation of noxious "vitiated" air was a particular obsession of doctors, public-health experts, architects, and most every other practical and moral authority of the time. The double hung was preferable to the casement window because it could provide fresh air without admitting rain or snow. Furthermore, by sliding the sashes halfway past each other, the outside of the window could be cleaned from inside the house.

But for some reason, once a window was painted shut, it tended to stay that way. If the upper sash is caulked on its outside or otherwise fastened to the jambs (look for wood blocks under the corner of the meeting rail, it was either never intended to move in the first place or was fixed at some later date. Even so, you may wish to restore its operability. In any case, freeing a frozen sash is not only important for its own sake but is also a prerequisite for any other repairs.

For obvious reasons, the sill is the most vulnerable surface of any window. Neglecting routine painting and caulking allows water to soak into the wood, opening fissures and splits that harbor rot. The weathertightness of the joint between the bottom of the jamb and the top of the sill depends on the integrity of its caulking. If unchecked, the decay will work inward, infecting the sheathing, the studs, and all the way down to the sills. Rotted sills and jambs are ideal candidates for epoxy consolidation and patching. Otherwise, the rotted sill must be torn out and replaced with a new one.

Assuming that the sill and jambs are basically sound, the outside face of the sash is next most likely to show the ravages of weather and time. Fissures in the wood will show through the flaking paint of the bottom rail. The joint between the rail and the side stiles may be completely rotted. The glazing putty that once anchored the panes to their muntins will have cracked and fallen out. The panes themselves may be cracked or missing. Or, while the sash and glazing itself may be in good shape, the ropes, springs, or other tension hardware that held it in place may be broken or missing. The sashes may rattle about in their jambs, leaking air and water, or, as is more likely, be painted or even nailed tight.

FIRST FREE THE SASHES Because sash and glazing repair are best undertaken in the workshop, the ability to remove a sash without damaging it or the rest of the window is a fundamental skill of window repair.

First dampen the sash area with a mister to contain any lead dust and then carefully score the joint between the stiles and the stops of the lower sash with a utility knife to keep the paint from chipping. Work a wide stiff putty knife along all four edges of the sash. You may have to coax it along with gentle hammer taps. If possi-

Very few old windows are so badly deteriorated that it isn't worth taking the time to rebuild them. In this case, reglazing the sashes, brushing the woodwork with epoxy consolidant, and using some putty and paint will restore this window's appearance and usefulness.

The joint between the windowsill and casing is the most vulnerable part of the window frame. Neglecting timely repainting and caulking allowed the damage to progress to the point at which the entire sill and casing must be replaced.

ble, break the paint along the outside of the sash, too. Then slide the putty knife under the corner of the sash rail at the sill and lever it upward. Pry up the opposite corner, and then alternate lifting between corners until the sash frees up. If necessary, you can increase the leverage with a flatbar. To protect the wood, insert it between the knife and a scrap block. To break the seal on the upper sash, insert the knife be-tween the stiles and the parting beads and pry downward between the top rail and the head jamb.

REMOVE THE STOP Examine the stop for evidence of painted-over or filled-in screws. Chip the paint out of the slots and unscrew them. If the slot is stripped, you may be able to cut a new

Tips for Freeing the Sash

■ **Check for sash pins *before* you try to move a frozen sash.** These spring-loaded pins project through the stiles to catch in holes on the jambs, holding the window up. Any pins immobilized by encrusted paint will usually loosen up if you rotate them with a pair of gripping pliers. Replacement sash pins can be special-ordered by your local hardware store.

■ **If a sash refuses to move, it may be nailed or screwed shut.** The offending fasteners are typically driven through the edge of the sash and into the jambs or stops. You can feel them with your putty knife. Screws may be countersunk and filled. If you can't unscrew them or pull the nails, cut them with a mini-hacksaw inserted between the jamb and sash.

■ **Don't force the sash by hammering on a block of wood held against the meeting rails.** The rail joints may break before the sash moves.

■ **Be careful when freeing an upper sash.**
If the sash balances are missing or broken, it can drop suddenly and break the glass. If the bottom rail is badly deteriorated, it can fall off when you raise the sash. Lift carefully and hold the glass so that it doesn't fall out and break. Check that the glass isn't loose and tape any cracks (on both sides) so that the pane doesn't fall apart.

Sash pins that hold the lower sash up are often so encrusted with paint as to be inoperable. Check for broken-off sash pins before you try to force the sash.

one with your mini-hacksaw. If it is nailed instead, carefully pry it loose with your putty knife or a wide chisel (use an old one, not your best bench chisel). Most of the time, the wood is brittle and will split anyway. Don't worry, stop molding is a stock item or else easily duplicated. Remove only one stop molding, tap the sash gently with a rubber mallet to break any remaining paint seal, lever it up above the stool, and pull it sideways toward you.

REMOVE THE PARTING BEAD The parting bead must be removed to release the upper sash. If you're really careful and really lucky, you just might extricate the parting bead from its groove in the jamb without breaking it. Otherwise, split it out of the slot with a narrow chisel and plan on making a replacement. Predrill the new stops for wood screws and countersink the heads in tapered brass grommets for a traditional touch that also makes future sash removal a lot less destructive.

DETACH THE CORDS Carefully detach any sash cords, cables, or tape balances before lifting the sash free of the jambs. To avoiding snapping them, slowly release any tensioned steel cables or tapes. Check that the knots on the ends of the sash are fat enough to keep the cords from pulling past the pulleys and falling down into the weight pocket behind the jamb. Otherwise, push a finish nail through the end of the cord.

Repairing Rails

A rotted bottom sash rail or corner joint can be rebuilt with epoxy filler and consolidant or a dutchman patch. You can also mill a replacement rail. Drill out any remaining wood dowels that secure the stile (which, because of the end grain resting on the sill, tends to rot out first), and remove it. Most lumberyards carry standard sash stock. If yours is a unique pattern, a rail,

stile, or even the entire sash can be duplicated at a local woodshop. Square off the stub of the rail tenon and join it to the new stile with wood dowels and waterproof glue. (Unlike screws, wood dowels won't destroy your saw or plane blade when you need to shave down an edge.) If the joint is wobbly but still basically sound, stiffen it with galvanized drywall screws driven through the tenon. As a last resort, use flat angle irons.

Sash Balances

A sash that is heavy to lift and won't stay up has a balance problem. The old-fashioned counterweighted sash balance was ingeniously simple and efficient: Cast-iron weights concealed in a hollow space behind the jambs are matched to the weight of the sash, making it effectively weightless and allowing it to move easily and stay open at any desired point. The only weak link is the cord that connects the weights to the sash, which—being cotton—eventually wears out and breaks. For this reason, sash chain was sometimes used instead of cord, especially with a large, heavy sash.

Because cord replacement seems more complicated than it actually is, the average homeowner never ever attempted it. The top sash was nailed or blocked shut and the bottom sash was held open by the traditional wood stick or whatever else happened to be handy. The weights were simply left in the bottom of their hidden pockets.

Most counterweighted balances were abandoned inadvertently, when the cord broke or rotted old sashes were replaced. Beginning with the fuel crises of the 1970s, sash cords were deliberately cut, weights discarded, and the weight pockets stuffed with insulation in the name of energy efficiency. Usually, the sash runs were retrofitted with spring metal sash clips or new vinyl or aluminum tubular balance tracks. Because radiation and infiltration account for

Reglazing a Sash

To replace a broken pane of glass or reglaze a window, first chisel out the old glazing putty. You can use a stiff putty knife or chisel, but if you have a lot of windows to reglaze, consider a Prazi Putty Chaser, a carbide cutter with a guide bushing that is operated by your electric drill. In any case, to avoid cracking the glass, don't push on its edge; work against the wood instead. The pane is held against the muntins and sash by small metal wedges called glazier's points. Jamming a chisel into one full-tilt is a good way to crack the glass, so feel for them as you chip out the putty. Pry out the points and remove the pane.

If you are using oil-based paint, you can paint the glazing putty immediately. Otherwise, let it dry for at least 1 week. Leaving the putty unpainted hastens its premature failure. To make a watertight seal, the paint bead should just run slightly onto the glass.

1 Clean the rabbet down to bare wood and give it a coat of linseed oil.

2 Technique is the secret to cutting glass. Hold the cutter firmly between middle and index fingers and make a single cut with a smooth, uninterrupted motion. Cut the glass ⅛ in. smaller in both dimensions than the sash opening.

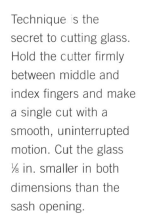

3 Immediately after scoring, grip the glass on both sides of the cut line and apply firm pressure to snap it. Use electrician's pliers or tile nippers when snapping off a narrow piece.

the lion's share of the heat loss associated with windows, the benefits of this conversion are questionable. On the other hand, some of the track systems were undeniably more weathertight.

A sash that was once counterbalanced will have grooved stiles that end in a circular bore where the knot was anchored. Ideally, both the sash cord pulleys and the weights were left behind when the cords were disconnected.

Replacing Rotted Sills

Neglecting routine painting and caulking will eventually rot out the sills and outside casings of any window. If unchecked, the decay will progress inward, attacking the wall, the studs, and even the foundation sills.

REMOVE THE OLD SILL If the windowsill is too far gone to be saved by an application of epoxy wood filler—that is, if it's nothing but dust held together by dirt—the window can be reconstructed. Before removing the sashes, scribe the line of the stiles against the parting bead and inside stop. This way you'll be sure of an exact duplicate for the sash run when you reinstall the sashes. Because the sill must be destroyed in order to remove it, record the details of its construction and measurements first. Then cut the sill in half with a reciprocating saw and then saw through the nails at the jambs. Since there's a good chance that the bottom ends of the jambs have also decayed, you may have to patch in a dutchman or epoxy putty.

MAKE A NEW SILL Old windowsills were typically fashioned from thicker stock than is used today, sometimes as much as 3 in. or 4 in. thick; finding a small timber of dry clear pine or fir stock is neither easy or inexpensive. Duplicate the sill (and the jambs if need be). Otherwise cut

Repairing Counterweighted Sash Balances

Although the quality of modern pressed pulleys is inferior to the original cast pulleys, replacement sash cord, pulleys, and possibly even weights are still available from specialty suppliers. (New weights are hard to find. Sometimes you can find discards at scrap yards or at dealers in architectural antiques.)

Push the replacement sash cord over the top of the pulley and down into the weight pocket where it can be fished out of the access hole. (If the window lacks an access hole, remove the inside jamb casing.) Usually you can fish the weight out through the access hole or position it close enough to the opening to tie off the sash cord.

The other end of the cord is knotted (and sometimes fitted to a split metal ring) and fits into a circular pocket in the sash. When properly adjusted, the weight should be 3 in. above the sill when the sashes are fully raised. If the weights are properly sized, the sash will stay put and not creep up or slither down when opened. You can tweak the weight by adding washers or pieces of lead or grinding off any extra. A length of 1½-in. polyvinyl chloride (PVC) pipe capped and filled with lead shot makes a pretty good substitute for a missing weight.

The parting bead and stop must allow enough room for easy movement of the sash. A putty knife makes a good spacer gauge. After removing or sanding down any paint buildup, coat the runs and the edges of the stiles with paraffin wax to ensure smooth operation. If the sash pulleys are bound up with layers of paint, remove them and dip them in paint stripper.

▲ Rebuilding a Rotted Windowsill from Inside

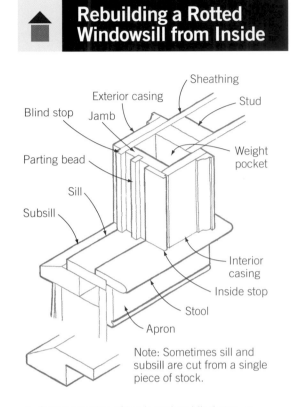

Note: Sometimes sill and subsill are cut from a single piece of stock.

1. Scribe location of jamb against blind stop or exterior sash. Scribe location of inside stop and parting bead on jamb.

2. Remove inside stop and parting bead. Take out sashes (not shown).

3. Cut paint or wallpaper against trim to prevent tears.

4. Carefully remove interior casings, stool, and apron.

5. Split or cut sill/subsill horns as needed to aid removal. Record size first.

6. Pry jambs free of exterior casing with flatbar, pulling window frame into room.

7. Fill unused weight pocket with solid blocking or insulation.

8. Replace unit. Nail to studs, hiding nails under stops.

the new sill from standard dimension lumber and add a filler piece to its outside edge to mimic the original depth.

INSTALL THE NEW SILL Because the bottoms of the casings and jambs are angled to fit the bevel of the sill (12 degrees is standard) the new sill cannot simply slide into the existing opening. (The opening at the front is narrower than the opening at the back and the sill is thicker at the back than at its front.) Inserting the sill from the inside of the window resolves the problem and creates new ones since the stool and apron must be removed. A workable compromise might be to mill the sill so that its maximum depth is equal to the minimum opening and wedge it upward against the jambs after it is installed. Fill the gap with expandable foam caulk and nail an unobtrusive filler strip under the sill or join it to the underside of the sill as described above.

DOORS

Some of the techniques for repairing windows apply to doors as well. A door has a sill (the threshold) and head and side jambs. The jambs are fitted with stops, weatherstripping, and hardware that enables the door to open inward like a large casement window. Like a window sash, most wooden doors have rails and stiles. Some entry doors have glass, but most have thin panels of wood that float freely in the frame. Because these panels can expand and contract without affecting the width or height of the door, the stability of the rail-and-stile door is unequaled by any other wood door, and its construction has changed very little since its first appearance around 1700. (Earlier doors were usually windowless board-and-batten style.)

The formal entry of any house is a much too important aspect of its facade to neglect its maintenance. Unfortunately, this rather charming entry is rotting into the pavement. Portions of the arched ceiling have already fallen down.

An exterior door suffers from the same general debilities as do windows. But because it is in constant daily use, a door rarely reaches the point of disintegration before someone is forced to fix it.

Replacing a Threshold

A worn, wobbly threshold is the first symptom of trouble. The sill under a threshold is especially vulnerable to rot. The worst situation is when stone steps trap snow and water against the band of trim under the lip of the door sill.

Replacing a worn or rotted threshold is similar to repairing a windowsill.

REMOVE THE DOOR First, remove the door by driving out the hinge pins and set the door aside. Measure the overall dimensions of the threshold from horn to horn. Check the width, because thresholds often taper. Also determine whether its ends are at right angles to its length or at some weird taper to suit a set of skewed jambs. Thresholds are usually cut from red oak, which is durable, heavy, and expensive. Unlike softwood, you can't expect to force hardwood into too tight a space—the cut and fit must be exact. Take the time to lay out the cuts properly; you can't afford to make a mistake.

REMOVE A STOP The doorstop molding generally fits flush to the top of the threshold. At least one side must be taken off to pry up and remove the threshold. If the stop is a rabbet cut into the jambs, this step won't be necessary. Use the threshold as a template to guide layout of the replacement piece. New unpleasantries and hidden rot may be exposed when the threshold is removed. Sometimes the finish floor, subfloor, portions of joists, and a good section of underlying sill have decayed. A simple hour's job can explode exponentially into a major repair project. But armed with perseverance and bitter resignation, you can rebuild all the rotted structure and finally, several days later, get back to installing the new threshold.

FIT THE NEW THRESHOLD Flash the front face of the new sheathing and the portion of the new subfloor under the threshold and up onto the wall studs with Bituthene® membrane to reduce the chance of new rot. Check the threshold for fit against the jambs. Then rehang the door and see if it closes properly. Now's the best time to find out if you need to shim up the threshold a bit or plane it down. As a general rule, thresholds should be laid parallel to the subfloor even if the floor is not level.

It's better to trim the bottom of the door to fit the threshold than to tilt a threshold to fit the door. Sometimes, though, you'll have to split the difference for the best overall appearance. If

everything is satisfactory, run several beads of silicone caulk over the membrane and especially where the ends of the threshold will butt the jambs, and set it back in place. Drill the wood for finish nails or countersink and plug screws. Seal the threshold with a penetrating oil finish, because any varnish will soon scuff off.

Taking Care of Doors

Wood doors that stick are one reason why so many insulated steel doors are sold. I suspect that if more attention were paid to proper preparation and maintenance of the door, dimensional stability wouldn't be such an issue. A rail-and-stile wood door is an investment. Protect all faces and edges, especially the bottom and top, with three coats of high-quality exterior spar varnish. Apply the finish when the humidity is low. Renew the finish as soon as it starts to show signs of wear, and recoat any deep scratches immediately. The idea is to prevent the wood from absorbing the moisture that causes seasonal changes in dimension—and sticking. Two coats of an oil-based enamel over a suitable primer is equally effective. The finish should be applied to the door before the hardware is installed and to the jambs as well.

Doors that stick are doors that haven't been taken care of. After decades of erosion by generations of scratching dogs and the tumultuous comings and goings of daily life, the rails and stiles pull apart. A loose-jointed door can change shape, perhaps becoming wider at the bottom or sagging onto the threshold. When the latch starts missing its strike, the door must be slammed to close. A panel splits, cold air rushes in unhindered. Finally, the exasperated homeowner planes down the sticking edge. Unpainted, it swells again in the wet fall air and twists so that the door no longer closes against its stop.

A Solid-Wood Threshold

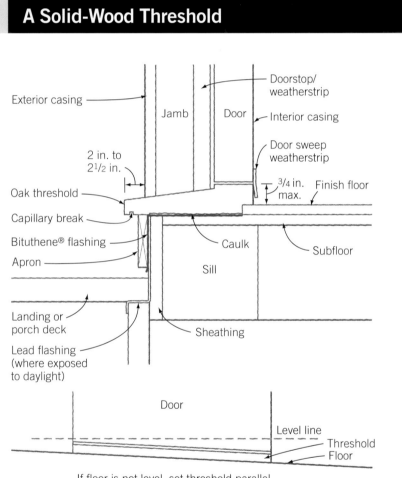

Exterior casing

Jamb

Door

Doorstop/ weatherstrip

Interior casing

Door sweep weatherstrip

2 in. to 2 1/2 in.

3/4 in. max.

Finish floor

Oak threshold

Capillary break

Bituthene® flashing

Apron

Caulk

Sill

Subfloor

Landing or porch deck

Sheathing

Lead flashing (where exposed to daylight)

Door

Level line

Threshold

Floor

If floor is not level, set threshold parallel with floor (do not shim level). Trim door bottom to match.

Furniture clamps and glue will squeeze open joints back together. Pin the rail tenons with countersunk galvanized wood screws. Check the corners for square before fastening them; years of slack may have allowed the door to fall from rectilinear grace. Panels can be mended with caulk or epoxy filler. The bead molding or even a missing panel can be replaced.

Other than a new door, there's no cure for a warped edge but to remove the stop and renail it to follow the actual rather than ideal edge. Sanding the old door smooth and repainting is more than a facelift; by keeping the door from swelling or joints from drying out and becoming unglued, future problems are prevented. If the door still sticks, the hinge screws might be loose, allowing the door to fall toward the jamb. Replace loose screws with longer or thicker ones. If the screws go through the jamb and into the space behind it without a solid purchase, hammer tapered slivers of pine (golf tees or toothpicks work well, if you have them) dipped in glue into the old screw hole until it won't take any more. These restored holes will hold screws as well as any new wood.

Storm Doors

In cold climates, an entrance door should never open to the outside. A tight storm door creates an air lock that helps keep in heat, especially if it is a wood door rather than a cheap aluminum one. (This doesn't apply to top-of-the line foam-core aluminum storm doors, such as the Larsen line, which are both handsome and efficient.) In general, painted or stained wood storm doors tend to be more durable and are certainly more historically compatible. Quite a cottage industry in reproduction fancy Victorian storm doors has developed since the first edition of this book came out. A door equipped with interchange-able storm and screen panels will provide summer cooling as well.

Planing a Binding Door

To plane down the leading edge of a door that binds, first rub the jambs with chalk and force the door against them. The chalk will transfer to the door, indicating the places to shave down. Give the edge a slight bevel (about 3 degrees or $\frac{3}{32}$ in.) to ensure a good fit. If you remove the latch bolt and mounting plate first, all but the bottom edge can be planed with the door still hung. Seal the raw edges as soon as the final fit is made.

Before you decide to plane down a door, be sure that the problem isn't caused by something other than the swelling of the door or its jambs. Wood swells in humid weather and shrinks in dry weather. A door that closes fine in the summer but always sticks in winter is not swelling. Examine the gap between the top of the door and the head jamb. If one side is higher than the other, the door frame (and the whole wall) is being lifted by frost heave. Planing down the door to fit in winter will make it too loose in summer. You have a foundation problem, not a door problem.

When installing a storm door, take care that the latch handle does not interfere with the doorknob of the entrance door. Another common mistake is to set the latch so close to the edge of the door that you pinch your knuckles against the stop or jambs as you turn the inside handle. Screen doors are usually hung flush to the entry door casing. If the reveal on these casings is increased to $\frac{3}{4}$ in. or slightly more, the jamb itself provides a stop.

TIP

No Storm Doors with Steel Doors

Storm doors should not be installed with insulated steel doors. The heat trapped between the two doors can warp and degrade the plastic trim of the insulated unit (especially if it has been painted a dark color) and warp the door itself. ■■ ■■ ■■

7

Porches, Verandas, and Additions

In all countries like ours, where there are hot summers, a veranda, piazza, or colonnade is a necessary and delightful appendage to a dwelling house, and in fact during a considerable part of the year frequently becomes the lounging apartment of the family.

—ANDREW JACKSON DOWNING, *COTTAGE RESIDENCES*

More than just shelter from the elements, porches and verandas enclose a social space. They balance privacy and neighborliness, inviting intimacy, but not too much—a perfect place from which to watch the world go by.

The porch is as much a part of the iconography of the American house as the fireplace. The word and the form are derived from the Latin *porticus*, an architectural element designed to draw attention to the formal entries of the aristocratic townhouse or country manor. Although it did provide some protection from roof runoff and winter winds, the portico, with its fluted open columns and classically detailed triangular pediment, was never intended as an outdoor living space. It was too small.

The influence of Andrew Jackson Downing's naturalistic theories transformed the portico from an ornament into a "necessary and delightful appendage." As the passion for porches swept across the country, old farmhouses and stately manors alike were "modernized" by the indiscriminate addition of porches, verandas, and piazzas. No new house was considered complete without one.

Repairing Porches and Verandas

Properly speaking, a porch is a roofed gallery supported by columns that does not cover an entire wall. A veranda covers one or more walls. The term *piazza* is synonymous with both.

In northern climates, the porch can screen the house from the direct force of the wind and, when glassed in during the winter months, help reduce heating bills through solar gain. It is a place to hang clothes to dry on a rainy day or to start trays of seedlings in early spring. A glassed-in porch also makes an ideal winter workshop, where heavy power tools can be set up and boards cut while the main areas of the house are both rebuilt and lived in, safe from sawdust. If the door between the house and the porch is left ajar, the porch will reach a comfortable working temperature—any heat loss is offset by stoking the stove with construction scrap. In hot, sticky Southern climates, a veranda catches and encourages the slightest breezes.

Open or enclosed with glass or screen, a porch or veranda is a place to gather or sleep, a cool and shady refuge. Though the usefulness of a porch is counteracted to some extent by the diminished light level of the rooms behind it, this is not altogether undesirable: The rooms will seem cooler in summer and cozier in winter.

Common Problems

Although porches are psychologically part of a house's living space, they are physically outside the domain of the house. Thus their routine maintenance is often neglected until repair or demolition is unavoidable. This is unfortunate, because with proper construction and upkeep, a porch should last as long as the house

Porch Trouble Spots

Wherever water can enter and collect will eventually become a site for decay.

- Side wall
- Leaking or damaged flashing
- Worn-out roll roofing/rusted tin/bubbled or dried-out tar
- Rafter
- Leaking gutter
- Ceiling joist
- Rotted ceiling boards
- Fascia
- Dried-out caulking

Rain gets into columns through fascia, roof, and gutter leaks. Moisture condenses beneath paint film and is trapped at base of column. Drill 1-in. vent holes to prevent condensation, and pop in plastic midget louvers.

- Column
- Knots, splits
- Open joints
- Torus
- Plinth (pillow block)
- Runoff from deck
- Joist
- Exposed end grain
- Rim joists or girder
- Heaving foundation post, steel or masonry pier
- Rotted lattice (in direct contact with ground)

Water destroys porches; the greater exposure of a porch to rain and snow demands special protective features. The drawing at left shows some typical sites of structural damage.

THE PORCH ROOF A well-built porch begins with a tight roof that is properly flashed to the side wall. Because of the relatively shallow pitch, which encourages snow and ice buildup, porch roofs are susceptible to leakage and the effects of wind-driven rain. Early porches were often roofed with tin sheets, soldered at the seams; unless the metal was kept painted, it eventually rusted. Asphalt coatings not only have the unfortunate effect of hastening corrosion but also dry out and crack fairly quickly. Leaks in porch roofs soon cause structural decay. Sagging, warped, or water-stained ceiling boards are a telltale sign of a chronic leak. It may take extra blocking between the ceiling joists to screw distorted boards back down after the leak and any structural damage have been repaired.

Today, half-lap mineral-surfaced roll roofing applied over a Bituthene membrane is cheaper and easier to use than metal. Fiberglass-asphalt shingles could also be laid over the same membrane (which is superior to a cemented felt underlayment), even on roofs with slopes lower than 4 in 12. Organic felt shingles however, should not be used, because they would rot as they soaked up the moisture inevitably trapped between their undersides and the waterproof membrane.

The porch roof should be joined to the side wall of the house with copper or galvanized enamel-coated steel flashing. This flashing must extend up under the siding and down over the last course of roofing, with the bottom edge of the flashing embedded in flashing cement. More than on any other part of the house, gutters are a mandatory feature of porch roofs, because rainwater should not be allowed to splash against the porch skirts, foundation posts, and steps.

VULNERABLE JOINTS The floorboards, which are so exposed to the weather, are likely to be at least partially rotted. This decay can often infect the underlying framing. The bottoms of the posts or columns and rails and balusters are also likely victims of climate and neglect. Wherever a joint has opened up or end grain is left exposed, there is an opportunity for water to seep in and for fungi to begin their insidious work. Preventing joint failure and rot is as much a matter of attention to proper construction as it is to timely maintenance.

Disassembling the Porch

Unless a multistory porch is involved, the load carried on porch columns is quite light. No special jacking or support is needed to carry the roof while the columns, floor, and joists are removed. Use 4x4 jack posts, lifting from the porch deck to relieve the roof load. Then lower the roof back down onto 4x4 posts jammed between the ground and the underside of the porch headers. (These posts should be set at an angle to facilitate framing removal.)

Don't worry if the roof sags some during repairs; it's a simple matter to jack it back to level from the rebuilt porch deck. Use 2x12 pads above and below the posts to distribute the force. Often, as the roof is lifted, the porch columns or posts and their attached railings come up with it. It's safer to remove these elements than to leave them dangling. Removing railings and columns also makes it a lot easier and more comfortable to strip, repair, or repaint them on a sawhorse or in the workshop.

Repairing Porch Framing and Flooring

Replace rotted framing with pressure-treated lumber. Don't forget to pitch the joists about ⅛ in. per foot so the porch floor can drain. Because the flooring joints must follow the direction of the water flow, the floor joists must run perpendicular to the width of the porch.

When flashing is installed *over* rather than *under* siding, it will eventually and inevitably leak. Water can seep into the building walls as well as the porch ceiling and cause a great deal of hidden rot before the leak becomes obvious.

It takes very little to support a single-story porch roof. In this case, "strongbacks" of 2x6s nailed together in a T do the job.

TIP

Pressure-Treated Lumber

The advent of pressure-treated lumber in a wide variety of stock widths and styles, including ornamental turnings specifically designed for outdoor structures, has dramatically increased porch longevity and simplified repair work and upkeep. To take advantage of its benefits, use only kiln-dried-after-treatment (KDAT) wood. The standard grades typically have a high moisture content and will warp, twist, and split as they dry out. ■■■ ■■■ ■■■

TIP

Porch flooring

Tongue-and-groove porch flooring is not available in pressure-
treated wood. If your porch floor
will be exposed to excessive
moisture, you can use a router
or shaper to mill your own very
rot-resistant flooring from
square-edged pressure-treated
¾-in. boards (not radius-edged
5/4 decking). Always wear a
dust mask and observe recommended safety precautions
when working with pressure-
treated wood. ■■■

Use strings to establish level and straight lines
for the sills and joists. These will also show the
amount of correction needed to straighten sags
and bows in the existing framing caused by settled or lifted foundation posts or structural failure. An automobile screw jack will provide all
the lift you'll need.

If the existing floor framing is still relatively
sound, treated joists can be sistered alongside
partially decayed old wood. To extend the usefulness of the existing joists, coat their top edges
with preservative and a layer of flashing cement.
Joists can also rot along their bottom edges if
they are too close to the ground—8 in. is the
minimum recommended clearance for untreated wood.

Cut any sections of decayed flooring back to
sound wood over the middle of the nearest joist
and replace with similar stock. The traditional
material for porch decks is 1-in.-thick by 4-in.-
wide clear-grain Douglas fir or yellow pine
tongue-and-groove flooring. A good widely
available substitute is mahogany porch flooring,
which is cost-effective, rot resistant, and stable.
Use ¾-in.-thick flooring when the joists are
16 in. on center, or 5/4 (1⅛-in.-thick) flooring
when the joists are 24 in. on center. Soak each
board in a trough filled with wood preservative

The end grain of porch-floor boards is particularly
vulnerable to rot.

for at least 3 minutes, and let it dry for 2 days
before you paint it.

Use two coats of oil-based porch-and-deck
enamel on both sides and all edges of the board.
When installing the flooring, seal each tongue-
and-groove joint with a good-quality paintable
siliconized latex caulk as the pieces are installed.
This tedious and messy step will greatly reduce
water penetration and paint failure. The exposed
ends of the flooring boards can be protected
from water exposure by nailing a bullnose molding cut from an extra length of flooring over
them. Apply a third coat of enamel to the finished deck.

Repairing Porch Posts

Fortunately for the porch restorer, the typical
ornamental turned-wood porch post has a
squared section at top and bottom. Replacing
these rotted areas with a prosthetic section
requires a lot less skill than duplicating the
carved portions. Mate the new section to sound
old wood with a wood dowel or rebar pin.
Should complete replacement be necessary,
lumberyards stock turned hemlock, fir, and

▲ Protecting Exposed End Grain of Porch Decking

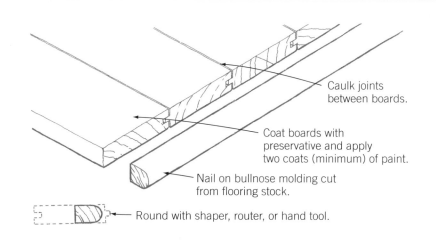

Caulk joints
between boards.

Coat boards with
preservative and apply
two coats (minimum) of paint.

Nail on bullnose molding cut
from flooring stock.

Round with shaper, router, or hand tool.

pressure-treated posts. Salvage yards specializing in architectural antiques are another source, if the standard patterns are not a good enough match. If all else fails, an exact replacement can be custom-turned at a woodworking shop. There are also firms that specialize in reproduction Victorian millwork and porch trim of all sorts.

Once the paint peels, hollow round columns start to split. These splits admit water, as does the exposed end grain at the column base and any open joints between elements of the capital. Water can then collect in the interior of the column and cause the staves to swell and bow or rot. These surfaces should be stripped, sanded, and sealed with preservative. Then they need to be primed, caulked, and given two top coats of latex paint (latex films are slightly more permeable than oil and will thus permit some vapor migration from the interior of the column).

Hollow columns will last a lot longer if vented. Drill several 1-in. holes in an inconspicuous part of the column just below the capital, away from the prevailing wind. Cover the openings with pop-in plastic midget louvers. Drill a hole up through the floorboards and column base from underneath the porch to allow trapped water to drain. Or drill ¼-in. weep holes around the base of the column, just above its plinth block (the square base on which the column sits).

Repairing Porch Railings

Because of their many joints, balusters and railings are especially prone to decay. A lot of future repair can be prevented by ensuring that the railings are properly supported by blocking inserted between the bottom rail and the deck every 3 ft. or 4 ft. This prevents the rails from sagging under stress and the joints from opening. Timely caulking and repainting will preserve untreated wood for a long time. If the railing needs to be replaced, use kiln-dried-after-

The Torus and the Plinth

Because water is easily trapped under them and sucked into the cracks between their joints, the plinth block and the torus (an ornamental wood disk between plinth and column proper) will almost always rot first, especially when caulking and painting are neglected. A common mistake is to fashion replacements from a solid block of wood, which leaves too much end grain exposed. Whether treated or not, any exposed end grain should be covered with miter-jointed moldings. This is one place where epoxy consolidation is easier and probably more economical than the highly skilled shopwork demanded by the repair of severely deteriorated columns. For one thing, the work can be done on site.

Given their intimate contact with the ground and shrubbery, the lattice panels that skirt the porch bottom are usually the first part of the porch to rot. Prefabricated pressure-treated lattice has simplified repairs; the panels are easily sandwiched between treated boards.

Bracing Porch Steps

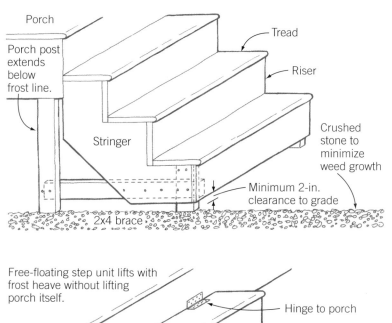

Porch

Porch post extends below frost line.

Tread

Riser

Stringer

Crushed stone to minimize weed growth

Minimum 2-in. clearance to grade

2x4 brace

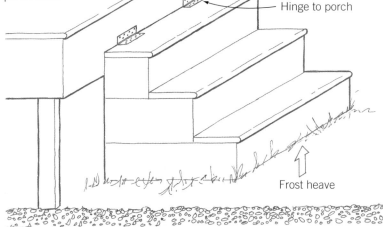

Free-floating step unit lifts with frost heave without lifting porch itself.

Hinge to porch

Frost heave

treatment (KDAT) lumber and turnings for the new work.

It's not unusual for porch railings to terminate at a turned post sawn in half and set directly against the wall over a trim board. If this board has rotted, or worse, was omitted, the new one should be made of treated wood.

Repairing Steps

Steps are another problem area, but their longevity has been greatly improved by pressure-treated wood. At the very least, the undercarriage and riser boards should be cut from treated stock even if the treads are made with ordinary fir or yellow pine.

Even so, never simply set the risers on a board or stone resting directly on the earth. Ideally, steps should be supported at the bottom by a footing that extends below the frost line to protect them from frost heave. If there are only two or three steps, you may be able to suspend the unit from the porch so frost heave won't be an issue. To do this, provide strong attachment under the top tread and add braces between the porch posts and the bottom of the stringers as shown in the drawing at left. For less formal setting, build the steps as a separate unit that simply rests against the porch. Then they are free to rise and fall without damage. If this independent stair is hinged to the porch frame, it can move, but not too much.

Repairing Porch Foundations

Very often the problem with a porch is not so much rotted framing, as it is unstable foundation supports. Porch sills and posts often rest on rocks or concrete blocks set directly on the ground. Sometimes they are carried by steel pipes driven into the earth. The seasonal lift and settlement of such foundations can sometimes rack a porch so badly that it starts to tear loose from the house.

A scary situation: Because the stones rest on top of the ground, frost has heaved this porch column off-kilter. Unchecked, the movement could eventually cause the column to kick out.

One solution to frost heave is a footing that extends below the frost line. There are two ways to provide this footing—posts on piers or posts directly in the ground. Because the ground under a porch isn't insulated with a snow cover, frost penetration is deeper than normal. Any postholes or pier should be dug 1 ft. deeper than the standard frost depth.

POSTS ON PIERS Dig holes below the local frost line and insert round paperboard forms, such as Sonotubes®. Cut the forms off a couple of inches above grade. Fill the forms and sink J-bolts into the wet concrete. Attach post anchors to the J-bolts and then pressure-treated posts between the piers and porch framing.

POSTS IN THE GROUND Dig postholes that are at least twice as wide as your posts. Pour about ½ cu. ft. of concrete in the hole to make a pad. An 80-lb. sack of concrete mix (such as Sakrete®) will make footing pads for two posts when poured into the hole. Let the concrete harden a day or two before setting any posts.

PERIMETER DRAINAGE Another way to prevent frost heave is to excavate a trench along the entire porch perimeter and set precast footing blocks on a layer of crushed stone. This technique is particularly effective in wet soil. Lay perforated drain pipe and provide an outlet at grade as for a standard perimeter drain system (see p. 106). Backfill with more crushed stone around the bases of the porch support posts and then with gravel to grade. Ideally, the porch drainage should be teed into the rest of the foundation drainage system, especially if it is part of a general foundation overhaul.

Repairing Stoops

Despite a preponderance of porches, the formal portico never became extinct. The *stoop*, a platform or small set of steps at the front entry sheltered by a small triangular roof, is its vestigial descendant.

Most porch stoops are not as elegant as this one.

The success of these additions is questionable. Sometimes utility triumphs over good taste, and a perfect facade is marred by a clumsy, ill-matched stoop. But then, a trellised stoop and its climbing vines or roses are certainly part of the charm of a country cottage. Because country people rarely use their front doors anyway, it's better to tear off a decayed or ugly stoop rather than rebuild it—or move it around back to the kitchen door where it will do some good. In the country, it's not unusual to find the front door walled over with a polyethylene sheet, sometimes even year-round. In the city, the back door is the service (delivery and servants') entrance; the front door retains its formal character and remoteness even today. City people new to the country can be identified by which door they walk up to first.

Proper flashing of a stoop roof to the side wall of the main house is the key to preventing rot. One detail that is often overlooked is the need for some sort of backing board between the roof brace (or bracket) and the siding. Scribe and cut away the siding so that this piece (use pressure-treated stock) can lie flat against the sheathing. Backers should always be used under anything that would otherwise be mounted directly against the siding, such as light fixtures and rail or baluster supports. An exception might be covered electrical outlets or outside water spigots, if they fit into a single clapboard. Otherwise water and debris can collect behind the fixture or seep into splits opened by its fasteners and rot the siding. Bevel the top edge of such trim boards to shed water. Backers also provide a much firmer attachment for porch railings.

The more usual case: This hastily and poorly built stoop is a true remuddling disaster that seriously mars the otherwise pleasing appearance of the facade.

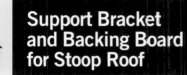

Support Bracket and Backing Board for Stoop Roof

1. Scribe backing-board profile on siding and cut out clapboards using fine toothed saw and utility knife.

2. Screw backing board into sheathing (try to catch stud if possible).

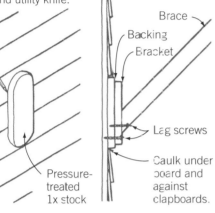

Brace

Backing

Bracket

Lag screws

Caulk under board and against clapboards.

Pressure-treated 1x stock

Step flashing cut into clapboards is a very important detail.

Here is a truly unique approach to the problem of diverting roof runoff away from arriving guests.

These custom-made sectional overhead garage doors look exactly like traditional side-hung double doors. Unfortunately, at around $3,000 each, such a high level of architectural fidelity and operational convenience does not come cheap.

TIP

Attic Conversions

The attics of many old houses can be turned into valuable living space. But if you want to leave beams, rafters, and roof boards exposed you'll have to install insulation on the outside of the roof deck and devise a new roof to cover it. An easier alternative is to install rigid foam insulation board between the exposed rafters and then finish with a drywall ceiling. Be sure to nail 1x2 cleats along the rafters against the underside of the roof deck to provide a ventilation channel behind the insulation with an outlet to a ridge vent. ■ ■ ■

SHED AND GARAGE ADDITIONS

Like the seed at the heart of a fruit, the core of an old house is often buried under an accretion of later additions. Unfortunately, such additions were not always conceived as a harmonious whole. In fact, thoughtlessly attached wings, sheds, garages, and walled-in porches are some of the best examples of "remuddling" you can find.

Renovate or Remove?

The question of whether to renovate or remove an addition depends on architectural and structural considerations. Additions were not always built with the same care and skill as the original house. Attached sheds, in particular, usually lack real foundations and often have settled, racked, and rotted beyond reasonable hope of repair. It may prove more economical to tear the thing down than to tinker with it. Or you can always

live with it until nature takes its course, as long as its continued decline does not threaten the health of the main house.

Conversely, because its framing is accessible and relatively light, a small barn or shed on the threshold of collapse is more easily rescued than a house in similar condition. Concrete foundations are not necessary. Any rotted sills are simply replaced with pressure-treated timbers carried on treated posts set below frost. If the structure provides useful space and the bulk of its framing is still sound, it's probably worth shoring up.

A sound but ill-fitted structure, such as a twentieth-century garage attached to a nineteenth-century house, can be retrofitted to the main house by replacing discordant architectural details, sidings, and window styles with historically appropriate materials and siding. If an exact match is not affordable, a stripped-down version won't strike an inharmonious note, as long as it captures the essence of its more ornate prototype. In hope of sidestepping the ideological crossfire of preservationists, restorationists, and renovators, I suggest this as a guiding philosophy for undoing the "improvements" wrought on a house by insensitive remodeling.

Avoid Technological Trashing

Along with remuddling, the editors of *The Old House Journal* warn against what they call "technological trashing," where, in an attempt to increase energy efficiency, the beauty of a house is destroyed by an ill-conceived passive-solar retrofit. Other than installing solar hot water heating panels flat against the roof slope where they will not be too obtrusive, foisting a solar-heating system on an old house without destroying its character is almost impossible. I have seldom seen a felicitous mating of old and new.

With attention to detail and a lot of money, a modern greenhouse could be integrated into a Victorian mansion (glass-walled conservatories were all the rage during that era), but the sloped glazing of a contemporary sunspace indiscriminately tacked onto farmhouses and townhouses alike is seldom harmonious. If energy efficiency is that important, build a new house, don't trash an old one.

A traditional sun porch addition makes a more harmonious match with an old house than a contemporary sun space, with only a slight tradeoff in potential solar gain. Because the additional space is under a roof, you can use conventional windows that match the rest of the house instead of the glaringly inharmonious look of fixed sloping glass. In the sun porch shown in the photo at right, classic detailing creates a seamless transition to the main house. These details include stock half-round plastic gutters and shadow lines from the layers of wood and moldings that suggest formal columns and cornices. Painted moldings and trim boards layered on top of medium-density overlay plywood create a classic relief.

Its benefits notwithstanding, it is hard to imagine a way to felicitously retrofit a passive-solar Trombe wall to an old house.

A classic sunroom addition blends much better with an old house than a slanted-glass greenhouse.

8 Insulation and Ventilation

The houses built by our ancestors were better ventilated in certain respects than modern ones, with all their improvements. . . . The great majority of the American people, owing to sheer ignorance, are, for want of pure air, being poisoned and starved; the result being weakened constitutions, frequent disease, and shortened life.

—CATHERINE E. BEECHER AND HARRIET BEECHER STOWE, *THE AMERICAN WOMAN'S HOME*

The polyethylene sheet battened over the foundation is a modern version of traditional banking. Practitioners of this New England autumn rite would pile hay bales or spruce boughs or lay tarpaper over the drafty foundation stones to keep their cellars from freezing.

The nineteenth-century notion that consumption and a host of other ills both physical and moral were caused by breathing "vitiated" air fueled a mania for ventilation that was both scientifically baseless and remarkably persistent. The idea originated in Antoine Lavoisier's experiments with combustion and oxidation during the 1770s. The father of modern chemistry mistakenly theorized that an increase of "carbonic acid" (carbon dioxide) caused a deleterious atmosphere in which the body's ability to absorb oxygen was decreased. Coupled with the prevailing miasma theory that poisonous "organic effluvia" exhaled by putrefying matter from both within and without the body was the cause of disease, ventilation became a major public health concern.

VENTILATION
FACT AND FANCY

The general acceptance of the germ theory of disease in the waning years of the nineteenth century ended the association between ill health and vitiated air. It was realized that germs could be carried by fresh air as easily as by stale. At the same time, scientists proved that excess carbonic acid had nothing to do with the discomfort or healthfulness of crowded and close rooms and that comfort was correlated to the levels of temperature and humidity. By 1925, the accepted

ventilation standard was 10 cu. ft. of fresh air per person per minute, which is still the consensus among HVAC engineers today. The goal of ventilation shifted toward removing odors for aesthetic comfort. The kitchen and bathroom exhaust fans became the only provision for ventilation beyond that provided by the cracks and openings in the building envelope.

Control Is the Key

Today, the perception of the problem is not how to provide enough ventilating air but rather how to reduce the unnecessary and uncontrolled air flow that makes the typical old house uncomfortable to live in and expensive to heat.

It's a common misconception that heavy insulation is the most important requirement for a warm house. However, heavily insulated walls are not as important as tight walls. It's been estimated that the cumulative heat loss through all the cracks and gaps in the envelope of a typical old house is about the same as leaving the front door wide open 24 hours a day. It takes a lot of caulking to fill a hole that big. The infiltration of cold outside air is the main cause of drafts, high heating bills, and (as will be made clear) a host of other problems.

Controlled infiltration is ventilation; uncontrolled infiltration is expensive, discomforting, and potentially unhealthy. A certain amount of air exchange is necessary for health. The current wisdom is that a complete exchange of household air every 3 hours or 4 hours—six to eight exchanges per day or 0.25 to 0.33 air changes per hour (ACH)—will vent excess moisture, indoor pollutants, and other unhealthy by-products of cooking, breathing, and living without intolerable heat loss or the need for mechanical assistance (other than a simple bathroom or kitchen exhaust fan).

Deciding on the Right Amount of Fresh Air

A good rule of thumb for calculating the fresh air requirement for a house is to multiply the number of bedrooms plus 1 by 10 cu. ft. Following this rule, a three-bedroom house requires at least 40 cu. ft. of fresh air per minute.

A 1,800-sq.-ft. (14,400-cu.-ft.) house with 0.33 ACH would deliver a more-than-sufficient 80 cu. ft. of fresh air per minute (4,800 cu. ft. divided by 60 minutes) of fresh air. This applies only to non-smoking households, with no other unusual source of moisture or internal pollution. Otherwise the requirements are at least doubled.

Despite the jeremiads of the nineteenth-century fresh air fetishists, a typical "tight" house of that period cycled through 24 to 48 air changes per day (1 to 2 ACH). Although some modern superinsulated houses are

The Energy-Efficient Old House

There are many ways to increase the energy efficiency of an old house without retrofitting solar panels or other high-tech options.

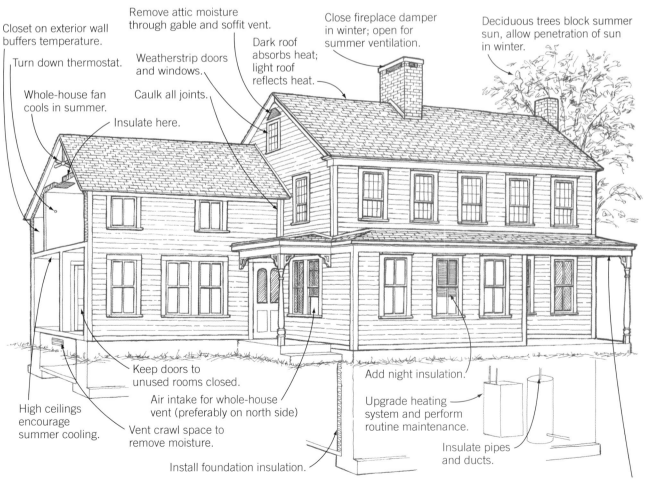

Closet on exterior wall buffers temperature.

Turn down thermostat.

Whole-house fan cools in summer.

Insulate here.

Remove attic moisture through gable and soffit vent.

Weatherstrip doors and windows.

Caulk all joints.

Dark roof absorbs heat; light roof reflects heat.

Close fireplace damper in winter; open for summer ventilation.

Deciduous trees block summer sun, allow penetration of sun in winter.

Keep doors to unused rooms closed.

Air intake for whole-house vent (preferably on north side)

High ceilings encourage summer cooling.

Vent crawl space to remove moisture.

Install foundation insulation.

Add night insulation.

Upgrade heating system and perform routine maintenance.

Insulate pipes and ducts.

Porch blocks high summer sun, allows entry of low winter sun.

designed to begrudge only one tenth of their indoor air per hour (requiring the assistance of powered air-to-air heat exchangers to prevent the buildup of truly vitiated air), bringing an old house up to the current ideal requires a rigorous program of retrofitted weatherization measures that would be unusual even in the average newly built house today. Nevertheless, relying on knotholes, loose siding, and rattling sashes for ventilation is no longer a wise or cost-efficient policy.

ENERGY AUDITS, CAULKING, AND WEATHERSTRIPPING

When buttoning up a house, it helps to know where the buttonholes are. Some homeowners will be more comfortable with a professional energy audit than hit-or-miss do-it-yourself weatherization measures. Finding an energy auditor is easy; but finding one who is both objective and competent is likely to prove a good deal harder. While some utility companies and fuel oil dealers offer energy audits, the resulting recommendations may be cursory at best. Although disinterested agents may exist, weatherization, HVAC, and insulation contractors who also perform energy audits are likely to have a built-in conflict of interest.

Your best bet may be to hire a member of the American Society of Home Inspectors or to have an audit done by the non-profit Energy Rated Homes of America. In any case, a professional auditor will use a special test (see the sidebar at right) to pinpoint air leaks and estimate the rate of air exchange and will plug the numbers into a computer program to perform a cash-flow and cost-benefits analysis of possible conservation measures. Some banks now factor

The Blower Door Test

The blower door test uses a calibrated high-speed fan mounted in a frame that seals to the main entrance door of the house. All windows, other doors, and vents are closed. The fan then either forces air out or in (depressurization or pressurization) while workers go from room to room moving smoke pencils along the exterior walls and windows and noting where the smoke is sucked out or blown in. After major leaks are caulked or plugged, the test is run again to find minor leaks.

You can rig a less sophisticated version of this test yourself with an ordinary window fan. Seal it to the sash opening with tightly packed rags and tape and make sure all other windows and doors are closed. (Stuff a towel against the door bottom). Set the fan to suck the air out of the room, which will increase outside air infiltration through cracks in the wall. Light an incense stick and move it slowly along baseboards, around window casings, ceiling lights, outlet covers and other suspect areas and note where the smoke blows inward. Repeat from room to room.

On the other hand, you can simply assume that any place that could leak, does. Next, search out and seal all possible points of entry.

reduced energy costs into home-improvement loan calculations based on the principle that an estimated savings on energy that's greater than the finance costs of the improvements will yield a positive cash flow over the life of the mortgage. Of course, any potential savings depend on local energy costs, payback period, and how long you actually live in the house.

Sources of Air Infiltration

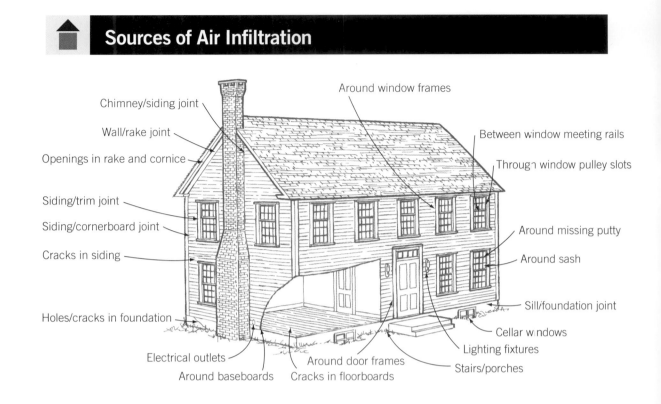

Chimney/siding joint

Wall/rake joint

Openings in rake and cornice

Siding/trim joint

Siding/cornerboard joint

Cracks in siding

Holes/cracks in foundation

Electrical outlets

Around baseboards

Cracks in floorboards

Around window frames

Between window meeting rails

Through window pulley slots

Around missing putty

Around sash

Sill/foundation joint

Cellar windows

Lighting fixtures

Stairs/porches

Around door frames

Plugging the Leaks

Modern technology has created a veritable arsenal of anti-infiltration tools. No longer does the homeowner have to laboriously replace dried-out linseed oil–based caulking every couple of years. Today, you can select high-tech polymers that can be applied over a wide temperature range, don't degrade in sunlight, adhere to almost any substrate, can be painted, and remain flexible for 50 years or more. (This is especially attractive if you need to caulk a high cornice and never want to do it again.) Over the long term, only the best caulk is the cheapest.

CAULK OUTSIDE The best time to caulk a house is when you repaint it, just after the walls have been scraped, cleaned, and primed—even the best caulk won't stick to loose, flaking, or dirty surfaces. Begin by caulking obvious outside problem areas. Search out and fill any gaps at the joints of door and window frames, especially where clapboards fall short of trim. Joints

between corner trim boards, cornice returns and the wall, and under thresholds are also likely targets. Use a paintable caulk to fill any splits in clapboards (yes, it's not the ideal fix, but it works for the short term).

One of the worst infiltration pathways is the gap between the top of the foundation wall and the sills—plug it with spray-foam polyurethane. Point or parge the above-grade portion of dry-mortared stone foundations. Seal cellar window frames and sashes.

Caulk penetrations for service entrance cables, telephone and TV cables, and sill cocks as well as exhaust fan and dryer vent covers. Reroute any antenna or cable wires that enter under window sashes through a new hole drilled through the wall and then caulked. If you wait to caulk until the sun has burned off any morning frost or dew and the temperature is above 50°F, the compound will spread and adhere better.

Choosing the Right Caulk

Time was when the selection of caulking compounds was like the choice of colors for a Model T Ford: "Any color you want so long as it's black." But like basic black, linseed oil–based caulking compound (which is what glazing compound still is) has been supplanted by a cornucopia of exotic high-tech offspring of chemical wizardry. There are now caulks for every niche, compounds for every specialized application. Here's a simple tour of the chemical zoo. As a rule of thumb, always use the best-grade (most-expensive) caulk for each application that you can afford.

Latex (Acrylic Latex). Latex is your basic, all-purpose, not-too-special, and inexpensive caulk. (Siliconized latex is a bit more expensive and a bit more durable than standard acrylic.) It is water soluble when uncured, for easy cleanup and tooling. Latex caulk is paintable and is available in white, brown, tan, clear, black, bronze, and gray. It is good for 15 years to 35 years or more, depending on the formulation and silicone content. This caulk is only fairly flexible; hence it's best for sealing between similar materials. The least-expensive grade, "painter's caulk," should be used only on interiors for sealing gaps between baseboard and other trim and wall surfaces for a neat paint job.

Acrylic Co-polymer. A typical representative of the acrylic co-polymers is Geocel®. These materials are clear, extremely sticky, and highly flexible, making them very well suited for sealing between materials with different rates of thermal response, such as metal to masonry or wood to glass.

Butyl Rubber. Butyl rubber–based caulks are black and, like co-polymers, are extremely sticky and messy to work with. However, they are superior to most caulks for sealing glazing to a substrate and asphalt roofing to metal flashings.

Silicone. There are now almost as many varieties of silicone caulking compounds as latex ones. These caulks are the most durable and versatile of all common and affordable products. Although at least twice as costly as latex, their performance more than justifies the expense. Silicone should be your first choice for general exterior work. Choose a paintable type, when necessary, because paint does not stick to regular silicone caulk.

Adhesive Caulks. Products such as Phenoseal® are both a caulk and a glue. When cured they are not particularly flexible, but this type of caulk is durable, waterproof, and very strong.

Polyurethane Expanding Foam. Expanding foam caulks are ideal for sealing gaps between windows and walls, for filling the cracks between sills and foundations, and for all the myriad gaps between penetrations and the building envelope of an old house. The uncured foam is impossible to clean off your hands so wear rubber gloves during application. Use low-expansion foams around window casings, as excessive expansion can push the casings out of true.

Although caulking the outside of the house does contribute to reduced air infiltration, it can be argued that it is actually more important for preventing water infiltration. Open joints between exterior trim pieces allow water to sneak into the walls or under the roofing and eventually rot the structure. Preventing water infiltration is just as important as preventing heat loss.

Good Caulking Technique

The average 11½-oz. cartridge of caulk will fill 50 ft. of ¼-in.-deep crack or two door or window frames, if it's properly applied. As many homeowners can testify, running a neat bead of caulk is not as easy as it looks. The trick is to keep a steady even pressure on the plunger, and to ease off just before reaching the end of the bead.

It helps to use a high-quality caulking gun ($10 to $12 as opposed to $2 to $3) and to clip the nozzle at a 45-degree angle. Some experts recommend pushing the bead forward with the gun as opposed to pulling it as you draw the gun backward; I never noticed enough of a difference to recommend one method over the other. Use whichever you feel most comfortable with.

If the gun doesn't force the caulk all the way into the gap or if the caulk rounds up at the edges, tool it into a concave profile with a moistened fingertip. As when using the gun, keep a steady pressure and don't stop until you reach the end of the bead. Wipe your finger clean before smoothing the next bead. Keep a damp rag handy for cleaning up smears and over-runs. Stuff any holes or cracks wider or deeper than ⅜ in. with a filler. Oakum, the traditional crack filler, is too oily to bond well with modern polymer-based caulks. Use polyethylene backer rod, rope caulk, or expanding polyurethane foam.

SEAL INTERIOR LEAKS Drafts of cold air can't flow into your house unless warm air is leaking out. For this reason, sealing the inside walls is even more effective at stopping air leakage than caulking the outside. Caulk baseboards, cove moldings, and window and door casings to the wall finish. Install gaskets behind outlet covers in the exterior walls. Add or repair weatherstripping on windows, storm windows, and doors. Seal HVAC supply and return air duct runs with professional duct-sealing mastic (not duct tape, which eventually falls off). Caulk the trim of light fixtures to ceilings under the attic.

SEAL THE TRICKY SPOTS The job becomes trickier after the obvious sources of air leakage have been plugged. All penetrations in the building envelope provide a channel for air movement between heated and unheated spaces. Finding the hidden ones is the challenge. Look for hollow walls and plumbing chases that connect the basement with the attic. The wall cavities of some mid-nineteenth-century balloon-framed houses were deliberately designed to circulate air warmed by the cellar furnace to the attic in the mistaken belief that this would help heat the living areas. (Because the walls were uninsulated, this succeeded only in increasing heat loss to the outside.)

Unsealed penetrations for electrical cables and pipes at the top and bottom of partitions, around chimneys and exhaust fans, and at recessed lights are some typical problem areas. The stairwell walls and the door or hatch between the house and an unheated attic or garage require the same attention to weatherization as any outside wall.

CAULK UPPER SASHES Because in most cases, there's no compelling reason for the upper sash of an old double-hung window to open in the first place, the infiltration problem is easily remedied by caulking the sash to the jambs. Chances are, it's already been glued to the jambs by decades of paint. Along this line, you may be able to find a special removable caulking that offers a quick fix for the lower sash. Applied in the fall, the transparent gum-like bead seals the window during the heating season and is simply peeled off the following spring.

Applying Weatherstripping

Like caulking, modern weatherstripping products are much more sophisticated than the leather listing and wool felts of the nineteenth century. Choosing the right product for a particular application can be confusing. Except for temporary quick fixes, avoid adhesive-backed foam, spring-plastic, and wool-felt weatherstripping. Foam and plastic soon degrade, becoming crumbly or brittle and splitting apart. Adhesives dry out and the weatherstripping falls off; wool felt soaks up moisture and rots. Inspect your doors and windows and renew or install weatherstripping on every surface that opens, closes, or moves against another.

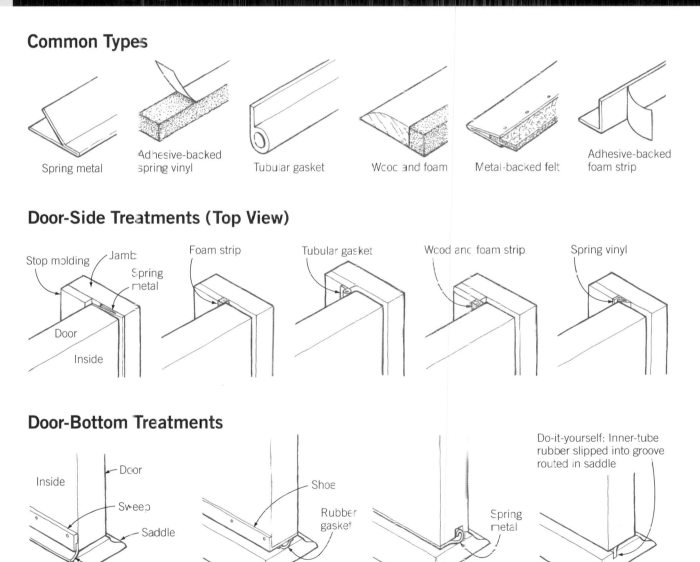

Weatherstripping

Common Types

Spring metal

Adhesive-backed spring vinyl

Tubular gasket

Wood and foam

Metal-backed felt

Adhesive-backed foam strip

Door-Side Treatments (Top View)

Stop molding Jamb Spring metal Door Inside

Foam strip

Tubular gasket

Wood and foam strip

Spring vinyl

Door-Bottom Treatments

Inside Door Sweep Saddle Rubber or plastic blade

Shoe Rubber gasket

Spring metal

Do-it-yourself: Inner-tube rubber slipped into groove routed in saddle

Rather than attempt to retrofit adequate weatherstripping, the owners sealed this cellar entrance door permanently shut with expanding foam caulk. Note the fiberglass insulation stuffing.

Except for the newer spring vinyl, most inexpensive weatherstripping is not suited for use where it will be subjected to friction. Instead, use heavy-duty tubular vinyl or ethylene propylene diene monomer (EPDM) gasketing. These are durable and easy to install, although their clumsy appearance (the exposed metal mounting flange shows naked nail heads) is a definite disadvantage in room decor. One solution is to install them on the outside of windows.

Another alternative is to use a wood-backed vinyl gasket such as Porta-Seal. The 1½-in.-wide strip seals doors; the narrower ¾-in. strips are used against window sash. Tubular gaskets mounted in an adjustable metal shoe are an excellent choice for sealing under doors and are far less obtrusive than the typical cheap rubber or plastic sweep. Interestingly enough, spring metal, which is the oldest kind of weatherstripping, also happens to be among the tightest and most durable.

THE GOOD, THE BAD, AND THE UGLY: INFILTRATION, CONDENSATION, AND INSULATION

A wall is a relatively porous membrane. In cold weather, the air inside the house is much warmer than the outside air, so heat will move through the walls by conduction and convection in an attempt to establish equilibrium. When the air inside your house is heated, it becomes less dense and rises. And because warm air molecules zing around more, it also pushes (that is, it is pressurized) and will try to move from an area with greater pressure to one with lesser. As buoyant warm air rushes up the chimney or leaks out through the attic ceiling, it depressurizes the interior of the house, drawing cold outside air in through cracks around windows and doors and between the siding boards, in what is known as the *stack effect,* and robbing your house of its hard-earned warmth.

The fact that the strength of the stack effect is proportional to temperature difference was the reason the open fireplace was such an efficient engine of wintertime ventilation and why something else had to be done to cool the house in summer when there is little difference between indoor and outdoor air temperatures.

Wind blowing against a house creates pressure differentials regardless of any temperature difference. On the windward side, the pressure is positive, and outside air is forced inside (infiltration). On the leeward side, the pressure is negative, and inside air is sucked out (exfiltration). Wind-driven exchanges are highly variable and specific to site and exposure. But taken together, experts agree that infiltration losses account for 25 percent to 30 percent of the total heat (or cooling) load of the typical not-too-tight house.

These are losses that extra insulation will not mitigate. Insulation basically retards the conductive and convective heat transfers from the warmer to the cooler side, which are driven by the temperature difference across building surfaces (heat loss in winter, heat gain in summer). Although it depends on the cost of energy, the severity of the heating and cooling climate, and the existing level of insulation, the payback for reducing the total air changes per hour of an old house is usually greater than that for upgrading windows or adding extra insulation.

Infiltration Problems

While the extra cost of infiltration heat loss may be something you can live with, infiltration also causes problems that you can't afford to ignore. Because people and plants live in the house, the inside air is heavy with water vapor and moisture. (Although the terms are often used interchangeably, *vapor* is water in a gaseous state, whereas *moisture* is actually microscopic droplets of liquid water diffused in the air—that is, fog.) Warm air holds more water vapor than does cold air. When air is holding all the vapor it can at a given temperature, it is said to be saturated. Its vapor content, together with the air temperature, determines the dew point, which is the temperature at which saturated air gives up its water by condensation. Relative humidity is a measure of the amount of vapor the air is holding compared to the amount it could hold at a given temperature, expressed as a percentage.

The more water vapor the air contains, the higher its vapor pressure—that is, the harder it will push to get to someplace with a lower pressure. *Diffusion* is the process whereby differences in vapor pressure and temperature push water vapor through solid but permeable materials, like wood siding and masonry, from an area of

higher pressure to one of lower and from the warm side of a building to the cold side. Warm, moist air will always move toward cool, dry air. Because the amount of water vapor that air can hold increases as it is heated, vapor pressure and thus vapor transport by diffusion is ultimately a temperature-driven phenomenon. Because vapor transport by diffusion is an entirely different process than vapor transport by air movement (infiltration), it can occur in the opposite direction simultaneously under the right circumstance. For example, hot humid summer air will move into an air-conditioned house even if the indoor air is at a higher pressure and moving outward.

Condensation: A Modern Problem

In the days before insulation, condensation inside walls was not usually a problem. Most of the vapor was carried off to the outside by convection currents. Moisture that did condense on cold interior surface of the outside wall instantly froze. Much of this frozen water would sublimate (return to gas without going through a liquid phase) as soon as the temperature rose above the dew point. The water that didn't sublimate would drip down the studs to collect on the sill, but this wasn't usually a problem because the warm, dry air pumped out by redhot stoves and fireplaces would heat the wall cavities enough to evaporate the water before it could cause wood to rot. The fact that most old houses did not rot away in a few years shows that condensation within the walls was not a common occurrence.

Theoretically, all this changes when the wall cavity is filled with insulation. Convection currents are considerably diminished (especially with tight sheathing or sheathing paper). So is the temperature of the cavity surfaces, which raises the dew point to levels at which condensation is much more likely. Because the insulation

Insulation, Vapor Barrier, and Condensation

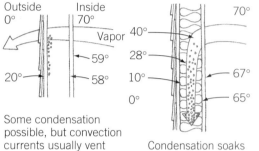
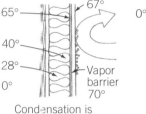
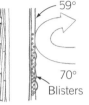

Uninsulated Wall without Vapor Barrier

Outside 0°　Inside 70°

Vapor

59°

20°　58°

Some condensation possible, but convection currents usually vent moisture to outside.

Insulated Wall without Vapor Barrier

70°

40°

28°

10°

0°

67°

65°

Condensation soaks insulation.

Insulated Wall with Vapor Barrier

65°　67°

40°

28°

0°

Vapor barrier 70°

Condensation is deflected, absorbed by household air, although water may condense on cold surfaces.

Uninsulated Wall with Vapor Barrier

59°

0°

70°

Blisters

Condensation forms behind interior surfaces under conditions of high humidity.

Relative Humidity

Although it might seem sensible to lower household relative humidity as much as possible to prevent condensation, this is not a good idea. Studies and common sense have shown that people feel most comfortable and are healthiest at a temperature of about 70°F, with a relative humidity ranging from 35 percent to 50 percent. When interior humidity is low it takes more heat for us to feel warm, because moisture evaporates faster from the skin in dry air, lowering body temperature. Maintaining proper humidity enables the homeowner to turn down the thermostat, feel warm, and keep the family's mucous membranes from drying out.

will also warm up slowly, sublimation does not occur and liquid water soaks the insulation, coincidentally reducing its insulation value and increasing the likelihood of further condensation.

STOPPING THE VAPOR When an impermeable film is installed on the warm side of the wall under the finish surface, water vapor cannot diffuse through to the cold side. Heat can still move through the wall by conduction and also by infiltration, but the incoming cold air tends to reduce the humidity of the escaping warm air.

The key concept is *impenetrability:* With a continuous barrier, the water vapor stays inside, where it is absorbed as new air is warmed by the heating system. If there's too much vapor present—that is, if the relative humidity is high—the water will condense on any convenient cold surface, especially windows and cold pipes. Water can hold a lot of heat. When it condenses, it loses this "latent heat," which means that the room becomes a little bit colder every time a drop of water runs down the window-pane to collect on the sill. A vapor barrier installed against an uninsulated wall will cause condensation on interior surfaces where high humidity is present, such as bathrooms and kitchens. Because high-gloss oil paints applied over plaster make a fairly good vapor barrier, paint always peels off the bathroom ceiling first.

The Tight House: Striking a Balance

The possibility of excessive levels of indoor humidity during the heating season would have been inconceivable to our ancestors. It is an entirely modern problem, ironically arising within the last 50 years or so as a consequence of the improvements in building technology that have made our homes so comfortable. The insulation that keeps our houses warm in winter and cool in summer also prevents escaping heat from drying out moisture in wall cavities and attics, making dry rot a real possibility. Heat that once escaped through the ceilings or floorboards of an uninsulated attic kept the underside of the roof warm enough to prevent condensation. But during the energy crisis of the 1970s, added attic insulation turned that surface into a condenser.

Caulking, weatherstripping, and tight sheathing and sealed-combustion or power-vented heating appliances (in lieu of chimneys and fireplaces) lower rates of air exchange, causing interior humidity to increase and indoor pollutants to build up to the unhealthy levels that our great-great grandmothers warned us against. While a tight house is not the *cause* of indoor air pollution, it does prevent the dilution of pollutants produced or introduced into it.

Like old-fashioned fireplaces, old inefficient heating systems with their grossly oversize furnaces and boilers sucked in huge amounts of dry outside air, keeping humidity low and diluting pollutants. Modern combustion appliances draw less air. Finally, forced-air heating and air-conditioning systems combined with a tighter building envelope have increased the problems caused by pressure differentials. Leaky supply and return ducts can pressurize or depressurize the living areas, causing infiltration of moisture-laden air in summer or exfiltration of moisture into attic and wall cavities in winter. Depres-

The mold and rot in this attic ceiling was caused by moisture transported from chronic standing water in the cellar.

surization also causes infiltration of radon and moisture into the cellar and backdrafting in chimneys and combustion chambers. Besides causing condensation that rots out window sills, wall cavities, and attic ceilings, excessive indoor humidity breeds mildew and dust-mites and exacerbates asthma and allergies.

When an old house is tightened up to modern standards, health and safety depend on the elimination of egregious sources of moisture. Fortunately, this can be accomplished without seriously affecting lifestyle, if not pocketbook.

Eliminating Cellar Moisture

Because the cellar is normally the primary pathway by which excess moisture enters the house, proper grading and foundation drainage, coupled with gutters and downspouts that drain roof runoff away from the foundation, are critical. Make sure to lay a polyethylene vapor barrier over earth-floored crawl spaces and cellars and seal it to the foundation walls, as discussed in chapter 3. Although an existing old slab floor may appear dry, particularly during the heating season, it is still wicking moisture from the ground into the cellar air. But because the heated air of a leaky house tends to be dry, that moisture is absorbed without condensing on the surface of the concrete. Tape a 2-ft.-sq. piece of polyethylene to the slab and leave it overnight. When you check it the following day, you'll notice beads of moisture condensed on its underside. (If the slab has a vapor barrier the poly will be dry.) The most effective cure is to cover the existing concrete with poly and pour a 2-in.-thick new slab over it.

Using Exhaust Fans

Make sure you run the exhaust fans in bathrooms and kitchens while showering or cooking, especially when cooking with gas. Studies have shown that ventilation fans that exhaust or draw no more than 50 cu. ft. per minute will not upset the pressure balance of even a tight house (that is, they won't cause or exacerbate negative or positive pressurization). The latest kitchen and bath fans are quieter and have relatively air-tight dampers than older ones. The fan should have a *sone rating* (a measurement of its noise level) of 3 for bathrooms and 5 for a range hood.

To reduce friction, keep the duct run as short and straight as possible. Rigid aluminum duct is better than corrugated flexible duct, which has more resistance to air flow and tends to sag, col-lecting dirt and moisture. If possible, select a fan or fan controller with infinite speed. Variable controllers allow the fan to run slow in winter so that it will ventilate without causing drafts and at high speed in summer to exhaust hot kitchen air. It's better to spend extra on the best-quality fan you can afford than to buy the budget model. (Expect to spend $75 to $150 for a good bath exhaust fan and anywhere from $150 to $300 for a range hood.)

There is a trade-off: Keeping the humidity high enough to ensure comfort will inevitably cause some condensation. Replacing single glazing with insulated sashes or storm windows contributes to comfort by increasing the surface temperature of the room-side glass, which lowers its dew point. The tighter the house, the easier it is to strike a balance between comfortable humidity and minimal condensation. This is one of the best arguments for a general program of caulking and tightening up and for adding an exterior air barrier when residing an old house.

VAPOR BARRIERS AND AIR BARRIERS

Ever since the 1920s, when the idea that water vapor gets into wall cavities by diffusion was first promulgated, vapor barriers (or, in the argot of architectural pedantry, *vapor diffusion retarders*) have been controversial, widely misunderstood, and all too often, incorrectly applied. The official doctrine was "seal the warm side, vent the cold side." The barrier is placed on the warm side because that's where the highest pressure exists. There should be nothing on the exterior side of the wall to prevent any moisture that has gotten past the vapor barrier from venting to the outside.

The Controversy

Despite being enshrined in the canons of the building code, many builders continued to dispute the need for vapor barriers in the first place. Tales of walls that metastasized in a few short years into masses of sodden rot and congealed insulation beneath fatal shrouds of polyethylene were a stock bogeyman of contractor horror stories. And renovators wondered how the walls of old houses stuffed with mineral wool or blown-in fiberglass and sheathed with tarpaper and asphalt shingles on the outside, but lacking any kind of vapor barrier on the interior, could be perfectly dry, showing no signs of rot after 50 years or 60 years, if the theories were true. Other builders noted that installing rigid foam insulation boards (an effective vapor barrier) on the exterior of the sheathing did not cause the condensation problems that this violation of the basic rule predicted.

Part of the problem is that the thermal performance of houses in the real world is more complicated than the performance of test houses in laboratories. Condensation is affected by many variables. There must be a source of water, a cold condensing surface, an air passage between the source and the surface, pressure to drive the moist air through the passage, time for sufficient contact, and a diffusion barrier to retard drying or sublimation of condensation.

The quantity of vapor available, the dew-point temperature, the nature of the wall cavity, the ability of the insulation to absorb water, the severity of the climate, the tightness or looseness and permeability of the sheathing and siding, the presence or absence of paint, and how much moisture the wood can absorb all determine whether condensation causes structural damage. Different climates and temperature extremes require different strategies. A one-size-fits-all prescription can't work. But the biggest difficulty is that, until very recently, there had never been a clear understanding of the difference between air barriers and vapor barriers and hence, the roles played by infiltration versus diffusion in the origins of condensation problems.

A New Understanding of the Role of Air Movement

In the late 1970s, researchers in Canada and Norway began to suspect that the majority of moisture condensing on the cold side of the building envelope was dumped there by air movement and not, as was previously believed, by diffusion. In fact, further research established that because the volume of vapor transport by diffusion depends on surface area, minor tears and rips in the barrier actually have no significant effect on its performance. If 5 percent of the surface area of the barrier is full of holes, the barrier is still 95 percent effective. This is why the kraft paper covering of fiberglass insulation still retards vapor passage even when ripped and puckered.

But unlike the inherently slow process of diffusion, air movement is a rapid and efficient means of transporting water vapor. The number and size of leaks do not matter. The greater the difference in pressure (and temperature) between the cold and warm sides of a wall, the faster the rate of infiltration. It's like turning the spigot on your garden hose—the hose diameter stays the same, but the increased pressure forces water through at a faster rate. One hundred times more water vapor is transported through a hole in the vapor barrier by air leakage (infiltration) than by diffusion.

Thus retarding air movement through walls and ceilings is now seen to be much more important than retarding diffusion. What is needed is not a vapor barrier (or vapor diffusion retarder) so much as an air barrier (or air flow retarder).

Climate Zones

LEGEND

Severe Cold
8,000 heating degree days or greater

Cold
4,500–8,000 heating degree days

Mixed Humid
More than 20 in. of annual precipitation; 4,500 heating degree days or less; monthly average outdoor temperature drops below 45°F during winter

Hot Humid
More than 20 in. of annual precipitation; monthly average outdoor temperature remains above 45°F throughout year

Hot Dry or Mixed Dry
Hot dry: less than 20 in. of annual precipitation; monthly average outdoor temperature remains above 45°F throughout year
Mixed dry: less than 20 in. of annual precipitation; 4,500 heating degree days or less; monthly average outdoor temperature drops below 45°F during winter

Because it was permeated and punctured with holes for electrical outlets and pipes and with rips and tears, polyethylene sheeting made a fairly good vapor diffusion retarder and a very poor air flow retarder. Builders and researches struggled to devise strategies by which the poly could retard the flow of vapor *and* air, but most methods required too much attention to detail and cost too much to be practical in the real world.

In the 1980s, building scientists like Joseph Lstiburek pioneered the airtight drywall approach (ADA), which uses drywall sealed and gasketed to the floor and ceiling as an air retarder to block infiltration. The vapor retarder could be vapor-impermeable paint (one brand is Glidden Insul-Aid) or polyethylene behind the drywall or even foil-backed drywall. (The foil side should always face the wall cavity.) Ideally, if there were no penetrations in the air retarder, no vapor retarder would be needed. Although the ADA system made for a very tight house, it did not stop the convective heat loss that occurred when cold air washed through the insulation within the wall cavities. Placing a tightly sealed air flow retarder on the outside of the building wall did. Materials such as Tyvek® are impermeable to air passage but allow vapor diffusion. One advantage of placing the air barrier on the outside of the building is that it is easier to seal it against penetrations, which is a good reason to install it when replacing old siding.

Deciding Where and When to Block Vapor and/or Air

The consensus among experts now seems to be that the question of whether and where to use a vapor diffusion retarder, an air flow retarder, or an air and vapor retarder depends on your climate. Thus the experts distinguish between heating climates, mixed climates, and cooling climates. Lstiburek delineates five different climate zones that determine the applicability of various infiltration control strategies.

The tune that seems to emerge most clearly from the current cacophony of learned opinion is that a polyethylene vapor diffusion retarder should be used on the inside walls and ceilings in severe-cold climates, as defined on the map on the facing page. In cold climates, the value of vapor diffusion retarders is ambiguous: sometimes useful, sometimes not. Some experts advise using them only on ceilings or only on bathroom and kitchen ceilings. In mixed-humid climates, vapor diffusion retarders are superfluous. And in hot-humid climates, they should be applied, if at all, only on the exterior of the house. Here, and in mixed-humid climates, some experts feel that permeable walls may actually dry better than walls with a vapor diffusion retarder, since the walls can dry to either side. For the same reasons, they caution against using impermeable vinyl wallpapers and recommend unfaced insulation instead of paper or foil faced.

Where seasonal temperatures do not vary greatly, rates of infiltration and diffusion will be naturally low, and vapor barriers are not necessary, except under floor slabs and crawl spaces. But there is general agreement that an air flow retarder is a good idea and should be used in every climate zone and is absolutely essential in extremely hot and cold regions. Without an air flow retarder, vapor diffusion retarders are basically useless. And a leaky air flow retarder is not an effective one. The question of whether it

Installing Vapor Diffusion Retarders

It's not possible to install a perfectly continuous barrier in an old house, since there's no way to retrofit the membrane around floor joists and over partitions. Nevertheless, even without resorting to ADA sealing, it's still important to be as thorough as possible.

- Patch any rips or holes with polyethylene tape.
- Overlap seams between sheets at least the width of a bay (the space between studs).
- Seal the edges with tape.
- Cut an X over electrical outlets and tape the plastic to their sides.

should be applied to the outside or the inside of the building envelope has proponents and detractors for each. Ultimately, wherever it is placed, it should be as tight as possible.

HOUSEWRAPS Even though studies have shown that housewraps are no more effective as an air flow retarder than plywood or rigid foam sheathing with taped joints, building codes now require them for all new construction. Even if you plan to cover old sheathing boards with new plywood or foam, there's still one good reason to use housewrap anyway. Although housewrap allows vapor to escape, it is impermeable to moisture and so acts like traditional tarpaper to create a rain screen or *drainage plane*, beneath the siding that keeps moisture out of the wall cavities and from being absorbed by the sheathing. In the humid Deep South, the warmth of sunlight after a downpour has been shown to push water through the siding and into the sheathing.

Insulation and Venting: A Dissenting Opinion

Fred Lugano, a Vermont weatherization contractor, believes that building codes and code officials have yet to catch up to the very latest science. He notes that myriad penetrations in the attic ceiling allow warm air to move right through even the heaviest blanket of insulation. Adding more insulation or venting the soffit will not prevent ice dams. In fact, venting the attic only increases the exfiltration of warm moist air from the living areas and makes the condensation problem worse. Lugano actually blocks gable vents and removes the ridge vents above sloped ceilings. He then methodically and meticulously pulls back the attic floor insulation and seals every penetration through the ceiling he can find. He uses metal flashing and high-temperature silicone caulk (used to seal combustion exhaust pipes) to seal the framing to masonry at chimney penetrations.

Then he fills the attic ceiling with blown-in cellulose insulation. On sloped insulated attic or cathedral ceilings, he fills any existing air channel behind the insulation and the rafter bays full of high-density cellulose to form an impervious and continuous air barrier. Although

Pulling back the attic insulation reveals a multitude of cracks in a plaster-and-lath ceiling.

this violates code writ and shingle manufacturer's warranties, Lugano says that unlike conventional approaches to air sealing and moisture control, his method always works and hasn't caused any degradation of the shingles.

Lugano also sides with the school of thought that does not believe in venting crawl spaces. He argues that, in summer, the crawl space will always be cooler than the outside air so venting it just draws in more moist air from outside, which fosters mold and mildew and condensation buildup. He lays down a poly groundcover and seals the space tight. Code and many other experts disagree about closing up vents in summer.

The insulation filters dust out of warm air leaking through a hole in the ceiling, leaving a telltale black stain. The penetration will be sealed with expanding polyurethane foam. (Photo by Fred Lugano)

Once potential air leaks are sealed, blown cellulose fills the irregular spaces of framing better than batt insulation. Sealing the ceiling and the roof and soffit vents prevents air washing of the insulation.

In fact, some investigators feel that moisture entering the walls from outside the building is a bigger problem than transport from the interior. The tarpaper or housewrap also makes a *capillary break* across which moisture cannot travel. (Like housewrap, 15-lb. tarpaper is permeable to vapor but to not moisture.)

Attic Ventilation

Based on a 1947 experiment, all current building codes require a minimum net free vent area (NFVA) of 1 sq. ft. for every 300 sq. ft. of attic floor area. In 1996, the Certainteed Corp. (a major manufacturer of roofing and insulation) sponsored extensive tests on the performance of attic insulation and ventilation. The results revealed that condensation would not occur in a full attic above an insulated ceiling, even if it were unvented, so long as the ceiling beneath the attic floor was sealed with an intact air and vapor retarder (airtight drywall with or without poly). However, penetrations through the ceiling as small as the gap around a 1½-in. vent pipe allowed enough moist air into the attic to cause condensation under some conditions. Because it is difficult if not impossible to build or maintain a perfect ceiling air and vapor retarder, venting the attic would seem to be good insurance. The combination of ridge and soffit vents always provide the most effective ventilation for the attic.

The tests also showed that condensation would occur on cathedral ceilings in every case when the insulation was not supplied with an air channel under the roof deck. Interestingly enough, condensation did not occur on cathedral ceilings that had a vent channel between the insulation and the underside of the roof deck but did not have a ridge or soffit vent outlet and inlet. For some reason, the dead air space alone seemed to be enough to prevent condensation.

The bath fan is caulked to the ceiling, and the plumbing vent stack is sealed with expanding foam.

TIP

Energy Conservation

Insulation is *not* the most important element of the old-house energy-conservation program. It's more cost effective to reduce infiltration heat loss than to beef up existing insulation beyond whatever the existing wall cavities and attic joists can easily accommodate (typically, R-11 to R-15 for walls and R-38 to R-54 for flat ceilings). ■ ■ ■

INSULATION THEORY AND PRACTICE

It's important to have a thorough understanding of the art and science of insulation, because as much damage can be occasioned by incomplete comprehension as by incorrect application.

The passage of heat through solid materials is called *conduction*. An *insulator* is anything that retards this movement. Trapped (dead) air is an excellent insulator. A hollow wall itself is not a dead-air space, because the volume of air is large enough to allow the transfer of heat by convection. Currents of air, which arise whenever a temperature difference exists across an enclosed space, transfer heat between moving molecules—any air space wider than ¾ in. will permit the formation of convection currents.

The old-timers applied the principle of dead air when they filled the walls of their houses with corncobs, seaweed, sawdust, straw and mud, and even bricks. Fibrous insulation works because its tangled web of fibers retards air circulation (and hence, convective heat transfer). Foams insulate because they contain closed cells filled with inert gases that resist conductive heat flow.

The Importance of R-Factor

The effectiveness of insulation is rated by its ability to slow heat transfer, as measured by its R-factor. Because the R-factor varies according to the density and other properties of a material, it is also related to thickness—an important consideration when determining the cost effectiveness of a given insulator for a particular application. Generally, the price of insulation is directly proportional to its R-value per inch. The synthetic foams are the best insulators but also the most expensive. Loose-fill material is cheap, but professional application is not.

The chart on pp. 268–269 describes commonly used insulation materials and their applications. When first introduced in the 1920s, the typical insulation blanket was only ¼ in. to 1 in. thick. Yet even this marginal amount of insulation significantly increased the comfort of the house and lowered heating costs. The bottom line is, as heating costs rise, more insulation is more cost-effective. There is, however, an economic point of diminishing returns: just 2 in. of fiberglass installed in a bare wall may decrease heat loss by 80 percent; 4 in. will save 90 percent; but 8 in. will save only 95 percent.

Is the extra cost of the insulation and/or the added wall thickness justified by the fuel savings over a short enough payback period? Today the answer is yes, for that last 10 percent anyway. In the 1960s, when architects and engineers recommended values of R-11 for walls and R-19 for ceilings and oil was cheap as dirt, it wouldn't have been. At the height of the energy crises of the 1970s, the minimum jumped to R-19 and R-38, respectively, and superinsulated homes with values up to R-40 and R-60 were built throughout the snowbelt. Today, these heavily insulated houses seem a bit extreme, but who knows when the next fuel price hike will make that last 3 percent of heat-loss resistance worth the price.

Insulation Strategies for Old Houses

The existing structure of an old house limits the amount of insulation you can stuff into the walls and the options you have for doing it. Because, after the windows, most of a house's heat loss is through the roof rather than the walls, insulation retrofit dollars are best invested in the attic, where it's usually easiest to add extra depth.

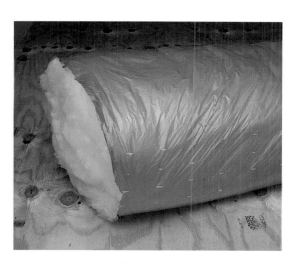

A number of new forms of batt insulation have come onto the market in recent years, including "itch-free" Miraflex fibers, which won't get into your lungs (top); encapsulated fiberglass, which is wrapped up to stay put (upper middle); new cotton insulation made from cotton-mill waste (lower middle); and wool insulation blankets, which come from New Zealand (bottom).

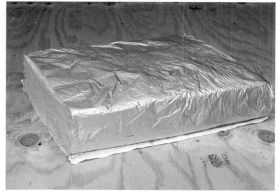

Of course, if there is no insulation in the walls at all, it definitely pays to add it, even if you are leaving the interior walls undisturbed and need to blow in insulation from the exterior. But if the walls are insulated with the 2-in.-thick Thermite fiberglass batts of the 1940s and 1950s, the cost of stuffing the wall cavities full might be better spent on tightening up air leaks (unless you plan to gut the plaster anyway).

ROLLING IT IN: A LOOK AT FIBERGLASS

BATTS One of the reasons I became a renovation contractor was so that I could hire other people to install the fiberglass. There are few experiences truly less enjoyable than stapling fiberglass insulation batts overhead on a hot humid summer day in a 140°F attic. The fibers stick to the sweat on your face and arms and build up until you begin to resemble a large poodle or less-than-cuddly teddy bear.

Yet fiberglass insulation is undeniably cheap, easily installed, and versatile. It is suited for almost every application in both old and new houses. Recently, manufacturers have begun to address the irritation problem by producing fiberglass batts that are encapsulated in a continuous perforated polyethylene wrapper that ostensibly contains the fibers so they can't get into the air and under your skin and into your lungs. Encapsulated fiberglass batts cost about 5 percent more than standard batts.

Residential Insulation Characteristics

Material	Description	Application	R-Value per Inch (avg.)	Comments
Fiberglass	Continuous rolls and precut batts for framing that is 16 in. or 24 in. on center. Standard thicknesses are 3½ in. (R-11), 5½ in. (R-19), 8½ in. (R-25), and 12 in. (R-38). Also, high-density batts for R-15, R-21, R-30 and R-38 (@ 10¼ in.), respectively. Available unfaced or with aluminum foil or kraft-paper vapor retarder. Also loose fill for blowing or pouring; 1-in. rolls for pipe-wrap; and rigid panels for sheathing.	Used in walls, floors, and ceilings, fitted or blown between studs, joists, and rafters. Faced batts or rolls are stapled through flanges. Unfaced batts or rolls are friction-fitted and covered with polyethylene vapor barrier. (In severe cold climates, recommended over faced insulation as well.) Loose fill blown by machine into wall cavities or poured between attic floor joists.	3.2 (batts) 3.8 (high-density) 2.2 (loose fill)	Least expensive, most versatile, and easy to install. Short-term skin and lung irritant, possible long-term carcinogen; wear respirator, goggles, gloves, and loose-fitting clothing. (Newly available Owens-Corning Miraflex and other "encapsulated" fiberglass batts don't itch or release fibers into the air and lungs.) Preferred nesting material of rodents (absorbs feces and odor). Noncombustible, nontoxic, will not rot, but holds water like a sponge. Blown-in tends to settle in wall cavities.
Mineral or rock wool	Mineral wool (manufactured from steel mill blast-furnace slag) precut paper-faced batts in thickness from 3 in. to 8 in. Loose-fill rock wool (manufactured from basalt or diabase rock). Will withstand temperatures in excess of 500°F.	Stapled through flanges, poured into attic bays, blown into walls.	3.2 batts 3.1 loose-fill	More expensive than fiberglass. Finer, sharper particles, same health concerns and precautions. Noncombustible, won't rot. Holds water. Superior heat-resistance and acoustical properties well suited to commercial and industrial applications. Only one U.S. manufacturer of mineral wool batts at time of publication.
Organic fiber batts, blankets, and loose-fill (3.2/inch)	Insulcot: 75% recycled textile-mill waste cotton 25% polyester, Kraft-faced batts, and loose-fill; Thermofleece Natural Wool Insulation: industrial wool waste mixed with other polymers.	Fitted or stapled between studs and joists or poured into attics.	3.2	Nontoxic and nonirritating. As easy to install as unfaced fiberglass batts, without the potential health problems. Limited distribution network for cotton insulation restricts availability to mostly southeastern U.S. No domestic manufacturer of wool insulation at time of publication. Import from New Zealand or Germany prohibitively expensive.
Loose-fill cellulose	Shredded newspaper (with various additives). Loose fill for blowing or pouring into cavities and attics.	Poured from bag into attic bays, blown into wall cavities from exterior with rented or contractor-supplied machinery. Mainly used for retrofitting old houses (better than nothing) and for capping attics. Typical density 1.5 pcf (pounds per cubic foot).	3.2	Inexpensive, though professional installation is not. Can settle in walls if not enough blown in. Flammable. Some condensation problems reported in retrofits without proper vapor barrier. Soaks up water. Does not itch. Wear dust mask and eye protection; additives are hazardous if breathed in.
Adhesive cellulose fiber (K-13)	A mixture of cellulose, glue, and whitening agents.	Machine-sprayed directly over walls, into stud cavities, over masonry, and onto steel sidings and beams. It can be left exposed or covered over as desired. Will adhere to almost any dry surface.	5.5	Excellent for insulating metal buildings and problem surfaces such as the cellar side of brick or stone foundation walls. Needs masking to protect adjacent areas. Can be used as combination insulation and finish ceiling. Will flake off when rubbed. Noncombustible, water-resistant. Not cheap.
Wet-spray cellulose	Cellulose fibers moistened with a small amount of water and acrylic binder that allows insulation to adhere to cavity and itself. High density (up to 3.5 pcf) makes tight seal and greater R-value.	Contractor-installed system. Blown into open wall cavities between stud bays, excess shaved flush with power trimmer. For both renovation and new construction.	3.5	High-density cellulose does not settle, blocks infiltration better than fiberglass. Dust and fire-retardant chemicals possible irritants; wear dust mask during application. Like similar contractor-installed or proprietary systems, more costly than standard loose-fill application.

Material	Description	Application	R-Value per Inch (avg.)	Comments
Blown-In Blanket System (BIBS)	Cellulose fiber augmented with binders (to ensure good seal and prevent settling).	Blown dry into open wall cavities faced with plastic mesh screening.	3.5 to 4.0	Proprietary system. Professional installation required.
InSealation, Icynene Polyurethane spray foam	Open-cell, carbon-dioxide-blown, expansive polyurethane spray insulation.	Thin layer sprayed into open wall cavities, expands 100-fold in seconds. Excess trimmed with handsaw.	6.2	Installed by licensed contractors. Cost-competitive with wet-spray cellulose stems. Sticks well to most surfaces, makes tight air seal. Non-ozone-depleting. Also available in a type for expansion in closed cavities.
Extruded polystyrene foam: "blueboard" (Styrofoam), "pinkboard" (Foamular), et al.	2x8 tongue-and-groove sheets, 1 in., 1½ in., and 2 in. thick (other thicknesses also available). Cells filled with air.	Glued to surfaces or friction fit. Used extensively for insulating outside of foundations, under concrete slabs, exposed crawl spaces. Also used on interior basement walls, between attic joists, and over roof decks.	5.0	Water-resistant, rigid. Releases toxic gases when burned; must be covered with fire-rated drywall for interior use. Nontoxic, nonirritating. No installation precautions. Degrades in sunlight. Since early 1990s, manufacture no longer involves use of ozone-depleting foaming agents.
Expanded polystyrene foam "beadboard" (Durovon)	2x8 and 4x8 sheets, 1 in. to 6 in. thick.	Used on interior of basement, crawl space, between studs and joists with appropriate fire-rate drywall.	4.0	Not for burial or outdoor use, will absorb water, easily broken or crushed. Burning emits toxic gases. Less expensive than extruded foams. Very popular mouse-nesting material.
Polyurethane foam	4x8 sheets, unfaced or kraft-paper covered. Cells filled with Freon, gas instead of air.	Same as for expanded polystyrene foam.	6.2	Expensive, releases toxic gases when burned. Possible long-term thermal degradation (loss of R-value).
Polyisocyanurate foam (Thermax, High-R, R-Max, et al.)	4x8 sheets, ½ in., ¾ in., 1 in., 1½ in., 2 in., and 4 in. thick. Aluminum-foil faced both sides, fiberglass-fiber reinforced, closed-cell, gas filled. Sandwiched with waferboard drywall panels to make stress-skin panels, used for prefabs and energy-efficient timber framing.	Installed by nailing, gluing, friction-fit. Widely used as exterior wall sheathing, over-roof deck insulation, and for maximum R-value where space is at a premium. Often used under drywall for a vapor barrier over fiberglass batts.	7.4 to 8.0	Most expensive. Greater fire resistance, lower toxicity when burning. Irritating fiberglass fibers and dust released when material is cut and handled. Not for exposure to weather or sunlight. Will absorb water. Thermally stable. New product, test results need long-term verification in field.
Impregnated fiberboard (Celotex)	4x8 sheets, ½ in. thick. Made from ground corn husks, other organic and vegetable waste fibers, sometimes impregnated with asphalt as a moisture repellant.	Widely used for nonstructural sheathing, occasionally found under drywall or plastic wall tiles in remodeled old houses.	2.0	Nonasphalt types will absorb water easily and hold it against the framing until the whole mess rots. Fiber "IB" panels will smolder if ignited. Sawdust is an irritant.
Perlite, vermiculite	Perlite is a natural mineral foam of volcanic origin. Vermiculite is a kind of mineral "popcorn" made from mica-rich rock.	Both are loose fill, poured into cavities. Widely used to insulate cores of concrete block walls.	2.5	Both are nonflammable, rot-proof. Perlite dust is hazardous. Vermiculite will absorb water. Contains asbestos, can cause lung and liver cancer. Should not be used as attic insulation (a very common use). Wear respirator when handling.
Sawdust	Widely used as early form of insulation.	Loose fill.	1.0	Soaks up water, causing wall framing to rot. Also settles and is flammable. Solid wood has the same R-value as sawdust.

Where to Insulate

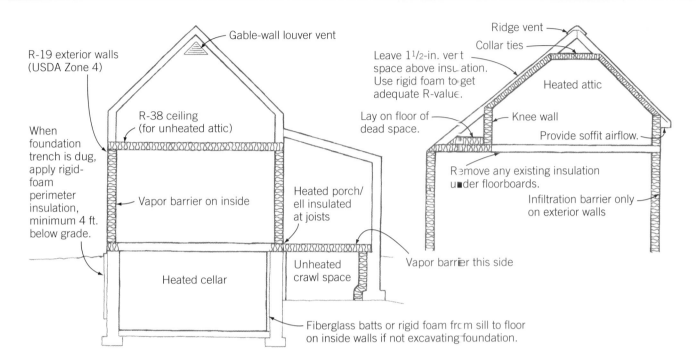

R-19 exterior walls (USDA Zone 4)

Gable-wall louver vent

When foundation trench is dug, apply rigid-foam perimeter insulation, minimum 4 ft. below grade.

R-38 ceiling (for unheated attic)

Vapor barrier on inside

Heated porch/ell insulated at joists

Heated cellar

Unheated crawl space

Fiberglass batts or rigid foam from sill to floor on inside walls if not excavating foundation.

Ridge vent

Collar ties

Leave 1½-in. vent space above insulation. Use rigid foam to get adequate R-value.

Heated attic

Lay on floor of dead space.

Knee wall

Provide soffit airflow.

Remove any existing insulation under floorboards.

Infiltration barrier only on exterior walls

Vapor barrier this side

Owens Corning has also begun producing Miraflex® batts, which feature a long fiber that feels as soft as cotton and that lacks the binders that give fiberglass insulation its distinctive pink or yellow color (and contribute mightily to its irritability). At present, this added comfort and safety comes at a hefty premium, up to 30 percent more than regular fiberglass.

Together with rigid polyisocyanurate foam panels, it's possible to add more than enough heat-loss resistance without spending a fortune or seriously compromising the old house's original features (granted, if gutting the walls is considered only a minor compromise). The drawing above shows the general areas where insulation should be installed in the thermal envelope of an old house.

FOIL-FACED BATTS Although it might seem that foil-faced insulation would increase the total R-value (the reflective surface is supposed to bounce radiated heat back toward the room

from which it escaped), the advantage is mostly theoretical. To be effective, the foil must be separated from the back of the interior wall surface by at least ¾ in. Ideally, stapling the flanges of the batts to the inside edges of the studs accomplishes this; in reality, the batts sag forward. The only way to maintain a dead-air space is to nail spacers to the studs over the insulation, which is a great deal of trouble and expense for a questionable benefit, because once the shiny surface tarnishes, it loses its reflectivity.

PAPER-FACED BATTS Some builders insist that kraft-paper-faced insulation be stapled over the studs to prevent "fish mouths" (puckers in the batt flange) that would act as holes in the vapor retarder. Others maintain that the batts should be stapled to the sides of the studs to prevent the paper from lumping up behind the drywall. But still others say stapling to the stud sides compresses the insulation, reducing its R-value. I'm not sure that this effect is significant enough to worry about. But bunched up paper can cause nails in the drywall to pop out later. Besides, even if it were possible to staple the paper perfectly flat, without rips and tears, asphalt-backed kraft paper is not much more of a vapor barrier than ordinary plywood and it is totally ineffective as an air barrier. The only reason to use paper-faced insulation is to decrease the amount of fibers floating around the room and into your clothing and lungs. Paper flange batts are also the only kind available for ceiling insulation.

UNFACED BATTS Unfaced insulation is actually much easier to cut to size and faster to install than faced batts or rolls. Because it can be cut to fit odd spaces or to lay in horizontally across wide bays, there's less waste. It also fits tighter. Hardly any more fibers are released than from faced insulation. The batts are simply pressed into the stud cavities and then cut and folded around obstructions.

HIGH-DENSITY BATTS New high-density unfaced batts are even better than standard unfaced insulation. The fiberglass is stiffer, which makes for a tighter fit and produces less airborne fibers. The 3½-in. batts have an R-value of R-15 instead of R-11; and 5½-in. batts top out at R-21 instead of R-19. An 8½-in. R-30 batt and a 10¼-in. R-38 batt (for 2x10 and 2x12 ceilings where an airspace is required) are also available.

Insulating an Attic

An attic space large enough to consider converting into living area can be a mixed blessing. Sloped ceilings are difficult and expensive to insulate adequately, and preventing condensation in cathedral ceilings is always a challenge. The most effective strategy, which is also the most expensive, is to insulate on top of the roof deck. This completely eliminates the need for an air channel but does create problems with retrofitting cornice trim.

Whether to staple the batt inside the bay or on the face is one of those eternally controversial questions (like whether to use oil or latex paint). Whatever the thermal drawbacks, stapling inside the bay makes it a lot easier to finish the walls since the studs are not hidden beneath lumpy paper.

On the other hand, insulating an unfinished attic is both economical and easy. But before adding extra insulation, seal all the obvious air leaks (as described earlier) and attempt to retrofit a reasonably effective vapor retarder. Ideally, this could be done when old ceilings are gutted. Otherwise, vapor-resistant paint could be used.

Another option (assuming either that existing attic floorboards can be easily pried up or that there are no attic floorboards) is to fit the barrier between the attic floor joists. Pull up any existing batt insulation or scoop up and bag any loose fill (wear a respirator). Cut strips of poly long enough to lay between the joist bays and overlap each other at the sides of the joists. Seal the overlap with caulk or polyethylene tape (such as Tyvek® tape) before stapling the poly across the tops of the joists.

If the old insulation is in good shape, it can be reused. Any additional batts or new insulation should be unfaced and laid perpendicular

Do's and Don'ts of Installing Fiberglass Insulation

Never mash fiberglass batts to fit under or around a pipe or electrical cable. Compressed fiberglass loses its R-value because its dead-air space is drastically reduced. Instead, split the batt to half its thickness. Slide half of the batt behind the pipe or cable and lay the remaining piece on top.

To insulate around an electrical box, split the insulation so you can loosely tuck some behind the box and then carefully cut the remaining insulation around the box. The same split-and-cut technique is used wherever insulation encounters obstacles and changes in depth, such as where a ceiling joist splices into a rafter. Simply butting the insulation against the resulting bump-out creates a gap and squishes the batt at the same time. Both conditions should be scrupulously avoided. Don't leave any gaps at the top or bottom of the bays or where the batts butt together.

Also, don't pack fiberglass insulation into the gaps around windows and doors—fill these gaps loosely. (A wood shingle makes an excellent stuffing spatula.) Urethane spray foam does a much better job of insulating and sealing these trouble spots. It's expensive and messy to use, but its superior R-value and infiltration resistance are well worth the trouble. Use the low-expansion foam for filling around window and doorjambs. Highly expansive foams can bow the jambs and cause the window or door to stick.

If you insulate above ceiling-mounted light fixtures, make sure they are designed for that purpose (rated IC); otherwise, the buildup of trapped heat could start a fire. (Don't use fixtures that can't be covered with insulation.)

Splitting the batt in half is a good way to fit fiberglass batts around wires and pipes.

to the existing batts. Take care not to block soffit vent intakes and to add baffles to establish or extend the requisite air channel. A 2-ft.-long piece of 2-in.-thick XPS rigid foam is ideal for this purpose.

Insulating over a Cellar or Crawl Space

Adding insulation between the floor joists of an unheated cellar or crawl space presents several difficulties. Short of taking up the floorboards, there's no way to install an effective vapor barrier over the insulation. (Depending on your climate zone, if the crawl space is tightly sealed and has a ground sheet of poly, there may be no significant temperature difference between it and the living areas, and a vapor diffusion retarder is thus not necessary.)

The common wisdom calls for stuffing fiberglass batts, paper-side up, against the flooring and stapling chicken wire or springing lengths of metal strapping (like the kind used to band palettes of lumber together) between the bottoms of the joists to keep the stuff from falling down. Sliding the batts up between rows of furring strips is another suggestion. Metal hangers (such as E-Z Hanger)—available up to 4 ft. long—are also a possibility; they are hammered between the joists to support the insulation.

Having eaten more fiberglass than I'd like to think about, I long ago decided that this is the kind of situation that rigid foam was made for. Because of the vapor-barrier effect of the aluminum facing, use a layer of ½-in. rigid polyisocyanurate foam board, followed by two 2-in. layers of less expensive extruded polystyrene blueboard or expanded polystyrene beadboard. An alternative vapor retarder could be fashioned from strips of polyethylene cut to fit between the joists and taped to their edges. But the best solution might be to insulate the crawl space walls instead of the floor and bring the crawlspace into the heated building envelope.

Don't pack the gaps around windows. The insulation should be able to expand just enough to fill the cavity without compressing. A serrated bread knife is a good tool for both cutting and stuffing fiberglass.

Never stuff insulation behind an electrical box. Split the batt to fit neatly behind the box and then cut the rest to fit around it.

Designer Insulation

If your schedule and budget won't permit immediate finishing, and you find yourself living with kraft-paper or aluminum-foil decor for a time, it is imperative to cover the insulation with a poly film. Faced (as opposed to unfaced) decor has a way of growing more pleasing day by day, as the urgency to do more slips away: The house is warm, why bother? I remember a particular brand of insulation I used back in the 1970s that was printed with a woven-mat pattern, almost as if the manufacturer had expected it to double as temporary wallpaper. I remember spending the night in such a house, sleeping on a guest bed next to the wall; I woke up feeling as though I'd spent the night in a nettle patch. A fine rain of fiberglass slivers had fallen into the blankets and from them, onto me.

If one were condemned to use fiberglass, I'd apply the polyethylene, staple the insulation paper-side out, and then—to permit moisture release—cut a series of diagonal slashes through the facing. Close the joist bays with sheets of fiberboard (or other vapor-permeable material) to prevent a drizzle of glass fibers into the household air. When the crawl space is exposed to the outside (as with a heated porch or house on piers), protect the insulation against infestation by rodents or insects by nailing asphalt-impregnated fiberboard or pressure-treated plywood to the bottoms of the joists.

Insulating between Widely Spaced Studs

In some old houses, the wall studs might be spaced as much as 32 in. on center, much too far apart to support drywall or plaster base, without the original wood lath or some kind of supplemental framing. (This is an ideal application for horizontally laid unfaced batt fiberglass.) It's quite common to find pole or timber rafters spaced as much as 4 ft. on center. An alternative

to adding an extra stud or rafter between each bay is to nail 1x4 spruce strapping over the framing, spaced horizontally on 16-in. centers. Although the vapor barrier will keep the insulation from falling out of the bays, the strapping prevents the whole thing from bulging into the room like an unbelted beer belly until the wallboard is applied.

POURED AND BLOWN-IN INSULATION

Fiberglass batt and blanket insulation is most effective when installed between regularly spaced studs and joists in walls and unobstructed attics. Otherwise, loose fill insulators will do a better job, particularly in attics where fiberglass batts compress under their own weight when laid down in layers thicker than 12 in.

Loose-fill insulation is ideal for increasing the R-value of a poorly insulated attic. However, the material should not be dumped on top of existing batt insulation. Instead, pull up the old material and seal any air leaks, as already described. Even if you took the time to carefully slice through the flanges at the bottoms of the joists so that the batts could be removed with their paper facing relatively intact, the stuff is likely to contain more dust, seeds, and mouse-droppings by weight than insulation and probably isn't worth salvaging. Because any batts, new or old, would have to be laid on top of the loose-fill material, filling the attic to the appropriate depth with new loose fill insulation is a lot less trouble. A piece of plywood notched to fit over the tops of the joists makes a gauge board for checking the depth of the fill, which is typically 6 in. to 12 in. higher than the top of the joists. Likewise, a strip of plywood wired to a garden rake makes a useful spreading and leveling tool.

Vermiculite

The attics of many old houses are often insulated with vermiculite, a mineral "popcorn" made from expanded mica or perlite (a mineral foam of volcanic origin). These materials have an R-value of about 2.5 per inch and are light, nonflammable, rot- and vermin-proof, and non-irritating (although perlite dust is hazardous to breathe). On the downside, vermiculite absorbs water like a sponge, which is why it is a major component of potting soils and growing mediums and problematic under a leaky roof (although the vermiculite manufactured for insulation purposes is treated with a water repellant).

But the biggest problem is that 70 percent of the vermiculite ore mined in the world came from one particular mine in Libby, Montana, which happened to be naturally contaminated with asbestos. Usually, when vermiculite is isolated in a vented attic, there's not much chance of any asbestos getting into the household air. So the best thing to do with vermiculite insulation is to leave it alone. (You may want to send a sample to a testing laboratory to determine its asbestos content just for your own peace of mind. Wear a dust mask and gloves and wet down the sample when collecting it.) Like all asbestos-containing materials, professional removal of vermiculite is both mandatory and expensive.

The real danger of asbestos exposure arises when your renovations include tearing out an old attic ceiling or wall cavity that has been filled with vermiculite. This is one case where it's probably not a good idea to scoop up the old insulation to air-seal the attic ceiling or retrofit a vapor barrier. Encapsulating the existing vermiculite by pouring new (noncontaminated) vermiculite or other loose fill insulation on top of it is a better solution. Since both perlite and vermiculite are relatively expensive, their main use is for insulating the cores of concrete blocks rather than attics.

Fiberglass or Cellulose

That leaves either fiberglass or cellulose. The problem with all loose-fill insulations (poured or blown in) is settlement. As loose-fill insulations settle, their density increases and their overall thickness decreases which translates into a drop in R-value. It is critical to install enough material to attain the intended R-value when the insulation finally stops settling. Fiberglass settles relatively little (0 percent to 8 percent) and its R-value drops only about 0.5 percent for every 1 percent of settlement. On the other hand, cellulose settles 15 percent to 25 percent over time, with a 1 percent drop in R-value for every 1 percent loss in thickness. Unfortunately, many irresponsible or unscrupulous contractors will pour (or blow in) only enough insulation to meet the installed value, not the settled value. Some manufacturers now list both values on their labels.

For best results, always overfill loose-fill cellulose by 25 percent. (And specify the settled R-value when hiring an insulation contractor.) If blowing rather than pouring insulation into the attic, set the machine at low pressure and low speed. When blown into wall cavities at the proper density of 3.5 lb. to 4 lb. per cubic foot (twice the conventional density of loose fill), cellulose does not settle at all.

Tests have also shown that when the attic air temperature falls below 30°F, convection currents arise within loose-fill fiberglass, resulting in a loss of R-value that increases to 50 percent at 10°F and lower. Since the phenomenon does not occur in loose-fill cellulose at any temperature, this would seem to rule out the use of loose-fill fiberglass attic insulation in cold climates. However, there is no evidence of convection currents within fiberglass batts. So laying high-density fiberglass batts over loose fill is one way to preserve the R-value of deep insulation while preventing convective R-value drop.

FIBERGLASS AND CELLULOSE PROS AND CONS

The manufacturers of cellulose and fiberglass insulation have been waging a long-standing propaganda war for the hearts and minds of the consumer. While the cellulose industry cites studies suggesting that fiberglass may be carcinogenic, the fiberglass producers allege that cellulose is a fire hazard and can rot walls because of its absorbency. The fiberglass people claim that the very chemicals used to imbue the cellulose fibers with fire resistance can corrode electrical boxes and cables, thereby igniting electrical fires. While that might have been true of some of the compounds used by fly-by-night operators during the heydays of the 1970s energy crises, the borax used today is noncorrosive.

Personally, I vote for insulating with blow-in cellulose—which is only a dirty job, as opposed to the dirty and itchy job of blowing in fiberglass.

PROBLEMS WITH BLOWING IN Ultimately,

both kinds of blown-in insulation have always been inherently problematic. Unless sources of excessive moisture (chiefly a damp cellar) are eliminated, blowing the walls full of cellulose or fiberglass without the ability to retrofit an effective vapor barrier all too often causes condensation, particularly when impermeable oil-based paint covered the exterior. (That particular source of trouble was apt to be short lived, however, since the migrating moisture would soon peel the paint off the siding.)

The other major difficulty with blown-in insulation is that the application was necessarily blind. Without an expensive infrared scan ($150 to $300 extra), it was impossible to be absolutely certain that all the cavities were actually filled with insulation. Only a very conscientious contractor who was willing to take the time to carefully probe each wall cavity could come reasonably close to certainty.

Blown-In Blankets

If you intend to gut the walls in any event, much of the rationale for blowing in cellulose or fiberglass disappears because it is far easier, faster, and cheaper to insulate exposed walls with ordinary fiberglass batts. On the other hand, since it fills every nook and cranny within the wall cavity, blown-in high-density cellulose or any of the wet-spray or blown-in blanket (BIB) systems form a much more effective air barrier and perform generally better than batt insulation.

There are several professionally installed proprietary systems that allow cellulose or fiberglass mixed with a binder to be sprayed into open wall cavities. As shown in the top photo on the facing page, the excess insulation is shaved off with a special roller. Other BIB systems use a mesh-reinforced plastic membrane (for example, ParPac) stapled across the studs to contain the cellulose until the binder sets up. (The mesh can also be used with dry cellulose to cover open bays at lower density.) There is also a BIB system that mixes adhesive with fiberglass or cellulose with a special nozzle to form fast-drying foam that fills the stud bay behind a special leveling trowel as it is moved up the wall. These methods offer the advantage of visual inspection throughout the entire procedure.

Wet-spray cellulose is trimmed with a special roller and the excess is reused (top). Reinforced nylon
netting allows cellulose mixed with a binder to be blown into open wall cavities. Both systems yield a
much tighter air barrier than standard batt insulation provides (bottom). (Top photo courtesy Green Stone
Industries; bottom photo courtesy ParPak)

Walls, Ceilings, and Floors

It has been said that "dirt is matter out of place," but if it has come to be in the right places through the long years, we call it "patina" and admire it.

—HERBERT WHEATON CONGDON,
EARLY AMERICAN HOMES FOR TODAY

As with the sagging features of the formerly young and beautiful, a facelift is futile if it renews only exterior appearance without a corresponding improvement on the inside. For tired faces, we deal with self-esteem; for old houses, with plaster.

In North America, from the earliest colonial days until just after World War II, plaster was an almost universal interior wall finish. It was cheap, the raw materials were readily available, and the craft was highly developed. Plaster also made a tight, strong wall with fairly good air flow resistance, a fact of no small importance in the era before modern insulation and caulking. It could be argued that plastered walls contributed to the longevity of old houses in cold

It's a rare old house that doesn't need at least some plaster repair— but with luck, not as much as this one.

climates by helping reduce excessive condensation in wall cavities.

But the plasterer's craft was demanding and expensive, both because of the skill it required and the amount of time it took to finish a house. The prefabricated plasterboard panel (also known as drywall) was introduced to the building trade in 1915 as a time- and labor-saving alternative. This truly revolutionary product was so successful that within a few years after World War I, the traditional "wet wall" plastered house was as obsolete as the braced frame. It is only since the last two decades of the twentieth century with the burgeoning interest in authentic renovation and nostalgia for traditional techniques and styles that the craft of traditional plastering has enjoyed a definite renaissance in both high-end new construction and old house renovation.

Today, in urban areas at least, there are enough plasterers willing to compete with drywall installers that the price of a traditional plaster job may be not as high as one might expect. Machine sprayers and other technical advances have also helped bring down the cost.

Seen from behind, this is what good keying and a solid plaster finish look like.

WHAT TO DO ABOUT PLASTER?

The first major question the old-house renovator must answer is, What to do about the plaster? How bad is it and how feasible are the repairs? Are there any historic features that should be conserved at all costs? Should the walls be gutted or does it make more sense to leave them intact? Are there any reasonable alternatives between traditional plastering and drywall? Are professional subcontractors required?

Conservationists will argue that the original plaster finish should be repaired or restored with new material mixed and applied according to traditional recipes and finishes. Preservationists are not averse to using modern materials to repair the original plaster or, should repair prove impractical, to hiring a professional plasterer to duplicate the original texture. Likewise, they suffer no qualms over using modern latex ceiling paints in place of the traditional calcimine or whitewash finishes. Utilitarian remodelers, depending on their sensitivity (or lack of it), will not hesitate to gut the entire house at the first

sign of a bulge in the ceiling and wrap every available surface in drywall and texture paint.

Except for the house whose plaster ceilings are distinguished by ornamental medallions and cornice castings worthy of professional restoration, I confess that my feelings about plaster lie somewhere between the liberal preservationists and the conservative remodelers. I'd favor traditional plastering techniques for minor repairs and opt for modern alternatives when facing wholesale replacement. In other words, unless

Causes of Plaster Failure

There are ancient houses whose original plaster is still sound and solid after the ebb and flow of centuries. And there are others, much younger, in which the plaster has fallen from the ceilings and crumbled to dust behind the wallpaper, having given up the ghost long before the rest of the house grew into its age.

If properly mixed and applied and protected against moisture and structural movement, a plaster wall finish is as close to eternal as any building material can ever hope to be. That this ideal was so seldom attained has more to do with faulty workmanship and structural deficiencies than any inherent shortcomings of the material itself. Some of the causes of plaster failure are the following:

■ **Dry lath.** Insufficiently moistened wood lath will suck water out of the plaster, preventing a good cure.

■ **Running joints.** The joints between lathes should be staggered in blocks of six to eight to prevent stress cracks.

■ **Low humidity and temperature.** Plaster has to be kept moist and prevented from freezing while curing, a process that takes several days.

■ **Drafts, overly rapid drying.** Ventilation is necessary to remove moisture from the building, but direct drafts dry the plaster before it cures, causing cracks.

■ **Bad mix.** Plaster and water must be fresh and clean and mixed in the proper proportions to make strong keys.

■ **Undersized ceiling joists.** The weight of plaster causes sagging or cracking and can even pull the lath off a ceiling if the joists are too bouncy.

■ **Frame shrinkage and building settlement.** The most common and most readily repairable causes of stress cracks.

■ **Vibration.** Over time, heavy traffic on a nearby street can loosen plaster bonds.

■ **Water damage.** Moisture from leaking plumbing, walls, roofs, and windows or from condensation within wall cavities causes irreversible and fatal disintegration of plaster.

there was a compelling reason not to, I'd be more likely to gut old problem plaster rather than fuss with the tedium of repairing it. But, as I explain below, it doesn't necessarily follow that I'd recommend replacing traditional plaster with drywall.

Repairing Cracks and Holes

Hairline cracks, which are the most innocuous form of plaster failure, usually result from the normal settling of a house over time. Assuming that the settling has stabilized (and there are no foundation problems), such cracks are easy to repair. Superficial cracks can be patched with a coat of all-purpose drywall joint compound reinforced with fiberglass mesh joint tape. To patch a deeper or wider crack, first use the blade of a stiff putty knife or a utility knife to cut back its edges to form a keyway (see the drawing below). This helps lock the patch into place.

Then, with a taping knife, trowel joint compound into the crack and embed a strip of fiberglass-mesh joint tape in the compound. Knock off any ridges or bumps in this coat after it dries and apply a second coat, smoothing it outward with a wide taping paddle. Sand this coat to blend in with the rest of the surface. A third coat feathered out at least 2 in. beyond the undercoat and sanded smooth will make the repair all but invisible.

When walls settle and floors sag, the plaster cracks. Stresses tend to concentrate above doors and windows, which is where cracks are most likely to appear. To achieve a lasting repair, any movement must first be arrested.

 ## Patching Hairline Cracks

Undercut edge of crack with putty knife to form keyway (exaggerated for clarity).

Using 5-in.-wide taping knife, cover crack with joint compound and bed joint tape into it.

Joint compound
Joint tape

Apply second coat with 12-in. taping paddle. When dry, apply third coat, feathering out edges.

Quick-Set Compound

Ordinary joint compound will shrink or crack when used in holes deeper or wider than about ⅛ in. Use shrink-resistant quick-set joint compound instead. Depending on the number of cracks to patch, choose either 60-minute, 90-minute, or 120-minute drying time. One important caveat: Quick-set compound dries too hard for easy sanding and hence should be used only as a base coat. Use standard joint compound for the finish coat.

Refurbishing Damaged Plaster

Crack repair is tedious and time-consuming when, as is often the case, a goodly part of the wall or ceiling is mottled with a web of cracks. Yet, if the plaster itself is still firmly keyed to the lath, it still makes more sense to repair it than to remove it. The tried-and-true method for refurbishing sound but threadbare plaster is to reinforce it with a canvas lining that is designed to be covered with paint or wallpaper. This method is described below. Old-house restorer Mario Rodriquez has developed an alternate system that is more work but produces a finish that more nearly mimics the original plaster. (See "A Novel Method for Refurbishing Plaster Walls" on pp. 284–285).

REINFORCE PLASTER WITH LINING CANVAS

Lining canvas has a long history as a cure for cracked and peeling but basically sound plaster walls and ceilings. Although canvas cloth can still be had, most modern lining materials are made from polyester or fiberglass fabrics of varying thickness coated or saturated with a white acrylic latex primer. These are typically glued to the substrate with vinyl adhesive.

The thicker liners can bridge deep cracks and grooves and are also suitable for use over rough masonry and concrete block. Because they do have a surface texture, they are generally finished with wallpaper or texture paint. Thinner liners furnish a smooth surface suitable for painting. Loose and flaking paint should be scrapped off, and cracks and holes deeper than ¼ in. should be filled with a patching compound (such as Spackle®).

Heavier liners are also an alternative to removal if you need to redress the atrocity of wood paneling visited on a room by a bout of past remodeling. On walls, the liner is hung vertically, with seams butted, not overlapped. Like wallpaper, it is smoothed with a sponge or brush from the center outward a little at a time to eliminate air bubbles. Use gentle pressure to avoid forcing the liner into cracks. Allow the liner to dry for 4 days or 5 days before applying finish paint or wallcovering.

LEAVE EXISTING WALLPAPER

Because layers of wallpaper may actually reinforce the stability of the underlying plaster, you might consider painting over the paper instead of trying to remove it. This is a good quick-and-dirty intermediate strategy to brighten up a dingy room and make an old house habitable in the interim before you can afford to get down to serious renovation. Because of its irrevocability, the strategy described here applies only to generic wall coverings. If you suspect that the wallpaper either covering the plaster or hidden beneath later wall coverings is historically significant, do nothing without consulting a preservation professional. Remove an exploratory patch in an inconspicuous area first.

Remove any loose pieces of wallpaper or plaster with a putty knife. Then prime the entire wall with a pigmented shellac sealer (such as B-I-N® or Kilz™). Fill in holes with patching plaster and hairline cracks with latex caulk or ultralight spackling compound.

Prime all the patches and check the wallpaper for new bubbles that may have been raised by the primer. (Cut them out and patch and prime them, too.) Finish the patched and primed plaster (or wallpaper) with latex paint. Some remodelers (this is remodeling, not renovation) will lay down a coat of heavy texture paint or add texturing compound to the wall paint to obscure the outlines of the patches and wallpaper seams.

Repairing Sagging Ceilings

In an old house, a wallpapered ceiling is an ominous sign: Suspect a quick fix for powdery plaster. When the paper is stripped, what's left of the ceiling could come with it. Nevertheless, the wallpaper should be stripped, if only to assess the state of the underlying plaster. Fortunately, the bond between wallpaper and old plaster is seldom tenacious. Assisted by occasional sponging with warm water, the paper should lift off easily with a scraper. Stubborn paper can be dislodged with a rented wallpaper steamer. If most of the plaster is still on the ceiling or wall after the paper has been removed, crumbled areas can be patched and sags and cracks repaired.

REATTACH LATH TO JOISTS Sometimes a ceiling will sag because the nails anchoring the plaster lath to the joists have rusted away. A chronic water leak or corrosion caused by countless generations of mouse droppings is the usual cause. Use drywall screws to secure the fallen lath back in place and reduce the problem to one of simple crack repair and patching.

REATTACHING PLASTER TO LATH A ceiling also sags when the plaster separates from the underlying lath. This happens when, for a variety of reasons, the keys that bind the plaster to the lath have broken off. Use plaster washers, which are perforated metal discs with a countersunk screw hole, to pull the sagging plaster back tight against the lath. Unfortunately, bits of broken plaster and a truly remarkable quantity of rodent droppings and seed husks often make it all but impossible to flatten out the sag without some delicate surgery first.

The separated plaster might be amenable to repair with plaster washers. The adjoining blowout must be patched.

Textured Surfaces

Beware of textured ceilings or walls. Although the effect was sometimes worked into the finish coat of the plaster itself, from the 1920s until about 1935, textures were more often created with so-called plastic paints that typically contained asbestos. Stripping asbestos-laden texture paint is a complicated and hazardous operation. Unfortunately, plastic paints were often promoted as a cure for failing plaster ceilings. Although they did mask the cracks, the added weight of these heavy joint-compound-like products actually tended to accelerate the problem. This could be a good thing insofar as asbestos removal may already have occurred, albeit inadvertently.

A Novel Method for Refurbishing Plaster Walls

House restorer Mario Rodriguez has developed an elegant system for refinishing walls to mimic the original plaster. It involves using a reinforcing mesh that is coated with joint compound. Begin by stripping any old wallpaper. Then clean any debris from the cracks. Cut out loose areas and patch them with drywall. Use 80-grit sandpaper to rough up glossy paint for better bonding.

■ Apply the mesh. Before applying the mesh, coat the walls with a polyvinyl acetate (PVA) bonding agent to ensure good adherence (available from your local lumberyard

Loose plaster is dug out and the edges of the crack are chamfered with a taping knife before patching with fiberglass mesh tape and joint compound.

or a masonry supplier). Once the walls are prepped, reinforce them with Perma Glas-Mesh, a 3-ft.-wide version of ordinary self-sticking fiberglass mesh joint tape. It takes two people to unroll the mesh and keep it from sagging as it's stuck onto the wall. The mesh also serves as a base for the fortified joint compound that will be troweled over it.

■ Prepare the first-coat mix. Remove about one quarter of the contents of a 5-gal. pail of all-purpose joint compound and replace it with five 1-lb. coffee cans full of #00 mason's sand (a fine-grained pebble-free sand available from masonry suppliers). Blend the mixture with a mixing paddle powered by a low-speed heavy-duty drill.

■ Apply base coats. Trowel the fortified compound thinly onto the mesh, filling holes and cracks, covering seams and patches, and otherwise leaving the mesh just barely showing through. Allow the first coat to dry and then trowel on a second coat of fortified compound over any depressions or defects. After the second coat dries, level

Fiberglass mesh reinforces the previously patched and prepped old plaster.

A troweled-on base coat of joint compound fortified with mason's sand fills in cracks and holes and covers patches and the mesh.

Lumps and ridges in the sandy-textured base coat are knocked down with a taping knife.

Regular joint compound is applied to smooth out the base coat.

out the corners with the edge of a trowel and then use a taping knife to knock off any ridges or lumps left by the troweling.

Apply the finish coat. Trowel standard joint compound over the fortified base coat to fill in and smooth out its textured appearance. Apply additional thin coats until any remaining roughness is no longer visible. Because each coat is quite thin, the compound dries quickly and multiple coats can be applied within hours.

Polish the compound. Finally, moisten the compound with a sponge to slightly soften the dried compound; polish it with a ceramic-tile grout float to a smooth finish that is almost indistinguishable from true lime-putty gauging plaster.

The final coat is polished with a grout trowel.

With a sharp utility knife, carefully cut through the center of the bulge and delicately pry the edges of the incision away from the lath with a spatula. Hold the crevice nozzle of a vacuum cleaner directly under the cut. Gently move the spatula around to help the vacuum cleaner suck up the rubble. The worst that could happen is that a section of plaster will fall down and you'll need to do some unanticipated patching. After the bulge is cleaned out, drill pilot holes through the plaster and screw the washers into the lath with drywall screws to pull the sagging plaster tight to the lath. Then patch the crack and the washers with high-gauge plaster or drywall compound, as described above.

Replacing Sections of Plaster

If the plaster has deteriorated beyond the ability of washers to keep it together or pieces of the ceiling have actually fallen down, cut any loose or dangling plaster back to a solid area and undercut the margins of the damaged area to furnish a key for the patch.

SECURE THE EDGES AROUND THE MISSING PLASTER
Secure the edges of the plaster adjoining the patch to the lath with drywall screws spaced 6 in. apart and set just slightly below the surface. (If the screws are turned too far, the plaster will break apart under the screw heads. Ideally, the paint film should pull in slightly.) Alternatively, use plaster washers. Unless the lath is directly over a joist, don't use nails. The lath will bounce and you could suddenly have a much larger repair job on your hands.

SECURE ANY LOOSE LATH
Screw down any loose lath and replace any broken sections as necessary. Once the old lath is secure, cut a piece of expanded metal lath to fit the patch and attach it to the existing wood lath with wire ties. (Metal lath provides a better grip for the new plaster than the dried-out old wood.) Loop a 6-in. piece of wire around the wood lath and through the metal and twist it tight with needle-nose pliers. Space the ties 6 in. apart.

APPLY THE SCRATCH COAT
Wet down the lath with a spray bottle so that it won't suck water out of the plaster and weaken it. Mix a wetting agent (available from a photographic-supply store) with the water to help it penetrate the dusty old lath. Working from a *hawk* (a square metal or wood plate equipped with a handle), cut off a wad of plaster and sweep it onto the

Three Coats of Plaster

A traditional three-coat plaster wall is ¾ in. to ⅞ in. thick and consists of a *scratch* coat, *brown* coat, and *finish* coat. If the plaster is only about ½ in. thick and the plaster base is neither wood nor metal but something resembling drywall, you have a two-coat wall (which appeared around 1880 and became increasingly common in the last days of plastering before the almost total triumph of drywall).

The base, or scratch coat, so-called because its surface is grooved with a serrated trowel or wire brush before it hardens, stiffens the lath and provides a solid underlayment for the second, or brown, coat. Old-fashioned scratch coats typically contained horsehair as a binder to impart strength to the plaster. The brown coat had more sand in it, hence the name.

Today, plasterers, amateur and professional alike, use premixed perlited gypsum-base coat plaster (you just add water, as opposed to the kind you mix yourself from sand and hydrated, or slaked, lime), such as Gypsolite® or Structolite®, for both scratch and brown coats. Because plaster has a fairly short shelf life (less than 1 year), it may be difficult to find a building-products distributor who stocks it. Masonry suppliers are the best bet. The finish coat plaster is composed of fine white gauging plaster mixed with lime and troweled to a hard polished finish. In two-coat plasterwork, a plaster base like Rocklath (a 16-in. by 48-in. gypsum-board panel that has gypsum crystals embedded in its paper facing to facilitate plaster bonding) substitutes for the scratch coat.

lath in an arcing motion, forcing it well into the keyways of the lath. Work from the wet edge outward. Hold the hawk below the trowel to catch falling plaster. (Because plaster is inherently sloppy, quite a bit will escape anyway. Protect existing finish floors with a dropcloth.) The completed scratch coat should be about ⅜ in. thick. As the plaster begins to set, score it with a trowel or a rake-like *scarifier* and then let it set for 48 hours. To ensure proper curing, maintain the room temperature above 55°F while providing plenty of air circulation to vent moisture from the wall cavities.

APPLY THE BROWN COAT Dampen the scratch coat with a spray bottle and trowel on the brown coat to within ¹⁄₁₆ in. to ⅛ in. of the finish surface. After the patch is completed, run a slicker over the entire surface to smooth and level it off. This flexible straightedge can be a 2-ft.-long length of cedar bevel siding or an ordinary paint edger. Use a sponge or scraper to clean any wet plaster off the adjacent original plaster. Use a sharp edge to knock down any remaining high spots in the brown coat before it sets up hard and then let it damp cure for 2 days (spray it with a mister every 3–5 hours). Too-rapid drying causes hairline cracks. For the same reason, protect fresh plaster from direct exposure to drafts. (The old-timers hung burlap over the open windows.)

APPLY THE FINISH COAT The finish coat is where plastering gets tricky. Even with a 1:3 mix of gauging plaster to lime, beginners will find it daunting to mix the plaster quickly enough to leave sufficient time for troweling it onto the wall before it sets up and becomes unworkable. You can increase the working window (or *open time*) by adding an approved retarder to the gauging plaster water. Follow the directions on the bag.

Trowel the finish coat directly over the brown coat. Unless you are patching over an old brown coat, it's not necessary to wet the undercoat down to keep it from absorbing water and cracking the finish coat. The finish coat will stiffen as you work it, making it fairly easy to bring it to a smooth and level finish. To achieve that professional slick appearance, gently mist the almost set-up plaster with water and polish it with a few more passes of the trowel. Use an angle trowel or margin trowel to clean up and straighten out any edges and corners.

Mixing Patching Plaster

Professionals mix their plaster in a mortar tub with a mortar hoe (or on large jobs, with a power mixer). But for patching, a clean 5-gal. plastic bucket makes a convenient container. If you mix only enough plaster to fill half the bucket, you won't run the risk of the plaster setting up before you can use it all up. Wait until you get a feel for the process and how fast you can do it before graduating to the mortar tub.

Cleanliness and mindfulness are two of the most important requirements for successful plastering. Keep your tools scrupulously clean by rinsing them after each use. Change the rinse water frequently and never use it to mix plaster. Likewise, to prevent premature setting, do not allow bits of set-up plaster to contaminate a fresh batch, use a clean bucket for mixing each type of plaster, and don't mix more than you can use up in about 1 hour. Never retemper plaster that has begun to set by adding more water to it. The result will soon crumble off the wall.

To mix a small batch of base-coat plaster, pour about ½ gal. clean cold potable water into a 5-gal. bucket and dump in about a third of a bucket of plaster. Stir it with a mixer paddle (fitted in a ½-in. low-speed electric drill). Add a splash of water or a handful of plaster until the mix has the consistency of mayonnaise or pudding (that is, until it's fairly stiff).

This is what happens when oil or latex paint is applied over untreated calcimine.

Patching with Two Coats

Two-coat plastering offers a labor-saving alternative to traditional three-coat patching. As before, the damaged plaster is cut back to sound material, and the patch is made as square as possible to simplify fitting the plaster base (such as Rocklath®). Make a paper template for complex pieces. Screw the plaster-base patch to the lath, and then trowel on the perlited gypsum brown coat and lime putty finish coat as above.

Because a traditional ¾-in. or ⅞-in. two- or three-coat plaster can be matched with two layers of ⅜-in. or ½-in. plus ⅜-in. drywall, respectively, it might seem to be a lot less trouble to simply use drywall and joint compound for all plaster patching, both large and small. In fact, those for whom convenience matters less than authentic appearance have often employed just such a strategy. The problem is that, unlike a small patch or crack filled in with drywall compound, there is no satisfying way to completely hide the mismatch between the textures of drywall and plaster, even beneath several coats of paint and/or joint compound.

Dealing with Calcimined Ceilings

Throughout the late eighteenth and much of the nineteenth centuries, ceilings were whitened with calcimine, a mixture of powdered chalk, glue (sizing), and water. Although a single coat will easily wash off with water, over many years and repeated applications the glue becomes hard as rock, making its removal considerably more difficult. A solution of warm water and trisodium phosphate is often quite effective at removing built-up layers of calcimine. The problem becomes worse when, instead of being washed off to provide a clean, flat plaster ceiling for recoating, the original calcimine was painted over with oil or latex paint.

This combination of strong film over weak base causes the inevitable flaking that gave calcimines their undeservedly bad reputation among old house restorers. Moisture leaking into the ceiling will also cause calcimine to break down and peel. The only cure for painted-over and peeling calcimine is to strip the accumulated layers down to the original plaster using heat or chemicals. The tedium of that task might be reason enough to tear down the entire ceiling instead.

Calcimine should not be confused with whitewash, which is a thin, brushable gruel of lime and chalk dissolved in water, usually without the sizing. Paint will not adhere to plaster surfaces that have been treated with lime whitewash unless first coated with a latex alkaline-resistant primer formulated for use with plaster or masonry. Wallpaper paste, brushed onto calcimine or whitewash, is often an effective remover. As the paste dries, it shrinks and curls, pulling the paint off the plaster as it does.

Gutting the Plaster

When plaster is truly unsalvageable, there's no choice but to strip the interior walls and ceilings down to the lath and replaster or apply some other finish material. In fact, some might argue for the complete removal of all plaster regardless of its condition, on the grounds that it's the only affordable way to revamp the wiring, plumbing, and insulation and make other major interior changes. Except for museum-quality historic houses, where the owners are obligated to make every effort to retain or restore the original finishes, the average old-house owner must decide whether to save the plaster strictly on the basis of personal taste and budget.

BE AWARE OF HEALTH HAZARDS Should you decide to gut the plaster, the job is best done all at once. Piecemeal removal only means extended mess and continued inhabitability. Walls that may have appeared sound on initial examination will begin to crumble the first time a molding is removed, a window casing pried, or a door slammed. Start with the attic and work toward the cellar. Plaster by itself is dusty and gritty. The airborne dust can be contaminated with decades of carcinogenic coal soot or lead from lead-based wall paint. Mixed with mouse droppings and decades of house dust and pollen, it can be a potent and possibly life-threatening allergen.

In some buildings, particularly urban rehabilitations, there is also the possibility of contracting histoplasmosis, a potentially fatal lung infection transmitted through pigeon droppings. Asbestos fibers, which were sometimes added to the plaster as a binder or, more often, as fireproofing and acoustical insulation in commercial buildings, can also be released. If the wall cavities or ceilings contain old blown-in fiberglass or mineral wool or cellulose, the material most likely has settled enough to make it worthless.

The itch and choking dust of insulation removal adds a piquant spice to the delights of plaster removal. To make matters even more interesting, some insulation installed between the 1930s and 1950s also contained asbestos. (Be especially wary of vermiculite.) Whether or not your old plaster and insulation contain asbestos fibers or lead dust and, if so, in a form and at levels high enough to constitute regulated hazardous waste can be confirmed only by laboratory testing.

This devil's potpourri of plaster, dirt, detritus, and insulation will seem to expand as it pours from the walls, until the entire house is full of it. Days later, you'll feel it in your clothes and between the sheets and taste it in your food. The insidious itch becomes more psychological than physical—you can never be quite sure if you are imagining it or not. If the house gutting coincides with foundation repair, lighten the load you'll have to lift by throwing the stuff out the windows and into the trench (assuming it is not regulated asbestos-containing material). Otherwise, you'll have to rent a construction trash container or arrange to haul the debris off to your local transfer station. In rural areas, you may be able to bury it somewhere out back. In any case, deal with the stuff before it gets rained on and reduced to pudding.

Safety Precautions

When gutting plaster, at the very least it makes sense to act as if you were dealing with a less-than-benign material. Wear an Occupational Safety and Health Administration (OSHA) approved respirator and disposable coveralls. Where plaster and insulation are being removed, seal the rooms off from the rest of the house. Vacate the premises during the operation and do not allow children or pets back on site until the cleanup is complete. All surfaces should be damp-mopped and cleaned with an HEPA-filter vacuum cleaner.

Patching Plaster with Drywall

Holes in plaster that are more than a few inches square can be readily repaired with a drywall patch, as described here. But be advised that this type of repair trades ease for authenticity; it's nearly impossible to get the texture of the drywall patch to match the surrounding plaster. Also, depending on the thickness of the plaster, you may need to screw a layer of drywall, plywood, or other shim material to the lath so that the finish patch ends up flush with the plaster. For ceiling repairs, the patch should be screwed to the drywall in any case because tape and paper alone won't keep the patch up. Also, to prevent cracking, don't apply the mud in layers thicker than about $1/16$ in. at a time.

1 Square up the hole to make the patch easier to fit.

2 Cut the patch oversize, score it on the back, and peel the gypsum away to leave a paper border.

3 Spread joint compound on the back of the patch and flanges and insert the patch before coating with more compound.

4 Remove excess compound and smooth the paper flange to blend into the old plaster.

In the country at least, a pickup truck is the renovator's best friend.

At this point, a pickup truck is a real handy tool. Ideally, the plaster is funneled from the upper story into the truck via a chute rigged out of old boards. What can't be thrown out the windows and into the truck is carried over plank ramps with a wheelbarrow. If you don't already have a pickup or don't want to trade in the family Volvo® for one, you'll have to funnel the stuff out the window into a rented trash container. If the demolition will stretch out so long that container rental is impractical, pile or bag the debris as neatly as possible and hire someone to haul it away.

DEMOLISH THE WALLS Although smashing through walls with the hooked end of a crowbar and ripping down great chunks of plaster and lath is a great outlet for fantasies of destruction or revenge, it's better to knock the plaster off first, dispose of it, sweep up, and then pull off the lath and pile it up for disposal. (Owing to their enhanced vulnerability to lead poisoning, children under six should be kept away from the job site.) Use snow shovels to scoop up the fallen plaster. The destruction is best done in summer, when an afternoon's dip in the pond will wash away the memories and grime of a miserable day's work.

Partial Gutting and Blown-In Insulation

Even without the justification of major repairs, gutting the plaster is one sure way to deal with the problem of retrofitting new insulation to an old house. Insulation can be blown into the stud cavities from outside the building, but that's not necessarily the best way to do it. When blindly blowing the fill in, it's virtually impossible to fill every stud cavity completely. Cold spots, as evidenced by frost on the inside walls, are not unusual.

Even conscientious contractors can't always fill every hole or pack the cellulose at a high-enough density to prevent settling and air washing. But a high-density installation is certainly more costly than the more lax standards acceptable to less scrupulous operators. Otherwise, at low densities, condensation either through vapor diffusion or air infiltration remains a real threat. Insulation contractors will assure you that the cellulose fibers have been treated to be water resistant, vermin proof, and fire resistant. What this actually means is that if water condenses in the wall, the insulation will soak it up like a sponge so that the wood can start to rot.

Vapor-retarder paints (such as Glidden Insul-Aid) can be applied over intact old plaster, but these don't solve the cold-spot problem or prevent moisture movement through areas that can't be painted (for example, behind wood baseboards, wainscoting, and casings). Vapor-retarder paint is still better than ripping out sound old plaster, but it's no cure-all.

If the lath is left intact after stripping off the plaster and then covered with a polyethylene vapor retarder, the stud cavities can be blown from the inside, allowing the insulator to see how well the spaces are filling. Since the lath supports the insulation much better than polyethylene alone, the cavities can be packed at higher densities. If the new wall finish is to be traditional plaster, attach expanded wire mesh or gypsum plaster base over the poly after the insulation is blown in.

Although electrical outlets and cables can be worked behind the lath, horizontal strapping nailed to the studs allows the cables to be run outside of the vapor retarder (or air barrier) and restricts penetrations to the outlet boxes while eliminating the need to drill studs. Because cables can be run after the insulation is installed and will remain visible at all times, keeping track of circuits is a lot easier. The spaces between the strapping can also be fitted with rigid-foam panels to increase the R-value of the walls. And a formerly uneven wall surface can be straightened out by inserting wood shims behind the strapping.

Once the rubble is removed and the floors are vacuumed and mopped clean, the walls can be reinsulated with fiberglass batts in preparation for the new wall finish. This also the time to begin the rewiring and make other structural repairs.

Applying New Walls over Old

Applying a new wall finish on top of the existing plaster is an alternative to complete removal of interior plaster; it's worth considering when the walls are already insulated or will be by blowing in from the exterior. First staple a polyethylene vapor retarder over the plaster. For best results, remove existing baseboards, ceiling moldings, and window and door casings. Next, screw drywall into the underlying studs or joists whenever possible.

If, as is likely, the original plaster was butted against the baseboards, shim out the studs behind them so that the baseboards line up with the face of the drywall when they are reattached. Likewise, install extension jambs to bring the window and door jambs flush with the new wall. Prime and paint the drywall before replacing the casings and other surface trim.

Successfully removing and replacing old trim without damaging it won't be easy. You might

How to Install Drywall without Removing Casings

L-bead prevents joint compound from cracking.

New drywall

Existing trim

Old plaster

Wood band molding wraps edges of casings for enhanced profile.

Avoid having to remove casings by butting new drywall to trim.

Outlet box

Old wall

New wall

Extension ring

Extend electrical box with extension ring to bring box flush with new wall surface.

Hire a Plasterer or Do It Yourself?

A professional-looking polished and perfectly flat traditional plaster finish isn't easily achieved by beginners. If that's what you want, hire a professional. Otherwise, replace the gutted plaster with some other material such as drywall, veneer plaster, or wood paneling that is more tolerant of inexperience.

If, on the other hand, a trowel-scarred and wavering finish is something you actually desire, the results are guaranteed by doing it yourself. Just be aware that no old-time plasterer worth at least his weight in gypsum would ever settle for anything less than a dead-flat and level wall. The crude texture of some genuine early colonial or old European plaster was likely the best effort of unskilled peasant artisans or the equivalent of seventeenth- and eighteenth-century do-it-yourselfers.

consider simply butting the drywall to it instead. The objection that this treatment flattens out the trim profile is solved by wrapping the edges of the casings with a narrow band of molding of slightly greater depth and/or using ¼-in. drywall (bonded with construction adhesive, which consolidates the plaster and requires fewer screws). To prevent cracking of joint compound, the edges of the drywall panels butt against the trim into metal L-beads. Use extension rings to bring existing electrical boxes flush to the new wall.

Installing new drywall over old plaster also offers the advantage of extra sound deadening, a bit more thermal mass, and a lot less debris. But these methods are a lot slower than wholesale plaster removal, so you may want to reserve them for use in individual rooms or on single walls.

ALTERNATIVES TO PLASTER

Time—as in the great deal of it required for plaster to cure, both between coats and before painting—is probably the single greatest factor contributing to the precipitous decline of plaster's importance in residential construction. Traditionally, painters or paperhangers would wait up to a year before touching fresh lime plaster. (This helps explain the widespread popularity of paints like whitewash and calcimine, which, unlike oils, could be applied immediately after the initial cure.)

While the development of fast-curing gypsum-based plasters and the two-coat system significantly trimmed the downtime, prudent painters still waited 2 weeks to 3 weeks before priming new plaster. Even the reduced amount of lime in the thin finish coat would cause paint to peel if not perfectly dry. The old-timers used the "match test" to tell when the plaster was ready to paint: If a match didn't light when struck on new plaster, it was still too wet.

Because both lime and gypsum plaster release large quantities of water that must be gradually removed for a good cure, indoor humidity will remain quite high for some time, even with good ventilation. Excessive moisture is not only uncomfortable for inhabitants but can be detrimental to household furnishings. Hence traditional two- and three-coat plastering may not be the best choice for an occupied house.

Wallpaper

Ordinary drywall finished with wallpaper instead of paint strikes me as a very workable alternative to replastering (for walls at any rate). Wallpaper is certainly more suited to an old house than the monotonous uniformity of roller- or spray-painted drywall. Machine-made wallpaper has been used in the United States since 1837 (hand-painted wallpapers had been imported by wealthy homeowners since the mid-1700s), so it's hard to argue against it on traditional grounds. And because the joints are covered, the taping needn't be as flawless as for paint. You'll most likely need to fur out the wall studs or leave the old wood lath in place to maintain the original reveal against the trim.

VENEER PLASTER Veneer plaster is a recently developed system that can provide an acceptable labor- and cost-saving alternative to traditional plaster and is only slightly more expensive than drywall. (Drywall requires three coats of joint compound and a lot of sanding. It's messy, time-consuming, and a lot harder than it looks. Then it has to be primed and painted.)

The base for veneer plaster is commonly called *blueboard* (one brand is Calwall). These are ½-in.-thick, 4x8 drywall-like panels with a blue paper coating treated to bond with the plaster. Joints between the panels are lapped with a special blue fiberglass mesh tape and skimmed over with plaster. A ⅟₁₆-in.-thick coat of high-strength veneer plaster (not perlited gypsum plaster) is troweled onto the blueboard. The finish coat is either a second layer of veneer plaster or standard gauged lime. Even though it's

Sometimes all that holds the old plaster into place are layers of wallpaper covering it. When removing wallpaper, samples of every layer should be saved as they may be of historic value.

This one-coat Structolite plaster finish exploits the do-it-yourselfer's lack of plastering skill to advantage. Many people find the resulting rough and rustic texture quite pleasing, historical veracity notwithstanding.

TIP

Alternative to Paint

An interesting alternative to paint is suggested by Herbert Wheaton Congdon, in his classic treatise *Early American Homes for Today*. Writing about matching new plaster to old, he recommends two coats of thinned-down "cheap varnish" (use turpentine and don't try this with urethane) to recreate the mellow and pleasing patina of aged, unpainted plaster. ■ ■ ■

only ⅛ in. thick, veneer plaster has a compressive strength of 1500 psi, the same as conventional three-coat plaster. Because it is so thin, veneer plaster releases much less moisture and dries quickly, often overnight. It is then ready for painting.

Veneer plaster can also be troweled over a ⅛-in. brown coat of ordinary gypsum plaster (such as Structolite) augmented with two shovels of sand per bag. The sand makes a compatible "hard" brown coat that prevents differential cracking of the veneer coat. I've also found that a single coat of this plaster that's between ⅛ in. and ¼ in. thick will produce a satisfactory rustic finish on blueboard or even ordinary drywall treated with a polyvinyl acetate (PVA) bonding agent. Misting and protection against drafts are especially important with one-coat plaster if poor set and cracks are to be avoided.

If a rustic or primitive texture is what you want, single-coat gypsum plaster (for example, Structolite) is the fastest, easiest, and least expensive way to get it. It looks and feels more like real plaster than the same effect attempted in joint compound, because it *is* real plaster. It's also the only possible finish you can produce with this method.

DRYWALL

Unlike their predecessors, modern homeowners are faced with a bewildering choice of materials for interior wall finish, almost all of them inappropriate. To me, materials such as imitation bricks, plastic beams, acoustical ceiling tiles, and prefab paneling have no soul; they negate whatever spirit the house may be struggling to articulate. If people could feel the emptiness of these products, they would never consider living with them.

With some reservations, I would maintain that these objections don't hold for drywall, an undeniably versatile material. It is not so much the nature of the product itself that sometimes may be offensive, but rather the way it is thoughtlessly used. Drywall is, above all, a neutral material. If used with wood or a contrasting surface, the tension between texture and space is highlighted. Dramatic planes are defined; dark

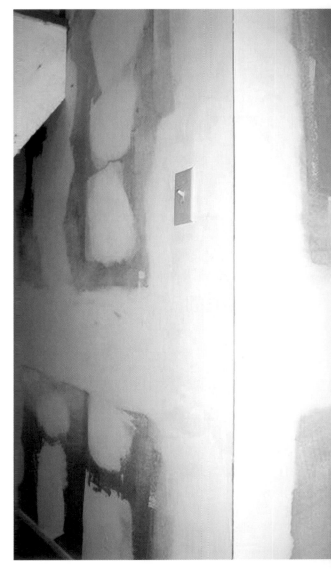

The difference between a clumsy amateur taping job and a smooth professional job is the degree to which the joint compound is feathered out over the joint. A good taper spreads relatively little compound over a large area, avoiding the lumpy buildup that telegraphs through the paint of an amateur finish.

rooms, lightened. Drywall can be a noncompetitive background for furniture and artwork and can offer relief in what might otherwise become a tyranny of busy wood.

Nevertheless, the only advantage drywall offers over traditional or veneer plaster is a dubious economy paid for by sacrificing a very real and satisfying solidity and organic texture (in the sense of hand-worked imperfection as opposed to machine-made perfection). Drywall is unmatched, however, as a base for wallpaper.

Installing Drywall

Although *hanging* (that is, screwing—no one uses nails anymore) drywall panels to the framing is a relatively easy operation with a fairly generous margin of error, *taping* (that is, hiding the joints behind several coats of joint compound or mud) isn't. Despite the popular image of a smiling woman, trowel in hand, wearing tailored jeans and neat bandana—if she can do it, anyone can—it's not a job for rank beginners. Patience, a steady hand, and lots of practice are the recipe for successful taping. Nothing looks worse than a poor taping job, which is all that most neophytes succeed in accomplishing. This is a strong argument for hiring a professional drywall contractor, or else figuring out a clever way to avoid the issue altogether.

The nuts-and-bolts of hanging and taping drywall are widely available in other books. Aside from a few general caveats, I confine my discussion here to those aspects of drywall installation specifically relevant to the renovator.

ADJUSTING FOR OUT-OF-SQUARE CEILINGS

With old houses in particular, the run of the ceiling joists should be checked for square (that is, perpendicularity) with the plane of the walls. Because the ends of each sheet must fall on the middle of a joist, the edges of the first sheets that butt the walls may have to be trimmed.

Line up the edge of the first panel with the joist and measure the width of the gap (if any) that opens up between the sides of the panel and the wall. Assuming that the wall is not curved, convert the measurement to a ratio. For example, a 1-in. gap over 8 ft. means that the wall is running out of square ⅛ in. per foot. Thus a 13-ft.-wide room will require an adjustment of 1⅝ in. Mark a point on the ceiling at 48 in. from the ending corner, make another at 46⅜ in. from the beginning corner, and snap a chalkline between them. Trim the edge of the panels that abut the wall so that they fit to the chalkline.

Trimming a full sheet is always easier than patching in a tapered piece. Depending on how skewed the walls are, the long, the short, or even both ends may need to be adjusted keep the sheets falling over the joists.

USING STRAPPING When the ceiling joists are spaced on 2-ft. centers and the space above is used for living, the ceiling should be strapped. Screw 1x3 furring on 16-in. centers across the joists. The strapping need not be perfectly perpendicular to the joists, because the sheets will line up to it and not the joists. Strapping is also the method used to flatten out an uneven ceiling. Strings set on blocks indicate where shingle shims must be wedged between the joists and the strapping to bring the ceiling into the same plane.

There's another reason to use strapping: Sometimes the spacing of joists is something other than the 16 in. or 24 in. that works with 48-in.-wide drywall panels. The spacing may not even be very regular. After all, the carpenters who built the house didn't have to worry about providing nailing for plywood and drywall.

TIP

Drywall Corners

Granted that drywall lacks the quality of a good plaster finish, the difference is not so noticeable that one couldn't learn to live with it. In fact, the rounded quality of plastered edges can be duplicated with quarter-round wood molding or rounded-profile metal bead in place of conventional square-edged metal corner bead. ▪▪ ▪▪ ▪▪

Back-Saving Ways to Hang Drywall on a Ceiling

Unlike most new construction, the ceiling of an old house may not be square to the walls of its rooms. Drywall panels may have to be put up, tried, taken down, trimmed, and fitted again. This can be very much a pain in the neck, back, and other parts of the anatomy. Thus mechanical assistance—lifting and holding the panels up against the ceiling while they are adjusted—is a good idea.

The pros use a panel lift (right photo below). These can be rented, or you can make a couple of deadmen out of 2x4s, as shown in the left photo below. Make the deadmen a few inches taller than the distance between the floor and the joists. This will allow you to wedge them in with a couple of kicks at the bottom. Even with the deadmen, it takes two people to put up ceilings, especially with panels over 8 ft. long.

The deadman should be slightly longer than the ceiling height, so that it can be wedged up tight against the drywall panel. Hanging panels this way is still awkward without a helper.

HANGING THE WALLS If you hang the wall panels horizontally from the top down, any cut edges will be hidden behind the baseboard molding and the tapered long joints will be at a convenient height for finishing. Staggering the vertical joints between the panels also eliminates hard-to-finish *crossroads*. While hanging the sheets vertically does eliminate butt joints entirely, it's harder to get a good taping job when you have to climb up a ladder or squat down to floor level with your trowel. The first sheets may also require trimming where they butt against the ceiling, to square up with the studs.

Cleaning Up

Sweep and vacuum the floor area after all the drywall is hung and the scraps are disposed of. The dust has a way of appearing all over the house. The stuff is so fine that it can ruin a household vacuum cleaner and soon clog the filter of a shop vacuum. Small crumbs of drywall seem to have a special affinity for joint compound. They're forever showing up as streaks and gouges under the taping knife.

A rented drywall lift makes it possible for one person to lift and fasten drywall sheets to the ceiling without undue strain.

REPAIRING STAIRS

The staircase is perhaps the hardest-working part of a house. However sturdily built, generations of use can result in loose and worn treads, risers, balusters, and newel posts. Here are some ways to tune up an old staircase.

Treads and Risers

The treads and risers of housed stringers cannot be removed unless you gain access to the underside of the stair carriage. If this has been plastered over, it must be stripped. Fortunately, for the novice stair repairer, at least, housed stringers were used only for first-class jobs. The treads and risers of most stairs were simply face-

Stair Rails, Balusters, and Newel Posts

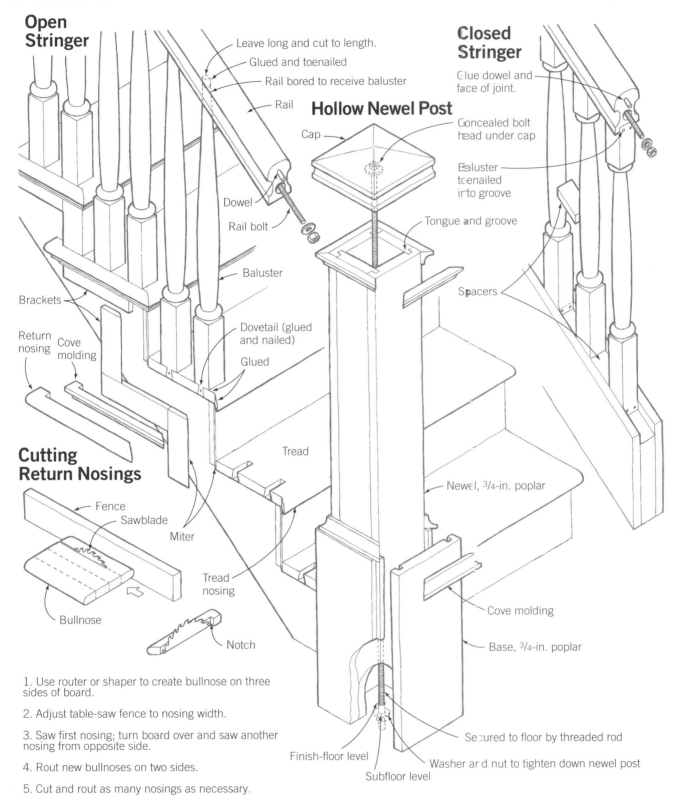

Open Stringer

Leave long and cut to length.

Glued and toenailed

Rail bored to receive baluster

Rail

Dowel

Rail bolt

Brackets

Return nosing

Cove molding

Baluster

Dovetail (glued and nailed)

Glued

Closed Stringer

Glue dowel and face of joint.

Concealed bolt head under cap

Baluster toenailed into groove

Tongue and groove

Spacers

Hollow Newel Post

Cap

Cutting Return Nosings

Fence

Sawblade

Miter

Tread

Tread nosing

Bullnose

Notch

Newel, ³/4-in. poplar

Cove molding

Base, ³/4-in. poplar

Secured to floor by threaded rod

Washer and nut to tighten down newel post

Finish-floor level

Subfloor level

1. Use router or shaper to create bullnose on three sides of board.

2. Adjust table-saw fence to nosing width.

3. Saw first nosing; turn board over and saw another nosing from opposite side.

4. Rout new bullnoses on two sides.

5. Cut and rout as many nosings as necessary.

6. Notch each nosing for bracket with table saw; hide overrun underneath nosing on back side.

nailed into the stringer and set flush to the skirtboards. In such cases, damaged treads and risers are simply pried up and replaced as needed.

Some renovators look at a set of treads worn by the scuffing of generations of feet, and buried under iron-hard layers of porch and deck enamel, and conclude that the only alternative to tedious stripping and peeling is complete removal and replacement with new material. This is a tragic mistake. New material can never match the unique and satisfying sculpture that a worn tread has become, the visible evidence of the house's connection to the past. If the treads and risers are carefully disassembled, they can be much more easily stripped of the old, caked-on finish.

The treads and risers butt into skirtboards, which are much more accessible to the scraper or sander with the treads and risers removed. I remember discovering exquisite cherry hidden under brown paint so ugly the owner was about to have me tear the old stairs out. Quite by accident, a helper had found a stock of triangular cherry boards that looked a lot like the pieces left over from a skirtboard, hidden in the attic. This got us to wondering what was under the paint.

Repairing Balusters

There are only a few repairs to the newel posts, the rail, and balustrade that anyone but a skilled carpenter should attempt. Fixing broken or loose balusters is one of them. These often decorative but quite necessary pieces are typically dovetailed into the tread in an open stringer. The joint is hidden behind a strip of bullnose *return nosing* nailed to the end grain of the tread. When this is removed, the joint is exposed. The drawing on the facing page shows an easy way to make bullnoses, should any be damaged or missing.

Sometimes the damaged baluster is identical to a stock pattern, or you may find a replacement at a salvage warehouse. If a baluster has sheared off at the dovetail instead of at the top where it plugs into the rail, a new dovetail can be fashioned and doweled into the bottom of the baluster. You might even be able to remove the old dovetail in one piece and dowel it back to its baluster. Driving glue-coated wood shims into the dovetail joint tightens loose balusters. Remove any loose balusters and clean off the old dried-out glue before regluing.

When balusters are inserted into a closed stringer, they are locked into place with flat pieces of wood that fit into the baluster groove at the top of the stringer. Pry up these pieces or replace any missing ones. The balusters are secured by toenailing into the stringer. Predrill nail holes in hardwood, to prevent splitting the wood or bending nails.

TIGHTENING NEWEL POSTS Newel posts are either solid or boxed (hollow). Turned newels are usually solid. To tighten a solid newel, drill through its face and screw it to the underlying stringer. Plug the bore hole with a dowel. Boxed newels are normally secured to the floor by a threaded rod. Gain access by removing the newel cap. Turn the nut at the top of the rod to stiffen the newel post. If such a rod is missing, it can be retrofitted by bolting it through a metal bracket screwed into the floor. Rail repair usually involves finding and removing the wood plugs that give access to the various stair nuts and concealed rail bolts that tie the railings together. These bolts are either tightened or replaced.

WOOD PANELING

Wood and plaster are a traditional coupling. The interior partitions of many of the earliest American houses consisted of vertical planks finished with whitewash. This explains why a renovator will sometimes find a painted wall under the plaster lath. Around the last quarter of

The lucky renovator may sometimes uncover antique paneling or "ceiled" boards under encrustations of wallpaper or plaster. The paneling requires little more than a good scrubbing and a coat of boiled linseed oil to restore its beauty.

Although it looks like traditional colonial paneling, this wainscot is actually built up from moldings and boards appliquéd over paint-grade plywood.

the eighteenth century, plank walls gave way to vertical boards nailed to studs. These "ceiled" boards were often given a decorative bead along their edges.

Early American Paneling

Walls that were not plastered were often paneled. Early American wood paneling bears no resemblance to its modern namesake. Instead, it was more like a continuous door; thin beveled panels of remarkable width floating in grooved rails and stiles. (Boards cut from virgin forests were much more stable than modern lumber.) Indeed, any door set in such a wall was designed so that its rails matched the rails of the wall paneling. The term *wainscoting* was also applied to this floor-to-ceiling paneling.

Although wainscoting is technically rail-and-stile paneling run up a wall, in modern popular use the term refers to almost any wood boarding applied either horizontally or vertically partway up a wall and capped with a *chair rail*. The height is somewhere between 30 in. and 42 in. The treatment of the chair rail varied from a simple rounded molding to elaborate pseudo-cornices.

It wasn't until the middle nineteenth century that rail-and-stile wainscoting was supplanted by the narrow edge- and center-beaded (E&CB) tongue-and-groove *matchboard* that we have come to regard as traditional wainscoting. From about 1880 to 1920, matchboard wall paneling, wainscoting, interior and porch ceilings, and kitchen cabinet doors were the hallmark of inexpensive interior finish. Today, stripped of shellac or darkened varnish and refinished, the clear Douglas fir and southern yellow pine of these once pedestrian floors, walls, and cabinets are irreplaceable and beautiful treasures.

CEILING TREATMENTS

In the old days, exposed ceiling beams were a sign of poverty. Those rough-hewn timbers were cased with planed boards or plastered over as soon as the householder could afford to hire a plasterer or carpenter. A successful man celebrated his wealth with successive layers of plaster and paint, demonstrating, perhaps, the pioneer's mastery of nature with artifice and ornamentation. Our present fascination with exposed ceiling beams may belie a longing for reconnection with the natural world. The undeniable feeling of security that emanates from the rude strength of these old timbers is a revelation of structure in harmony with nature.

Ceilings with Exposed Beams

Exposing the ceiling beams creates the problem of how to finish the spaces between them. Some folks are quite enamored of the rough-sawn subfloor boards now revealed. They simply brush them clean, cut off any protruding nails with a pair of nipping pliers, and leave it at that. But, eventually, the ceiling begins to grow a beard, as the household dust is snagged from the air by the rough boards; then the particles rain down from the cracks in the floor above. The dark wood becomes dingy and the room seems dense and almost gloomy. This cave-like atmosphere may suit a den or private retreat, but it almost defeats the reason the beams were exposed in the first place; the timbers are lost in the gloom.

The intensity of the sunlight entering the house, the height of the ceiling, and the finish of the floors and walls contribute to the effect of the ceiling. Bright walls and light floorboards may benefit from the counterpoint of a dark ceiling. Another possibility is suggested by the colonial practice of whitewashing the unsheathed interior walls: Simply paint the subfloor boards with a thinned-down white latex

Despite the objections of purists, old-house aficionados have been stripping off ceiling plaster to expose hand-hewn ceiling beams at least as far back as the colonial revival at the turn of the twentieth century.

ceiling paint or semitransparent white stain. (Brushing on cheap ceiling paint and immediately wiping it off with a rag works quite well.) This preserves the texture of the boards and brightens the room at the same time.

Keep in mind that exposing the ceiling beams means you will have to live with more noise downstairs, since there is no ceiling to muffle footsteps and other sounds. If this approach is a little too rough or if the subfloor boards are too shabby to leave uncovered, there are several ways to construct a new ceiling between the exposed beams. Choices of material include wood paneling, drywall, and plaster.

Cleaning the Beams

One rather tedious but necessary task that must precede the installation of a new ceiling is the cleaning of the beams. A stiff bristle brush removes clinging dust and cobwebs. Scrub the beams with detergent (TSP) and hot water. If, after the beams dry, the results are pleasing, no

TIP

What's under the Plaster Ceiling?

If a plaster ceiling is removed to reveal closely spaced pedestrian sawn joists rather than hewn beams, it would have been best left undisturbed. How do you know what to expect? Unless the visible framing in the attic and cellar is timbered, don't expect to find buried treasures under the plaster. If the floor joists are sawn lumber, the ceiling joists will be, too. ■■ ■■ ■■

further treatment is necessary. But a lot more can be done. They can be stained to a uniform tone; darker colors look good against light ceilings, especially if the beams are roughsawn rather than hand hewn. Experiment with turpentine and tinting colors to find a suitable shade.

Old beams darken with age, often so much so that the wood appears featureless. A drill-mounted wire brush will remove this accumulated obscurity. It also wipes out the bulk of the stains left by plaster lath. Short of sanding, there's no practical way to remove all of the plaster stain. Sanding would take forever and would leave the surface unnaturally smooth to boot. A wire brush does a really good job. It removes the grime and scale and, because of its rapid rotation, leaves only minute scratches. The dark grain of the wood is left to contrast with its lighter background in a swirling dance of delight. A coat of boiled linseed oil or other penetrating sealer will accentuate this play of structure and light. It's an exhausting, dirty, and tedious job, but the results are worth the effort.

Dirt Can Be Beautiful

The pigment in many stains is basically dirt. With that in mind, here's a method that can bring out a rich brown or reddish color in your old beams. Try it in a small area first to see if you like the results.

Brush the beams liberally with linseed oil—you may need two or three coats if the beams are really dry and porous. Then scrub the beams with a stiff scrub brush. This will loosen the dirt and mix it with the linseed oil, perhaps producing exactly the color and patina you are after.

Installing Tongue-and-Groove Boards

Tongue-and-groove boards installed at a right angle to the exposed beams can make a handsome ceiling, particularly if the boards have a V-groove profile. The smooth new wood is light in color and, when rubbed with linseed oil or a tung oil varnish, takes on a soft, warm luster much more pleasing than the hard gloss of polyurethane varnish.

ADD NAILER CLEATS FOR THE BOARDS Once

the beams are clean, nail 1x1 cleats directly to the sides of the beams up against the subfloor; 1x3 spruce strapping ripped in half makes a good cleat. So do strips ripped from leftover trim boards and pine paneling. Spruce holds nails better than pine, but splits easier.

Use 6d or 8d box nails (not screws) and blunt the tip so the nail will crush the wood fibers rather than wedge them apart. Box nails are thinner than common nails and less likely to split thin wood. They also bend more easily. If the wood is old and hard, you may have to predrill pilot holes to get the nails in. Run any cables through the ceiling as needed. Use a "nail-biter" electrician's bit when boring through at the top edge of a beam, which is likely to contain more than a few flooring nails. Use ½-in.-deep *pancake ceiling boxes* screwed to wood support blocks between the beams to allow for the installation of ceiling light fixtures.

ATTACH THE BOARDS

Hold the boards up against the cleats and drive two finish nails through their ends angled up toward the beam. It would be quite a chore to scribe and fit each board to the uneven contours of a hand-hewn beam. Unless the timber is sawn, don't try for a perfect fit; the results won't be encouraging and the joints will open up anyway due to seasonal shrinkage. Instead, nail a ¾-in. quarter-round molding or a flat ½-in. by 1-in. band molding against the beam to conceal the ends of the ceiling boards. The ceiling

Three Types of Ceiling Finishes Used between Exposed Beams

Wood Paneling over Cleats

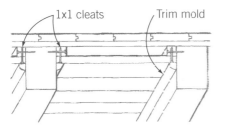

1x1 cleats   Trim mold

Drywall (or Gypsum Lath for Plaster)

Protective polyethylene sheet   1x1 cleat

Cut plastic after ceiling is painted.

Metal Lath and Plaster

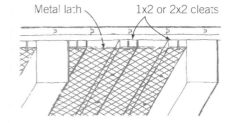

Metal lath   1x2 or 2x2 cleats

---

boards can also be toned down with thinned-down oil stains, which won't deny or mask the nature of the wood. A light gray or sandy wash could be very soothing.

Installing Plaster or Drywall between Beams

There can be such a thing as too much wood. Wood floors and wood walls may be fine, but a wood ceiling can overdo it. Painted drywall or the rougher texture of perlited plaster may be more appropriate between the ceiling beams.

Although it is possible to screw drywall directly to the subfloor, it isn't a good idea. Not only will you lose the opportunity to run wiring across the ceiling but the boards will flex and bounce as the floor is walked on, and the fairly wide boards will expand and shrink seasonally, causing taped joints to crack and nails to pop. Unlike wood paneling, drywall cannot be toenailed.

You could screw the drywall along a cut edge without all the screws breaking through the paper but, given that the beams are likely to be spaced at least 32 in. on center, the long-term prospects for such a wide sheet of otherwise unsupported drywall remaining on the ceiling are questionable. Even if this weren't a problem, the screws would be likely to split a ¾-in.-wide cleat, unless the screw holes were predrilled.

ADD CLEATS FOR DRYWALL OR LATH Rip a 2x4 into 2x2 cleats or, if the extra depth is troublesome, glue a 1x2 cleat flat against the subfloor and secure it to the beam with 12d box nails or 3-in. drywall screws driven through pilot holes. Attach cleats perpendicular to the run of the beams wherever there is a joint between the sheets of drywall. If, as is often the case, the beams are spaced 32 in. or more apart, screw another cleat to the subfloor, down the middle of the bay between them, to help support the drywall.

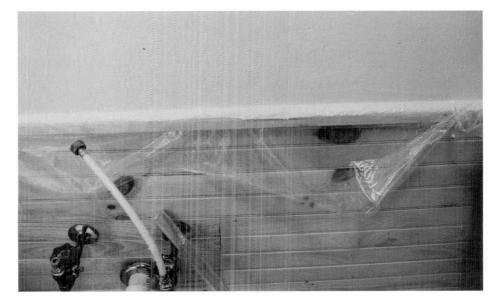

To dramatically streamline the otherwise tedious job of cutting in plaster and paint against abutting wainscoting or an exposed ceiling beam, first lay a strip of plastic food wrap behind the drywall or plaster base. Use a sharp matte knife to cut out the film after the paint has dried.

Don't Make Drywall Joints Parallel to the Beams

When the space between the exposed beams is greater than half the 4-ft. width of a full drywall sheet don't try to piece together the leftovers in a mistaken effort to avoid waste. This may seem extravagant, but a poor taping job shows up more clearly on a ceiling than on any other surface. Plaster base, such as Rocklath®, is an alternative; but the thin, narrow panels will require a continuous center cleat for proper support. This tends to transmit the bounce from the floor above directly to the plaster, which will probably cause a fair amount of joint cracking.

Before nailing any cleats to the beams, staple a strip of 4-mil poly (not the 6 mil used for insulation) film against the top edge of the beams, wide enough to hang down past the bottom. This will protect the beam during painting and save painstaking cleanup when the edges of the drywall are filled with joint compound. Force the point of a utility knife at a slight angle up into the joint to cut the polyethylene when the job is finished.

USING PLASTER OVER DRYWALL Plaster bases such as Rocklath and Calwall have specially treated paper surfaces that bond to gypsum. Theoretically, plaster applied over drywall, even when treated with a PVA bonding agent, won't hold as well, especially on a ceiling. I agree that this might be true for a two- or three-coat job, but one coat of gypsum plaster (for example, Structolite) or veneer plaster seems to stick to PVA-treated drywall just fine.

CUTTING THE DRYWALL Variations in the width of the bay and inwardly tilted beam faces conspire against a snug fit for the drywall or plaster base. Measure between the beams at sev-eral places along the run of the drywall, to determine whether the sheet must be tapered and by how much. A ¼-in. tolerance at each side will ease its fitting. Fill the gaps and screw heads with joint compound. It may take several coats, since there is no effective way to install L-bead or joint tape.

Drywall ceilings are usually finished with a flat (or matte) latex ceiling paint. These are formulated for extra brightness and more covering power than regular wall paint. To diffuse light and soften glare and, most important, to hide blemishes in the taping job, sanded texture paint is often used as a ceiling finish. In my opinion, if texture is desired, use the real thing and trowel on rough plaster. No taping is required at all and the finish is, if not architecturally quite correct, at least well suited to exposed beams.

Tin Ceilings

Falling plaster was a problem for turn-of-the-century renovators, too. Stamped sheet-steel or iron "tin" ceiling panels were widely promoted as a cheap, safe, and decorative way to conceal damaged plaster and to imitate the decorative patterns of a classic plaster ceiling. (*Tin* is a misnomer; pure tin was never used. In most cases, the steel or iron sheet metal was not even tin plated.)

At the height of their popularity—from the 1850s until 1930—more than 400 patterns were available, including cornice moldings, floor-to-ceiling wall panels, and a cornucopia of decorative medallions and borders. By 1910, embossed steel panels cost less than plaster or wood paneling, making them the wall and ceiling treatment of choice for residential and commercial buildings (where they had been widely used from the beginning).

Surprisingly, tin ceilings are not obsolete. Although the selection of patterns and accessories is far less varied, tin ceilings made from the original molds are still available and still an easy-to-install (but no longer exactly inexpensive) cure for damaged plaster ceilings or for replacing an inappropriately remodeled ceiling with a historically accurate one. It's not uncommon to find a more-or-less intact 1890s tin ceiling hidden beneath a 1960s dropped ceiling.

Restoring an Existing Tin Ceiling

Metal panels were protected against rust by the buildup of multiple layers of paint. An open seam or a crack in the protective paint film is a common symptom of hidden water damage. Since the typical 30-gauge sheets are only about $\frac{1}{100}$ in. thick to begin with, loose and peeling paint or rust spots must be carefully removed to avoid further damage to the delicate metal.

REMOVE LOOSE PAINT With a brass or medium-bristle steel rotary brush mounted in an electric drill, apply just enough pressure to dislodge loose paint without scratching or crushing the pattern. Use medium-grit aluminum oxide sandpaper or steel wool to remove only the flaking or scaling rust that prevents paint from adhering. It's not necessary to clean down to bare metal. (The old paint is very likely lead based. Seal off the room, wear protective gear, and follow the general procedures and precautions outlined earlier for dealing with lead paint on windows and trim.)

PATCH HOLES Patch any pinholes with paintable silicone-latex (not pure latex) caulk. Large holes can be repaired or sculpted to match the pattern with auto-body filler compound, reinforced by a backing of ¼-in. wire mesh (*hardware cloth*). You can also make rubber molds of intact sections of the pattern for casting repair patches from body filler.

REPLACE BADLY DAMAGED PANELS If a panel is badly rusted or otherwise damaged, you can often order an exact match from a supplier's catalog. Use a tack-puller prybar to take out the cone-head nails that secure the damaged piece.

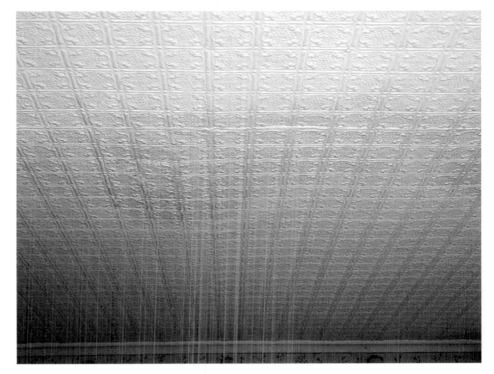

Tin ceilings were a popular coverup for old plaster in the era before acoustical ceiling tiles and drywall.

Flatten any buckled edges of adjoining panels. If not preprimed, the replacement should be primed on both sides and given two coats of oil-based paint on the exposed side before it is installed.

Never use latex or calcimine on metal panels: The aqueous vehicle will cause instant rust. Secure the sheet to the existing strapping with 1-in. cone-head nails, driven into the preformed "buttons" distributed throughout the pattern.

Installing a New Tin Ceiling

Nail the 2x2, 2x4, or 2x8 panels to strapping laid right over the old plaster and screwed into the joists. A helpful hint: Staple 4-mil polyethylene to the old ceiling first to keep dust and grit from falling on your head while you install the strapping.

STRAP THE PERIMETER Begin by screwing strapping around the perimeter of the room. Next, snap chalklines diagonally between the corners to locate the center of the room. The

Tin-Ceiling Installation

1. Screw strapping to perimeter; snap chalklines to find ceiling center.

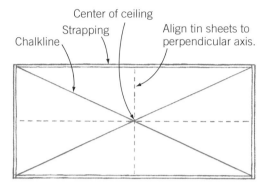

Center of ceiling
Strapping
Chalkline
Align tin sheets to perpendicular axis.

2. Install first course of strapping to follow centerline; continue with parallel courses on 12-in. centers.

Pieces of strapping fastened perpendicular to vertical strapping on 8-ft. centers secure ends of sheets.

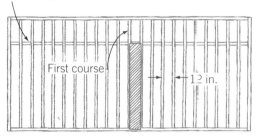

First course
12 in.

3. After ceiling sheets are installed, nail strapping to wall to support cornice trim.

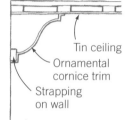

Tin ceiling
Ornamental cornice trim
Strapping on wall

layout is similar to that used for floor tiles: The panels are aligned to perpendicular axes radiating from this point. This ensures that the last sheets will be the same width on both sides of the ceiling.

FILL IN THE STRAPPING AND ATTACH THE TIN

Run the first course of strapping along the centerline of the ceiling, followed by parallel courses on 12-in. centers. Fasten short pieces of strapping perpendicular to these on 8-ft. centers to secure the ends of the sheets. If necessary, shim the strapping to level out the ceiling. Attach the tin with 1-in.-long cone-head nails or brads driven into the preformed nailing beads.

Experienced installers can put up a ceiling working unaided. They literally use their heads (and a piece of strapping) to hold up the loose end of the sheet being nailed. A novice would probably find it more comfortable to work with a helper. A word of warning: Wear thin leather gloves when handling tin; the edges can be razor sharp.

INSTALL CORNICE TRIM

Once the ceiling sheets are installed, nail strapping to the wall to support the cornice trim. Flatten any open seams by gently tapping them with a hammer and a blunt chisel or nail head. Stubborn seams can be filled with paintable caulk.

APPLY PAINT OR FINISH

Wipe the tin with paint thinner to remove any factory oil coating and apply oil-based metal primer followed by two coats of oil-based white or metallic paint. Metal ceilings can also be left unprimed and then finished with a clear lacquer or multi-purpose sealer like Masury Oil. Or, for a special touch, you can emphasize the embossed pattern by highlighting it with contrasting, complementary or darker or lighter shades of color. Start by applying the chosen highlight color first and then, after it has completely dried, brush or roll on the base color. Use a sponge or rag to wipe the paint off the raised areas, leaving the highlight color to draw attention to the relief.

Board Ceilings

If wallboard, new plaster, or tin seem like too much trouble for your ceiling, there's always wood. I'd suggest using edge-and-center-beaded matchboard (⅜-in.- to ½-in.-thick boards about 5½ in. wide with a center bead pattern that makes them look like two conjoined strips). This was a common treatment for turn-of-the-last century commercial buildings. Locally available species are generally less expensive. Depending on where you live, these may be spruce, white or yellow pine, or Douglas fir.

Another option that still has much the same feeling as traditional matchboard at a slightly lower cost is 1x3 V-groove board. Board finishes are easily installed over 1x3 strapping nailed over the ceiling joists. (Once again, it's not necessary to remove the original ceiling.) The boards can be either varnished or painted.

STRIPPING TRIM

Many old-house owners, in the belief that natural must always be better, are convinced that all interior woodwork and trim should be liberated of its paint, so that the bare wood can express its true character, fortified by an oil or varnish finish. But unless the underlying wood is inherently beautiful, such as cherry, walnut, mahogany, oak, or other semiprecious hardwood, stripping is usually not worth the effort. Most woodwork was painted because it lacked any particularly interesting grain in the first place. With many softwoods and even some hardwoods, the paint is absorbed into the surface so that it cannot be entirely removed without sanding away a great deal of wood.

Trim that has accumulated so much paint that its detail is lost and trim that has been the victim of previous careless stripping effort can benefit from stripping before repainting. A little detective work will determine whether the underlying work is worth rescuing. Select an inconspicuous piece of trim and, with a single-edged razor blade, carefully excavate the paint strata, one layer at a time. If it's paint all the way to the bottom, the wood is probably only worth painting. If you uncover a layer of varnish or shellac, the wood was probably interesting enough that someone had left it unpainted.

Stripping trimwork in situ is one of the least-stimulating tasks imaginable. It's easier (and, given its likely lead content, safer) to remove the trim, number and record its location, and take it to a commercial strip shop. Although the hot-dipping process does leave a fuzzy grain that will have to be sanded smooth, this isn't a major problem (except for precious antiques, which must always be cold-stripped to avoid raising the grain). To stiffen the fibers, seal hot-dipped wood with shellac before sanding.

Removing Trim

The key to removing moldings and other painted trimwork without splitting them is to break the paint bead first with a putty knife inserted along the margin of the molding. A trick experts use to loosen the piece is to insert a chisel, heavy screwdriver, or small prybar between two putty knifes and lift up. This opens a crack into which a larger prybar can be inserted, without damaging the edges of the trim piece.

A flatbar (one brand is Wonder Bar®) is the tool of choice for the actual removal. Place a flat block of wood between the bar and the wall or ceiling to prevent damage, and gently pry along its length, gradually widening the gap. Don't hurry and try to pull off the piece too quickly. As you work along, attempt to pry close to the nails to avoid breaking the molding.

REMOVE THE NAILS Many of the nails will pull through the back of the wood. Cut those that won't budge with a hacksaw blade. Drive any protruding nails into the wall rather than risk damaging the finish by trying to remove them. To avoid splintering the face side, pull out any remaining nails in the trim piece from the back side with nipping pliers. The curved edge of some locking pliers, such as Vise-Grip®, will lever out the most stubborn nail. Last, scratch or stamp an identifying mark into the back of the piece. Pencil or markers will not withstand the stripping process. (Note that glass cannot be hot stripped; if you strip old window sashes, remove the glass first or else apply cold stripper yourself.)

FINISHED AT LAST: THE FLOORS

Linoleum is making a comeback. Once derided as suitable only for battleships, after a decade-plus hiatus, linoleum is once again being manufactured. It is presently available in more than 80 colorful patterns in both sheet and individual tile form. It makes a durable, comfortable, and environmentally benign floor well suited to late-nineteenth- and early-twentieth-century houses.

The floors of an old house are an archaeological (or perhaps geological) adventure. The various dynasties of a house's past are chronicled in the flooring strata. Rare is the old house without at least one layer over the original floorboards. Some houses have them all, laid down one upon another in successive waves of modernization, like the sedimentary deposits of advancing and receding seas.

Tired of scrubbing at the scars left by years of heedless boot heels, progressive housewives of the post–Civil War era soon had the old hard pine or utilitarian spruce floors of the much-trafficked first-story rooms covered over with new and readily available hardwood strip flooring. Upstairs floors, much less abused, were only painted—with countless coats of steel gray, iron-hard paint.

In the next cycle of improvement, the wood floors—not only of the kitchen and bath but often of every room of the house—were covered with water-resistant and easy-to-mop-and-clean linoleum, a composite of linseed oil, rosin, ground cork, wood "flour," limestone, and natural pigments pressed onto a jute fiber backing. Since this wildly popular flooring material remained in use for over a century (invented in 1863, it remained in continuous production until 1974), there's a good chance you'll need to dig through more than one layer of the stuff.

Beginning in the 1950s, linoleum in the kitchen and bath was taken up or covered over—first, with asphalt composition tiles and, later, with vinyl composition tile and resilient vinyl sheet flooring. During that same period, wood or linoleum throughout the rest of the house was interred under the wall-to-wall carpet that had become the hallmark of the well-appointed floor.

It's best not to take up all the overlying flooring before the walls and ceilings are refinished. The battered old linoleum protects the original wood floor from damage during renovations.

Taking Up Linoleum and Composition Flooring

Usually, the topmost layer of flooring is worn and scuffed vinyl sheet or tile—something like the fashion equivalent of plaid pants. This will be glued to an underlayment of ¼-in. plywood or ⅛-in. hardboard (such as Masonite®), which is in turn nailed over one or more layers of older tiles that themselves may be glued down to one or more layers of linoleum that cover the original floor. Sometimes, the topmost floor is glued directly to the earlier floors, without an intervening underlayment. It may even be glued directly to the original floorboards. Floorboards that have telegraphed through the vinyl aren't always the good sign that they first appear to be. It's a lot harder to remove adhesives from wood flooring than to take up linoleum, which was normally cemented to a tacked down tarpaper underlayment and not directly to the wood.

REMOVING UNDERLAYMENT Flooring cemented to an underlayment is best removed by taking up the underlayment itself. Force a flatbar under an accessible edge at a threshold or where a baseboard can be removed. Work along the edge and then pry the underlayment up, levering it with a length of 2x4 or pulling it up by hand, popping and pulling nails as you go. Cut through the overlying flooring to expose seams in the underlayment.

REMOVING COMPOSITION TILE Old vinyl composition tile or its precursor, asphalt composition tile, is usually quite brittle and the adhesive is usually dried out and loose. The flooring yields readily to a wide, stiff putty knife, although a square-edged shovel or a long-handled ice scraper, sharpened with a file, will be faster as well as easier on the back. (The same method of attack works for glued-down carpet.) Some close work with a paint scraper should remove any stubborn patches of old adhesive, revealing the same hardwood strip floor that someone couldn't stand to wax or wash one more time.

BEWARE OF ASBESTOS IN ADHESIVES
Although you might be able to take up an old composition floor with no particular difficulty, you could create a very big problem for yourself by so doing. Unlike modern vinyl tile and sheet flooring, asphalt and early vinyl goods and their adhesives often contained a significant amount of asbestos, which is released into the home air

From the most recent self-stick vinyl composition tile, through sheet vinyl and asphalt composition tile, to ancient linoleum the epochs of bathroom remodeling can be read in the strata of its flooring

Frozen Floor Removal

There are some old composition and linoleum floors that don't come up at all easily. The cement still maintains a robust grip or leaves a thick, sticky asphalt film on the substrate. The traditional solution was to apply blowtorches, heat guns, scrapers, and long hours of backbreaking elbow grease and then to sand any remaining residue.

Freezing with dry ice is a lot faster and more effective. A chunk of dry ice is placed on a flat metal tray, like a cookie sheet fitted with wooden handles (the tray should be steel, not aluminum, which is a poorer conductor of cold). Once the flooring freezes solid, it will shatter and chip and pull loose from the wood. You'll still need to do a little hand scrapping or sanding to remove any lingering adhesive.

when the flooring is disturbed (or sanded). Have a sample of the flooring tested. It's worth the $25 to $30 cost and 3-day or 4-day wait. If the report is negative, then rip and tear to your heart's content—and your back's despair.

There are two options if the report is positive. The less troublesome and possibly less expensive method is to simply cover the old flooring over with new material. If this is unacceptable and you really want to expose that old curly birch strip flooring, sign up for a course to become a certified asbestos abatement contractor. Then, wearing the proper protective gear and following all the relevant protocols for handling and disposal, wet down the floor and take it up. After all is done, clean the containment area with a HEPA-filtered vacuum cleaner. For the cost of professional removal, you could afford to lay down a very fine hardwood strip or antique heart-pine floor.

Repairing Wood Floors

Squeaks are usually caused by slightly warped or shrunken boards that rock up and down in response to weight. The cure is to drive finish nails at an angle into *both* sides of the tongue-and-groove joint.

To tighten down a loose, not warped, floorboard, simply drive a flooring nail through the board and into the underlying joist; then set and fill the nail hole. If a joist is not convenient, drive two nails at opposing angles through the top of the floorboard and into the subfloor. Drill pilot holes first. Screws will usually work where nails fail. Make the pilot hole through the floorboard slightly wider than the screw, so that it pulls the board into the subfloor rather than pushing it up. Countersink the head and fill with a dowel plug. If the floor can be accessed from underneath, the screws won't show.

REPLACING A DAMAGED STRIP OF FLOORING

The only practical way to replace a cracked or rotted strip of flooring is to split it out. Use a carbide blade in a circular saw set to the depth of the flooring and saw down the middle of the board to be removed. Finish the cut at the ends with a chisel. Pry up the split pieces. Oak, birch, maple, and fir strip flooring are readily available. Other species or nonstandard widths can be custom-milled from square-edged stock. To fit the replacement piece, saw off the bottom edge of the groove. Spread a bead of construction adhesive on the subfloor and face-nail the patch with finish nails—attach cleats to the faces of the joists to support replacement subflooring if needed. Set the nails and fill with colored putty.

Removing Strip Flooring

Personally, I despise strip flooring. Perhaps because of childhood associations with school corridors, the stuff somehow just seems too hard for comfortable living. Curiously, wider plank floors don't have that impersonal feel. I don't know why the width of floorboards should

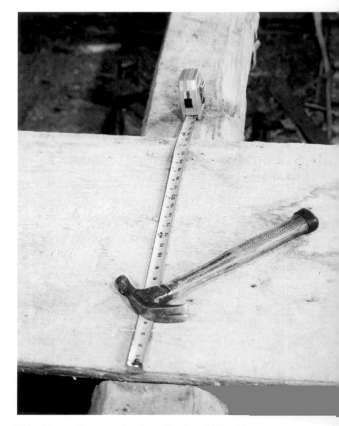

This old-growth spruce floorboard is almost 2 ft. wide.

make such a difference, but it does. Why is it that wide-board floors are prized above all others? Perhaps it is the difference between the signature of the machine and a filet of a living tree; there's more life to the wood.

Nevertheless, unless the flooring is warped and damaged beyond repair, there is no structural reason to take up a hardwood strip floor—especially since it might be covering a really bad softwood floor. Hardwood strip flooring is historically appropriate for houses dating from the middle nineteenth century to the present. Repairs are generally not hard to make. And, I confess, that I've seen some hardwood strip floors that actually look quite pretty.

If you share my feelings about hardwood strip floors and investigations in other parts of the house have revealed softwood floors beneath, salvage the old hardwood—for reuse on a countertop, a workbench, or for someone else's floors—and dig farther to uncover the underlying original flooring. Old-growth pine, spruce, and hemlock are denser and have a higher resin content than second-growth lumber; the characteristic patina of old softwood flooring cannot be reproduced with new wood, even after years of mellowing. To my mind, the value of this treasure is so great that it should not remain hidden under a plebeian hardwood strip floor that belongs to a later century.

Strip flooring is removed with the least damage if it is pulled up from the tongue side. Because flooring is always laid tongue out, the last board laid (which is usually narrower than the first board) is where you start. Remove the baseboard and insert the curved end of a flatbar into the gap between the edge of the board and the wall (if there's room). If the gap is too tight, split the flooring apart at the next joint. If you're lucky, the old nails will be more rust than metal, and most of the strips will lift up without splitting. As long as the face side is intact, the pieces are reusable. When you have room enough to

work, stand facing the flooring and drive the blunt end of a pinchbar under the boards. Lift up and push them away from the nails; pulling with the curved end of the bar tends to cause more damage. Pull out any protruding nails and sweep the area clean.

Refinishing Floors

The original wide boards, sawn from trees larger than any growing today, won't look like much. It takes an act of faith to see the clear grain masked by the grime of years, pocked with nail holes, and separated by wide rubble-filled gaps. It takes more than faith to exhume the wood hidden under that cladding of paint.

PREPARE FOR SANDING Prepare the floor for refinishing before you go out and rent a drum sander. Nail down any loose boards. Set all nail heads at least ⅛ in. below the surface. Use a screwdriver to clean out the old caulk or other debris from the cracks between boards. Patch in missing boards. If there are more than a few badly split or rotted boards, or if the gaps between them are excessive, it might be possible to take up the entire floor and re-lay it without too much trouble. Check the attic or barn: These are often partly floored with boards of the same age and species as the main floor. Otherwise, new wood must be colored (as best you can) to blend in with the old. Applying a chemical paint stripper to loosen the first few layers of old paint will save a lot of sandpaper and sweat.

RENT A DRUM SANDER Although rented drum sanders are not always as powerful or easy to use as those employed by professionals, the careful amateur can still do a reasonably good job. If you are unusually lucky, the rental agent may actually know more about running the machine than just how to tighten the belts. In any case, take home more belts than you think you'll need; until you get the feel for the machine, you'll tear several to pieces the moment the drum hits the floor. Besides, unused belts are returnable and you don't want to run short.

START WITH COARSE PAPER On painted floors, start with 32/0 coarse open-coat paper, which won't clog as fast as other grits. The same grade is also used for badly worn and pitted, cupped, and irregular floors where a great deal of material must be removed. This is the grade you'll need the most of. Cupped and dipping floors will level faster if the initial pass is made diagonally to the grain. Make a second diagonal pass perpendicular to the first and then a final pass with the grain.

SWITCH TO MEDIUM GRIT Once the wood is paint- or varnish-free and level, the rest of the job is dedicated to smoothing out the scratches left by this initial sanding. Start the restoration with 60-grit or 80-grit paper. On unpainted and

Sanding wood floors requires patience and skill. Here, the gouges left by inept use of the edger are highlighted by the stain. The surface has also been dished out by sloppy work with the drum sander.

Tips for Running a Drum Sander

■ **Always work with the grain.** Cross-grain sanding not only leaves hard-to-remove scratches but makes the sander follow the dips and humps in the floor instead of leveling them. The speed at which the machine pulls itself across the floor will determine the depth of the cut. Never let it linger in one place or it will scoop out the wood. Ease the sanding drum into and out of action by leaning it on its backstop. It should be running at full speed when it contacts the floor and shut off only after contact is broken. To avoid abrading the drum sander cord, sling it over your shoulder.

■ **Controlling sawdust.** At the end of a pass, pull the sander backward over the cut to pick up sawdust and smooth it out. Overlap each pass 3 in. to 4 in.

If the dust bag is emptied before it fills up, a lot less dust will escape into the rest of the house. Even so, seal off the room from the rest of the house by taping plastic over doorways and air ducts. Enclose switch plates and outlet covers to prevent the infiltration of fine dust that could cause a short circuit.

■ **Play it safe.** Painted floors, (as opposed to varnished floors) are almost certain to contain lead. Wear an approved respirator and take the usual precautions for lead dust control. Use a damp mop and a HEPA-filter vacuum cleaner to thoroughly clean up the residue of this first pass before further sanding. Likewise, dispose of the contaminated sanding dust properly: Don't use it for mulching the shrubbery.

more-or-less level floors (especially hardwood), the coarser of these can often be used for the cutting coat. If the 80 grit clogs too quickly, use 60 grit.

SAND TO FINAL FINISH When the scratches have been reduced to faint swirls and the grain is beginning to stand out from the background, the floor is ready for fine sanding; 100 grit will generally do for softwood floors, but hardwood may require an additional pass with 150-grit paper. Wear crepe-soled shoes or socks while finish sanding, or you risk marring the wood. The finished floor will be smooth to the touch. Look at the floor obliquely under strong light to check for dished-out areas left by the sanding drum or any renegade scratches. The job is done when you can see clear, unscratched grain in the knots.

USING THE EDGE SANDER An edge sander is used in corners, along walls and in areas too small or awkward for the drum sander to reach. The edger follows each pass of the drum sander using the same grits. Remove the baseboards first. Use a sharp chisel or scraper to pare down the arc at the inside of each corner where the edger can't reach, and smooth it with a finish sander or a piece of sandpaper wrapped around a block of wood. Sometimes, especially when the grain runs in the wrong direction, the edge sander is the only machine that can reach into closets and hallways. If you're lucky, there won't be too many places like this, since no better torture for the lower back could be imagined than the stooped-over position demanded by the edger.

CLEAN THE FLOOR Clean the finish-sanded floor with an industrial-strength vacuum cleaner, paying particular attention to the cracks between the boards. Go over the floor once more with a tack cloth; you'll be surprised how much dust the vacuum cleaner left behind.

Selecting a Finish

The selection of a floor finish defies easy resolution. In colonial times, repeated washing of unfinished wood with hot water and lye eventually imparted a soft silvery gray finish. The dense and resinous heartwood was pretty much impervious to water. Although floors were also painted as far back as the mid-1700s in New England, the practice did not become widespread until well into the first decades of the nineteenth century. Colors that didn't show dirt, such as brick or "Indian" red, gray, brown, and green were typical. Surprisingly bright colors such as yellow, light blue, and ochre were also quite common.

The practice of painting floors to mimic carpet patterns and other often quite extravagant decorative motifs continued well past the mid-1800s. Inexpensive pine flooring was often stained to mimic more costly woods like walnut and cherry. Linseed oil was applied to floors starting in the early nineteenth century. But the glossy hard finish of shellac and other varnishes (derived from natural resins such as copal, amber, and tung nuts) are only about a century and a half old. First coming into wide use around 1850, glossy finishes remain popular today, although today they are achieved with synthetic varnishes such as polyurethane rather than natural resins.

The true warmth and character of this floor lie hidden beneath the polyurethane varnish brushed over a haphazardly applied brown stain on cursorily sanded boards. In addition to the usual scrapes and scratches, the boards are disfigured with an acne of paint splotches.

PENETRATING OILS VERSUS SURFACE RESINS

Every type of floor finish has its partisans, who recommend it above all others and condemn any alternatives. Basically, there are only two kinds of floor finishes: penetrating oils and surface resins. A penetrating finish (such as linseed oil, tung oil, and "Danish oils" such as Watco® brand) is generally easy to renew by simply cleaning and adding another coat. Surface coatings (such as natural varnishes, polyurethane, and other synthetic resins) have more resistance to scratches but look the worse for it and can be renewed only by stripping and sanding. Traditional shellac is brittle and damaged by alcohol and water, but it's easy to repair. The choice comes down to soaking your floors in oil or covering them with plastic.

A penetrating oil finish will help maintain the patina of a fine, old softwood floor, so long as it is given a coating of paste wax to help it resist moisture. Spar (marine) varnish makes an excellent finish for hardwood strip floors. A splintery softwood floor can be rescued with a polyurethane glaze. The real problem with polyurethane is its unpredictable bonding to previously finished wood (even after sanding) and response to temperature and moisture conditions, which can cause a cloudy finish. The recently developed water-based polyurethanes are easier and healthier to apply—they don't release flammable and toxic volatile organic chemicals (VOCs). Plus, they dry so fast that you can finish three coats in a single day. But safety and speed come at a premium: Water-based polyurethane is at least twice as expensive as the oil-based kind.

URETHANE Three or four coats of gloss urethane is the most wear-resistant finish a nonprofessional can safely apply over hardwood, especially for floors that aren't subjected to heavy traffic. There are products such as moisture-cured oil-modified polyurethane and urea-formaldehyde-based Swedish varnish that produce a very hard, very high gloss "gym-floor" finish. But the high VOC content and (in some cases, high toxicity) of these products restricts them to professional application only.

Given three coats of ordinary polyurethane, or four or five coats of water-based polyurethane, bedroom floors will remain like new forever, whereas kitchen floors will need refinishing every 4 years to 5 years unless people get into the habit of taking off their shoes at the door. Never wax polyurethane, as it makes refinishing impossible.

APPLYING FINISH Whatever finish you choose, religiously follow the directions on the label. And give some thought as to where you'll live while the finish cures. Not only must the rooms be kept heated and ventilated (which is hard to do in the winter) but a house full of evaporating hydrocarbons is neither pleasant nor healthy to live in. This is a strong argument for using water-based polyurethane.

In spite of your efforts with the vacuum cleaner, the cracks between wide boards will still contain sanding grit and flakes of debris that are easily picked up by the brush bristles. To imprison the dust and reduce further frustration, first flood the cracks with floor finish as you start to coat the floorboards proper. Wider cracks can be filled after the first sealing coat is dry with lampblack-tinted glazing compound. Force the material into the cracks with a putty knife and then wipe the surface clean with mineral solvents before applying the second and third finish coats. Hemp rope can also be packed into the cracks with a caulking iron or blunt chisel.

The beauty of old floorboards is worth the effort of uncovering, sanding, and refinishing. New wood, even when stained, cannot duplicate their tone. More than a color, it is a palpable warmth distilled from the heart of the wood.

Any work you perform on old wiring is a compromise, trading less expenditure of money and mess against safety. . . . How can you assure safety in dealing with old wiring? The only solid advice that can be offered without any hedges is this: Rewire from the service drop on, rather than touch anything that another has done or begun— whether yesterday or yesteryear.

—DAVID E. SHAPIRO,
OLD ELECTRICAL WIRING: MAINTENANCE AND RETROFIT

L ying in bed on some cold nights, poised on the edge of sleep, I hear a noise that seems to come from within the walls of the house. It is the 60-cycle hum of electric current, the sound you hear when there is no other sound. Sometimes the sound fills the entire house, pounding like an idling diesel engine outside the windows. The very walls vibrate. I wake my wife and ask her if she can hear it too. She can. We both lie awake, stomachs tight, listening to the walls pulse. Adult as we are, it is still frightening, and the point is that electricity itself can be frightening. There are those who cannot fix a plug, who react to a spark with the same terror as they react to a

The entrance panel is the heart of the household electrical system.

lightning bolt. And then there are others who find it a mystical and irrational force.

Indeed, there is reason to fear electricity. Handled incorrectly, electricity can electrocute you or burn down your house. The good news is that when installing new wiring there are no gray areas. If you educate yourself about the right cables and devices to use in each situation, making the right connections is very straight-forward. This is why the ideal approach is to take David Shapiro's advice and rewire from the service drop.

Unfortunately, unless you are gutting all the walls, it is not usually practical to rewire an old house from scratch. While any good wiring man-ual will tell you all you need to know about new materials and techniques, they won't give you much guidance about dealing with old wiring. So in this chapter I focus on what you are likely to find when you open an old electrical box and on how to snake wires through old walls. This will help you decide what you can tackle your-self and when it is time to call an electrician who knows his or her way around old wire.

BASIC ELECTRICAL THEORY

If electricity is thought of as invisible water, it becomes friendlier—electrical problems are remarkably similar to plumbing problems, with one important difference: Leaking pipes won't drown you, but leaking wires can kill you.

Although shop-worn almost to the point of a cliché, the water analogy for electrical current is still the best way to understand it. So here it is: Water flowing through a pipe exerts pressure, which is expressed in pounds per square inch. The pressure of electricity flowing through a wire is expressed as volts. The rate of flow for water is measured in gallons per minute; the rate of flow for electricity is measured in amps. The friction of water against the walls of the pipe is

measured in poises; with electricity, this friction is called resistance and is measured in ohms.

The longer the wire, the greater the resist-ance. To reduce friction and the need for stronger pumps, larger pipes are needed to carry increased volumes of water. The same is true of wires: They must increase in diameter to carry larger currents over longer distances. The elec-trical analog to the loss of pressure that occurs in water pipes over long distances is called a *voltage drop.* Heat is the by-product of electrical resistance, which is why an undersize extension cord can melt down.

The relationship between these aspects of electrical flow is contained in Ohm's law: Volts times amps equals watts. Watts are a measure of the work done by electricity, convertible both to horsepower (kinetic energy) and BTUs (thermal energy). Water is sold by the cubic foot, electric-ity by the kilowatt hour (kWh), with 1,000 watts being used over 1 hour.

Just as water flows through the empty space contained within waterproof pipes, electricity flows through the spaces between atoms in con-ductors, bound by an electrically impermeable insulator. In a water circuit, such as an outdoor fountain, water is pumped from a reservoir and then collected and returned. In an electric cir-cuit, a current flows because of a difference in potential (that is, *charge*) between the source and a region of zero potential, the *ground.*

Think of water flowing downhill. (The term is both literal and figurative since the "ground" is ultimately the ground.) A lightning bolt is nothing more than a very big spark that marks the completion of a circuit between positively charged clouds and negatively charged earth. Thus, if the generating station is conceived of as a reservoir, electrical current flow is more analo-gous to a gravity-flow water supply than a pumped supply. Although the current flow must be in a closed loop, the electricity flowing from the generator to your house actually doesn't return to the generator. It just flows through the most direct and least-resistant path to ground.

Of Shocks and Shorts

An electric current flows whenever there is a continuous path between its source and a ground. Along the way, it will perform tricks like turning motors, heating coils, and emitting light, or electrocuting you, according to whatever device or part of your body is inserted in the circuit.

When a pipe springs a leak, the water will flow until the reservoir is emptied. An electrical reservoir is, for all practical purposes, infinite. If a leak occurs in an electrical circuit, all the power, all the way back to the generator, will flow through it to ground, unless some protective device intervenes first. This is a *short circuit*, or more properly, a *ground fault*.

A short circuit allows more current to flow through a wire than it can hold, increasing resistance and heat until the insulation melts and the wires and the house surrounding them burn up. A fuse is simply a thinner wire that vaporizes first, breaking the circuit and preventing the flow of current. A circuit breaker is a heat-sensitive switch that opens when a preset current limit is exceeded. Proper circuit protection and grounding are critical—consult an electrical wiring manual for details. The key to safety is to make absolutely sure that the shortest and best path to ground can never run through you.

LOW-RESISTANCE SHORTS Short circuits are a state of low resistance and high current flow. The current has found an easier path to ground than the intended one. The current flow may be great enough to manifest as a visible arc, as when a hot wire accidentally touches its steel enclosure.

In most cases, unless the overcurrent protection is defective or somehow bypassed, the fuse will blow or the circuit breaker will trip before the fault causes a fire. But sparks from an arcing short have all too often kindled fires by igniting dust and debris in electrical enclosures. Shorts are also an inadvertent connection between the hot and neutral conductor, such as when you saw through a live cable and "cross" the conductors with the blade

What makes a low-resistance short particularly dangerous is the time lag between its occurrence and the shutting down of the circuit by its protection device. If the current flow to ground happens to be through you, you could be dead before the breaker trips. Depending on how well grounded you are vis-à-vis the rest of the circuit, enough current can flow through you to electrocute you without ever approaching the trip point of the breaker. At the very least, you could get a nasty shock by allowing yourself to become an electrical device.

HIGH-RESISTANCE SHORTS While low-resistance faults cause electrocution, they rarely cause houses to burn down. The culprit behind most electrical fires is a particularly insidious fault characterized by high resistance and low-current flow. If you think of low-resistance faults as acute events, high-resistance faults are chronic conditions. This kind of fault is usually caused by corrosion or a loose connection.

The Ground Conductor

Minimizing the possibility of shorts and electrocution is the rationale behind the National Electrical Code (NEC) requirement for bonding all the conductive elements of a circuit together by a continuous ground conductor. This bare copper wire, it is hoped, offers a more attractive path to ground for short circuits than your body and ensures that breakers will trip and fuses will blow before things get out of control.

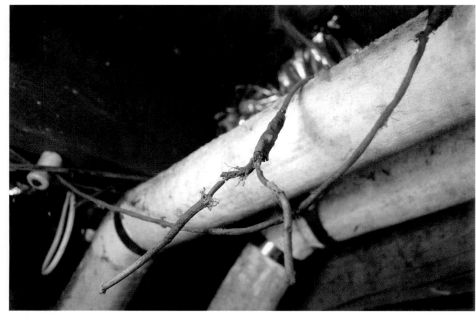

The rubber-and-cloth insulation of vintage wiring becomes brittle with age and cracks. The exposed bare conductors, if left live, are hazardous and a leading cause of house fires.

Aluminum wires connected to copper-only terminals, exposure to moisture, and the pitting caused by intermittent arcing of a loose connection all hasten the buildup of high-resistance oxide films on electrical terminals. Because resistance equals heat, as the corrosion thickens over time, the connection can become hot enough to melt and char the insulation on the wires, igniting surrounding combustibles, all the while never drawing enough current to trip the breaker or blow a fuse, unless the exposed hot conductor finally shorts to ground or the naked neutral. Dry air has high resistance so a hot conductor of ordinary household current must be in microscopically close proximity to a ground for it to arc.

A SHORT HISTORY OF HOME WIRING

Up until 1897, when pressure from insurance companies and fire marshals led to the adoption of the first National Electrical Code (NEC), the installation of house wiring was haphazard and frequently unsafe. But in urban areas, by the close of the 1920s the electrical appliances that we take for granted today had become standard features of the American household, and electrical wiring had advanced to the point to which it would not be unrecognizable to a modern electrician.

In the hinterlands, however, the only homes that had electrical power were those that produced it themselves. Gasoline-powered generating plants (many of which produced only DC power) supplied power for lighting as early as the 1890s. But it wasn't until the Rural Electrical Administration program of the 1930s that electricity began to be a household item in rural America.

Early Exposed Systems

Because most early electrical work was confined to retrofitting wiring in existing houses, rather than installing it in new ones, the first wiring systems were exposed. The direct current system developed by Thomas Edison used three paper-and-cloth insulated conductors mounted on wooden cleats spaced about 4 ft. apart. The conductors were routed along walls and up staircases between floors. It wasn't long before the wooden cleats were replaced with safer porcelain in the 1880s.

The drawbacks of exposed wiring, both from the standpoint of safety and appearance were soon apparent. But the first attempt to conceal wiring by embedding it in the wall and ceiling plaster was even more problematic. Not only was it difficult to find and repair problems but the lime in the plaster ate away the insulation, causing dangerous shorts. It seemed only natural to snake wires through abandoned iron gas pipes. While this early form of conduit offered excellent mechanical protection, the insides of the pipes often contained moisture and rust that ate away the insulation, allowing the copper conductor to contact the pipe. Galvanizing the inside of the pipe helped, but it wasn't until the invention of vinyl insulation in the 1940s that metallic conduit became safe and practical.

Greenfield Conduit

Given the need for elbows and other fittings and the inherent difficulty of retrofitting rigid conduit within the walls and floors of an existing building, many kinds of flexible conduit appeared on the market around the turn of the twentieth century. Lumped together under the generic name *Greenfield* (after the inventor of one of the most successful brands), this spiral-wound galvanized tubing could be snaked like cable through walls and ceilings. While it provided the superior mechanical protection of rigid conduit and was much easier to use, Greenfield conduit suffered from the same problems caused by the vulnerability of the conductor insulation to moisture and degradation. Furthermore, unlike jointed piping, the multiple sections of flexible conduit did not provide a continuous path to ground, which could be both lethal and a fire hazard.

Knob-and-Tube Wiring

The knob-and-tube system was the first widely used concealed wiring system that was both cost effective and safe. Even though the rubber insulation would deteriorate or be nibbled away by rodents, the physical separation between the parallel conductors offered a fair degree of protection, so long as the conductors were adequately supported and did not sag.

Electricians would wire a house by prying up the floorboards of the second floor to expose a foot-wide channel parallel or perpendicular to the joists, giving them access to the ceiling of the floor below. Then they would bore through the joists or wall studs as needed to run a feed wire to a dead-ended fixture box in the middle of each room, often at the center of a plaster medallion. A ceiling light was hung from a length of former gas pipe threaded into the box or else the fixture was screwed directly to the box.

The conductors of knob-and-tube wiring systems were protected by woven cloth *loom* where they passed through an obstruction or into a fixture box. (Here, the loom on the right is missing.) Even though this porcelain lamp socket has been grandfathered, the exposed conductors and lack of an enclosure render it unsafe by today's standards. The wiring and the fixture should both be replaced.

Wires to power wall outlets (and occasionally, wall switches) radiated outward like octopus tentacles from this central junction. More often, pull chains controlled the ceiling lights, making for one less set of wires to snake down through the walls. Ideally the two conductors were mounted to knobs on the sides of opposing joists, rather than on the face of a single joist. To reduce labor, circuits were run through cellars and across attics whenever possible.

Surface-Mounted Raceways

The expense of taking up and replacing flooring boring holes, patching plaster, and snaking wires through walls and behind baseboards, made retrofitting concealed wiring prohibitively expensive for many families. Wood and metal surface-mounted raceways were a popular, easy-to-install alternative to exposed wiring at half the cost of concealed knob-and-tube systems. The wood raceway was a two-part system, featuring a base plate grooved for two or three conductors that was attached along the baseboard or ceiling line and a decorative cap molding. The runs were planned to look like interior

The Aluminum Hazard

There is one especially hazardous condition, which professional electricians inadvertently helped create. Throughout the 1960s, aluminum was promoted as a low-cost alternative to expensive copper cable. The wiring devices for connection to this cable, although listed as safe, turned out not to be. The connections would corrode and heat up. It wasn't until 1971 that the Underwriter's Laboratories (UL) called for stricter listings. In the meantime, many houses and lives were lost to fires that could have been avoided.

trim. Unfortunately, the wood was in such close proximity to the conductors that it could ignite if the circuit was overloaded. If the wood became wet, it would soak the primitive insulation and cause a short. Finally, later remodelers sometimes mistook the wire mold for simple wood molding, and would drive nails through the wires. For all these reasons, wood raceways were outlawed in the early 1930s.

Inconspicuous oval or rectangular galvanized metal wire mold was also introduced around 1900 and supplanted wood by the 1920s. Although often embedded in plaster, the metal was susceptible to rust and dampness and its use was eventually restricted by code to surface wiring only. Improved versions of metal raceway are still widely used today.

HOW IT ALL WORKS

Because alternating current (AC), unlike direct current (DC), can be transmitted over large distances without excessive voltage drop, it is the most commonly used form of power. In this country, the current changes polarity 60 times (or cycles) per second. Power comes into the home through two hot wires and a neutral wire.

At a given moment, the charge on one of these wires with respect to the ground is 110 volts positive while the other is 110 volts negative. But if these current pulses are properly timed (in phase), the voltages will add together instead of canceling out, which means that the power coming into the house is 220 volts, measured across both hot wires.

A 220-volt service makes it possible to deliver two different voltages into the house: 110 volts for devices that consume relatively little power, and 220 volts for those with a greater appetite. Electricity travels from the power station at high voltage (typically 7,000 volts) to a step-down transformer mounted on the pole outside your house, where it is reduced to 220 volts.

The Service Drop

The electric company's meter measures power through the *service drop,* the connection between pole and house proper, before it feeds into the service entrance panel. This box contains a safety device, the main disconnect, which will shut off all the power to the house, and a number of *overcurrent protection devices* (that is, circuit breakers or plug-base and cartridge fuses) to protect and distribute power at the appropriate voltages and amperages to the individual circuits that radiate out from the service panel.

Inadequate wiring usually begins at the service drop. The earliest systems, devoted exclusively to illumination, required only a 20-amp or 30-amp service drop. Homes wired before the advent of electric ranges and clothes dryers might have had a 60-amp service. I've even seen isolated farmhouses still wired for 30-amp service. Today, the bare minimum is 100 amps and any home of size (or more than 300 ft. from the power pole) is better off with a 200-amp service.

The electric company runs its wires from the transformer to a wall or mast-mounted weatherhead or runs your underground service cables up their pole in conduit you have provided. The rest of the service installation is your responsibility. Ask your utility company for a copy of their service entrance specification booklet. This will show you exactly what type (and brand name and catalog number) of equipment they will accept and how they want it to be hooked up so that it will pass their inspection. Don't be afraid to ask, if the specs aren't clear. Otherwise hire an electrician—this is one place where you absolutely want to get it right.

The Entrance Panel

From the meter box, the entrance cable is supposed to proceed to the entrance panel by the "most direct path." Considering the cost of the cable, there's an incentive to comply with this code directive. Depending on code specifications, the meter box and/or the service panel are grounded to a buried steel water main or an 8-ft.-long copper-clad steel rod driven fully into the earth. (The former won't work if your water main is plastic.) To ensure a continuous ground path, the water meter should have a *jumper,* from the pipe on the inlet side to the outlet side. There should also be jumpers on any *dielectric unions.* Typically located at the inlet and outlets of electric water heaters or where a copper pipe mates with a galvanized main, these unions contain a nonconductive bushing that prevents galvanic corrosion by isolating the dissimilar metals.

Entrance cable is almost always aluminum. Although the terminals inside the panel are not supposed to react with this metal, the connections sometimes corrode or loosen, especially if an antioxidant coating (such as No-Al-Ox) was not applied first. Corrosion increases resistance, which leads to a potentially dangerous heat buildup or arcing to ground, which can cause the neutral wire to become sporadically energized. Circuit breakers can also become corroded, especially in damp cellars. This has the effect of increasing the amount of current needed to trip the breaker. When a circuit designed for 20 amps

is overloaded to 25 amps before the breaker opens, the fire hazard is more than theoretical. Routinely tripping the breakers once a month will help prevent corrosion buildup

The service cable feeds into the entrance panel. Each conductor is connected to lugs on the main breaker, which also functions as a disconnect switch. In older systems, the disconnect

In some jurisdictions, the electric company installs the service wiring from the pole to the meter box and the homeowner takes it from there. In others, the homeowner is responsible for all the wiring from the weatherhead down. This meter box is ready for the service drop. Note the braided copper ground conductor.

Don't Mess with the Meter

The utility company has the sole legal right to tinker with the meter they install in your meter box. They own it. There is a plastic seal affixed to the lock, and if it is broken, they can hold you liable and impose all sorts of penalties, especially if they think you were trying to tamper with the meter to cheat them out of their rightful profits. If you need to turn off the power to the meter, let the utility company handle it or ask for permission to do it yourself.

switch was typically separate from the service panel. Subfeed boxes usually don't have disconnects either. The strands of the aluminum jacket are twisted together to form a wire, which is fastened to the main grounding lug. Flat metal bars (the *bus bars*) deliver the current to the individual circuit breakers. The hot (black) wires from each circuit are connected to the breaker terminals. The neutral bus is fitted with screw terminals for the neutral (white) leads and is mechanically bonded to the steel box itself.

The bare ground conductors also are connected to a separate bonded grounding bus or share the neutral bus. This holds true, however,

Circuit Design Basics

What determines whether or not you can perk the coffee at the same time you toast your muffins?

There are some basic NEC rules that pertain to residential circuit design. The most important is that the total current draw on a circuit must not exceed 80 percent of its capacity. Recalling Ohm's law, it's obvious that this requirement determines wire sizes, lengths of circuit runs, the number and wattage of fixtures, and circuit-breaker ratings.

Because normal household circuits (not including heater, range, or dryer type) use either 15-amp breakers with 14-gauge wire or 20-amp breakers with 12-gauge wire (the smaller the number, the larger the wire diameter), circuit design is basically a matter of adding up the wattages of each proposed fixture or appliance and seeing if the total is within the 80 percent of maximum capacity specified by the code (actually, the total is adjusted by a demand factor, since it's unlikely all the fixtures will be in use at the same time). The current-carrying ability of a wire depends not only on its gauge but also on the length of the circuit. A good electrical handbook will include tables for sizing wires to loads.

To answer the important question posed above, given a 20-amp breaker, can you run a coffee maker and a toaster oven at the same time? The plate on the bottom of the toaster oven says 1,050 watts, the one on the percolator says 700 watts. The maximum capacity of a 20-amp circuit is 20 amps times 110 volts, which equals 2,200 watts. The 80-percent allowable load is 1,760 watts. You can toast and brew without blowing a fuse and have the satisfaction of knowing that you are also complying with code. Adequate capacity is the rationale for two or more separate kitchen outlet circuits.

One more example: What size breaker is required for an electric clothes dryer? The dryer contains two elements that draw 5,000 watts at full tilt. The dryer is wired for 220 volts. Thus 5,000 divided by 220 equals 23 amps, which is the current it will draw. And 80 percent of the capacity of a 30-amp breaker is 24 amps (30 times 0.8 equals 24) so the dryer should have a 30-amp breaker. Standard tables tell us a 30-amp circuit should use 10-gauge wire for the connection. If the dryer had been wired at only 110 volts, it would have drawn more than 45 amps, twice the current, which is why it's more economical to use higher voltages to meet large demands.

Here are some other considerations and code requirements to keep in mind when upgrading your system:

■ Kitchens must have at least two 20-amp appliance circuits.

only in the service panel. In subfeed panels downstream of the main panel, the neutral bus must "float"—that is, it is electrically isolated and never bonded to the box. Here, the ground wires always connect to a separate bonded ground bus. Proper grounding and bonding of main panels and subpanels can be very confusing. Most amateur electricians are unaware of the difference between the two and often overlook the requirement to bond the neutral in the main panel. Remember: *Neutral is not the same as ground!*

Finally, special ganged breakers enable both black and white leads, or black and red leads, to tap 220-volt instead of 110-volt power.

███ Circuits for kitchen outlets must be separate from the lighting circuit.

███ Anything with a motor of ⅓ hp or more (such as a refrigerator, dishwasher, freezer, water pump, or air-conditioner) or a large heating element (water heater, electric range, or clothes dryer) is required to have its own individual circuit with wire size and capacity determined by the wattage or horsepower of the appliance.

███ The 15-amp lighting circuits for bedrooms, living rooms, and hallways can have no more than 9 outlets and/or fixtures (12 with a 20-amp circuit).

███ All outlets in the bathroom, at kitchen counters within 4 ft. of a sink, in the garage, or in an accessible basement, and all outdoor outlets must be protected by a ground-fault circuit interrupter (GFCI). This device automatically breaks the circuit within microseconds at the slightest flow of current from hot to ground, which means that you won't fry if you are standing in bare feet on the wet floor and touch an appliance that is electrically live.

███ Keep lighting circuits separate from appliance circuits.

███ Provide one 15-amp general-purpose circuit for every 500 sq. ft. to 600 sq. ft. of floor space.

███ Don't put all the lights on a given floor on the same circuit.

███ Paddle fans cannot be hung from ordinary fixture boxes. Use listed boxes that attach directly to structural members.

███ Provide at least one wall switch for at least one ceiling light in each room. Pull chains are no longer permitted.

███ Use three-way switches at each end of a hallway and at the top and bottom of a stairwell.

███ Use 12-gauge wire for general use circuits. Although 14-gauge wire is still permitted for 15-amp circuits, it's a better idea to use 12 gauge throughout to accommodate any future circuit revisions and extensions.

███ No part of a wall should be more than 6 ft. from a receptacle (that is, provide at least one outlet for every 12 ft. of uninterrupted wall). All walls at least 2 ft. wide should have an outlet.

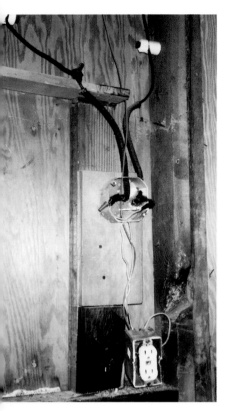

An accident waiting to happen: Someone grafted a new bathroom circuit onto part of this old knob-and-tube wiring. Moreover, this unprotected *flying splice* hidden behind the wall is very dangerous and completely illegal.

THE PERILS AND PITFALLS OF OLD WIRING

According to the National Association of Home-builders, almost half of all single-family homes in the United States were built before 1940. This means that the original wiring in almost half of all U.S. homes has outlived its service life. It also means that a lot of homes may have been hap-hazardly rewired or improperly modernized, so that potentially hazardous, if not actually life-threatening, conditions may be much more common than anyone would like to think.

As successive owners struggled to adapt their house wiring to the demands of increased elec-trical usage, the wiring often became tangled up in a web of overextended circuits and mis-matched cables that radiated outward like tenta-cles from the undersize service panel to satellite subfeed panels or distribution boxes, stuffed with the fuses, breakers, switches and splices dedicated to the burgeoning circuitry. For the sake of simplicity and aesthetics, if not safety, these jungles should be clear-cut and a new entrance panel with adequate capacity installed.

Modern Isn't Necessarily Safe

Sometimes, previous attempts to "modernize" the wiring resulted in situations more dangerous than the ones they replaced, especially when unknowing homeowners or unlicensed "mid-night electricians" performed the alterations. Even relatively recently upgraded installations can sometimes cause trouble. Most people assume that upgrading the electrical system is simply a matter of ripping out the old fuse box and replac-ing it with a circuit-breaker panel. The more pru-dent homeowner may even replace the service entrance so that the adequate power can safely be delivered to the new panel. But unless the old wiring is also upgraded, adding more capacity can actually make the existing wiring less safe. See also "Fuse Box or Breaker Box?" on p. 59.

A lot of old wiring was never designed to carry the loads that modern electrical usage demands. Many old general-purpose circuits were run with 14-gauge cable. Grafting a "daisy chain" of extensions onto an existing circuit, even when run with heavier 12-gauge cable, can overload the existing 14-gauge cable, resulting in dangerous overheating and harmful voltage drops. And, given the aforementioned weakness of prethermoplastic insulation, unless the cables themselves are no older than 1960s vintage, they can be unsafe under any load.

Bulbs aren't the only electrical components that burn out. Switches and splices and devices subject to mechanical fatigue and thermal stress make up one of the most common causes of electrical troubles. The other is sloppy or wrong-ful installation, either originally or at a later date. Corrosion, usually caused by exposure to moisture or the improper conjunction of dis-similar metals, is also the cause of potentially very dangerous conditions.

Repairing Cracked Insulation

Old ceiling lights of any sort are always prob-lematic. The shallow (½-in.- to ¾-in.-deep) *pancake* boxes they are typically mounted on are jammed so full of wires and splices that heat cannot dissipate, hastening the degradation of the old rubber insulation. This is especially so in the kitchen. Here, ceiling lights are more likely to have been "overlamped" (for example, with a 100-watt bulb screwed into a 60-watt fixture) in the first place, and there is already a lot of hot air rising to the ceiling from cooking and baking.

Cracked insulation won't necessarily cause a short, unless it crumbles and exposes the con-ductor. This usually occurs whenever the wires are jiggled, as for example if the canopy is moved or the box is opened for some reason. Sometimes, even changing a light bulb can twist the wires when a decrepit lamp holder turns with the bulb. Over time, heat damage can cause open connections or intermittent arcing.

Suspect the light fixture first; then look to the switch, if the light flickers or you hear a sizzling sound when it is switched on.

Except for direct mechanical injury, conductors within a cable don't crack or crumble along their run. (This isn't true for the exposed conductors of knob-and-tube wiring.) The outer sheathing protects the conductor insulation against the deleterious effects of exposure to air. On the other hand, in damp locations, it also traps moisture, which certainly does rot the internal insulation. But normally, any breaks are almost always to be found within an enclosure where the wires are exposed to both heat and light.

The problem with old wiring is that what you can't see *can* hurt you. Here, crumbling old wires unprotected by any kind of enclosure, fed a ceiling light fixture. The fixture canopy was hung from a mounting bracket illegally nailed to the joist. (The bracket is supposed to be screwed to mounting ears on the missing fixture box.)

Adding a Junction Box to Cure Cracked Insulation

If insulation inside a box is cracked and there isn't enough slack to pull more cable into the box, you can fix the problem by adding a new section of cable. Because it is illegal to splice wire together outside of an electrical box, cut the wire back and make the splice in a junction box as shown in the drawing at right. It's best, of course, if you can put the box someplace inconspicuous, such as the basement or attic. But if you must put it in a wall, don't bury it. Code requires that you leave it accessible and covered with a removable plate. This same technique can be used when rerouting circuits.

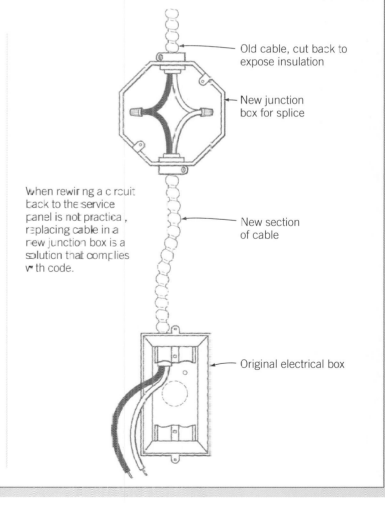

Old cable, cut back to expose insulation

New junction box for splice

When rewiring a circuit back to the service panel is not practical, replacing cable in a new junction box is a solution that complies with code.

New section of cable

Original electrical box

Replacing a Fixture Box

Even if you don't do a complete rewire, it's still a good idea to swap the shallow pancake box for a roomier 1½-in.-deep modern ceiling box. Although an existing box is grandfathered, as long as it was legal back when it was first installed, there are strict code limitations on the number and size of conductors that an old box can contain. In many cases, two 14-gauge conductors is the maximum. It's up to your local code enforcement official to decide whether you can replace an old pancake box with a new one or can install a new pancake box anywhere at all.

INCREASING THE BOX DEPTH Unless there is a risk of damaging historic ornamental plaster, it's a good idea to replace the old box or to add an extension ring to increase its depth. Depending on the diameter and type of box, you may find new parts that fit it. But one of the more annoying frustrations of working with old outlet boxes in general is that quite a few of them will not match up with modern covers and extension rings.

Because the canopies of most lighting fixtures are belled, they can usually accommodate a projecting new box. Sometimes, the original box will have been recessed deep behind the plaster (this is illegal) and the new box or extension ring will bring it flush, killing two birds with one stone. Failing this, notch the joist to receive the new box. Work carefully when cutting through wood or plaster lath. The vibration of a sawblade as it pulls through springy lath can break adjoining plaster keys.

Some pancake boxes have internal clamps for non-metallic (NM) or BX cable; others rely on knockouts and external clamps. The center knockout is often used to mount an old work bracket or stud for a *hickey* (basically an adapter that looks like a U laid on its side). The threaded stem or nipple from the lamp canopy screws into

TIP

Take Precautions

When removing old ceiling pans and opening up old ceiling boxes, be wary of any debris that can rain down on you. Wear eye protection and a dust mask. Potent allergens and even toxic contaminants and lethal viruses can lie dormant in the detritus of old wiring. ■ ■ ■

Shallow Boxes for Old Work

For Direct Attachment

For Use with Old-Work Hanger

For Heavy Ceiling Fixtures

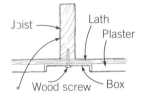

Install on substantial timber where possible.

For Lighter Ceiling Fixtures

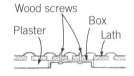

Mount box to two laths, not just one, to distribute weight of fixture.

Old-Work Hangers (most reliable)

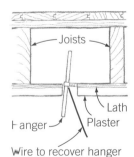

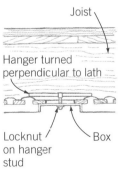

the bottom leg of the hickey, while the other leg is threaded onto the center stud. This is how ceiling fixtures were mounted on old round boxes (especially pancake boxes) that had a raised center fitting instead of fixture-mounting ears.

ATTACHING THE FIXTURE All modern ceiling boxes intended to support light fixtures have two ears diagonally across from each other, tapped for 8/32 screws. A flat steel strap with slotted openings is typically supplied with the light fixture. This is screwed to the mounting ears on the box. The fixture canopy is secured to threaded holes in the strap with longer 8/32 screws. If the canopy is designed to mount with a stem nipple instead, the strap will have a threaded hole in the middle to accommodate it. Modern straps also have a tapped hole for attaching the green ground conductor screw.

PROVIDING SUPPORT FOR THE BOX Whether antique pancake or modern octagon, ceiling boxes should be screwed through the plaster lath directly into a ceiling joist to support a heavy fixture such as a chandelier or paddle fan. With lightweight canopy lights, the box can be screwed directly to the lath. If an old-work hanger is used, the weight of the fixture will be distributed over numerous laths. The hanger is simply inserted up into an access hole, and then rotated perpendicular to the lath so that the threaded mounting stud slips into the center knockout of the box, which is then secured to it by tightening down a locknut. If you attach a piece of wire to the hanger when slipping it into the hole there's no danger of losing it between the ceiling joists or wall studs.

SECURING THE CABLES

When inspecting the box, check to make sure that all the internal or external cable clamps are both present and tight. (This applies for all boxes throughout the system.) The clamps should also be of the correct sort for the type of cable used. External connectors for non-metallic cable have opposing flattened plates that clamp the cable sheath when their screws are tightened. Armored cable clamps have a screw that tightens against the cable's steel jacket to make both a mechanical and an electrical bond. An internal clamp for non-metallic cable (*BN clamp*) in a steel box is basically a flat angled plate that screws down against the cable jacket. Make sure that the clamp is not pressing against exposed conductors instead.

Internal clamps, called *X clamps*, for armored cable (a.k.a. BX), have an L-shaped plate with circular openings for the conductors and a flange that tightens down to grip the armor. Check armored cable to make sure that its cut end is fitted with a red plastic or fiber antishort bushing (a *red hat*) to protect the exposed conductors. Finally, check for open *knockouts* (the dime- or nickel-size circular openings that admit the cable and external clamps). These must be plugged with spring-tab knockout seals. Otherwise, mice and detritus can nest within the box.

Refurbishing a Fixture

In addition to defective conductors in the box, old light fixtures often suffer from deteriorated lamp sockets or frayed wiring leads (this is often the case with swag-type fixtures). If the fixture was legal at the time of its installation, the code allows you to rebuild it. But when you replace the original brittle Bakelite or scorched paper lamp socket, either replace it with a base that does not have a built-in pull-chain switch (which is no longer legal) or remove the pull chain so the switch is inoperable and in the on position.

If the lamp is not being rebuilt, replace the metal pull chain with a nonconductive plastic chain or link. This precaution protects you against a shock should there be a short to the metal of the canopy and its attached chain.

It's almost always better to rehabilitate an antique light fixture than to replace it with a modern one. Repair parts are readily available at any well-stocked hardware store, and the process is pretty much obvious. (It helps to make a sketch of the order in which the various nuts and nipples and bushings were put together.) The wisdom of this course will be apparent when you check out the price of reproduction replacements.

This antique fluorescent ceiling light is a treasure worth keeping.

Modern Light Levels from Old Fixtures

Historically, the earliest ceiling fixtures had unfrosted carbon filament lamps that drew 15 watts to 40 watts, providing an ambient light level that we would find unbearably dim today. Sometimes, the only fixture was a bare bulb dangling from the ceiling. Nevertheless, it's possible to re-create the ambiance of period electric lighting using original or reproduction fixtures without compromising utility. Equip the ceiling fixture with modern unfrosted lamps and use a dimmer switch set at about 25 percent of full power to simulate the glow of antique carbon filament lighting. Wall sconces and table and floor lamps can furnish task lighting. Reproduction lamps that mimic old-fashioned styles while providing modern light levels are also available.

Always use thermally rated or protected wires designed to withstand the heat that builds up behind the canopy when replacing the fixture leads.

DEALING WITH CLOSET FIXTURES The traditional bare bulb and porcelain socket with a pull chain is no longer legal in clothes closets. Many fires have been started by unattended exposed lamps that were left on. (This prohibition does not apply to pantries and cleaning or other utility closets.) Incandescent clothes closet lamps can be replaced only with cool-burning fluorescent fixtures installed on the wall above the door and not the ceiling above or in front of a shelf.

Is the Wire Hot?

Unlike modern color-coded black and white and sometimes red conductors, whose function is usually obvious, with old wiring it's difficult if not impossible to distinguish between the hot and neutral conductors. Sometimes both conductors are black. Quite often, a conductor which may have originally been white will have faded and crumbled away to an indistinguishable dark gray. Even though you can never absolutely rely on color-coding to determine if current is flowing through a wire or not, it's at least an assumption to cautiously begin with.

Even more than modern wiring, never assume that antique wiring conforms to standard safe practices. It's not uncommon to find a switch installed across the neutral conductor instead of the hot. Thus, even though the lamp is off, current is still flowing through the hot to it. When you accidentally touch the metal shell of the lamp socket and complete the path to ground, you'll be made excruciatingly aware of it.

Watch Out for Carter System Circuits

You may discover, quite by accident, that what appeared to have been a standard three-way switch circuit was actually a *Carter system* circuit. Also known as "lazy neutral" wiring, this once legal and quite commonplace wiring method allowed you to control a light from two points using only two-wire cable instead of three-conductor cable. Normally, the hot wire from the feed goes to the common terminal of a three-way switch, which then routes power through one of two *traveler* wires to the second switch. In a Carter system, the current is switched between the hot and the neutral conductors. Sometimes, the neutral is actually the hot. You can get shocked when you remove a lamp (the technical term for a light bulb) because both the center contact of the lamp holder and the threaded shell will be hot.

Is It Grounded?

As discussed in chapter 1, you can't assume that the presence of three-pronged outlets indicates updated wiring. The jumper from the ground terminal on the outlet may indeed be bonded to a screw in the enclosure, but the cable entering the enclosure may still be two-wire cable, lacking the bare ground conductor. Because there is no ground return path, a fault can still shock you without tripping the breaker. Armored cable—as long as the armor is intact and its electrical bond to the box at the clamp is not compromised by rust—does provide a good ground return. (If the armored cable run is an extension of an ungrounded non-metallic cable run, the protection is lost.)

In the best of all possible worlds, the missing bare conductor may be found wrapped around the cable at the clamp. As mentioned earlier, ground conductors were available long before a lot of electricians knew what to do with them. Uncoil it from the incoming (feed) cable and splice it to the jumper from the device to the box and the outgoing (run) cable with a copper crimp connector or a green twist-on solderless connector (one brand is Wirenut).

It's Not Always Black and White

Even when you are dealing with modern color-coded wiring, it is not safe to assume that black is always hot and white is always neutral. There are cases when it is within code to use a white wire as the hot wire. Code requires such wires to be marked with a wrap of black tape at the connection, but this precaution may have been neglected. Or the person doing the wiring may have simply gotten the wires crossed.

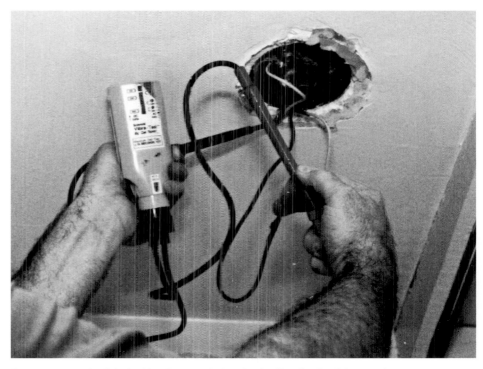

Never assume a circuit is dead just because the breaker is off or the circuit is unused. Always test every conductor before making any changes to the wiring.

The round "crowfoot" receptacle on the left has been illegal for a long time. (The shape of the slots will accept a 20-amp male plug backwards, thereby energizing the neutral side of the circuit.)

FIXING A CLIPPED GROUND In the worst of all possible worlds, you'll be stuck with either ungrounded cable or a ground that has been clipped off just outside the box. Code says that you can remedy the former by running an "adequately protected" grounding conductor to the nearest good ground. But what constitutes a good ground and adequate protection are open to question. It's safer to replace the old cable with grounded cable.

If the ground has been clipped off just inside the box, you can splice a bare conductor onto the stub of the existing conductor with a crimp connector. While any sort of *flying* splice (a splice outside an enclosure) is now illegal, an inspector would probably let this one pass. Soldered and taped flying splices were once quite legal with knob-and-tube wiring. So long as the splice was mechanically well made and well soldered, and its tape intact, it was apt to remain safe. Poorly made and badly soldered splices, on the other hand, are a prime locus of high-resistance faults. If you're lucky, there may be enough slack in the cable to pull it farther into the box and cut back the sheathing to make a legal splice.

SPOTTING IMPROPER GROUNDS Look also for extensions using grounded cable from outlets fed by ungrounded cables. These are particularly dangerous, because any fault in the ungrounded outlet will not trip the breaker since there is no return path to ground. Instead, it will energize the grounded enclosure box and any metallic cover plate and its mounting screws. Beware, too, of the ubiquitous bootleg ground. Here, the ground jumper is spliced into the white neutral in lieu of the absent ground wire. Besides being able to electrocute you or burn the house down, a bootleg will also cause ground-fault circuit interrupters to trip and electronic equipment plugged into the circuit to act weird.

Poor grounds can cause power to appear to be off when it is in fact feeding through the ground to the enclosure. *Backfeeds,* whereby power appears in a circuit that should absolutely be dead, are a problem in some older apartment buildings where somehow the circuits supplied by one meter got crossed with another or a meter was bypassed to steal power. In old house wiring, the circuit you cut off may not supply power to all the wires in a box. Sometimes, the switch you think controls a light doesn't. Sometimes a black isn't hot or a white isn't neutral or a ground isn't grounded. If you "kill" part of a circuit without ripping out the cable, leave it accessible and do not disconnect its ground conductor.

When removing a fixture or cutting a cable at one end of a run, trace the other end back to its source at a junction or outlet box or the panel and disconnect it there, too. If you rip a cable out of a box, always close the opening with a knockout seal or tighten down the internal cable clamps to block off the opening. Never assume the bare end of a dangling cable cannot be hot or that an apparently dead outlet actually is. Always check the wiring with a circuit tester before replacing wiring devices or adding and removing circuits.

A Few Old Wiring Crimes

Dangerous junction boxes, like the one shown in the photo below, are a far too common sight in old-house basements. The enclosure is badly corroded, armored cable shouldn't be used in a damp cellar, and a cable clamp is missing—all of which can cause a potentially lethal poor ground.

The lack of protective bushings where the conductors exit the armored cable can lead to abrasion and a short; dampness could corrode the unsoldered taped splices, causing a high-resistance fault and further exacerbating the deterioration of the already crumbling antique rubber and cloth insulation.

Finally, there are just too many wires stuffed into this little box. Considering that this is just one box in the galaxy of an entire antique electrical system, it's a wonder the house hasn't burned down.

The top right photo shows an illegal flying splice. For obvious good reasons, the NEC doesn't allow any connections between conductors outside of a protective enclosure.

Splicing wires outside of an enclosed box violates code.

Don't assume that wiring is correct just because it is modern. The surface-mounted receptacle shown in the photo below is completely acceptable, but the cables feeding it must be enclosed within metal or plastic wire mold. Unenclosed cable is allowed only in unoccupied spaces like attics, basements, and garages.

This overstuffed junction box is a fire waiting to happen.

Code does not allow exposed cable within living spaces.

Tools for Rewiring

Here's a run-down on the tools you'll need for rewiring.

■ **Fishwire.** Used to pull cables through walls and around corners, this flexible wire is indispensable. Although you can manage with only one, there are cases where two are useful.

■ **Contractor-grade drill.** You'll also need a ½-in. right-angle-drive heavy-duty drill. Ordinary home handyman ⅜-in. drills don't have enough torque and power to drive the 16-in. or longer electrician's augers you'll need to bore through multiple layers of framing or between floors. The angle-drive feature makes it possible to bore between stud cavities, which you couldn't do with a regular straight-drive drill. Since a contractor-grade drill can cost upward of $200, you may want to rent one if your rewiring is not extensive.

■ **Nail-eater bit.** For close work, you'll need a 7½-in. "nail-eater" bit. The hardened steel chews through the inevitable hidden framing nails with ease. Fitted with one or more extension bits, your drill will fearlessly bore through just about anything.

■ **Circuit testers.** A neon bulb tester will show you if a wire is live, but a pocket-size multitester is a lot handier, since it gives voltage and resistance readings as well. Plug-in circuit analyzers are also useful. When plugged into an outlet, the combination of glowing lights indicates whether the circuit is correctly wired or, if not, what is wrong with it. This will prove invaluable when troubleshooting the handiwork of the previous home electrician, who may have been colorblind when it came to observing the wiring color code.

■ **Miscellaneous tools.** Finally, you'll need a wire stripper/crimping tool, insulated lineman's pliers (a.k.a. *dykes*), diagonal cutters (for heavy cable), an NM cable sheathing splitter, an insulated screwdriver, needle-nose pliers, and the usual basic carpenter's tools.

Some basic electrician's hand tools (*from left to right and top to bottom*): electrician's pliers, needle-nose pliers, diagonal cutters, nippers, service-cable cutter, fishtape, stud finder, neon bulb tester, plug-in circuit analyzer, multitester, wire stripper/crimping tool, wire strippers, telephone wire modular connector tool, electrician's augers, extensions, nail-eater bits, armored cable jacket splitter, octagon box template for drywall, NM cable sheath splitter, hex-key wrench for service panel lugs, insulated screwdriver, outlet box screw-thread/tap tool, and conduit bender.

The many ways that old wiring can go wrong could fill a book. (*Your Old Wiring* by David E. Shapiro, McGraw Hill, 2001, is one of the best.) Short of pulling the meter (and this doesn't always work), the only way to be sure that a circuit you wish to work on is dead is by careful testing (and retesting). *Learn how to use a tester properly.*

REWIRING AN OLD HOUSE

If your house was rewired with aluminum cable, it's a good reason to rip out and redo the electrical system. If the walls are already gutted, you have an excellent opportunity to ensure your safety and peace of mind by renovating the wiring, whatever type of cable it may contain. Renewing the electrical system without removing the walls can be done, but I'd hate to hire an

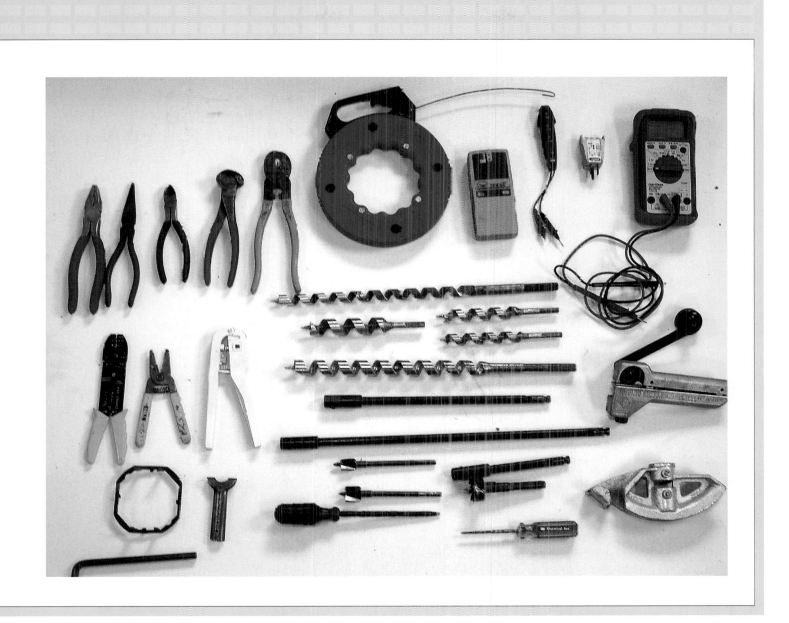

electrician to do it. It's slow work, and unless you are funded by a historic preservation grant, too costly for the average budget.

Rewiring old houses has always been more a problem of carpentry than electricity. It's a game of hide-and-seek, where you look for hidden wires and reroute them through or around unseen obstacles. If, as they say, one picture equals one kw (kiloword, not kilowatt), then the rule book for this sometime frustrating game is found in the drawings in the rest of this chapter.

Surface-Mounted Wiring Systems

If you're less than excited at the prospect of trying to hide wires behind fragile moldings and crumbling plaster or by crawling through dusty insulation and attic cobwebs to fish the lost end of a cable up a blind hole, you can resort to a time-tested and traditional alternative. You can add a fixture, switch, or outlet with one of the numerous readily available surface-mounted wiring systems. In these systems, single-conductor wire (type THHN) or regular plastic-jacketed cable is routed through metal or plastic raceways between boxes that hold the individual wiring devices. All the components are screwed to walls, ceilings, and baseboard moldings by mounting tabs, and are usually painted to match the wall finish. Where exposed cable is not objectionable (garages, cellars, attics, and outbuildings), the familiar dark brown Bakelite® surface-mounted device is an inexpensive alternative.

Personally, I think of surface-mounted raceways as a means of last resort, just the thing a preservationist might approve of if forced to electrify a historic house or the simplest way to power the light fixture the electrician forgot to wire without tearing down the finished ceilings. Otherwise, I feel that wiring is best hidden behind the walls where it looks better and where it is safe from being bumped (which can loosen connections).

Fishing Expeditions

There are special old-work outlet boxes with beveled rear corners and internal cable clamps designed to make it easy to reroute non-metallic cable into the box without disturbing a finished wall. The square corners of the boxes used for new work (installing wiring in the easily accessible bays of exposed framing, as opposed to the old work of retrofitting it to finished walls) punch the cable against the sides of the opening in the wall when you try to push the box into it, especially if cables enter at both the top and the bottom of the box. By contrast, the sloped shoulders of old-work boxes permit the cables to slip back into the wall opening. But check your local code requirements before installing these boxes. Their smaller volume limits the number of connections and wires they can contain, and they may be illegal. Use a *cut-in* box or standard box that has a knockout for rear entry.

An Elegant Alternative to Tearing into Walls

An alternative to removing baseboards, tunneling behind walls, or resorting to the unsightliness of surface-mounted wiring is to incorporate wiring into retrofitted wainscoting. A 1½-in.-deep outlet box will just fit flush to the surface of the baseboard if applied over ¾-in.-thick paneling. (Check with your local electrical inspector first to see if such shallow boxes are still allowed.) When the wainscoting panels are applied over horizontal furring, standard-depth boxes can be used instead.

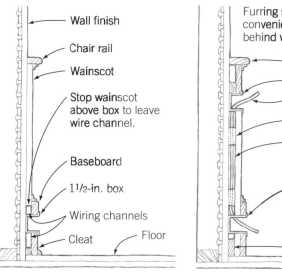

Wall finish
Chair rail
Wainscot
Stop wainscot above box to leave wire channel.
Baseboard
1½-in. box
Wiring channels
Cleat
Floor

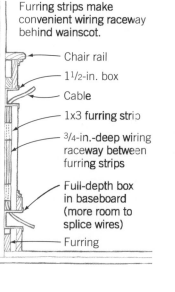

Furring strips make convenient wiring raceway behind wainscot.
Chair rail
1½-in. box
Cable
1x3 furring strip
¾-in.-deep wiring raceway between furring strips
Full-depth box in baseboard (more room to splice wires)
Furring

Beveled-Corner Outlet Box for Old Work

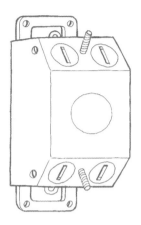

An outlet box with beveled corners and internal cable clamps simplifies retrofitting wiring to finished walls.

The plastic box on the left is for new work and mounts with built-in nail holders to a stud. The plastic Veco Adjust-A-Box has a face-mount bracket that automatically sets the box at the correct depth. The standard steel *gem box* has adjustable plaster ears that can be screwed into lath or wood paneling. The box second from right is a steel equivalent of the plastic new-work box. And the *utility box* on the right is intended for surface mounting in indoor locations.

CUTTING A HOLE FOR A NEW BOX You can use an electronic stud-finder to locate the framing, though I've found that, for electrical work at least, all you need is to listen for the change from a hollow to a sharper tone while rapping along the wall with your knuckles. Make a Masonite template and use it to mark the location of the new outlet box about 4 in. or 5 in. away from a stud (see the the top left drawing on p. 338). Before you get carried away, drill a test hole through the underlying plaster lath. Since the box is best supported when only one complete lath piece is cut away, you may need to relocate the opening slightly. You will also need to notch the laths above and below the one you have removed.

Boxes that are designed to be ganged have protruding ears on the top of one side and the bottom of the other for the screws that hold them together. If you are using this kind of box, once you've determined the exact location of the outlet, drill ½-in. holes at the points indicated on the template. Insert the tip of your keyhole saw and support the plaster with your hand while gently sawing through the lath. Stick masking tape along the guidelines to help prevent the plaster from crumbling.

The cut-in box is just one of several styles of old-work boxes that allow you to add a switch or receptacle without tearing out the wall. The ears on the front of the box and the bracket on its back clamp it to the wallboard.

Installing an Outlet Box in a Plaster Wall

1. Locate studs. Drill test hole to find lath center and position template.

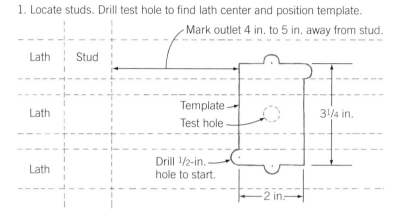

Mark outlet 4 in. to 5 in. away from stud.

Lath | Stud

Lath

Lath

Template
Test hole
Drill ½-in. hole to start.

3¼ in.

2 in.

2. Cut box outline with keyhole saw. Cut away one lath and part of each of two others, never through two complete laths. Hold plaster to prevent it from breaking. Fish cable from opening into box.

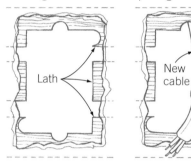

Lath

New cable

3. Install box and secure cable.

Cable into box
Screw box to lath.

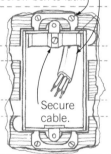

Secure cable.

INSTALLING A NEW BOX WITH BX CABLE If you are using armored BX cable, you'll have to slip a connector clamp over the cable before you pull it into the box. Sloped boxes with internal clamps aren't available for BX cable, so there's no way to pull the box into the opening without pinching against the cables. Leave about 1 ft. of wire sticking out of the cable and into the box, and use this to pull the clamp up into the knock-out after the box is installed, as shown in the drawing below. Then secure the clamp by slipping a locknut over the wires and onto the clamp.

Box-Mounting Options

Unlike new-work boxes, which are designed to fasten directly to the studs with spikes, there are at least four ways to mount square-cornered or bevel-cornered old-work boxes in the wall, depending on whether the attachment is to wood, lath, plaster, or drywall. The drawing on the facing page shows how the mounting ears can be reversed to suit plaster or wood, how special compressible spring clamps (Griptite™ box) anchor boxes to walls too flimsy to hold screws, and how steel Madison clamps pull the boxes against the back of drywall panels.

Installing BX Cable in a Box

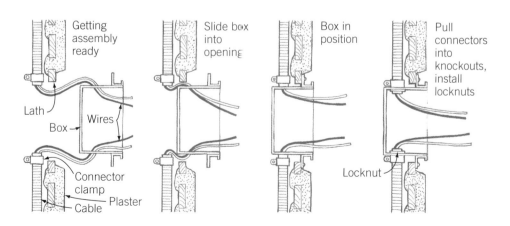

Getting assembly ready

Lath
Box
Wires
Connector clamp
Plaster
Cable

Slide box into opening

Box in position

Pull connectors into knockouts, install locknuts

Locknut

Old-Work Boxes in Existing Walls

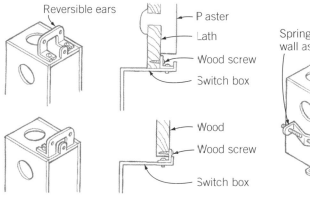

Reversible ears

Plaster
Lath
Wood screw
Switch box

Wood
Wood screw
Switch box

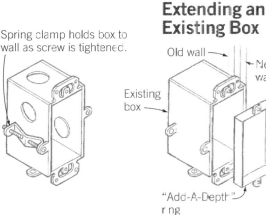

Spring clamp holds box to wall as screw is tightened.

Extending an Existing Box

Old wall
New wall
Existing box
"Add-A-Depth" ring

Cable Extensions: Adding a Switch or Receptacle

One of the most annoying things about old houses is their lack of outlets and switches. Not only is a thicket of extension cords sprouting from a single baseboard outlet unsightly, it's also a fire hazard. And anyone who has groped in the dark for the pull chain on a ceiling lamp would certainly appreciate the convenience of a wall switch to control room lights.

The feed to a fixture controlled by a pull chain is always live, so you can rewire the connections to add a switch leg. Or, if it is convenient, you can use the live feed as a power source to extend the circuit with one or more new receptacles. In many cases, you may want to add both a switch leg and additional receptacles, although adding two more cables to the fixture box is very likely to require installation of a larger box. In any case, the hard part is snaking the new cable or cables to the new box or boxes.

ADDING A BOX DIRECTLY UNDER A WALL-MOUNTED FIXTURE The job's degree of difficulty depends on where the switch or new receptacle is located relative to the fixture and what's behind the walls you must fish the wire through. For example, adding a switch or recep-

Ganging Boxes

It's often desirable for more than one wiring device to be included in an outlet box. Make sure that the boxes you use can be ganged together; there are some that won't permit this option. Ganging two or more boxes together (six is the most that cover plates are made for) is simply a matter of loosening a screw to remove one side plate on each box and then hooking them together and tightening down the screws.

Another type of ganging occurs when a new outlet is added back to back to an existing one. Unless the existing box has an internal cable clamp, the only way to protect the wires running between the two boxes is to join them with a length of threaded ½-in. galvanized pipe nipple.

Running Cable across Wall Studs

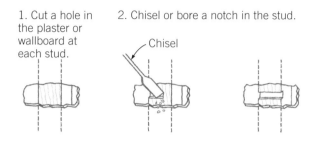

1. Cut a hole in the plaster or wallboard at each stud.

2. Chisel or bore a notch in the stud.

Chisel

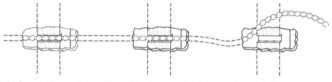

3. Feed the cable inside the wall from one hole to the next.

4. Cover the notch with a 1/16-in. steel plate and patch the opening.

tacle directly beneath a wall-mounted fixture is straightforward: With the power off, cut the opening for the new box and remove the existing fixture to expose its box. If you're very lucky, the box will be screwed into the lath and not nailed into a stud. If it is a nailed box, you can probably lever it loose with a flatbar.

Knockouts are much harder to remove from inside a box than from outside, so if you can pull the box out of its hole, adding the new cable will be a lot less trouble. Push the cable down into the stud cavity. If the wall is filled with insulation, slip the cable between the face of the vapor barrier and the back of the wall finish so that the barrier is not punctured. Reach into the hole for the new box and snag the cable with a bent coat hanger or fishtape. Then install the new box and device.

ROUTING CABLE BEHIND BASEBOARDS If the switch or receptacle will be on the same wall, but at some distance away from an existing wall-mounted fixture, the new cable can be routed behind the baseboard or across notches cut in the face of the wall studs.

To run cable across the wall behind a baseboard, first cut the opening for the new switchbox. Then remove the baseboard and cut two more holes in the wall where they will be hidden behind the trim, one directly below the existing fixture and the other beneath the switchbox opening.

With the power off, remove the fixture. Then slide a fishwire through a knockout in the box and down the wall until it comes out at the hole at the baseboard. Attach the cable to the fishwire and pull it up into the fixture box. Next, run the fishwire from the new outlet box hole down to the other baseboard hole and snake the other end of the cable up into the opening. Install the new switch box, and then make the appropriate connections. Before replacing the baseboard, cut a groove in the plaster and/or lath deep enough to accommodate the cable. The code calls for 1¼ in. minimum clearance between the cable groove and top and bottom edges of the baseboard. Since the baseboard has already been removed, it is a good idea also to remove a strip of lath to accommodate the cable. Nail the usual nail-proofing plates over the cable wherever it crosses a stud or use armored cable.

Fishing between Floors

Wiring changes are a lot less trouble if the new cables are run across the attic floor or between ceiling joists. Then, the only wall openings are for the new wiring devices. Drop the fishwire into a hole bored through the wall plate. Pry up attic floorboards (if any) and drill the underlying joists to run the cable. There is no danger of splitting baseboards or cracking plaster where it could show. Just make sure you have correctly located the underlying partition before drilling. You don't want to find the point of an auger sticking out of the ceiling or the face of the wall. Because partitions are usually built to the joists before the ceilings are put up, the top of the wall should be plainly visible from the attic, once any insulation has been pushed aside.

Wiring a Ceiling Fixture to a Wall Outlet

1. To get cable from A to B, make a temporary hole at C.
2. Feed first fishwire through C and out A.
3. Feed second fishwire through C and out B.
4. Hook fishwires together at C. Push into hole.
5. Attach cable to fishwire and pull from A out B.

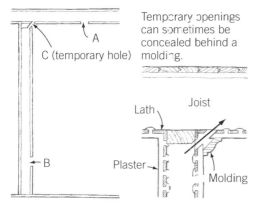

Temporary openings can sometimes be concealed behind a molding.

C (temporary hole)

A

B

Lath

Joist

Plaster

Molding

Because cellars are even more accessible than attics, it might seem easier to make first-floor wiring changes by simply boring up into the partitions from below. As long as you can accurately locate interior partitions from below boards (look for nails protruding through the subfloor or take measurements from known points), this is certainly the case. But when the wire must run through an outside wall, the foundation and sills will obstruct any simple boring. Instead, bore up into the wall cavity at an angle from the cellar or, if the space between the floor joists is inaccessible, down from above, after removing the baseboard.

Fishing through Partition Walls

Things get more complicated when a cable must run between floors and into partitions. Since it's likely that a plate will block the top of the partition, you'll need to make a temporary opening at the top of the wall, as shown in the drawing above. If there is a ceiling crown molding, it can

be removed and the hole concealed behind it. Otherwise, you'll have to patch the hole later.

RUNNING CABLE FROM A CEILING FIXTURE TO A WALL OUTLET To run a cable from the ceiling fixture to the wall outlet (or down into the cellar), feed one fishwire into the temporary hole and wiggle it along the joists until it can be pulled out of the ceiling opening. Feed a second fishwire into the temporary hole and out through the wall opening. To do this right, you'll have to use a fishwire with hooks at both ends, not the single-ended kind that rolls up into a dispenser. Hook the fishwires together at the temporary opening and pop them back into the wall. Pull one of the wires until you have a continuous loop from ceiling to wall outlet. Then attach the cable and, feeding it into the ceiling hole, pull it out the wall with a fishwire.

Wiring between Floors with Stacked Partitions

1. Remove upper-floor baseboard. Bore down through top plate of lower wall.

2. Bore second hole through sole plate of upper wall.

3. Insert fishwire and work down through plates.

4. Pull out fishwire at B to run cable from A to B, or . . .

5. Bore up into partition from cellar at C, insert second fishwire to hook first wire.

6. Attach cable to fishwire and pull from A to C.

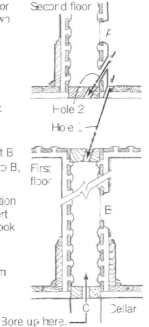

Second floor

F

Hole 2

Hole 1

First floor

E

C   Cellar

Bore up here.

RUNNING CABLE BETWEEN FLOORS WITH PARTITIONS ABOVE EACH OTHER To run cable between floors when the partitions are directly over each other, first remove the baseboard of the upper partition and bore a hole down through the top plate of the lower partition, as shown in the bottom right drawing on p. 341. Then bore a second hole through the sole plate of the upper partition. (Two holes are necessary to make the holes at the angles you'll need to stay in the wall.) Push the fishwire through this hole and work it down into the lower partition. You'll probably need to snag it with a second fishwire worked up from the outlet opening in the wall below. (This can be tricky, especially if the wall is insulated. See the drawing below for an old-timer's trick.)

If the upper outlet is to be mounted in the baseboard, use the fishwire to pull the cable from that point down and out of the opening in the lower partition. Otherwise, push the end of the first fishwire back into the upper partition and snag it with yet another fishwire (a bent coat hanger can also do the job) fed into the wall from the new outlet opening.

RUNNING CABLE BETWEEN FLOORS WITH OFFSET PARTITIONS When the partitions on the two floors are offset from each other, bore a temporary access hole at the top of the lower partition and another behind the baseboard of the upper wall, as shown in the drawing at left. Then, as with the installation of a ceiling fixture, use two fishwires to run the cable. The operational principle is always to end up with a single loop of fishwire between the two points for pulling cable.

RUNNING CABLE THROUGH JOISTS In the previous examples, we have assumed that the cables were run parallel with the ceiling joists. Since you obviously can't push a fishwire or cable through solid framing, a length of the overlying flooring must be removed to run cable perpendicular to the joists. As any 1920s electrician will testify, it's generally easier to take up flooring than to refinish a plaster or drywall ceiling. Square-edged softwood boards are not hard to pry up with an ordinary chisel. Attic floorboards are often not even nailed down. But lifting tongue-and-groove hardwood strip flooring isn't so easy. Once the joists are exposed, they can be notched or drilled for the cable. Fill any holes bored through the flooring with plugs of matching hardwood.

RUNNING CABLE AROUND CORNERS Not all wiring obstructions are between floors. Sometimes a cable has to turn a corner. If you can't run the cable in a protected groove behind

Wiring between Floors with Offset Partitions

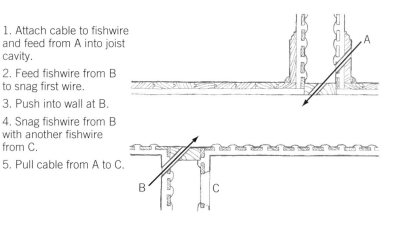

1. Attach cable to fishwire and feed from A into joist cavity.

2. Feed fishwire from B to snag first wire.

3. Push into wall at B.

4. Snag fishwire from B with another fishwire from C.

5. Pull cable from A to C.

Belling the Fishwire

When fishing blind, old-timers *belled* the fishwire. Hook one terminal of a cheap doorbell or buzzer to a 6-volt dry cell battery. Connect the other terminal to one of the fishwires with 18-gauge automotive wire and electrical tape. Then tape another wire from the other bell terminal to the second fishwire. When the fishwires touch each other inside the wall, the bell will ring.

the baseboard, make two temporary holes in the plaster so you can bore through the corner posts with the holes meeting at a right angle. Poke a fishwire in one hole, and then snag it with a fishwire through the other hole to pull the first fishwire around the corner. Then use the fishwire to pull the cable through.

GETTING AROUND A DOOR When a door interrupts the wall, the cable can either be looped down into a cellar or into the ceiling joist cavity. Otherwise, remove the door casings, cut a channel into the jack studs and across the header and run the cable around the door. To be safe, I'd use armored cable here or, code permitted, plastic or EMT conduit to protect it from unwitting puncture. Otherwise, NM requires a continuous 1/16-in.-thick protective plate. (This would also be a good idea for behind-the-baseboard runs.)

In new work, studs are bored for cables (at least 1/4 in. from the edge) to reduce the likelihood that a trim or paneling nail will pierce the wire. Even then, carpenters typically note the location of the wires and avoid nailing near them. I have already mentioned the need for nail-proof plates. When a cable must be concealed in a notch cut across the top of an exposed ceiling beam, run it through a length of galvanized steel pipe or EMT conduit. If you need to fit more than a single cable in this pipe, use individual type THHN wires instead. You can fit up to five conductors in the same space occupied by a single Romex wire.

LIGHTNING PROTECTION

Given the quote at right, the reader couldn't be blamed for assuming that the introduction of electrical wiring has eliminated the need for those iconic antique lightning rods perched high atop the ridgelines of many a solitary old farmhouse. However, the reader, like Roger Whitman,

The only thing obsolete or unnecessary about lightning rods are the ornamental glass balls.

When current is purchased from a central station, the power lines are so well grounded and protected against lightning that the wires form the most efficient type of lightning protection known.

—ROGER B. WHITMAN,
FIRST AID FOR THE AILING HOUSE

would be dangerously wrong. Lightning strikes still cause many millions of dollars of damage to buildings every year. Whole-house lightning protection is still a prudent investment today wherever thunderstorms are common. Without it, the electrical wiring of a house can actually attract lighting strikes, with disastrous and possibly fatal results. If your old house also has an old lightning protection system, there is every reason to make sure it is working properly and no reason to remove it.

While more properly regarded as a part of the electrical system, the first and often only contact most renovators have with their lightning protection system is when they are installing a new roof. This is often the only opportunity they will have to inspect and evaluate the system.

Lightning protection systems have changed very little since Benjamin Franklin invented the first lightning rods. His were made from wrought iron and extended 5 in. to 10 in. above the house and the same distance into the ground. This rudimentary system was refined over the course of the nineteenth century. But the basic principle remains the same. The lightning rod (or *air terminal*), which must be ⅜-in.-thick solid copper and project at least 10 in. above the roof surface, is connected via a *conductor,* a heavy braided copper cable (30-strand 17-gauge) to a ground rod buried in the earth. The idea is to provide a more desirable path to ground for the lightning bolt than some other element of your house, such as its chimney or roof peak or a nearby tree.

Without the rod, the lightning bolt seeks the next sharpest object on the roof, such as the chimney or the edge of a metal gutter. Because these are poor grounds, they do not propagate

an upward arc, and the result is a direct hit. Seeking the best ground, the current jumps to metal pipes, downspouts, and—worst of all—the house wiring. House wiring can't handle a surge current of several million amps so it fries, along with all the appliances connected to it. A nearby tree, full of sap (whose sugars make it a conductive electrolyte) is also an attractive path to ground.

Checking the System

When you are up on the roof, inspect the lightning rods. They should be tightly connected to the conductors. Corroded connections are poor grounds. The bonding clamps between conductors should also be tight. The cable itself should not be frayed or broken. As with house wiring, the conductors must run unbroken to ground. Make sure there is at least one rod on each chimney. (In the old days, rods were mounted next to, rather than on top of, chimneys.) Chimneys more than 4 ft. sq. require an additional rod. Otherwise, the rods are spaced 20 ft. apart along the ridge. There should also be a rod at the front peak of any dormer or any other ridge or projection of the roof more than 2 ft. long. They should not be bent, broken, or crooked.

Any tree within 10 ft. of the house that is taller than the house must have special tree terminals on its major branches. Any metal objects on the roof or the walls of the house, such as cast-iron vent stacks, television antennas, metal gutters and eaves, snowbelt flashing, metal roofing, aluminum siding, or an outside A/C condenser, must all be bonded to the grounding conductors.

Surge Protection

The conductors should be laid out so that each lightning rod has two possible paths to ground. The bronze or copper clamps used to crimp the cables together must be able to withstand 200 lb. of pull (electrical distributors carry heavy-duty crimping tools). Although the connection to the ground rod may be intact, the ground rod itself may no longer be doing its job. Ground rods corrode over time and lose their conductivity. For safety's sake, assume that any ground rod more than 30 years old should be replaced. It's not necessary to pull up the old rod. Drive a new one next to it and switch (or jump) the conductor to it. Ground rods used for lightning protection should be 10 ft. long, instead of the standard 8-ft. rods used for system grounding, and should be driven 1 ft. below the surface. The house electrical, plumbing, and telephone systems grounds should also be bonded to the lightning protection ground.

Because a lightning strike can induce huge electrical currents in nearby wiring, even at a considerable distance, code now requires surge protection to protect sensitive solid-state electronic devices. Surge protectors can be installed by the utility company at the meter. You can also install surge protection at the main breaker in the service panel. Even with whole-house protection, it's still a good idea to install lightning-rated surge suppressors at the individual outlets that your electronics plug into.

Although lightning protection as outlined here may seem simple enough to implement, just like the rest of you house's wiring, there are a lot of details that can make the life or death difference in safety and performance. For this reason, fire insurance companies and experts alike uniformly recommend that you hire a certified professional installer.

A solid mechanical bond is a prerequisite for a good electrical bond. This cast-iron vent stack is not effectively connected to the lightning protection system.

Household Plumbing

Antique plumbing fixtures are often worth preserving for their beauty alone.

Plumbing is a vast body of knowledge composed of little bits and pieces. This is what makes plumbing seem so complicated—all the different kinds of pipes, valves, faucets, fittings and fixtures, each requiring simple, yet somewhat different treatment to assemble, join, and repair. When you realize that a plumbing system is put together much like an Erector set, you will have no hesitancy in tackling the problems that arise.

—MAX ALTH,
DO-IT-YOURSELF PLUMBING

The word *plumber* is derived from the Latin word for lead, *plumbum*. The basic principles of the trade have changed very little since the ancient Romans circulated their household water and wastes through lead pipes. Plumbers, like masons, have jealously guarded their secrets. And until recently, there was perhaps some justification for the aura of mystery in which plumbers cloaked themselves. They worked with ancient and heavy elements, with lead, cast iron, copper, bronze, and tin. They were heirs to the alchemists; they plied their trade in dark and moldy cellars. You can't expect a wizard to come at your beck and call.

Plumbers have a sizable investment in specialized tools: pipe threaders, reamers, cutters, wrenches, torches, augers, and drills. They must carry a warehouse of fittings and connectors, pipes, solders, and fluxes. No wonder then, that plumbers place themselves at the apex of the blue-collar elite and adjust their wages accordingly.

But the introduction of plastic pipe has shaken the foundations of the plumber's hoary hegemony. The plumbers' unions and trade associations, which help enforce and write plumbing codes, fought bitterly against the adoption of the new materials. What latex paint did to the professional painter, plastic pipe has done to the plumber. Today, except for special cases where codes still require cast-iron or galvanized-steel pipe for drainage lines, in new work, professionals and homeowners will rarely have to deal with these intractable materials. The old house is a different matter, of course; you'll have to work with old materials all the time, if only to replace them or marry them to new materials.

Especially for old work, all the reasons that justify the employment of an electrician apply equally to plumbers. They have the tools, the right parts, and the experience. As with wiring, local building codes and mortgage regulations may require the work to be performed by a licensed plumber or inspected for compliance with the Uniform National Plumbing Code. The subject of codes, permits, and inspections as they pertain to home plumbers and electricians is likewise as complex a tangle as it is for house wiring, because local codes can limit or take precedence over the requirements of the national codes.

Many municipalities have laws that prohibit anyone from engaging in the business of plumbing or wiring without a license. A bona fide homeowner, plumbing or wiring his or her own house, is definitely not engaged in the business. Legal precedent has established that people can plumb or wire their own homes. What they can't legally do is pay someone else who does not hold a valid license to plumb or wire their house for them. (This is moot if you live in a town that does not require plumbing or electrical permits.)

If you do your own work, and permits are required, you will need to obtain one from the relevant city, county, or state offices. Obtaining this permit automatically engages the inspection process. Until the local inspector is satisfied that your work complies with code requirements and signs off on the permit, a certificate of occupancy won't be forthcoming. If you decide to do your own work, spend some time with a good guidebook and become familiar with the requirements for a safe and legal installation. An excess of confidence bolstered by sublime ignorance cannot be overcome by a lack of experience.

How Plumbing Works

A domestic plumbing system is actually two subsystems. The supply system is the distribution network that moves water from a source to the fixtures where it is used. The waste system collects the used water and takes it somewhere else, along with any pollutants it has acquired along the way. As with electricity, which demands absolute separation of neutral and hot conductors, for the plumbing system to work safely and efficiently, supply and wastewater must never mingle. If clean water becomes contaminated with wastewater, anyone who uses it could get very sick.

Of Pipes and Parts

The invention of plastic plumbing pipe is one of the great revolutions in the building trades. But not all plastic pipe is equal. Some can be used only for drainage, others for supply, and some are good for nothing. Following are descriptions of the most common pipes in use today.

BLACK PIPE FROM THE WELL In rural areas, flexible polyethylene pipe (*PE,* if you prefer hip architectural jargon, or *black plastic pipe* if you don't) is widely used to bring water from the well into the cellar. You hope that's what you'll find in your cellar instead of a stub of corroded galvanized iron or, even worse, dull gray toxic lead poking through the foundation stones. Iron pipe eventually succumbs to clogged arteries, especially with hard water. As the diameter of the pipe decreases, friction increases; the pump has to work harder to draw less water, shortening its life. But minerals don't adhere easily to the slippery and chemically inert surface of polyethylene pipe. It can be buried directly in the ground, is impervious to corrosion, will expand when frozen without breaking, and since it is available in coils of up to 1,000 ft. long, it's possible to eliminate potentially leaky spliced joints.

However, plumbing codes prohibit the use of polyethylene pipe beyond the supply main because it softens at about 120°F. Because the temperature of domestic hot water runs from about 120°F to 150°F, it wouldn't take a fire to turn the stuff into limp spaghetti. It isn't used for cold-water lines because it is prone to failure at the joints. The nylon fittings used for connections are secured with stainless-steel clamps; over time, in pressurized systems, the momentum of water slamming into a joint when the flow is stopped can force it apart or break the nylon fitting. But since both the pipe and the fittings are inexpensive and easy to work with, it is often used for simple unconcealed supplies in barns and other outbuildings. Even though the pipe itself will not burst if frozen, the fittings are not as flexible. Ice can crack or pull them apart. Black plastic should not be installed in unheated spaces where it cannot be drained or protected by a suitable heat tape.

The only reason you might find black plastic pipe inside an old house is if the plumbing has been blithely cobbled together over the years by ignorant or willfully heedless homeowners making do with whatever they had on hand that was cheap and easy to use.

PEX PIPE FOR SUPPLY In another incarnation, polyethylene pipe has entirely different capabilities. Cross-linked polyethylene (PEX), which has been used throughout Scandinavia and Germany for almost a half century for both radiant heating and household plumbing, has recently been adopted by heating and plumbing contractors in North America. The physical structure of the polymer is such that it is able to withstand wide temperature swings without softening or becoming brittle. Lined with an integral oxygen diffusion barrier, PEX tubing can be directly buried in concrete without succumbing to the corrosion that made earlier copper and iron radiant floor hydronic heating impractical.

PEX without the oxygen barrier is used for both hot- and cold-water piping. It can withstand temperatures up to 180°F, well above the operating range of a radiant heating system (105°F to 130°F) and domestic hot water. The big advantage of PEX tubing over other kinds of water piping is its flexibility and ease of installation. Although the tubing itself costs less than copper, the solid brass fittings (which are typically crimp fitted) are expensive.

CPVC AND PVC PIPE Rigid chlorinated polyvinyl chloride (CPVC)—one brand is Genova—or polyvinyl chloride (PVC) plastic pipe and fittings were once widely promoted as the low-cost and easy-to-work-with alternative to conventional copper tubing. (The difference between PVC and CPVC is that the latter is stronger and approved for water up to about 180°F. PVC should not be used for pressurized water hotter than 100°F.)

But CPVC water piping is an idea whose time has come and gone. Although the evidence is not conclusive, there is a real possibility that over time, aided by the solvent power of hot water, CPVC can break down into its parent monomer, vinyl chloride, a proven potent carcinogen. To make things worse, CPVC gives off toxic fumes when ignited.

If these aren't big enough drawbacks, CPVC pipe will shatter when frozen even more readily than copper will split. True, it is easily cut, and the fittings are quickly installed, but as the price of copper has fallen and the price of oil has climbed, it is no longer as economical as before. Also, if a joint springs a leak or was misaligned, unlike copper, it cannot be taken apart and reassembled. Instead, the piece must be cut out and replaced with a coupler and new fittings. Unfortunately, there's a good chance that you'll find CPVC water lines somewhere. I'd rip them out as soon as you can budget time and money to replace them.

White PVC pipe in 1½-in., 2-in., 3-in., and 4-in. diameters is extensively used for drainage, waste, and vent (DWV) lines. Gray UV-stabilized PVC is used exclusively for underground (UG) and exposed electrical conduit. Note that only the thicker-wall Schedule 40 pipe is approved for DWV use; the thinner Schedule 20 is the familiar foundation drainpipe.

ABS PIPE Although it does not withstand high temperature or pressure any better, black acrylonitrile–butadiene–styrene (ABS) pipe is structurally stronger than PVC and CPVC. It is also reputed to be less toxic if burned. In some jurisdictions, ABS is the only plastic pipe permitted for DWV use. What non-metallic cable did for wiring, plastic DWV pipe has done for plumbing. Because drainage-diameter copper pipe is prohibitively expensive and traditional cast iron is both too expensive and too heavy for most nonindustrial uses, even professional plumbers, albeit reluctantly at first, have been won over and now use the plastic almost exclusively. Plastic DWV has made do-it-yourself plumbing practical and possible.

POLYBUTYLENE PIPE In the last few years polybutylene pipe (PB)—for example, Qest®—has also won grudging acceptance for supply pipe.

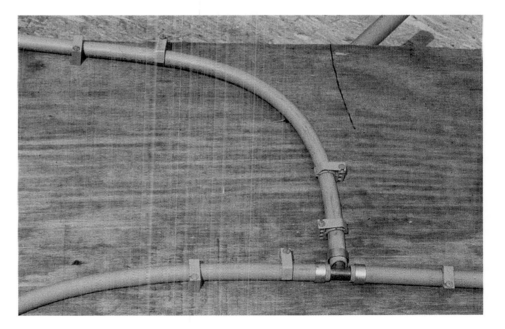

Flexible polybutylene pipe is a good choice for supply retrofits because it can be easily snaked through walls with a minimum of fittings. However, fittings must be carefully installed to prevent leaks. (Photo by Rex Cauldwell)

In some regions, most notably the Southwest, the material is widely used in new construction. In other areas, like New England, you'll be lucky if the distributor has even heard of it. This is unfortunate, since it is well suited to the demands of remodeling. Unlike PVC plastics and more like PEX, the material is approved as safe for drinking water and food processing. It is freezeproof down to 50°F and heat stable in pressurized systems up to 180°F.

PB pipe is available in 5-ft. rigid lengths or flexible coils of up to 400 ft. Indeed, flexibility is one of its most attractive features (½-in.-diameter pipe can be bent to an 8-in. radius without kinking). The pipe can be snaked through walls like electrical cable, run through holes drilled in the studs, and bent around corners with a minimal number of fittings. Since, like PEX, the solid brass fittings themselves are relatively expensive, this is a good thing.

Compression-type fittings are the most commonly used with PB pipe, but they are also the most problematic. Whether because of poor design or improper installation, leaky fittings initially gave PB installations a bad reputation. But when barbed fittings are attached with a crimped-on copper ring, the joints have proven strong, stable, and leakproof. Nevertheless, crimps must be carefully made if they are not to fail.

The fussy nature of the process is one reason why PEX is a more attractive system. The other is cost: PEX tubing is less expensive and can be had in 1000-ft.-long coils. PEX systems also use solid-brass barbed fittings and a kind of compression ring, but assembly is much simpler and virtually foolproof, and the joints themselves are basically indestructible. But the joint-making tools are proprietary and quite expensive (my Rehau toolkit cost about $400 in 1999). The tools can be rented by the day from the distributor; but if you've got an entire house to replumb or a radiant heating system to install, the tool more than pays for itself in labor savings and

peace of mind. And you won't have to worry about hurrying to get the job done so you return the rental on time.

COPPER TUBING Traditional copper tubing is still considered the hallmark of a first-class plumbing system—and with good reason. It is strong, noncorroding, unaffected by heat, and safe. Sweat-soldered joints seldom pull apart and are not difficult to make once the art is mastered. Copper plumbing also contributes to a higher resale value. Because its use is so widespread, almost any fitting is available and most fittings are fairly inexpensive.

The design of a domestic plumbing system and a discussion of the many fittings available and techniques used are beyond the scope of this book. In any case, the system in your house is a fait accompli. The information that follows is intended only as a guide to the basic principles and repairs.

THE OLD-HOUSE PLUMBING SYSTEM

The drawing on the facing page shows a generic plumbing system likely to be found in any house 25 years old or more. It takes no account of any connections with a heating system, which is considered completely separate from the plumbing, both in theory and in practice.

In new construction, a plumbing system can be laid out rationally, with consideration given to the proper sizes and installation of pipes and fixtures. In an old house, plumbing is limited to repair and upgrading of existing facilities—unless all the plumbing has burst (when the house was abandoned) or its galvanized-iron pipe has rusted out so that the entire system needs replacing.

Anatomy of an Old-House Plumbing System

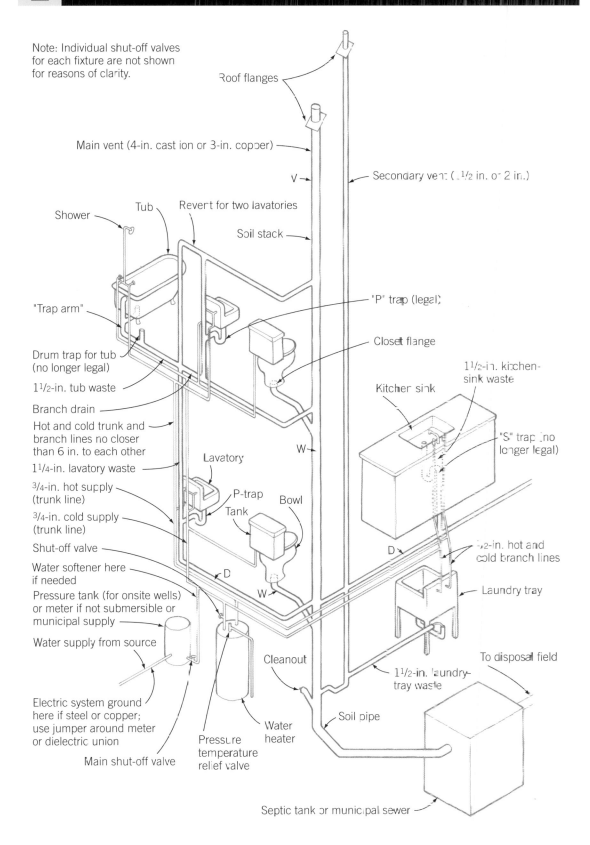

Note: Individual shut-off valves for each fixture are not shown for reasons of clarity.

Roof flanges

Main vent (4-in. cast iron or 3-in. copper)

Secondary vent (1½ in. or 2 in.)

V

Shower

Tub

Revent for two lavatories

Soil stack

"P" trap (legal)

"Trap arm"

Closet flange

1½-in. kitchen-sink waste

Kitchen sink

Drum trap for tub (no longer legal)

1½-in. tub waste

Branch drain

Hot and cold trunk and branch lines no closer than 6 in. to each other

"S" trap (no longer legal)

1¼-in. lavatory waste

Lavatory

W

¾-in. hot supply (trunk line)

P-trap

Bowl

¾-in. cold supply (trunk line)

Tank

Shut-off valve

D

½-in. hot and cold branch lines

Water softener here if needed

D

Pressure tank (for onsite wells) or meter if not submersible or municipal supply

W

Laundry tray

Water supply from source

Cleanout

To disposal field

1½-in. laundry-tray waste

Electric system ground here if steel or copper; use jumper around meter or dielectric union

Water heater

Soil pipe

Pressure temperature relief valve

Main shut-off valve

Septic tank or municipal sewer

Why carpenters hate plumbers: This is not a good thing to do to a floor joist.

Plumbers, at least as a carpenter would describe them, have always been wanton and heedless destroyers of houses. Even worse than the electricians who, after all, bored only small holes through joists and studs for their concealed cables, plumbers were legendary for hacking and hewing through structural beams to set toilet bowls and then loading them down with a cast-iron bath tub for good measure. Unfortunately, since drains must run downhill, they're a lot more troublesome to retrofit than wiring or even supply pipes, which could be (and often were) run over the existing walls rather than inside them. The challenge for the old house restorer is how to replace worn-out piping without gutting walls. Pipes can be routed through chases hidden behind false walls, inside closets, or alongside chimneys or even boxed-in corners.

One usually learns to live with whatever insanities of design come with the house. The existing plumbing will be a weedlike tangle, having been patched together during the tenure of the house's previous owners. It can take half a day just to discover that there is no shut-off valve for the toilet supply. The rule is that if it doesn't leak, don't fix it. There is little point in renovating a plumbing system just to make it more sensible.

Preventing Frozen Pipes

To prevent frozen pipes, never route water lines inside exterior walls. A drainable system can be emptied out when the house must be left vacant and unheated for a while. After the supply is shut off and the tank has been flushed, pour 1 pint of methanol-based RV antifreeze (the glycol antifreeze will harm septic-tank bacteria) into the toilet bowl to keep the water in the trap from freezing and cracking the bowl. Pour some more antifreeze down each sink trap.

Upgrading the Supply System

Cold water entering the house from a well or municipal supply is separated into a hot-water supply and a cold-water supply, pipes for which are run to all fixtures. When more than one fixture is on a given line, the supply feeder should be ¾-in. pipe and the fixture feeders, ½ in. If all lines are only ½ in., a pressure drop occurs when, for example, you run the shower and flush the toilet at the same time. The increased diameter allows more water to be delivered, preventing one fixture from pre-empting another and you from being scalded as cold water is suddenly drawn off to refill the toilet.

PROVIDING SHUT-OFF VALVES Individual shut-off valves should be installed between the hot and cold feeds for all fixtures and the main supply pipes. In the event of repairs, the defective fixture can be isolated without shutting down the entire system and inconveniencing the household. Whenever possible, supply lines should slope slightly so that the entire system can be drained if necessary. Long lines can pitch toward a drain valve in the center of the line. In-line stop and waste valves are fitted with a threaded drain cock. Use boiler drain valves at the lowest points of the system and on water storage tanks and heaters. These can be coupled to a garden hose to empty the entire system into a basement floor drain.

Repairing Galvanized-Iron Supply Line

If the plumbing has not been renovated in the last half century or so, the galvanized-iron distribution lines will probably be plugged with rust and begging for replacement. If water barely trickles out of the faucets, you can count on it. Don't replace old iron pipe with new. Change over to copper or PEX pipe instead.

CHECK THE MAIN CONNECTION Check the connection between the incoming water main and the house supply. Since the old main is usually galvanized iron and the house plumbing is copper, the joint will often be severely corroded because of the galvanic action between the two metals. If the main is still usable, the union should be refitted with a dielectric union that isolates the two metals with a nonconductive gasket. (Don't forget to attach a jumper across the union for the grounding electrode.)

PATCHING PINHOLE LEAKS Sometimes basically sound galvanized pipe suffers from spot corrosion, which causes a pinhole leak. Factory-made repair patches are a simple and an effective cure. The patch consists of a rubber sheet gasket that is tightened between two curved metal clamps. Of course, it's unlikely that you'll just happen to have a clamp of this sort lying around waiting for a leak to happen. When you're awakened in the middle of the night by the hiss of high-pressure water streaming out of a pipe between the cellar floor joists, you can't dash off to the hardware store either. But you might just happen to have a curved piece of metal (bend one if you don't) and a piece of rubber cut from an inner tube or a deflated basketball. The drawing on p. 354 shows how these can be combined with wire and a wooden wedge to make a temporary patch that will hold until you can get to the hardware store.

A stainless-steel hose clamp or automotive radiator clamp will also permanently tighten a rubber and metal gasket over the leak. Whatever you use, turn off the water before patching (if you can—you may discover that there is no working shutoff valve).

PATCHING HAIRLINE CRACKS When the pipe leaks through a hairline crack instead of a pinhole, pipe-sealing cement may work better than a rubber gasket. The pipe must be dry first. Before applying the sealer, drill a small hole at each end of the crack and several more along its length. The end holes stop the crack from opening farther and the others help the cement grip the pipe.

TIGHTENING LOOSE JOINTS Galvanized pipes usually leak at threaded joints because the joints

When sweat soldering, protect wood framing and electrical cables from the heat of the torch with a heat-resistant woven glass cloth or a heat-diffusing square of sheet metal.

Diagnosing Water Stains

Water stains on ceilings, floors, or walls are a sign of plumbing trouble, a leaky roof, or condensation problems. If the stain is dormant, the problem has probably been fixed. But if actual water shows up, you've got trouble. Obviously, if the leak is active only during a rainstorm, especially when the wind is blowing from a certain direction, the roof or exterior siding is leaking. When the moisture buildup occurs seasonally, during the coldest winter months, condensation or an ice dam on the eaves is the culprit. If the water stain manifests suddenly and continues to grow, you've got a plumbing problem. You also have a carpentry problem, because you'll have to tear out a section of wall or ceiling to find the source of the leak. Fortunately, since much of the plumbing is concentrated in the cellar, most of the leaks will be, too. Finding the leak is the first step toward fixing it.

Repairing Leaks in Galvanized Pipe

1A. Seal leak in thick-walled pressurized pipe with gasket and clamp assembly. Shut of water before repairing.

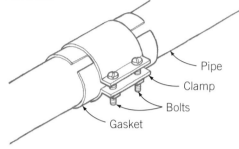

Pipe
Clamp
Bolts
Gasket

1B Or use an automotive-type clamp, a curved piece of metal, and some rubber or gasket sheeting.

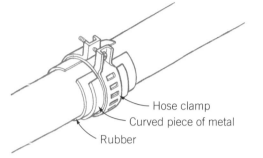

Hose clamp
Curved piece of metal
Rubber

1C. This temporary patch will hold until you can get to the hardware store to buy the clamp and gasket. Drive wedge farther under the wire after fastening the coils, then drive a small nail into wedge at X to secure it.

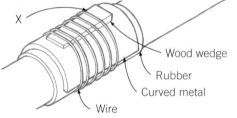

X
Wood wedge
Rubber
Curved metal
Wire

2. To repair a hairline crack in thick-walled pipe, drill holes at crack ends and a few along its length. After roughening the surface with a file, apply pipe-sealing cement, which will enter holes and fill the crack.

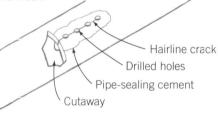

Hairline crack
Drilled holes
Pipe-sealing cement
Cutaway

3A. To fix a small leak at a threaded joint, try tightening the pipe into the joint. If you're lucky, you'll be able to back out the thread at the other end of the pipe without causing another leak.

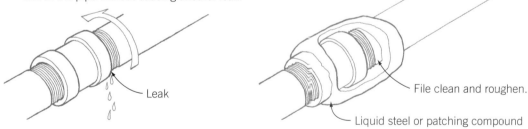

Leak

3B. An alternative is to dry and roughen the outside of the joint, then seal with liquid steel or plumber's epoxy patching compound.

File clean and roughen.

Liquid steel or patching compound

3C. A sure-fire method is to cut the leaking pipe at an angle, swing the cut ends out of line, and unscrew them. Make a new section from a union and two pipe nipples of appropriate lengths.

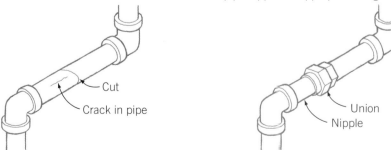

Cut
Crack in pipe

Union
Nipple

are not tight enough. Unfortunately, unless the pipe is fitted with a union somewhere along its length, you can't tighten one connection without loosening the other end. If you're lucky, the good joint might be so well made that it can be backed off just enough to tighten up the leak without leaking itself. Failing this, you can disassemble the joint, which typically involves taking apart an entire series of joints all the way back to something you can unscrew without tightening something else.

Threaded joints loosen for a number of reasons. If pipe-joint compound (*pipe dope*) wasn't applied to the threads when the joint was originally assembled, the pipe can expand from the heat generated by turning unlubricated metal surfaces against each other. When the joint cools off, the threads are loose. Sometimes loose joints will hold for years until a change in water pressure causes them to leak. Sometimes corrosion will eventually plug a leaking joint until something disturbs it.

FIXING DEFORMED THREADS A joint that was overtightened and then taken apart for some reason and reassembled will often leak, because the metal deforms so much that it can never be tightened properly again. Rethreading is a sure cure for deformed pipe threads. The fittings should be replaced with new ones. Before heading out to rent a pipe threader, try cleaning the threads and coating them with automotive gasket cement. If this doesn't stop the leak, roughen the outside of the pipe with a file, let it dry and then coat it generously with liquid steel or plumber's epoxy patching compound.

ADDING A NEW UNION There is an alternative to taking apart a lot of joints (which might create more leaks to fix) that is also foolproof. Cut the leaking pipe at an angle so that the ends of each section can be swung out of line and unscrewed. Make a new section up from two pieces of threaded pipe and a union joint. If stock *nipples* (short lengths of threaded pipe) won't

bridge the distance, have a piece cut to length and custom threaded at the hardware store.

When it is the union itself that is leaking, check the ground faces of the joint for corrosion or scouring. If cleaning and reassembly doesn't work, try inserting a rubber or lead gasket between the faces. Otherwise, the union will have to be replaced.

Repairing Copper Pipe

In some ways, copper pipe is a lot easier to repair than thick-walled galvanized pipe, but in one way it isn't. Before a leak can be soldered shut, the pipe must be emptied of water. Otherwise, the metal won't heat properly and the solder won't stick. Steam will also blow out through the molten metal. In theory, it should be easy to drain the pipe. In practice, it always seems that the shut-off valves never quite do, allowing just enough water to trickle through to prevent the solder from taking. Sometimes there aren't any shut-offs on the troubled line. Sometimes, the pipe is run so that it cannot be drained.

REPAIRING PINHOLES IN COPPER Pinhole leaks in copper pipe caused by a careless carpenter or drywall installer can usually be repaired with a simple solder patch. Drain the pipe and open a valve somewhere along the line to vent steam. Clean the area around the leak with steel wool and apply paste flux and a dab of solder. A well-bonded solder patch will hold under pressure.

If the hole is bigger than $\frac{1}{16}$ in., solder will fall into the hole instead of plugging it. In such cases, clean around the pipe and solder a curved piece of copper or small section of copper pipe over the hole.

REPAIRING SPLIT PIPES Pipes that have split because of frost damage can sometimes be repaired with patching compound. The only sure cure is to cut out and replace the damaged section. Fortunately, frozen copper pipes usually break apart at the solder joint before they split. When a pinhole leak appears at a fitting, it is

Tightening Compression-Ring Fittings

Compression-ring fittings are the most common joint for toilet and lavatory supply risers. Most leaks respond to tightening. Some leaks will stop when packing thread is wrapped above the compression ring. Short of stripping the threads off the fitting, you can't damage a compression ring by overtightening. But because the metal is soft, use a wrench on both sides of the fitting to prevent twisting it apart.

If the leak doesn't stop, you can't take the joint apart and try to retighten it. The metal will be too deformed. Install a new riser pipe and ring instead.

It's a better idea to seal up and insulate a cold basement than to rely on heat tapes, such as those shown here, to keep pipes from freezing. Frost-damaged pipes are difficult to fix without replacing the damaged sections. Because frozen copper pipe usually pulls apart at solder joints before bursting, there's less damage than with threaded iron pipe.

sometimes possible to repair the joint without taking it apart. As earlier, drain the pipe and open a valve. Heat the fitting and sweat acid-core solder (which cleans out any contaminants) into it. If the leak persists or gets worse, you'll have no choice but to take the joint apart, clean it thoroughly to dislodge the offending speck of dirt or oxide, and resolder it with ordinary solder and nonacid flux.

If the fitting is part of a valve or close to it, take the faucet apart and remove the core to protect its rubber washer from the heat. If the pipe cannot be drained, cut it apart (you may need a special mini-cutter designed for tight spaces) and rejoin the pieces with a coupler after the leaking fitting is successfully soldered.

If, despite everything, one side of the pipe still dribbles water, you can solder the coupling to the dry side first. Then prepare the dripping side, pack the pipe with a ball of white bread, and quickly solder the coupling together. By the time the bread has absorbed enough water to soften, the joint should be completed.

FIXING A LEAKING FLARE JOINT A leaking flare joint in a copper or chrome-brass pipe (which is usually used to connect kitchen faucets and toilet supplies and also extensively with LP gas tubing) is ideally fixed by cutting out the old flare and reforming a new one. The local hardware store should carry the flaring tool that you'll need for making new joints. If there isn't enough tubing left to allow this, the alternative is to apply a bead of trusty automotive gasket cement to the flared end and retighten it. Faucet-packing thread wrapped around the pipe under the flange nut might also do the trick. Short of complete replacement, the final solution is to solder the flare to its fitting, file off the excess, and screw the flange nut back down.

THE DRAINAGE SYSTEM

Since at least 1870, all drainage systems have had three parts: drainpipes to carry waste water away, a vent to aid drainage and exhaust toxic sewer gases, and fixture traps to prevent them from leaking into the household air. Like a tree that increases in size from the upper branches down to its trunk, a drain system must always increase in diameter as it flows downstream. Branch lines are always smaller than the main stack, and always enter it at an angle to prevent clogging and to aid cleanout.

The gases produced by the decomposition of human and household wastes include hydrogen sulfide, which is poisonous and smells like rotten eggs; methane, which is explosive and smells even worse; and carbon monoxide and other nasty gases. In addition to letting these gases escape, the vent introduces fresh air, which prevents corrosion and limits the growth of bacterial slime. But the vent's primary purpose is to prevent siphoning. If a drainpipe were ever to fill completely with water, the momentum of its falling could suck the water out of the trap. The longer the pipe, the greater is the likelihood of siphoning. The importance of keeping traps full and preventing soiled water from backwashing into fixtures is the reason behind the complicated code prescriptions for proper venting.

Drain systems clog when pipes are not properly pitched or are too narrow, or when too much greasy kitchen waste is dumped into them. Plastic has such a strong affinity for grease molecules that it's not unusual to find a branch drain plugged solid with a butter-like sludge after only a few years. Of course, some drains clog because someone has thrown insoluble objects like hair, toys, bobby pins or construction debris into them. Plaster and mortar sand are not soluble, and will often collect at the bottom of a trap if tools are washed out in the sink.

Repairing Drain Lines

Leaks in drain lines are easier to repair by patching than are leaks in supply lines. For one thing, a drain line (if properly sloped) has water in it only when a fixture is actually in use. Because drain water is not pressurized, patches are not likely to loosen or spring a leak several hours later.

The joints and fittings of old-fashioned *hub-and-spigot* cast-iron drainpipes (or soil pipes) were sealed (or caulked) with a packing of oakum and molten lead (see the drawing at right). As the house settled over the years, some

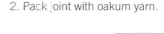

Making a Vertical Caulked Lead Joint

1. Center spigot of one cast-iron pipe inside hub of another.

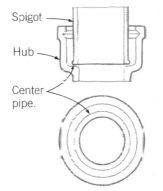

Spigot

Hub

Center pipe.

2. Pack joint with oakum yarn.

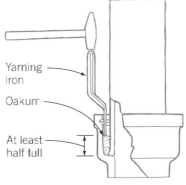

Yarning iron

Oakum

At least half full

3. Pour molten lead into joint.

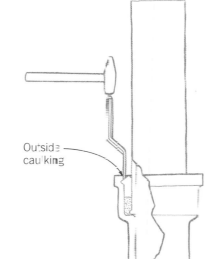

About 1 in

Lead

Oakum

4. Caulk joint; expand with inside caulking iron, which has a beveled edge.

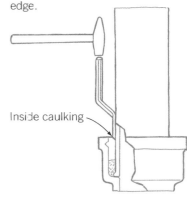

Inside caulking

5. Caulk outside circumference with outside caulking iron. Note difference in bevel angle.

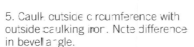

Outside caulking

6. Trim ridge of caulk left on lead surface, if desired.

Flatten or leave.

For horizontal joint, use an asbestos joint runner clamped around pipe and pushed up against hub, as shown. This forms a small opening through which you pour hot lead into the pocket.

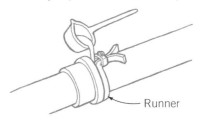

Runner

of these rigid joints might have shifted and cracked open.

Most of the time, a leaking joint is easily fixed by hammering on the lead gasket with a plumber's caulking iron to mash the soft metal tightly against the hub. Ideally, you'd use an inside iron first and then an outside iron to form the lead into the proper ridge. (The bevels on the edges of these are reversed.) If you can't borrow, rent, or even find these tools, a cold chisel, prybar, or length of steel bar will probably make a serviceable substitute.

Even if the joint is too loose to recaulk with an iron or if pieces of lead are actually missing, there's still no need to reform it with molten lead. With a chisel, remove the rest of the failed lead gasket to expose the underlying oakum yarning. This rope-like substance, when tightly packed, forms the actual waterproof seal—the lead gasket just locks it in place and prevents the pipes from shifting or pulling apart. Replace any charred or rotted yarning or add new material to

TIP

Lead Substitutes

If your local hardware store doesn't stock lead wool, use one of the water-based lead substitutes (Genova's Plastic Lead, for example). Use a trowel to pack the hub with this putty-like compound, and don't run any water through the drain or allow the joint to flex until the compound has completely cured. ▪▪▪

Working Safely with Poured Lead

Although making a poured-lead joint is not difficult, it can be dangerous. If you let it sit too long before pouring the lead, the oakum packing could absorb moisture, which then instantly turns to steam, splattering hot lead out of the joint. Leather gauntlets (gloves with sleeves) are a must for working with hot lead.

When pouring, hold the ladle at arm's length and to one side. Heat the lead in a well-ventilated area and wear a respirator; the fumes from boiling lead are very toxic. Fortunately, unless you're adding and changing fittings or rerouting and extending hub-type cast-iron pipe, there's no need for the plumber's lead pot. Modern hubless cast-iron pipe eliminates the need for poured lead joints altogether. Unfortunately, not all local plumbing codes allow it.

An Alternative Leaded Joint

Repack the joint with oakum yarn, then seal with lead wool. Braid the wool into a rope, press into pipe hub, and caulk with an iron, as for molten lead. This method eliminates the need to use molten lead, but it's costlier and more time-consuming.

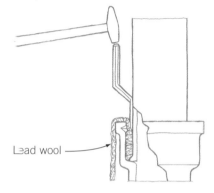

Lead wool

tighten up a loosely packed joint. Tightly pack the oakum with a blunt-edged yarning iron.

Seal the joint with lead wool. Braid the soft, heavy strands into a rope; press it into the hub; and caulk it with an iron, as for molten lead. The only reason lead wool isn't used by plumbers for all joints is that it costs about twice as much as ordinary lead and takes more time to work with. This isn't an issue if you're repairing only a joint or two.

FIXING HAIRLINE CRACKS IN CAST IRON

Settling can also cause the barrel of otherwise sound sections of pipe to crack. These cracks can range from minor hairlines to major abysses. Sometimes a small crack will become enlarged as its exposed edges corrode away.

The procedure for fixing a hairline crack in cast iron is similar to that for fixing splits in galvanized pipe. Drill a hole at each end of the crack to arrest further growth. Clean out debris and scaled rust with a wire brush or steel wool forced into the edges. Apply rust remover (naval jelly) and let it dry for several hours before rinsing the area with a wet paintbrush. When dry, spread plumber's epoxy patching compound (one brand is Epoxybond Plumber Paste) over the crack with a putty knife, forcing it into the crack. The material is workable for 20 minutes to 30 minutes at room temperature and cures permanently in 3 hours.

FIXING WIDER CRACKS IN CAST IRON Cracks up to 1 in. across can be patched with a stiffer epoxy putty (such as Epoxybond Plumber Seal). Prepare the edges of the crack as before, chipping out any rusted edges. With your hands protected by disposable plastic gloves, work a ball of the putty into ³⁄₁₆-in.-thick ropes about 6 in. or 8 in. long. Press the ropes firmly against the rough edges of the crack to form an anchor bead. Once this bead has set firm, close the crack by adding more layers of bead, keeping your hands moist to aid smoothing. The putty will set on a wet surface, which is useful if you can't stop the pipe from dripping.

Very large cracks or outright holes should be patched with fiberglass cloth, as in auto-body work. Coat the margins of the hole with the epoxy paste and embed the cloth patch in it, spreading more paste over the edges of the cloth. When the paste is dry, coat the rest of the cloth with paste and continue building up successive layers until the shape and thickness of the pipe are approximated.

REPLACING CORRODED PIPE Because naked cast iron is quickly attacked by rust, cast-iron pipe owes its longevity to the factory-applied asphalt-based coating, which normally doesn't wear off. Inferior grades of cast iron tend to corrode more readily. When struck with a hammer, corroded pipe makes a dull thunk instead of the sharp ring of sound pipe. Corrosion also presents itself as scaling patches of rust and ill-defined pits that crumble into ever larger holes when you try to clean them out for patching. Other than fixing a small rusted-out area in an otherwise sound cast-iron pipe, corroded pipe cannot be patched; it must be replaced.

The existing copper male adapter made it easy to splice a new PVC drainpipe into this cast-iron hub.

If wholesale replacement is called for, switch over to ABS plastic, which is a lot cheaper, lighter, and easier to work with. Remove the entire drain system up to the point where the sewer enters the foundation or disappears under the cellar slab. Adapters are available for mating plastic and cast iron (or just about any other combination of materials, if necessary). These are usually caulked to the joint with oakum and sealed with a product such as Plastic Lead.

Adding a Drain Line

Other than repair work, the only other occasion you might have to take apart cast-iron drainpipes would be to install a tee or wye fitting for a drain-line extension to new or relocated fixtures.

USING A SADDLE TAP Where the new drain line is smaller in diameter than the main drain, use a saddle tap instead of adding a tee, as shown in the top drawing on p. 362. Be aware that some codes don't permit saddle taps. Drill a circle of closely spaced holes in the face of the

Rerouting Drain Lines

To relocate the stool for a renovated bathroom, the existing cast-iron drain line was cut with a reciprocating saw equipped with a tungsten-grit blade. The lead was chiseled out of the joint, and an ABS to cast-iron adapter was inserted. The new drain was made with ABS. The water supply lines had to be rerouted to accommodate the change as well. Because of the tight and awkward working conditions and a sweat fitting that kept leaking even after being stuffed with bread, the changeover took the better part of an entire day.

 Once the upper section of cast-iron pipe was cut out, it was fairly easy to chisel and chip the stub end out the leaded joint. The danger is that overzealous pounding can shatter the part you want to reuse.

1 The toilet was removed and the lead chiseled and pried out of the joint between the drain and stool flange so that the rest of the pipe below the floor could be removed.

4 A flexible rubber coupler that could fold back over on itself was used to fit the new ABS wye between the inflexible cast-iron pipes.

3 The wye fitting is removed and ready for fitting the new pipe. Note the broken edge of the remaining vent stack. (Fortunately, it will be covered by the new fitting collar.) The original galvanized adapter was left in place on the sink drain-double wye. Note also the saddle tap on the copper supply line.

Saddle Tap

Use where drain line is smaller in diameter than main drain.

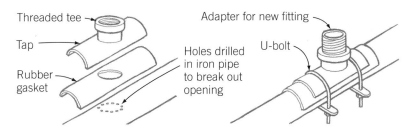

Threaded tee
Tap
Rubber gasket
Adapter for new fitting
Holes drilled in iron pipe to break out opening
U-bolt

pipe and tap it until the circle breaks out. File down the rough edges, install the rubber gasket, and clamp the saddle over the hole by tightening down its U-bolts. Insert the appropriate adapter for connection to ABS pipe.

TAPPING INTO THE CLEAN-OUT WYE The brass plug that covers a clean-out wye is also an ideal place to add a drain-line extension. Installing an entirely new drain line could be preferable to taking apart an existing line. Since you can avoid tearing up floors and walls and the possibility of damaging joints in the existing pipe as you work loose its upper sections, the added expense of the new pipe is well worth it. Screw a bushing into the opening and install a new clean-out wye and elbow for the new drain.

> **TIP**
>
> ## Support Pipe before Cutting
>
> When removing a section of vertical pipe, make sure that the upper sections can't slide down. Wrap heavy steel pipe straps around one or two hubs and fasten them to the wall studs. Horizontal pipe should also be supported before cutting. ■ ■ ■

Adding a Drain Extension

Remove and replace threaded section that holds plug. Screw bushing into opening and install new clean-out wye and elbow.

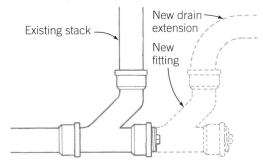

Existing stack
New drain extension
New fitting

Installing a Tee

If you have no choice but to tap into the main stack or sewer line with a tee, at least try to run the extension into the horizontal sewer line in the cellar rather than the vertical stack in the walls. The sewer line is accessible, which is unlikely to be the case with the vent stack, unless a substantial chunk of wall covering, ceiling, or flooring is removed first. Modern cast-iron pipe uses no-hub joints. The sections and fittings are joined together by neoprene rubber gaskets secured by an overlapping stainless-steel clamp. The no-hub system does away with caulking and lead sealers and makes assembly so fast and simple that anyone can do it.

To install a hubless fitting in an existing bell-and-spigot cast-iron line, cut out a section of pipe 1 in. longer than the length of the fitting to be installed. Slip the hubless connectors over the ends of the fitting, folding the rubber gasket back over on itself so that the fitting can be inserted between the stubs of the old pipe. Loosen the clamp so that it slides below the gasket. With the fitting in place, unfurl the rubber, position the clamp and tighten it down.

CUTTING THE PIPE Cutting cast iron in place is a lot harder than cutting a section of pipe in the open. Because there probably won't be enough room to use a pipe cutter, you'll have to resign yourself to making the cut by hand. Make a cut at least 1/16 in. deep completely around the pipe with a coarse-bladed (16 teeth per inch) hacksaw (or a reciprocating saw and tungsten carbide-grit blade. Gently hammer along this line with a cold chisel until the pipe breaks. If a jagged piece is left, don't use the chisel. Cut it off with the hacksaw instead. Getting to the back of the pipe with a hacksaw may prove challenging. If it is impossible, remove the entire section of pipe first by chiseling out its caulked lead joints. Tilt the section sideways to lift it out of the hub.

It's not strictly legal, but sometimes you have to improvise: The renovator drilled into the side of this cast-iron stack, punched out a circular hole, filed its edges as smooth as possible, and threaded and caulked an ABS male adapter for a new lavatory drain into it. (The alternative, a saddle tap, was not allowed by code either.) Removing a section of the stack without destroying the wall would have been impractical and too time-consuming.

A stainless-steel clamp tightened over a flexible neoprene rubber gasket is used to join modern hubless cast-iron pipe to old-fashioned bell-and-spigot pipe. Couplers, such as these by Fernco®, are available in a wide variety of sizes and types for mating almost any conceivable combination of similar and dissimilar DWV piping.

Two couplers (Fernco brand) were used to insert new PVC drain connections into the existing cast-iron sewer line.

USING A SISSON FITTING When local codes won't allow hubless pipe, use a *sisson fitting* to enable the new fitting to slip into the hubs of the existing pipe without raising it up. Cut and remove a section of pipe. Save the hubbed end, cut it to length, and reinsert it in the bell of the lower pipe. The sisson fitting is next, followed by the new hubbed fitting. Once everything is in place, the bell of the sisson fitting is expanded so that all the joints are tight and ready for caulking.

REPAIRING LEAKS IN PLASTIC DRAIN LINES

Leaks in plastic drain lines can be repaired with a plumber's poultice. Wrap alternating layers of cloth (an old bed sheet ripped into strips will do just fine) and wet plaster of Paris over the damaged area and allow it to set up. This bandage should last for years and be completely watertight. If the drainpipe is dry, coating the entire rim of the joint with a thick layer of solvent cement can sometimes stop a small leak at a fitting. Scrape out as much of the edge of the fitting as you can before applying the cement.

REPAIRING LEAKS IN BRASS DRAIN LINES

The thin-walled chrome-plated brass tubing used for sink drains will leak either because a slip nut is too loose or cracked or because a washer is missing or defective. If simple tightening of the slip nuts doesn't solve the problem, take apart the joints and inspect the washers. Replace any frayed or cracked ones and retighten. Take care to align the pipes evenly, since misalignment is also a cause of leaks.

If the leak is in the pipe itself (usually at the bottom of the trap), the pipe has corroded or split. Water left to freeze in traps lacking a drain plug can split the pipe. These splits can be soldered, although it's easier to just replace the whole piece. A corroded pipe cannot be patched. It just falls apart. Brass will corrode when another kind of metal is in contact with it, as for example, if a nail or hairpin happens to fall into the sink and lodge in the bottom of the trap.

Cast-Iron Connections

When using no-hub fittings to add a drain, make the two pipe cuts 1/2 in. farther apart than the length of the new fitting.

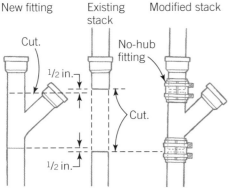

To connect plastic to cast-iron pipe, insert plastic spigot into cast-iron bell and seal with appropriate compound.

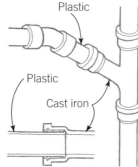

Where hubless pipe isn't allowed by code, add a drain using a sisson fitting. The sisson fitting, which requires that you caulk four joints, expands after it is in place.

Add stack fitting by lifting and tilting top portion of pipe, allowing it to protrude above the roof.

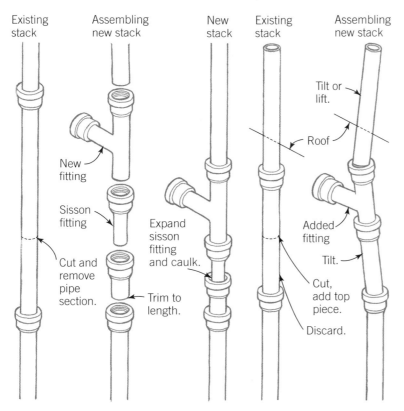

Special Fixes for Water-Closet Connections

You can learn more than you ever wanted to know about replacing a water closet, repairing a leaking faucet, setting a sink, and making minor plumbing repairs and changes by consulting any reasonably complete "Big Book of Fix-It-Yourself Home Improvement Skills." But while these books are undeniably handy (I have a half-dozen or so on my bookshelf), they usually aren't much help when something unexpected happens. And, when working with old plumbing, and old houses in general, the unexpected and the unusual are unremarkably ordinary.

For example, resetting the toilet after a new floor is laid is one of the more common annoyances. The closet flange effectively sinks relative to the new floor level. The usual quick-and-dirty fix is to use an extra-thick wax ring, or even two rings one without a plastic funnel stacked on top of one with a funnel to raise the flange

height. What eventually happens is that the wax squishes sideways as the toilet wiggles back and forth under the load of its occupant, and the seal leaks. The photos shown here offer two better alternatives and a handy repair fitting for a broken cast-iron flange.

The bottom of a connector (Ultra-Seal is shown here) seals to the drain line with an O-ring. A rubber boot at the top seals to the horn of the toilet. This type of connector won't slip sideways or leak when ruptured by the pressure of a toilet plunger. The grooves allow the O-ring to be adjusted up and down.

A galvanized steel repair flange (such as the Span-It one shown here) repairs a broken cast-iron closet flange. It screws into the existing bolt holes.

Use a PVC closet-flange spacer to bring the old flange up to the new floor level.

PLUMBING AND STRUCTURAL CHANGES

Because, as with electrical wiring, water-supply pipes and drainpipes are usually concealed within the walls, most plumbing renovation problems are really carpentry problems. How to find concealed pipes, gain access to walls with minimal damage, remove old and fit new piping into inaccessible places are just some of the difficulties you'll encounter.

As the number of rules devoted to it in most codes suggests, proper venting of drain lines is very important for health reasons and for trouble-free operation. Depending on the location and types of fixtures and the local code requirements, adding a new bathroom can require raising floors, dropping ceilings, and tearing out walls. Destruction and reconstruction can be minimized if you concentrate new plumbing in the same areas as the existing plumbing, by adding them back-to-back or one above the other. Then, at least, the supply pipes and the vent stack are already in place or near at hand. But if a new bathroom has to be installed at a great distance from the existing drain stack, it's usually a lot easier to run a new stack than to extend a new drain across a ceiling (see the drawing below).

Hiding Pipes in Floors and Walls

A cast-iron bathtub, filled with water and an average-size person, can weigh as much as a ton. It seems obvious that if any floor joists have to be cut, notched, or bored for drain lines, proper measures must be taken to ensure the safety of the floor framing. It's amazing how often the obvious is ignored and how both wall and floor frames have been indiscriminately hacked apart by heedless plumbers—amateur and professional alike.

As with concealing electrical wiring, there are a number of ways to hide pipe under floors and in walls. If you are lucky, your supply and drain lines will all run parallel to joists and studs. If there is no way to avoid running drain pipes perpendicular to joists you have two choices: You can add headers and trimmers flanking the pipes as for any structural opening, to support the cut joists, or you can install a false floor.

Because supply pipes are much smaller in diameter than drain pipes, you also have the option of notching joists and studs to accommodate them. While you can safely bore joists for supply lines, with old work you won't often have the luxury of exposed framing, so you won't be able to slide lengths of supply pipe through the holes. Sometimes, you can use several short lengths, spliced together with couplers or add false floors. Another option is to thread flexible PEX or PB through bored holes.

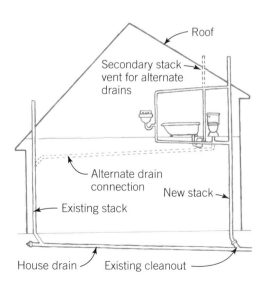

Installing a New Stack

Roof

Secondary stack vent for alternate drains

Alternate drain connection

New stack

Existing stack

House drain

Existing cleanout

Notching Joists for Pipe

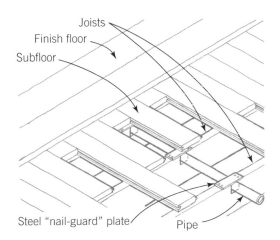

Joists
Finish floor
Subfloor
Steel "nail-guard" plate
Pipe

NOTCHING JOISTS AND STUDS FOR SUPPLY LINES Flooring can be taken up and the joists notched to receive supply pipe. (Make sure not to nail through the pipe when putting the floor back down! Protect plastic and copper pipe where they cross joists with steel nail-guard plates; isolate the copper from the steel with a strip of plastic or old inner tube.) Notched joists can be stiffened by nailing 2x4s alongside them as shown in the drawing below. When it's the studs of a load-bearing wall that are notched, extra stiffening studs should be nailed flatwise

alongside the cut ones, as shown in the drawing below right.

INSTALLING A FALSE FLOOR If a step up into the bathroom is not objectionable, a high-ceilinged Victorian house has sufficient headroom to allow concealment of new drains under a false floor. This avoids dealing with structural problems entirely. Just run the pipes between new joists placed across the existing the joists. Because drainpipe must pitch downward at ¼ in. per foot, the thickness of the new joists will depend on the length of the pipe run. Likewise, if you are running drainpipe parallel to existing joists, this pitch requirement determines whether the joists are wide enough to let you run the pipe in the existing bays.

Strengthening Notched Load-Bearing Studs

2x4 nailed flatwise for support

Steel "nail-guard" plate

Stiffening Notched Joists

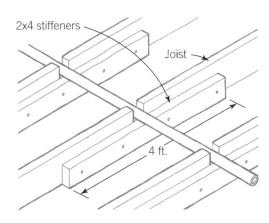

2x4 stiffeners
Joist
4 ft.

Concealing Drain Lines between Joists

15 ft.

12-in. joist

12 ft.

10-in. joist

4 ft.

8-in. joist

Drain is 4-in. cast-iron (you'll get longer runs with 3-in. plastic).

Concealing Large-Diameter Drain Lines

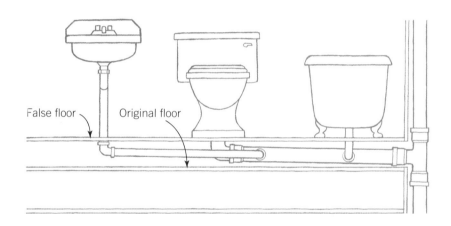

False floor   Original floor

Raised Floor or Dropped Ceiling?

In most cases, you need to run bathroom drainpipe only a short horizontal distance to get to a down pipe on a bathroom wall. In these cases, a raised floor in a relatively small bathroom is almost always preferable to a dropped ceiling in a larger room below. But if you do have to make a long run parallel to joists, a dropped ceiling may be the only alternative to get the depth you need. Dropped ceilings usually aren't an option for pipe runs across and under joists; the ceiling would have to be too low.

Pipes can be run between floors without tearing into the walls by hiding them behind built-out corners and false walls. Even better, they can be placed inside closets or in the corners of built-in bookcases.

A WATER-PUMP PRIMER

The owner of a country home that is not tethered to the municipal water supply may discover that the spring that never ran dry in the living memory of man suddenly has, causing the faithful pump, in a fit of burning wires, to give up the ghost. Such are the trials and tribulations of rural life.

Gravity-Feed Systems

There are four basic pumping systems for on-site water supply. The simplest (and in some ways, most efficient) is gravity feed. When a source, such as a spring, is located sufficiently high enough above the house, the water will flow downward through a pipe into the house. The higher the source, the greater the pressure.

This difference in pressure points out the disadvantage of a gravity system as well. Because the pressure decreases as the water rises within the house, a second-floor fixture may not get sufficient flow to operate. Since the pressure in a gravity system equals ½ lb. per square inch (psi) for each foot of drop, a source 40 ft. above the house will supply 20 lb. of pressure in the basement. But 20 ft. higher than that, up in the second-floor bathroom, 10 lb. of pressure won't operate a clothes washer and will give a rather unsatisfactory shower.

In the days before rural electrification, gravity-feed water systems were common. The pipes for these old installations were galvanized (and even made of lead); and since the trenches had to be dug by hand, they were seldom buried below frost line. Usually, the snow cover kept the ground from freezing. A tap was also left open since moving water won't freeze as easily. So long as the source was higher than the cellar, water would flow into a concrete cistern for storage. From there it could be pumped (by hand in the days before electricity) up to an attic storage tank that pressurized the entire system.

MAINTAIN OR REPLACE? Other than digging up the old pipe and replacing it with polyethylene in a new trench below the frost line, there is no reason not to continue using a gravity-feed supply. Adding a simple electric piston pump in the cellar will solve the pressure problem. Install a check valve (a one-way valve) in the incoming line before the pump to prevent pressurized water from flowing back up the line to the spring.

To reduce friction, gravity systems require oversize pipes. Use 1½-in. pipe for runs over 100 ft. instead of standard 1-in. pipe. Where the pipe cannot be buried below the frost line because of an underground ledge, cover it with 2 in. of rigid foam and a layer of straw mulch topped with burlap and at least 1 ft. of soil. If this fails to prevent freezing, wrap the pipe in electric heat tape.

Artesian Wells

The rich uncle of the gravity-feed system is the artesian well. Here, a drilled well or spring strikes a vein of water confined between sloping impervious soil strata. The water supply is self-pressurized. Depending on the location of the house relative to the slope, the pressure can be just enough to bring the water to the surface, or so great that a pressure-reducer must be installed before it can be used in the house.

Shallow-Well Pumps

The shallow well pump is far more common than gravity-feed systems or artesian wells. The hand-powered pitcher pump and the windmill-driven piston pump—veritable icons of country life—have been replaced by an electrically powered piston pump, but otherwise the principles of operation have stayed the same for more than a century and a half. Because a shallow-well pump pulls water by suction (which is less efficient than pushing) its effective vertical lift is limited to about 25 ft. Horizontal pull, however, is limited only by friction, especially if the run is slightly downhill.

CENTRIFUGAL PUMPS A more powerful version of the shallow-well pump, which also requires less maintenance, is the centrifugal pump. The pump operates by drawing water through an impeller (a set of spinning blades in a sealed chamber). It is less noisy and a lot more efficient than a piston pump. Never let a centrifugal pump run dry the heat generated by the friction between the closely fitted nylon blades and the walls of an empty pump chamber will quickly ruin them.

Jet Pumps

A jet pump will bring water up from wells as deep as 125 ft. The pump requires two pipes to operate: one for the water coming up from the well and another that returns some of that water to the bottom of the well, where it is jetted

This shallow-well centrifugal pump is mounted directly on top of the tank that maintains system pressure.

through a special orifice at high pressure to force water up into the intake pipe. Thus the jet pump pushes water up by boosting its pressure, instead of pulling on it by suction. A jet pump uses more power than a piston or centrifugal pump, but it is the only kind that will work for sources below 25 ft. Since it is located in the cellar and not the well, it is as easy to service as the other pumps.

Submersible Pumps

When a well is more than 100 ft. deep, a submersible pump, which can force water up from depths of 500 ft. or more, is the only practical choice. A submersible pump (as its name implies) is lowered to the bottom of the well by the black plastic "drop" pipe to which its power cable is taped. Although installation and replacement are not beyond the ability of a homeowner, the peace of mind provided by a warranty that includes repairs in case of pump failure is probably worth the extra cost of a professional installation.

Repairing a Water Pump

A properly installed top-quality submersible pump is virtually trouble-free. Barring a direct hit by lightning or a well that runs dry or fills with silt, it will run dependably for decades. When it eventually wears out, it is easily replaced.

Shallow-well pumps, on the other hand, fall prey to several common ailments. The intake opening at the bottom of the well is fitted with a foot valve, a species of check valve attached to a strainer that prevents debris from being sucked into the line and the pump. The foot valve prevents the water in the line from flowing back down into the well whenever the pump shuts off. Sometimes, especially if the well is pumped almost dry, an accumulation of gravel, twigs, or mud can prevent the valve from closing, causing the pump to lose its prime.

Protecting Deep-Well Pumps from Lightning

Because the buried 220-volt power cable that connects the motor to the house is about as good a ground as could be imagined, deep-well pumps are susceptible to damage from lightning strikes. Motors encased in an insulating oil bath are less easily damaged. Because lightning can travel underground to the power cable and into the house from quite a distance, you should protect the pump and the household electrical system by installing a lightning arrester across the line from the service panel to the pump-control relay. This is a kind of one-shot fuse that literally goes off with a bang when a nearby lightning strike sends a power surge into the system. It's also a good idea to turn off the pump during severe thunderstorms. Polyethylene pipe rated for 140 psi can be safely used to depths of about 250 ft. Beyond this, stronger pipe or even galvanized iron is needed to withstand the pressure exerted by a very long column of water.

DIAGNOSING THE PROBLEM Pumps are designed to suck or push water, not air. But they'll keep trying until the pump or the motor itself overheats and seizes. When a pump runs continuously and no water flows out of the tap, the pump has either lost its prime or its piston or impeller has failed. An empty water line will feel warm and light and lack a pulse (you can feel water moving through the intake pipe). The pump chamber will also feel warm to the touch. Working pumps sweat with condensation on their ground-water-cooled surfaces. If the pump is cold and running, the problem is not lost prime, but lost suction. A pump that takes forever to reach shut-off pressure is probably suffering from this kind of problem.

REPLACING OR REJUVENATING THE LEATHER WASHERS Like a bicycle pump or the familiar camp stove, a piston pump pushes air out of a chamber with a rod (the piston) creating a vacuum that sucks water up the line on its backstroke. The piston is sealed to the sides of the air chamber by flexible leather washers, which eventually dry or wear out. Replacement kits, available from the manufacturer or distributor, will give new life to a pump that runs a lot but doesn't seem to draw much water. Dried-out leather washers can sometimes be rejuvenated by soaking them in light machine oil or mineral oil.

REPLACING AN IMPELLER Centrifugal pumps lose their suction when overheating wears down their nylon or brass impellers. Abrasion from dirt sucked into the pump chamber when the well ran too low or was flooded with surface debris will also damage the impellers. Because this is not a far-fetched occurrence, these parts are designed to be easily replaced.

CLEANING OR REPLACING THE VALVE If the pump has lost its prime and you can see water in the bottom of the well or spring, examine the foot valve. If the intake strainer is not choked with dead leaves or mud, unscrew the strainer and see if any dirt has lodged between the spring-loaded flapper valve and its gasket. Check the spring itself for proper operation. Clean or replace the valve as necessary.

Fixing Excessive Pump Cycling

Water pumps are set to switch on automatically when water pressure falls below a preset limit and to turn off when it reaches the desired pressure. A pressure-sensing diaphragm (it looks like a flying saucer tethered to a thin copper tubing) is connected to a relay that switches the pump motor on and off. There are adjusting screws on the relay to change the high and low limits. These should be set so that the pump cycles on at 20 psi to 25 psi and off at 40 psi. Although shut-off pressure can be increased slightly to supply a third-story bathroom, exceeding the normal working range of the plumbing system will cause joints and fittings to spring leaks. Faucets that constantly sputter when opened or a pump that runs and runs is a symptom of a split nylon connector in the black plastic supply pipe; air is being sucked into the line.

If the pump cycles constantly whenever the smallest amount of water is drawn off, the problem is in the pressure tank, not the pump itself. Piston pumps are usually mounted directly on top of the pressure tank. Centrifugal and jet pumps (and, of course, submersibles) usually have a separate pressure tank. To reduce excessive pump cycling, water in the tank is pressurized by a cushion of compressed air at the top of the tank.

Draining Waterlogged Tanks

Old-fashioned (usually plain or rather rust-pitted galvanized steel) pressure tanks gradually lose their pressure as the air dissolves into the water. When the air cushion no longer exerts enough pressure, the pump comes on whenever water is drawn off, and the tank is said to be *waterlogged*. Shut off the pump, close the main valves to prevent backflow into the tank, and allow it to drain.

Repriming a Shallow-Well Pump

A 1-in. line 300 ft. long takes 30 gal. to fill; to reprime a pump, all the air between the foot valve and the pump must be replaced with water.

The first step is to shut the valve between the pump output and the pressure tank (if there is one) or the main system shut-off (you don't want to fill all the pipes in the house too).

■ **Pour water into the line.** Unscrew the priming plug located on top of the pump head (usually a ½-in.-square plug, top dead center of the impeller housing or pump chamber). Insert a funnel and slowly pour water into the line, allowing the air to bubble out. This will take a long time. If you can't get any water in at all, look for a check valve at the inlet side of the pump and remove it.

■ **Start the pump.** When the line will accept no more water, screw the plug back in loosely, and turn on the pump. You should hear a whooshing sound, and the intake pipe will jump as slugs of water lurch up the line. Air should bubble out the sides of the plug along with water. When only water squirts out of the plug, you've recaptured the prime. Most often, it will take several (sometimes dozens) of tries before the line is emptied of enough air for the pump to grab water.

■ **Priming with a force pump.** If there are high spots along the line (for example, where it rises to cross a ledge), no amount of priming can clear the resulting air lock. Suspect this condition if the pump won't prime and yet refuses to take any more water through its priming plug. In this case, you'll need a force pump.

A force pump—a kind of oversize bicycle pump that can be rented from your local plumbing store—will take up water from a pail and push it into the line with enough force to dislodge the offending air bubble. Ideally, it should be connected to the end of the intake line, with the foot valve removed and its intake hose let down into the well. It will also work, with a bit less efficiency, at the pump end, connected to the priming hole. When re-laying a water-supply line, anticipate priming problems and install a tee connected to an aboveground priming valve at any high spot. Maintaining a constant pitch (upward or downward or level) will also prevent problems.

If the problem persists after the tank refills, check the air valve (which is exactly the same as a tire valve) at the top of the tank to be sure it is not loose or leaking air.

REPLACING A PRESSURE TANK It's a good idea to replace the old-style pressure tank with a modern diaphragm-type pressure tank in any case. Your system will require less maintenance and will work more efficiently, prolonging the life of the pump. These (typically) bright blue enameled steel tanks have a rubber diaphragm that maintains a permanent separation between the water and the air. They are usually factory charged and do not require recharging. If the tank loses pressure, it isn't just waterlogged, it's defunct; the diaphragm has sprung a leak, and the tank must be replaced.

Because a submersible pump is not inside the house, other than the click of the pump relay contacts, you won't necessarily notice that it is cycling excessively. But weird gurgles, sighs, wheezes, and moans emanating from within the pressure tank are definitive communications from a dead tank.

Home Heating Systems 12

There's an old New England saying—"What with the high cost of heating, the average icicle on a roof costs about five dollars a foot."

—ERIC SLOANE,
A REVERENCE FOR WOOD

A lthough the installation of anything but the most basic new heating system is generally a job best left to a knowledgeable professional, it's still a good idea to understand how your home heating system works and to be familiar with its components and routine maintenance and simple repair procedures. Too often, we are at the mercy of the machines that are our slaves, and we live our lives surrounded by systems whose functioning is beyond our comprehension, leaving us feeling powerless and abused by forces outside our control. Our colonial forebears, who made almost everything they needed with their own hands, would wonder at the state we've come to.

This modern high-efficiency gas boiler heats an entire two-story, 10-room house and occupies only a fraction of the space of the old boiler it replaced.

HOT-AIR SYSTEMS

Gravity-flow hot-air heating is elegantly simple in theory and seriously inefficient in practice. Air circulating between a firebox and an outer enclosure is heated and rises into a plenum (a sort of sheet-metal cap that sits on top of the furnace) where, being lighter than ordinary air, it rises through ducts to circulate throughout the rooms of the house. Denser cold air flows into a return duct or falls down the stairs into the cellar.

To rise fast enough, air has to be heated to high temperatures. Even so, the overall heat transfer is not very great. Unless it is full of water, which, given the relationship between relative humidity and outside infiltration, would be unlikely in an uninsulated, drafty old house, air is a poor heat-transfer medium. (Water can hold 3,000 times more heat than air.) Some of the little heat it can contain is also lost to radiation through the metal ducts as it rises to the upper stories. And, because the pressure differential is not impressive to begin with, large-diameter ducts with a minimum of gentle bends are required to reduce friction and even more heat loss. Cool air moves down walls and across the floor while hot air rises from floor ducts to the ceiling, creating uncomfortable drafts. These same air currents probably circulate as much, if not more, household dust as heat.

Forced Hot-Air Systems

The only thing primitive gravity hot-air systems had going for them is that, compared to steam and hot water, they were cheap and simple. Modern hot-air systems, driven by electrically powered blowers that greatly increase the circulation rate and efficiency of the system (by pulling the cold air down into the plenum, not by forcing hot air out), outfitted with filters to reduce dust, with ducts carefully balanced to minimize drafts, and automatic dampers to create zoned control, still maintain their ancestral advantages as well. Forced hot-air systems account for almost two thirds of all systems today. You can still find surviving coal- and wood-burning *octopus* furnaces converted from gravity to forced circulation with grafted-on 1940s or 1950s oil burners, free-standing blower cabinets, and cold-air return plenums. (The earliest gravity furnaces used a trench in the cellar floor as the cold-air return.)

The drawing on the facing page shows the layout of a typical furnace and fuel tank, which have remained basically unchanged since the 1940s. Routine maintenance (such as oiling shafts, checking and replacing drive belts and filters) is well within the province of the average homeowner and should not be ignored. If you are lucky enough to have an owner's manual to accompany your furnace, read up on the details of maintenance and specifications.

Other than such routine maintenance, there isn't much else that can go wrong that the average homeowner will be able to fix—other tasks are best left to the professionals who perform the annual fall tune-up. Cleaning and adjusting the burner orifices for maximum efficiency is precise work.

Fuel-Saving Tip

Here's a trick to save a good deal of fuel with a forced hot-air system. In an attempt to mask any deficiencies in system performance that could otherwise be prevented by more meticulous design and installation, some heating contractors set the fan limit switch to turn the blower on at a profligate 135°F and off at an equally wasteful 90°F. By resetting the switch set points to 110°F and 90°F, the homeowner can save fuel without a noticeable sacrifice of comfort.

Simple Forced Hot-Air Heating System and Typical Maintenance Problems

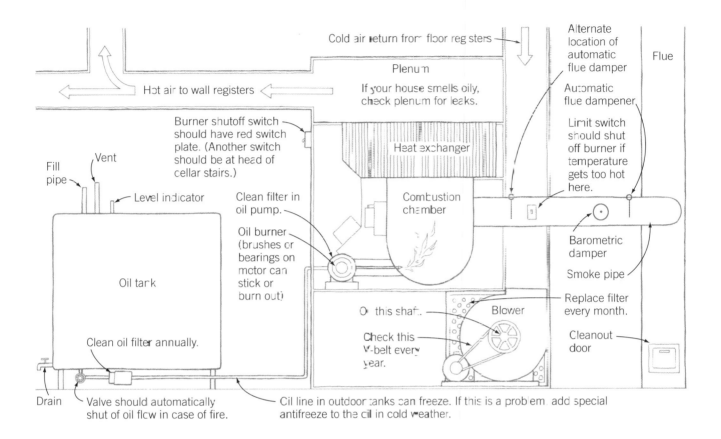

Cold air return from floor registers

Alternate location of automatic flue damper

Flue

Plenum

If your house smells oily, check plenum for leaks.

Automatic flue dampener

Hot air to wall registers

Burner shutoff switch should have red switch plate. (Another switch should be at head of cellar stairs.)

Heat exchanger

Limit switch should shut off burner if temperature gets too hot here.

Fill pipe

Vent

Level indicator

Clean filter in oil pump.

Combustion chamber

Oil burner (brushes or bearings on motor can stick or burn out)

Barometric damper

Smoke pipe

Oil tank

Replace filter every month.

On this shaft.

Blower

Check this V-belt every year.

Cleanout door

Clean oil filter annually.

Drain

Valve should automatically shut of oil flow in case of fire.

Oil line in outdoor tanks can freeze. If this is a problem, add special antifreeze to the oil in cold weather.

STEAM HEATING SYSTEMS

For those who could afford it, steam heat was the epitome of Victorian-era heating technology. The elegance of a naturally pressurized system, combined with its superior heat-transfer capacity, raised home-heating systems to a heretofore unimaginable level of comfort and efficiency. (Hot water will circulate—that is, *thermosyphon*—by gravity, too, but not much more efficiently than hot air. It required the addition of an electric circulator pump to make hot-water heat practical for single-family homes.) Because steam (and hot water) heat by radiation rather than convection, drafts and dust are much reduced. Other than advances in con-

trols and heating engineering, which improved safety, convenience, and overall system responsiveness, the same two basic steam-heating systems developed back in the mid-nineteenth century are still used today.

One-Pipe and Two-Pipe Systems

The earliest and simplest system was the one-pipe system (see the drawing on p. 376). In this system, water is turned to steam in a boiler, expanding more than 1,000 times in volume as it does so. The hot steam rises up a pipe to a radiator, where it condenses back to water on striking the cold metal, giving up its heat. The spent water (condensate) then flows back down the same pipe by gravity to the bottom of the boiler, where it is reheated to begin the cycle again. Because steam is ascending through the same pipe that water is descending, the one-pipe system requires

One-Pipe Steam System

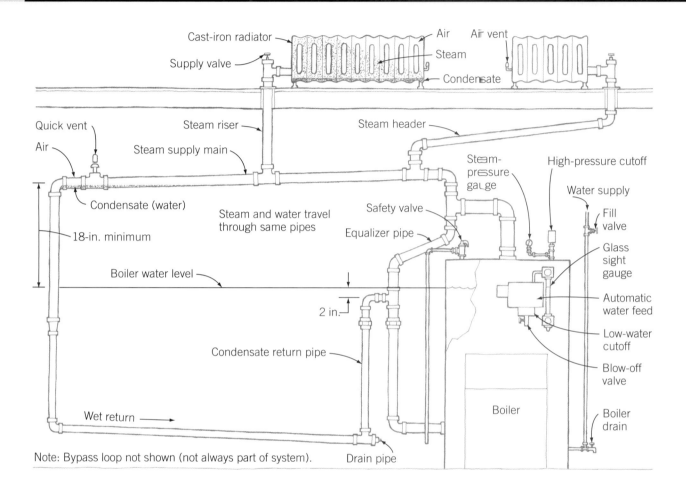

Cast-iron radiator

Supply valve

Air   Air vent

Steam

Condensate

Quick vent

Air

Steam riser

Steam header

Steam supply main

Condensate (water)

Steam-pressure gauge

High-pressure cutoff

Water supply

Fill valve

18-in. minimum

Steam and water travel through same pipes

Safety valve

Equalizer pipe

Glass sight gauge

Boiler water level

Automatic water feed

2 in.

Low-water cutoff

Condensate return pipe

Blow-off valve

Boiler

Wet return

Boiler drain

Note: Bypass loop not shown (not always part of system).

Drain pipe

fairly large-diameter pipes. Even so, a lot of heat is transferred to the cooled water by the counter-flowing steam. The knocking sound traditionally associated with rising steam is caused as it pushes against pockets of water trapped in the pipes.

Around 1905, the two-pipe system was developed to eliminate the drawbacks of using just one pipe. In the two-pipe system, the steam rises to the radiators through one main, and the condensate flows back down another. Smaller pipes can be used, knocking is eliminated, and more heat is transferred to the radiators. But because it uses twice as much pipe (and labor), a two-pipe system is more expensive.

Steam Venting

Before a radiator can fill with steam, the air it contains must be expelled. Getting this to happen reliably was a problem that plagued heating contractors until 1912, when George Hoffman of Waterbury, Connecticut, patented his Number One automatic air vent, which is basically still in use today. Hoffman's vent, located halfway up the side of the radiator opposite the supply valve, is designed to stay open until the incoming steam heats it to about 180°F.

VENT RATINGS How fast a radiator can heat up and how hot the room will get before the boiler shuts down are controlled entirely by the air vent. Air vents have two ratings: the maximum operating pressure (usually 10 lb. per square inch; psi) and the drop-away (or operating) pressure. The drop-away pressure is critical. Because not all the air will vent from the radiator when it first fills with steam, unless the drop-away pressure of the vent is higher than the cut-in setting of the boiler's pressure control (the control that regulates the operating steam pressure; one brand is Pressuretrol®), the vent won't open and trapped air will prevent the steam from filling the entire radiator. Air vents are available in five speeds— very slow, slow, fast, very fast, and fully variable. The faster the vent, the lower its drop-away pressure. Thus carelessly installing a quick vent without adjusting the pressure control can actually make your entire system perform more poorly.

VENTING FOR ONE-PIPE SYSTEMS In a one-pipe system, steam must necessarily reach the radiators closest to the boiler before those farthest away, hence the system is unbalanced. The most distant rooms will never get hot and the nearest rooms will overheat. The solution was to install faster vents (ones with larger holes) at the end of the line and slower vents at its beginning. Unfortunately, this means that the radiators with the slow vents are forced to heat less efficiently. *Double-venting* is the time-honored cure. Drill and tap a hole to match the thread on the vent nipple (⅛-in. National Pipe Thread; NPT) just below the existing vent and install a second vent. This allows the remaining air to continue venting after the uppermost vent has closed down. This not only balances the radiator but also slows the venting rate, preventing water hammer.

VENTING FOR TWO-PIPE SYSTEMS The radiators of a true two-pipe steam system *do not* have air vents. Instead, the air vents are located only near the ends of the steam mains. (Vents are also located on the mains in one-pipe systems, as well as on each radiator.) Instead of entering at the bottom as in a one-pipe system, the steam enters through a riser pipe into the top of the radiator and moves across the top.

There is usually a steam trap where the condensate pipe exits the radiator. These automatic temperature-sensitive valves prevent steam from sneaking into the condensate return line. In lieu of a steam trap, there may be a check valve of some sort. Sometimes, in an attempt to fix a radiator that refused to heat, a homeowner, ignorant of the existence of these controls, added an air vent (radiators often had standard taped and plugged openings that could be used for this purpose) instead of freeing up the stuck check valve or clogged steam trap that was the true cause of the problem. Putting an air vent in the wrong place can create problems that reverberate throughout the entire system. Replace any malfunctioning steam traps

The sections of steam radiators used in one-pipe systems are coupled together by nipples that run across the bottom only. The steam always enters at the bottom and, being lighter than air, rises rapidly, displacing the air out the air vents as it does so. The two-pipe systems use a radiator that is coupled together at both top and bottom, which is the same radiator used in hot-water systems. Because hot water does not rise as fast as steam, the doubled nipples increase circulation and efficiency. In steam systems, the steam enters at the upper nipples and the condensate exits at the lower nipple. While either type of radiator can be used with hot-water heat, it makes a difference which type you use for steam.

Two-Pipe Steam System

The radiator on the left is configured for a true two-pipe system. The radiator on the right represents an earlier arrangement in the development of two-pipe steam.

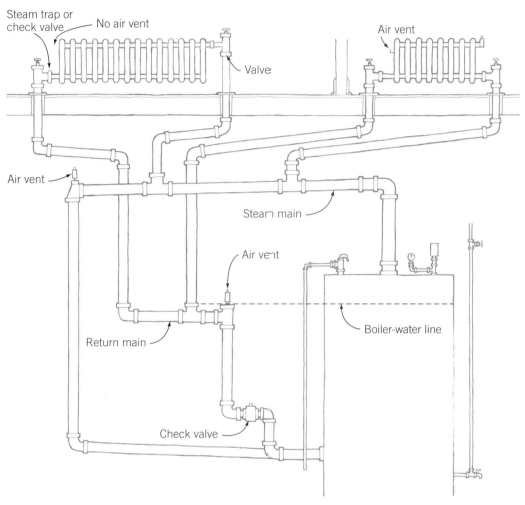

Vacuum-Flow Steam

To make matters more confusing, midway between the one-pipe and the evolution of the true two-pipe steam system, there was also a two-pipe air-vent steam system that used bottom-coupled radiators fitted with an air vent. Look for two pipes, entering and exiting at the bottom, each fitted with a hand valve.

Vacuum-Flow Steam

For all its simplicity and basically efficient action, gravity-powered steam heating does suffer from one drawback that was not fully remedied by the two-pipe system and variable venting: When the boiler shuts off and the radiators begin to cool down, the air that is drawn back into them cools them off even faster, and the thermostat soon calls for more heat. Thus gravity steam heat tends to be uneven, with frequent cycles of hot and cold, rather than a steady heat output.

The solution resorted to by old-timers was to convert the system to a *vacuum flow*. The air vents were replaced with vacuum vents and the hand valves, with special *packless* (airtight) valves. The vacuum vents allow air to escape but not re-enter as the system cools. In the resulting airtight loop, the condensing steam creates a partial vacuum, drawing more hot steam into the radiators and thereby maintaining a more even temperature. And because water in a partial vacuum boils at a lower temperature, less fuel is burned to produce the steam. Finally, filling the radiators with lower-temperature steam (typically 180°F vs. 215°F) tends to make the rooms more comfortable.

This "natural" vacuum system worked fine with the coal-fired boilers of yore. Because a coal fire heats up and burns down gradually, there is plenty of time for steam to fill the radiators and push the air out before the vacuum arises. But when the old coal burners are converted to gas and oil burners, the fire comes on and goes out instantly. For all practical purposes, when the fire is out there is no heat in the firebox, and when it is on, the heat is ferocious. The vacuum forms before all the air has a chance to be pushed out of the radiator. The result is a very unmanageable heating system.

Steam Boiler Maintenance

Because the boiler feed water will always contain some air, which is released as it is heated, the oxygen in this air plus the air drawn in by the radiators (in a nonvacuum system) cause a buildup of rust and scale throughout the system, especially in the boiler. These flakes of corrosion can interfere with the proper functioning of the safety and control valves and lead to premature boiler failure. Mineral buildup also reduces heat-transfer efficiency. Opening the blow-off valve (usually located on the automatic water feeder) once a month (a *blowdown*) during the heating season to drain off these constantly accumulating sediments is a routine part of operating a steam-heating system. Drain the rusty water into a bucket until it runs clear.

Before purchasing an old house with an antique steam-heating system, give the boiler a test run. The most common maladies that afflict steam systems are usually easy to diagnose and cure. Unless the boiler and the steam mains have corroded to the point of no return, there's no compelling reason to replace the entire system.

A steam boiler has several important attachments that must be checked at frequent intervals for proper operation. These include the glass sight gauge, the steam gauge, and the safety valve—and in updated systems, the high-pressure limit switch, the low-water cut-off switch, the automatic water feed, and the blow-off valve.

In the days before automatic water feeds, keeping the boiler filled with water was much more than just a bothersome chore. The safety of the house depended on constant attention to the boiler. Modern safety controls provide no security if they don't work. Not only should all the controls be checked at the beginning of each heating season but the conscientious homeowner will also get in the habit of glancing at the sight gauge every time he or she walks by the boiler. The water feed should be checked as part of the monthly blowdown.

CHECKING THE SIGHT GAUGE Never fire up a boiler before checking the sight gauge, which is a vertical glass tube mounted on the side of the boiler that shows the water level inside the boiler. It should read about half full, slightly more when cold, slightly less when hot. If no water is showing, either the boiler is empty, the gauge is plugged, or both. Don't turn the boiler on! Open the water feed and see if the gauge fills. If not, open the draincock at its bottom end until the water runs clear. If the valve is still clogged close its shut-off valves, unscrew the gauge-retaining nuts and remove the sight glass for cleaning.

Replace a nonfunctioning gauge. If the sight glass fills, the boiler is safe to turn on. Sometimes, a boiler is fitted with try-cocks instead of a sight gauge. These are two small faucets near the top of the boiler. Open the lower one carefully; water should stream out. With the boiler running, open the upper cock;

steam should rush out, indicating that the water level is somewhere between the two try-cocks.

CHECKING THE STEAM GAUGE The steam gauge is a meter that shows the pressure (in psi) of the steam at the top of the boiler. Normal safe operating range for small domestic steam boilers is around 5 psi. The danger zone begins above 12 psi. (Of course, the gauge for a vacuum system will have a negative scale.)

CHECKING THE SAFETY VALVE The boiler should also be equipped with a safety valve, similar to the pressure-relief valve required at the top of a water heater. The safety is preset to open at 15 psi, to prevent a runaway boiler from building up explosive force (at 50 psi, 30 gal. of water will blow the boiler and the house apart with the same force as a pound of nitroglycerin). Check the valve for proper operation yearly. With a long stick (to prevent scalding), gently lift up the release lever until steam escapes. Repeat until all debris is cleared out. If the lever has rusted shut, replace the entire unit after the boiler has cooled down.

CHECKING THE PRESSURE CONTROL Modern boilers are also equipped with backup safety controls that regulate the steam pressure in the boiler and determine its firing cycle. A small metal box connected to the burner, controlled by an electric cable, contains the steam pressure control (one type is Pressuretrol). Inside the twin unit are two lever-type switch contacts, with adjusting screws. The first set of contacts is marked *cut-in* and determines the steam pressure at which the burner will turn on when the thermostat calls for heat. The second switch, marked *differential,* is adjusted to set the pressure at which the burner will shut down. This is a safety switch, since it will override any other control if pressure goes over the safe limit. The cut-in and the differential limit the normal operating range of the boiler. The switches are calibrated by fiddling with their adjustment screws until the desired cut-in and cut-out points match the reading on the steam pressure gauge. Normal cut-out pressure should not exceed 5 psi.

CHECKING THE LIMIT SWITCH The same boiler that heats hot water for steam can also be used to heat it for domestic use. During the summer, when the thermostat is turned off, the cut-in switch won't work. Instead, the limit switch (for example, Aquastat) responds to the water temperature inside the boiler. When it falls below the setting on the limit switch dial, the boiler fires until the water is heated a few degrees warmer than its upper setting, at which point the switch shuts the boiler off. The boiler heats water circulating through a heat exchanger to an external storage tank. Drinking water is never allowed to mix with boiler water, because the latter often contains chemical corrosion inhibitors.

CHECKING THE HIGH-PRESSURE LIMIT SWITCH The high-pressure limit switch automatically shuts off the boiler when the steam pressure exceeds 10 psi. An easy way to test its operation is to crank the thermostat up to the top of the dial and watch the steam-pressure gauge as the boiler struggles to answer the call. If the pressure goes over 10 psi and the boiler is still running, turn it off manually, using the red-colored emergency shut-off switch. Call a repair person.

CHECKING THE LOW-WATER CUT-OFF SWITCH The low-water cut-off switch is usually part of the automatic water feed and blow-off system located on the side of the boiler. To test the switch, close the manual water feed so that the boiler cannot get more water. Open the blow-off valve with the boiler running. Just about when the water level drops below the bottom of the sight gauge, the boiler should shut off. If it does not turn off the boiler immediately. Don't forget to reopen the feed valve so the boiler will fill back up. Call a repair person. If you must run the boiler in this potentially dangerous mode, check the sight gauge at least four times a day until the level switch is repaired.

CHECKING THE AUTOMATIC WATER-FEED
CONTROL In the unlikely event that your boiler is still supplied by a manual feed, don't use it before you have added an automatic water-feed control. This control looks like a cross between a circulating pump and a water meter, and is attached to a loop in the cold-water feed line so that its center is at the same level as the desired water level in the boiler.

Like the float in a toilet tank, a control valve opens when the boiler water level drops and closes when it reaches the correct height. One cause of gurgling and knocking pipes is an over-filled boiler caused by a sticking automatic feed shutoff. The water is pushed up into the steam main from the top of the boiler and will eventually begin to dribble out the radiator vents. This turns your steam heat into a lukewarm water system, and the circulation must be fixed and the system drained back to the proper water level.

Test the automatic feed with the boiler off. First, make sure all the control valves are properly set—someone may have inadvertently shut down or partially opened one of the bypass valves. If the boiler water level reads too low, close the outfeed gate valve C (see the top drawing at right) and crack open union #2 just in front of it. Water should squirt out under pressure if the feeder's internal float valve is operating properly. If water doesn't squirt out, the float valve is probably stuck closed or clogged. If there's nothing wrong with the float, check the water line for blockage. If the water level is too high, close infeed gate valve A and open union #2 again.

REPAIRING A STUCK FLOAT If water continues
to trickle out, the float is stuck open. Check the float action by trying to lift the float valve stem on the side of the feed control with a screwdriver blade (see the bottom drawing at right). If it won't move or holding it open

Automatic Water-Feed System

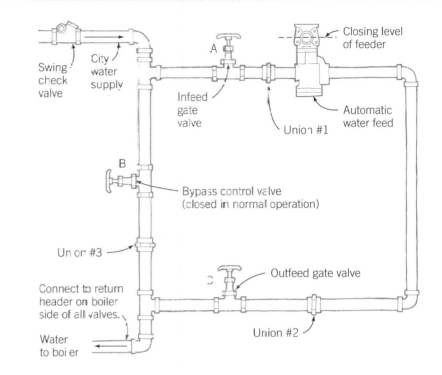

Closing level of feeder

Swing check valve

City water supply

A

Infeed gate valve

Union #1

Automatic water feed

B

Bypass control valve (closed in normal operation)

Union #3

Outfeed gate valve

Connect to return header on boiler side of all valves.

Union #2

Water to boiler

Testing and Cleaning the Float Valve Stem

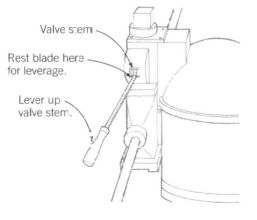

Valve stem

Rest blade here for leverage.

Lever up valve stem.

doesn't flush the valve seat clean, take the control apart and replace the valve and all the gaskets. Bypass control valve B allows water to flow into the boiler if you need to isolate the circulation loop (by closing valves A and C and opening B), as if, for example, you have to fix it during winter, when you don't want to shut down the system.

DRAINING THE BOILER Finally, to reduce corrosion buildup, drain the boiler completely once a year to flush out sediment. Check the sight glass. Unless the automatic fill control is defective or the boiler has a manual fill, the glass should show half full. If you need to add water manually, let the boiler cool down for a few hours before you do. Letting cold water into a hot boiler could cause the boiler to crack.

Spits, Dribbles, Knocks, and Other Impolite Radiator Behavior

The only sound a properly operating steam-heating system should make is the hiss of steam escaping out the vent just after the radiator fills. It should not spit, dribble, or hiss continuously. If it does, the vent should be replaced or cleaned. Air vents are subject to chronic clogging. You can remove the vent and soak it in vinegar and boiling water to loosen the caked-on sediment or buy a replacement for about $10.

Repacking a Stem

When water or steam leaks out the radiator shut-off valve, the stem packing is worn out. With the system shut down, unscrew the valve stem and wrap new packing thread around the stem in the direction it turns down. If you have a vacuum system, the packless valve has lost its seal, allowing air to leak back in. The valve should be repaired or replaced.

Solving Trapped Water Problems

Gurgling, sloshing, and thumping in the lines or radiators are caused by trapped water. Steam lines should always slope downward. Sometimes a broken pipe strap causes a section of steam pipe to drop, creating a water trap. Or an inexperienced home plumber may have run a steam line below an obstruction (like a joist); always route pipes over obstructions. Radiators should also slope toward the return line. If the floor has settled, a radiator can sometimes tilt in the wrong direction and trap water inside itself. Wood shims added under the feet on the low side will cure this problem.

Broken support

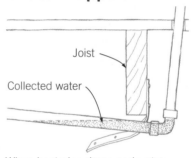

When heat pipe drops and water collects, noise occurs when steam enters pipe.

Incorrect pipe installation

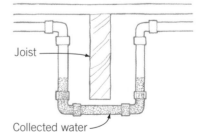

Trapped water obstructs steam line. Pipes should go through or over obstructions.

With the boiler full, turn up the thermostat so that it comes on. Then hold a bucket under the draincock at the bottom of the boiler and draw off water and sludge until the low-water safety switch kicks in and shuts off the boiler. Let some fresh water drain through the system before closing the valve and allowing the boiler to refill. Continue to refill and drain off until the water runs clear. Once the boiler is completely filled, add a corrosion-inhibiting compound through the safety-valve tap hole. Really sludgy boilers should be power-flushed by a professional who will use super-heated water and detergent chemicals.

HOT-WATER HEATING SYSTEMS

The constant maintenance required to keep a steam-heat system in healthy condition, and the danger of explosion when these chores are ignored or a safety valve rusts shut, is probably the main reason why hot-water heat became so popular. Unlike a steam system, it is almost impossible to run a hot-water boiler to danger-ous pressures, because all the water in the lines and radiators would have to boil off before the boiler could become dangerously low. And as the water turned to steam, it would harmlessly vent out of the radiator air vents.

In addition, hot water heat provides a more comfortable, even warmth. Because water has a greater latent heat than steam, the radiators in a hot-water heating system will give off heat for a longer time, which means the boiler doesn't cycle off and on as much and the heat can be steady. Also, because of its latent heat capacity, water does not have to be heated to as high a temperature as steam. Although they take longer to heat, rooms warmed by hot water do not tend to overheat like they do with steam heat. The radiators never get as hot. Thus hot water heat became renowned for its gentle evenness.

Identifying your System

It can be hard for the uninitiated to tell the difference between a two-pipe steam system and a hot-water heating system. Both steam and hot-water radiators are fitted with a hand valve. (These allow the radiator to be shut off or partially opened as needed to balance the system.) The radiator vents are the giveaway: The bleeder valve on a hot-water system is tiny, whereas the air vent on a steam radiator is domed and fairly large.

A steam boiler will often have the same general configuration as a hot-water boiler. But the hot-water boiler will never have a sight glass. It will have an altitude gauge (indicating the height of the water in the topmost radiator) as well as a temperature and pressure gauge. (Sometimes the altitude, temperature, and boiler pressure gauges are combined into a single gauge called a tridicator.) Open the bleeder valve to let out water and note the needle reading when that radiator is full. If it drops below that figure, the system is getting low on water.

Gravity-Flow Hot Water

As with steam heat, the oldest hot-water heating systems were gravity flow. The drawing on p. 384 shows the principal parts of this type of heating system. Basically, water is heated in a boiler; it rises up through a pipe to the radiator, gives up its heat and flows back down another pipe to the boiler. Because water expands when it is heated, the extra water rises up a pipe to an expansion tank somewhere up in the attic. This tank has an open drain, usually a pipe venting directly out onto the roof, to discharge any overflow.

At the same time that hot water is expand-ing, it gets lighter. The radiators above are filled with heavier cold water, which flows down the return pipes, pushing the lighter hot water up into the radiators. Because a gravity system is an open one, explosive pressure cannot build. The boiler could burn out, but it wouldn't blow up. But the constant loss of water via the

Simple Gravity System

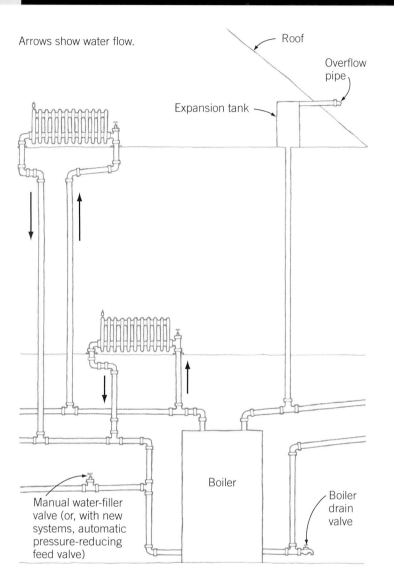

Arrows show water flow.

Roof

Overflow pipe

Expansion tank

Boiler

Manual water-filler valve (or, with new systems, automatic pressure-reducing feed valve)

Boiler drain valve

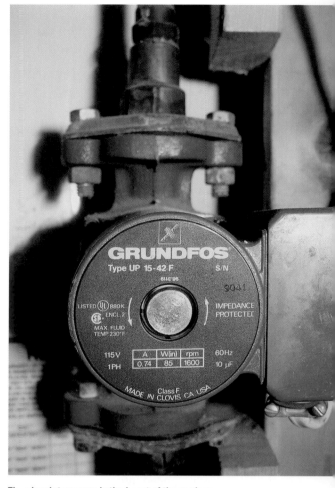

The circulator pump is the heart of the modern forced-flow hot-water heating system. Hydronic circulation is much faster and more efficient than the earlier gravity-flow systems these pumps replaced.

expansion overflow is also a heat loss. Since the difference between the hottest water (about 190°F) and the coolest water (170°F) is not great, the circulation and heat-transfer rate is slow, and large pipes are needed to overcome friction. The air brought into the system by the open expansion tank and the new replacement water also fosters relatively rapid corrosion. These drawbacks ensured the continued popularity of steam heating well into the 1930s.

Forced-Flow Hot Water

Forced-flow (hydronic) hot-water heating systems eliminated the drawbacks of the gravity-flow systems. An electric pump circulates hot water at a rapid rate, greatly increasing the speed and efficiency of the heat transfer to the radiators and allowing the use of much smaller pipes. Hydronic heat typically uses ¾-in. copper tubing instead of a 2-in. black iron steam pipe. Forced systems are also closed systems. Because no water (or very much heat) is ever lost through the expansion tank, no new water need be added. Corrosion is reduced, and system efficiency is increased.

SINGLE-PIPE AND TWO-PIPE SYSTEMS The so-called single-pipe (or *loop*) system is the most economical and widely used hydronic installation. Unlike single-pipe steam radiators, single-pipe hot water radiators have two pipes entering them. (No hot-water system of any kind ever has just one pipe entering a radiator.) In a single-pipe hot-water system, both the radiator supply pipe (the *riser*) and the return pipe are teed into a single pipe that makes a circuit of the house, returning to the circulator pump on the boiler. When the hot water enters a special directional, or *scoop*, tee at the riser, a portion of its flow is diverted into the radiator.

The more expensive two-pipe system uses a separate main feed and main return line. In the one-pipe system, the radiators closest to the boiler get the hottest water, and the ones at the end of the line get the coolest. The two-pipe system is more even, since the same-temperature water is equally available to every radiator.

ZONED SINGLE-PIPE SYSTEM A modern variation is the zoned single-pipe system. In this system, the house is divided into two or more zones, each served by its own loop and accompanying thermostat. In addition to allowing more control over the heat, zoned systems also mitigate the cool radiator problem inherent in

Forced-Flow Hot-Water System

Single-Pipe System

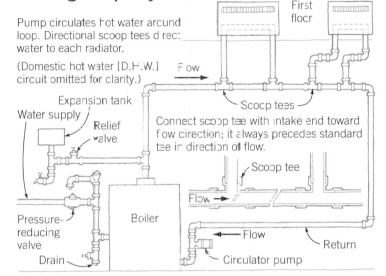

Pump circulates hot water around loop. Directional scoop tees direct water to each radiator.

(Domestic hot water [D.H.W.] circuit omitted for clarity.)

Connect scoop tee with intake end toward flow direction; it always precedes standard tee in direction of flow.

Two-Pipe System

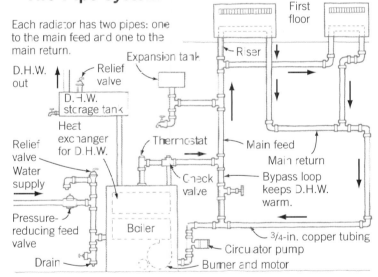

Each radiator has two pipes: one to the main feed and one to the main return.

The small bleeder valve at the top left corner confirms that this 1930s to 1940s vintage cast-iron radiator is hooked up to a hot water system. The much larger steam radiator air vent would have been mounted halfway up the side. Note the thermostatic valve at the bottom right that allows for zone control of each radiator and replaces the two hand valves of steam and early hot-water systems.

No Power, No Heat

One disadvantage of a heating system that depends on electric power is the potential havoc wrought by a power outage during the heating season. In the old days, when heating with a coal- or wood-fired furnace meant keeping the coal bin or wood shed full, there was little danger of losing the heat or of the resulting frozen pipes. Because it is a closed system, a modern hydronic system is usually no longer filled with water. Instead, a heat-transfer fluid (a nontoxic propylene-glycol-based antifreeze) circulates through the system and protects it both from corrosion and freezing.

TIP

Air Separators

If you don't relish the inconvenience of having to bleed the radiators, an alternative is to install an air separator (such as a Spirovent) at the head of the boiler manifold (where the riser from the boiler becomes the main supply pipe and the water is the hottest). This device removes the air from the system before it enters the pipes. Not only does this eliminate the need to bleed the radiators, it also prolongs the life of the system by removing corrosive oxygen. ■ ■ ■

single-pipe systems, since the water has a shorter loop back to the boiler. An efficient modern furnace with new multizone pipes retrofitted to existing radiators is an elegant upgrade that does no damage to the character of an old house.

Hot-Water Heat Maintenance

Despite all their advantages, hot-water heating systems, like any mechanical arrangement, are subject to the infirmities of age. The most common problem with hot-water systems is a cold radiator. As with steam heat, in order to work, old-style hot-water radiators must be purged of air. (Modern baseboard hot-water systems radiate heat through the fins attached to the water pipe—they don't contain any air.) Purge the radiators before the heating season, when the boiler is drained down and everything else is checked. Open the bleeder valve at the top of the radiator with a small socket wrench or radiator valve key (you can get them at a hardware store) until all the air is out and the water flows free of bubbles. Replace any valves that leak or don't drain. The radiators must also be purged of air whenever the system is drained down for repairs and refilled and, since dissolved air is always coming out of

solution when the water is heated, often at frequent intervals throughout the heating season.

CHECK THE CONTROL VALVE Both steam and hot-water radiators are also fitted with a hand valve, allowing the radiator to be shut off or partially opened as needed to balance the system. These valves often require repacking. Suspect a partially closed zone valve if all the radiators on a line are too cold.

CHECK THE EXPANSION TANK Like the old-fashioned pressure tank of the water-supply system, a non-diaphragm expansion tank should be drained yearly to prevent waterlogging. Look for a horizontal steel tank 3 ft. to 5 ft. long hanging above the boiler. Close the tank inlet valve and attach a hose to the drain valve and open it. If there is a vacuum-breaker plug on the drain valve, open it too. (As with well-water systems, in the long run, replacing an old-fashioned expansion tank with a sealed diaphragm type will guarantee more efficient operation of the system.)

CHECK THE THERMOSTAT VALVE Some hot-water systems are controlled by a thermostat valve, similar to the one in a car radiator, installed in the hot-water main exiting the boiler. This valve is supposed to open at about 150°F to prevent the circulator pump from forcing cold water into the radiators when the system first cycles up. If the furnace and the circulator both appear to be running and all the radiators are still cold, the thermostat may be stuck closed. Shut the system down and drain it. Remove the thermostat. Set it in a pan of water and heat it on the stove. If the thermostat doesn't open long before the water boils, it's defective and should be replaced.

CHECK THE LIMIT SWITCH Instead of a thermostat, most fairly modern boilers use a limit switch (Aquastat, for example). This switch is basically a safety control that cuts the power to the burner when the water temperature reaches a preset high point (typically 180°F). In this function, it is acting as a high-limit switch. Some also act like a thermostat, not switching the circulator on until the boiler water warms up. There is also a low-limit function, which cycles the boiler back on when the water temperature drops to a preset low point. Use a multimeter to see if the switch is working.

CHECK THE CHECK VALVE The one-way check valve is located right before the thermostat and is supposed to prevent water from running backward through the system when the lever on its side is set in the normal position. In the closed position, the flow to the radiators is blocked so that the boiler can heat domestic hot water without heating the house in the summer. The open position, in which the water can flow either way, is used to drain the system. Remove the valve and make sure that the flapper inside moves freely.

CHECK THE CIRCULATOR PUMP If the circulator pump doesn't run, hot water can't get to the radiators. Use a circuit tester or test meter to check that current is flowing across the limit switch. Then check the circulator itself. If it is humming and feels warm, the pump is probably frozen. Fortunately, a burned-out motor is unlikely. Shut off the system and the furnace breaker and try to turn the pump with a pair of pliers. If it won't move or turns hard, someone has neglected to oil the pump bearing and it has run dry. Soak the frozen pump shaft with a silicone lubricant (such as WD-40), and see if you can get it to turn. If not, drain the system, disassemble the pump and replace the shaft and bearing. The impellers may also be damaged. Replacement parts are usually available for most makes of circulator pumps. The spring-loaded coupling between the pump and the motor may also be broken; it, too, is easily replaced.

DRAINING THE BOILER Another beneficial side effect of the change from open gravity systems to closed hydronic systems is the reduction in the buildup of scale and sludge in the boiler and radiators. (This benefit distinguishes closed-loop hot-water heating from steam heating as well.) Since dissolved air is introduced only when fresh water is (infrequently) added to the boiler, corrosion within the piping and boiler is minimal. Nevertheless, you should check your boiler annually, and drain any sediment that may have collected. When you move into an old house, you can assume that draining the boiler is part of the deal.

Turn off the boiler and the automatic or manual feed and let the water cool down for a few hours. Then open the draincock and draw off water and sediment into a bucket. When the water runs clear, close the draincock, reopen the supply valve, and restart the boiler. Let it run for a while to drive off any air dissolved in the fresh water.

Sometimes, as when an antique boiler in an unoccupied old house has been left idle for a protracted period or when bleeding the radiators was seriously neglected, enough sludge may have collected in the boiler that the entire system should be drained. Also, unlike plain water, hot-water systems filled with antifreeze must be drained every few years as a matter of course, since old antifreeze becomes corrosive.

To drain the system, connect a garden hose to the draincock and run it into the cellar sump convenient floor drain, or outside. Open the air vents on the highest radiators to relieve air lock and then open the drain valve. When all the radiators and the boiler are fully drained, close the air vents. Let the boiler fill until clear water runs out the drain, then close the drain and allow the system to refill. Turn on the boiler, and heat the water to drive its dissolved air out of solution. If the boiler lacks an air separator, bleed off the radiators.

TIP

**Remember
the Antifreeze**

Just about any repair of a hot-water boiler or its attached controls requires draining the system. Be sure to add boiler antifreeze when refilling, if your system doesn't run on plain water. ▆▆ ▆▆ ▆▆

REPLACING BOILERS AND FURNACES

Even running in top form, the average old boiler is only about 50 percent to 60 percent efficient. Boilers eventually wear out and need to be replaced. When the inevitable happens, replacing the old boiler with a modern boiler that can attain an efficiency of 80 percent to 90 percent will quickly pay for itself in reduced fuel costs. But swapping boilers and converting from steam to hot water or gravity to forced circulation isn't always a simple and straightforward operation. Sometimes, even heating contractors can unwittingly or carelessly create problems worse than the ones they sought to fix.

Removing the Old Unit

The first problem with replacing an old boiler or furnace is taking it apart and getting it out of the cellar. Most boilers are sectional, constructed, like a cast-iron radiator, in modules bolted together. Thus a boiler could literally be carried down into or up out of a cellar in more-or-less manageable pieces. There's the rub. When I disconnected the four 1-in.-diameter threaded rods that held the six sections of my antique hot-water boiler together, it was obvious that each single section weighed at least two or three times what I and a helper could conceivably carry. I resorted to the tried-and-true boilersmith's secret method—with sledgehammer and sweat, I reduced the sections into manageable chunks.

Unlike boilers, hot-air furnaces are not sectional. While you may be able to reduce the overall bulk by disassembling some or all of the enclosing cabinet, what's left is still likely to be more than you can easily maneuver out of the cellar. But armed with two rollers—lengths of 1½-in. polyvinyl chloride (PVC) pipe—a lever or helper, an inclined plank, and patience, you can relocate the heaviest furnace without strain or danger. I've used PVC rollers to move 900-lb. steel beams and 700-lb. furnaces with equal aplomb.

Choosing a Replacement

Before you remove the dead boiler you need to decide whether to replace it with the same type of boiler or convert it to a different type of heating system. There are good reasons for either option. You can replace a steam boiler with a new steam boiler or a hot-water boiler. The existing pipes and radiators can be adapted to either system. Likewise, gravity systems can generally be converted to forced systems without major readjustments.

Watch Out for Asbestos

The disassembly of an antique boiler or furnace becomes seriously complicated if it happens to be swaddled, as most were, in a blanket of asbestos plaster. In the dark ages, before we knew about the perils of asbestos, heating contractors would just bust out the asbestos with the cast iron. Homeowners of a more enlightened age, would often seal the boiler in a polyethylene envelope, wet down the plaster, and tear it off, tossing it into plastic bags and disposing of it with the rest of their household garbage, hoping that no one would notice. The efficacy and the ethics of that approach were both suspect. If an antique boiler still lurks in your cellar, the most cost-effective solution might be to ignore it and install the new boiler alongside it, integrating as much of the old piping or ductwork as practical.

But changing from a steam or hot-water system to a hot-air system would normally be impractical and pointless. And, generally, unless you are still burning coal, it's not cost-effective to switch fuels, as for example, from oil to gas or vice versa, because the fuel tank is either already installed and paid for or will have to be. Be aware that if you do install a gas-fired heating appliance in a region where oil-burners are the norm, you may find it hard to find a heating contractor or service person who knows enough about gas to competently install and maintain the equipment. The same holds true in reverse in regions where gas is the standard fuel.

CONVERTING FROM STEAM TO HOT WATER

Nowadays, most moribund steam boilers are replaced with hot-water boilers, and the system is changed over to hydronic heat. Hot-water installation usually costs less than steam, even with a complete changeover.

The most difficult part of converting one-pipe steam heat to two-pipe hydronic is adding new return lines. One way to make the job easier and to avoid gutting walls is to use flexible cross-linked polyethylene (PEX) tubing for the returns (see p. 348). PEX is more readily snaked though walls than is rigid copper. Replace the radiator air valves with bleeder valves, and replace the hand valves with thermostatic valves. Because hot water is cooler than steam, the heat output of each radiator will drop by at least 30 percent. The only way to compensate for this drop is to reduce the overall heat load of the house. Given that the steam radiators were initially sized for a house that was uninsulated and quite leaky, simply adding insulation and weatherstripping will likely make up the difference.

INSTALLING A NEW STEAM SYSTEM

Nevertheless, there's still nothing wrong with replacing your moribund steam boiler with a new one. Unlike sizing a hot-water boiler, sizing a steam boiler is not a straightforward calculation, because significant heat loss through the pipes must be considered. This is a job for a heating contractor who has lots of experience with steam heat.

When replacing a boiler it's a good idea to also plan on replacing all the air vents on the radiators and mains. If the original boiler lacked one, this is the time to also install a drain valve in the *mud leg* at the bottom of the boiler for removing sediment.

REPLACING A HOT-WATER BOILER
Like steam boilers, in the days before insulation and tight windows, hot water boilers were casually oversize to compensate for unpredictable heat losses. Replacing an old boiler with a new one of the same rated output will waste fuel. Although not absolutely necessary, insulating the piping is still cost-effective.

REPLACING GRAVITY HOT WATER WITH FORCED CIRCULATION
If you are replacing gravity hot water with forced circulation, be sure to add a flow-bypass line around the new boiler. This prevents cold water from entering the hot boiler and corrosive flue gasses from condensing inside the boiler, where they can destroy it. The manufacturer's installation instructions typically specify the appropriate bypass configuration for each particular boiler.

A competent heating contractor knows that any system changeover can upset the balance of the system. It should be obvious that the large-bore pipes required for efficient distribution of hot water or low-pressure steam in a gravity system will perform differently under forced circulation. As mentioned above, the

TIP

Residual Cellar Heat

Replacing an inefficient old boiler with an efficient modern one can cause an unexpected side effect. Because new boilers and former steam pipes converted to hot water don't leak a lot of heat into the cellar, pipes may freeze. You may have to heat the cellar to cure the problem.

Combustion Air-Supply Problems

Although a nineteenth-century hot-air furnace installation often included a duct to supply outside air, the motivating principle was mainly to ensure fresh air for ventilation. There was no attempt to create what heating engineers would call a closed combustion loop. Bringing in outside air without controlling infiltration was both costly and unnecessary. The leakage of air through the cracks and crannies of the foundation and house walls supplied more than enough combustion air, and fresh air to boot.

But now that tightening up the heating envelope of an old house is a routine part of any renovation, the provision of sufficient combustion air is a concern, particularly when the furnace or boiler must compete against other combustion appliances such as a gas water heater, range, or clothes dryer as well as an air-guzzling fireplace. After a new boiler or furnace is installed (or after the house has been weatherized) have a heating contractor or energy auditor test its combustion efficiency and calibrate the barometric damper. Insufficient combustion air not only strangles the fire but can cause backdrafting of carbon monoxide into the house. That possibility is reason enough to outfit the heating plant with an outside combustion air supply.

On the other hand, establishing a closed combustion loop in a tight house can actually increase indoor air pollution and humidity problems. Without the appetite of the heating plant to fuel outside air infiltration, an exhaust fan may be needed to remove polluted air.

The bottom line is that the perambulations and proclivities of pressurized fluids such as air, water, and steam are subtly complicated, often counterintuitive, and a lot more consequential than you or even quite a few heating contractors could ever imagine. This is something to bear in mind when you're trying to decide whether to install a new heating system yourself or hire someone to do it for you.

efficient operation of a gravity system was keyed to the slow fires characteristic of coal-fired boilers and furnaces. Replacing a coal burner with a gas or oil burner is more disruptive to a steam system than to a hot-water or hot-air system. But corrosive by-products and moisture produced by these fuels do create potentially serious problems of another sort in the chimney.

Likewise, when replacing the gravity-feed octopus in the cellar with a sleek new cabinet furnace, the existing overlarge ductwork will be incompatible with forced circulation, and, among other ills, the supply and return air systems will be thrown out of balance.

CAST-IRON RADIATORS

Unless they spring a pinhole leak at a nipple or crack because they were allowed to freeze in an unheated house, cast-iron radiators are close to immortal. Because of their intimate exposure to air, antique steam radiators tend to have more rust and scale deposits than radiators used in closed hot-water systems. Fortunately, most of the time, the sludge just sits in the pockets at the very bottom of each section and doesn't cause any problems. However, should you decide to pitch a one-pipe radiator toward its inlet valve, as was often done to improve condensate

The ornately scrolled cast-iron radiators manufactured between 1880 and 1920 are unappreciated works of art, all too often junked when an antique steam or hot-water system is replaced by modern forced hot-water and low-slung and utilitarian baseboard radiation. Happily (or not, depending on whether you are buying or selling), enough folks have lately begun to realize their value that what could once be had free for the hauling is now becoming a scarce and pricey item.

drainage and reduce water hammering, the sludge can clog the valve, and the radiator will have to be removed and flushed clean. Likewise, if you are recycling salvaged radiators, flush them out to get rid of any loose scale and rust flakes before installing them.

Fixing Cracked Radiators

Cracked cast iron is very difficult to repair. Attempting to weld a crack usually only makes it worse. Because the iron contracts and expands, patches don't stay put. Some folks have successfully stopped cracks by packing them with flexible lead wool. Others have had good luck with patching compounds used for fixing leaks in cracked cast-iron engine blocks. To have even a chance of holding, the patch site must be sanded down to bare metal. This assumes you can find the leak and be able to reach it with a grinder or sander, which will probably require you to disassemble the radiator sections. Only a very special radiator is worth that much trouble.

The Efficient Radiator

Any house heated by radiators will benefit by having a radiant reflector installed on the wall behind the radiator or baseboard convector. This is typically a piece of foil-faced rigid insulation or galvanized sheet metal (ordinary aluminum foil will do in a pinch) that reflects the heat back into the room and reduces heat loss to the outside walls. Keeping radiators dust-free and unobstructed will also improve their output. Radiator enclosures or grilles, on the other hand, will do anything but. These were promoted as a way to hide "ugly" old radiators that clashed with notions of modern decor. While that result may be debatable, the fact that they replaced radiant heat output with convection was not. If your antique radiators have been hidden behind these misbegotten devices, you'd do well to liberate them.

Moving Radiators

As with boilers, one of the biggest problems of working with old radiators is moving them. They are back-wrenchingly heavy: 300 lb. to 400 lb. for a typical 38-in.-tall unit. If you've got radiators to move, rent a hand truck or dolly. And if the move involves a flight of stairs, get helpers, strap the radiator to the hand truck, and use chocks and caution to keep it under control. A runaway radiator and a staircase make a deadly combination.

Disconnecting Radiators

Use care when disconnecting an antique radiator. Cast iron is actually quite brittle. Yanking on a union joint with a pipe wrench can snap the radiator at the tap for the fitting. Use two pipe wrenches, one to turn the fitting and another to hold the pipe and prevent it from twisting.

There are at least two reasons why you might wish to remove or add sections to an antique radiator. Radiators ideally are placed in front of windows and are as wide as those windows. If you have a cache of identical salvaged radiators, you might need to shrink or expand them to fit. Or you might need to reduce or increase the output of an existing radiator to match it to the demands of a new location or new boiler. For example, because hot water is typically about 35°F cooler than steam, the heat output of a radiator converted from steam to hot water will drop by 30 percent or more. Other than replacing it with a finned baseboard convector, the only effective way to increase the radiation of an antique radiator is to add on sections.

On the other hand, given that our nineteenth-century forebears slept with the windows wide open so that they wouldn't be poisoned by vitiated air and miasmas in their sleep, radiators were about 30 percent larger than they needed to be if the windows had been kept shut. This is why we moderns find steam-heated bedrooms so stiflingly hot that we turn off the radiator hand valves. Either way, depending on when it was manufactured, taking a radiator apart can be a real bear.

DISASSEMBLING A RADIATOR For a time, radiator sections were joined together by unique threaded nipples that had both right- and left-handed threads. Turning the nipple pulled the opposing sections into each other. After a while, corrosion would weld the nipples and the radiator sections irredeemably together. There is no way to pry them apart.

Later manufacturers employed beveled two-piece push nipples. The beveled nipples slip together, and threaded rods running through the sections lock everything snug and watertight. Thus removing or adding sections is a matter of removing the nut that locks the threaded rod, applying penetrating oil to the nipple, and—with a pry bar and careful application of leverage—prying it apart. If you discover a damaged nipple, you can get a replacement by sending the original as a sample to the Oneida County Boiler Works, the only place in the United States that still makes them. Assuming all else goes well, remove the unwanted section and reassemble the radiator.

For all practical purposes, the radiators used for steam and hot-water heat are identical, except for the vents. When converting from steam to hot water, check for leaks, remove the steam valves or traps, and replace them with bleeder valves. Plug any openings and, for one-pipe systems, add return piping.

Adding and Subtracting Radiators

In the course of remodeling, it may be necessary to add or remove radiators. To add a radiator with steam heat, simply add a standard tee in the main at any point. For a two-pipe system, tap into the return main as well. To remove a radiator, replace the tee with a coupler or simply

The supply and return pipes of this former two-pipe steam system radiator were retrofitted with tees to extend pipes up to new hydronic radiators installed on the upper floor. While antique cast-iron radiators may not work as fast as modern finned baseboard convectors, they are much better suited to the aesthetics of an old house.

remove the riser, insert a short nipple into the existing tee, and screw a cap onto it. If the radiator you wish to add happens to have been made for hot water, screw a plug into one of the unused openings and replace the bleeder valve with an air or vacuum vent. Insert a gate valve in the riser before the radiator.

ADDING A HOT-WATER RADIATOR Adding a radiator to a hot-water system is basically the same as for a steam system. Add a scoop tee for the inlet and a standard tee for the outlet, spaced so that the risers go straight up to the radiator. When cutting and capping the supply and return to remove the radiator in a one-pipe system, remove the scoop tee and install a coupler. The return tee can be capped. But don't leave sections of riser, which will trap air or steam, sticking up into the floor joists.

LOCATING RADIATORS Ideally, radiators, like hot-air registers, should be located under windows. The top of the radiator should be just below the windowsill, never above it. Sometimes, as with tall radiators and low windowsills, this isn't always feasible. The next best choice

is against the wall alongside the window. The worst is on an interior wall opposite it. In any case, position the radiator so that its back is 2½ in. in front of the wall for maximum convective airflow.

Finned copper radiators have a higher heat output than cast iron; and they work faster. But cast-iron heaters hold more water and thus give off heat for a longer time. They're also more suited to an old house. Thermostatic radiator valves ($35 to $75 each) work with either steam or hot water to allow radiators to be zoned (so long as they are not connected in series).

Does Color Matter?

Although it seems obvious that painting a radiator black would maximize its radiant output, studies have established that with one exception, the color of a radiator has no discernible effect on its heat output. The only thing that sandblasting to expose the raw, dark cast iron will increase might be your aesthetic satisfaction.

But paints containing powdered aluminum or bronze pigments will definitely reduce radiation by about 20 percent. Old-timers used this curious phenomenon to reduce the heat output of oversize radiators. But the effect applies only to the topmost coat of paint. Painting over aluminum or bronze with any other color negates it. And the number of layers doesn't have any effect on heat transfer either. Thus there's no reason not to indulge yourself by replicating the often elaborate paint schemes typical of pre-1920s radiators.

COOLING OLD HOUSES

It wasn't until after World War II that the room air-conditioner as we know it became commonplace and that whole-house air-conditioning using the ductwork of the hot-air system was introduced. Thus, unlike heating, the majority of mechanical cooling systems are of necessity, convective. And, unlike heating, the relatively late adoption of mechanical cooling means that it is not native to old houses. Thus old houses and air-conditioning are always a retrofit.

The same logistical drawbacks that encouraged the retrofitting of steam and hot-water heating rather than hot air apply to central air-conditioning. Unless there are existing ducts to take advantage of, or the house will be entirely gutted, installing the ducts necessary for central air wreaks unacceptable violence on an old house. Thus, until recently, most old house owners living in regions with hot and humid summers and mild short winters had to content themselves with the time-honored cooling strategies of ceiling fans, whole-house fans, shady porches, tall ceilings, and open windows that might catch a blessed breeze; failing these, they installed a room-size window-mounted air-conditioner.

But within the last decade, high-velocity air-conditioning systems have made it possible to install central air in an old house without doing violence to the walls and ceilings. The key is a fan that delivers chilled air at about three times the velocity of standard air-conditioners and uses mufflered mini-ducts. Similar to the flexible plastic hose used to vent clothes dryers, this 3-in.-diameter spiral of metal wrapped in sound-deadening nylon fabric is easily snaked between walls and joist. In single-story houses, rooms are easily accessed from the attic or basement by outlets in the ceiling or floor. In two-story houses, attic ducts feed ceiling outlets for cooling the upper floor, and basement ducts feed floor outlets for the first story. Ducts can also be snaked through pipe chases and stacked closets between floors. Whenever possible, the ducts are snaked through nonbearing interior walls, to avoid structural damage, the insulation that would get in the way, and the loss of cooled air to the exterior. The outlets themselves are 2 in. in diameter, and so can be unobtrusively located in ceilings, woodwork, and floors.

One outlet is required for approximately every 100 sq. ft. of floor space. The outlets are typically located along the walls and in corners to limit drafts. Care must be taken that they are not placed near sitting and working areas or doorways. Allow a minimum of five and a maximum of seven outlets per ton of refrigeration (12,000 BTUs per hour, which is the cooling equivalent of a fan blowing air across a 1-ton block of ice for 24 hours—the way they used to do it in the old days). Although the mini-duct components cost about 20 percent more than conventional systems, the labor is significantly less, and so professional installation is competitive with a standard whole-house system.

REPAIRING AND RESTORING CHIMNEYS

Combustion gases, whether from wood, coal, oil, or gas, must be vented to the outside. A proper stovepipe installation and a workable chimney are crucial to the safety of the household as well as to the efficient functioning of the heating appliance. An unsafe chimney is a structural problem that must join foundation and roof problems as top-priority repairs.

The first chimneys were temporary expedients, built of sticks plastered with a mix of mortar and manure, as crude as the rough cabins they heated. These were soon replaced with

Cleaning a Chimney

Never use an old chimney or fireplace before you or a professional inspect and clean it. Hold up or dangle a light down the flue; use a mirror to find obstructions and offsets hidden behind walls and to inspect the brickwork and flue lining for soundness. Chimneys and fireplaces that have been unused or covered for a long time are often clogged with fallen bricks, birds' nests and even dead birds—especially at the bottom slope of an offset or on the fireplace smoke shelf. Creosote buildup in these places can completely close off the flue.

Loosen a brick on the side of the offset by gently tapping along its mortar joints with a brick chisel. Remove another brick so that you can reach in and clean out the obstruction, bit by bit, or push it down the rest of the flue to the cleanout at the bottom of the chimney.

Creosote stains and efflorescence caused by moisture leaching salts out of the mortar are evidence that this chimney lacks flue tiles and should be relined for safe use.

more substantial stone or brick chimneys, whose flues were coated with refractory (heat-resistant) mortars.

Clay flue liners did not come into use until after World War I. Because of their smooth surfaces, clay liners don't slow the ascending smoke as much as do rough masonry joints. The smoke doesn't cool as fast, creosote buildup is reduced, the chimney has a better draw, and downdrafts are less frequent. There are fewer joints through which flue gases can leak into the rooms, and if a chimney fire does occur, it is usually contained safely within the flues. A fire in an unlined chimney could crack the mortar between bricks and burst out into the framing; before this happens, the bricks will become so hot that the surrounding wood catches fire. Flue liners are such a good idea that an unlined chimney should never be used. The only possible exception might be a chimney that has an intact fireclay parging. This treatment will be adequate to handle the relatively low temperature and moisture content of the exhaust from oil-fired heaters.

Reopening a Chimney

It often happens that in the course of renovations, an old unused fireplace or chimney will be found entombed under the plaster. Some of these can be real treasures, well worth restoring. A competent mason can reconstruct old fireplaces. (The original may have been covered because it smoked too much; early fireplace and chimney designs were sometimes flawed or incorrectly built by unskilled masons.) At the end of the eighteenth century, there was quite a cottage industry devoted to the "Rumfordizing" of smoky fireplaces. One common cure is to retrofit a smoke shelf and damper at the chimney throat.

If you decide to reopen a closed-off chimney, be sure that it hasn't been taken down below the roof and that openings weren't cut into it—old-timers weren't too fussy about running more than one stovepipe into a single flue.

Relining a Chimney

Chimneys can be relined with clay tiles, with a proprietary cementitious mix, or with rigid or flexible stainless-steel chimney pipe. These materials are all expensive and/or time-consuming to install, and the work typically requires skills beyond those of the average homeowner. The choice of method depends on the type of chimney and the combustion products it will vent.

METAL LINERS ARE FOR OIL OR GAS Coal and wood pose special problems. Coal flue gases are extremely corrosive, and although some manufacturers claim their products are corrosion resistant, metal liners should never be used for a coal-burning system. Likewise, the stoke-and-starve cycle of wood burning encourages creosote formation, which often leads to chimney fires. Even clay flue liners can crack in a really bad chimney fire. A metal liner will burn through long before the flue gets hot enough to destroy flue tiles.

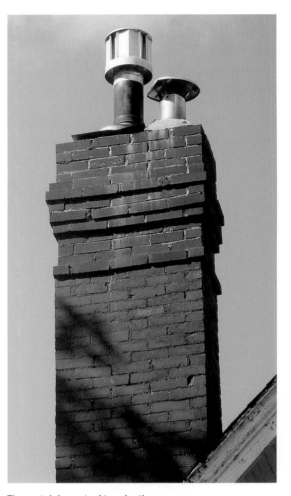

These stainless-steel termination caps are obvious evidence of a relined chimney.

When wood is burned only sporadically, as in a fireplace, the likelihood of a chimney fire is low, and stainless-steel flue liners could be used. Even so, these liners won't last for more than 4 years to 10 years when used in wood-burning chimneys. Although a cementitious or a standard clay liner might cost three or four times as much as a metal liner to install, it will last at least 50 years. Metal liners are only cost-efficient and safe with the relatively low flue-gas temperatures and the clean burn of oil and gas fires.

CEMENTITIOUS LINING Overall, for reasons of safety and longevity, the best choice for relining a chimney is either with a cementitious mix or clay tiles. The former is more expensive. In this patented process, which was first invented in

Installing a Corrugated Stainless-Steel Flue Liner

One-piece flexible stainless-steel liners are easy to feed into a chimney, particularly one that has offsets in it. After sweeping the chimney, chip out the chimney pot and mortar cap. Drop a strong weighted line down the flue and attach its top end to the conical termination of the liner.

Have a helper pull gently from below while you feed the liner down the chimney from the rooftop.

When the termination emerges, disconnect it and attach the closure plate to the liner. Seal it to the chimney throat or attach it to the outlet of the heating appliance and seal the joint with fire cement and nonasbestos packing. Attach the top closure plate and set it into a bed of mortar. Lay extra mortar to match the original cap. Then cap the liner with an approved cowl.

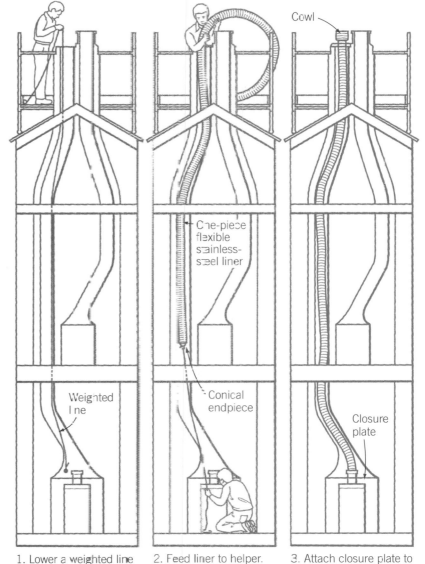

Cowl

One-piece flexible stainless-steel liner

Weighted line

Conical endpiece

Closure plate

1. Lower a weighted line into the flue.

2. Feed liner to helper.

3. Attach closure plate to liner and seal to the outlet of the heating appliance.

4. Attach top closure plate, set in mortar, and cap liner.

Retrofitting Flue Tiles

Flue tiles can be lowered down from the top of the chimney using a rope and a block of wood with an offset hole that allows the block to grab against the sides of the flue, as shown in the drawing at right. Butter the joints at the top of each section with refractory cement before lowering into place. You'll have only one chance to make sure it sets properly on the previously installed tile without mashing the mortar. Use a mirror and light to inspect the joints. Wipe them smooth by gently lowering a sawdust-filled burlap bag down the flue.

When a chimney has an offset section, relining is much more complicated (and expensive), as it takes a skilled mason to remove enough of the offset so that the mitered flue liners can be inserted without collapsing the chimney. It is usually necessary to open up the offset even when using a poured liner, to ensure that the form is properly positioned. Flexible steel liners can avoid this bottleneck, at least for gas and oil burners.

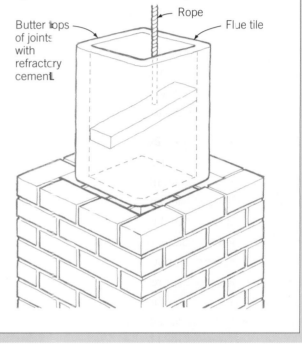

2x4 block with offset hole—tilted block pinches against sides of flue while it is being lowered.

Rope

Flue tile

Butter tops of joints with refractory cement.

England in the 1960s and is available only through franchised dealers—National's SUPA-FLU and the British Poured Flueliner (BPF) systems are two of the better known—a special rubber form is inserted into the chimney and inflated to the desired diameter. Spacers keep the form from touching the walls of the chimney. A special mix of perlited refractory mortar is pumped into the space between the form and the chimney walls. After 10 hours to 12 hours, the form is deflated and extracted. The relined chimney can withstand temperatures of 2,000°F and has superior insulating qualities, which helps reduce heat loss and creosote buildup. But the process is not recommended for multiflue chimneys.

CLAY LINERS The main disadvantage of clay liners is that it is usually necessary to tear out a face of the chimney at several points to slide the liner up or down in the flue. To gain access to the chimney, sections of walls must also be torn apart. Disposing of several tons of broken brick and crumbled mortar is a dirty, messy job. Wear a dust mask to avoid breathing in hazardous soot and creosote dust. Rebuild the brickwork before tearing out another section.

Old-Time Brick Needs Old-Time Mortar

Up until the middle of the nineteenth century (and even later in some regions) bricks were made as they had been since prehistory, by hand-packing clay into wooden molds to be fired in wood-burning or, later, coal-burning kilns. The resulting bricks were as irregular and inconsistent as the fires that produced them.

They were also quite soft. Beginning in the 1830s, a variety of machines and processes for pressing clay into bricks were developed, and improvements in drying and firing techniques resulted in a much more uniform size and density. At the end of the century, dry clay was being extruded under high pressure into a slab that was sliced by piano wire into individual bricks. Fired in the circular, continuous-process Hoffman kiln (invented in Germany in 1858, but not employed in the United States until the 1890s), these *wire-cut* bricks are identical to the hard, regular bricks in use today.

SOFT MORTAR FOR SOFT BRICKS Old brick and new mortar do not mix. Antique "soft" lime mortar, in use up until about 1850 (and in some areas until the end of the century) has a compressive strength measured in the mere hundreds of pounds per square inch, which is less than that of the bricks it bound together. This allows the mortar to compress slightly when the harder bricks expanded in hot weather and stretch when they contracted in cold. This very desirable elasticity was paid for in durability. Lime mortar gradually weathered away long before the brickwork.

Twentieth-century "hard" Portland cement mortar, on the other hand, contains very little lime and has a compressive strength measured in thousands of pounds per square inch. Together with equally hard-fired brick, this durability and strength made it possible to build the multistory masonry curtain walls of fin-de-siècle office buildings. But when modern hard mortar is used to repoint the crumbling lime mortar of antique soft brick, as is often done by unwitting homeowners and ignorant masons, the mortar lacks the give to accommodate seasonal changes in the brick. Instead, the brick suffers, spalling at the edges in hot weather and cracking in cold.

Modern Portland cement mortar is harder than old brick and old lime mortar. Incapable of cushioning seasonal contraction and expansion, the rigid mortar causes the faces of the brick to chip off.

Identifying the Mortar

The key to restoring weathered masonry successfully is to identify the brick and to reproduce, as closely as possible, the composition of the original mortar. With the exception of architecturally significant masonry, you shouldn't need to enlist the specialized expertise of a historic masonry consultant or a mason who specializes in restoration to accomplish this. Following are some helpful hints for the amateur masonry sleuth.

CHECK COLOR AND CONSISTENCY Lime mortar is pure white. Portland cement mortar is basically gray. How easy is it to dislodge? The easier you can chip out the mortar with a chisel or old screwdriver, the more lime it is likely to contain; the harder it comes, the more Portland cement. If you can carve a hole in it with a penknife, it's all or mostly lime. If you can't, it's not.

Drop a chunk of mortar onto the sidewalk. If it makes a dull thud, it contains a lot of lime. If it rings you've got mostly Portland cement. Likewise, lime mortar will crumble in your hand but it takes a hammer to bust up Portland cement mortar, and even then, it doesn't crumble. Lime mortar also tends to fall apart if you wet it down with vinegar and water. Portland cement remains intact.

THE ACID TEST Once you've ascertained that you have lime mortar, it needs to be broken down for further analysis so that you can match the original as closely as possible. Put about ½ cup of pulverized mortar in a glass jar and cover it with a 3-percent solution of muriatic acid. (Wear goggles and rubber gloves and don't breathe the fumes.) The acid will dissolve the lime, leaving a residue of sand on the bottom and a scum of dirt and other impurities floating on top. Note the size and color of the sand grains; they give the mortar its texture and color; the dirt also plays a lesser role. Somewhere within the circle of a dray horse's easy haul, the original source of sand might still be found.

MATCHING THE COLOR Laboratory microscopic and chemical analysis notwithstanding, even experts can't always match the exact color

That Old-Time Mortar

For antique preindustrial soft brick, a good general recipe is 2½ parts to 3 parts sand and 1 part slaked lime. This basic mix was sometimes augmented with crushed oyster shells, pulverized brick, or clay. High-lime mortar should be kept covered and wet for 3 days (72 hours) to fully cure. Adding a bit of Portland cement will speed up the curing process.

A good recipe for early industrial brick made in the early to middle nineteenth century, is 1 part white Portland cement (used in restoration work to match the color of lime mortar), 3 parts lime, and 10 parts to 12 parts sand. Machine-made pressed brick can withstand a slightly harder mortar: Use 1 part white Portland cement, 2 parts lime, and 8 parts to 9 parts sand.

To re-create turn-of-the-twentieth-century mortar, use 1 part white Portland cement, 1 part lime, and 6 parts to 7 parts sand. Or use standard gray premixed type N Portland cement mortar (ask for *brick mortar* at your lumberyard) to replace modern mortar. One of the nice things about lime mortar is its long working time: 4 hours to 5 hours per batch. Unlike plaster, mortar that starts to dry out can be retempered by mixing in a bit of water.

Lime mortar is mixed correctly when it's stiff enough to hold its shape if you roll it into a ball in your hand. You should be able to hold the trowel upside down without the mortar falling off.

When mixing up a recipe for replacement mortar, it's better to err on the side of softness and use more rather than less lime. The consequence may be an extra round of repointing in your or the next owner's lifetime, which is a lot less trouble than replacing cracked and spalted bricks.

of either replacement bricks or mortar. The materials weather at different rates in response to chemical composition and time. This is where experience definitely helps. Some experts try to stain the mortar or brick with colorants of one kind or another (coffee grounds added to the mix is one suggestion), but these additives fade away and so are only a temporary fix. The best solution is to match the mortar as closely as possible to the original, match the age of the bricks if you can, and let it all blend with time.

Repointing a Chimney

The mortar joints between old brick never last as long as the brick itself. They need to be renewed every few generations or so by repointing (or *tucking*). With a cold chisel, rake out crumbling mortar to sound material, usually about 1 in. below the surface. This is painfully slow work. Don't be tempted to speed things up by cutting out the joints with a circular saw or power grinder—you'll ruin the edges of the bricks. (On the other hand, a pneumatic chisel works fast and isn't as likely to damage the brick.) Dampen the joints with water to soften the mortar and square off the backs of the cuts with a pointing slicker.

Gently chip out and remove damaged bricks and replace them with used brick of similar size and (with luck) age. Wet down the bricks and joints with water before re-pointing. Old brick is very dry and will suck moisture out of the mortar before it properly cures. For the same reason, soak any replacement bricks in a tub of water for a few minutes before laying them. Be sure to place used brick weathered-side out, as the protected face will be much different in color and texture.

Force new mortar into the joints with a narrow-bladed tuck-pointing trowel. Tool the joint with a joint raker to a concave profile, just inside the rounded-over edges of the old brick.

After chipping out the decayed mortar down to sound material, blow the joints free of dust and debris and wet down with a garden-hose sprayer.

Fill the vertical joints (head joints) first with a sliver of mortar and a pointing slicker. The horizontal (bed) joints follow.

Strike the excess mortar from the joints, and shape it to match the original joint work.

Clean the finished joints with a bristle brush.

Afterword

Old houses, I thought, do not belong to people, ever, not really, people belong to them.

—GLADYS TABER, *STILLMEADOW DAYBOOK*

If one clear theme has emerged from the preceding 400 pages or so, it's that taking care of an old house is a lot like taking care of your teeth. A schedule of regular maintenance is the equivalent of daily flossing and brushing. If you neglect either, your house and your teeth will both decay. And like the health of our bodies in general, much of what goes wrong can be attributed to neglect if not willful abuse.

Moisture is the enemy. Water + wood = rot. (It's almost that simple.) Keeping moisture out of the walls and away from wood is a goodly part of what a house is supposed to do. Again, it's almost that simple.

Water is an insidious foe. It's a shape shifter, harmful in all its phases—solid, liquid, and gaseous—it probes at the house's defensive membranes, insinuating itself into the smallest hidden breach. Rising from the foundation stones by capillary attraction, condensing on cool surfaces, leaking, sweating, overflowing, evaporating, falling and splashing, piling up, and oozing between. Ice and snow buckle roofs and frost heaves walls, soggy clay squeezes out from under building corners. Creosote distills in the flues, mortars spall, plaster crumbles, metals corrode, pipes burst, and wood swells. Molds and fungus bloom and carpenter ants tunnel, digesting the house around you, antagonizing your immune system into allergic alert.

The symptoms of water damage are a call to action. I hope your renovation program has addressed the root causes of the problems and you have rebuilt any fallen ramparts. Most

people wouldn't think of driving their automobile without changing the oil or servicing it at regular intervals. Yet most house owners somehow assume that the place will just keep itself together without any attention on their part. But unlike a car with a blown engine, which won't take you an inch farther down the road, people can blithely continue living in an old house that is literally falling down around them, more or less quite comfortably, for generations or until it's problems are passed on to the next owner. Other than the relatively small portion devoted to greasing, oiling, cleaning, and adjusting the domestic machinery to keep it humming smoothly along until it wears out, the main focus of an old house maintenance program is to keep up the defenses against moisture.

The charts in chapters 1 and 2 established a triage system for deciding which tasks needed to be addressed immediately to arrest further deterioration or to repair conditions that threatened either life and safety or habitability and comfort and which repairs could be safely put off until later. But there is a difference between neglect and deferred maintenance. Things fester in the cellar while you wax the kitchen floor.

Small nagging seasonal chores, if faithfully performed, prevent extensive damage and expensive repairs. Cleaning the gutters and sweeping the chimneys are two prime examples. Washing lichen off roofing shingles, repainting metal roofing, painting and caulking window sills, trimming overhanging tree branches and pruning shrubs crowding the foundation, touching up peeled paint, caulking and patching open gaps in the trim and siding all add to the longevity and comfort of any house. Old houses are ongoing reincarnations. One of the responsibilities of owning them is to further them along into the next cycle.

Readings

A lot of books have been written about renovating, restoring and, remodeling old houses. No single volume could possibly cover every aspect of the subject, but a lot of books on the market don't even do justice to the basics, and some are so utterly lacking in any sensitivity to the special character of old houses that no one should ever read them. Unless they have some other merit, my suggested reading list won't include books that tell you to look for another house at the first sign of a crack in the foundation or worms in the woodwork—if you could afford a perfectly restored old house, you probably wouldn't be reading this book in the first place. But the list does include various handbooks for skills associated with renovation that are by necessity only touched on in this book.

For those whose interests range beyond the mere how-to, I've suggested some background readings in the historical, architectural, and philosophical aspects of the subject. The reasons for building new houses are fairly obvious; rebuilding old houses involves a peculiar form of masochism and dedication that is worthy of further exploration.

Building History and Architectural Styles

Brand, Stewart. *How Buildings Learn.* New York: Viking Penguin, 1994.

Thought-provoking and insightful inquiry into the life of buildings over time and of use and adaptive reuse.

Brierton, Joan M. *Victorian: American Restoration Style.* Salt Lake City: Gibbs-Smith, 1999.

Five different styles of Victorian decoration are analyzed via a room-by-room case study of authentically detailed restorations. Lots of color photos of interior decoration and details.

Carpenters' Company of the City and County of Philadelphia, eds. *Building Early America.* Radnor, PA: Chilton, 1976.

Articles on the development of central heating, masonry methods, house framing, early roofing materials, and window glass.

Condit, Carl W. *American Building: Materials and Techniques from the First Colonial Settlements to the Present.* Chicago: University of Chicago Press, 1968.

The title says it all—a comprehensive history of American building

Congdon, Herbert Wheaton. *Early American Homes for Today.* Dublin, NH: Bauhan, 1985.

A reprint of the original 1963 edition, this book is a practical restoration manual, an architectural history, and a sourcebook of decorative details, written by the son of the famous Gothic Revival architect, himself a practicing architect and lover of old Vermont country houses.

Elliot, Cecil D. *Technics and Architecture.* Cambridge, MA: MIT Press, 1992.

An always interesting and sometimes amusing, well-illustrated, and quite thorough history of the evolution of building materials and systems of Europe and North American from the Industrial Revolution to the present.

Garrett, Elizabeth Donaghy. *At Home: The American Family 1750–1870.* New York: Abrams, 1990.

What was it like to live in an eighteenth- or nineteenth-century house? Using diaries, letters, household manuals, contemporary paintings and prints, Garrett answers the question, room by room, chore by chore, day by day.

Hale, Jonathan. *The Old Way of Seeing.* New York: Houghton Mifflin, 1994.

Answers the question I posed at the beginning of this book, "What is it about old houses, anyway?" Uncovers the principles of harmonious design hidden behind Classical Revival facades and interiors of old houses.

Hubka, Thomas C. *Big House, Little House, Back House, Barn: The Connected Farm Buildings of New England.* Hanover, NH: University Press of New England, 1984.

An engaging architectural and social history of a style of building that is unique to northern New England.

Ierley, Merritt. *The Comforts of Home: The American House and the Evolution of Modern Convenience.* New York: Clarkson Potter, 1999.

A well-illustrated and enjoyably readable historical study of domestic technology from the end of the eighteenth century to the present.

Kelly, John Frederick. *Early Domestic Architecture of Connecticut.* New York: Dover, 1953.

A reprint of a classic work, full of details and lore about seventeenth- and eighteenth-century timber-frame houses. An excellent companion to the Congdon volume.

May, Jeffrey C. *My House Is Killing Me.* Baltimore: Johns Hopkins University Press, 2001.

After you read this book about indoor pollutants and allergens, you'll be afraid to breathe indoors, never mind tear into the walls of an old house. The author strikes me as the kind of person who would wear a safety helmet in bed. Yet chemical sensitivity is an undeniable fact of modern life. Catherine Beecher Stowe and the fresh-air crusaders may have had a point.

McAlester, Virginia, and Lee McAlester. *A Field Guide to American Houses.* New York: Knopf, 1984.

An encyclopedic taxonomy of American housing from the seventeenth century to the present.

McKee, Harley J. *Introduction to Early American Masonry.* Washington, DC: Preservation Press, 1973.

A historical study of the technology of stone, brick, mortar, and plaster from European antecedents up to about 1860. Good background reading.

Miller, Judith. *Period Kitchens: A Practical Guide to Period-Style Decorating.* London: Mitchell Beazley, 1995.

An idea book full of inspiring color photographs, the usual planning and layout advice, and practical sections of period finishes such as wood graining, color washing, and stenciling.

Moss, Roger W. *Paint in America: The Colors of Historic Buildings.* Washington, DC: Preservation Press, 1994.

An exhaustive history of exterior and interior paint in America. It also includes case studies and a detailed and technical analysis of paint composition and restoration.

Powell, Jane, and Linda Svendsen. *Bungalow Kitchens.* Salt Lake City: Gibbs-Smith, 2000.

Lavish color photographs show how turn-of-the-twentieth-century Arts and Crafts style kitchens are perfectly adaptable to a wide range of modern homes. Particularly useful are the "Obsessive Restoration" vs. "Compromise Solution" sidebars.

Rybczynski, Witold. *Home: A Short History of an Idea.* New York: Viking Penguin, 1986.

A study of the development of the idea of comfort, which partly answers the question, "What makes a house a home?" The author is an architect who also happens to be a fine writer.

Walker, Lester. *American Shelter.* Woodstock, NY: Overlook Press, 1997.

Clear line drawings describe and illustrate the evolution of every significant style of American housing from the Native Americans to the mobile home. The exploded floor plans are particularly valuable.

Wright, Lawrence. *Clean and Decent.* Buffalo, NY: University of Toronto Press, 1960.

An engaging history of the bathroom. Insights into cultural attitude toward bodily functions, sewerage systems, and plumbing.

Nineteenth-Century Sources

Dover Publications specializes in publishing facsimiles of nineteenth-century stylebooks, catalogs, and architectural classics, as does the American Life Foundation and Study Institute of Watkins Glen, New York. I find these publications enjoyable reading for their insights into the thinking of bygone times, both because of what is still remarkably similar and what is now outmoded, quaint, and curiously wrongheaded. They are also a first-hand sourcebook for historical architectural details. Here are some of my favorites.

Cleaveland, Henry W., William Backus, and Samuel D. Backus. *Village and Farm Cottages.* Watkins Glen, NY: American Life Foundation and Study Institute, 1982.

Unabridged reprint of the 1856 edition originally published by D. Appleton and Company.

Cook, Clarence. *The House Beautiful.* New York: Dover, 1995.

Unabridged republication of the 1881 edition of *The House Beautiful: Essays on Beds and Tables, Stools and Candlesticks* published by Charles Scribner's and Sons. (Original edition published by Scribner, Armstrong and Company, in 1877.)

Downing, Andrew Jackson. *Architecture of Country Houses* New York: Dover, 1969.

Unabridged republication of the 1850 edition originally published by D. Appleton and Company.

Downing, Andrew Jackson. *Victorian Cottage Residences.* New York: Dover, 1981.

Unabridged republication of the 1873 edition of *Cottage Residences; or, A Series of Designs for Rural Cottages and Cottage Villas, and their Gardens and Grounds, Adapted to North America.*

J. L. Mott Iron Works. *Mott's Illustrated Catalog of Victorian Plumbing Fixtures for Bathrooms and Kitchens.* New York: Dover, 1987.

Unabridged republication of the 1888 *Catalog "G" Illustrating the Plumbing and Sanitary Department.*

Palliser, Palliser & Co. *American Victorian Cottage Homes.* New York: Dover, 1990.

Unabridged reprint of 1878 edition of Palliser's *American Cottage Homes*

Mulliner Box and Planing Company. *Turn-of-the-Century Doors, Window and Decorative Millwork.* New York: Dover, 1995.

Unabridged republication of the 1893 catalog *Combined Book of Sash, Doors, Blinds, Mouldings, Stair Work, Mantels, and All Kinds of Interior and Exterior Finish.*

Sloan, Samuel. *The Model Architect: A Series of Designs for Cottages, Villas, Suburban Residences, Etc. Accompanied by Explanations, Specifications, Estimates, and Elaborate Details.* Philadelphia: Butler, 1865.

Stowe, Catherine E., and Harriet Beecher Stowe. *American Woman's Home.* Hartford, CT: Harriet Beecher Stowe Center, Library of Victorian Culture, 1998.

This is the eighth printing of the original 1869 edition published by J. B. Ford and Company.

Woodward, George E. and Edward G. Thompson. *A Victorian Housebuilder's Guide.* New York: Dover, 1988.

Unabridged reprint of the 1869 edition of *Woodward's National Architect.*

Conservation Methods and Philosophy

Bullock, Orin Jr. *The Restoration Manual.* Norwalk, CT: Silvermine, 1966.

A book for the conservationist, devoted to ferreting out the original beauty of antique buildings and rescuing them from the ravages of modernization. Written by a sensitive architect.

Historic Preservation. Washington, DC: National Trust for Historic Preservation.

Nontechnical preservation journal, good for professional contractors.

Kirk, John T. *The Impecunious House Restorer.* New York: Knopf, 1984.

An essay in attitude adjustment designed to foster reverence for old homes. Good on researching and documenting the age of a house.

Stephen, George. *New Life for Old Houses.* Washington, DC: Preservation Press, 1989.

An update of the 1973 volume *Remodeling Old Houses without Destroying Their Character,* published by Knopf. Good on design and planning, with a thoughtful and sensitive appreciation for the spirit of old houses. Stresses nondestructive remodeling. Good information on restoring brownstones as well as wood-frame buildings.

Hands-On Renovation

Brann, Donald R. *How to Rehabilitate an Abandoned Building.* Briarcliff Manor, NY: Easi-Bild Pattern, 1974.

A good book for the urban renovator, because it addresses problems rural home owners seldom encounter.

Evers, Christopher. *The Old-House Doctor.* Woodstock, NY: Overlook Press, 1986.

I like this guy—we think alike. I can't tell how many ideas he borrowed from me, and I'm sure he can't tell how many I've borrowed from him, but the diagnostic approach and the historical asides, coupled with generally solid techniques based on his experiences, make this a useful book.

Hawkins, R. R., and C. H. Abbe. *New Houses from Old.* New York: McGraw-Hill, 1948.

This out-of-print book was intended as a guide for modernizing the old houses of an earlier generation. It's another treasury of obsolete details and techniques one is likely to encounter in today's old houses.

Hutchins, Nigel. *Restoring Old Houses.* New York: Grammercy, 1985.

A bit thin on details, but good on historical analysis and on renovation of log and masonry structures. I like it because it has lots of black-and-white photos of old houses in Ontario and Quebec, which are distinctly different from American houses.

Labine, Clem, and the staff of *The Old-House Journal,* eds. *The Old-House Journal Compendium.* New York: Overlook Press, 1980. Poore, Patricia, and Clem Labine, eds. *The Old-House Journal New Compendium.* New York: Doubleday, Dolphin Books, 1983.

These two books are compilations of articles that previously appeared in *The Old-House Journal* (Brooklyn, NY). The magazine also publishes the annual *Old -House Journal*

Catalog, which is an indispensable source-book for all kinds of hard-to-find hardware, fixtures, and fittings for old houses. No one in the old-house business should be without at least one of these volumes.

Litchfield, Michael W. *Encyclopedia of Home Improvement.* New York: Sterling, 1997.

Originally published in 1982 as *Renovation: A Complete Guide* (New York: Wiley). A fat volume on residential renovation by the founding editor of The Taunton Press's *Fine Homebuilding* magazine.

Northead, Mary H. *Remodeled Farmhouses.* Boston: Little, Brown, 1915.

If you can find this book in your library, you'll enjoy hours of fascinating reading with these case studies of the remodeling of 22 farmhouses back before electricity and pumped water systems were considered standard. Contains a lot of practical old-time information and decorative details, as well as a fascinating perspective on how the craftsmen of an earlier era dealt with renovation problems.

Poore, Patricia, ed. *The Old-House Journal Guide to Restoration.* New York: Penguin Group, 1992.

A comprehensive manual of practical advise and a hands-on guide for restoring houses of every style from foundation to roof.

Time-Life Books staff. *The Old House.* Alexandria, VA: Time-Life, 1980.

As with all the volumes in the "Home Repair and Improvement" series, this book has excellent drawings and good how-to information. Strictly for timid amateurs, *The Old House* covers the basics, with one or two hints that even an experienced professional might find useful.

Whelchel, Harriet, ed. *Caring for Your Historic House.* New York: Abrams, 1998.

Published in conjunction with the Heritage Preservation and National Park Service, this is a collection of authoritative articles on preservation-oriented philosophy, methodology, and hands-on detailed how-to of particular relevance to the historically significant house. It is an excellent source of information for evaluating the condition of any old house and developing a repair and maintenance strategy.

Whitman, Roger B. *First Aid for the Ailing House.* New York: McGraw-Hill, 1934.

I collect old guidebooks to renovating for the same reasons that I collect nineteenth-century stylebooks. Also, knowing how and why they did things 50 or 75 years ago is most helpful when dealing with what you're likely to find lurking in the cellar or behind the walls of your old house. Whitman's book is still quite handy and is also an intriguing snapshot of building practices on the cusp of the modern age, when coal was just beginning to be replaced by gas and oil, and insulation was coming into wide use.

Williams, Henry L., and Ottalie K. Williams. *Modernizing Old Houses.* New York: Doubleday, 1948.

These guys are the pioneers of do-it-yourself renovation. Lots of drawings and descriptions of funky rural water supply machinery as well as heating and kitchen appliances.

Williams, Henry L., and Ottalie K. Williams. *Old American Houses: 1700–1850. How to Restore, Remodel and Reproduce Them.* New York: Coward-McCann, 1957.

Information on genealogy of hardware and other components of old houses, useful for dating, restoration, and preservation. The only book I've come across with a serious discussion of how to move a house.

Materials and Specifications

Dunlop, Carson and Associates. *Structure, Roofing and the Exterior; Electrical, Plumbing, Insulation and the Interior; Heating and Air Conditioning* volumes in *The Illustrated Home Series.* Toronto: Stoddart, 2000.

If a picture is worth a thousand words, these three volumes, with over 1,500 illustrations, make up a library. No text, just clear line drawings of what repairs and renovations should look like. Don't renovate home without it.

Philbin, Tom, and Steve Ettlinger. *The Complete Illustrated Guide to Everything Sold in Hardware Store.* New York: Macmillan, 1988.

This book tells you the names of all those widgets and fittings that the novice will need to ask for at the hardware store.

Vila, Bob, with Norm Abrams, Stewart Byrnes, and Larry Stains, *This Old House Guide to Building and Remodeling Materials.* New York: Warner Books, 1986,

An encyclopedia of building materials very useful for nonprofessionals to learn how to choose the right materials for the job.

Warner Books. *The Brand New Old-House Catalog.* New York: Warner Books, 1980.

A superb sourcebook.

Watson, Donald, ed. *Architectural Details: Classic Pages from Architectural Graphics Standards 1940–1980.* New York: Wiley, 2001.

This is a compendium of "lost pages" of the graphic details of mid-twentieth-century architectural practice that have been dropped over the years from the *Architectural Graphics Standards,* the bible of accepted architectural standards, now in its 10th edition. Architects and designers specializing in commercial and residential renovation and restoration will find it enlightening and more useful than its modern progeny.

Carpentry Skills

There's more to know about building, repairing, and maintaining a house and everything in it than one book or one brain can contain. When you need to fix a faucet, repair a clothes dryer, set up a router, or sharpen a chisel, somewhere in these books you'll find the answer to your questions. The nice thing about old houses and old stuff is that the repair manuals are never out of date. Here's a few on my shelf of late:

DeChristoforo, R. J. *DeChristoforo's Complete Book of Power Tools, Both Stationary and Portable.* New York: Harper & Row, 1972.

Everything you always wanted to know about your radial-arm saw and table saw.

Knox, Gerald M., ed. *Better Homes and Gardens Complete Guide to Home Repair Maintenance and Improvement.* Des Moines, IA: Meredith, 1980.

McClintock, Mike, ed. *Home Book: The Ultimate Guide to Repairs, Improvements, and Maintenance.* Upper Saddle River, NJ: Creative Homeowner Press, 2000.

Reader's Digest. *Reader's Digest Book of Skills and Tools.* Pleasantville, NY: Reader's Digest, 1993.

Reader's Digest. *Reader's Digest Complete Do-it-Yourself Manual.* Pleasantville, NY: Reader's Digest, 1973 (later editions).

Reader's Digest. *Reader's Digest Home Improvement Manual.* Pleasantville, NY: Reader's Digest, 1982.

Shakery, Karin, ed. *Ortho's Home Improvement Encyclopedia.* San Ramon, CA: Ortho, 1985.

Zmetana, Katherine, ed. *Complete Fix-It-Yourself Manual.* New York: Time-Life, 1989.

And for actual carpentry books, here's the only three you'll need:

Nash, George. *Do-It-Yourself Housebuilding.* New York: Sterling, 1992.

If you were marooned on a desert island and had to build yourself a house, this is the one book you'd want to have with you. This 703-page tome is oriented specifically to the real-life owner–builder, not the trade-school carpenter. It teaches you not only how to build right but how to fix things when they inevitably go wrong.

Syvanen, Bob. *Carpentry and Exterior Finish: Some Tricks of the Trade from an Old-Style Carpenter.* Chester, CT: Globe Pequot Press, 1982.

Syvanen, Bob. *Carpentry and Exterior Finish: More Tricks of the Trade from an Old-Style Carpenter.* Chester, CT: Globe Pequot Press, 1993.

Tells you how to take those shortcuts that every experienced carpenter knows.

Index